BASIC ETHICS IN ACTION

Business Ethics

MICHAEL BOYLAN

Prentice
Hall

Upper Saddle River, New Jersey 07458

10-16

Library of Congress Cataloging-in-Publication Data

Boylan, Michael (date)
  Business ethics / Michael Boylan.
    p. cm.—(Basic ethics in action)
  ISBN 0-13-773839-0
    1. Business ethics—Case studies. I. Title. II. Series.

HF5387.B686 2001
174'.4—dc21   00-042747

Editor-in-Chief: Charlyce Jones Owen
Acquisitions Editor: Ross Miller
Assistant Editor: Katie Janssen
AVP, Director of Manufacturing
  and Production: Barbara Kittle
Senior Managing Editor: Jan Stephan
Production Liaison: Fran Russello
Project Manager: Linda B. Pawelchak
Manufacturing Manager: Nick Sklitsis
Prepress and Manufacturing Buyer: Sherry Lewis
Cover Director: Jayne Conte
Cover Design: Bruce Kenselaar
Marketing Manager: Ilse Wolf
Copy Editing: JaNoel Lowe
Proofreading: Maine Proofreading Services

Acknowledgments begin on page 422, which
constitutes a continuation of this copyright page.

This book was set in 10/12 Palatino by Pub-Set
and was printed and bound by R.R. Donnelley and Sons, Inc.
The cover was printed by Phoenix Color Corp.

© 2001 by Michael Boylan
Published by Prentice-Hall, Inc.
A Division of Pearson Education
Upper Saddle River, New Jersey 07458

Printed in the United States of America
10 9 8 7 6 5 4 3 2 1

ISBN 0-13-773839-0

Prentice-Hall International (UK) Limited, *London*
Prentice-Hall of Australia Pty. Limited, *Sydney*
Prentice-Hall Canada Inc., *Toronto*
Prentice-Hall Hispanoamericana, S.A., *Mexico*
Prentice-Hall of India Private Limited, *New Delhi*
Prentice-Hall of Japan, Inc., *Tokyo*
Pearson Education Asia Pte. Ltd., *Singapore*
Editora Prentice-Hall do Brasil, Ltda., *Rio de Janeiro*

For Éamon

Contents

Preface

This book aspires to introduce the student to important ethical issues that arise in the world of business. As such, it fits into that branch of ethics referred to as Applied Professional Ethics. *Business Ethics* is the third book in the series *Basic Ethics in Action*. The series includes this book and two other anthologies on applied professional ethics: *Environmental Ethics* and *Medical Ethics*. The series (for which I am the general editor) also features other (generally single author) titles in Normative and Applied Ethics. These will include social and political philosophy, professional ethics, human rights, and legal ethics (among others in an expanding list). The series will also include focus books that are about half as long as the current one on particular moral issues, such as genetic engineering, international business, and informed consent. *Basic Ethics in Action* includes both types of book. The series aspires to the pattern set by Prentice Hall's influential *Foundations of Philosophy* series of the 1960s and 1970s.

The series is anchored by *Basic Ethics*, an essay on Normative Ethics and Metaethics. Instructors and students of ethics can use (1) *Basic Ethics* alone or with other primary texts in an ethics course, (2) *Basic Ethics* with one of the applied texts in the series in an ethics course that emphasizes an integration of theory and practice, or (3) one or more of the applied texts in courses concentrating on practice.

DISTINCTIVE FEATURES OF THIS BOOK

This book includes an original interview with a prominent person who faces the practical challenges of ethical issues in business daily; a discussion of competition and a linking principle to decision making; an ethical methodology for linking theory to action; a discussion of gender issues as they relate to business, E-business, and the Internet; and a method for students to follow to write an essay using the information presented.

The book begins by introducing the student to my theory of worldview, or *Weltanschauung.* This concept is one of the unifying themes of *Basic Ethics.* I believe that acknowledging one's worldview and its relation to the common worldview (the worldview created by a particular community) is a crucial element in explaining and justifying what we value. This critical model, in turn, leads to what I call a linking principle to action. In the case of Business Ethics, I have constructed criteria that describe fair competition that I believe will allow students to move from theory to practice. A full exposition of this principle is found in my essay "The Principle of Fair Competition" in Chapter Four.

Chapter One also presents an interview with Mel Streeter, who runs the largest African American–owned architectural firm in the Pacific Northwest. This interview is presented to help students gain some perspective on the central themes in this book from the point of view of a successful practitioner in the field.

Chapter Two presents four ethical theories, which are not meant to be exhaustive. For readers who desire a more complete treatment of the major ethical theories, I suggest *Basic Ethics* or another source that explores some of the more prominent ethical theories.

Chapter Three addresses the nature of the corporation. Is a corporation a nameless piece of property—a shield behind which employees, stockholders, directors, and officers can hide from the responsibility for their actions? Certainly, that was part of the *raison d'être* of its creation. But *should* it be that way? Are there models by which to understand the corporation—such as its being an individual or including various entities (stakeholders) that interact with the company in some meaningful way? This chapter examines several ways to view the corporation to understand ethical issues related to it.

Chapter Four discusses the issues of professional practice. Since I believe that understanding professional practice is essential to understanding and developing guidelines for fair competition, Chapter Four is a key chapter in the book. After a section on the concept in general, several articles examine one established profession, advertising. Next the chapter examines the amorphous, emerging area of information technology and the Internet. Advertising and information technology offer practical applications of the key linking principle in the book: the standards of professionalism within business.

Chapter Five extends this discussion to issues within the corporation, specifically working conditions, affirmative action, and gender issues. Each of these addresses situations affecting the status of the employee within the corporation and the way she or he is treated. Intracorporate ethical issues operate together to create what has been termed *corporate culture.*

Finally, Chapter Six examines the corporation in the national regulatory environment and the international environment. The reasons that regulation is needed and what groups should provide it are discussed. The second topic involves moral absolutism and how to compete adequately in markets that have morally corrupt practices.

Beginning with Chapter Three, each chapter ends with a section on how to respond to case studies that contain ethical issues. Each section presents one step in this process so that by the end of Chapter Six, the student should have developed the ability to write an essay responding to case studies involving ethical issues.

A part of these sections in the core chapters of the book presents case studies depicting situations related to topics discussed in the chapter's readings. These case studies are separated into two groups, macro cases and micro cases. The macro case takes the point of view of someone in a managerial or supervisory role who considers business ethics from a systemic perspective. The point of view in the micro cases is of salespeople, secretaries, and middle managers who must make decisions that have ethical implications. Through these case studies, the student has an opportunity to react to the readings and test his or her own attitudes by writing an essay.

Basic Ethics in Action has an argument-based style and tone and intends to challenge the reader to think about some of the various ethical implications involved in specific situations. I have found that discussion of the more controversial premises focuses debate in a way that is satisfactory for both instructor and student.

Many may wish to read *Business Ethics* along with an ethical theory text (such as *Basic Ethics*). Others will want to delve more deeply into issues of practice by finding topics that interest them and then doing their own interview of people in the field. I believe that getting a sense of what real life is like is important. It puts these cases and principles into a context that can be more easily integrated into the students' worldview. This is, after all, the purpose of a course on Business Ethics. It helps students refine their practical decision-making skills so that they might be better able to live following a worldview that is, above all else, good.

ACKNOWLEDGMENTS

As in all projects of this sort, there are many to thank. First, I would like to thank the following reviewers: David Griffith, Ouachita Baptist University; Michael J. Olivette, Syracuse University; and David Redle, University of Akron (Ohio).

Next I would like to thank Ross Miller, my editor, for his support on this book and on the series *Basic Ethics in Action.* The series is already bearing the marks of his insightful judgment. I am also grateful to Katie Janssen, assistant editor, and to my able production editor, Linda B. Pawelchak.

I would also like to mention the help I have received both from Marymount University's research librarians, especially Margaret Norden and Marge Runge, and from Pat Milmoe McCarrick and the staff at the National Reference for Bioethics Literature (they also have a good collection on business ethics).

Finally, I would like to mention my family: Arianne, Seán, Éamon, and Rebecca. Their lives and the values they teach me are a constant source of strength and sustenance.

Michael Boylan

Contributors

John B. Matthews Jr. is a professor at the Graduate School of Business Administration, Harvard University.

Nani L. Ranken is professor emerita of philosophy at Indiana University at Kokomo.

Peter A. French is professor of philosophy at the University of South Florida.

Thomas Donaldson is professor of business ethics at the Wharton School, University of Pennsylvania.

Stakeholders

Kenneth E. Goodpaster is Koch Professor of Business Ethics at the University of St. Thomas.

Stephen Cohen is professor of philosophy at the University of New South Wales.

CHAPTER FOUR: WHAT ARE PROPER BUSINESS PRACTICES?

Competition and the Practice of Business

Alan Malachowski is a member of the Department of Philosophy in the Faculty of Letters, Reading University.

Michael Boylan is professor of philosophy at Marymount University in Arlington, Virginia.

Advertising

Barbara J. Philips is assistant professor at the University of Saskatchewan.

Geoffrey Sher, M.D., is on staff at the Pacific Fertility Medical Center/Los Angeles, California.

Michael Feinman, M.D., is on staff at the Pacific Fertility Medical Center/Westlake, Oregon.

Tonly L. Henthorne is director of the Institute for Service Excellence and associate professor of marketing at the University of Southern Mississippi and director of the Institute for Service and professor of marketing at the University of Southern Mississippi.

Michael S. LaTour is associate professor of marketing at Auburn University.

Information Technology

Duncan Langford is a computing fellow, University of Kent at Canterbury.

Peter W. F. Davies is a senior lecturer in strategic management and business ethics at Buckinghamshire Business School, Buckinghamshire College, United Kingdom.

Joseph L. Badaracco Jr. is John Shad Professor of Business Ethics at Harvard Business School.

Jerry V. Useem is former research associate at Harvard and currently on the editorial staff of INC. Magazine.

Michael D. Myers is in the Department of Management Science and Information Systems, University of Auckland, New Zealand.

Leigh Miller is at Loughlin McGuire, Auckland, New Zealand.

CHAPTER FIVE: ETHICAL ISSUES WITHIN THE CORPORATION

Working Conditions

William W. Lowrance is a consultant on health policy, benefit/risk, and medical privacy issues and is based in Geneva, Switzerland.

Sheila M. Neysmith is on the faculty of social work at the University of Toronto.

Jane Aronson is on the faculty at McMaster University in Canada.

David M. Schilling is a United Methodist minister and director of Global Corporate Accountability at the Interfaith Center on Corporate Responsibility in New York.

Affirmative Action

Judith Jarvis Thomson is professor of philosophy at M.I.T.

Robert Simon is professor of philosophy at Hamilton College.

Michael Boylan is professor of philosophy at Marymount University in Arlington, Virginia.

Gender Issues

Rekha Karambayya is associate professor in the Schulich School of Business at York University.

S. Gayle Baugh is assistant professor of management at the University of West Florida.

Ronald J. Burke is professor of organizational behavior, Faculty of Administration Studies, York University, Canada.

CHAPTER SIX: THE CONTEXT OF BUSINESS

Government Regulation

Michael J. Clarke is a member of the Department of Sociology, University of Liverpool, United Kingdom.

John C. Ruhnka is professor of management at the Graduate School of Business Administration at the University of Colorado at Denver.

Heidi Boerstler is associate professor of health administration, law and ethics at the Graduate School of Business Administration at the University of Colorado, Denver.

Eric W. Orts is on the faculty at the Wharton School, University of Pennsylvania.

The International Marketplace: Bribery

Michael Philips is professor of philosophy at Portland State University.

Thomas L. Carson is associate professor of philosophy at Loyola University of Chicago.

Scott Turow was deputy chief at the Criminal Receiving and Appellate Division of the U.S. Attorney's Office. He is now in private legal practice.

The International Marketplace: Universal Codes of Conduct

Larry R. Smeltzer is professor and chair of the Business Administration Department at Arizona State University.

Marianne M. Jennings is professor of legal and ethical studies at Arizona State University.

John Blake is professor of accounting in the Department of Accounting and Financial Services at the University of Central Lancashire, United Kingdom.

Julia Clarke is a member of the Department of Business Studies, Manchester Metropolitan University, United Kingdom.

Catherine Gowthorpe is principal lecturer in the Department of Accounting and Financial Services at the University of Central Lancashire, United Kingdom.

Timothy K. Larrison is completing his MBA at London Business School after having spent some years working on several continents in the development industry.

chapter one

Introduction: Worldview and the Link to Moral Action

I. THE STRATEGY OF APPLIED ETHICS.

Applied Ethics assumes a theory of normative ethics and a linking principle or principles by which the ethical principles or maxims can be applied in real-life situations. It is a very difficult branch of ethics because it assumes a certain facility with the subject matter of ethics and with the general practical imperatives involved. The series of books, *Basic Ethics in Action,* addresses practical imperatives of the professions. This book examines issues facing the world of business-related professions. Other books in the series address other professional issues such as medical ethics.

I believe that the logical order of presentation begins with an ethical theory that we have chosen, moves to "linking principles," and finishes with a practical directive to action. However, as neat and logical as this order of presentation is, we live in the genetic order of existence that is constantly changing and developing. We also find ourselves changing in order to keep up with these alterations and developments. This means that we must regularly take time to engage in an assessment of our personal understanding of professional practice and ethical theory. Both work together in Business Ethics to create an interdisciplinary attitude. Like all interdisciplinary perspectives, one side is often developed to the exclusion of the other.

For your study of this book, a certain amount of ethical material is prerequisite. This material concerns normative ethical theory. Although some of those issues are briefly addressed here, the discussion is not meant to be comprehensive. My book *Basic Ethics*, the anchor volume of this series, addresses in more detail the material questions that will help you better consider the problems inherent in Applied Ethics. Other books on ethical theory also address these issues. It would be very useful for the student to avail himself of one of these books in order to prepare for studying Applied Ethics. The section "Evaluating a Case Study," a series of essays that follow the core chapters in this volume, gives some help to the student in this regard.

After studying the various ethical theories, you must choose which one to adopt. I believe that this choice is quite important and depends on some self-conscious understanding of your personal worldview. The next section of this chapter briefly discusses some important features of the personal worldview along with the Personal Worldview Imperative, which gives direction to the nature of the worldview a person should adopt.

Finally, after presenting the worldview, the Personal Worldview Imperative, and some key ethical terms, I discuss how these might be integrated with action. At the end of this chapter I present more specifics relating to professional business practice through the interview with Mel Streeter. Later, in Chapter Four, I present one example of a very useful linking principle through my essay on "The Principle of Fair Competition."

II. The Personal Worldview Imperative.

A.

The World was all before them, where to choose
Thir place of rest, and Providence thir guide:
They hand in hand with wand'ring steps and slow,
Through Eden took their solitary way.
                    —Milton, *Paradise Lost*

This is the way the world ends
This is the way the world ends
This is the way the world ends
Not with a bang but with a whimper.
        —T.S. Eliot, "The Hollow Men"

B.

Little Lamb, who made thee?
Dost thou know who made thee?
    —William Blake, "The Lamb"

That bit of filth in dirty walls,
And all around barbed wire,
And 30,000 souls who sleep
Who once will wake
And once will see
Their own blood spilled.

> —Hanus Hachenburg, "Terezin" (1944, just before his death in a Nazi concentration camp at the age of 14).

In these two groups of paired poems, each has a definite *point of view*. Group A begins with an optimistic view of a tragedy (The human fall in the Garden of Eden at the beginning of the world) followed by an angst-ridden view of the end of the world.

Group B presents an innocent view of gentle questioning about the causes of life from the mind of a carefree rural child followed by the queries of a soon-to-be Holocaust victim about the nature of life in death and death in life.

Each passage reflects a different set of assumptions held by the past. In literature, we call this *voice*. As a writer of poetry and fiction (and occasional reviewer of literary novels), myself, I can attest to the fact that the ultimate judgment that we make when reading a piece of fictive literature revolves around the author's voice.

Charles Dickens did not achieve fame on his stylistic writing. In fact, his sentences are often clumsy, and he uses many words improperly. His characters are often wooden and his plots predictable. What sets Dickens apart from others in his century (who were his superior in these departments) is his voice. Dickens's voice is that of a champion for the rights of children and for the rights of the oppressed and against those who through their machinations seek to overreach themselves and grasp goods meant for others. A reader of a Dickens novel is impressed with the clarity of moral vision that suffuses the pages. This sense of literary voice is what I will call the worldview, or *Weltanschauung*.

Voice demarcates the world we enter when we open the covers of a fiction book. The world it presents is an escape, and we assent to it or not according to a myriad of factors. The act of reading is a knowing *suspension of disbelief*. We willingly enter into the author's worldview and test what it is like to be there. This is more than merely becoming a murderer (in a mystery story); a member of the opposite sex; or a person of a different race, religion, or culture; it is accepting a network of beliefs that together express values concerning the critical concerns of life: ethics, politics, religion, aesthetics, and so forth. When the world we enter is welcoming (meaning that it *accords* with some deeply held tenets within our own worldview), we feel comfortable and react positively. When this world is foreign and hostile (meaning that it does not accord with our deeply held tenets within our own worldview), we are uncomfortable and react negatively.

The composition of this worldview web of beliefs is not the same in everyone. Some (probably very few) may have a tree-structured logical pyramid of axiomatic primitives at the top and derivative theorems that follow from them. Others (many more) have an edifice that is *aporitic* in nature (meaning that a number of separate constructs owe their existence to specific problems that have arisen in each person's life). These aporitic constructs often exist in isolation from one another. I am reminded of Wemmick in *Great Expectations,* who had a life in Jaggers's office and another life with the aged-one in the "castle." Wemmick often advised Pip to bring up certain topics with him at one arena or the other, depending on the answer Pip wanted to receive because in each place, Wemmick took on a different worldview. There was (almost) no integration between the two.

I am also reminded of the metaphorical descriptions used by John Ruskin in *The Seven Lamps of Architecture,* in which he declares that the composition of a building should reflect all of the architect's values. Under this view, if the architect's worldview is not well integrated, during the process of design the architect must create a single vision that is true to her materials, function, and execution (or else the project will ultimately be a failure). The construction of the building is a metaphor for how we are to construct *ourselves.* It speaks to personal values and their relationships within our lives. In this way, we can be viewed as the architects of ourselves. Some might believe that this is rather ephemeral for hard-nosed philosophy, but I believe that the ideas of the worldview rest at the edge of traditional philosophical discourse.

It is important for the position I am defending that it be possible for an individual to evaluate his worldview and life plan in a holistic fashion as one of several key components. This holistic approach means that a person cannot separate worldview from philosophy. Some analytic philosophers have suggested that somehow it is possible for philosophy to work independently of any worldviews.[1]

These various views of analytic philosophy depict it as an objective tool that anyone can employ without assuming any of the characteristics, values, or worldview of the practitioner. This position seems wrong to me. I believe that the philosopher always brings her worldview along with her. This is not a position of epistemological relativism but merely an admission that the subjective and objective do not neatly segregate.[2]

Although they are subjective in nature, these worldviews are themselves subject to evaluative criteria. They are formal and logical principles that are virtually devoid of empirical content. Together, these criteria can be put

---

[1]Kai Nielsen discussed this briefly in his article "Philosophy and *Weltanschauung*," *The Journal of Value Inquiry* 27 (1993): 179–186.

[2]This is similar to Quine's insistence that analytic and synthetic truths do not easily segregate. See Willard Quine, "Two Dogmas of Empiricism," *From a Logical Point of View* (Cambridge, MA: Harvard University Press, 1953).

together to form the Personal Worldview Imperative: *"All people must develop a single, comprehensive and internally coherent worldview that is good and that they strive to act out in their daily lives."*[3] In my opinion, every agent acting or potentially acting in the world falls under the normative force of the Personal Worldview Imperative. This principle could probably be analyzed to cover a wide range of axiological issues and may be the topic of some future work, but here I simply highlight three separate criteria that I believe are embedded within the Personal Worldview Imperative and that bear closer examination.

The first criterion is this: *We have a duty to develop and to act out our worldview.* This means that we are expected to choose and fashion a point of view that will do much to condition our day-to-day consciousness. It is not enough merely to accept another's general beliefs and attitudes about ethics, politics, aesthetics, and religion. Doing so would be tantamount to becoming the slave of another. If some modicum of freedom and autonomy is a part of our human nature, and if ultimately we are content only if we act out our human nature (assuming that all wish to be ultimately content), then we should all seek to exercise our freedom in the most practically fundamental way by choosing and fashioning a worldview.

Our power of choice in adopting a worldview may not be absolute, but that does not prevent us from exercising freedom within a limited domain. Let us use another metaphor. Having a limited choice in adopting a worldview would be akin to moving into someone else's house. Suppose that the house had many features that we decided we did not like. We have some money, so we might remodel the house a room at a time, taking care the remodeling concept is in accord with some larger plan or aesthetic point of view. The word *fashion* is meant to embody some of this sense of re-creation or remodeling.

Depending on our circumstances, this process of fashioning a worldview, like remodeling the house, could take a considerable length of time, especially given difficult exterior or interior factors. No two people's tasks are identical.

The second criterion is this: *We have a duty to develop a single worldview that is both comprehensive and internally consistent.* This second duty involves rather prudential concerns of what would count as a serviceable worldview. A worldview that is not unitary and comprehensive might not give us direction at some future time when such direction is sorely needed. We cannot depend on a worldview that is not comprehensive to help us grow and develop in life.

---

[3]Some might contend that my depiction of this imperative places an overreliance on form over content. It is a procedure and thus cannot have normative "content." Against this attack, I reply that although the prescription, by itself, is procedural, it will result in some content. And, if taken in the Socratic spirit of living an examined life, then the force of the normativity is toward participation in a process that must be sincere because it represents each of our very best versions of the "good, true, and beautiful."

Likewise, a worldview that is not internally consistent in the future might offer us contradictory directions of action because each area of inconsistency (call them A and non-A) might develop a line of reasoning that maintains its original character (logical heritability). The resulting "offspring" of A and non-A would also be opposed. If these offspring are imperatives of action, then we are in a dilemma.[4] Such a worldview is inadequate because it may not be able to offer clear direction for action at some time in the future.

The third criterion is this: *We have a duty to create a worldview that is good.* This final criterion is the most difficult to justify in moral terms. Clearly, the word *good* in this instance may mean merely good for the agent's prudential interests. Certainly, we would not want to create a worldview that is self-destructive. Few would argue against the premise that our worldview ought to support a plan of life and development that will be personally advantageous to us. But I assert that the sort of worldview I am talking about should be morally good as well. Such a moral interpretation of the Personal Worldview Imperative is essential if this principle is to be of use in moral analysis.

III. WORLDVIEW INTEGRATION.

The basic approach to worldview integration was suggested in *Basic Ethics*. In that book, I argue that in constructing our worldview, we might combine personal inclinations toward other essential values such as the principles of aesthetics, feminism, religion, and professional practices into a general system of ethics.

Many people actually reside in several self-contained worlds that dictate how they should act in this or that situation. These specifications can often be contradictory. For example, I have been a volunteer baseball coach for youth sports for a number of years. One day I had a baseball game scheduled on a field that was occupied by another team holding a practice. I approached the man running the practice and showed him my permit for the field. He refused to leave and continued with his practice. When the umpires arrived for our game, they confirmed our reservation for the field. But the man holding the practice told us that we would have to call the police to have him evicted from the field.

I was not keen on calling the police[5] and began to exhort the usurper in rational terms. First, I mentioned that he was not setting a good example of reasonableness and good will in front of the children of both teams. Both

---

[4] A moral dilemma occurs when one, through no fault of his own, finds himself in the situation in which the only available choices of action are both evil.

[5] I thought that calling the police to force the man from the field was merely to fight force with force and would represent a defeat for reason. Instead, I presented an argument in a controlled and level tone.

teams that rightfully had the field were being bullied by someone without a permit whose only claim for the field was that he was using it. I asked the man if he believed in societies without the rule of law—for that was what a *krateristic* (might makes right) position amounts to. Then I started naming various *krateristic* regimes in the twentieth century, starting with Joseph Stalin and Adolf Hitler. At the mention of those two names, the man yielded the field.

I found out later that he was the coach of a church-sponsored team and was a prominent lay leader in that church. He was a respected corporate tax lawyer. I believe that when he was doggedly holding a field for which he had no permit, he was in the worldview of the aggressive corporate tax lawyer. However, when I began speaking about lawlessness and historical instances of how *kraterism* has resulted in tyranny, the worldview of the church leader took over and he yielded the field.

This man lived in at least two different worlds. Each world contained its own practices and endorsed different approaches to solving problems. It was also probable that each of these worlds had little interaction with the other. The Personal Worldview Imperative calls for us to create a single worldview. This means that people who hold multiple worldviews that refer, in turn, to multiple and contradictory practices must work to create unity and coherence among these worldviews. By integrating these various beliefs, general attitudes, and life values, these people confront the world more authentically than they did when their worldviews were fragmented. Such a process of integration obviously requires introspection and self-knowledge.

Another similar example occurs when someone who has a serviceable single worldview makes certain exceptions now and again for activities that the worldview explicitly forbids. This is not an instance of weakness of the will (in which the person maintains her worldview but fails to carry out its prescriptions because she is overwhelmed by contrary desires) but is a set of ad hoc amendments to the worldview that are patently inconsistent with its other tenets. Consider a person who has a general rule against belittling people because of their national origin or religion. But this person harasses an employee in a manner that directly contradicts his general rule. He forms a new amendment to his worldview that allows him to act in this way. Obviously, this is an instance of incoherence and thus disallowed by the Personal Worldview Imperative.

In the process of integration, we relate the empirical world (in which we live and make sense of by continually wrestling and striving with these issues) to various more abstract principles in such a way that life becomes rationally comprehensible. I compare this process to an artist painting a picture or a poet writing a poem. In each case, we are (as Hamlet said) holding a mirror up to nature. However, the imitation itself—the artifact—may vary. Thus, Jan Van Eyck, Claude Monet, and Wassily Kandinsky might all paint one particular scene differently.

Consider John Donne, John Dryden, or Anthony Hecht. Each would create a poem describing a common event[6] in his own way. The reason for this is that (a) each views the event in an objective way as to the measurement of sounds and colors but (b) each also arranges these details somewhat differently according to an order based on a value-laden worldview. The result is an artifact about which the group could come to some factual agreement if queried in a court of law but which each would describe differently. The significance of the whole and of the way the parts are arranged to make up the whole varies.

Also consider the way different peoples have reacted to the human condition to create religion. If such a reaction were a transparent process of merely translating either a revelation (of God) or a reaction to some common human need, then one would expect that there would be one and only one religion, but this is obviously not the case. The reason is that (as with the painters and the poets) people react to the same revelation or human need differently.[7] Thus, we have various religions in the world (their number is almost as great as that of the variety of artistic schools of expression).

These examples express some of the relationships among (a) worldview, (b) empirical events, and (c) other theoretical constructs. Together, I call these *interactions:* integration through the process of dialectical interaction.[8]

This integration will have two important manifestations in the way we apply ethical theories: First is the way we integrate empirical events into theoretical categories (dialectical subsumption) given our worldview. Second is the way we match our ethical imperatives with our worldview. Let us discuss each of these briefly and then examine the process of applying an ethical theory.

The first manifestation is the way we integrate empirical events into theoretical categories (dialectical subsumption) given our worldview. Dialectical subsumption is the interactive process by which objects are schematized into our consciousness. The best way to describe dialectical subsumption is to contrast it to mechanical subsumption. In mechanical subsumption, a class, alpha, has certain membership requirements (e.g., possession of trait phi). When any x has phi, it belongs to alpha. The entire process is termed *mechanical* because it is a simple mechanism of sorting things where they belong according to some preestablished set of rules. The decision procedure is certain so that the procedure could be performed on a sample space so that it would be exhaustive

---

[6]Obviously, this is a thought experiment. The point of putting people of different styles and historical eras together is to highlight how important the component of worldview is in the way we process empirical data.

[7]This analogy may be objectionable to advocates of a religion who believe that their particular version is the only one of any true value. They would object to the aesthetic model I am creating here and prefer a more scientific one.

[8]See *Basic Ethics*, Chapter Eight, for an exposition of the various sorts of dialectical processes relevant here.

and complete. This model of mechanical subsumption may be possible in mathematics and computer modeling. It is often used to give fullness to certain theories in some of the social sciences (especially economics!).

Unfortunately, mechanical subsumption is largely a priori in character.[9] This means that instead of interacting with the data in a carefully refining, bootstrapping operation, the practitioners intend a simple process of observing whether x possesses phi and, if it does, putting it into alpha.

Dialectical subsumption is more complicated than this. Let us consider two further arguments along this line: (a) ascription of properties to some object is a complicated process involving the worldview of the observer and (b) the manner by which the observer inserts the object into a category is also theory laden (meaning that it is connected to the observer's worldview).

A. First Form.

My first argument is that the ascription of properties is not a simple procedure. Although the painters Cranach and Turner may agree that the sunset is red, they may mean different things by this. Cranach may consider the sunset as a carefully circumscribed aspect of the third ground or background of the painting's composition while Turner may say that there is only one ground and that the sunset affects everything. The "what it is" is intricately connected to the "way it behaves." Thus, the ascription of properties includes more than a simple list of properties in some mechanical, objective manner. Instead, how the properties exist within the entire composition and the interaction of these into some environmental context must be considered. Both of these conditions are necessary to really understand the properties of some object.

An example of the linkage between the object and its activity is the identification of function along with morphology in evolutionary biology. Without function, the shapes, colors, and sizes are not completely described. The what it is is conditioned by the way it behaves. Both are necessary to understand homology in an evolutionary context. This means that the ascription of properties is not a simple, objective procedure without a connection to the observer's worldview. In the examples cited, a person's theoretical dispositions condition the way the person depicts the object itself.

These examples illustrate that the ascription of properties is not as straightforward as the mechanical subsumptionists would have us believe. Dialectical subsumption is a procedure that is informed by an individual's

---

[9]Although mechanical subsumption is widely used in diverse fields from legal positivism to econometrics to some theories of zoological systematics, it has been attacked by others as well. The reader is invited to examine some of these in context. Two diverse examples can be cited: in law by Ronald Dworkin, *Taking Rights Seriously* (Cambridge, MA: Harvard University Press, 1977), chaps. 2 & 3; and in evolutionary biology by Ernst Mayr, *Toward a New Philosophy of Biology* (Cambridge, MA: Harvard University Press, 1988), pt. 5.

worldview. The way that the observer understands the object is colored by the way the observer understands the object to behave. The way that the object behaves is conditioned by the observer's theoretical assumptions about this object and objects like it. Finally, an individual's theoretical assumption about general laws governing existing entities is a major component of that person's worldview.

B. Second Form.

The manner by which we insert the aforesaid object into a category is also theory laden (meaning that it is connected to the worldview of the observer). In many ways, this second form is similar to the first. The second form involves fitting unknown individuals into preestablished categories. This contrasts with the first form that seeks to identify objects and to ascribe to them certain traits and properties.

In biology, the second form is called *taxonomy* and the theory governing the process is called *systematics*. A person identifying some individual to determine what group it belongs to ascribes certain traits to it and uses that description to match (or approximate) its membership into some higher class (thus employing the first form). Sometimes this task is rather delicate; often the individual object is not clearly in a single subspecies but may possess traits of two or more subspecies. In these cases, the observer must make a judgment about the physical traits that are most significant, which is relative to the function of the part in question. Thus, the observer is ranking morphological traits based on theoretical assumptions about functional efficacy.

This is just like the first form in which the observer harbored certain more general theoretical assumptions to help form a judgment about what traits an object possessed and how they were to be described. In the second form, also, the observer uses a more general context (i.e., theoretical assumptions, a part of one's worldview), which is the justification for putting the object into this or that taxonomological category.

Thus, both the ascription of properties to the object (the first form) and the act of placing the object into its appropriate category (the second form) are connected to the observer's worldview. This means that the mechanical subsumption model is false.

The alternative to the mechanical subsumption hypothesis is the *dialectical subsumption* thesis. According to it, the observer moves back and forth between the object and her understanding of the object (including all of her theoretical assumptions) until the nature of the object can be determined. When a dissonance occurs between the object as preconceived and the object as dialectically understood, the latter trumps the former.

The second manifestation *is the way we match our ethical imperatives with our worldview.* The dialectical process of matching ethical imperatives with our worldview is outlined in Chapter Eight of *Basic Ethics*. What is the driving force behind this dialectic? What might cause an individual to accept certain courses of action and to reject others? For the answer to these questions, we must return to the Personal Worldview Imperative. This dissonance may occur when a theory suggests that the individual do x, but x is contrary to certain core values that this person holds. Let us examine two examples to see how this dissonance occurs.

Example One.

Max is a guard at a Nazi concentration camp. His superiors have given him a directive to shoot a dozen Jewish prisoners because the camp needs to meet its production requirements. Max marches the prisoners to a corner of the camp that is under repair and from which they could escape if he would turn away. He would never be detected if he shot his gun in the air and allowed them to escape because little attention is paid to the disposal of bodies (since this camp kills hundreds each day).

Max has been taught by his mother that human life is sacred. He knows that these Jews have committed no crimes except being at the wrong place at the wrong time. Therefore, Max believes that killing these people is wrong; he also knows that he has a prima facie duty to obey his superiors. It is a time of war and he has his orders. He is inclined to let the prisoners escape, but the law says that he should not.

Example Two.

Sally is an American woman who has grown up in poverty in Appalachia. She had always been close to her mother, who told her that African Americans and Affirmative Action were responsible for her father losing his job and committing suicide as a result. Sally is now a sergeant in the Army and has some African Americans under her command. Military regulations require that all soldiers be treated equally regardless of race. However, she has the opportunity to make the lives of these African Americans in her command very difficult as payback for what happened to her father. She is inclined to "give them hell"; regulations say that she should not.

These two examples are complementary. In the first case, Max's personal worldview may cause him to disobey the law to do the right thing. In the second case, Sally's personal worldview may cause her to disobey the law to do a bad thing. What are we to make of this?

The first question to be asked is whether the Personal Worldview Imperative has been engaged in either case. If Max and Sally had never examined their convictions, should they break the law, they probably would act according to some idea of punishment and reward. In other words, if both are convinced that the law would not punish them, they would probably follow their worldview. But what of this worldview? How responsible are they for it? Was it not merely handed to them by another?

Socrates' dictum—the unexamined life is not worth living—lies at the heart of the Personal Worldview Imperative. I contend that if Max had examined his worldview as suggested by the Personal Worldview Imperative, he would have assumed ownership for his values. In that case, clearly he would not have performed the dissonant action of killing his prisoners. The conflict would be resolved in favor of the worldview.

Sally's case is more challenging; her worldview is incoherent. If she were to consider everything she believes in, that is, (a) that no biologically significant difference between the races exists, (b) that what happened to her father was an instance of an individual affected by a large government policy (which was not established by African Americans), and (c) that no logical link exists between what happened to her father and these people now in her command. Such an introspective inventory would surely cause Sally to change her worldview. According to the Personal Worldview Imperative, we must strive to make our worldview coherent. If Sally accepts this challenge, she would alter her beliefs.

What if Sally does not alter them? In this case, she would be a pawn of her mother's value system. Her responsibility for her immoral treatment of her subordinates would still fall to her because she failed to examine her life (via the Personal Worldview Imperative). Her real flaw would be living an inauthentic existence as a slave to another (in this case her mother). All the consequences of this initial choice also may be attributed to Sally. She is actually responsible even if the paradigm she used to guide her actions came from another.[10] This is the description of the material conditions of agency. How we treat Sally as to her culpability of action is another issue. We may determine that circumstances influenced her failure to examine her life.

I believe that all immoral worldviews that are examined according to the Personal Worldview Imperative will be revised. This is so because I believe that only moral worldviews will satisfy the conditions of rationality, such as those described in the Personal Worldview Imperative.

In this way, the Personal Worldview Imperative offers a necessary basis for any moral theory. Therefore, I can write this introduction without knowing the moral theory of a practitioner. If he has adopted the Personal Worldview Imperative completely, then it will condition the version of any ethical theory into one that will be serviceable to him or any other agent.

This does not mean that all theories are to be judged as equally correct (see my earlier discussion of painters and poets). No, an individual's world-

---

[10]Of course, some would disagree that we really have as much choice as I have portrayed. A pointed rebuttal of my position in this regard has been made by Anita Allen, "Confronting Moral Theories: Gewirth in Context" in Michael Boylan, ed., *Gewirth: Critical Essays in Action, Rationality, and Community* (New York: Rowman and Littlefield, 1999).

view will dictate that Deontology, Utilitarianism, Intuitionism, or Virtue Ethics is *the* correct theory. The Personal Worldview Imperative allows this judgment to be made. However, the version of this theory (whichever is chosen) will also be conditioned by the Personal Worldview Imperative. An example of this is the emphasis on both understanding and justification (see *Basic Ethics*, Chapter Eight).

In this way, the Personal Worldview Imperative is not a full-blown theory, but an important element to consider when considering questions of metaethics, Normative Ethics, and Applied Ethics. It may offer a bridge between often inaccessible theories and the real lives of people who wish to consider ethical issues.

IV. Decision Making.

Figure 1.1 is a version of the process that I believe should be performed when an individual decides to apply an ethical theory. The process begins when the individual must make a decision that has ethical implications. The process is a rather simplified version of how I believe we should apply any ethical theory.

What can be highlighted about this process is that it emphasizes the sincerity of the individual in following his conscience. "Con-science" means the gathering of a person's exact understandings. This congregation of knowledge is really one form of worldview. Thus, to act according to conscience (in this sense) means to act so that the person's core beliefs are not violated by the proposed action.

It is important to relate the gravity of the proposed action to the primary nature of the core beliefs. For example if an individual were considering parting her hair from behind or eating a peach, the intended action is clearly rather trivial. If such actions were ethically offensive to the person's core beliefs, then there would be no question that they would be prohibited. Likewise, if the action in question were serious (e.g., Sally's dilemma discussed earlier) and the worldview impediment were relatively trivial, the decision would be easy.[11]

When the ethical issue is serious and the conflicting value is primary (e.g., abortion, the death penalty, euthanasia), the situation is most challenging. When this occurs, the individual must do his best to be true to his conscience/worldview. If the worldview has been carefully crafted according to the steps listed in Figure 1.1, then this touchstone should represent the person's own best approximation of those values that together are most important in life.

---

[11]A further discussion of this type of analysis can be found in each of the accompanying volumes to this series. See: the Evaluating a Case Study series of essays.

Step One: The agent identifies the problematic situation in all its particularity, including any possible ethical issues.

Step Two: The agent identifies relevant moral rules in which he believes.

Step Three: The individual engages in dialectical subsumption of the ethical issues in step one, relating them to the rule identified in step two (see the last section for a discussion of dialectical subsumption).*

Step Four: The operation of step three will produce a provisional action directive (i.e., an ethical imperative for action).

Step Five: The individual matches his provisional action directive from step four with his worldview (as discussed in the last section).

Step Six (a): If the provisional action directive fits with his worldview according to the criteria of the Personal Worldview Imperative, he has an ethical imperative for action.

Step Six (b): If the provisional action directive does not fit with the individual's worldview according to the criteria of the Personal Worldview Imperative, he must return to step three.

Step Seven (a): If the difficulty can be resolved by further dialectical subsumption (following his worldview examination in step five), he has an ethical imperative for action.

Step Seven (b): If the difficulty cannot be resolved by further dialectical subsumption, the individual must return to step five and repeat the process.

Step Eight (a): If the difficulty can be resolved, he has an ethical imperative for action.

Step Eight (b): If the difficulty cannot be resolved, steps six (b) and seven (b) should be repeated until the problem is resolved or an impasse is reached.

Step Nine: In the event of an impasse, the individual returns to the process of choosing an ethical theory and repeats that process.

*When step three occurs as mechanical subsumption, the model is more similar to logically abstract single principled theory models discussed in *Basic Ethics*, Chapter Eight.

Figure 1.1 The Process of Applying an Ethical Theory

If there truly are a right and a wrong in human conduct, then we can imagine the four situations shown in Figure 1.2. In the first alternative, the individual has a good motive [it is fully consonant with her worldview and the relevant ethical principle(s); see steps three and five in Figure 1.1] and a good action.

	Motive/Action	
Motive/Action	1. Good/Good	2. Good/Bad
	3. Bad/Good	4. Bad/Bad

FIGURE 1.2 A Matrix of Actions and Motives

The second alternative suggests a good motivation with a bad action (the person sincerely believed that what he was doing was correct, but it really was not).[12] The significance of this second alternative contrasts with the third alternative (bad motivation and an accidentally good action). The real issue is engaged at this point. I believe that acting in accordance with one's worldview is the most important criterion. If this means that he commits a bad action, at least he is doing the best he could; it was sincerely executed. The possibility that the action might turn out to be the best does not lend any credit to the individual who has acted against his best inclinations.[13]

The basis of this judgment is the Personal Worldview Imperative. When an individual accepts the fact that she must examiner her life and develop a single, comprehensive, and internally coherent worldview that she must strive to act out in her life, then she has self-consciously agreed that this exercise of autonomy and freedom is what we should do. Such behavior defines us as humans in a more comprehensive way than even saying that we are "rational animals" because the Personal Worldview Imperative specifies the *manner* of executing our rationality. It is more holistic and ties people to abstract, atemporal logic, to an intellectual tradition, and to various cultural and personal values that jointly describe who we are.

As Figure 1.2 illustrates, an individual goes through this process by engaging in both dialectical subsumption (which commits that individual to create a bridge between the particular action at hand and various principles that enrich and give meaning to his understanding of that action)[14] and in the worldview check. This check is analogous to the procedure of balancing a checkbook. We all do some quick mental arithmetic to estimate what our total

---

[12]Whether something is or is not a good action in this context is a thought experiment to make a point about the relationships between conscience/worldview and the act itself. Some would contend that the only way to determine whether an action is right or wrong is to apply the appropriate operational criteria to it. In this case, there is no right or wrong apart from the successful execution of said operation. This point of view could negate the force of my thought experiment unless one were willing to allow the posit that an action *was* actually right apart from some agent's deliberations on the subject.

[13]For an example of this, see the excerpt from H.G. Wells's *The History of Mr. Polly*. Michael Boylan, ed., *Perspectives in Philosophy* (New York: Harcourt Brace, 1993), pp. 379–88. Mr. Polly intends to commit suicide and ends up a hero. Was it right to treat him as a hero?

[14]This process is also similar to Paul Ricoeur's view of the role of the productive imagination in the A-version of Kant's schematicism.

should be and then we go through the mechanics of adding and subtracting. If our mechanical total is quite different from our original guess, we suspect a mistake and repeat the procedure. This process is similar to the worldview check, which offers a check and balance against improper calculations. This is so because we live in our worldview, and we accept it as being what we want—even if we do not always fully execute its demands.

We could use the vernacular expression, "Is this really *me?*" to describe this interaction in another way. If it is not me, then I should not do it—or I should redefine who me is. Thus, the ultimate authority of action is always the subject (the "me") because the me will be responsible. It is the "me" who will have to live with the action taken.

Thus, the short answer to how to apply an ethical theory is that an individual should strive to be (a) true to the moral theory she or he has chosen, (b) as thorough as possible (according to some sort of scale of proportionality of ethical gravity) in her or his application process (especially steps one through five in Figure 1.1) and (c) as open as possible to altering or changing his or her ethical theory according to the interactions of the *entirety* of her or his worldview. It seems to me that this is what we can and should expect of everyone. No more. No less.

Interview with Mel Streeter, AIA

Mel Streeter has more than forty-two years of experience as an award-winning architect. He first established his own architectural practice, known then as Mel Streeter Architects, in 1967; it has since been renamed Streeter and Associates. With a staff of many colors and cultures, the firm collaborates with clients and engineers in designing public facilities that reflect the diversity of the region's communities. The firm is the largest African American–owned architecture practice in the Pacific Northwest.

Notable public projects designed by Mr. Streeter's firm include the Auburn City Hall, the Federal Aviation Administration Building at Boeing Field, all administrative and maintenance facilities at the West Point Treatment Plant, and three buildings at the Everett Naval Station. Under Mr. Streeter's guidance, Streeter and Associates has been responsible for the design of the new African American Academy for the Seattle School District and is on the team designing Seattle's new baseball and football stadiums.

THE INTERVIEW

Part One: The Origin of Values

Q: So where do we begin when we discuss ethical issues in business?
A: I would say that it is the formation of what you term the Personal Worldview. Everyone forms a worldview of sorts when he or she is growing up. In my own case, I was very lucky to have been schooled in values by my mother and grandmother. They taught me a number of lessons that shaped my worldview. Of particular note would be my mother's maxim that we should always trust our fellow man until he proves himself to be untrustworthy. That is an important principle that covers a wide range of cases.

Many (perhaps most) people take just the opposite position. They distrust you until you prove yourself. But this is too narrow a view, in my opinion. There may be many good people who can be lost under that attitude and it encourages prejudice. Thus, I would rather allow myself to be burned a certain number of times in the hope that I am giving everyone I meet an even break.

A second principle that comes to mind comes from my grandmother. She taught me to always search for the good in people. If a person looks for the good in a difficult business situation or personal conformation, then it can be a means of building bridges and creating community. When a person is always looking for the bad, then he isolates himself and we dismantle community. As an architect of public buildings, I like to think of myself as a facilitator of community, not one of its enemies.

Q: In this way, a moral principle (looking for the good in people) actually helps you to be better at your profession.
A: That's right. It reinforces my personal professional vision—which gets back to worldview again.

Q: So for you, having a good, solid upbringing has helped form your values as an adult.
A: Yes. It is always easier when one has such lessons at a young age from those he trusts. For those lacking such a background, it is harder—not impossible, but harder.

However, a good background is not enough. A person needs to validate those principles in his experience. As he lives his life, things happen to him. These events demand to be interpreted. In that process, one can see whether the principles he has been given as a child are true or not.

Q: Do you think everyone interprets the events that happen to him?
A: Yes, to a greater or lesser degree, depending on the person. It is this process that I understand your Personal Worldview Imperative to be about: checking one's personal values against hard lessons of life. Do they support those principles or is an adjustment in order? This is subject to constant revision.

Q: Has this process of revision caused you to create or highlight any new principles?
A: "Highlight" is a better word for it than "create" in my case. Certainly, the concepts of justice and fairness come to mind as having been brought to the fore as a result of my experiences in life.

Q: Can you cite a concrete example that illustrates your understanding of justice and fairness?
A: Yes. One contemporary issue is the compensation of corporate executives. I am certainly an advocate of capitalism, but even capitalism seeks to reward people on how much they produce. You cannot convince me that American executives produce that much more than their Asian counterparts to be paid three to five times more. There is no legitimate reason based on capitalism that can justify this. It goes contrary to that theory of justice (capitalism) and in doing so, it is unfair.

Q: Why does it happen?
A: Greed and power. Those at the top of corporate America are very powerful and their position often generates enormous greed. As a result, those executives do not look toward the real good of the company (and the community it represents) but instead look only to their own pocketbooks.

Individualism in most contexts is a good thing, but it becomes malignant when it transforms into selfish egoism. In these cases, the individual forgets the greater good of the community. He's so involved with himself that the universe has only one authentic member.

Since justice (the way I conceive of it) is inclusive of others in its very formulation, this would counteract such selfish egoists.

Part Two: Applied Ethical Issues

Q: Perhaps we could consider briefly some of the major themes that will be discussed in this book. First is the question of how we should think of a corporation. Is it merely some abstract piece of property that is meant to shield everyone who is associated with it, or should we create a different model?

A: I think you point to a real difficulty that exists. Often people want to shift responsibility away from themselves. The "buck" always stops somewhere else. But this is wrong. Obviously, *people* make the operating decisions within any corporation. People create the strategic goals. People implement those goals. Therefore, people must be responsible when things go wrong. In your introduction, you cite an example from the Holocaust. This was a classic instance of people who committed horrific actions without taking any responsibility: "I was only following orders." Or take the case of lynching in the South. Somehow, if a group did the deed, no single person was responsible. The action happened, but no one is accountable! This is ridiculous. We must find a way to create accountability.

One way to do this might be to hold the directors and officers of a corporation personally responsible for its misdeeds. There are limits, of course, to this suggestion. In today's America, many frivolous lawsuits are filed by shareholders and others against corporate boards (generally because share prices have gone down or because someone wants to get rich by a tidy settlement), but these civil cases could be accommodated by insurance. The real meat of this would be criminal accountability: up and down the line of command of everyone who has implemented criminal policies. If everyone's head were on the block, people might not act as if they left their humanity at the door when they reported to work.

Q: What about the role of competition in business? Do you think that it often drives people away from honest business practices?

A: There is no question about it. If you are competing with fewer constraints on your bottom line (because you are unethical), you can come in with a lower bid. Or you come in with a lower bid intending not to fulfill everything you promised. Both of these approaches are wrong—but the reason they continue is that those who employ this strategy often win the contracts.

All of this seems rather gloomy; however, let me tell you that I think most of these types get caught. I have a personal anecdote about a large contractor who operated in this fashion and was an unabashed racist. This man would tell nasty jokes about minorities at "public" social gatherings such as cocktail parties where important figures were invited. Despite the public nature of the gatherings, this man would joke and smear minorities in a thoroughly deprecating fashion. This man cheated on his public business and as a private person he held these ignorant views and flaunted them!

You can imagine how I felt as an African American when he would slur people of my race in his bigoted tirades. Well, this character flaw came home to roost. You might say he failed the Personal Worldview Imperative. The man's sins finally caught up with him, and he went bankrupt. Those he had cheated and those he had ridiculed shed no tears at his demise.

I think that this is more often the situation than not. There is some defect in these folks that will generally bring them down—but this is not always the case. Some will "get away with it" forever.

Q: And do you think these people are happy?
A: Happy, no. They have a bigger house than they had five years ago—maybe with a pool. That's all they care about. When that's all you care about, you are never truly happy.

Q: Perhaps in that way they have traded their own humanity for a house with a pool?
A: That's right.

Q: But would you agree with me that such individuals try to compartmentalize themselves? At least, that is their fiction. They say, "I am one person at the office and another person at home."
A: They may say it; they may think it; but it isn't so. A person's character is more powerful than that. You can't turn it on and off. As I've said, most will fall, but those who don't, unfortunately, give a bad example to others.

Q: One of the issues I raise in Chapter Four concerns particular business practices as seen in the light of a professional standard. What do you think about the concept of a professional standard by which to judge business ethics?
A: Well, of course, it is commonplace to think of professional standards in terms of normal job performance. If you are an apprentice carpenter, we can expect certain things of you and likewise of a journeyman and master carpenter. I would not be averse to applying such standards to ethical considerations, as well. I think that the community in which one lives makes such judgments and bases opinions on something. What I find intriguing is the mixing of normal job criteria with moral judgments. They are a seamless whole, and that's the way it has to be.

Q: What if we took an example—say advertising. What would the application of this be like?
A: One example might be a gun manufacturer. Say I was head of an advertising agency and a potential client approached me ready to pay top dollar for my services, but the problem was that he was a gun manufacturer and I personally believe in tight gun control laws. Well, this potential client's business

is squarely against my ethical beliefs and personal values. I cannot take him on as a client.

Q: Won't he say that his money is just as green as someone else's?
A: Money alone has never been the bottom line with me. That is the problem with many businesspeople. They try to fit ethics in around making money. First of all, you have to live with yourself, your spouse, your family, and the community in which you live. This is the true bottom line.

If that person offends my ethics and personal values, then I cannot take him as a client. And I'll tell you that in my forty-plus years in business, I've tried to hold to just that. Now I know that some say that I shouldn't be the one to judge a potential client—that's not my role. Many lawyers and accountants make such arguments. But that's not the way I see it. I cannot relegate myself to being some automatic puppet for someone else. First and last, I am a person. And that person believes in values.

Q: What about the issue of employee working conditions?
A: This issue begins with the people you hire. You may know that the field of architecture is dominated by white males. Most firms are very homogeneous. I believe that America is a diverse country so that if I want to serve people properly, I should be diverse as well. And that is what I have done. I go to great lengths to recruit personnel to achieve a gender, racial, and ethnic balance. I believe this is right to do and it makes good business sense. Diverse perspectives yield excellence.

When you go out of your way to hire the right personnel and you treat them as people, then most of your working condition problems vanish. Better to emphasize the right general attitude than to worry about a myriad of sometimes conflicting regulations. When you act in good faith, you will not have employee disgruntlement.

Another point that can cause bad feelings among employees is too great a disparity in wages from the bottom to the top of the company. You were mentioning Plato's idea to me earlier about ten times being a good differential to which to adhere.[1] I could buy into that. It is all a part of building a community in your company. People are willing to work hard when they feel that the whole system is set up fairly.

Compensation is an important component of this.

Q: Where do you stand on the issue of government regulation?
A: I guess you would say that I take a middle-of-the-road position regarding government regulation. On the one hand, everyone knows that each time you

---

[1]A ten times differential would mean that if the lowest-paid person in the company was making $25,000, the highest-paid person in the company would make $250,000 (maximum).

pass a regulation, you create an inefficiency. There is one more hoop to jump through and more paperwork to execute. This can be burdensome—especially on small businesses.

Also, if you let government bureaucracy grow (as unchecked regulation is apt to do), then you can get a situation in which nonprofessional bureaucrats are telling professional businesspeople what they should do. We need only look at the situation in health care today (in which doctors are being told what to do by insurance company bureaucrats) to see the danger in this approach.

On the other hand, you cannot let the marketplace run free without check. This is tantamount to allowing the powerful to do whatever they want. In such a situation, greed and selfish egoism will run rampant. This is totally unacceptable. In such a situation, business ethics will be the province of only those lucky survivors.

I believe that the balance between these has to be justice and fairness. There must be a sensitivity to efficiency, but in the end, the rule of right must trump all other considerations.

Q: It is a given that the future economy will be (if it is not already) a global economy. What are some challenges that face businesspeople in this new environment?
A: Let me answer your question in two ways: (a) the present and (b) the future.

First, let's address the present. At this moment, the world is filled with people who have constructed worldviews—many according to the Personal Worldview Imperative. These worldviews are really diverse. Many conflict with each other on key points. This can pose interesting problems for philosophers like you, but for businesspeople, it poses difficult problems. One of these is the issue of bribes. Quite a few countries require paying a bribe to do business. For them, it is only the fulfillment of a societal custom. For a U.S. businessperson, it constitutes a possible violation of U.S. law and an unethical creation of an uncompetitive business practice. When one accepts money from a client, he has an automatic bias toward awarding the contract to that individual. This seems to leap frog the normal, expected contract process. Thus, bribes are uncompetitive.

Whenever one creates a bidding situation in which certain ground rules are laid, anything that undermines the process is unfair to the process. As I've said earlier, fairness is one of the key principles of business ethics. Thus, bribes undermine business ethics at an important point.

I can tell you straight out that I have had several lucrative business opportunities in Asian countries that I had to bow out of because they expected me to participate in the bribing process. Ultimately, it's not just a cultural custom, it's unfair. Remember that the bottom line is not making the most money.

Q: What about the future of international business?
A: Of course, I do not possess a crystal ball, but I do believe that some sort of consensus on the ground rules of doing business is in order. This would constitute a large-scale endeavor and would take years, but once established, it would allow for fair competition in the international arena. Obviously, part of the process would have to be enforcement mechanisms.

Q: How realistic is such standardization of business practice?
A: It is not as far fetched as you may think. This is because of the process of socialization between countries. As people meet and interact, they come to some common understandings. These understandings occur when the various peoples do as my grandmother advocated and see the good in each person. Once this occurs, a trust is formed, and my mother's maxim that we should always trust our fellow man until he proves himself to be untrustworthy will come into play. At that point, real progress on the international level can become possible.

chapter two

Four Ethical Theories

I. Overview.

This chapter introduces the reader to some basic terminology and a brief sketch of Intuitionism, Virtue Ethics, Utilitarianism, and Deontology. Each theory section is followed by an exercise intended to facilitate the reader's understanding of how to integrate that theory into her day-to-day understanding of how life might be if she went to adopt that particular theory. At the end of this chapter are some additional exercises. I believe that this worldview approach is essential in authentically choosing an ethical theory.

II. Some Key Ethical Terms.

A. Metaethics.

Metaethics refers to the most general investigation about how to go about creating and applying a theory that prescribes how we should act. Many issues and discussions have developed in this area of ethical study—more than can be set out in such a brief treatment as this; however, in the depiction of the ethical theories, themselves, the reader should refer to Chapters One through Four of *Basic Ethics*.

One central issue concerns the *origins* of the theories. This, in turn, engenders several related questions: How do we know these theories are correct? How are these theories justified? What do these theories tell us about the world?

These (and other) questions are important because they set the stage for our being able to construct a normative theory of ethics. In this way, metaethics serves Normative Ethics just as philosophy of science serves those who create theories of science. There is a sense of creating the boundaries of acceptable discourse.

One of the principal questions in metaethics in the twentieth century was whether you could derive an "ought" statement from an "is" statement. If you cannot, then "oughts" occur from nonfactual (i.e., nonrational) sources. Why do people hold such a position? Let us examine this through an example.

Premise—John says to Mary, "There is a poisonous cobra under your chair."

Conclusion—John then says, "You ought to get out of your chair and run" or, more simply, "Get out of your chair and run!"

What is the relationship between the premise and the conclusion? On first glance, it might seem as if the factual premise 1 implies the normative action-guiding conclusion. In this case, we would have an "is" (or factual statement) implying an "ought" (or prescriptive statement).

However, others might demur. They would say that there are suppressed premises in this paradigm. These might include the following:

1′.   A poisonous cobra will kill you.
1″.   You do not wish to be killed.
1‴.   The only way to avoid being killed is to get out of your chair and run.

Premise 1′ and 1‴ are both factual statements, but 1″ is a suppressed premise that is also normative. The whole argument would go differently if one were to assert that *he or she were indifferent to being killed.* This means that 1″ is really equivalent to "You *ought* not wish to be killed." In this way, the detractor would contend that a hidden *ought* has been smuggled into the premises. If this is true, then one has not derived an ought from an is but an *ought* from an *ought.*

Thus, the detractor of there being a derivation of an ought from an is would assert that in every supposed example of such a purported derivation, there is a suppressed premise that contains a "hidden 'ought.'"

There are other important questions in metaethics. For example, per-haps the basis of ethical value cannot be determined rationally. Those who would make such an assertion fall into two camps: (a) the cognitivists who emphasize the role of rationally informed emotions such as sympathy and care (as in ethical feminism) and (b) the noncognitivists.

The noncognitivists believe that the basis of ethical theory is not legiti-mately in knowledge. In a deep sense, it is a matter of "taste." For example, few of us would contend that there is an intellectual basis for liking Fortnum and Mason's Irish Breakfast Tea over Brewley's variety of the same. Some pre-fer the softer taste of the former, while others choose the sharper, tannic aspect of the latter.

The noncognitivists contend that no matter how hard one tries, mat-ters of value cannot be traced back to matters of fact. For example, in the pre-ceding example concerning tea, one could say that good tea has a sharper, tannic taste; therefore, Brewley's is better. However, the critic would con-tend, how do we know that sharper and tannic are better and how do we measure them? This can be a problem, the noncognitivists contend. There is *no* pure standard for good tea to which all would agree; this is why we have so many types of tea!

I will not elaborate on various other noncognitivist strategies here—such as linguistic analysis and emotivism. For a more detailed treatment, I refer the reader to *Basic Ethics* or other general books that treat issues of metaethics.

B. Normative Ethics.

Normative Ethics concerns itself with creating[1] norms or standards of human conduct. Each of the theories in Normative Ethics comes complete with its own internal justification and metaethical assumptions. There are many important normative theories, but this abbreviated treatment presents only four: Intuitionism, Virtue Ethics, Utilitarianism, and Deontology. In ad-dition to these traditional theories, various modifications of these theories have been made that include Feminism, Religion and Ethics, and Professional Ethics.[2] Each case has a prescriptive set of directives that are designed to offer judgments about our actions.

---

[1]I use the word *creating* here because (like Kant) I believe that we legislate moral maxims over a universal sample space. Those who would advocate Virtue Ethics or Utilitarianism would demur because for them the process is not one of creating but one of scientific discovery. Emo-tivists would also concur.

[2]It should be acknowledged that many advocates of Feminism, Religious Ethics, and Pro-fessional Ethics would criticize me here by saying that their theories are not "overlays" to some other theory but should stand by themselves. I would concur that this is one way to view these theories. However, I would add that in my treatment, their status would be as an overlay to en-rich other theories.

C. Applied Ethics.

Applied Ethics covers ethics in action. Actual ethical decision making occurs on this level. Ethics in action is a study of the way we *ought* to make decisions in the business world in dealing with problems that have ethical content (i.e., touch on the right and wrong in human action). Just what counts as "right" and "wrong" is determined by a normative theory. Thus, Applied Ethics is an interdisciplinary arena in which all the rules of prudent professional decision making are confronted with another parameter—ethical considerations. Thus, from the outset, Applied Ethics deals with all the realities of real business decisions.

The context that enables this choice to occur effectively is normative theory. Thus, Applied Ethics bounces back and forth between the front line of decision making and the Normative Ethics that supports this process. This series of books, *Basic Ethics in Action*, embodies this dynamic. It consciously moves back and forth between Normative and Applied Ethics.

III. INTUITIONISM.

Ethical Intuitionism can be described as a theory of justification based on the immediate grasping of self-evident ethical truths. Ethical Intuitionism can operate on the level of general principles or on the level of daily decision making. In this latter mode, many of us have experienced a form of Ethical Intuitionism through the teaching of timeless adages such as Look before you leap, and Faint heart never won fair maiden. The truth of these sayings is justified through intuition. Many adages or maxims contradict each other (as these two do) so that the ability to apply these maxims properly is also understood through intuition.

A Quick Exercise to Understand Intuitionism.

In practice, Ethical Intuitionism works from an established list of moral maxims that have no other justification other than they are immediately perceived to be true. To understand better how this ethical theory works, try the following exercise:

Step One: Make a list of general moral maxims that you believe will cover most moral situations (e.g., don't lie.). Choose at least three but no more than ten.

Step Two: Establish a hierarchy among the maxims that applies for the most part.

Step Three: Create a moral situation that involves at least two moral maxims from your list. Determine which moral maxim best applies in the situation and state the reasons for your choice. How would you respond to someone who disagrees with your choice?

IV. VIRTUE ETHICS.

Virtue Ethics is also sometimes called *agent-based ethics.* Its position is that in living, a person should try to cultivate excellence in all that he does and all that others do. These excellences or virtues are both moral and nonmoral. Through conscious training, for example, an athlete can achieve excellence in a sport (nonmoral example). In the same way, a person can achieve moral excellence. The way these habits are developed and the community that nurtures them are all under the umbrella of Virtue Ethics.

Virtue Ethics works from an established list of accepted character traits called *virtues.* These traits are acquired by habit and guide the practitioner in making moral decisions. Aristotle described these character traits as being a mean between extremes. According to him, the good man so habituates his behavior to these virtues that he will carry out the good actions over and over again throughout his life.

A Quick Exercise to Understand Virtue Ethics.

To better understand what Virtue Ethics means, complete the following exercise.

Step One: Make a list of traits that you believe to be virtues. Make sure you have at least three virtues but no more than ten.

Step Two: Establish the mean by outlining how the virtues in Step One are really somewhere in the middle of two extremes.

Step Three: Describe how you might ingrain this trait into your character. What consequences would this virtue have?

Step Four: Create a moral situation and show how Virtue Ethics would help you to resolve it. How does Virtue Ethics make a difference in this situation?

V. UTILITARIANISM.

Utilitarianism is a theory that suggests that an action is morally right when that action produces more total utility for the group as a consequence than any other alternative does. Sometimes this has been shortened to the slogan, "the greatest good for the greatest number." This emphasis on calculating quantitatively the general population's projected consequential utility among competing alternatives appeals to many of the same principles that under-lie democracy and capitalism (which is the reason that this theory has al-ways been very popular in the United States and other Western capitalistic democracies).

A Quick Exercise to Understand Utilitarianism.

Since Utilitarianism commends the moral choice that produces the great-est happiness for the greatest number of people, under this system we must have a mechanism for determining (a) the alternatives involved, (b) a list of possible outcomes of the alternatives, (c) a clear definition of the population sample to be affected by the alternatives, and (d) a way to measure the pos-sible impact each alternative would have on the population sample so that it will become clear which alternative will yield the most pleasure/utility. The test chosen must be one that can be carried out and have relatively uncontro-versial units by which the happiness impact can be measured and examined. To better understand what is involved in choosing Utilitarianism as a moral theory, try the following exercise.

Step One: Create a moral situation that involves a difficult choice of alternative actions. (Cases, which pit the majority interests against rights of the minority, are often good for this exercise.)

Step Two: List the possible alternatives and their projected outcomes.

Step Three: Define the population affected by your case.

Step Four: Propose a way to measure the happiness of the parties involved. Be sure that your measuring system can be quantified. What criticisms of your test could people make? How would you respond to their criticisms?

Step Five: Test your sample population and give the actual numbers of the hap-piness coefficients that each group will possess according to each alternative.

Step Six: Justify your choice from step five against possible criticism.

VI. DEONTOLOGY.

Deontology is a moral theory that emphasizes one's duty to do a particular action because the action itself is inherently right and not the result of any calculation about the consequences of the action. Because of this noncon-sequentialist bent, deontology is often contrasted with Utilitarianism, which defines the right action in term of its ability to bring about the greatest aggregate utility. In contradistinction to Utilitarianism, Deontology rec-ommends an action based on principle. Principle is justified through an

understanding of the structure of action, the nature of reason,and the operation of the will. The result is a moral command to act that does not justify
itself by calculating consequences.

The moral principle is derived from and justified by the nature of
reason and the structure of human action. Both its justification and its scope
are general. The principle defines duty concerning moral situations in general. One way to understand this level of generality is to compare it to a scientific law, which is universal and absolute, covering all societies in all
historical epochs.

One difficulty people often face with such a general principle is that
moral cases are presented to us as particulars. In logic, general or universal propositions are contrasted to particular or individual propositions.
They are different logical types and cannot be directly compared. The moral
problem must be "translated" into general language at the same level as
the moral principle, which allows a definitive outcome to be determined.
However, this translation is not so easy. For example, consider Maria, who
is contemplating an abortion. All particulars of her individual situation
must be translated into the form of a general moral principle or general
moral law.

For this example, let us assume Kant's Categorical Imperative as our
general principle. This principle states that we should act only on that maxim
through which we can at the same time will that it become a universal law.
This principle prohibits murder[3] because a universal law allowing murder in
some society is logically contradictory. (If everyone murdered everyone else,
there would be no society.) Logically contradictory universal laws are immoral; therefore, murder is immoral.

Autonomy, however, is also dictated by the Categorical Imperative and
becomes its cornerstone of a formulation of the Categorical Imperative that addresses people as ends, not means only.

An example of the problem of moving from the particular to the general
level (necessary for applying the moral laws/principles of Deontology) is in
the translation of abortion. Is abortion an instance of *killing* or of *autonomy*? If
it is the former, it is prohibited. If it is the latter, it is permitted.

The real debate rests in the translation. Once a moral situation is translated, the application to the moral law is easy. The moral law determines our
duty in the situation, and we must do our duty or else we repudiate our
human nature; we are, after all, rational beings.

---

[3]The mode of this prohibition is that all moral maxims generated from the notion of a
universal society of murderers are shown to incoherent. This means that a moral maxim such
as "It is permissible to murder" is found to contain a logical contradiction. Like Plato, Kant believes that logical contradictions indicate immortality because morality means the right and
wrong in human action. *Right* and *wrong* are determined by reference to logic. Illogic, therefore,
is wrong. This is the driving force behind the universality of the Categorical Imperative in its various forms.

A Quick Exercise to Understand Deontology.

To better understand how Deontology works, try the following exercise.

Step One: Choose a universal moral principle (it can be Kant's or any other principle stated in general "lawlike" terminology).

Step Two: Create a particular moral situation that seems to involve a difficult choice of alternative actions. (Cases, which pit two moral duties against each other, are often good for this exercise.)

Step Three: Determine the possible alternative ways to translate the particular case into more general language (i.e., as an instance of truth telling, murder, autonomy).

Step Four: Justify your translation and point out the flaws in alternative translations.

Step Five: Show how your translation fits a general corollary of the universal moral principle. Explain how you arrived at the corollary and the outcome of translation to the corollary. What criticism of your translation, corollary derivation, or outcomes application could people make? How would you defend yourself against these criticisms?

The criteria for deciding between ethical theories are elaborated by metaethics. Once you endorse a theory, you must determine how to apply it. One commonly held principle of application states that similar cases are to be treated similarly. Let this principle be termed the *just implementation of rules.* This principle is a purely formal principle of distributive justice.[4] (Distributive justice is that subbranch of morality that provides criteria by which goods and services may be parsed to recipients.) As a formal principle, this tells us that no matter what the content of the rule all things being equal, it is just to treat like cases the same way.

The just implementation of rules is a necessary but not a sufficient principle. For example, if the Nazis held that the right to live is to be distributed only to non-Jews, then the application of the just implementation of rules would suggest that all Jews be killed!

What is needed are specifications on the *content* of the rule. When the content of the rule is included (as per the Personal Worldview Imperative), it is obvious that the imperative is inconsistent since no morally relevant difference exists between Jews and non-Jews. Since the Nazis contended that such a difference existed, they can be accused of being logically inconsistent.

---

[4]Distributive justice is only one form of justice. The other most prominent form is retributive justice, which outlines how we are to punish others and the conditions on which these decisions are made and justified.

Some might contend that makes no difference. These bestial creatures could care less. The answer would be that they diminish themselves—whether they know it or not—by violating the Personal Worldview Imperative.

Specifications on the content of the rule also address issues of what is the best system of distributive justice. Traditional candidates of distributive justice have included *capitalism* (to each according to her production), *socialism* (to each according to his need), *egalitarianism* (to each equally), *aristocracy* (to each according to his inherited station), and *kraterism* (to each according to her ability to snatch it for herself).

There are other candidates for distributive justice, but this list provides various approaches that are often used to answer the question of how goods and services are to be distributed.

Once one has argued for and accepted a theory, then according to the just implementation of rules, he must apply it in a like manner to all similar cases.

In the preceding example, the theory of justice one adopts constitutes the material element in the theory while the just implementation of rules represents merely a formal implementation rule.

This example is meant to illustrate the types of issues with which Normative Ethics concerns itself. In this domain, we are interested in creating norms for conduct, including a justification and defense of all issues involved with the creation, understanding, or general application of such ethical norms.

In subsequent chapters of this book, we extend our exploration of both Normative Ethics and its interaction with actual decision making, which is Applied Ethics. At the end of the core chapters of the book are exercises to integrate this process with the ability to create a coherent written evaluation of these case studies (a simulated action situation).

EVALUATING A CASE STUDY: DEVELOPING A PRACTICAL ETHICAL VIEWPOINT

Your goal in this book is to respond critically to case studies on various aspects of Business Ethics. To do this, you must be able to assess the ethical impact of some critical factor(s) in situations that pose ethical problems. One factor in accessing the case is the ethical impact of the project/policy/action. At the end of the Reacting to a Case Study essays, you should be better prepared to do just that. This chapter and Chapters Three through Six end with an "Evaluating a Case Study" section that focuses on a particular exercise. These sections include case studies to which you can apply the insight you gained from the readings and discussions in the chapter. Because the information presented in the "Evaluating a Case Study" is cumulative, you should be able to write a complete critical response to a case study by the end of Chapter Six.

These essays seek to bridge the gap between Normative Ethics and Applied Ethics. Skill in Applied Ethics is very important, for this is where the practical decision making occurs. My approach in these essays is to allow you to employ techniques that you have been taught elsewhere along with those found in this text. Depending on your background in business, you can write a critical response to a case study that demonstrates your professional acumen along with your sensitivity to the ethical dimensions found in the situation you are examining. Classes that have few students with business backgrounds will deemphasize the business fundamentals and concentrate instead on a less technical response.

Businesspeople often become so enmeshed in the practice of business that they lose the ability to discern and react to possible ethical dilemmas, a difficulty experienced in all professions.[1] But this is wrong. The "Evaluating a Case Study" sections will help you analyze both ethical and practical situations. The approach will invoke a technique that rates a proposal as having three levels of complexity: surface, medium, and deep. The level of interaction allows you to see at a glance how the competing areas of interest and ethical value conflict.

The five essays in this series are intended to sequentially lead you to develop the abilities to write a critical response to a case study: (a) Developing a Practical Ethical Viewpoint, (b) Finding the Conflicts, (c) Assessing Embedded Levels, (d) Applying Ethical Issues, and (e) Structuring the Essay.

At the end of Chapters Three through Six, you will be presented case studies to which you can apply your newfound skills. By the end of the term, you should be able to create an ethical impact statement of some sophistication.

Let us begin first by choosing an ethical theory and then proceed to developing a practical viewpoint. Few people bother to choose an ethical theory, most pick up a few moral maxims that they apply when the occasion seems appropriate. The manner of this acquisition is often environment dependent, that is, having to do with their upbringing, friends, and the community(ies) in which they live. As such, their maxims reflect those other viewpoints.

The Personal Worldview Imperative enjoins us to develop a single comprehensive and internally coherent worldview that is good and that we strive to act out in our lives (see Chapter One). One component of this worldview is an ethical theory. Thus, each of us must *develop* an ethical theory. This does not mean we must all start from scratch. Those before us have done too much good work. But we must personally choose an ethical theory and assume ownership for it as being the most correct theory in existence. It is not enough merely to accept someone else's theory without any active work on our part. We must go through the process of personal introspection and evaluation to determine what we think is best and to be open to ways we can improve the theory (in concept or in practice).

This process of making an ethical theory our own can take years. This course lasts only a few months. Does this pose a problem? Not really when you

---

[1]For a fuller discussion of this, see *Basic Ethics*, chap. 7.

consider that part of the process of making an ethical theory our own involves provisional acceptance and testing of various moral maxims. Obviously, this testing has a limit. We should not test whether it is morally permissible to murder by going out and murdering various people. The testing I am advocating is a way to examine various moral commands and evaluate whether their application is consonant with other worldview values we hold. The process will perhaps go back and forth in a progressive dialectic until we have accepted or rejected the commands.

To begin this process of testing, we must read about some of the most prominent ethical theories. We must identify the major ethical theories and their tenets. Many books survey and evaluate the major ethical theories. In this series of textbooks, *Basic Ethics in Action,* I have written one such survey entitled *Basic Ethics.* I would suggest that you either refer to that book or another like it to obtain enough information to enable you to begin the process of choosing an ethical theory.

For the purposes of this book, I will highlight four major theories: Utilitarianism, Deontology, Intuitionism, and Virtue Ethics. To begin the process, I recommend that you choose a single theory from these four (or from others your instructor may suggest) as your critical tool as you prepare for class. You might ask, How do I know which viewpoint to choose? This is a difficult question. It concerns the justification of the various ethical theories.

Many criteria can be used to justify an ethical theory. One criterion is Naturalism. Each theory presupposes a naturalistic or nonnaturalistic epistemological standpoint. Naturalism is complicated; for our purposes, let us describe it as a view that holds that no entities or events are in principle beyond the domain of scientific explanation. Cognitive claims are valid only if they are based on accepted scientific modes.

Ethical Naturalism states that moral judgments are also merely a subclass of facts about the natural world that can be studied scientifically. From this study, we can determine moral correctness as a corollary of certain facts that can be scientifically investigated (e.g., how much pleasure various alternatives will produce for the group). Thus, utilitarians believe that moral judgments *are* judgments about which alternative will be most beneficial to some group's survival.

A utilitarian might point to the scientific study of nature and say that the instinct to seek pleasure is evidenced in all species. Furthermore, an evolutionary advantage seems to exist for those species that act for the benefit of the group that does not exist for those who do not act in this way.

Many sociobiologists make this sort of claim. The main imperative is that a person's own genes be passed on to another generation. If passing a person's genes is impossible, the next best thing is to pass on the genes of the individual's relatives. Thus, seemingly altruistic behavior (such as a bird that stays behind in dangerous situations so that the group might survive) is really selfish because helping the group *is* helping the bird to pass on its genes (or those of its relatives).

Sociobiology, of course, is not universally accepted, nor is it necessary for a utilitarian to be a sociobiologist. However, this example does illustrate a type of justification that the utilitarian might make. He could move from the concept of group happiness in animals and extrapolate to humans. The supporting data are scientific; therefore, the theory is naturalistic.

Deontologists may or may not be naturalists. Since Deontology involves a duty-based ethics, the key question to be asked concerns how we know whether a binding duty exists to do such and such. Are all moral "oughts" derivable from factual, scientifically ascertainable "is" statements? If they are, then the deontologist is a naturalist. If they are not, then the deontologist is not a naturalist.

In his book *Reason and Morality*, Alan Gewirth claims to derive ought from is. There is no reference to knowledge claims that are not compatible with the scientific inquiry of natural objects. This would make Gewirth a naturalist. Kant and Donagan are somewhat different. Each refers to supernatural entities that are not scientifically supported. Kant spends considerable effort trying to define those boundaries in the "Transcendental Dialectic" section of his book *The Critique of Pure Reason*. This aside, neither Kant nor Donagan considered that a problem about integrating the factual and the normative existed.

If you are inclined to view reality as an extension of evolutionary biology or to believe that group advantage immediately entails a moral ought, then you are leaning toward Utilitarianism. If you think that people should act from pure duty alone without reference to anything except the rightness of the action, however, then Deontology is probably your preference.

The is-ought problem was sharpened by intuitionist G.E. Moore,[2] who rejected Ethical Naturalism because he believed it contained a fallacy (which he dubbed *the naturalistic fallacy*). This fallacy claims that it is false to define goodness in terms of any natural property. This is so because good is not definable and because good is not subject to scientific examination. This is true because the factual is realm is separate from the normative ought realm. The chasm between the two cannot be crossed.

Good for Moore is a unique, unanalyzable, non-natural property (as opposed, for example, to yellow, which is a natural property). Clearly, scientific methods are of no use. Science can tell us things about yellow but can tell us

---

[2]I cannot stress too much the impossibility of completely pigeonholing philosophers. In some important ways, Moore was an intuitionist. "Good" had to be accepted as an unanalyzable, unnatural fact. Toward the end of *Principia Ethica,* he sounds much like an agathistic utilitarian, however, one who wishes to maximize the group's good. This mixture of labels among philosophers shows only that labels are limited in what they can do.

Ross and Rawls have deontological and intuitionistic aspects to their theories. Therefore, one label alone cannot adequately capture the spirit of their philosophy. In an introductory text, such as this one, labels are used to simplify—but hopefully not obfuscate—the dynamics present in these thinkers.

nothing about the meaning of good. Other intuitionists also hold that we understand important moral terms and/or moral maxims by cognitive means that are not scientific. Generally, these are immediate and cannot be justified in factual "is" language.

Intuitionism is therefore a non-naturalistic theory. Still, it has some remote connections to Naturalism. For example, one can point to the *plausibility* of accepting certain common moral maxims—such as a prohibition against murder—by reference to other societies. (In other words, since all societies prohibit murder, the prohibition against murder must be immediately apparent to all.) However, plausibility is not the same as exhaustive scientific demonstration. Justification in Intuitionism lies in its alleged unarguable truth that can be grasped in principle immediately by all.

If you are having trouble adopting any of the theories and believe that acceptance or rejection of an ethical theory comes to some sort of brute immediate acceptance, then you will probably want to accept Intuitionism as your ethical theory.

Finally, we turn to Virtue Ethics. This theory seems at first to be naturalistic. Aristotle lends credence to this when he talks about relying on the common opinions of people about what is considered to be a virtue. The common opinions could be gathered and reviewed much as a sociologist or anthropologist might do, and this "scientific" method would yield definitive results. Aristotle believed that some common agreement about a core set of virtues existed.

Justification, therefore, was not an issue for Aristotle. If we accept a worldview such as Aristotle presents, then we would all agree that everyone considers courage (for example) to be a virtue. The confirming data can be gathered and scientifically studied; ergo, it is naturalistic. The proof depends on the community that values these traits. This emphasis on community makes Virtue Ethics a favorite theory among those who call themselves *communitarians*. The communitarian begins with the group and its intuitions and depends on individual members to submit to the authority of the group (or to change the group in ways acceptable to the group).

How does Communitarianism affect today's pluralistic society? Some might argue that consensus about the virtues no longer exists, nor does a single community to which we all belong. If there is no consensus as Aristotle envisioned, then what constitutes a virtue may collapse into a form of Intuitionism. For example, I think that X is a virtue. You think Y is a virtue. X and Y are mutually exclusive traits. You and I come from different communities/societies; therefore, we cannot come to an agreement. All each of us can say is that I am right and you are wrong. Personal insight (Intuitionism) is all we have to justify our practices (to ourselves and to others).

If you believe that courage, wisdom, self-control, piety, and so forth are virtues in every society, then perhaps you will choose Virtue Ethics as your model.

To help you choose an ethical theory, try the following exercise. Examine one or more of the following moral situations and (a) interpret what is right and wrong according to each of the four theories, (b) then give an argument that each theory might provide, and (c) state your own assessment of the strengths of each theory.

Situation One.

You are the constable in a small, remote, rural town in Northern Ireland that is divided into the Catholics (20 percent minority) and the Protestants (80 percent majority). All Catholics live in one section of town on a peninsula jutting into the river just east of the main part of town.

One morning a young Protestant girl is found raped and murdered next to the town green. According to general consensus, a Catholic must have committed the crime. The Protestants form a citizens' committee that demands the following of the constable: "We believe you to be a Catholic sympathizer, and we don't think you will press fast enough to bring this killer to justice. We know a Catholic committed the crime. We've sealed off the Catholic section of town; no one can go in or out. If you don't hand over the criminal by sundown, we will torch the entire Catholic section of town, killing all 1,000 people. Don't try to call for help. We've already disabled the telephone."

You made every effort to find out who did it, but you made no progress. You could not find out. At one hour before sundown, you do not know what to do. Your deputy says, "Why don't we just pick a random Catholic and tell them he did it? At least we'd be saving 999 lives."

"But then I'd be responsible for killing an innocent man!" you reply. "Better one innocent die and 999 be saved. After all, there's no way the two of us can stop the mob. You have to give them a scapegoat," the deputy responds.

Describe how each ethical theory might approach this situation. Which one is most consonant to your own worldview, and why?

Situation Two.

You are a railroad switcher sitting in a tower and controlling a switch that allows trains to travel over the regular track or switches them to a siding. One morning you face a terrible dilemma. The N.Y. Zephyr is traveling at high speed on the main track, and a school bus filled with children (at least fifty) has stalled on the main track as it crosses Elm Street. The bus driver is trying to restart the engine, but the ignition will not turn over. It is clear to you that the bus will not get off the track in time. On the siding track is a homeless man who has fallen down and caught his foot on a rail tie. It is clear that he also is stuck.

In fifteen seconds, you must decide whether to use the switch to send the train to the siding—thereby killing the homeless man—or to do nothing and allow the train to take its normal course and thereby hit the bus and probably kill most if not all of the fifty schoolchildren on board.

Describe how each ethical theory might approach this situation. Which one is most consonant to your own worldview, and why?

Situation Three.

You are on the executive committee of the XYZ organization of health care professionals. Each year the committee gives an award to one of its members who display high moral character in his or her work. This year you are among the four judges for the award. There is some disagreement among the judges, however, about what constitutes a good person. The judges, besides yourself, are Ms. Smith, Mrs. Taylor, and Mr. Jones. The candidates for the award are Mr. Little and Mrs. Big.

Ms. Smith said that the award should go to Mrs. Big because she saved a man from drowning. However, Mr. Jones demurred, saying that Mrs. Big's motives are suspect because the man she saved was in the midst of a very big financial deal with Mrs. Big. If the man had been allowed to drown, Mrs. Big would have lost a lost of money. Ms. Smith said motives are not important but that the goodness of the act counts and the man who was saved runs a big business in town. Many people besides Mrs. Big would have been hurt if Mrs. Big had not saved the man.

Mr. Jones said the award should go to Mr. Little because he performed a kind act of charity in chairing the town's United Way Campaign last year. Surely such an act could not be said to benefit Mr. Little in any way (unlike Mrs. Big).

Mrs. Taylor said that she is somewhat unsure about either Mrs. Big or Mr. Little because both of them have been recommended on the basis of a single good act. Mrs. Taylor believed that it would be better to choose a candidate who has shown over time to have performed many good actions and to be of good character. "After all," she said "a single swallow does not make a spring." Mr. Jones and Ms. Smith scratched their heads at this remark and turned to you. Who is right?

Describe how each ethical theory might approach this situation. Which one is most consonant to your own worldview, and why?

Choosing an ethical theory is only the first step in developing a practical ethical viewpoint. A link between the Normative Theory and application of the theory is needed. In Chapter One, I outlined my basic position concerning personal worldview and how it might be utilized when applying an ethical theory. In the last section Chapter One, I outlined a principle of fair competition that I believe can be used to apply the general theory chosen and to the moral decision at hand.

The point is that one important aspect of developing a practical ethical viewpoint is to challenge ourselves to think about and provisionally accept certain necessary tenets to effectively apply ethical principles to practice. These concepts should allow professionals to connect normative theories to the real-life problems that confront them.

Before addressing ethical cases, try first to provisionally accept one moral theory. Then try to determine what connecting principles or concepts are necessary to translate theory to practice. Concentrate your efforts on these connections. They will be useful to you as you address what you see as the important issues resident in each case.

chapter three

What Is a Corporation?

GENERAL OVERVIEW.

One important element that is fundamental to our study of business ethics is to determine the nature of a corporation. Is a corporation merely a piece of property owned by its shareholders? Is it a combination of the shareholders, directors, and top executives? Perhaps a corporation is an abstract entity that belongs to all of those who are affected by its activities (the stakeholders, discussed later in this chapter)? These are some traditional thoughts on this subject.

Another way to look at a corporation is as a moral agent in its own right. This ascription can be merely metaphorical, or it can be true in a very literal sense.

The duties and responsibilities of a corporation depend on the way we view it and the way it views itself. This is not merely an abstract problem without practical ramifications; it may be that viewing the corporation as a moral person will increase its ethical accountability and afford it additional rights in the exchange. For this reason, we begin our inquiry with an exploration of this central question.

The Corporation as an Individual.

Overview.

One goal in defining a corporation as an individual is to be able to create a model that requires it to be morally responsible for what it does. The "corporate veil" originally created to absolve directors, officers, and stockholders from personal liability resulting from the company's actions has often created a situation in which *no* person/entity is ever responsible for anything.

In the article by Kenneth E. Goodpaster and John B. Matthews Jr., the authors contrast two different imperatives that might guide corporate decision making: the invisible hand and the government hand. In the former imperative, the sole obligations of the corporation are to make money and obey the law. The forces of the market will control the corporation's activity. If the public is upset with the company's behavior, then the public will vote with its pocketbooks and force the company to change or go under.

The imperative of the government hand marshals the activity of the corporation toward the common good. In this model, government policy can involve ethical concerns and therefore a corporation is held responsible for its actions for the general good of the society in which it operates.

Such an account depicts the corporation (in a loose way) to be rather like an individual. This attribution of individuality is the result of a moral projection based on similarities between an individual and her moral duties and the moral duties that a corporation ought to recognize.

Nani L. Ranken replies that Goodpaster and Matthews's moral projection fails because the analogy between persons and corporations breaks down at a crucial point. This critical flaw concerns the concept of moral improvement. Corporations do not "feel" or have sympathy as persons do. These feelings are important for character development, which, in turn guards against the excesses of some super entity that is supposed to tell us what is right but may end up doing just the opposite.

Peter A. French advances the concept of the corporation as a person *from* an analogy *to* a position that asserts that a corporation really is a moral person. He bases his argument on a theory of personhood that is rooted in the action theory of Donald Davidson and the functionalism of Daniel Dennett. If we can identify the structural features of an action description, then we can ascribe agency to the alleged actor. This does not depend on biology (such as a living, breathing organism).

French believes that if the corporation is a moral actor, metaphysical personhood follows as well. He cites two theories to prove his point: the fiction theory and the reality theory. The former has a thorough legal grounding of the person; the latter is prelegal. He contrasts these views with standard theories (as characterized by the legal aggregate theory) that identifies a corporation with its human stakeholders. French's argument is important because the rights and responsibilities that a corporation enjoys are a function of its metaphysical and moral status.

Thomas Donaldson replies to French by emphasizing that a corporation does not have the same rights as a person (such as the right to vote) and that the origin of the corporation's rights (unlike human persons) cannot be natural. Natural rights are important because some oppressed people (such as African Americans in the United States) were legally denied rights but surely possessed them despite the fact that legal institutions did not recognize them. If they had these rights, then how did they possess them? Presumably, they possessed them by natural right. If natural rights are more basic than legal rights, then how can we explain that corporations have natural rights?

These arguments are meant to engage the reader in considering how to find legitimate ways to include corporations in the moral universe in which moral responsibility accompanies action.

Can a Corporation Have a Conscience?

Kenneth E. Goodpaster and John B. Matthews Jr.

During the severe racial tensions of the 1960s, Southern Steel Company (actual case, disguised name) faced considerable pressure from government and the press to explain and modify its policies regarding discrimination both within its plants and in the major city where it was located. SSC was the largest employer in the area (it had nearly 15,000 workers, one-third of whom were black) and had made great strides toward removing barriers to equal job opportunity in its several plants. In addition, its top executives (especially its chief executive officer, James Weston) had distinguished themselves as private citizens for years in community programs for black housing, education, and small business as well as in attempts at desegregating all-white police and local government organizations.

SSC drew the line, however, at using its substantial economic influence in the local area to advance the cause of the civil rights movement by pressuring banks, suppliers, and the local government.

"As individuals we can exercise what influence we may have as citizens," James Weston said, "but for a corporation to attempt to exert any kind of economic compulsion to achieve a particular end in a social area seems to me to be quite beyond what a corporation should do and quite beyond what a corporation can do. I believe that while government may seek to compel social reforms, any attempt by a private organization like SSC to impose its views, its beliefs, and its will upon the community would be repugnant to our American constitutional concepts and that appropriate steps to correct this abuse of corporate power would be universally demanded by public opinion."

Weston could have been speaking in the early 1980s on any issue that corporations around the United States now face. Instead of social justice, his theme might be environmental protection, product safety, marketing practice, or international bribery. His statement for SSC raises the important issue of corporate responsibility. Can a corporation have a conscience?

Weston apparently felt comfortable saying it need not. The responsibilities of ordinary persons and of "artificial persons" like corporations are, in his view, separate. Persons' responsibilities go beyond those of corporations. Persons, he seems to have believed, ought to care not only about themselves but also about the dignity and well-being of those around them—ought not only to care but also to act. Organizations, he evidently thought, are creatures of, and to a degree prisoners of, the systems of economic incentive and political sanction that give them reality and therefore should not be expected to display the same moral attributes that we expect of persons.

Others inside business as well as outside share Weston's perception. One influential philosopher—John Ladd—carries Weston's view a step further:

> It is improper to expect organizational conduct to conform to the ordinary principles of morality. We cannot and must not expect formal organizations, or their representatives acting in their official capacities, to be honest, courageous, considerate, sympathetic, or to have any kind of moral integrity. Such concepts are not in the vocabulary, so to speak, of the organizational language game.[1]

In our opinion, this line of thought represents a tremendous barrier to the development of business ethics both as a field of inquiry and as a practical force in managerial decision making. This is a matter about which executives must be philosophical and philosophers must be practical. A corporation can and should have a conscience. The language of ethics does have a place in the vocabulary of an organization. There need not be and there should not be a disjunction of the sort attributed to SSC's James Weston. Organizational agents such as corporations should be no more and no less morally responsible (rational, self-interested, altruistic) than ordinary persons.

We take this position because we think an analogy holds between the individual and the corporation. If we analyze the concept of moral responsibility as it applies to persons, we find that projecting it to corporations as agents in society is possible.

DEFINING THE RESPONSIBILITY OF PERSONS

When we speak of the responsibility of individuals, philosophers say that we mean three things: someone is to blame, something has to be done, or some kind of trustworthiness can be expected. (See the *Exhibit.*)

Holding Accountable

We apply the first meaning, what we shall call the *causal* sense, primarily to legal and moral contexts where what is at issue is praise or blame for a past action. We say of a person that he or she was responsible for what happened, is to blame for it, should be held accountable. In this sense of the word, *responsibility* has to do with tracing the causes of actions and events, of finding out who is answerable in a given situation. Our aim is to determine someone's intention, free will, degree of participation, and appropriate reward or punishment.

Rule Following

We apply the second meaning of *responsibility* to rule following, to contexts where individuals are subject to externally imposed norms often associated with some social role that people play. We speak of the responsibilities of parents to children, of doctors to patients, of lawyers to clients, of citizens to the law. What is socially expected and what the party involved is to answer for are at issue here.

Decision Making

We use the third meaning of *responsibility* for decision making. With this meaning of the term, we say that individuals are responsible if they are trustworthy and reliable, if they allow appropriate factors to affect their judgment; we refer primarily to a person's independent thought processes and decision making, processes that justify an attitude of trust from those who interact with him or her as a responsible individual.

The distinguishing characteristic of moral responsibility, it seems to us, lies in this third sense of the term. Here the focus is on the intellectual and emotional processes in the individual's moral reasoning. Philosophers call this "taking a moral point of view" and contrast it with such other processes as being financially prudent and attending to legal obligations.

To be sure, characterizing a person as "morally responsible" may seem rather vague. But vagueness is a contextual notion. Everything depends on how we fill in the blank in "vague for _____ purposes."

In some contexts the term "six o'clockish" is vague, while in others it is useful and informative. As a response to a space-shuttle pilot who wants to know when to fire the reentry rockets, it will not do, but it might do in response to a spouse who wants to know when one will arrive home at the end of the workday.

We maintain that the processes underlying moral responsibility can be defined and are not themselves vague, even though gaining consensus on specific moral norms and decisions is not always easy.

What, then, characterizes the processes underlying the judgment of a person we call morally responsible? Philosopher William K. Frankena offers the following answer:

> A morality is a normative system in which judgments are made, more or less consciously, [out of a] consideration of the effects of actions . . . on the lives of persons . . . including the lives of others besides the person acting. . . . David Hume took a similar position when he argued that what speaks in a moral judgment is a kind of sympathy. . . . A little later, . . . Kant put the matter somewhat better by characterizing morality as the business of respecting persons as ends and not as means or as things. . . .[2]

Frankena is pointing to two traits, both rooted in a long and diverse philosophical tradition:

1. Rationality. Taking a moral point of view includes the features we usually attribute to rational decision making, that is, lack of impulsiveness, care in mapping out alternatives and consequences, clarity about goals and purposes, attention to details of implementation.

2. Respect. The moral point of view also includes a special awareness of and concern for the effects of one's decisions and policies on others, special in the sense that it goes beyond the kind of awareness and concern that would ordinarily be part of rationality, that is, beyond seeing others merely as instrumental to accomplishing one's own purposes. This is respect for the lives of others and involves taking their needs and interests seriously, not simply as resources in one's own decision making but as limiting conditions which change the very definition of one's habitat from a self-centered to a shared environment. It is what philosopher Immanuel Kant meant by the "categorical imperative" to treat others as valuable in and for themselves.

It is this feature that permits us to trust the morally responsible person. We know that such a person takes our point of view into account not merely as a useful precaution (as in "honesty is the best policy") but as important in its own right.

These components of moral responsibility are not too vague to be useful. Rationality and respect affect the manner in which a person approaches practical decision making: they affect the way in which the individual processes information and makes choices. A rational but not respectful Bill Jones will not lie to his friends *unless* he is reasonably sure he will not be found out. A rational but not respectful Mary Smith will defend an unjustly treated party *unless* she thinks it may be too costly to herself. A rational *and* respectful decision maker, however, notices—and cares—whether the consequences of his or her conduct lead to injuries or indignities to others.

Two individuals who take "the moral point of view" will not of course always agree on ethical matters, but they do at least have a basis for dialogue.

Projecting Responsibility to Corporations

Now that we have removed some of the vagueness from the notion of moral responsibility as it applies to persons, we can search for a frame of reference in which, by analogy with Bill Jones and Mary Smith, we can meaningfully and appropriately say that corporations are morally responsible. This is the issue reflected in the SSC case.

To deal with it, we must ask two questions: Is it meaningful to apply moral concepts to actors who are not persons but who are instead made up of persons? And even if meaningful, is it advisable to do so?

If a group can act like a person in some ways, then we can expect it to behave like a person in other ways. For one thing, we know that people organized into a group can act as a unit. As businesspeople well know, legally a corporation is considered a unit. To approach unity, a group usually has some sort of internal decision structure, a system of rules that spell out authority relationships and specify the conditions under which certain individuals' actions become official actions of the group.[3]

If we can say that persons act responsibly only if they gather information about the impact of their actions on others and use it in making decisions, we can reasonably do the same for organizations. Our proposed frame of reference for thinking about and implementing corporate responsibility aims at spelling out the processes associated with the moral responsibility of individuals and projecting them to the level of organizations. This is similar to, though an inversion of, Plato's famous method in the *Republic,* in which justice in the community is used as a model for justice in the individual.

Hence, corporations that monitor their employment practices and the effects of their production processes and products on the environment and human health show the same kind of rationality and respect that morally responsible individuals do. Thus, attributing actions, strategies, decisions, and moral responsibilities to corporations as entities distinguishable from those who hold offices in them poses no problem.

And when we look about us, we can readily see differences in moral responsibility among corporations in much the same way that we see differences among persons. Some corporations have built features into their management incentive systems, board structures, internal control systems, and research agendas that in a person we would call self-control, integrity, and conscientiousness. Some have institutionalized awareness and concern for consumers, employees, and the rest of the public in ways that others clearly have not.

As a matter of course, some corporations attend to the human impact of their operations and policies and reject operations and policies that are questionable. Whether the issue be the health effects of sugared cereal or cigarettes, the safety of tires or tampons, civil liberties in the corporation or the community, an organization reveals its character as surely as a person does.

Indeed, the parallel may be even more dramatic. For just as the moral responsibility displayed by an individual develops over time from infancy to adulthood,[4] so too we may expect to find stages of development in organizational character that show significant patterns.

EVALUATING THE IDEA OF MORAL PROJECTION

Concepts like moral responsibility not only make sense when applied to organizations but also provide touchstones for designing more effective models than we now have for guiding corporate policy.

Now we can understand what it means to invite SSC as a corporation to be morally responsible both in-house and in its community, but *should* we issue the invitation? Here we turn to the question of advisability. Should we require the organizational agents in our society to have the same moral attributes we require of ourselves?

Our proposal to spell out the processes associated with moral responsibility for individuals and then to project them to their organizational counterparts takes on added meaning when we examine alternative frames of reference for corporate responsibility.

Two frames of reference that compete for the allegiance of people who ponder the question of corporate responsibility are emphatically opposed to this principle of moral projection—what we might refer to as the "invisible hand" view and the "hand of government" view.

The Invisible Hand

The most eloquent spokesman of the first view is Milton Friedman (echoing many philosophers and economists since Adam Smith). According to this pattern of thought, the true and only social responsibilities of business organizations are to make profits and obey the laws. The workings of the free and competitive marketplace will "moralize" corporate behavior quite independently of any attempts to expand or transform decision making via moral projection.

A deliberate amorality in the executive suite is encouraged in the name of systemic morality: the common good is best served when each of us and our economic institutions pursue not the common good or moral purpose, advocates say, but competitive advantage. Morality, responsibility, and conscience reside in the invisible hand of the free market system, not in the hands of the organizations within the system, much less the managers within the organizations.

To be sure, people of this opinion admit, there is a sense in which social or ethical issues can and should enter the corporate mind, but the filtering of such issues is thorough: they go through the screens of custom, public opinion, public relations, and the law. And, in any case, self-interest maintains primacy as an objective and a guiding star.

The reaction from this frame of reference to the suggestion that moral judgment be integrated with corporate strategy is clearly negative. Such an integration is seen as inefficient and arrogant, and in the end both an illegitimate use of corporate power and an abuse of the manager's fiduciary role. With respect to our SSC case, advocates of the invisible hand model would vigorously resist efforts, beyond legal requirements, to make SSC right the wrongs of racial injustice. SSC's responsibility would be to make steel of high quality at least cost, to deliver it on time, and to satisfy its customers and stockholders. Justice would not be part of SSC's corporate mandate.

The Hand of Government

Advocates of the second dissenting frame of reference abound, but John Kenneth Galbraith's work has counterpointed Milton Friedman's with insight and style. Under this view of corporate responsibility, corporations are to pursue objectives that are rational and purely economic. The regulatory hands of the law and the political process rather than the invisible hand of the marketplace turns these objectives to the common good.

Again, in this view, it is a system that provides the moral direction for corporate decision making—a system, though, that is guided by political managers, the custodians of the public purpose. In the case of SSC, proponents of this view would look to the state for moral direction and responsible management, both within SSC and in the community. The corporation would have no moral responsibility beyond political and legal obedience.

What is striking is not so much the radical difference between the economic and social philosophies that underlie these two views of the source of corporate responsibility but the conceptual similarities. Both views locate morality, ethics, responsibility, and conscience in the systems of rules and incentives in which the modern corporation finds itself embedded. Both views reject the exercise of independent moral judgment by corporations as actors in society.

Neither view trusts corporate leaders with stewardship over what are often called noneconomic values. Both require corporate responsibility to march to the beat of drums outside. In the jargon of moral philosophy, both views press for a rule-centered or a system-centered ethics instead of an agent-centered ethics. In terms of the *Exhibit*, these frames of reference countenance corporate rule-following responsibility for corporations but not corporate decision-making responsibility.

The Hand of Management

To be sure, the two views under discussion differ in that one looks to an invisible moral force in the market while the other looks to a visible moral force in government. But both would advise against a principle of moral projection that permits or encourages corporations to exercise independent, noneconomic judgment over matters that face them in their short- and long-term plans and operations.

Accordingly, both would reject a third view of corporate responsibility that seeks to affect the thought processes of the organization itself—a sort of "hand of management" view—since neither seems willing or able to see the engines of profit regulate themselves to the degree that would be implied by taking the principle of moral projection seriously. Cries of inefficiency and moral imperialism from the right would be matched by cries of insensitivity and illegitimacy from the left, all in the name of preserving us from corporations and managers run morally amok.

Better, critics would say, that moral philosophy be left to philosophers, philanthropists, and politicians than to business leaders. Better that corporate morality be kept to glossy annual reports, where it is safely insulated from policy and performance.

The two conventional frames of reference locate moral restraint in forces external to the person and the corporation. They deny moral reasoning and intent to the corporation in the name of either market competition or society's system of explicit legal constraints and presume that these have a better moral effect than that of rationality and respect.

Although the principle of moral projection, which underwrites the idea of a corporate conscience and patterns it on the thought and feeling processes

---

EXHIBIT: THREE USES OF THE TERM *RESPONSIBLE*

The causal sense	"He is responsible for this." Emphasis on holding to account for past actions, causality.
The rule-following sense	"As a lawyer, he is responsible for defending that client." Emphasis on following social and legal norms.
The decision-making sense	"He is a responsible person." Emphasis on an individual's independent judgment.

---

of the person, is in our view compelling, we must acknowledge that it is neither part of the received wisdom, nor is its advisability beyond question or objection. Indeed, attributing the role of conscience to the corporation seems to carry with it new and disturbing implications for our usual ways of thinking about ethics and business.

Perhaps the best way to clarify and defend this frame of reference is to address the objections to the principle found in the ruled insert here. There we see a summary of the criticisms and counterarguments we have heard during hours of discussion with business executives and business school students. We believe that the replies to the objections about a corporation having a conscience are convincing.

LEAVING THE DOUBLE STANDARD BEHIND

We have come some distance from our opening reflection on Southern Steel Company and its role in its community. Our proposal—clarified, we hope, through these objections and replies—suggests that it is not sufficient to draw a sharp line between individuals' private ideas and efforts and a corporation's institutional efforts but that the latter can and should be built upon the former.

Does this frame of reference give us an unequivocal prescription for the behavior of SSC in its circumstances? No, it does not. Persuasive arguments might be made now and might have been made then that SSC should not have used its considerable economic clout to threaten the community into desegregation. A careful analysis of the realities of the environment might have disclosed that such a course would have been counterproductive, leading to more injustice than it would have alleviated.

The point is that some of the arguments and some of the analyses are or would have been moral arguments, and thereby the ultimate decision that of an ethically responsible organization. The significance of this point can hardly be overstated, for it represents the adoption of a new perspective on corporate policy and a new way of thinking about business ethics. We agree with one authority, who writes that "the business firm, as an organic entity intricately affected by and affecting its environment, is as appropriately adaptive . . . to demands for responsible behavior as for economic service."[5]

The frame of reference here developed does not offer a decision procedure for corporate managers. That has not been our purpose. It does, however, shed light on the conceptual foundations of business ethics by training attention on the corporation as a moral agent in society. Legal systems of rules and incentives are insufficient, even though they may be necessary, as frameworks for corporate responsibility. Taking conceptual cues from the features of moral responsibility normally expected of the person in our opinion deserves practicing managers' serious consideration.

The lack of congruence that James Weston saw between individual and corporate moral responsibility can be, and we think should be, overcome. In the process, what a number of writers have characterized as a double standard—a discrepancy between our personal lives and our lives in organizational settings—might be dampened. The principle of moral projection not only helps us to conceptualize the kinds of demands that we might make of corporations and other organizations but also offers the prospect of harmonizing those demands with the demands that we make of ourselves.

NOTES

1. See John Ladd, "Mortality and the Ideal of Rationality in Formal Organizations," *The Monist,* October 1970, p. 499.

2. See William K. Frankena, *Thinking About Morality* (Ann Arbor: University of Michigan Press, 1980), p. 26.

3. See Peter French, "The Corporation as a Moral Person," *American Philosophical Quarterly,* July 1979, p. 207.

4. A process that psychological researchers from Jean Piaget to Lawrence Kohlberg have examined carefully; see Jean Piaget, *The Moral Judgment of the Child* (New York: Free Press, 1965) and Lawrence Kohlberg, *The Philosophy of Moral Development* (New York: Harper & Row, 1981).

5. See Kenneth R. Andrews, *The Concept of Corporate Strategy,* rev. ed. (Homewood, Ill.: Dow Jones-Irwin, 1980), p. 99.

Corporations as Persons: Objections to Goodpaster's "Principle of Moral Projection"

Nani L. Ranken

Much current work in business ethics is based on drawing analogies between persons and corporations. Just as we expect persons to be morally responsible agents, so too corporations should be expected to be moral. This is taken very seriously, and taken far, perhaps by none more than Kenneth Goodpaster who urges us to base a good portion of the enterprise of business ethics on the fruitfulness of the analogy. In 'The Concept of Corporate Responsibility' (Goodpaster, 1983) he argues for a "principle of moral projection" which states: "It is appropriate not only to describe organizations (and their characteristics) by analogy with individuals, it is also appropriate normatively to look for and to foster moral attributes in organizations by analogy with those we look for and foster in individuals."

I wish to argue that it is not appropriate to think of corporations as moral agents, and that proposals directed at making corporate activity more beneficent should be based on the recognition that the individual members of the corporation, acting in various capacities, are the relevant moral agents. Neither the corporation as an entity nor the organizational structure should be treated as having independent moral status. In particular, I shall argue that Goodpaster's project may obscure more than it reveals, distracting us from other promising approaches to enhancing the role of ethics in business. I shall end by briefly attacking the person analogy as dangerous.

Goodpaster proceeds as follows: (a) decisions are made for and in the name of the corporation—these are correctly described as corporate decisions. (b) we should expect corporations to be morally responsible agents, just as we expect persons to be responsible. (c) a responsible person (in the relevant sense, which he terms the "decision-making sense") exhibits certain "cognitive and emotional dispositions . . ." (p. 7) whose elements can be identified as perception, reasoning, coordination, and implementation (p. 8), functioning in the service of the moral point of view which is described as having two components—rationality and respect. The function of the person analogy now becomes one of guiding us in "tracing" the elements of responsibility in the decision-making processes of corporations by identifying analogies.

I have no criticism of the analysis of moral responsibility ("decision-making sense") nor, on the whole, with Goodpaster's application of the concept to corporate decision-making. But I do not see that the *analogy* really plays a role, except in the thinnest way: institutions, we are told, are actors—in fact, they have "become the primary actors on the human stage, ..." (p. 9). Therefore, it makes sense to ask what it would be for a corporation to be morally responsible, and ". . . to foster moral attributes . . . by analogy with those we look for and foster in individuals." But the analogy does not suggest to Goodpaster anything *special* about the responsibility of corporations: what is required of individuals is straightforwardly transferred to corporations. Thus, they too must gather and process information, taking account of morally important impact on others; they too must reason, and include moral considerations in their reasoning; they too must try to coordinate interests that appear to conflict; and finally they too must match means to ends and do whatever is necessary to carry decisions through to implementation.

But how is all this to be done? As soon as this question is raised the unfruitfulness of the person analogy becomes apparent. In fact, if the analogy provides a special insight it may be precisely to call attention to the consequences of the corresponding *dis*analogy: While an individual, to become responsible, must develop certain habits and dispositions—what we generally refer to as a good character—a corporation must go about it another way: it must *institutionalize* the traits that we associate with responsibility (informing oneself, anticipating impact on others, etc.). The pay-off of the person analogy would then appear in the way it suggests institutional features—actual structures and procedures—that are to be set up to function like the good character of the responsible individual (information nets, etc.). But, while the development of habits is something a person might be motivated to undertake, the "institutionalizing" of anything is not something a corporation can be motivated to do. It is an institution, created by persons using another institution (the law). It can be changed by persons, from the outside; but *it* has no inner springs of change analogous to the motives of natural persons. Of course a manager can make decisions for the corporation under conditions which permit us to call these decisions *of* the corporation. But his or her inner springs of change, the cluster of motives that underlie those official actions—surely we should not attribute these to the corporation!

The parallel suggested by the analogy holds only superficially: people, to be responsible, must develop proper habits and dispositions; and corporations, to be responsible, must institutionalize the analogue of such habits and dispositions. Beneath the linguistic surface, it seems to me, the parallelism vanishes: corporations themselves *are* institutions; *they* cannot institutionalize anything. It must be people, inside or outside the corporation, who will have to decide how to institutionalize the elements of moral responsibility. The point I wish to make is that the actual process of setting up the structures and procedures that institutionalize responsibility is, necessarily, a process carried out by persons. It must therefore stem from the character of the persons who occupy the relevant positions. To the extent that these persons are responsible, in Goodpaster's sense, they will decide to fill their positions conscientiously. In implementing their own responsible decisions—step four of Goodpaster's analysis—they will in fact be setting up the structures that will have the effect of institutionalizing corporate responsibility. As structures are developed and procedures followed through, individual persons will be implementing, or failing to implement, or sabotaging decisions. Implementations, as we are told, involves fitting means to ends, setting up incentives and controls, etc. This is exactly what must be done to institutionalize values. It would seem, therefore, that if "institutionalizing" moral responsibility means anything, it is just identical with (not analogous or parallel to) the process of implementation of decisions arrived at by morally responsible individuals, as they develop and enact their roles as board members, executives, supervisors, or others who decide on structures and job descriptions.

Goodpaster himself is perfectly clear about that whenever he is dealing with concrete cases. He is very insightful in advising managers on what must be done in institutionalizing ethics. But if indeed we must all agree that it is *people* who will do the job (albeit "in the name of the corporation"), then must we not also agree that the principal question is: What can motivate people to choose and implement the institutionalizing of ethics?

The person analogy is irrelevant to this question. In fact the question illustrates the weakness of the analogy for the practical purposes at stake: while we can give a rough account of the human faculties and experiences that underlie character-development (and therefore motivation) we can find no analogues of such faculties and experiences in corporations as such. A slight digression into conditions for character-development might help to make this point clearer: Human beings develop and maintain a responsible character through exposure to a great variety of experiences that have both cognitive and affective aspects. Thus, we become aware, as we mature, of the causal connections between our wants, our behavior, and their effects on things and people external to us; and, for reasons that have been variously described, some of these effects matter to us. It is this affective element that provides the necessary motivation to bring about effects on others that we see (and feel) as good, and avoid those that we see as harmful. However one explains this, persons can be moral agents in part because they develop internal reinforcers of responsibility by seeing and emotionally reacting to the flow of events that results from their own concerns and dispositions.

What this seems to amount to is that the potential growth in moral traits such as conscientiousness, depends on eminently *human* faculties: we are capable of *valuing* some things, of *preferring* them to others, and therefore of *seeing* them as having moral weight. But if the analogue of character-development in persons is the institutionalization of certain functions in the corporate makeup, as the person analogy suggests, then what is the analogue of the facilities that *make for* character development? The corporation which, we are told, must institutionalize responsibility, does not in itself value or give moral weight to things. And so I would argue that the analogy breaks down.

Perhaps the best way to show that the above account of character-building cannot be transferred to an artificial person, is to appeal once more to Goodpaster's project: we are told that the responsible corporation, like the responsible person, must assure against moral "blindness" in the gathering and processing of information; this is defined as failure to recognize moral issues *as* moral issues (p. 8). But what guards against moral blindness? Is it not precisely the capacity of people to feel for others, the sympathy that Hume found to be a natural bond, making moral life a psychologically plausible reality? Must we not respond affectively to the good and harm that comes to others, before we can recognize it as morally relevant? And if this is so, how can we speak of a *corporation* guarding against moral blindness? Whatever qualities we attribute to that artificial being, surely it cannot be supposed to have a capacity for human sympathy. It must therefore lack the independent *internal* motivating force which is precisely what we rely on when we speak of a person of good character, a *conscientious* person.

The point is, again, that the human faculties which *make for* character development, including the development of our ability to recognize issues as having moral import (guarding against "moral blindness") have no analogue in corporations. They serve as internal motivators just because they are bound up in the very *nature* of persons. No corresponding motivating factors can be part of the nature of corporations, for in *their* case all motivators are externally imposed—as was said before, by persons implementing their own conscientiousness (or other) ends. Just as corporations cannot act except through persons, so they cannot change (or improve) except as *persons* change or improve, and implement their own changed goals.

In supporting his project Goodpaster makes a passing reference to a topic that has received much attention in recent writings about corporations—namely that of "corporate cultures". Goodpaster suggests that discussions of corporate *culture* may be taken to indicate that 'personality' (and therefore what I have called "character") can reasonably be attributed to corporations (*ibid*, p. 10). Now it is true that a "corporate culture" does function to some extent like a character: We think of a person's character as the enduring source of motivation and direction, just as the culture of a corporation is thought of as providing the enduring source of values that determine goals and major policies, as well as day-to-day modes of interacting. The culture of a corporation can be defined by the values used to justify decisions. Peters and Waterman in their book, *In Search of Excellence* argue strongly in favor of "value-driven" cultures that give everyone a sense of purpose and meaning beyond mere profit (Peters *et al.*, 1982). But they do make it clear that there is after all a purpose behind their apparently idealistic appeals to goals outside the traditional business values: a corporate culture, they say, is a management tool. As such, its purpose is ultimately to improve productivity and efficiency; and the "values" of the culture are seen to be just another instrument for good management. But for *our* purpose, we are interested in that aspect of culture which is the analogue of the character traits that we refer to as conscientiousness, moral responsibility, disinterestedness; and these cannot be mere management tools without their very essence being corrupted. It seems therefore that if we rely on "corporate culture" as an analogue of character, then we do not have what we need for the purpose of moral improvement. We have, instead a set of goals which may change, indeed, but whose elements remain tied to their function as instruments for achieving management goals. Whereas the potential for moral growth in a human character depends, as we said, on being *affected* (and thereby changed) by what happens to others as a result of our own actions.

To sum up: corporations are real enough—they are systems for the joint (usually cooperative) activity of people; to implement decisions about the outcome of such activity, people must take into account the system and shape it so that it embodies conditions for the actions of people that are best suited (means-ends) to aim at the desired outcome. Therefore what we most need to know is how *people* can become more morally responsible in shaping the institutions in which they play controlling roles. It is humans only, not corporations, who feel fear, shame, and pity; and they do so because they can see and react affectively to the flow of events in which they are causally involved, whether in personal life or in work roles. It is just such experiences that build and reinforce a responsible character. Changes of corporate goals and structures will come from experiences of *persons*. Therefore, to repeat, we must focus attention on experiences that would lead persons, in their corporate roles, to make the desired changes. To think of the institution itself as an independent actor obscures this need and distracts from the task. In concentrating on persons we gain the practical advantage of dealing with subjects of behavior whom we know to be capable of a moral life; so that moral arguments can reasonably be expected to make a difference; and so that praise and blame and the whole range of incentives and disincentives available to society can reasonably be applied to change morally dangerous intentions and dispositions; while corporations have "no pants to kick or soul to damn" (Mencken, 1942).

It may well be that Goodpaster's own position, as expressed in a more recent article (Goodpaster, 1984) would naturally lead to a similar conclusion: He refers to a study by Herman Gadon, in which Gadon concludes that moral improvement in corporate personnel policies depends on external pressures; and that this result undermines the "moral agent" model of corporations. Goodpaster argues (p. 38) that the need for external pressures, even if real, is not sufficient to show that there can be no disinterested internal perspective, i.e., no corporate conscience. In fact, he says, the analogy with persons holds: just as persons respond internally to an externally provided "prod" or "call" to ethical behavior, so too ". . . corporations might be stimulated to take the moral point of view by external events: judicial decisions, social pressures, regulatory and legislative actions, etc. The 'inner call' of conscience may be heard as differentially among organizations as among individuals." I would certainly agree that the presence of external pressures to moral change are no indication of an absence of conscience. But surely the moral response to such external pressures is a response made by individual persons. (Goodpaster is quite clear on that, as he refers, in the preceding paragraph, to "the operating assumptions of key managers as they defended or rejected various policy alternatives . . . ".) Now the response to external pressures can be motivated by prudential or "interested" considerations alone (maximizing the financial security of the firm, etc.) or it can be motivated by the individual's *moral* (disinterested) response to the facts brought to light by the external pressures. In the latter case, "the inner call of conscience" must refer to the struggle of the key managers in question to incorporate a *disinterested* perspective into the decision. But what could possibly serve as a motive for that, other than the individual's own sense of the value of such a perspective? And if this is correct, then why introduce the notion of a "corporate conscience," thereby suggesting an independent entity which could somehow be directly moved?

In a slightly earlier article (Goodpaster, 1982) Goodpaster suggests a more limited use of the person analogy: "The real force of the moral person analogy lies in legitimating the use of ethical categories for guiding corporate policy . . ." (p. 103). This is such a modest claim that one wonders why any special conceptual machinery (such as the moral person analogy) is even appealed to. Why not say simply that since corporate decisions and actions may radically affect the well-being of persons, the individuals who structure the decision-making process, make the decisions, and carry them out, are morally bound to take such effects into account. Ethical categories are relevant, whether one acts on one's own behalf or as agent for a corporation. And this is so, not because corporations are like moral agents, but just because corporate decisions, like personal decisions, can have serious consequences.

So far I have argued that the person analogy is not fruitful. Let me now briefly go on to the attack and show that it can have downright negative effects, insofar as it encourages the view that the corporation deserves to be served and protected for its own sake. People, of course, have intrinsic value— their survival and welfare are valuable for their own sake. But a corporation is an artificial instrument, a human tool with no *intrinsic* value. (Similar points have been made by several writers, e.g., Velasquez, 1983.) To the extent that employees (all the way up to the CEO) see themselves as serving the company in a sense where "The Company" is perceived as a superperson with a life and interest of its own; to that extent some morally important issues will be screened out of their considerations as irrelevant. If, furthermore, they perceive their own security and advancement to be dependent on just such a view of their role, then even when moral considerations become obvious, they will be less likely to be acted upon because of conflict with self-interest. A comparison with service professions should help make the point: hospitals employ doctors and nurses, and these see their role as one of service to the patients (we hope!). If they were to see the *hospital* as the "person" whose interest they are to serve, we should find this most unfortunate. The closer the employees approach the ideal of seeing themselves as freely engaged in a labor whose outcome they recognize as valuable in human terms, rather than "for the Company", the more natural it is for them to use ordinary moral categories in noticing, evaluating, and choosing alternatives in the course of their work. In the ideal situation of freely chosen work, there is a natural readiness to assume responsibility for the consequences of one's actions.

Another way of looking at the issue is to see that the person analogy naturally encourages what has been called "strong role-differentiation" for business managers. Alan Goldman argues at length against such role-differentiation, that is, against managers being seen by others and by themselves as having primary professional duties to serve the corporation, which supersede ordinary morality. (Goldman, 1980) He argues convincingly that such a view would encourage "occupants of the roles in question to become insensitive to the common moral rights of others . . . but departure from common moral principle in favor of professional norms would be most dangerous perhaps in the case of business, in which the central norm is linked to personal gain, rather than directly to justice or the good of others, as in law and medicine."

In conclusion, the person analogy appears to do more harm than good, first, in distracting us from the critical task of motivating *persons* to develop habits of responsible action in their work roles; and secondly, in its tendency to obscure the fact that corporations ought not to be served for their own sake.

NOTE

I am grateful to Larry May of Purdue University for his comments on an earlier draft of this paper.

References

Goldman, A.: 1980, 'Business Ethics: Profits, Utilities, and Moral Rights', *Philosophy and Public Affairs* **9**, 260–286.
Goodpaster, K.: 1982, 'Review of Thomas Donaldson, *Corporation and Morality', Business and Professional Ethics Journal* **1**, 101–105.
Goodpaster, K.: 1983, 'The Concept of Corporate Responsibility', *Journal of Business Ethics* **2**, 1–22.
Goodpaster, K.: 1984, 'Testing Morality in Organizations', *The International Journal of Applied Philosophy* **2**, 35–38.
Mencken, H. L.: 1942, *A New Dictionary of Quotations on Historical Principles from Ancient and Modern Sources*, Knopf, New York.
Peters, T. J. and Waterman, R. H.: 1982, *In Search of Excellence*, Harper and Row, New York.
Velasquez, M.: 1983, 'Why Corporations Are Not Morally Responsible for Anything They Do', *Business and Professional Ethics Journal* **2**, 1–18.

The Corporation
as a Moral Person

Peter A. French

In his *New York Times* column, Tom Wicker expressed his aroused ire at a Gulf Oil Corporation advertisement that "pointed the finger of blame" for energy shortages and high prices at virtually every element of our society except the oil companies. Wicker, as might be expected, attacked Gulf Oil and the petroleum industry as the major, if not the sole, perpetrators of that crisis and most every other social ill, with the possible exception of venereal disease.

In a courtroom in Winamac, Indiana, in 1979–80, the Ford Motor Company was tried for reckless homicide in the deaths of Judy, Lyn, and Donna Ulrich. The three teenagers were incinerated when the Ford Pinto in which they were driving was hit in the rear at a speed differential of around thirty miles per hour. One of the law professors who worked as a consultant for the prosecution recently wrote: "What we were saying is that a corporation like all other persons must be forced at times to look at the very personal tragedies it causes."[1] The prosecution's case was directed at demonstrating the moral and criminal capacity for responsibility of the Ford Motor Company. No attempt was made to prosecute individual Ford executives or engineers. We need not concern ourselves with whether Wicker was serious or merely sarcastic when he made his charges against Gulf. Most certainly the prosecution in the Pinto case was serious and, although Ford Motor Company was acquitted of the charges, the concept of corporate moral and legal responsibility was not discredited. Indeed, it was provided with a landmark of courtroom precedent and popular acceptance. In this essay I will examine the sense ascriptions of moral responsibility make when their subjects are corporations. I hope to provide the foundation of a theory that allows treatment of corporations as full-fledged members of the moral community, of equal standing with the traditionally acknowledged residents: human beings. With such a theory in hand we should treat moral-responsibility ascriptions to corporations as unexceptionable instances of a perfectly proper sort and not have to paraphrase or reduce them. Corporations as moral persons will have whatever privileges, rights and duties as are, in the normal course of affairs, accorded to all members of the moral community.

It is important to distinguish three quite different notions of what is it to be a person that are frequently entangled throughout the various aspects of our tradition: the metaphysical, moral, and legal concepts of personhood. The entanglement is clearly evident in John Locke's account of personal identity. He writes that the term "person" is "a *forensic* term, appropriating actions and their merit; and so belongs only to *intelligent agents,* capable of law, and happiness, and misery." He goes on to say that by consciousness and memory persons are capable of extending themselves into the past and thereby become "concerned and *accountable.*"[2] Locke is historically correct in citing the law as a primary origin of the term "person." But he is incorrect in maintaining that its legal usage entails its metaphysical sense, agency; and whether or not either sense, but especially the metaphysical, is interdependent on the moral sense, accountability, is surely controversial.

There are two distinct schools of thought regarding the relationship between metaphysical and moral persons. According to one, to be a metaphysical person is only to be a moral one; to understand what it is to be accountable, one must understand what it is to be an intentional or a rational agent and vice versa. According to the other, being an intentional agent is a necessary but not a sufficient condition of being a moral person. Locke appears to hold the interdependence view, with which I agree, but he roots both moral and metaphysical persons in the juristic person, which is, I think, wrongheaded. The preponderance of current thinking in moral and social theory, however, endorses some version of the necessary precondition view. Most of those holding such a position do exhibit the virtue of treating legal personhood as something apart from moral and metaphysical matters.

It is of note that many contemporary moral philosophers and economists both defend a precondition view of the relationship between the metaphysical and moral person and also adopt a view of the legal personhood of corporations that excludes corporations per se from the class of moral persons. Such philosophers and economists tend to champion the least defensible of a number of possible interpretations of the juristic personhood of corporations, but their doing so allows them to systematically sidestep the question of whether corporations can meet the conditions of metaphysical personhood.[3]

John Rawls is, to some extent, guilty of fortifying what I hope to show is an indefensible interpretation of the legal concept and of thereby encouraging an anthropocentric bias that has led to the general belief that corporations just cannot be moral persons. As is well known, Rawls defends his two principles of justice by the use of a thought experiment that incorporates the essential characteristics of what he takes to be a premoral, though metaphysical population and then derives the moral guidelines for social institutions that they would accept. The persons (or parties) in the "original position" are described by Rawls as being mutually self-interested, rational, as having similar wants, needs, interests, and capacities and as being, for all intents and purposes, equal in power (so that no one of them can dominate the others).

Their choice of the principles of justice is, as Daniel Dennett has pointed out,[4] a rather dramatic rendering of one version of the compelling (though I think unnecessarily complex) philosophical thesis that only out of metaphysical persons can moral ones evolve.

But Rawls is remarkably ambiguous (and admittedly so) regarding who or what may qualify as a metaphysical person. He admits into the category, in one sentence, not only biological human beings but "nations, provinces, business firms, churches, teams, and so on," then, perhaps because he does not want to tackle the demonstration of the rationality of those institutions and organizations, or because he is a captive of the traditional prejudice in favor of biological persons, in the next sentence he withdraws entry. "There is, perhaps, a certain logical priority to the case of human individuals: it may be possible to analyze the actions of so-called artificial persons as logical constructions of the actions of human persons. . . ."[5] "Perhaps" is, of course, a rather large hedge behind which to hide; but it is, I suppose, of some significance that in *A Theory of Justice* when he is listing the nature of the parties in the "original position" he adds as item c "associations (states, churches, or other corporate bodies."[6] He does not, unfortunately, discuss this entry on his list anywhere else in the book. Rawls had hold, I think, of an important intuition: that some associations of human beings should be treated as metaphysical persons capable, on his account, of becoming moral persons, in and of themselves. He shrunk, however, from the task of exploring the implications of that intuition and instead retreated to the comfortable bulwarks of the anthropocentric bias.

Many philosophers, including (I think) Rawls, have rather uncritically relied upon what they incorrectly perceive to be the most defensible juristic treatment of corporations as a paradigm for the treatment of corporations in their moral theories. The concept of corporate legal personhood under any of its popular interpretations is, I want to argue, virtually useless for moral purposes.

Following a number of writers on jurisprudence, a juristic person may be defined as any entity that is a subject of a right. There are good etymological grounds for such an inclusive neutral definition. The Latin *persona* originally referred to *dramatis personae*, but in Roman law the term was adopted to refer to anything that could act on either side of a legal dispute. (It was not until Boethius' definition of a person: *"Persona est naturae rationabilis individua substantia"* [a person is the individual subsistence of a rational nature] that metaphysical traits were ascribed to persons.) In effect, in Roman legal tradition persons are creations or artifacts of the law itself, i.e., of the legislature that enacts the law, and are not considered to have, or only have incidentally, existence of any kind outside of the legal sphere. The law, on the Roman interpretation, is systematically ignorant of the biological status of its subjects.

The Roman notion applied to corporations is popularly known as the Fiction Theory. Frederick Hallis characterizes that theory as maintaining that "the personality of a corporate body is a pure fiction and owes its existence to a creative act of the state."[7] Rawls' view of corporate persons, however, is not a version of the Fiction Theory. The theory draws no dichotomy between real and artificial persons. All juristic persons, on the theory, are creations of the law. The Fiction Theory does not view the law as recognizing or verifying prelegally existing persons; it maintains that the law creates all of its own subjects. Second, the theory, in its pure form at least, does not regard any juristic persons as composites. All things which are legislatively created as subjects of rights are nonreducible or, if you will, primitive individual legal persons. It is of some note that the Fiction Theory is enshrined in English law in regard to corporate bodies by no less an authority than Sir Edward Coke, who wrote that corporations "rest only in intendment and consideration of the law."[8]

The Fiction Theory's major rival in American jurisprudence and the view that does seem to inform Rawls' account is what I shall call the Legal Aggregate Theory of the Corporation. It holds that the names of corporate organizations are only umbrellas that cover (but do not shield) a specific aggregate of biological persons. The Aggregate Theory allows that biological status has legal priority and that a corporation is but a contrivance, the name of which is best used for summary reference. (Aggregate Theorists tend to ignore employees and identify corporations with directors, executives, and stockholders. The model on which they stake their claim is no doubt that of the primitive partnership) . . .

The third major rival interpretation of corporate juristic personhood resides in Germanic legal tradition. Primarily because of the advocacy of Otto von Gierke, the so-called Reality Theory recognizes corporations to be prelegal existing sociological persons. Underlying the theory is the view that law cannot create its subjects; it can only determine which societal facts are in conformity with its requirements. Law endorses the prelegal existence of persons for its own purposes. Gierke regards the corporation as an offspring of certain social actions and as having a de facto personality, which the law declares to be a juridical fact.[9] The Reality Theory's primary virtue is that it does not ignore the nonlegal roots of the corporation while it, as may the Fiction Theory, acknowledges the nonidentity of the corporation and the aggregate of its directors, stockholders, executives, and employees. The primary difference between the Fiction and Reality Theories, that one treats the corporate person as de jure and the other as de facto, turns out to be of no real importance, however, in regard to the issue of the moral personhood of a corporation. Admittedly the Reality Theory encapsulates a view at least superficially more amenable to arguing for discrete corporate moral personhood than does the Fiction Theory just because it does acknowledge de facto personhood, but theorists on both sides will admit that they are providing interpretations of only the formula "juristic person = the subject of rights," and as long as we stick to legal history, no interpretation of that formula need concern itself with metaphysical personhood or intentional agency. The de facto personhood of the Reality Theory is that of a sociological entity only, of which no claim is or need be made regarding agency, or rationality, or any of the traits of a metaphysical person. One could, without contradiction, hold the Reality Theory and deny the metaphysical or moral personhood of corporations. What is needed is a Reality Theory that identifies a de facto metaphysical person not just a sociological entity.

Underlying all of these interpretations of corporate legal personhood is a distinction, embedded in the law itself, that renders them unhelpful for our purposes. Being a subject of rights is often contrasted in the law with being an administrator of rights. Any number of entities and associations can and have been the subjects of legal rights. In earlier times, animals have been given legal rights; legislatures have given rights to unborn human beings; they have reserved rights for human beings long after their death; and in some recent cases they have invested rights in generations of the future. Of course such recipients of rights, though, strictly speaking, legal persons, cannot dispose of their rights. They also cannot administer them, because to administer a right one must be an intentional agent, i.e., able to *act* in certain ways. It may be only an historical accident that most legal cases are cases in which "the subject of right X" and "the administrator of right X" are coreferential. It is nowhere required by law, not under any of the three theories just discussed or elsewhere, that it be so. Yet, it is possession of the attributes of an administrator of rights and not those of a subject of rights that constitutes the generally accepted conditions of moral personhood. It is a fundamental mistake to regard the fact of juristic corporate personhood as having settled the question of the moral personhood of a corporation one way or the other.

Two helpful lessons are learned from the investigation of the legal personhood of corporations: (1) biological existence is not essentially associated with the concept of personhood (only the fallacious Aggregate Theory depends upon reduction to biological beings), and (2) a paradigm for the form of an inclusive neutral definition of a moral person is provided: a subject of a right. I shall define a moral person as a referent of any proper name or of any noneliminatable subject in an ascription of moral responsibility. The noneliminatable nature of the subject should be stressed because responsibility and other predicates of morality are neutral as regards person and person-sum predication.[10] I argued [elsewhere] that ascriptions of moral responsibility involve the notions of accountability and being held liable for an answer. These notions presuppose the existence of responsibility relationships, and one of their primary foci is on the subject's intentions. To be the subject of an ascription of moral responsibility, to be a party in responsibility relationships, hence to be a moral person, the subject must be at minimum an intentional actor.[11] If corporations are moral persons they will evidence a noneliminatable intentionality with regard to the things they do.

For a corporation to be treated as a moral person, it must be the case that some events are describable in a way that makes certain sentences true: sentences that say that some of the things a corporation does were intended by the corporation itself. That is not accomplished if attributing intentions to a corporation is only a shorthand way of attributing intentions to the biological persons who comprise, e.g., its board of directors. If that were to turn out to be the case, then on metaphysical if not logical grounds, there would be no real way to distinguish between corporations and crowds. I shall argue, however, that a Corporation's Internal Decision Structure (its CID Structure) provides the requisite redescription device that licenses the predication of corporate intentionality. . . .

The important point is that metaphysical personhood depends on the possibility of describing an event as an intentional action. Often a single event can be correctly described in a number of different and nonequivent ways. With respect to some events, there are layers of nonintersubstitutable true descriptions. Some layers merely describe the event as a movement or a piece of behavior. Other layers describe the same event as the effect of prior causes that are reasons or desires and beliefs. Significantly, a single event may be described as the effect of different sets of reasons, even of different kinds of reasons, so there may be more than one layer of true descriptions of an event at which it is appropriate to identify it as an intentional action. At every layer at which it is proper to describe an event as an intentional action, there is a metaphysical person, an actor.

Certainly a corporation's doing something involves or includes human beings doing things, and the human beings who occupy various positions in a corporation usually can be described as having reasons for *their* behavior. In fact, in virtue of those descriptions, they may be properly held responsible for their behavior, ceteris paribus. What needs to be shown if there is to be corporate responsibility is that there is sense in saying that corporations and not just the people who work in them have reasons for doing what they do. Typically, we will be told that corporate reasons are to be identified with the reasons and desires of the directors or of certain high-level managers and that, although corporate action may not be reducible without remainder, corporate intentions are always reducible to such executive intentions. Such a view is, in fact, captured in English legal precedent, specifically in the 1971 case of *Tesco Supermarkets Ltd. v. Nattcass.* The supermarket company was charged under a section of the Trade Descriptions Act of 1968. The case involved false price advertising. An assistant had replaced reduced-priced soap boxes with those marked at regular prices. The assistant did not notify the store manager who is responsible for seeing that sales items were properly priced. The manager failed to check the pricing on his own. The company argued that it had exercised due diligence and that the negligence was that of a person too far down in the corporate hierarchy to be identified with the intentions of the corporation itself. The House of Lords found in the company's favor, thereby endorsing the idea that corporate reasons are the reasons of senior executive staff members. Such a view, I shall argue, is not adequate to the understanding of corporate intentionality. It should, however, be strikingly plain that finding directional negligence, for example, is not necessarily finding corporate negligence. If an underling can act for personal, self-serving reasons, so can a director, and his doing so may have nothing to do with the corporation's business practices. In fact those practices may make his self-serving possible by creating a climate of trust and honesty in which he can operate.

Every corporation has an internal decision structure. CID Structures have two elements of interest to us here: (1) an organizational or responsibility flowchart that delineates stations and levels within the corporate power structure and (2) corporate-decision recognition rule(s) (usually embedded in something called corporation policy). The CID Structure is the personnel organization for the exercise of the corporation's power with respect to its ventures, and as such its primary function is to draw experience from various levels of the corporation into a decision-making and ratification process. When operative and properly activated, the CID Structure accomplishes a subordination and synthesis of the intentions and acts of various biological persons into a corporate decision. When viewed in another way, as already suggested, the CID Structure licenses the descriptive transformation of events, seen under another aspect as the acts of biological persons (those who occupy various stations on the organizational chart), to corporate acts by exposing the corporate character of those events. A CID Structure *incorporates* acts of biological persons. For illustrative purposes, suppose we imagine that an event E has at least two aspects, that is, can be described in two nonidentical ways. One of those aspects is "Executive X's doing y" and one is "Corporation C's doing z." The corporate act and the individual act may have different properties; indeed they have different causal ancestors, though they are causally inseparable. (I hope to show that the causal inseparability of these acts is a product of the CID Structure; X's doing y is not the cause of C's doing z; nor is C's doing z the cause of X's doing y; although if X's doing y causes event F, then C's doing z causes F and vice versa.)

J. K. Galbraith rather neatly captures what I have in mind, although I doubt he is aware of the metaphysical reading that can be given to this process, when he writes in his recent popular book on the history of economics: "From [the] interpersonal exercise of power, the interaction . . . of the participants, comes the *personality* of the corporation."[12] I take Galbraith here to be quite literally correct, but it is important to spell out how a CID Structure works this miracle.

In philosophy in recent years we have grown accustomed to the use of games as models for understanding institutional behavior. We all have some understanding of how rules in games make certain descriptions of events possible, which would not be so if those rules were nonexistent. The CID Structure of a corporation is a kind of constitutive rule (or rules) analogous to the game rules with which we are familiar. The organization chart of a corporation distinguishes players and clarifies their rank and the interwoven lines of responsibility within the corporation. An organizational chart tells us, for example, that anyone holding the title "Executive vice-president for finance administration" stands in a certain relationship to anyone holding the title "director of internal audit" and to anyone holding the title "treasurer," etc. In effect it expresses, or maps, the interdependent and dependent relationships, line and staff, that are involved in determinations of corporate decisions and actions. The organizational chart provides what might be called the grammar of corporate decision-making. What I shall call internal recognition rules provide its logic.

By "recognition rule(s)" I mean what Hart, in another context, calls "conclusive affirmative indication," that a decision on an act has been made or performed for corporate reasons.[13] Recognition rules are of two sorts. Partially embedded in the organizational chart are procedural recognitors: We see that decisions are to be reached collectively at certain levels and that they are to be ratified at higher levels (or at inner circles, if one prefers that Galbraithean model). A corporate decision is recognized internally, however, not only by the procedure is its making, but by the policy it instantiates. Hence every corporation creates an image (not to be confused with its public image) or a general policy, what G. C. Buzby of the Chilton Company has called the "basic belief of the corporation," that must inform its decisions for them to be properly described as being those of that corporation. "The moment policy is sidestepped or violated, it is no longer the policy of that company."[14]

Peter Drucker has seen the importance of the basic policy recognitors in the CID Structure (though he treats matters rather differently from the way I am recommending). Drucker writes:

> Because the corporation is an institution it must have a basic policy. For it must subordinate individual ambitions and decisions to the *needs* of the corporation's welfare and survival. That means that it must have a set of principles and a rule of conduct which limit and direct individual actions and behavior.[15]

Suppose, for illustrative purposes, we activate a CID Structure in a corporation, Tom Wicker's whipping boy, the Gulf Oil Corporation. Imagine that three executives, Jones, Smith, and Jackson have the task of deciding whether or not Gulf Oil will join a world uranium cartel. They have before them an Everest of papers that have been prepared by lower-echelon executives. Some of the papers will be purely factual reports, some will be contingency plans, some will be formulations of positions developed by various departments, some will outline financial considerations, and some will be legal opinions. Insofar as these will all have been processed through Gulf's CID Structure system, the personal reasons, if any, individual executives may have had for writing their reports and recommendations in a specific way will likely have been diluted by the subordination of individual inputs to peer group input and higher level review and recommendation before Jones, Smith, and Jackson deal with the matter. A vote is taken, as is authorized procedure in the Gulf CID Structure, which is to say that under these circumstances the vote of Jones, Smith, and Jackson can be redescribed as the corporation's making a decision: that is, the event "Jones, Smith, and Jackson voting" may be redescribed to expose an aspect otherwise unrevealed, quite different from its other aspects, e.g., from Jones's (or Smith's or Jackson's) voting in the affirmative. Redescriptive exposure of a procedurally corporate aspect of an event is not to be confused with a description of an event that makes true a sentence that says that the corporation did something intentionally. But the CID Structure, as already suggested, also provides the grounds in its other type of recognitor for such an attribution of corporate intentionality. Simply, when the corporate act is consistent with an instantiation or an implementation of established corporate policy, then it is proper to describe it as having been done for corporate reasons, as having been caused by a corporate desire coupled with a corporate belief and so, in other words, as corporate intentional.

An event may, under one of its aspects, be described as the conjunctive act "Jones intentionally voted yes, and Smith intentionally voted yes, and Jackson did so as well" (where a "yes" vote was to vote in the affirmative on the question of Gulf oil joining the cartel). Within the Gulf CID Structure we find the conjunction of rules that tell us that when the occupants of positions A, B, and C on the organizational chart unanimously vote to do something that is consistent with an instantiation or an implementation of general corporate policy and ceteris paribus, Gulf Oil Corporation has decided to do it for corporate reasons. The event of those executives voting is then redescribable as "the Gulf Oil Corporation decided to join the cartel for reasons consistent with basic policy of Gulf Oil, e.g., increasing profits," or simply as "Gulf Oil Corporation intentionally decided to join the cartel." This is a rather technical way of saying that in these circumstances the executives voting is, given its CID Structure, also the corporation deciding to do something. Regardless of the personal reasons the executives have for voting as they do, and even if their reasons are inconsistent with established corporate policy or even if one of them has no reason at all for voting as he does, the corporation still has reasons for joining the cartel, that is, joining is consistent with the inviolate corporate general policies, as encrusted in the precedent of previous corporation actions, and its statements of purpose as recorded in its certificate of incorporation, annual reports, etc. The corporation's only method of achieving its desires or goals is the activation of the personnel who occupy its various positions. However, if Jones voted affirmatively purely for reasons of personal monetary gain (suppose she had been bribed to do so) that does not alter the fact that the corporate reason for joining the cartel was to minimize competition and hence pay higher dividends to its shareholders. Corporations have reasons because they have interests in doing those things that are likely to result in realization of their established corporate goals, regardless of the transient self-interest of directors or managers. If there is a difference between corporate goals and desires and those of human beings, it is probably that the corporate ones are relatively stable and not very wide ranging, but that is only because corporations can do relatively fewer things than human beings, being confined in action predominantly to a limited socioeconomic sphere. It is, of course, in a corporation's interest that its component membership views the corporate purposes as instrumental in the achievement of their own goals. (Financial reward is the most common way this is achieved.) . . .

The CID Structure licenses both redescriptions of events as corporate and attributions of corporate intentionality, while it does not obscure the private acts of executives, directors, etc. Although Jones voted to support the joining of the cartel because she was bribed to do so, Jones did not join the cartel, Gulf Oil Corporation joined the cartel. Consequently, we may say that Jones did something for which she should be held morally responsible, yet whether or not Gulf Oil Corporation should be held morally responsible for joining the cartel is a question that turns on issues that may be unrelated to Jones' having accepted a bribe.

Of course Gulf Oil Corporation cannot join the cartel unless Jones or somebody who occupies position A on the organizational chart votes in the affirmative. What that shows, however, is that corporations are organizations or associations including human beings. That should not, however, rule out the possibility of their having metaphysical status, as being intentional actors in their own right, and being thereby full-fledged moral persons.

This much I hope is clear: we can describe many events in terms of certain physical movements of human beings, and we also can sometimes describe those very events as done for reasons by those human beings, but further we can sometimes describe the same events as corporate and still further as done for corporate reasons that are qualitatively different from whatever personal reasons component members may have for doing what they do.

Corporate agency resides in the possibility of CID Structure licensed redescription of events as corporate intentional. That may still appear to be downright mysterious, although I do not think it is, for human agency as I have suggested, resides in the possibility of description as well.

NOTES

1. Bruce Berner, "Letter to William Maakestad," published in "The Ford Pinto Case and Beyond." A paper presented by F. Cullen, W. Maakestad, and G. Cavender at the 1983 Meeting of the Academy of Criminal Justice Sciences, 1983.

2. John Locke, *An Essay Concerning Human Understanding*, P. H. Nidditch, ed. (Oxford: Oxford University Press, 1975) Book II, ch. 27, p. 346.

3. For a particularly flagrant example see Michael Jensen and William Meckling, "Theory of the Firm: Managerial Behavior, Agency Costs and Ownership Structure," *Journal of Financial Economics* (1976), 3:305–60. On page 311 they write, "The private corporation or firm is simply one form of legal fiction which serves as a nexus for contracting relationships."

4. Daniel Dennett, "Conditions of Personhood," in A. O. Rorty, ed., *The Identities of Persons* (Berkeley: University of California Press, 1976), pp. 175–96.

5. John Rawls, "Justice as Reciprocity," in Samuel Gorovitz, ed., *John Stuart Mill, Utilitarianism* (Indianapolis: Bobbs-Merrill, 1971), pp. 244–45.

6. John Rawls, *A Theory of Justice* (Cambridge: Harvard University Press, 1970), p. 146.

7. Frederick Hallis, *Corporate Personality* (Oxford: Oxford University Press, 1930), p. xlii.

8. *Coke's Reports* 253, see Hallis, *Corporate Personality,* p. xlii.

9. See in particular Otto von Gierke, *Die Genossenschoftstheorie* (Berlin, 1887).

10. See Gerald Massey, "Tom, Dick, and Harry and All the King's Men," *American Philosophical Quarterly* (April 1976), 13(2):89–108.

11. I am especially indebted to Donald Davidson, "Agency," in Robert Binkley, Richard Bronaugh, and Ausonio Marras, eds., *Agent, Action, and Reason* (Toronto: University of Toronto Press, 1971).

12. John Kenneth Galbraith, *The Age of Uncertainty* (Boston: Houghton Mifflin, 1977), p. 261.

13. H. L. A. Hart, *The Concept of Law* (Oxford, Oxford University Press, 1961), ch. 6.

14. G. C. Buzby, "Policies—A Guide to What A Company Stands For," *Management Record* (March 1962), 24:5–12.

15. Peter Drucker, *The Concept of Corporation* (New York: Crowell, 1972), pp. 36–37.

Personalizing Corporate Ontology: The French Way

Thomas Donaldson

The trickiest philosophical problems are those for which we choose alternative and self-contradictory solutions. The problem of corporate agency appears to be of this kind, at least insofar as leading theorists investigating it have divided their opinions dramatically, one side declaring the corporation to be an impersonal machine incapable of even modest moral attributes, and the other proclaiming it to be a person with similarities to human beings, similarities sufficient, indeed, to warrant sponsoring the development of moral faculties such as "consciousness" in the corporation analogous to those on the level of flesh and blood people.[1] Logic tells us that the corporation cannot be both machine and person, but which side of the dilemma are we to choose?

When a penetrating mind encounters a dilemma, it often refuses to be pigeonholed by either side. This seems to characterize Peter French who, despite subtle suggestions now and then that his view remains the same, began his writing on the subject strongly emphasizing the similarities between corporations and human beings—he began, one might say, as an unabashed moral person theorist—and has ever since been modifying his view in the opposite direction. In this article I investigate French's shift of view in detail, for I believe it provides a clue to a problem underlying his entire analysis. I argue that in the end he is driven to propose a modified set of conditions for moral personhood that are insufficient for his task, and that, although he manages to clarify key problematic issues, he nonetheless fails in his primary mission of bridging the conceptual gap between corporations and human beings. His mission fails, I believe, because it is a mission impossible.

Through a series of separate writings,[2] we find French moving from a view which presumes that the set of rights and duties held by traditional persons can be held by corporate "persons," to one that denies the legitimacy of presuming without independent evidence that rights and duties attaching to human beings have straightforward counterparts in the corporation. In an early writing, "The Corporation as Moral Person," for example, we find in the opening paragraph a statement of vigorous personalism: he writes "I hope to provide the foundation of a theory that allows treatment of corporations as members of the moral community, of equal standing with the traditionally acknowledged residents: biological human beings, and hence treats . . . responsibility ascriptions as unexceptionable instances of a perfectly proper sort without having to paraphrase them. In short, corporations can be full-fledged moral persons and can have whatever privileges, rights, and duties as are, in the normal course of affairs, accorded to moral persons."[3]

Now to assert that whatever privileges, rights, and duties are normally accorded to ordinary moral persons, can also be possessed by corporations is a vigorous assertion of moral similarity between corporations and people. It would appear that once we are happy with the list of rights and duties that we think characterize normal, adult human beings, we can then apply that list *en toto* to corporations—at least corporations that meet certain structural and procedural conditions.[4] Think of the list the average person would draw up for flesh and blood persons, and then think of it applied to Exxon or Union Carbide. Such a list would include, I suppose, all ten items in the U.S. Constitution's Bill of Rights, including rights to privacy, property, and freedom from cruel and unusual punishment, and also those rights highlighted in the preamble to the Declaration of Independence, e.g., to life, liberty, and the pursuit of happiness.

One almost begins to suspect that Professor French did not intend such a strong statement; in any case, he clearly wishes in later writings to establish limits on the ascription of rights to corporations. In his recent book, for example, he responds to a criticism I had made in this regard.

> (Donaldson) tells us "If, morally speaking, corporations are analogous to persons, then they should have the rights which ordinary persons have." The idea is that

we will be aghast at this notion and give up the theory as having an absurd corollary. But does it? . . . (Donaldson) claims that it would be implausible for corporations to have the right to vote and to draw Social Security benefits. Yes it would definitely be implausible, indeed it would be stupid.[5]

So one thing is clear. Professor French wants to deny attribution of at least some rights to corporations. Does he then wish to persist in maintaining that corporations are directly analogous to human persons? Apparently so. Notice that his question in the above paragraph, i.e., "But does it (have an absurd corollary)?" suggests that he is less than aghast at maintaining strong moral interchangeability. And in the next line he writes:

> But that proves absolutely nothing. Twelve-year-old human children do not have either the right to vote or the right to draw Social Security benefits. And why not? Because legislated rights are not always, in fact rarely are they, nonrestrictive. The fact that a perfectly competent sixteen-year old woman does not have the right to vote says nothing at all about her moral status.[6]

So now he appears able to defend the claim that corporations are directly analogous to human persons, since even in the instance of ordinary persons, not *all* rights are possessed by *all* persons. The key to his defense is the notion of the general restrictiveness of rights in application to persons. Sixteen-year old women do not have the right to vote, and corporations do not have the right to draw social security presumably because legislated rights typically have classificatory restrictions built into their application; and yet their not having such rights makes them no less "moral persons." Of course, he concludes, "Donaldson might have argued that corporations cannot be said to have natural rights. That, of course, is unexceptionable. To have natural rights something must be natural. Corporations are clearly not . . . (Hence) Donaldson's argument from rights is utterly beside the point, misguided, and irrelevant.[7]

Something is wrong here. The above remark implies both that corporations *do* have those rights that are granted to them by duly authorized legislative bodies, and do *not* have those rights that traditionally are classified as "natural." But *prima facie* this is niggardly from the perspective of corporate rights. Among the rights counted as "natural" are those such as the right to property and to free speech, ones which Professor French—and excepting Marxists everyone else—wants to grant. Surely corporations have rights to property and free speech, and surely we must, in turn, adjust our interpretation of Professor French's account to square with this obvious fact.

Now this problem can be remedied only by adding the caveat that corporations possess rights to, e.g., property and speech, but that in the case of the corporation these are not "natural" rights, but instead have their epistemological source elsewhere, perhaps in legislation. But the remedy in this instance is worse than the disease. For either it is the case that corporations have rights to all the things that normally are counted as the objects of natural rights, or it is not. If it is, then an obvious objection arises, namely, that it is silly to imagine corporations having rights to life or unhindered worship, since they have neither lives nor religious sentiments.

If it is not, then a plethora of interconnected difficulties arises. First this contradicts the earlier assertion that corporations "can have whatever privileges, rights, and duties as are, in the normal course of affairs, accorded to moral persons." The caveat that legislated rights are restrictively applied is of little help here; in other words, it will not do to claim that a corporation's lack of the right to freedom of religious worship is like a non-citizen's lack of a right to vote, or like an ineligible person's lack of a right to draw medicare benefits. Unlike legislated rights (which are usually called "legal" rights in the literature) those rights contained in the package known as "natural rights" are understood by scholars to apply without exception to all adult, rational human beings. The only exceptions Locke makes in the application of rights are for children and those lacking human rationality. Hence all adult persons have *all* natural rights, e.g., to life, liberty, property, and so on, with the result that, unless we wish to exclude corporations on grounds of being "children" or "insane," then a commitment to the idea that corporations are directly analogous to human persons will involve attributing to them the entire list of rights included in the package of natural rights (although we may refuse to call them "natural" rights on the ground that corporations are not natural entities). But, again, this fails because some members of that list are simply inappropriate for corporate entities.

Second, claiming that corporations possess some but not all the rights usually called "natural" prompts the obvious question of how we know *which* rights are included in the "some." The first answer that comes to mind, and the one French seems to be hinting at in the remarks above, is that they have precisely those rights granted to them by duly authorized legislatures, or duly convened court sessions. Hence, the answer comes by looking at statutory and common law in the legal jurisdiction the corporation happens to inhabit. But this answer must be rejected as French himself notes in other writings. To claim that corporations have only those rights granted through law would be to consider them simply as juristic persons, as persons with exclusively legal personalities from the standpoint of morality. And while this constitutes much of the rationale behind the traditional concept in law of the corporation as a "persona ficta,"[8] it fails utterly as a canon of moral analysis. Juristic rights and duties can be poor or misleading guides to the determination of moral rights and duties. For example, the deceased in a probate case is a juristic person with certain legal rights (to have his will executed properly, for instance), but this fact is inadequate for establishing that the deceased is a moral agent, because, except for his or her past deeds, a deceased person cannot be held *morally* responsible for anything. Legal rights are typically distinguished from moral rights and for good reason. Consider the best accepted current definition of a right, which is offered by Joel Feinberg. A right, says Feinberg, is a "valid claim *to* something and *against* someone which is recognized by the principles of an enlightened conscience."[9] In other words, any right makes a claim *to* something, as a right to free speech is a right to speak freely, or a right to equal treatment is a right to be treated as all others would be in relevantly similar situations. At the same time, any right makes a claim *against* someone, in the sense that my right to free speech must also be a claim against those who are obliged to allow me to speak, or my right to equal treatment is a claim against those who are obliged to treat me equally.

Now most important in this definition is the idea that rights are entities or attributes recognized by the principles of an enlightened conscience and not by courts or legislatures. The U.S. Congress did not recognize the right of American blacks to not be slaves in 1850, but blacks then had a right to be free nonetheless. And today, the Soviet Union may not recognize the legal right of its citizens to free speech, but they have a right to speak freely nonetheless. Indeed, it is this notion of a right as a claim or entitlement that is justified not by law but by the nature of reason and reality that lies behind the notion of some rights as being "natural," and not so much, as Professor French seems to suggest, the idea that humans have rights because they are biological, i.e., "natural," creatures. In any event, this is another reason why it is crucial to distinguish legal rights and duties from moral ones and not to suppose that we can determine the rights or duties of any moral agent, corporation or human person, by merely consulting the law books. If the corporation is to be a moral person, and not merely a juristic person, it must possess some of its moral characteristics *qua* moral person, and not *qua* legal person. Finally, and most important, this constitutes a second reason why the other side of French's dilemma, in which he is forced to grant that only some of those rights called "natural" apply to corporations, is unacceptable. It is unacceptable because, once cut free from the appeal to courts and legislatures, we are entirely at sea when it comes to saying which "natural" rights do, and which do not, characterize the corporation.[10] This is a shaky platform, indeed, from which to proclaim the profound similarity between corporations and ordinary moral agents.

Having seen the problem, it remains to identify its theoretical source. Where did French go wrong, and why is he driven in the end to moderate so completely his earlier assertions about corporate personalism? My own suspicion is that die is cast early, about the time he attempts to ground the moral agency of the corporation on its status as an intentional or Davidsonian agent. Now were it true that plain, unmodified Davidsonian agency were sufficient to ground moral agency, then given French's supplementary argument that corporations are Davidsonian agents, it is a short step to the conclusion that whatever basic moral attributes are possessed by people are also possessed by corporations. After all, it appears reasonable that the same set of conditions that ground the moral agency and fundamental moral properties of humans, will also, when shown to be operative in the instance of the corporation, ground a similar agency and set of moral properties. And so long as one simply uses the term, "moral person," as a convenient placeholder for the concept of a full-fledged moral agent—which French does throughout his writings—then the term "moral person" will be no less appropriate when applied to a corporation than to one's spouse.

And yet the search for a set of characteristics which both grounds moral agency and is possessed by corporations and humans has proven elusive. Here too French has altered his views, beginning with a straightforward inference from Davidsonian agency to moral personhood and ending with a reasonably complex constellation of conditions, complete with subsidiary caveats, meant to serve as a criterion and explanation of moral personhood. In this alteration of his original opinions, Professor French has been wise, for he has recognized problems that demanded solutions and provided them. Moreover, this increasing sophistication has tended, as we have seen, to soften the connection he sees between human and corporate agency, and to make his view more alert to the genuine differences between them. But the price of increasing sophistication has been a sacrifice of his original goal; for, as I shall show, he no longer is left with a theory that can explain moral personhood.

Let us review quickly a key transformation of French's views that occurred prior to the writing of the present article. It was prompted in part, interestingly, by a criticism of my own.

Willing to grant that his own view as articulated in his earlier writings entailed that anything that can behave intentionally, i.e., a Davidsonian agent, is a moral person, French confronted in Chapter Twelve of his *Collective and Corporate Responsibility* a counterexample I offered. I had written that "some entities appear to behave intentionally which do not qualify as moral agents. A cat may behave intentionally when it crouches for a mouse. We know that it intends to catch the mouse, but we do not credit it with moral agency . . . One seemingly needs more than the presence of intentions to deduce moral agency.[11] Now French first appears to reject this criticism, for he remarks: "With the dash of a philosophical swashbuckler, Donaldson cavalierly leaps from a somewhat noncommital 'may behave' to a very staunch epistemological claim about the way cats think."[12] But later, having acknowledged that respected philosophical psychologists such as Aristotle[13] and Daniel Dennett[14] do regard lower animals as intentional agents, he is persuaded to conclude:

> Rather than wasting time poking fun at Donaldson's example, we are in a position to offer our modification of the account of moral personhood to satisfy the concern that seems to have motivated Donaldson's comments, while yet preserving the basic theory of the corporation as a moral person. . . . Donaldson's cats and other lower animals are to be excluded from the class of moral persons because, although they may behave intentionally in some rather restricted way that I should not like to try to specify, they can neither appreciate that an event for which their intentional or unintentional behavior has been causally

responsible is untoward or worthy nor intentionally modify their way of behaving to correct the offensive actions or to adopt the behavior that was productive of worthy results. In short, they are just not full-blooded intentional
actors. Simply, they are not intentional actors.[15]

Clearly, French is wise to alter his account of personal moral agency so
as to exclude lower animals, and he is, I think, correct to say that a critical
difference is that merely intentional agents such as dogs and chimps cannot
"appreciate" the moral "untowardness" (irresponsibility) of their acts or intentionally modify their ways of behaving to correct the offensive actions.
French later suggests, I think also correctly, that this latter condition is linked
to his principle of responsive adjustment. And finally, there is nothing objectionable about redefining the notion of "intentional" so that the only agents
qualifying as intentional are those above the level of the lower animals.[16]

French's overall argument could be arranged in the form of a syllogism,
namely:

If A has x, then A is a moral person.
Most corporations have x.

Therefore, most corporations are moral persons.

Here x stands for the conditions of moral personhood, and it is crucial that
these conditions be sufficient, and not merely necessary ones, for if not the
syllogism cannot be constructed. French seems to forget this at one point when
he speaks of his conditions as only "minimal" ones and writes, "if . . . something is to be counted as a moral person, it must, minimally, be a Davidsonian agent with the capacity or ability to intentionally modify its behavior
patterns, habits, or modus operandi after learning that untoward events were
brought about by its past pieces of behavior."[17] But later he is more careful to
make the stronger claim: "How then does the concept of a moral person fare?
What entities ought to be included in the moral census? A moral person, we
should say, is a Davidsonian agent with the capacity to respond and respon-
sively adjust to moral evaluation."[18] Business corporations, he adds, "cannot
be locked into purely programmed decision structures."[19] Here, then, we seem
to have the characterization we are looking for. Stripped of its Davidsonian jargon it means:

A moral person is something that can act intentionally and respond to moral
evaluation.[20]

In this way French has finally provided substance to the value of "x" in his
premise, "If A has x, then A is a moral person." And, happily, so long as the
concept of x has been discovered without included as a precondition that x
must be a property held by corporations, then French's overall argument is not

circular. But is x a sufficient, and not merely necessary, condition? Again, it must qualify as a sufficient condition to make his argument go through, and yet I am afraid it fails on this score.

Can we imagine an entity able both to behave intentionally and respond to moral evaluation that is not a moral person? Let us grant that when considering the class of all existing biological agents known, so long as any known biological agent can behave intentionally and respond to moral evaluation (i.e., so long as it possesses x), then we may infer that the entity is a moral person. Quite simply, the only agents in this class that qualify are human beings. But this does not show that logically speaking there is a necessary inference to be drawn from the possession of x to moral personhood.

Imagine a hypothetical extraterrestrial being. Let us call him the Creature-without-a-heart, or for short, Heartless. Now Heartless, let us suppose, belongs to a species of creatures that is rational and intentional in every way. Heartless plans, schemes, worries, adjusts opinions to meet facts, and in every other way displays rational control over his behavior. Heartless plays chess like a demon, has an I.Q. of 160, and has read and thoroughly absorbed Kant's *Groundwork for the Metaphysics of Morals*. But Heartless hasn't a heart. He never concerns himself with others except insofar as their lives impact on him. He never worries about others but only about himself, and, indeed, it is natural for him to do so since all other members of the species to which he belongs are similarly disposed. And although Heartless knows that the essence of morality lies in acting in accordance with such maxims as "Act so that the principle of your act can be universalized," and "Do unto others as you would have them do unto you," and certainly *could* act in accordance with such maxims if he wished, he does not so wish. That is, he can see no reason why he *should* act in accordance with them because he places no value on the pains, desires, feelings, and existence of anyone other than himself.

Is Heartless a moral person? It strikes me that only the most extreme rationalists in ethics (of a kind that even Immanuel Kant was not) would answer "yes." Heartless is not a moral person because, as a matter of his innate nature, he lacks the ability to sympathize with others.[21]

And here is the rub for French. Do corporations have hearts? Do the rules and procedures of corporate decision-making, their "CID structures" as French calls them, entail that they recognize and respect the fact that other moral agents, in particular human beings, have value in themselves, value over and above the corporate ends they may aid or hinder? I am not at all sure how to answer such questions, but I am certain that I cannot claim to know that most corporations are moral persons in this sense. My inclination would be to say that the rules and procedures of some corporations push them close to the status of "having a heart" and others do not. But in any case, supporting such an inclination would be the subject of a lengthy investigation into the structure of corporations, and is a topic for another occasion. What the preceding analysis has shown is that French's attempt to posit the sufficient conditions of moral personhood misses the mark insofar as it fails to compass all requisite conditions. To put it in Kantian language, showing that an agent is able to act in *accordance* with true moral principles (principles Kant refers to as the "Moral Law") is not sufficient to conclude that an agent is able to act *out of respect* for true moral principles. Perhaps Professor French will respond that it is possible to infer from the fact that a corporation is made up of individual moral persons that the corporation, and not merely its individual members, can act *out of respect* for morality. I hope, indeed, that such a demonstration is possible; and yet, I think even French would grant that his work to date has offered no such demonstration.

Hence we are brought full circle in our investigation. Having started by questioning the stark parity French appears to grant in his early writings between corporations and human beings, we are once again asking about such parity. We asked at the beginning about the correctness of claiming that whatever rights and duties are possessed by ordinary moral agents are also possessed by corporations, a claim that French himself seemed later to moderate. And now at the end of our inquiry, we are asking about the correctness of claiming that the underlying conditions sufficient for moral personhood are actually present in corporations. It appears that, even if the set of conditions identified by French for moral personhood is present both in humans and corporations, the set he identifies is insufficient to guarantee moral personhood.

The two problems are not unconnected. French's motivation behind asserting a parity of basic rights and duties in corporate and human agents was no doubt tied to an underlying conviction that the essence of moral personhood was present in both instances, that, in other words, whatever makes something a moral person is equally present in corporate as well as individual human agents. Hence the difficulty of discovering a consistent, satisfactory account of the rights and duties of corporations and humans examined in the first part of the paper, is inextricably linked to the difficulty of articulating the essence of moral personhood examined in the second part.

Thus French has made a heroic attempt to bridge the conceptual moral gap between corporations and human beings, and yet the gap looms large as ever. One's recognition that this attempt, undertaken by a gifted scholar in a thoroughgoing way, has failed, may prompt one to look in another theoretical direction entirely. Instead of assuming that a single concept of moral agency underlies both human and corporation, why not consider the prospect of a double concept? Why not consider the possibility that both human and corporation qualify as moral agents, and yet refuse to reduce each agency to a common denominator? Such an approach would preserve the moral quality of corporate decision-making without sacrificing rational and moral consistency. The final acceptability of such a view would depend on its capacity to be worked out in detail; but *prima facie* it seems plausible. On such a view, Exxon, Incorporated, and Mr. John Jones would look like very different creatures indeed.

NOTES

1. John Ladd is a popular representative of the former view, see, e.g., "Morality and the Ideal of Rationality in Formal Organizations," in *The Monist*, 54 (1970), pp. 488–516; while Kenneth Goodpaster is frequently associated with the latter, see, e.g., "Morality and Organizations," in *Ethical Issues in Business: A Philosophical Approach*, ed. Thomas Donaldson and Patricia Werhane (Englewood Cliffs, N.J.: Prentice-Hall, Inc., 1983).

2. Three of these writings are: "The Corporation as a Moral Person," *American Philosophical Quarterly*, 16 (July 1979): 207–15. *Collective and Corporate Responsibility* (New York: Columbia University Press, 1984), and "Principles of Responsibility, Shame and the Corporation," (this volume).

3. *Moral Person*, p. 207.

4. See Thomas Donaldson, *Corporations and Morality* (Englewood Cliffs, N.J.: Prentice-Hall, Inc., 1982), Chapter 2.

5. French, *Collective and Corporate Responsibility*, pp. 169–70.

6. French, *Collective and Corporate Responsibility*, p. 170.

7. French, *Collective and Corporate Responsibility*, p. 170.

8. The view of juristic personhood has evolved from Roman law and seems well entrenched in legal practice.

9. See Joel Feinberg, "Duties, Rights and Claims," *American Philosophical Quarterly*, 3 (1966), 137–44. Also Feinberg, "The Nature and Value of Rights," *Journal of Value Inquiry*, 4 (1970), 243–57.

10. The only mode left for determining the class of rights and duties characterizing corporate entities is dead reckoning, a mode which Professor French finally relies upon. But appeals to our intuitions about corporations and their moral attributes are inappropriate if the purpose of one's argument is to show why corporations are on all fours with other moral agents and to provide a theory of corporate moral agency.

11. Donaldson, *Corporations and Morality*, p. 22.

12. French, *Collective and Corporate Responsibility*, p. 166.

13. French, *Collective and Corporate Responsibility*, p. 166.

14. See French, "Principles of Responsibility, Shame, and the Corporation," p. 16, in this volume; and Daniel Dennett, "Conditions of Personhood," in *The Identities of Persons*, ed by Amelie Rorty (Berkeley: University of California Press, 1976) p. 179.

15. French, *Collective and Corporate Responsibility*, p. 166.

16. This is the force of the transition from "full-blooded intentional actors" to "intentional actors" in the passage quoted from French, i.e., his remark that "In short, (lower animals) are just not full-blooded intentional actors. Simply, they are not intentional actors."

17. French, "Principles of Responsibilities, Shame, and the Corporation" in this volume, p. 27.

18. French, *Ibid.*, p. 29.

19. French, *Ibid.*, p. 29.

20. It is interesting to notice the striking similarity between this revised analysis of moral agency and the one I offered in *Corporations and Morality* that French has so frequently criticized. There I wrote that in order to qualify as a moral agent a corporation must have the capacity to use moral reasons in decision-making as well as the ability to employ such a moral decision-making process to control not only its overt acts, but the structure of its policies and rules. See Donaldson, *Corporations and Morality*, p. 30.

21. He may be able to empathize, but he cannot sympathize.

Stakeholders.

Overview.

Another way to view a corporation is as a collage of relationships that includes virtually any agent or group that works for, or is affected by the company or its policies. The *stake* is the interest, share, or claim that an agent or group has against a company. Those who possess these stakes, whether they be legal, economic, political, moral, or so on, are called *stakeholders*.[1] This view of the corporation is called *stakeholder theory*.

R. Edward Freeman depicts stakeholders as "any individual or group who can affect or is affected by the actions, decisions, policies, practices, or goals of the organization."[2] Under this model, we can distinguish between the company's primary stakeholders (owners, customers, employees, and suppliers) and secondary stakeholders (all other interested groups such as the general public, government, competitors). Primary stakeholders weigh more heavily in the decision-making process than do secondary stakeholders, but even primary stakeholders possess stakeholders of their own so that the societal web becomes very complex.

Proponents of stakeholder theory point to the way that it *situates* a company. That is, it forces the company to view itself as being contained in a series of environments that often intersect. In this way, a company must accommodate its actions with the needs and interests of all of its stakeholders. If morality is about ameliorating an individual's interests given those of the broader group (a crucial tenet of Utilitarianism), then stakeholder theory provides a way to integrate ethics into daily business decisions. Virtue Ethics (either by itself or integrated with Communitarianism)[3] is also a possible theory that distributes interests among stakeholders in an ethical fashion.

Stakeholder theory is meant to contrast with a traditional view of whose interests ought to be considered (viz., those of the owners of the company: the stockholders). Under traditional theory, a contract exists between the stockholders and the company's board of directors, which will do everything to continue its historical mission and make money for the stockholders. Such an agreement incurs a fiduciary responsibility on the part of the officers and directors of the corporation to the stockholders.

It is clear, however, that this fiduciary responsibility is *not* carte blanche. If the company were *merely* concerned with making money, it could engage in illegal gun sales, money laundering, and drug smuggling, for example. The stockholders do not have the right to expect the officers and directors to make *the most amount of money possible* because this could involve the company in illegal activity and is wrong on three counts: (a) the company would be breaking the law and faces fines and sanctions (a prudential reason) if caught,

---

[1]For more discussion of the definition of stakeholders, see Archie Carroll, *Business and Society: Ethics and Stakeholder Management* (Cincinnati, OH: South-Western Publishing Company, 1989); and Joseph Weiss, *The Management of Change: Administrative Logics and Actions* (New York: Praeger, 1986).

[2]R. Edward Freeman, *Strategic Management: A Stakeholder Approach* (Boston: Pitman, 1984), p. 25.

[3]A sketch of Virtue Ethics in the context of Communitarianism can be found in Michael J. Sandel, *Liberalism and the Limits of Justice*, 2nd ed. (Cambridge: Cambridge University Press, 1998), pp. 76–77, 88–89, 98–99.

(b) the company is veering away from its historical mission (the basis on which stockholders invested in the company—a moral reason of promise keeping), and (c) the company should not engage in an illegal or immoral activity (an ethical reason—but the basis is rather unclear without future justification).

Under traditional analysis, it is not entirely clear why a company should not "ride the line" of legality and illegality in an attempt to weigh the risk-rewards of extra profits versus the possibility of getting caught. If the company's sole mission is to make money for the stockholders, then it should do all it can to fulfill that mission. It should operate near the edge of the law, occasionally challenging that barrier when the risks/rewards calculus dictates that it is prudent to do so. Nobel Laureate Milton Friedman has been a proponent of this strategy.[4]

Thus, stakeholder theory is one alternative to the traditional stockholder model. (The corporation as a morally responsible individual is another.) One of the key issues that stakeholder theory must address is how it claims to be a normative theory. It is one thing to say that a company's actions affect many individuals and groups. One can describe the sociology of decision making and the dynamics of the political process. All of this is a *descriptive* exercise. It is another thing to be able to show how some claims *should* trump others and how sometimes a moral argument will carry the day. This latter mission of how ethics can trump other considerations is a normative exercise. In business ethics, we are ultimately interested in the normative exercise.

In the first article of this section, Kenneth Goodpaster takes the position that stakeholder theory, as generally presented, leads to a so-called stakeholder paradox. This paradox may be put into a dilemma situation (that one is both enjoined and not enjoined to perform some action). This paradox results from the phenomena of multifiduciary responsibilities that is the natural consequence of multiple (often conflicting) stakeholder interests. If Goodpaster is correct, then stakeholder theory must be corrected. The essence of this correction will revolve around the notions of different types of responsibilities. In other words, a fiduciary relationship is not the only type that directors should recognize, but there must be a way to adjudicate between these different types of obligations.

In his excerpted essay, Stephen Cohen offers a way to deal with various conflicting stakeholder interests (such as those mentioned by Goodpaster) through the concept of *consent,* which emphasized here is deliberate, future-oriented consent. What consent does to the decision making equation is to create a political framework through which problems might be solved among stakeholders. Cohen cites various criteria that are utilized in the process of group consent. The reader must determine for himself whether the normative question raised by Goodpaster has been satisfied.

---

[4]See Milton Friedman, "The Social Responsibility of Business Is to Increase Its Profits" *New York Times Sunday Magazine,* September 13, 1970, pp. 32–33, 122–126.

Business Ethics and Stakeholder Analysis

Kenneth Goodpaster

> So we must think through what management should be accountable for: and how and through whom its accountability can be discharged. The stockholders' interest, both short- and long-term, is one of the areas. But it is only one.
>
> Peter Drucker, *Harvard Business Review,* 1988

What is ethically responsible management? How can a corporation, given its economic mission, be managed with appropriate attention to ethical concerns? These are central questions in the field of business ethics. One approach to answering such questions that has become popular during the last two decades is loosely referred to as "stakeholder analysis." Ethically responsible management, it is often suggested, is management that includes careful attention not only to stockholders *but to stakeholders generally* in the decision-making process.

This suggestion about the ethical importance of stakeholder analysis contains an important kernel of truth, but it can also be misleading. Comparing the ethical relationship between managers and stockholders with their relationship to other stakeholders is, I will argue, almost as problematic as ignoring stakeholders (ethically) altogether—presenting us with something of a "stakeholder paradox."

DEFINITION

The term "stakeholder" appears to have been invented in the early 1960s as a deliberate play on the word "stockholder" to signify that there are other parties having a "stake" in the decision-making of the modern, publicly held corporation in addition to those holding equity positions. Professor R. Edward Freeman, in his book *Strategic Management: A Stakeholder Approach,* defines the term as follows: "A stakeholder in an organization is (by definition) any group or individual who can affect or is affected by the achievement of the organization's objectives."[1] Examples of stakeholder groups (beyond stockholders) are employees, suppliers, customers, creditors, competitors, governments, and communities. . . .

Another metaphor with which the term "stakeholder" is associated is that of a "player" in a game like poker. One with a "stake" in the game is one who plays and puts some economic value at risk.[2]

Much of what makes responsible decision-making difficult is understanding how there can be an ethical relationship between management and stakeholders that avoids being too weak (making stakeholders mere means to stockholders' ends) or too strong (making stakeholders quasi-stockholders in their own right). To give these issues life, a case example will help. So let us consider the case of General Motors and Poletown.[3]

THE POLETOWN CASE

In 1980, GM was facing a net loss in income, the first since 1921, due to intense foreign competition. Management realized that major capital expenditures would be required for the company to regain its competitive position and profitability. A $40 billion five-year capital spending program was announced that included new, state-of-the-art assembly techniques aimed at smaller, fuel-efficient automobiles demanded by the market. Two aging assembly plants in Detroit were among the ones to be replaced. Their closure would eliminate 500 jobs. Detroit in 1980 was a city with a black majority, an unemployment rate of 18 percent overall and 30 percent for blacks, a rising public debt, and a chronic budget deficit, despite high tax rates.

The site requirements for a new assembly plant included 500 acres, access to long-haul railroad and freeways, and proximity to suppliers for "just-in-time" inventory management. It needed to be ready to produce 1983 model year cars beginning in September 1982. The only site in Detroit meeting GM's requirements was heavily settled, covering a section of the Detroit neighborhood of Poletown. Of the 3,500 residents, half were black. The whites were mostly of Polish descent, retired or nearing retirement. An alternative "green field" site was available in another midwestern state.

Using the power of eminent domain, the Poletown area could be acquired and cleared for a new plant within the company's timetable, and the city government was eager to cooperate. Because of job retention in Detroit, the leadership of the United Auto Workers was also in favor of the idea. The Poletown Neighborhood Council strongly opposed the plan, but was willing to work with the city and GM.

The new plant would employ 6,150 workers and would cost GM $500 million wherever it was built. Obtaining and preparing the Poletown site would cost an additional $200 million, whereas alternative sites in the midwest were available for $65–80 million.

The interested parties were many—stockholders, customers, employees, suppliers, the Detroit community, the midwestern alternative, the Poletown

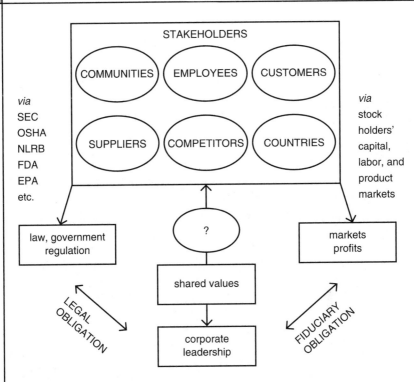

FIGURE 1 **Business decision-making and ethical values**

neighborhood. The decision was difficult. GM management needed to consider its competitive situation, the extra costs of remaining in Detroit, the consequences to the city of leaving for another part of the midwest, and the implications for the residents of choosing the Poletown site if the decision were made to stay. The decision about whom to talk to and *how* was as puzzling as the decision about *what* to do and *why*.

STAKEHOLDER ANALYSIS AND STAKEHOLDER SYNTHESIS

Ethical values enter management decision-making, it is often suggested, through the gate of stakeholder analysis. But the suggestion that introducing "stakeholder analysis" into business decisions is the same as introducing ethics into those decisions is questionable. To make this plain, let me first distinguish between two importantly different ideas: stakeholder analysis and stakeholder synthesis. I will then examine alternative kinds of stakeholder synthesis with attention to ethical content.

The decision-making process of an individual or a company can be seen in terms of a sequence of six steps to be followed after an issue or problem presents itself for resolution.[4] For ease of reference and recall, I will name the sequence PASCAL, after the six letters in the name of the French philosopher–mathematician Blaise Pascal (1623–62), who once remarked in reference to ethical decision-making that "the heart has reasons that reason knows not of."

1. PERCEPTION or fact-gathering about the options available and their short- and long-term implications;
2. ANALYSIS of these implications with specific attention to affected parties and to the decision-maker's goals, objectives, values, responsibilities, etc.;
3. SYNTHESIS of this structured information according to whatever fundamental priorities obtain in the mindset of the decision-maker;
4. CHOICE among the available options based on the synthesis;
5. ACTION or implementation of the chosen option through a series of specific requests to specific individuals or groups, resource allocation, incentives, controls, and feedback;
6. LEARNING from the outcome of the decision, resulting in either reinforcement or modification (for future decisions) of the way in which the above steps have been taken.

We might simplify this analysis, of course, to something like "input," "decision," and "output," but distinguishing interim steps can often be helpful. The main point is that the path from the presentation of a problem to its resolution must somehow involve gathering, processing, and acting on relevant information.

Now, by *stakeholder analysis* I simply mean a process that does not go beyond the first two steps mentioned above. That is, the affected parties caught up in each available option are identified and the positive and negative impacts on each stakeholder are determined. But questions having to do with processing this information into a decision and implementing it are *left unanswered*. These steps are not part of the *analysis* but of the *synthesis, choice* and *action*.

Stakeholder analysis may give the initial appearance of a decision-making process, but in fact is only a *segment* of a decision-making process. It represents the preparatory or opening phase that awaits the crucial application of the moral (or nonmoral) values of the decision-maker. So, to be informed that an individual or an institution regularly makes stakeholder analysis part of decision-making or takes a "stakeholder approach" to management is to learn little or nothing about the ethical character of that individual or institution. It is to learn only that stakeholders are regularly identified—*not why and for what purpose*. To be told that stakeholders are or must be "taken into account" is, so far, to be told very little. Stakeholder analysis is, as a practical matter, morally *neutral*. It is therefore a mistake to see it as a substitute for normative ethical thinking.[5]

What I shall call "stakeholder synthesis" goes further into the sequence of decision-making steps mentioned above to include actual decision-making and implementation (S, C, A). The critical point is that stakeholder synthesis offers *a pattern or channel by which to move from stakeholder identification to a practical response or resolution*. Here we begin to join stakeholder analysis to questions of substance. But we must now ask: What kind of substance? And how does it relate to *ethics?* The stakeholder idea, remember, is typically offered as a way of integrating *ethical* values into management decision-making. When and how does substance become *ethical* substance?

STRATEGIC STAKEHOLDER SYNTHESIS

We can imagine decision-makers doing "stakeholder analysis" for different underlying reasons, not always having to do with ethics. A management team, for example, might be careful to take positive and (especially) negative stakeholder effects into account for no other reason than that offended stakeholders might resist or retaliate (e.g. through political action or opposition to necessary regulatory clearances). It might not be *ethical* concern for the stakeholders that motivates and guides such analysis, so much as concern about potential impediments to the achievement of strategic objectives. Thus positive and negative effects on relatively powerless stakeholders may be ignored or discounted in the synthesis, choice, and action phases of the decision process.[6]

In the Poletown case, General Motors might have done a stakeholder analysis using the following reasoning: our stockholders are the central stakeholders here, but other key stakeholders include our suppliers, old and new plant employees, the City of Detroit, and the residents of Poletown. These other stakeholders are not our direct concern as a corporation with an economic mission, but since they can influence our short- or long-term strategic interests, they must be taken into account. Public relations costs and benefits, for example, or concerns about union contracts or litigation, might well have influenced the choice between staying in Detroit and going elsewhere.

I refer to this kind of stakeholder synthesis as "strategic" since stakeholders outside the stockholder group are viewed instrumentally, as factors potentially affecting the overarching goal of optimizing stockholder interests. They are taken into account in the decision-making process, but as external environmental forces, as potential sources of either goodwill or retaliation. "We" are the economic principals and management; "they" are significant players whose attitudes and future actions might affect our short-term or long-term success. We must respect them in the way one "respects" the weather—as a set of forces to be reckoned with.[7]

It should be emphasized that managers who adopt the strategic stakeholder approach are not necessarily *personally* indifferent to the plight of stakeholders who are "strategically unimportant." The point is that *in their role as managers,* with a fiduciary relationship that binds them as agents to principals, their basic outlook subordinates other stakeholder concerns to those of stockholders. Market and legal forces are relied upon to secure the interests of those whom strategic considerations might discount. This reliance can and does take different forms, depending on the emphasis given to market forces on the one hand and legal forces on the other. A more conservative, market-oriented view acknowledges the role of legal compliance as an environmental factor affecting strategic choice, but thinks stakeholder interests are best served by minimal interference from the public sector. Adam Smith's "invisible hand" is thought to be the most important guarantor of the common good in a competitive economy. A more liberal view sees the hand of government, through legislation and regulation, as essential for representing stakeholders that might otherwise not achieve "standing" in the strategic decision process.

What both conservatives and liberals have in common is the conviction that the fundamental orientation of management must be toward the interests of stockholders. Other stakeholders (customers, employees, suppliers, neighbors) enter the decision-making equation either directly as instrumental economic factors or indirectly as potential legal claimants. . . . Both see law and regulation as providing a voice for stakeholders that goes beyond market dynamics. They differ about how much government regulation is socially and economically desirable.

During the Poletown controversy, GM managers as individuals may have cared deeply about the potential lost jobs in Detroit, or about the potential dislocation of Poletown residents. But in their role as agents for the owners (stockholders) they could allow such considerations to "count" only if they served GM's strategic interests (or perhaps as legal constraints on the decision).

Professor Freeman appears to adopt some form of strategic stakeholder synthesis. After presenting his definition of stakeholders, he remarks on its application to any group or individual "who can *affect* or is *affected by*" a company's achievement of its purposes. The "affect" part of the definition is not hard to understand; but Freeman clarifies the "affected by" part:

> The point of strategic management is in some sense to chart a direction for the firm. Groups which can affect the direction and its implementation must be considered in the strategic management process. However, it is less obvious why "those groups who are affected by the corporation" are stakeholders as well . . . I make the definition symmetric because of the changes which the firm has undergone in the past few years. Groups which 20 years ago had no effect

on the actions of the firm, can affect it today, largely because of the actions of the firm which ignored the effects on these groups. Thus, by calling those affected groups "stakeholders," the ensuing strategic management model will be sensitive to future change.[8]

Freeman might have said "who can actually or potentially affect" the company, for the mindset appears to be one in which attention to stakeholders is justified in terms of actual or potential impact on the company's achievement of its strategic purposes. Stakeholders (other than stockholders) are actual or potential means/obstacles to corporate objectives. A few pages later, Freeman writes:

> From the standpoint of strategic management, or the achievement of organizational purpose, we need an inclusive definition. We must not leave out any group or individual who can affect or is affected by organizational purpose, *because that group may prevent our accomplishments.*[9]

The essence of a strategic view of stakeholders is not that stakeholders are ignored, but that all but a special group (stockholders) are considered on the basis of their actual or potential influence on management's central mission. The basic normative principle is fiduciary responsibility (organizational prudence), supplemented by legal compliance.

The question we must ask in thinking about a strategic approach to stakeholder synthesis is this: Is it really an adequate rendering of the *ethical* component in managerial judgment? Unlike mere stakeholder analysis, this kind of synthesis does go beyond simply *identifying* stakeholders. It integrates the stakeholder information by using a single interest group (stockholders) as its basic normative touchstone. . . .

Many, most notably Nobel Laureate Milton Friedman, believe that market and legal forces are adequate to translate or transmute ethical concerns into straightforward strategic concerns for management. He believes that in our economic and political system (democratic capitalism), direct concern for stakeholders (what Kant might have called "categorical" concern) is unnecessary, redundant, and inefficient, not to mention dishonest:

> In many cases, there is a strong temptation to rationalize actions as an exercise of "social responsibility." In the present climate of opinion, with its widespread aversion to "capitalism," "profits," the "soulless corporation" and so on, this is one way for a corporation to generate good will as a by-product of expenditures that are entirely justified in its own self-interest. If our institutions, and the attitudes of the public make it in their self-interest to cloak their actions in this way, I cannot summon much indignation to denounce them. At the same time, I can express admiration for those individual proprietors or owners of closely held corporations or stockholders of more broadly held corporations who disdain such tactics as approaching fraud.[10]

MULTI-FIDUCIARY STAKEHOLDER SYNTHESIS

In contrast to a strategic view of stakeholders, one can imagine a management team processing stakeholder information by giving the same care to the interests of, say, employees, customers, and local communities as to the economic interests of stakeholders. This kind of substantive commitment to stakeholders might involve trading off the economic advantages of one group against those of another, e.g. in a decision to close a plant. I shall refer to this way of integrating stakeholder analysis with decision-making as "multi-fiduciary" since all stakeholders are treated by management as having equally important interests, deserving joint "maximization" (or what Herbert Simon might call "satisficing").

Professor Freeman contemplates what I am calling the multi-fiduciary view at the end of his 1984 book under the heading "The Manager As Fiduciary To Stakeholders":

> Perhaps the most important area of future research is the issue of whether or not a theory of management can be constructed that uses the stakeholder concept to enrich "managerial capitalism," that is, can the notion that managers bear a fiduciary relationship to stockholders or the owners of the firm, be replaced by a concept of management whereby the manager *must* act in the interests of the stakeholders in the organization?[11]

. . . We must now ask, as we did of the strategic approach: How satisfactory is multi-fiduciary stakeholder synthesis as a way of giving ethical substance to management decision-making? On the face of it, and in stark contrast to the strategic approach, it may seem that we have at last arrived at a truly moral view. But we should be cautious. For no sooner do we think we have found the proper interpretation of ethics in management than a major objection presents itself. And, yes, it appears to be a *moral* objection!

It can be argued that multi-fiduciary stakeholder analysis is simply incompatible with widely held moral convictions about the special fiduciary obligations owed by management to stockholders. At the center of the objection is the belief that the obligations of agents to principals are stronger than or different in kind from those of agents to third parties.

THE STAKEHOLDER PARADOX

Managers who would pursue a multi-fiduciary stakeholder orientation for their companies must face resistance from those who believe that a strategic orientation is the only *legitimate* one for business to adopt, given the economic mission and legal constitution of the modern corporation. This may be disorienting since the word "illegitimate" has clear negative ethical connotations, and yet the multi-fiduciary approach is often defended on ethical grounds. I will refer to this anomalous situation as the *Stakeholder Paradox:* It seems essential, yet in some ways illegitimate, to orient corporate decisions by ethical values that go beyond strategic stakeholder considerations to multi-fiduciary ones. I call this a paradox because it says there is an ethical problem whichever approach management takes. Ethics seems both to forbid and to demand a strategic, profit-maximizing mindset. The argument behind the paradox focuses on management's *fiduciary* duty to the stockholder, essentially the duty to keep a profit-maximizing promise, and a concern that the "impartiality" of the multi-fiduciary approach simply cuts management loose from certain well-defined bonds of stockholder accountability. On this view, impartiality is thought to be a *betrayal of trust.*

Professor David S. Ruder, a former chairman of the US Securities and Exchange Commission, once summarized the matter this way:

> Traditional fiduciary obligation theory insists that a corporate manager owes an obligation of care and loyalty to shareholders. If a public obligation theory unrelated to profit maximization becomes the law, the corporate manager who is not able to act in his own self interest without violating his fiduciary obligation, may nevertheless act in the public interest without violating that obligation.

He continued:

> Whether induced by government legislation, government pressure, or merely by enlightened attitudes of the corporation regarding its long range potential as a unit in society, corporate activities carried on in satisfaction of public obligations can be consistent with profit maximization objectives. In contrast, justification of public obligations upon bold concepts of public need without corporate benefit will merely serve to reduce further the owner's influence on his corporation and to create additional demands for public participation in corporate management.[12]

Ruder's view appears to be that (a) multi-fiduciary stakeholder synthesis *need not* be used by management because the strategic approach is more accommodating than meets the eye; and (b) multi-fiduciary stakeholder synthesis should not be invoked by management because such a "bold" concept could threaten the private (vs public) status of the corporation.

In response to (a), we saw earlier that there were reasonable questions about the tidy convergence of ethics and economic success. Respecting the interests and rights of the Poletown residents might really have meant incurring higher costs for GM (short-term as well as long-term).

Appeals to corporate self-interest, even long-term, might not always support ethical decisions. But even on those occasions where they will, we must wonder about the disposition to favor economic and legal reasoning "for the record." If Ruder means to suggest that business leaders can often *re-formulate* or *re-present* their reasons for certain morally grounded decisions in strategic terms having to do with profit maximization and obedience to law, he is perhaps correct. In the spirit of our earlier quotation from Milton Friedman, we might not summon much indignation to denounce them. But why the fiction? Why not call a moral reason a moral reason?

This issue is not simply of academic interest. Managers must confront it in practice. . . .

THE PROBLEM OF BOLDNESS

What appears to lie at the foundation of Ruder's cautious view is a concern about the "boldness" of the multi-fiduciary concept ((b) above).[13] It is not that he thinks the strategic approach is always satisfactory; it is that the multi-fiduciary approach is, in his eyes, much worse. For it questions the special relationship between the manager as agent and the stockholder as principal.

Ruder suggests that what he calls a "public obligation" theory threatens the private status of the corporation. He believes that what we are calling multi-fiduciary stakeholder synthesis *dilutes* the fiduciary obligation to stockholders (by extending it to customers, employees, suppliers, etc.) and he sees this as a threat to the "privacy" of the private sector organization. If public organizations are understood on the model of public sector institutions with their multiple constituencies, Ruder thinks, the stockholder loses status.

There is something profoundly *right* about Ruder's line of argument here, I believe, and something profoundly *wrong*. What is right is his intuition that if we treat other stakeholders on the model of the fiduciary relationship between management and the stockholder, we will, in effect, make them into quasi-stockholders. We can do this, of course, if we choose to as a society. But we should be aware that it is a radical step indeed. For it blurs traditional goals in terms of entrepreneurial risk-taking, pushes decision-making toward paralysis because of the dilemmas posed by divided loyalties, and, in the final analysis, represents nothing less than the conversion of the modern private corporation into a public institution and probably calls for a corresponding restructuring of corporate governance (e.g. representatives of each stakeholder group on the board of directors). Unless we believe that the social utility of a private sector has disappeared, not to mention its value for individual liberty and enterprise, we will be cautious about an interpretation of stakeholder synthesis that transforms the private sector into the public sector.

On the other hand, I believe Ruder is mistaken if he thinks that business ethics requires this kind of either/or: either a private sector with a strategic stakeholder synthesis (business without ethics) or the effective loss of the private sector with a multi-fiduciary stakeholder synthesis (ethics without business).

Recent debates over state laws protecting companies against hostile takeovers may illustrate Ruder's concern as well as the new challenge. According to journalist Christopher Elias, a recent Pennsylvania antitakeover law

> does no less than redefine the fiduciary duty of corporate directors, enabling them to base decisions not merely on the interests of shareholders, but on the interests of customers, suppliers, employees and the community at large. Pennsylvania is saying that it is the corporation that directors are responsible to. Shareholders say they always thought they themselves were the corporation.[14]

Echoing Ruder, one legal observer quoted by Elias commented with reference to this law that it "undermines and erodes free markets and property rights. From this perspective, this is an anticapitalist law. The management can take away property from the real owners."

In our terms, the state of Pennsylvania is charged with adopting a multi-fiduciary stakeholder approach in an effort to rectify deficiencies of the strategic approach which (presumably) corporate raiders hold.

The challenge with which we are thus presented is to develop an account of the moral responsibilities of management that (1) avoid surrendering the moral relationship between management and stakeholders as the strategic view does, while (2) not transforming stakeholder obligations into fiduciary obligations (thus protecting the uniqueness of the principal–agent relationship between management and stockholder).

TOWARD A NEW STAKEHOLDER SYNTHESIS

We all remember the story of the well-intentioned Doctor Frankenstein. He sought to improve the human condition by designing a powerful, intelligent force for good in the community. Alas, when he flipped the switch, his creation turned out to be a monster rather than a marvel! Is the concept of the ethical corporation like a Frankenstein monster?

Taking business ethics seriously need not mean that management bears *additional* fiduciary relationships to third parties (nonstockholder constituencies) as multi-fiduciary stakeholder synthesis suggests. It may mean that there are morally significant *nonfiduciary* obligations to third parties surrounding any fiduciary relationship (see figure 2). Such moral obligations may be owed by private individuals as well as private sector organizations to those whose freedom and well-being is affected by their economic behavior. It is these very obligations, in fact (the duty not to harm or coerce and duties not to lie, cheat, or steal), that are cited in regulatory, legislative, and judicial arguments for

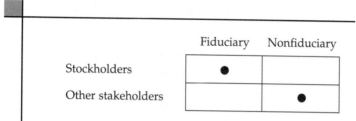

	Fiduciary	Nonfiduciary
Stockholders	●	
Other stakeholders		●

FIGURE 2 **Direct managerial obligations**

constraining profit-driven business activities. These obligations are not "hypothetical" or contingent or indirect, as they would be on the strategic model. They are not rooted in the *fiduciary* relationship, but in other relationships at least as deep.

It must be admitted in fairness to Ruder's argument that the jargon of "stakeholders" in discussions of business ethics can seem to threaten the notion of what corporate law refers to as the "undivided and unselfish loyalty" owed by managers and directors to stockholders. For this way of speaking can suggest a multiplication of management duties *of the same kind* as the duty to stockholders. What we must understand is that the responsibilities of management toward stockholders are of a piece with the obligations that *stockholders themselves* would be expected to honor in their own right. As an old Latin proverb has it, *nemo dat quod non habet*, which literally means "nobody gives what he doesn't have." Freely translating in this context we can say: I cannot (ethically) *hire* done on my behalf what I would not (ethically) *do* myself. We might refer to this as the "Nemo Dat Principle" (NDP) and consider it a formal requirement of consistency in business ethics (and professional ethics generally):

> (NDP)   Investors cannot expect of managers (more generally, principals cannot expect of their agents) behavior that would be inconsistent with the reasonable ethical expectations of the community.[15]

The NDP does not, of course, resolve in advance the many ethical challenges that managers must face. It only indicates that these challenges are of a piece with those that face us all. It offers a different kind of test (and so a different kind of stakeholder synthesis) that management (and institutional investors) might apply to policies and decisions.

The foundation of ethics in management—and the way out of the stakeholder paradox—lies in understanding that the conscience of the corporation is a logical and moral extension of the consciences of its principals. It is *not* an expansion of the *list* of principals, but a gloss on the principal–agent relationship itself. Whatever the structure of the principal–agent relationship, neither principal nor agent can ever claim that an agent has "moral immunity" from the basic obligations that would apply to any human being toward other members of the community.

Indeed, consistent with Ruder's belief, the introduction of moral reasoning (distinguished from multi-fiduciary stakeholder reasoning) into the framework of management thinking may *protect* rather than threaten private sector legitimacy. The conscientious corporation can maintain its private economic mission, but in the context of fundamental moral obligations owed by any member of society to others affected by that member's actions. Recognizing such obligations does *not* mean that an institution is a public institution. Private institutions, like private individuals, can be and are bound to respect moral obligations in the pursuit of private purposes.

Conceptually, then, we can make room for a moral posture toward stakeholders that is both *partial* (respecting the fiduciary relationship between managers and stockholders) and *impartial* (respecting the equally important nonfiduciary relationships between management and other stakeholders). As philosopher Thomas Nagel has said, "In the conduct of life, of all places, the rivalry between the view from within and the view from without must be taken seriously."[16]

Whether this conceptual room can be used *effectively* in the face of enormous pressures on contemporary managers and directors is another story, of course. For it is one thing to say that "giving standing to stakeholders" in managerial reasoning is conceptually coherent. It is something else to say that it is practically coherent.

Yet most of us, I submit, believe it. Most of us believe that management at General Motors *owed* it to the people of Detroit and to the people of Poletown to take their (nonfiduciary) interests very seriously, to seek creative solutions to the conflict, to do more than use or manipulate them in accordance with GM's needs only. We understand that managers and directors have a special obligation to provide a financial return to the stockholders, but we also understand that the word "special" in this context needs to be tempered by an appreciation of certain fundamental community norms that go beyond the demands of both laws and markets. There are certain class-action suits that stockholders ought not to win. For there is sometimes a moral defense.

CONCLUSION

The relationship between management and stockholders is ethically different in kind from the relationship between management and other parties (employees, suppliers, customers, etc.), a fact that seems to go unnoticed by the multi-fiduciary approach. If it were not, the corporation would cease to be a private sector institution—and what is now called business ethics would become a more radical critique of our economic system than is typically thought. On this point, Milton Friedman must be given a fair and serious hearing.

This does not mean, however, that "stakeholders" lack a morally significant relationship to management, as the strategic approach implies. It means only that the relationship in question is different from a fiduciary one. Management may never have promised customers, employees, suppliers, etc. a "return on investment," but management is nevertheless obliged to take seriously its extra-legal obligations not to injure, lie to, or cheat these stakeholders *quite apart from* whether it is in the stockholders' interests.

As we think through the *proper* relationship of management to stakeholders, fundamental features of business life must undoubtedly be reorganized: that corporations have a principally economic mission and competence; that fiduciary obligations to investors and general obligations to comply with the law cannot be set aside; and that abuses of economic power and disregard of corporate stewardship in the name of business ethics are possible.

But these things must be recognized as well: that corporations are not solely financial institutions; that fiduciary obligations go beyond short-term profit and are in any case subject to moral criteria in their execution; and that mere compliance with the law can be unduly limited and even unjust.

The Stakeholder Paradox can be avoided by a more thoughtful understanding of the nature of moral obligation and the limits it imposes on the principal–agent relationship. Once we understand that there is a practical "space" for identifying the ethical values shared by a corporation and its stockholders—a space that goes beyond strategic self-interest but stops short of impartiality—the hard work of filling that space can proceed.

NOTES

1. R. Edward Freeman, *Strategic Management: A Stakeholder Approach* (Pitman, 1984), p. 46.
2. Strictly speaking the historical meaning of "stakeholder" in this context is someone who literally *holds* the stakes during play.
3. See K. Goodpaster and T. Piper, *Managerial Decision Making and Ethical Values*, Harvard Business School Publishing Division, 1989.
4. See K. Goodpaster, "PASCAL: A Framework For Conscientious Decision Making," (1989). Unpublished paper, University of St. Thomas.
5. Actually, there are subtle ways in which even the stakeholder identification or inventory process might have *some* ethical content. The very process of *identifying* affected parties involves the use of the imagination in a way that can lead to a natural empathetic or caring response to those parties in the synthesis, choice, and action phases of decision-making. This is a contingent connection, however, not a necessary one.
6. Note that including powerless stakeholders in the analysis phase may indicate whether the decision-maker cares about "affecting" them or "being affected by" them. Also, the inclusion of what might be called secondary stakeholders as advocates for primary stakeholders (e.g. local governments on behalf of certain citizen groups) may signal the values that will come into play in any synthesis.
7. It should be mentioned that some authors, most notably Kenneth R. Andrews in *The Concept of Corporate Strategy*, 3rd edn (Irwin, 1987) employ a broader and more social definition of "strategic" decision-making than the one implied here.

8. Freeman, *Strategic Management*, p. 46.

9. Ibid., p. 52 (emphasis added).

10. Milton Friedman, "The Social Responsibility of Business is to Increase its Profits," New York Times Magazine, Sept. 13, 1970.

11. Freeman, *Strategic Management*, p. 249.

12. Ibid., pp. 226, 228–9. Ruder recently (in 1989) reaffirmed the views expressed in his 1965 article.

13. "The Business Judgement Rule" gives broad latitude to officers and directors of corporations, but calls for reasoning on the basis of the long-term economic interest of the company. And corporate case law ordinarily allows exceptions to profit-maximization criteria only when there are actual or potential *legal* barriers, and limits charitable and humanitarian gifts by the logic of long-term self-interest. The underlying rationale is accountability to investors. Recent work by the American Law Institute, however, suggests a rethinking of these matters. See appendix.

14. Christopher Elias, "Turning Up the Heat on the Top," *Insight*, July 23, 1990.

15. We might consider the NDP in broader terms that would include the relationship between "client" and "professional" in other contexts, such as law, medicine, education, government, and religion, where normally the community's expectations are embodied in ethical standards.

16. T. Nagel, *The View from Nowhere* (Oxford University Press, 1986), p. 163.

APPENDIX

The American Law Institute

PRINCIPLES OF CORPORATE GOVERNANCE: ANALYSIS AND RECOMMENDATIONS

Tentative Draft No. 2
(April 13, 1984)

Part II
THE OBJECTIVE AND CONDUCT OF THE BUSINESS CORPORATION

ANALYSIS AND RECOMMENDATION
§201. THE OBJECTIVE AND CONDUCT OF THE BUSINESS CORPORATION

A business corporation should have as its objective the conduct of business activities with a view to enhancing corporate profit and shareholder gain, except that, whether or not corporate profit and shareholder gain are thereby enhanced, the corporation, in the conduct of its business

(a) is obliged, to the same extent as a natural person, to act within the boundaries set by law,

(b) may take into account ethical considerations that are reasonably regarded as appropriate to the responsible conduct of business, and

(c) may devote a reasonable amount of resources to public welfare, humanitarian, educational, and philanthropic purposes.

Stakeholders and Consent[1]

Stephen Cohen

In this essay, I suggest that it might be fruitful to consider the notion of stakeholders from the perspective of consent-theory. Neither talk about stakeholders *per se* nor, particularly, talk about consent-theory is itself novel. However, I believe that the suggestion that consent-theory can shed some light on the position of stakeholders does provide something new, as does the suggestion that what I shall call "putative consent" and "future-oriented consent" both have important roles to play in discussions of stakeholders.

* * *

STAKEHOLDERS' INTERESTS

What is it, then, to take account of the interests of stakeholders? The simple answer is that it is to calculate the impact of an action or a practice on the stakeholders, and to figure into the overall calculation about what to do an element of the effect of the practice or action on the stakeholders. Standardly, this is conceived of as a matter of calculating the utility or disutility of a proposed practice for the stakeholders, recognizing that various stakeholders (or groups of stakeholders) have different stakes in the possible outcomes of some activity.[2]

Reaching a decision about whether a possible practice would be advantageous or disadvantageous to a particular group need not involve actual consultation with that group itself. Sometimes, the options available and the choices to be made are such that it is not presumptuous for someone other than the stakeholders to decide what is in the stakeholders' interest. If a certain practice would endanger the health of a group of stakeholders, and offer no prospects of advantage to them or to anyone else, it would not be presumptuous to calculate accordingly, without consulting with the stakeholders themselves. In such a case, we probably would not consider the decision not to endanger their health as being a paternal one or as preempting the decision of the interested parties. It would, rather, simply be deciding not to engage in some activity because of its possible harmful effects on some group—effects which are not offset by anything else.

More typically, however, decisions about whether to engage in an activity are based on trying to take account of the group's welfare in the context of some competing claims about that welfare, or at least in the context of there being both minuses and pluses associated with the activity (e.g., fluoridation of a community's water supply or stringing powerlines over the homes of numbers of the members of a community, at some risk to those residents). Here, to decide to act one way or another because of the benefit to the group can well be to engage in a paternalistic decision: "We'll do this, because it'll be for their good"; or, "we'll allow this risk, because the likely benefits are such as to make it a risk worth taking"; or "we'll do this, because the disadvantages or losses are outweighed by the benefits which will accrue." In such cases, someone decides the matter for those who will be affected by the activity. This differs from the earlier case (where there was nothing but disadvantage), inasmuch as in that case, there was, in effect, nothing to decide—because the proposed activity had no benefits to offset its likely disadvantages, and so nothing to raise the question of whether to engage in that activity. And it also differs from a case in which one decides that the possible disadvantage to one group is outweighed by the possible advantage to another, where, of course, the first group would dislike the activity, and where there would be no point in further taking their interests into account—precisely because one's calculation in the first place was to sacrifice that group's welfare for something else.[3]

As an alternative to paternalistic decision-making and the possibility of disinterested arm's-length calculation of utility by whoever has the power or the authority (governmental body, professional organization, business entity, or individual), it is important to keep in mind the possibility of taking account of the wishes or decision of the potentially affected group itself. It is important to recognize that stakeholders are not only to be taken account of, but, when appropriate, to be given a voice. Sometimes this is so (should be so) because the stakeholders can give a worthwhile opinion about the costs and benefits of the proposed activity—they have an opinion worth consulting about whether the benefits of the proposed activity do, in fact, outweigh the disadvantages. Further, there might be a real question of what that group would consent to. Given that there are some disadvantages or some risks associated with a possible gain for the group concerned, there might be a real question of whether incurring those disadvantages or those risks is worth the possibility of that gain—whether it is worth it *to them*. And there it should be recognized that it is not always the case (perhaps it is hardly ever the case) that only one decision is *the* rational (or even *the reasonable*) one. That being so, there is something to be decided, some choice to be made, on grounds other than simply, say, "the dictates of rationality." Here, very importantly, is an occasion for taking account of the interests of stakeholders. And here is an occasion where being informed of the actual view or the opinion of the stakeholders themselves is important for being able to properly take account of their interests.

Consent

Classical consent-theory in political philosophy argues that legitimate authority is exercised over people only with their consent. A central feature of human beings is their capacity to make decisions for themselves. Respect for agent autonomy is the hallmark of consent-theory. If this is so, then it is vitally important that the integrity of an environment in which human beings as agents engage in individual (and group) decision-making be maintained. This requires not only that a serious role be allowed for consenting, but also that the agents be in a position where their consent is meaningful and significant. In a word, it requires that the consent be "informed."

Informed Consent

The notion of "informed consent" has occupied an important position in discussions of the relation between individuals and medical procedures and to the medical profession generally, and also in discussions of people's relation to lawyers. The idea is that the only adequate justification for doing some things to people is that those people have been sufficiently informed about their situation, and have consented to the medical or legal activity concerning them. Without their consent, those activities are unjustified impositions on people. The context in which "informed consent" has been important has been where it is seen as unjustified, unacceptable behavior for a practitioner to judge that some proposed course of action would be for the subject's own good, or that it amounts to a risk worth taking (or avoiding), and hence, to unilaterally decide on that course. This paternalistic stance is seen to provide an insufficient justification; it does not allow the subjects themselves to make decisions for themselves, or even to be significantly involved in the making of those decisions which affect them. . . .

Consent and Stakeholders

Sometimes actual, express consent is not obtained (and need not be obtained), but is still the case that the subject could be said to have consented to something. The consent might be implied by something which the subject does. Sometimes implied consent can be explicit—it can be very clear that the subject consents, even though the subject never says "I consent," or words to that effect.

I suggest that the applicability of the notion of consent to a responsibility to take account of the interests of stakeholders is important, obvious, and largely neglected in discussions about stakeholders. Whether some risk or disadvantage should be imposed on some group for the purpose of some possible gain is a matter about which that group itself has an important opinion—possibly a decisive opinion. Imposition without the group's consent can be unjustified.

Discussions of stakeholders largely either neglect the possible role of stakeholders' consent or present stakeholder analysis as paternal, in contrast to consent theory. Mike Martin and Roland Schinzinger are exceptional in this respect. In suggesting that engineering should be viewed as social experimentation, they say,

> We believe that the problem of informed consent, which is so vital to the concept of a properly conducted experiment involving human subjects, should be the keystone in the interaction between engineers and the public.[4]

PUTATIVE CONSENT AND FUTURE-ORIENTED CONSENT

As I have indicated, sometimes consent can be literal and explicit, and sometimes it can be something else. There is also a place for what might be called "putative consent" and for what might be called "future-oriented consent," notions which are related but not identical, and which, I believe, should be particularly important with respect to taking account of stakeholders' interests. Putative consent amounts to imputing consent to someone. This might be because rationality requires consent to some particular thing, and so, of course this person consents to it. They needn't be asked whether or not they consent. Some such claims have played a role in arguments concerning the necessity of acquiring actual consent in matters relating to certain medical procedures: "only someone who was irrational or did not understand would refuse this procedure; therefore, the question need not actually be put." Putative consent also applies to imputation of consent to someone in situations where you know that they would consent if they were asked, not because consent is required by rationality, but rather because of the particular person that they are: "I went ahead and did such-and-such, because I knew that that's what you would want me to do"; or, "I went ahead and did such-and-such, because I knew that you would have agreed to it, if I had asked you." In such cases, application of putative consent requires that one know something about the particular person or group, because it is precisely in virtue of what one knows about them (perhaps their preferences, perhaps their desires, perhaps their character, perhaps their relation to the one who is wondering, . . .) that consent can be assumed or imputed.

I think that "future-oriented consent" is an important and useful notion here, as well:[5] I do something to you now, recognizing that you have not consented to it (either express or implied), and I claim as my justification not that I know what is best for you and am requiring that you do (or submit to) something which I know to be for your own good, but rather that if you had been in a position to know, etc., then you would have consented; or that when, in the future, you come to be in such a position, you will then consent to my having done this thing to (or for) you now—it is something that you will want that I have done. Future-oriented consent can differ from putative consent, in that an ascription of future-oriented consent does not necessarily carry with it a belief that if the consenter were asked now that he/she would consent. As an example of future-oriented consent, we might think of various things a parent might require that a certain child do. Some of those things are required simply because the parent knows best and requires that the child act according to the parent's will: "you simply have to take the swim lessons; I know they will be good for you." These are cases of pure justified paternalism. Other things, however, might be required of the child because the parent knows that particular child well enough to know that when the child reaches the "age of reason," the child will want that such-and-such had happened to him/her at that earlier age. The point here is that the parent knows the particular child well enough so that the parent might require something of the child or inflict something on the child or do something for the child—sometimes even contrary to the child's express wishes at the time—in the name of the child's consenting to it: "Given the kind of person you are, with your athletic and competitive nature, you will thank me for signing you up as a member of the tennis squad; you will want me to have done this—despite what you are saying now."

It is important to recognize a couple of features of—and some dangers associated with—future-oriented consent. It is something different from paternalism—different, at least, from any straightforward type of paternalism. Nevertheless, in invoking the notion of future-oriented consent, there is a particular danger of it functioning only as a "justification" for someone (e.g., a parent, a public utility, or a corporation) inflicting their preferences on someone else. There is a danger of someone's inappropriately taking licence, inflicting something on someone, while incorrectly claiming as a justification the presence of consent. We must be clear, however, that this would be a *misapplication* of the notion. It would be an *incorrect* claim about the consent of the subject. It is not a feature of future-oriented consent itself. Given the nature of future-oriented consent—in particular, that the subject's current preferences, etc. might legitimately be dismissed, while maintaining a legitimate reference to the subject's future preferences—there is the further danger of simply dismissing as irrelevant even explicit protestations by a subject that they do not consent. Perhaps the trickiest and most treacherous danger of all associated with the notion is the danger that in inflicting something on someone in the name of future-oriented consent, that which is inflicted is itself such as to produce the future consent of the subject. The extreme, of course, is brainwashing, where the activity itself might be designed specifically to achieve that result. This serious danger aside, however, I believe that there is an important place for considerations of consent—including putative and future-oriented consent—in discussion of the interests of stakeholders.

CONCLUSION

Reference to future-oriented consent, putative consent, and even, surprisingly, express consent have been largely absent from discussions of the relevant considerations which should be taken into account in having proper regard for the interests of stakeholders. The process of making a decision about what is to the advantage of a group or what advances *that group's* welfare should often (usually) involve considering *that group's* opinion. There are at least two reasons for this, the first (and maybe also the second) of which was advocated by John Stuart Mill.[6] (1) That group is usually particularly well-placed to evaluate what is and what is not in its own interest. By itself, this concern has nothing to do with respect for agent-autonomy. (2) In many matters involving some decision procedure, there is no single exclusively rational decision. There can be a number of possibilities. For example, the degree of risk which one or a group might be willing to take for some possible gain is, within limits, not a matter which can be specified as a directive of rationality. It can be a matter of preference, public policy, or any other of a number of other legitimate, appropriate concerns. And, I suggest, more often than not, it is the affected group itself which should have a major say in what course of action should be taken. What that group consents to should be an important element involved in arriving at a decision about matters concerning or affecting that group.

The process of making a decision about what is to the advantage of a group of what advances some group's welfare should often involve considering the opinion of the stakeholders in the activity which would bring about that effect. This is a broader claim, which involves eliciting the opinion of stakeholders in general, while realizing that from at least some perspectives (and perhaps from an overall perspective), it might be seen as desirable (or at least as satisfactory) that the interests of some be sacrificed for the benefit of some others. Even here, however, it seems to me appropriate that all the stakeholders have a say; even here, there is room for eliciting stakeholders' opinions and considering what they do actually or would consent to.[7] As with the situation in which the stakeholders are the ones for whose benefit an activity is proposed to be undertaken, here, too, the operable consent might be expressed, implied, putative, or future-oriented. Perhaps the groups can be consulted directly; but perhaps for any of a great number of reasons, some group cannot be so consulted. Either way, there is room for taking account of the important consideration of the groups' consent to the activity.

NOTES

1. I have benefitted from the comments and suggestions I have received at a number of points in the development of this essay from Damian Grace, Neil Harpley, and Michael Jackson, and for the ongoing dialogue about stakeholders which I have with Damian Grace. The general and specific critical comments from this journal's editor have been particularly helpful.

2. Kenneth Goodpaster in "Business Ethics and Stakeholder Analysis" (*Business Ethics Quarterly* 1 (1991), pp. 53–71) and Damian Grace in "Stakeholders" (unpublished) make the important point that merely identifying some group as stakeholders in some activity does not, by itself, point in any direction at all toward a correct or appropriate ethical analysis of the activity. It might be a significant prerequisite to moral reasoning, but it is not more than this. Further, Grace and I suggest that a danger with 'stakeholder analysis' is that as a phrase it might simply become synonymous with 'social responsibility,' while at the same time presenting a misleading impression (a) that there is some methodological substance to it as a *type* of analysis, and (b) that there should be a special status accorded to stakeholders, who as stakeholders have entitlements different from or additional to those present for society at large (*Business Ethics: Australian Problems and Cases* (Sydney: Oxford U.P., 1995), ch. 3). To talk about "stakeholder analysis" and "rights of stakeholders" without articulating what gives someone a stake can be misleading and dangerous. While I have nothing to add here to this general point, I do believe that the injection of a consent requirement into a stakeholder analysis amounts to recognition of a terribly important element in moral reasoning.

3. Perhaps this is not a good thing to do. Perhaps it could never be justified. Nevertheless, if it *were* the case, there would be no point in taking further account of the group whose interests were to be sacrificed. Nothing more could be learned about that group.

4. Mike W. Martin and Roland Schinzinger, *Ethics in Engineering*, second edition (New York: McGraw Hill, 1989), p. 68. It is not clear how far Martin and Schinzinger would be prepared to generalize this point to include other professions and, more importantly, to include other practices which do not so easily fit the model of social experimentation.

5. What I am suggesting here is a relative of Gerald Dworkin's "hypothetical consent." ("Paternalism, *The Monist* 56 (1972), pp. 64–84; and "Paternalism: Some Second Thoughts," in *Paternalism*, ed. Rolf Sartorius (Minneapolis: U. of Minnesota P., 1983), pp. 105–112.)

6. Mill, however, regarded these reasons as decisive. I am suggesting only that they are important considerations, and that they might, at the end of the day, be outweighed by other considerations on any particular occasion.

7. This would be a more easily supportable claim if made from a position analogous to John Rawls' claims about permissible inequalities within a society in general. We might argue that any satisfactory justification for advancing the welfare of one group above that of another must be such to help the lesser-advantaged groups, as well. And if this is so, then the consent of even the lesser-advantaged stakeholders might be gained from an appeal to their own self-interest alone.

EVALUATING A CASE STUDY: FINDING THE CONFLICTS

After establishing an ethical point of view (including a segue to application), we are ready to approach cases. The first stage in handling cases effectively is to analyze the situation according to normal practice and potential ethical issues. Obviously, sometimes ethical issues are involved in what one will do, and at other times they are not. It is your job to determine when ethical issues are involved. Let us consider specific cases.

Case 1.

You are a sales manager at a Fortune 1000 company. You have several large deals that are just about to close, but for some reason they have been hung up over some details. The sales in your division have been down for five consecutive quarters. If you show one more decline, you are history and many others in your division will be history, too. You could "fudge" your report and show two of the three pending deals as sold and thereby avoid being sacked. After all, you are very sure they will go through. Anyway, it buys you a little time even if they do not.

Does this case involve any ethical issues? If so, what are they? How do they affect normal practice?

Case 2.

You work in the accounting department of a small company. You notice that Mr. Jones has been "hitting on" Ms. Smith. This takes up a lot of time for both of them, and the other accountants must work even harder to make up for the time Mr. Jones and Ms. Smith lose. Your department is small, so this situation is especially difficult and irritating.

Does this case involve any ethical issues? If so, what are they? How do they affect prudential (self-interested) concerns? What about issues of professional practice?

CHECKLIST FOR DETECTING ISSUES CONCERNING PROFESSIONAL PRACTICE

Directions: Read your case carefully and determine what (if any) relevant points of professional practice are at stake. Identify the individual in the case from whose perspective you will develop your comments. Determine whether there are any clear violations of professional practice. Identify these violations and the various risks that such behavior entails. Next go through the checklist for detecting ethical issues.

CHECKLIST FOR DETECTING ETHICAL ISSUES

Directions: Read your case carefully. Determine your ethical viewpoint (as per "Developing a Practical Ethical Viewpoint," p. 32. Create one or more detection questions that identify ethical issues. These detection questions will follow your own ethical perspective. For example, from my own practical ethical perspective I have chosen the following two detection questions to bring ethical issues to my attention. These questions follow from a deontological viewpoint.

1. *Is any party being exploited solely for the advantage of another?* (Exploitation can include instances of lying, injuring, deliberately falsifying, creating an unequal competitive environment, and so forth.)
2. *Is every effort being made to assist and affirm the human dignity of all parties involved?* (Affirming human dignity can include instances of encouraging the fulfillment of legal and human rights as well as taking personal responsibility for results that are consonant with these principles. Thus, you cannot hide behind nonfunctioning rules.)

By asking these questions within the context of the case, I am able better to understand the moral dimensions that exist with other professional concerns.

A few other comments may be useful concerning my detection questions. Question 1 concerns "prohibitions" (i.e., actions that you must refrain from doing). Question 2 concerns "obligations" (i.e., actions that you are required to do). Anything that is not an ethical obligation or a prohibition is a "permission" (i.e., actions that you may do if you choose). Thus, if the case you present does not invoke a prohibition or an obligation, then you may act solely according to the dictates of your professional practice. It is often useful to group your detection questions as prohibitions and obligations, which emphasizes different types of moral duty.

Try creating detection questions and apply them to the two earlier cases. What do they reveal about the ethical issues involved in the cases? How do different detection questions emphasize different ethical issues? How different are these perspectives? How similar are they?

Once you have completed this preliminary ethical assessment, you can return to the ethical theory you have chosen and to determine *how* and *why* the prohibitions and obligations are applicable to this theory.

Read the following macro and micro cases and complete the steps outlined:

1. List the professional practice issues at stake.
2. Identify your practical ethical viewpoint including any linking principles.
3. Determine which character's perspective you will adopt.
4. Identify two or more detection questions that define obligation and prohibition within the ethical theory you have chosen.
5. Apply the detection questions to the cases to bring attention to the ethical issues.
6. Discuss the interrelationships between the dictates of the ethical issues and those of the professional practice. How might they work together? How might they be opposed?

Macro and Micro Cases.

The cases section of this book is divided into two categories, macro and micro. Each type of case employs a different point of view.

Macro Case. The macro case takes the perspective of someone in an executive position of authority who supervises or directs an organizational unit. His or her decisions will affect many people and resonate in a larger sociological sphere.

Micro Case. The micro case examines the perspective of someone at the proximate level of professional practice, such as a salesperson, accountant, or lower level manager. Obviously, this case applies to more people than does the macro case.

Case Development. This book suggests one way to develop critical evaluations of ethical cases. In the "Evaluating a Case Study" sections, you will be asked to apply a specific skill to the cases presented. At the end of Chapter Six, you will be able to write an essay concerning the application of an ethical perspective to a specific problem.

Please note that although the cases presented here have fictional venues, they are based on composites of actual business practice.

Macro Case 1.

You are the new chairperson of the board at Drummond Defense Contractors, which has experienced some ethical problems in the past. The company made its reputation through very cagey and aggressive business dealings. This means operating as far below the law as possible without being caught. These dealings have brought stockholders large profits. You want to change the company's dealings from being on the edge of legality to being fully compliant with the professional standards of good business practice. You realize that this suggestion is controversial since it could mean that the company's bottom line might suffer (most certainly will suffer is more accurate).

You know that you will need more than a whim to make your case to the other directors. You know that there are various ways to look at a corporation (i.e., as a moral agent, as the representative of stakeholders' interests, and as some other property-oriented aggregate, as you learned in college when you studied philosophy). You also know that the other directors think that philosophy is basically worthless (fit only for the feeble minded and the insane). You cannot present your case in philosophical terms or you will be out of a job. Instead, you must find a way to convince Drummond to revise its practices of doing anything to obtain specs on competitive bidding and to find out *beforehand* what other companies are bidding. Your job is to make the argument so that your board will accept it.

Macro Case 2.

You are the head of the federal Food and Drug Administration (FDA). You have learned that numerous vitamin companies are making claims about the efficacy of their over-the-counter products that are not entirely correct and in some cases are patently wrong. It has been agency policy to treat over-the-counter vitamins largely as unregulated so long as the products actually contain what the label says (e.g., vitamin E in a vitamin E pill).

The current situation worries you. More and more vitamins and herbal medications are available in increasingly potent amounts and pose health problems to people who use them improperly. Some affect heart rate, and others are mood altering. This poses a difficulty to your understanding of the professional responsibility incumbent in your position. You believe that your job is to protect the public; however, when you bring this up in a staff meeting, it becomes apparent that at least three clear positions emerge. First is the position that the marketplace will police itself and the media will inform the public of excesses and problems, which will result in putting financial pressures on those companies to reform themselves.

The second position is that only the government can treat corporations as moral entities with the moral (and legal) responsibility to act responsibly (with a high level of care and professionalism). Those who say that companies ought to be made accountable use language suggesting that these companies are persons in their own right.

A third position is to view the situation as the interface of stakeholders' interests.

Obviously, these three positions predict radically different solutions to what everyone agrees is a disaster waiting to happen. You have an appointment with the secretary of Health and Human Services to discuss this problem. Write a position paper noting the practical and professional issues and the way you characterize a corporation.

Micro Case 1.

You are the manager of a discount computer software and hardware store that is part of a chain. The final decision-making authority lies with the home office. Each store is rated against other stores in the chain, and those that score poorly experience lower pay and higher layoffs. It is a very competitive system.

One practice mentioned at a recent meeting of store managers is customer service exhaustion (CSE). Under CSE, the store classifies customer service requests as trivial and nontrivial. The classification depends on the cost to solve the problem. Problems costing the company $10 or less are trivial; all others are nontrivial. CSE has trivial requests processed promptly. Nontrivial requests are addressed under a calculated system of delay based on the "principle of five," which means that the client must be turned down at least five times. The rationale behind the principle of five is that few customers will have the endurance to continue the process of having a customer service associate meet with superiors and return time and again without approval to address the problem. The customer service associate assumes the role of the "good guy," and the superiors making the decisions are the "bad guys."

Employing CSE works; fully 70 percent of the customers walk away, saving the company the expense of seeking recompense from the supplier (a difficult operation at best). Stores that utilize CSE consistently outperform those that do not.

CSE does not fit the values of your personal worldview, however. You believe that CSE is simply a strategy to cheat the customer and make money for the company. You are a steward of the company's resources; the stockholders' money is in your hands. If you press forward your ideas of ethics and morality, you are concerned that you are adding a new element to your job description (preserving the company as a moral entity) and it is rather presumptuous of you to do so. Shouldn't you just do whatever is necessary to increase the profit of the company to the benefit of the real owners, the stockholders? What about the stakeholders?

You are very conflicted by this. Write a report for your own benefit to justify the action you will take. Be sure to take into account practical issues, professional issues, and your personal conception of what a corporation should be.

Micro Case 2.

You are a life insurance salesperson whose company has a new marketing campaign: "Rising to the Top of the Pyramid: Retirement Security." The essence of the campaign is to approach businesses and sell them on the fact that $50,000 of life insurance can be purchased by an employer and remain tax free. By "overpaying" a universal or variable life policy to the maximum under regulations, a person can create a pool of money that enjoys tax-deferred status. This is touted as an ideal plan for employers who wish to leverage their benefits as much as possible (in some cases, the corporation itself can be the beneficiary of the death benefit until the employee retires).

The problem is that although the life insurance policy is currently paying 5.5 percent and is guaranteed to pay 3.0 percent, this is deceptive in comparison to other investment vehicles. These figures are based on the net cost (i.e., before deducting the death benefit costs and administrative fees). Once these costs are deducted, the real return is approximately 0.75 percent.

You firmly believe that although life insurance is a legitimate financial planning tool and that every working person with a family should have 3 to 5 times the annual salary protected by life insurance, this campaign deceptively sells insurance as a retirement vehicle or an investment tool.

The problem is that you do not believe in the company's marketing plan. It violates the values supported by your personal worldview. Should you go along with the campaign? What do you owe the company? What do you owe the company's stockholders? Should you just continue to sell in your traditional way? What if everyone did that? If the company is wrong in its moral direction and if you think of the company as a moral entity, then perhaps you are doing the company a favor by not going along with its new campaign. If the company is a moral entity and is consciously moving in this direction, what does this say about the relationship between your own moral views and those of your employer? Does stakeholder analysis alter your evaluation?

This is a complicated set of questions. Choose the ones that seem most appropriate to you and write a report supporting your position. Be sure to make a copy and keep it in your safe deposit box in the bank in case there is an investigation.

chapter four

What Are Proper Business Practices?

GENERAL OVERVIEW.

In the first three chapters of this book, we explored moral theory and the world-view model, the perspectives of a highly successful business owner who wants to make money in the *right* way, and the nature of the corporation. In this chapter we explore actual practices, which are extremely important to understand the business environment and ethical issues that involve businesses. Readers are encouraged to consider these issues in view of their personal worldviews. This evaluation process is the first step in creating an integrated theory of value. When you have completed this process, you will be in a position to discuss these issues with others. These discussions can lead to a new shared community worldview that might better embody the values of its members (a bottom-to-top process). This endeavor never ceases and is subject to constant revision. Such is our lot if we seek to possess all aspects of our lives and authentically make them our own.

Competition and the Practice of Business.

Overview.

This section moves from the specific to the general in evaluating business practices in the context of competition.

Alan Malachowski opens this discussion as he examines the role of metaphor as it relates to competition in business. Malachowski focuses here on an evolutionary metaphor—not too unlike John D. Rockefeller Senior's use of Social Darwinism more than a century ago.

In the evolutionary metaphor, business goals are end-states to be achieved as efficiently as possible. Ethical values are merely an inefficient cost in this process. Thus, ethics are given as little attention as possible. Must this be the case? Can competition also bring out the best? This is a controversial issue, but Malachowski believes it can.

In the second essay of this section I seek to elucidate a principle of fair competition based on a superstructure of professionalism. Professionalism, broadly conceived, refers to a specialized notion of practice. To avoid relativism, practice must meet the standards flowing from a consistent worldview. Because competition and morality are often opposing forces, this essay seeks to define a direction for businesspeople that acknowledges these tensions and offers a clear action directive.

Focus: Ethics in Competition

Morality and Competitive Advantage

Alan Malachowski

The subject of competition in business raises a variety of subtle and complex moral issues. However, there seems to be a prevailing climate of opinion which prefers to gloss over, or even ignore, such issues. For, according to the cluster of views I am alluding to, the normal competitive behaviour of business practitioners and their organisations is, *in itself,* morally neutral. Such behaviour is nevertheless to be judged as worthy, all things considered, on account of its *beneficial consequences.*

The famous guiding thought here is that business is bound to achieve better results for society, even in moral terms, when it pursues self-interested, non-moral ends of a strictly commercial kind. Economists who initially fostered this famous line of thinking also professed a great deal of respect for the ways in which business practices and institutions *naturally evolve* over time. Unfortunately, that 'respect' appears to have been uncritically mirrored in the recent outlook of many politicians and members of the business community in the west. Their collective beliefs have begun to congeal into an 'evolutionary paradigm' of business practice, according to which survival of the fittest depends on adapting to prevailing circumstances.

Although I do not have space on this occasion to examine this evolutionary paradigm in detail, I want at least to try to show that it dogmatically obscures a number of vital questions about the morality of competitive behaviour in business. I shall begin by saying a little more about the general features of the 'paradigm', and then I shall indicate the sort of issues which it tends to obscure. My main aim is to stimulate reflection rather than to demonstrate any fixed conclusions on the issues at stake.

The Evolutionary Paradigm

> "Business is a survival game with its own set of rules."
> Verne E. Henderson, *What's Ethical in Business?* McGraw Hill, 1992

On a commonly accepted interpretation, evolution offers tests for survival in which 'the best' in some relevant sense (the strongest, smartest, fittest, fastest and so on) win out. When business is viewed in a similar light, it is tempting to look upon its individuals and organisations as having passed analogous 'tests' whenever they endure the trials of the marketplace.

Proponents of the evolutionary paradigm of business practice succumb quite easily to such temptations, but they are also inclined to push the analogies with natural evolution much further. Thus, a company which sustains competitive advantage in its markets is automatically deemed to be a 'better' company that its rivals, with little close attention being paid to the exact sense of 'better' which is involved. Moreover, in this scheme of things, *moral constraints* are believed to be fundamentally unhealthy. True business health—and, by reasonable extrapolation, the true health of society at large—is won, and maintained, by means of total competitive struggle using all *legally* sanctioned resources. Here, the law plays a minimal restraining role, and it is argued that the fetters of morality will inevitably lead to weaknesses on the part of competitors, thereby making the overall tests for survival less exacting. In such circumstances, or so it is contended, 'evolution' is liable to yield less than optimum results.

Notice that this picture has some morally disreputable attractions. In its grip, business practitioners can rationalise behaviour with which they might otherwise feel uncomfortable and which they would find difficult to justify. Indeed, they can take refuge in the fact that they will, at times, be *obliged* by competitive forces to give free rein to sides of their character that morality would have them suppress. And, finally, it goes without saying that politicians' lives become more inactive under the sway of evolutionary ideas. Business is simply to be left to get on with its own affairs in its own way, with the minimum of outside interference.

To reiterate, the central claims behind this evolutionary paradigm are:

i)   Business achieves the most beneficial end states for society by evolutionary means (these 'end states' are frequently cashed in terms of 'created wealth').

ii) Business modes of evolution necessarily involve forms of competitive behaviour which are, as far as possible, free from moral constraints.

We should note that the second claim is morally ambiguous as it stands, because the 'as far as possible' clause leaves room for equivocation over the extent of the moral constraints on business practice. Those who adhere to stricter versions of the evolutionary approach are willing to discard such qualifications. On their understanding, the law provides sufficient guidelines for business practice. They believe, as I mentioned earlier, that legally sanctioned competitive behaviour is morally neutral when considered in its own right.

Let us now turn to the issues which are obscured by the evolutionary picture we have just sketched.

KEY ISSUES

There are many moral issues which are obscured by evolutionary models of business, but for our present purposes, they can be slotted into the following three categories:

a)   Issues concerning the nature of business and the role of morality within it

b)   Issues as to whether business has any *special* moral responsibilities

c)   Issues regarding the moral character of business people and the moral significance of their organisations

We can now look briefly at each of these categories in turn.

a) The Nature of Business

According to the evolutionary outlook, business organisations should be treated as quasi-natural kinds. As such they should be left to evolve in their own style in line with their intrinsic competitive capacities. Putting moral constraints on the competitive behaviour of a business organisation is akin to placing a free-roaming animal in a cage. Under such constraints, the business world as a whole would end up like a zoo populated by denatured animals.

Leaving aside the questionable aspects of the 'macho rhetoric' here, it is worth stressing that the evolutionary thinking behind it tends to screen out important questions concerning the ways in which moral constraints might be fruitfully adapted by business *within competitive contexts*. Such questions importantly include those connected with the *strategic* significance of morality.

Current evidence suggests that the dogmatic equation

$$\text{moral constraints} = \text{unnecessary costs}$$

is simply false in many instances. There are cases where moral considerations can help *cut* costs (for example by enabling companies to avoid costly backlashes from punitive court proceedings or bad publicity). Furthermore, moral matters can help boost profits by playing a crucial role in the differentiation of products, services and employment conditions. The upshot is that morality has the potential to be a major factor in achieving and sustaining competitive advantage. Naturally, this provokes further interesting debate as to whether it is morally acceptable for business to deploy moral resources for competitive purposes.

Let me finish this section with a piece of 'counter-dogma' of my own (I hope to *argue* for the position on a separate occasion). Business organisations are not best described as quasi-natural kinds. They are *conventionally constructed* entities. This means that they have no 'essential' or 'intrinsic' properties (the same goes for 'functions'). It also means that the question of how much we should incorporate morality into business practice is a far more open question than the evolutionary paradigm allows.

b) Special Moral Responsibilities

The evolutionary paradigm confuses matters in this instance because it encourages the business community to hide from moral responsibility behind metaphors of evolutionary determinism ('it's a dog-eat-dog situation', 'it's a jungle out there', and so on). On this understanding moral responsibilities are a luxury which cannot be afforded in the struggle for survival. Again, the issues are complex and varied, but at least two levels of responsibility are likely to be screened out:

First, business blinds itself to its own responsibility for the conditions of competition which it faces. The conditions are not 'given'—like the so-called 'state of nature'—they are largely created by business organisations themselves.

Second, the metaphors of unavoidable struggle blind us all to legitimate, fine-grained questions concerning *which* moral responsibilities business ought to shoulder.

Again, in both cases, I wish to say that the issues are wide open, and that it is premature to endorse the negative conclusions of the evolutionary paradigm. No simplistic evolutionary conception of the nature of business should be allowed to dictate the extent of the moral responsibilities of business. Questions as to whether business has *special* moral responsibilities require more careful examination than the evolutionary approach usually leaves room for.

c) Moral Character

One reason why 'competition' is such an interesting topic, morally speaking, is that it can bring out both the best and the worst in human character. One apparent advantage of the evolutionary paradigm is that it seems to show how the darker sides of human nature can be harnessed. Self-interest, and greed in general, generate a beneficial economic outcome by means of competition in the marketplace, and this in turn leads to the most efficient production and use of resources.

However, the 'free-for-all' approach ignores important questions about the relationship between moral character and business practice:

a) In other areas of culture (think of sport or the arts), we try to fine tune the competitive conditions to produce *'the best'* in certain specific senses. Why should we not explore similar possibilities in business contexts rather than leave things to the 'laws of the commercial jungle'? And why should we not try to encourage particular habits and character traits by experimenting with the competitive conditions under which business operates? A spirit of open-ended experimentation in this respect could enable us to make important discoveries about the relationships between business activity and human character.

b) It is naive to believe that morally reprehensible actions can be 'limited' to, or contained within, the field of business, or disguised by the label 'neutral'. If we are pushy, advantage-seeking, competitors in our business lives this must create tensions in the moral fabric of our life as a whole. We need to explore questions as to whether the all-pervasive nature of business practice in modern developed communities makes it credible to claim a private/public division of the elements of the virtuous life.

In conclusion, I hope I have raised enough questions to show that the evolutionary paradigm needs an overhaul. First, its *empirical* credentials need checking: is it true that when left to 'naturally evolve', the business community will tend to produce the greater wealth? And, second its *moral authority* needs to be challenged independently of such empirical concerns: even if 'evolution' yields the greatest wealth, is it desirable from a moral point of view? I have undertaken neither of these tasks, but perhaps I have said enough to show that they need to be tackled with some urgency.

The Principle of Fair Competition

Michael Boylan

I believe that a businessperson faces the following factors when making a decision:

1. *Professional considerations (broadly conceived).* Here I follow Alasdair MacIntyre, who uses a sense of practice to develop the internal perspective of the shared community worldview.[1] MacIntyre says, "A practice involves standards of excellence and obedience to rules as well as the achievement of goods. To enter into a practice is to accept the authority of those standards and the inadequacy of my own performances as judged by them."[2] For our purposes, this definition provides the following.

First, to attain the products of the profession, a person must accept the internal rules to the practice. This means that she must accept the profession as being worthy, as being governed by rules, as having an authority, and that to enter into the profession, she must submit to its authority and its rules.

Second, accepting authority entails the following: (a) realizing that an individual is incapable as an agent to judge or alter the rules until that person has mastered them, (b) accepting the fact that to become a master of the rules, the individual must give herself over to the rules, and (c) that she must consequently give herself over to the rules.

Third, giving herself over to the rules entails (a) accepting the authority of the shared community's worldview over her personal worldview and (b) accepting the authority of the shared community's worldview when specific tenets of the shared community worldview conflict with her personal worldview.[3]

MacIntyre's design is to tie excellence in attaining the goods internal to the profession to turning oneself over to it. This excellence is virtue (in the traditional sense of Aristotle and Aquinas), and the internal structure of

---

[1] I develop the concepts of worldview, shared worldview, and the Personal Worldview Imperative in my book *Basic Ethics* (Upper Saddle River, NJ: Prentice Hall, 2000).

[2] Alasdair MacIntyre, *After Virtue: A Study in Moral Theory*, 2d ed. (London: Duckworth, 1985), p. 190.

[3] My comments here should clearly indicate that these consequences of accepting a practice, as defined by MacIntyre, come from my critical understanding of this process and are not meant to be an exact paraphrase of MacIntyre.

the profession ties together the practitioners (present, past, and future); therefore, the foundation of excellence is social. This constitutes an argument for Virtue Ethics.

I suggest that the internal practice constitutes the internal standpoint of the shared community worldview. In the context of Professional Ethics, this can be understood as the profession itself.

2. *Cost considerations.* These are self-evident (whatever will increase *benefit* on a cost-benefit analysis).[4]

3. *Worldview interactions.* Whatever personal worldview values an individual possesses interact with the shared community's worldview. The personal worldview dictates what each of us thinks are "fair" parameters for competition. The shared worldview dictates what is professionally acceptable for competition. These acceptable practices may vary from profession to profession.

For example, in one case an individual's personal worldview may dictate less restrictive guidelines than the professional shared worldview. In another case, the personal worldview may be more restrictive than the professional worldview. (In some cases—quite the minority, I believe—an individual's worldview may exactly mirror the professional worldview.) In the less restrictive and the more restrictive situations, the individual is at a disadvantage (in the former because he will possess a flawed worldview and in the latter because he will be at a competitive disadvantage).

In the first case, a salesperson, manager, or executive may exceed what is considered to be professionally acceptable to make the sale. Let us assume, for example, that a life insurance salesperson has created a computer printout as a marketing tool for a prospective universal life policy showing that particular interest rates will be credited to excess monies in the account. In our example, the salesperson has used interest rate assumptions that are higher than the company pays its current policies. Thus, the salesperson is acting contrary to the industry practice of quoting only what the company is currently paying for such policies.

By projecting higher interest rates than the company actually pays, the salesperson will probably make more sales, but what justifies the person's taking a less restrictive worldview in this situation? Clearly, the justification is a primary emphasis on cost considerations and personal gain. As a primary emphasis, this worldview trumps most other considerations and may express

---

[4]This is obviously a complicated issue. Many factors must be considered, such as the time frame of expected results, relation to strategic plan, crucial environmental effects, and so forth. For this analysis, let the benefit stand for (all things considered) the highest prudential consequential advantage to the company.

itself through selfish egoism.[5] I have detailed my problems with selfish egoism elsewhere.[6] In short, it seems to me that selfish egoism fails the consistency test of the Personal Worldview Imperative (PWI): All people must develop a single comprehensive and internally coherent worldview that is good and that we strive to act out in our daily lives.[7]

Therefore, unless we alter our worldview to become ethical egoists or adopt a complicated supernatural superstructure to support it,[8] we are involved in an inconsistent position when we assert an egoistic position. Individuals whose personal worldview violates the PWI will be forced (on the pain of being irrational)[9] to alter their position. They must conform (at least) to the minimal professional standard.

In the second case, individual values are more restrictive than the professional standard. In this situation, the individuals involved are at a competitive disadvantage, but this does not necessarily mean failure. In many environments, competition is not overly fierce and there is enough business for anyone willing to work hard and provide superior service. This strategy implies failure only when intense competition exists; in this event, entering an arena with one hand tied behind your back will put you at a disadvantage. I believe this to be a fact but this is not always bad, in my opinion. This is so because I do not believe that totally maximizing prudential benefits is an imperative (by itself alone) that is fruitful to follow. If a person found herself in a business so competitive (meaning many people working in a very limited market) that only those who violate standard professional practice (not to mention the law, in many cases) were able to succeed, then she should either discover a novel marketing slant (honestly outthinking her adversaries) or leave that field. There are always other ways for her to use her skills. Most business skills such as sales and customer relations are clearly transferable to other business venues and to more specialized endeavors, such as law and accounting.

The old adage that behind every challenge there is an opportunity may be pertinent here. By acting contrary to an individual's personal worldview, he will either hate himself or become so numb that much of what makes life worthwhile may disappear.[10] A person cannot authentically act contrary to

---

[5]I intend *selfish egoism* to refer to a decision-making mechanism that looks to personal, prudential benefit above all else when making an action decision.

[6]For a discussion of some of the most important issues involving egoism see the introduction to my text *Basic Ethics* (Upper Saddle River, NJ: Prentice Hall, 2000).

[7]I outline an argument for the Personal Worldview Imperative in *Basic Ethics*.

[8]I am thinking here of Plato's theory of reincarnation (very similar to Hinduism). One *could* by fiat create a situation in which the ethical action would always be to one's ultimate advantage. The issue is how much one must give up, logically speaking, to accept these added tenets?

[9]My position here is that to be irrational is to violate one's human nature. We are, by nature, rational animals. This is not to exclude other aspects of our nature, such as human love and sympathy, but these are always to be understood in relation to rationality.

[10]I also believe that many personally self-destructive behaviors, such as alcoholism and drug abuse, may begin this way.

her worldview because such action fragments who she is by forcing her to adopt multiple, conflicting personal and shared community worldviews. Thus, unless a person can find a legitimate approach by which to succeed (through honest innovation), she should move to something else, even if this entails temporary financial insecurity. Such an action promotes wholeness, that is to say, *integrity*.[11]

I view these relationships on a continuum of functional excellence. At one level is the *krateristic* group of people who live in a worldview of unbridled selfish egoism; in other words, they believe that might makes right. They would be very at home with Plato's depiction of Thrasymachus and Callicles.[12] These men believed that in life the powerful take what they can get; the more powerful restrained them. If someone could put them in jail, then they would pay attention to that person who had the power to do so. Otherwise, these men acted on the sole imperative of pleasing themselves and gratifying their personal whims.

The next level represents the law. All countries have legal principles to stop the most egregious selfish egoists. Of course, these laws must be enforced, but enforcement in many countries of the world (now and throughout history) has been the exception rather than the rule. The rich and powerful selfish egoists are allowed to have their own way even though they have broken the law.

The third level is based on the standards of professional practice. Our broad sense of profession outlined earlier stated that the hallmarks for professionalism are that one must accept that (a) the practice is worthy, (b) the practice is governed by rules, (c) whatever governs the practice has authority within the province of the practice, and (d) to enter into the practice, a person must submit to the authority of the practice and its rules.

Set in this way, the level of the standard of professional practice is more exacting that the legal standard (although in some cases the law may punish those who stray from the professional standard). Thus, in some instances, the legal and professional standards are the same. However, even in those instances there is really another, informal sense of the professional standard that separates itself from the *de jure* enforced standard and outlines what a good practice is.

Beyond the professional standard is another picture of an excellent member of the profession. This individual exceeds professional standards and is considered excellent to a high degree. This is the individual who has been able to compete in the world of business and still maintain wholeness. This is the person of integrity.

---

[11]This assumes, of course, that a person is not in a position to revise the system and expel those who are violating the professional standards. This would be an ideal answer but is rarely a practical alternative.

[12]These characters are famous advocates of might makes right and selfish egoism is all that counts. See Plato, *Republic* I and *Gorgias*.

The person of integrity stands as the most admired of all who value the standards of the profession. This person accepts the constraints and limitations of the profession—and more. Even with these constraints (and in some cases *because* of these constraints), the person still excels in the practice of the occupation.

This continuum can be depicted in Figure 1. Thus, those who choose to compete at the levels of X and Y are lawbreakers driven by selfish egoism. I am sorry to say that in many professions, this group of individuals represents (by far) the largest group of people. These people thrive because it is generally impossible to bring every lawbreaker to justice (barring a significant hundredfold increase in law enforcement personnel). Thus, this group plays the odds that they will not be caught. Because they have such a competitive advantage over those playing by the rules, this is the group that includes most tycoons of the world.

The next largest group of individuals operate between Y and Z. These individuals do not break the law, but they are not exemplary members of their profession. They look for a smaller competitive edge by acting within the law but sometimes unprofessionally.

The penultimate group consists of those who always strive to meet the professional standards. These people cannot be faulted for their behavior because they always seek to do exactly what a member of the profession should do. However, as good as this group is, it is not as high as those who rise to the level of integrity.

People of integrity seek to affirm all of their worldview values by their professional lives, which creates wholeness and requires them to fulfill additional standards in executing their professional roles (community worldviews).

It is not uncommon for a person who has a coherent, consistent personal worldview to seek to become a member of a community that shares the individual's worldview. Such a person exhibits a desire for wholeness; to be one person at work and another at home creates an unacceptable incoherence within the person's worldview. Therefore, a person should actively seek a business situation in which his personal and ethical values are not violated by working in the particular profession.

Such a depiction of the competitive arena underlies my Principle of Fair Competition, which can be stated formally: All businesspeople should strive

X	Y	Z	Z+
Selfish egoism standard	Legal standard	Professional practice standard	Integrity standard

FIGURE 1 **Standards for Competition**

always to compete at or above the level of accepted professional practice with a view toward advancing toward the level of integrity. This principle assumes several things. First, it assumes that the creation of the standard of professional practice occurs in a free and open way from the bottom up. That is, it is created by people who actually do the work involved. The personal worldview of these people interacts with the shared community worldview of the emerging profession. It is assumed that if the practices are open and responsive to the members of the profession, sound ethical rules that reflect the practical needs of the profession will develop.

Of course, one can imagine that in totalitarian top-down regimes, standards are *imposed* on the members of a profession and are shams. They are not authentic professional standards and thus do not fall under the purview of the principle of fair competition.

The principle of fair competition seeks to offer concrete direction as to how a person should behave as a businessperson. If a person is operating within a free and open society, then the person should first discover what the law is, second what the professional standard is, and third who the most admired practitioners are. A person should begin with the professional standard and seek to emulate the behavior of the most admired practitioners.

Some might say that this approach is rather idealistic. They might suggest that people who have jobs are lucky and jeopardize those jobs if they demand that their employers adhere to professional standards. This is a real problem. The power situation between employer and employee is vastly unequal, and good jobs are not easy to obtain.

This vast power inequality between employer and employee is the source of many problems in the workplace, including sexual harassment. For example, Mr. Big approaches a subordinate and interacts with her. His position of power eliminates any true sense of "consensual" behavior because what seems consensual to him is *not* necessarily consensual to her. The reason for this is that he holds a power advantage over her. Therefore, if she consents, she may do so because she is thinking of how much she needs her job to support herself and her family. She may be thinking that if she refuses, she might be fired (not for refusing sex, for no employer would fire an employee for that reason) but for some other reason. (When a boss wants to fire a person, she will find a way within the limits of the law.)[13]

In the rare (lucky) circumstance in which an employee is so valuable to his employer that he can dictate his own terms, this power dynamic is not a problem in the workplace. Even when it is the case, most employers try to pretend that many other people can perform the employee's job. The employer emphasizes how lucky the person is to have the job. This is a fact; we

---

[13]This scenario obviously works in the other direction, too. When one factors in homosexual situations, the possibilities increase, but the same principle still holds.

are all lucky to have the jobs we have. Does this mean, however, that we must abnegate our personal dignity to keep our jobs? Absolutely not. The basic rights we are entitled to morally are not a function of our bargaining position. If any person X deserves Y, then what X deserves does not depend upon Y's coming-to-be (based on some irrelevant set of circumstances or other fictions).

I believe that the essential point to be made in business ethics is that most cases in real life involve conflicts among professional values, cost issues, and our personal worldview (which determines all that we personally value, including ethics). Seldom are there easy, totally fair adjudications. People who obey the rules often lose to those who do not—this is a fact. However, this fact does not provide a license to do whatever selfish egoism dictates; instead, it is an admission that the final goals in life must be more than obtaining the most money and power. This is a state of balanced consciousness in which a person is content knowing that she is living within chosen guidelines that compose her individual worldview. Such a state of balanced consciousness supersedes the imperatives of winning.

I offer an analogy to sports to illustrate this point. I have been an athlete of sorts and a coach of youth sports for more than thirty-five years. The way athletes compete has always been a point of fascination to me. Some athletes openly violate the sport's standards. I once was in an AAU cross-country regional meet in which the runner just in front of me cut the corners on the turns and did not obey the flags posted to define the course. This runner's ability was probably equal to mine, but I lost because he cut the turns and I did not.

Other athletes adhere to a standard but push the envelope to enhance the professional practice standard. This is especially true in basketball. Basketball players are often trained to develop "tricks" (such as thrusting his hand into the abdomen of the shooter he is guarding to throw off the shooter's concentration or to "undercut" the shooter early in the game so that later he will fear injury on some crucial jump). Basketball players learn these and many other tricks to give them the competitive edge. Sports in general support the adages that nice guys finish last and that winning is not the most important thing—it is the only thing. Do we agree with this?

Most of us do not agree. We believe that fair competition begins at the standard of professional practice—this is the benchmark. Those who operate at any lower level are behaving badly and thus diminish themselves. When we exceed the standard of acceptable professional practice, we move toward the goal of professional or personal integrity, a level of excellence in which the practitioner exceeds the standard of professional practice by integrating her worldview into the shared community worldview. When one achieves the level of professional or personal integrity, she rises to a level of personal excellence that defines *telos* of all human endeavor.

In order to engage the reader further to the model I am presenting, let me pose some questions that have been put to me as I have lectured on this topic over the past few years.

Q: You describe the principle of fair competition as a linking principle to moral action. Describe in more detail just how it operates between the theoretical and the practical.

A: All moral linking principles (as I conceive of them) must have some logical origin in theory. However, they must also contain a high amount of empirical content so that everyone can readily apply them to action. This property must be very clear or the linking principle will be of very limited value.

First, in the case of the Principle of Fair Competition ("All businesspeople should strive always to compete at or above the level of accepted professional practice with a view toward advancing toward the level of integrity"), we must start with its link in moral theory. This link is established because the level of accepted professional practice is grounded in the fair and open interplay between individual worldviews (all of which will reflect various moral theories) and the shared community worldview (that will be the synthesis of the functional demands of the profession in light of the values of its members).

Second is the level of practice. Because the principle is also grounded in the functional demands of the profession, it will always be action guiding in its prescriptions.

Q: Isn't this theory of personal excellence (fair competition) rather remote for the average person?

A: Not really. It is a myth that people are most concerned with selfish egoism before all else. In my own experience on this earth (which includes a dozen years at or below the poverty level), I have found that people in lower economic circumstances are most often concerned with being true to their core worldview values. It is all that they have of any worth. Oddly enough, I believe that it is often the affluent who are overly concerned with maximizing their prudential gains.

This is not an overly idealistic prescription because it is something that is in our personal control. All of us can practice our jobs at the level of professional practice and above. Not all of us can become wealthy. Why not fulfill what is within our power when the rewards of personal harmony are there for the taking? This is a linking principle for everyone.

Q: What about the "owners" of the corporation—the stockholders—don't we owe them the highest possible return on their investment?

A: No. This is another myth. Investors deserve the highest possible return, all things considered. This caveat means the following:

1. Investors do not own the employees of the corporation. This means that the people who make up the company should be *expected* to express their highest values as they perform their jobs. Why sort of company would want less? Only one that wants to exploit its workers; only one that seeks to control people as if they were cogs in some giant machine. Such a company has an immoral purpose.

2. Investors cannot reasonably expect the company to break the law. They should not expect the company to operate only at the standard of the law. Such an attitude fosters a "wink-and-nod" mentality that is really nothing more than the standard of selfish egoism.

3. Companies that embrace the highest values within their employees' personal worldviews will foster a loyal and committed workforce that will honorably and fairly compete in the marketplace.

Thus, I believe that investors deserve to have everyone work hard, work honestly, work professionally, and, within those parameters, bring in the highest possible profit.

Q: When you say that people ought to leave overly competitive situations that are fraught with immoral business practices, aren't you really becoming part of the problem by not advocating a solution?
A: Perhaps. This is meant to be a practical prescription rather than a "perfect world" direction. Certainly, if one could *change* a widespread, immoral business practice, then she or he should do it. But most of us don't have such power; we are bits of sand in a landscape dominated by mountains. My point is that we should not just accept that the marketplace in which we are making our money is corrupt, and therefore, we should be corrupt, too (because that's the only way to make a living there).

It may be a fact that the marketplace is corrupt and that the only way to make a living there is to be corrupt also, but this fact does not compel *us* to be corrupt. We can get out of that marketplace. Even those with highly specialized skills can adapt their skills to a new venue. Unless they do so, they will fragment themselves and thus lead a life that is less satisfactory (assuming that the integrated personal worldview is more satisfactory than the disjointed, fragmented worldview).

Q: Since the Principle of Fair Competition depends on the accepted level of professional practice, isn't it really just another form of ethical relativism?
A: Not really. This is because, as a linking principle to moral action, the Principle of Fair Competition has ties to moral theory. I have described the societal circumstances that might foster proper standards for professional practice (free and open societies). In other situations, it is possible that professional standards that are ethically abhorrent might emerge. This is not the fault of the Principle of Fair Competition but of the oppressive totalitarian society. Any clear thinking, rational person will be able to see through such a sham.

The professional standard is functionally tied to the demands of the profession. From this, an *ethos* develops that considers the functional needs of the profession with the moral expression so that any and all practitioners can feel secure because clear guidelines have been established on how this job (all things considered) *ought* to be performed. Clear and fair rules mean that all businesspeople should strive always to compete at or above the level of accepted professional practice with a view to advancing toward the level of integrity.

The arena for this agreement will proximately occur in the national marketplace. It can also occur in our global economy. I believe that such agreement can spread across nations to create international standards of acceptable practice. It is when we achieve such agreement that the term *business ethics* will cease to be an oxymoron to many people and will instead express our highest aspirations about how people can and should act.

Advertising.

Overview.

The advertising industry is seeking to define its professional standards. Certainly, the general goal of advertising is to persuade the targeted audience to believe something or to take a specific action. Obviously, the purpose of advertising is dangerous since there are legitimate and illegitimate ways to persuade.*

If the level of professionalism described in the preceding article, "The Principle of Fair Competition," is to work, it is requisite that (at a minimum) people in the industry know what the standard is and agree to abide by the authority of that code in their practice.

In the first article, Barbara J. Phillips suggests that advertising is not an all-powerful tool that influences our behavior to the extent that consumption and materialism must inevitably rule our lives. In fact, she says, advertising is merely an expression of the underlying values of the shared community worldview of capitalism. *Capitalism* requires citizens to devote their attention to material goods, which will offer solutions to life's basic problems. Thus, capitalism, not advertising, is the "bad guy" for developing this materialism. Advertising merely reflects this underlying value structure. If the shared community worldview is flawed, then the shared community worldview needs to reinvent itself.

---

*I am assuming here that a legitimate way to persuade is through a rational linking of a basic human need to actual, proven features of a product. An illegitimate way to persuade is through using an irrational linking principle (also known as a logical fallacy) or by misrepresenting what is a human need.

In the second article, Geoffrey Sher and Michael Feinman move the question from the general to the particular. Their case involves advertising in vitro fertilization (IVF). IVF clinics often make and advertise claims about their successes in enabling infertile couples to conceive, but many of these claims have proven to be either false or highly inflated. The couples seeking treatment are obviously in a very vulnerable position and thus are ripe for exploitation.

Since IVF is not covered by most medical insurance, the potential to create unorthodox fee arrangements (such as tying fees to successful implantation) may actually violate the American Medical Association's code of ethics.

Watchdog groups performing independent audits of advertising and purported data claims may seek to correct this situation, but this particular problem indicates a conflict in advertising between the need to make a sale and the need to be open to external scrutiny to verify product claims.

In the last essay of this section, Tony L. Henthorne and Michael S. LaTour examine another specific issue in advertising, the use of sexually suggestive models to sell products, which consumers know is not a new phenomenon. The authors use a psychologically multidimensional scale to evaluate responses to such ads. For example, if it is taken as a given that a small erotic stimulus catches the audience's attention and (if the ad is sufficiently benign, according to the personal worldviews of those viewing the ad), attention is gained and may generate a positive feeling for the product. But if the advertiser goes too far, she risks a backlash on the part of the audience. Readers also may question the validity of even so-called successful uses of this strategy in the communication flow between media and intended audience.

In Defense of Advertising:
A Social Perspective

Barbara J. Phillips

> Advertisements are a pervasive part of the American aural and visual envi-
> ronment. It is impossible to ignore their wider role in providing people a gen-
> eral education in goods, status, values, social roles, style, and art (Schudson,
> 1984, p. 207).

For as long as there have been advertisements, there have been critics of advertising who have contended that advertising is harmful to society. Although
this topic has been argued from many perspectives, often the critics and the
defendants appear to talking at cross-purposes—each arguing narrow points
with little regard for the overarching question: what are the social effects of advertising? That is, what impact does advertising have on the collective attitudes, beliefs, and behaviors of our society? Critics tend to fixate on the most
common argument against advertising—that it manipulates or forces consumers to buy unneeded or unwanted products. Supporters counter that advertising plays an important role in providing information, and cannot force
sceptical consumers to buy anything that they do not want already. Stalemate.

Both this criticism and its rebuttal focus attention on the *individual* effect
of advertising—that is, on its power over each consumer's market behavior.
It diverts attention from the more fundamental and perhaps more important
issue concerning advertising's *collective* effect on society. The purpose of this
paper is to critically examine three negative collective effects that have been
attributed to advertising:

(a) the elevation of consumption over other social values,
(b) the use of goods to satisfy social needs, and
(c) general dissatisfaction with one's life.

These three effects can be grouped under the umbrella of increased materialism in society.

This paper will present a defense of advertising which argues that advertising is not the underlying cause of these negative effects. It will be argued
that a larger social factor, *capitalism,* is responsible for the growing materialism
in our society. Few critics or defendants of advertising have addressed materialism from this perspective. Thus, the primary contribution of this paper is

its explanation of the crucial role that a capitalistic economic system plays in creating the negative social effects that have attributed to advertising.

Before this argument is developed in greater detail, however, it is necessary to understand how advertising came to be seen as the institution responsible for society's rampant materialism. The next section of this paper explains how advertising gained its social influence. The third section examines the three social criticisms of advertising discussed above, and builds the argument that the underlying cause of these social conditions is capitalism. The final section offers suggestions for reducing the impact of capitalism's negative social effects.

A BRIEF HISTORY OF THE RISE OF ADVERTISING

> There is no single point in history before which we were all nature's children, after which we became the sons and daughters of commerce (Schudson, 1984, p. 179).

In traditional societies of the past, the family and the community were the most important social units. Because the social environment changed little from generation to generation, older community members had valuable knowledge about the opportunities and dangers in the outside world (Becker, 1981) and they instructed young people in the tasks and roles that they would be required to perform in society. Social guidance was provided by the family and the extended community, including the religious and educational authorities of the day.

At the beginning of the twentieth century, however, these social institutions began to change in the United States. Industrialization and urbanization split individuals from their communities as workers rushed to cities and factories (Harriss, 1991). Individuals were physically separated from their families, plucked from their isolated communities, and exposed to the wider world (Bell, 1976). In this rapidly changing society, older community members found that their experiences were out-dated and devalued (Bell, 1976); they had little relevant advice to offer. As geographic and social mobility increased, individuals became increasingly detached from traditional sources of cultural influence and authority, such as families, churches, and schools. Individuals were required to look elsewhere to receive the information that these institutions once had provided (Bell, 1976; Pollay, 1989).

Industrialization also caused a separation between individuals and the products they used. Because the manufacturing process was removed from individuals' daily lives, they had less personal knowledge of a product's production and its qualities. Consumers did not know how goods were made, nor by whom, nor for what purpose. At the same time, individuals had less time to spend seeking information about the increasingly complex goods in the market (Schudson, 1984). Consequently, consumers had a difficult time assigning social meanings to goods (Jhally, 1989). They were unsure what the goods they bought "said" about them; what messages were communicated to others by their choice of food, clothing, transportation, and gifts.

The sweeping social changes described above left individuals clamoring for a source of social guidance, and advertisers were happy to step into the void left by the decline of other institutions (Leiss *et al.*, 1986). As the tremendous consumer demand for advice grew, advertising in the U.S. began to change its focus from product attributes to the social meaning of goods (Leiss *et al.*, 1986). Around 1920, advertising began to take on a social guidance function, advising consumers in matters of morality, behavior, social roles, taste, style, and dress (Bell, 1976; Marchand, 1985). Consumers could turn to advertising for desperately-needed information that could help them reduce their anxiety in a complex and confusing world (Dyer, 1982). Although traditional sources of social guidance still exerted an influence, consumers responded to advertising because it was highly visible, readily available, and because it emanated authority and certainty (Cushman, 1990). "It tells us what we must do in order to become what we wish to be" (Berman, 1981, p. 58).

Since the 1920s, the importance of family, community, and tradition has continued to decline and the world has become more complex (Berman, 1981), while advances in technology have made advertising more pervasive and given it more impact (Leiss *et al.*, 1986). As a social institution with cultural influence and authority, advertising has a collective effect on society which Goldman (1992, p. 2) describes:

> Cultural hegemony refers to those socially constructed ways of seeing and making sense of the world around us that predominate in a given time and place. In the latter twentieth-century U.S. the supremacy of commodity relations has exercised a disproportionate influence over the ways we conceive our lives. Every day that we routinely participate in the social grammar of advertisements, we engage in a process of replicating the domain assumptions of commodity hegemony. These domain assumptions are important because they condition and delimit the field of discourse within which our public and private conversations take place.

That is, advertising helps to create our social reality (Dyer, 1982), thereby affecting the framework through which we view the relationships between society and ourselves (Berman, 1981), ourselves and others (Schudson, 1984), and ourselves and objects (Leiss *et al.*, 1986). By influencing our culture, advertising has the potential to affect our attitudes and values regarding the most fundamental issues in our lives, even when it does not affect our buying habits (Schudson, 1984).

It is important to note that advertising's collective effects on society, as opposed to its individual effects on buying behavior, do not require our beliefs in its claims (Schudson, 1984). For example, one advertisement for Dow bathroom cleaner presents a straightforward "reason why" claim for this low-involvement product: Dow clean makes cleaning the bathroom easier. At the individual level, a consumer can accept or reject the product claim, and then may choose whether or not to purchase the product. Regardless of whether consumers accept or reject the advertising message, they have been exposed to social information while viewing the ad. For example, the Dow ad implies that a sparkling clean bathroom is an important goal, and that this goal can be more easily reached through the purchase of a commodity. Even if consumers reject the advertising message as unbelievable, they are unlikely to reject, or even examine, the social information presented (Dyer, 1982). That information is implicitly accepted as "reality." And although a single ad may have little impact, consumers are exposed to similar social messages in hundreds of ads each day.

Thus, one of advertising's collective effects is that it helps to shape consumers' social reality. Consumers tend to accept the values and assumptions presented through advertising as "normal" without question because they live within the reality that advertising has helped to create (Pollary, 1989; Goldman, 1992). In the future, advertising's social influence may become more pervasive. The overused and often meaningless phrase of the 1990s, the "information superhighway," conjures up images of the future—a solitary individual barricaded in a room lit only by a flickering TV screen, isolated from the rest of society except for the information he or she receives through the surrounding mass-media. In modern U.S. society, individuals are increasingly isolated from others. Technology has contributed to the separation of the individual from traditional sources of social information. Perhaps in the future, all of our social guidance will be mass-mediated.

But putting science fiction scenarios aside, what does it matter if advertising is a major source of social guidance? The next section of this paper will examine the negative social effects that have been attributed to advertising because of its social guidance function, and will argue that these collective efforts are not caused by advertising, but by capitalism.

CAPITALISM: THE INVISIBLE UNDERLYING CAUSE

> Critics faulted advertising for its espousal of "materialism"—a venerable criticism, somewhat akin to criticizing a football player for aggressiveness or a model for concern with her appearance (Gold, 1987, p. 31).

As discussed in the preceding section, advertisers did not wrest control away from other social institutions in a calculated attempt to overthrow the traditional social order (Schudson, 1984); advertising gained social importance almost through default by responding to consumer demand for social information. Schudson (1984) notes that the religious, educational, and family forces that have lost much of their influence were often unwelcome and co-ercive, while advertising's growing influence on socialization was desired by consumers.

Despite Schudson's argument, however, critics contend that while advertising has immense social influence, it has no explicit social goals or social responsibility (Pollary, 1989). Advertising purports to have no social values beyond economic gain. We do not really know what advertising "believes" (Berman, 1991). This is in direct contrast with other social institutions such as educational systems or religions that explicitly state the social values they are trying to impart, and thereby open these values to public scrutiny and debate.

Defendants of advertising state that the primary job of advertising is to sell goods. Understandably, then, advertising practitioners concentrate on the effect advertising has on individual behavior and do not examine the collective effect that they are creating on society. However, they are trans-mitting a powerful social message. Every ad "addresses the dilemmas of modern life with a single, all-purpose solution: Buy something" (Gold, 1987, p. 25). And it is this collective message that critics say has unintended neg-ative effects on society.

As discussed earlier, three negative social effects have regularly been at-tributed to advertising: (a) the elevation of consumption over other social val-ues, (b) the use of goods to satisfy social needs such as the needs for self-identity and relationships with others, and (c) general dissatisfaction. Ad-vertising can defend itself against these compelling accusations only by show-ing that a social factor larger than advertising is responsible for these social conditions. There is such a factor—capitalism.

Capitalism is the accepted economic system that functions to maximize total productive output and relies on the self-interest of the individual who is intent on satisfying his or her own needs (Leiss, 1976; Rotzoll *et al.*, 1989). Our own capitalistic economic system directly *causes* the negative social condi-tions which lead to increased materialism. Advertising, as the mouthpiece for capitalism, presents values and assumptions that color consumers' percep-tions of reality. Therefore, advertising becomes a target for social criticism. However, advertising does not create the values it presents. Capitalism is the creator, and the cause of the negative social conditions underlying material-ism, perhaps encouraged by basic human nature.

Again, because individuals live within a capitalistic system, they take its "realities" for granted. That is, individuals are not aware of capitalism's effects on their cultural attitudes and beliefs because the capitalistic framework is largely invisible to those who operate within it. In addition, there are few al-ternative framework for contrast and comparison. Thus, individuals tend to displace capitalism's negative social effects onto more visible institutions, such as advertising. The sections below will examine the role of capitalism in the three materialistic trends that have been attributed to advertising.

The Elevation of Consumption

Because the ultimate purpose of advertising is to sell products, each advertisement promotes consumption of a specific brand. This may help consumers make individual market choices. However, on a social level, the promotion of consumption in many ads over time leads to a representation of goods as the solution to all of life's problems, and the way to achieve the "good life" of happiness and success (Pollay, 1989). Dyer (1982, p. 1) states that "Advertisers want us to buy things, use them, throw them away, and buy replacements in a cycle of continuous and conspicuous consumption." Beyond the negative environmental impact of this strategy, the promotion of aggregate consumption may lead to a preoccupation with material concerns at the expense of other values in society (Schudson, 1984). This is because individuals' attention is a scarce resource that social institutions organize and direct, and advertising directs attention towards consumption (Schudson, 1984). It tends to select and promote attitudes and lifestyles that are compatible with acquisition and consumption, and the unity and pervasiveness of this message focus consumer attention on those chose lifestyles (Dyer, 1982; Pollay, 1989). By directing consumers' attention towards consumption, advertising may contribute to the neglect of other social values considered important by family, government, or religious institutions. That is, this first criticism of advertising states that advertising makes individuals materialistic by focusing their attention on the consumption of goods and ignoring other values.

However, there is some evidence that our capitalist culture had materialistic leanings long before the rise of modern advertising (Pollay, 1989). Historians state that the belief in the worth of superior goods is an inherent part of American culture, and as early as 1830 writers note the rampant materialism of the colonies (Schudson, 1984). The production and consumption of goods are the most important activities in a capitalist economy, and a "capitalist society, in its emphasis on accumulation, has made that activity an end in itself" (Bell, 1976, p. xii). Capitalism directs attention towards consumption because it requires that a vast number of diverse commodities be produced and sold (Jhally, 1989). This cycle of consumption is necessary because the stability and authority of our society is not founded on inherited privilege or traditional associations, but on the achievements of economic production (Leiss, 1976). Therefore, permanently rising consumption is necessary for our capitalist society to retain its legitimacy and power (Leiss, 1976).

Capitalism requires that consumers' attention be directed to goods. In an expanding economy where all types of goods are widely available, this creates an inherent tendency for consumers to become fixated on exclusively material objects instead of seeking a more balanced mix of objects and other satisfiers such as interesting work or creativity (Leiss, 1976). Therefore, it appears that it is the importance of consumption and the abundance of products in a *capitalist* society that causes materialism; advertising is not the underlying cause.

Of course, there is no denying that advertising is one *tool* that capitalism uses to keep consumers' attention focused on goods. However advertising, as a tool, can be used to focus attention on any social value. This conclusion is supported by the rare instances when advertising is not used as a consumption tool, but instead is used to further a different social agenda. For example, the American Heart Association created print ads to encourage parents to turn off the TV and help their children exercise. In this case, advertising was used to promote *less* consumption of the mass media, and to focus attention on nonconsumption based activities. There are several other instances when advertising has been used to direct attention away from consumption and onto competing social values. For example, antismoking, drunk driving, and recycling campaigns have been successful in achieving these goals. These examples support the argument that advertising is just a tool for directing consumer attention; on what our attention is focused depends on the who is controlling the advertising. In most cases, advertising serves capitalism, suggesting that a capitalist agenda is the underlying cause of increasing materialism in our society.

The Use of Goods to Satisfy Social Needs

The second major criticism of advertising is that it presents goods not only as the solution to concrete problems (e.g., "Tough grass stains? Try Wisk!") but also as the solution to social problems. Ads tell us that we can buy happiness, success, and love, and over time, consumers may come to believe that their social needs can be satisfied by purchasing commodities (Schudson, 1984). Consumers may start to believe that they can use goods to define themselves, or their relationships with others.

As discussed in the previous section, advertising tells consumers what the goods they use "say" about them. Ads tell consumers that they can express their identifies through a pattern of preferences for the goods they consume (Leiss *et al.*, 1986). For example, recent Nike ads present the personalities of the individuals who wear each type of shoe. A Nike sandal wearer is "quiet yet aggressive" while a running shoe wearer is "strong and spunky." In this way, ads state that we tell the world who we are and to which groups we belong by purchasing certain goods. In addition, ads show us what we can become (Leiss, Kline and Jhally, 1986). For example, milk commercials show children that by drinking milk they can grow up to be strong, attractive, and popular. Consumption is extolled as a way of elevating ourselves into a superior position (Berman, 1981); we are not just buying a product, we are buying a way of life (Dyer, 1982).

The problem with this message is that when we think we can *buy* a self, we focus on the external trappings of identity instead of internal character. Critics contend that advertising finds reality in appearances (Bell, 1976; Leiss *et al.*, 1986). A focus on identity through consumption leads to building a life-style, not a character, and this means that our identity and perhaps our self-worth are directly related to our purchasing power. An example of equating self-worth with consumption occurred in the 1980s, when several boys in U.S. inner-cities were killed for their athletic shoes (Grimm, 1990). Although many social and environmental factors played a part in this behavior, it is an example of the consumption ethic taken to extremes. The perpetrator could not afford to buy an identity, so he stole one.

Advertising also presents consumption as the mediator in another social relationship—that between ourselves and others. Goldman (1992, p. 32) observes that "Ads obscure the fact that social relations, traits, and experiences are made by humans, suggesting that they come to us ready-made as part of the goods we purchase." Products become means for fulfilling social needs; when we buy a product we are also buying love, friendship, or respect from others. We will be able to "kiss a little longer," for example, if we buy Big Red gum. In addition, we can show our feelings for others through goods (Dyer, 1982). For example, a man can proclaim his devotion to his fiance by buying her an expensive diamond ring. Many ads promise to both create a social relationship, and make that relationship explicit to the rest of the world. One example of this type of advertising is a Coors Light ad which shows three young women painting a room. It suggests that buying the right beer will lead to closer friendships, and will also let your friends know how much you care.

The problem with ads that promote consumption as the way to social relationships is that consumers may ultimately come to believe that goods are the *only* means to this end. That is, social needs such as love, esteem, and friendship can be acquired or expressed only through purchasing a product, and not through other avenues such as concern for others and shared activities. The main point emphasized by advertising is that individuals' relationships have nothing to do with their personalities or characters; it is the product that makes it happen (Goldman, 1992). Therefore, individuals cannot build relationships; they must buy them. Again, this equates individuals' social worth with their purchasing power, and may focus attention on consumption to the detriment of actual relationship-builders such as communication.

Thus, the second major criticism of advertising states that advertising teaches us to define ourselves and our relationships with others through goods; that is, that advertising gives social meaning to goods. Critics of advertising feel that it causes us to buy products as means to social ends rather than as commodities that can perform utilitarian functions. In defense of advertising, however, researchers generally agree that every society establishes object meanings through which individuals can relate themselves to the world (Bell, 1976; Leiss *et al.*, 1986). This means that all needs are socially constructed in all human societies (Schudson, 1984), even when that society has no advertising.

The most basic human needs are socially constructed. For example, our culture dictates arbitrary rules about what is and is not an acceptable satisfier for our need for food. We are taught what we can eat, where, when, and with whom, and all of these rules are based on objects. For example, in American culture, we do not eat horse meat, brains, or insects. We cannot eat in a church, but it is fine for us to eat in our cars. If we invite guests over to eat with us in the dining room using fine china, silverware, and candles, we don't serve hamburgers. However, if we eat in the back yard on the picnic table, hamburgers would be perfectly acceptable. Jhally (1987, p. 4) sums up this view by stating:

> The contention that goods should be important to people for what they are *used* for rather than their *symbolic* meaning is very difficult to uphold in light of the historical, anthropological and cross-cultural evidence. In all cultures at all times, it is the relation between use and symbol that provides the concrete context for the playing out of the universal person-object relation.

It is the basic human practice to assign social values and social meanings to objects. For example, every society gives status to certain objects, whether they are beads or sports cars. All of these social meanings are transmitted through the social guidance institutions of the time (Schudson, 1984). Previously, social meanings were taught through religion, education, and family. Currently, they are taught also through advertising. The problem is not that advertising transmits social information about products, but that critics take exception to the type of social information that is being transmitted.

Once again, we see that the underlying social meanings being promoted by advertising are those that are required by capitalism. Capitalism organizes and specializes these social meanings according to its needs (Goldman, 1992) and dictates them to consumers to meet the market economy's requirements for continually expanding commodities (Leiss, 1976). A capitalist system would prefer all needs, including consumers' identities and relationships, to be purchased through the market. Again, advertising is a tool that capitalism uses to reach this goal; it is not the underlying cause. In support of this view, advertising has been used successfully to promote the social meanings dictated by other institutions. One example is a long-running television campaign for the Church of Jesus Christ of Latter Day Saints. These spots promote family relationships based on religious values and nonconsumption based activities. One commercial shows parents and children building a relationship by having a water-fight while washing their car. As with the first criticism, if advertising can present different social meanings based on its sponsor, it cannot be held solely responsible if the majority of those meanings promote consumption as a means of satisfying social goals.

Dissatisfaction

Advertising's purpose is to continually sell goods, which means that consumers have to continually buy them. To accomplish this, advertising must create "successive waves of associations between persons, products, and images of well-being" for possible routes to happiness and success (Leiss *et al.*, 1986, p. 239). For example, in the 1980s a "successful" woman, in general, was portrayed in ads as excelling in her career, helped by specific products like Charlie perfume or Secret deodorant. In the 1990s, a successful woman nurtures her family and the environment, and thus needs a whole new set of products. Just when consumers think they may have reached their consumption goals, advertising shows them new consumption goals. Thus, the third social criticism of advertising states that it causes general dissatisfaction with one's lot in life. Advertising tells us to search diligently and ceaselessly among products to satisfy our needs, implying that we should be somewhat dissatisfied with what we have or are doing now (Leiss, Kline and Jhally, 1986).

Consumers accept this command because the payoff is so appealing. We would all like to be the person and live the life that we see in advertisements. On some level, consumers know that ads idealize and falsify reality, but on another level, they know that such a reality is at least a possibility (Schudson, 1984). Moog (1990, p. 15) says about one of her patients: "Those brilliant commercials that were intended to make people like Amy thirsting for Pepsi were *actually* making people like Amy thirsty for a fantasy of a life." Our own lives pale in comparison to what ads show us we could have (Pollay, 1989), and so we become dissatisfied enough to buy the next product and the next.

The problem with crediting advertising for the creation of dissatisfaction is that dissatisfaction seems to be a basic human condition; comparing oneself to others has been occurring since the time of Cain and Abel. Dissatisfaction occurs because wants are psychological, not biological, and so are unlimited (Bell, 1976). To determine if their wants are being satisfied, consumers turn to their neighbors and define their needs relative to the standards of their society (Schudson, 1984). That is, we compare our consumption patterns to an average consumption norm to determine whether or not we are satisfied (Jhally, 1987). The problem with this method is that we take past increases in wealth and comfort for granted (Leiss, Kline and Jhally, 1986); as average national income increases over time, average levels of happiness and satisfaction stay the same (Jhally, 1987). Therefore, the manner in which we make comparisons dictates that many individuals will be somewhat dissatisfied.

Some critics may accept that advertising is not the fundamental cause of dissatisfaction, but may contend that advertising exacerbates it. However, increasing dissatisfaction appears to be directly related to a more basic aspect of capitalism; there are an increasing number of products available on the market to satisfy our needs. As the number of available products grows, each aspect of a consumer's needs is broken down into smaller and smaller components (Leiss, 1976). Think of the countless products, such as soap, moisturizer, and sunscreen, created just to meet the needs of one consumer's *skin*. It becomes hard to integrate all of these tiny subneeds into a coherent ensemble of needs, and it becomes increasingly difficult to determine if all of these complex subneeds are being met (Leiss, 1976). Consumers may become dissatisfied because they cannot monitor nor meet all of the various subneeds they have; at any time there will always be some subneeds that are not being satisfied. Thus it appears that the root of dissatisfaction is our basic method of comparison that only considers relative, and not absolute, satisfaction. The dissatisfaction that arises from this comparison is exacerbated by the availability of too many products in our capitalist economy that each address only one, fragmented subneed.

Overall, it appears that the above three conditions of materialism are levelled at advertising because it is a visible target of attack, while ignoring the true cause of these social conditions—capitalism. In a capitalist system, there is an abundance of goods in the market and the manufacture and consumption of goods are the most visible and important activities in society. The prominence of consumption in a capitalistic society causes a focus on these activities. Because an expanding economy is the source of its legitimacy and power, a capitalist system also prefers that all needs, including social, be mediated through the market. It uses advertising as one tool to achieve a fixation on goods above all else. Advertising, however, can also be used by other social institutions to achieve competing social goals. It is therefore a tool for directing consumer attention, but does not make the ultimate decision about where attention should be focused. In addition, capitalism is responsible for a flood of products in the market which fragment our needs to the point where we can no longer integrate these subneeds into a coherent ensemble, and dissatisfaction results.

Critics may be quick to point out that this argument seems to be splitting hairs—does it really matter whether advertising causes negative social effects or if capitalism causes these effects through advertising? It does matter, because by discovering the *actual* cause of these social problems we can begin to explore viable solutions to address them.

THE NEXT STEP

> One should not underestimate the elementary common sense of the general population just as one should not underestimate the degree to which individuals are dependent on social cues for guidance on how to consume things (Leiss, Kline, and Jhally, 1986, p. 242).

This paper has argued that capitalism is the underlying cause of several social problems that have been blamed on advertising. However, it is not enough to make this observation. The criticisms discussed above stem from growing materialism in our society that must be addressed. The overarching problem with materialism is that "commodities themselves, and the income to purchase them, are only weakly related to the things that make people happy: autonomy, self-esteem, family, felicity, tension-free leisure, friendship" (Leiss *et al.*, 1986,

p. 252). Capitalism obscures this fact and focuses consumers' attention on goods as the solutions to *all* of their needs. There are no easy answers to the problem of growing materialism in society.

Many critics of advertising call for increased regulation or an outright ban of advertising. However advertising is just one tool that capitalism uses to reach its goals. Other tools include the mass media, popular culture, and other economic enterprises (Schudson, 1984). Policies that only impact advertising would not affect the root of the problem; if advertising is stripped of its power to accomplish capitalist objectives, other tools will be used. However, it is also unlikely that we can attack the root of the problem by removing capitalism. In the modern world, there appear to be no viable alternatives. In addition, such an idea is untenable because it can create far more social problems that it can hope to correct. For better or for worse, we live in a capitalist economic system, and have to work within it to solve its problems.

One way to address these social problems is to create awareness of the capitalistic framework inside which we live. As discussed in the introduction to this paper, consumers tend to take for granted the social assumptions embedded in advertisements that reflect capitalist values (Goldman, 1992). By making these assumptions explicit, consumers are able to see how their attitudes, values, and actions are affected by the capitalist agenda espoused by advertising and other institutions. One way to create awareness is through consumer education, especially for children through the school system. Classes in understanding advertising and media are currently offered in some schools; an expanded program could bring about widespread awareness of the social values transmitted through the media. These programs would emphasize that individuals are not passive absorbers of ads but actively participate in constructing their meanings (Dyer, 1982). Consumers have the ability to look at ads and other sources of information critically, and accept or reject not only the product claims, but also the social assumptions. Information, education, and critical reasoning are the keys to solving these social problems (Moog, 1990).

Another way to combat these social effects is to create a greater number of advertisements that are based on alternative value systems. Several ads that present the values of religious and governmental institutions have been mentioned in this paper, but these types of ads make up a very small percentage of all of the ads seen. More nonconsumption based advertising is needed to present a balanced picture of the alternative ways consumers can satisfy their needs. A simple way to begin this remedy is for each advertising agency to increase the number of public service announcements that it creates and airs.

Both of these alternatives address the underlying cause of materialism, the requirements of capitalism, with viable and effective solutions that can work within the capitalist system. As researchers concentrate on the actual roots of the negative social effects described above, many other remedies will follow. As Moog (1990, p. 221) says, "more can be done to deal effectively with the reality of advertising rather than cursing its pervasiveness."

References

Becker, G. S.: 1981, *A Treatise on the Family* (Harvard University Press, Cambridge, MA).

Bell, D.: 1976, *The Cultural Contradictions of Capitalism* (Basic Books Inc., New York, NY).

Berman, R.: 1981, *Advertising and Social Change* (Sage Publications, Inc., Beverly Hills, CA).

Cushman, P.: 1990, 'Why the Self is Empty: Toward a Historically Situated Psychology', *American Psychologist* **45**(5), 599–611.

Dyer, G.: 1982, *Advertising as Communication* (Methuen, Inc., New York, NY).

Gold, P.: 1987, *Advertising, Politics, and American Culture: From Salesmanship to Therapy* (Paragon House Publishers, New York, NY).

Goldman, R.: 1992, *Reading Ads Socially* (Routledge, New York, NY).

Grimm, M.: 1990, 'New Games to Play, New Rules to Learn', *Adweek* **31**(38), S172.

Harriss, J. (ed.): 1991, *The Family: A Social History of the Twentieth Century* (Oxford University Press, New York, NY).

Jhally, S.: 1987, *The Codes of Advertising: Fetishism and the Political Economy of Meaning in the Consumer Society* (St. Martin's Press, Inc., New York, NY).

Jhally, S.: 1989, 'Advertising as Religion: The Dialectic of Technology and Magic', in I. Angus and S. Jhally (eds.), *Cultural Politics and Contemporary America* (Routledge, New York, NY), pp. 217–229.

Leiss, W.: 1976, *The Limits to Satisfaction: An Essay on the Problem of Needs and Commodities* (University of Toronto Press, Toronto, ON).

Leiss, W., S. Kline and S. Jhally.: 1986, *Social Communication in Advertising: Persons, Products, & Images of Well-Being* (Methuen Publications, New York, NY).

Marchand, R.: 1985, *Advertising and the American Dream: Making Way for Modernity, 1920–1940* (University of California Press, CA).

Moog, C.: 1990, *"Are They Selling Her Lips?": Advertising and Identity* (William Morrow and Company, Inc., New York, NY).

Pollay, R. W.: 1989, 'The Distorted Mirror: Reflections on the Unintended Consequences of Advertising', in R. Hovland and G. B. Wilcox (eds.), *Advertising in Society: Classic and Contemporary Readings on Advertising's Role in Society* (NTC Business Books, Lincolnwood, IL), pp. 437–476.

Rotzoll, K., J. E. Haefner and C. H. Sandage: 1989, 'Advertising and the Classical Liberal World View', in R. Hovland and G. B. Wilcox (eds.), *Advertising in Society: Classic and Contemporary Readings on Advertising's Role in Society* (NTC Business Books, Lincolnwood, IL), pp. 27–41.

Schudson, M.: 1984, *Advertising, the Uneasy Persuasion: Its Dubious Impact on American Society* (Basic Books, Inc., New York, NY).

Accountability, Representation, and Advertising

Geoffrey Sher and Michael Feinman

Advertising in medicine, whether we like it or not, is here to stay. So why are we debating the ethics and morality of advertising in the field of assisted reproduction? Is it because we regard this area of medicine that deals with the initiation of life as sacrosanct and above the fray of traditional product marketing? Or is it because the field is so prone to misrepresentation that any advertising not linked to accountability is by definition fraudulent?

Everyone agrees that the same couple walking into two different in vitro fertilization (IVF) clinics in the United States could face live birth rates that are five times higher in one program than in the other. Although the national average birth rate for IVF in women younger than age 40, who use their own eggs, is estimated to be approximately 21% per egg-retrieval procedure, this statistic ranges from single digits in poor programs to almost 50% in the best ones.

Because most health insurance companies refuse to cover IVF services, the majority of patients face enormous financial obstacles. Moreover, when turning to professional medical bodies such as the Society for Assisted Reproductive Technology (SART) to help them select an IVF program on the basis of its proven track record, they find themselves stonewalled.

Despite several false starts, aimed at accomplishing the important goal of achieving accountability in reporting clinic-specific success rates, there is still no verifiable outcome-based IVF reporting system in the United States.

In this article we review briefly the events that have led to his dismal state of nonaccountability. Then we demonstrate how we at Pacific Fertility Medical Centers of California have attempted to remedy this situation by having our own results audited by an outside agency and how immediate intervention is needed to restore consumer confidence. In so doing, we propose both interim and long-term solutions that, if implemented, could reestablish an ethical milieu in which we then could consider the other lofty issues confronting our field.

Using a specific aspect of advertising that relates to outcome-based fee structuring and thus is affected by issues of accountability and ethics, we demonstrate why, in the field of IVF, factual and informative advertising can provide consumers with an important source of disclosure and empowerment.

Finally, recognizing that 95% of couples who would benefit from IVF in the United States cannot afford it, we see how the resolution of these issues could lead to third-party payers reevaluating their current reluctance to reimburse for IVF services.

The Society for Reproductive Technology really was born in New Orleans at the annual meeting of the American Fertility Society in 1984. At that time, the future SART was named, perhaps not inappropriately, the IVF Special Interest Group. As one of its founding members and an elected member of its initial steering committee, one of the authors of this article (G.S.) strongly recommended that clinic-specific outcome data be provided on request. This motion was rejected, and until 1986 only pooled data were available. In that year, the Office of Technology Assessment held hearings to address consumer concerns over issues of quality and honesty in the field of IVF. As a result, Congressman Ron Wyden of Oregon generated a report that led to a congressional mandate for a one-time clinic-specific annual report of IVF outcomes that finally was completed in 1989.

This dragged the IVF Special Interest Group, by then renamed the Society for Reproductive Technology, into the practice of providing clinic-specific outcome data, starting in 1990. Though admirable, the data were still not peer reviewed and thus were subject to inaccuracy, whether intentional or not.

The following are a few actual examples:

- A few years ago, one of the California chapters of a national infertility consumer advocacy group known as RESOLVE held a public symposium in which a number of leading IVF programs were invited to present and distribute information regarding their most recent ongoing pregnancy statistics. There were a number of cases in which the results could not be reconciled, and RESOLVE subsequently requested of the participating IVF programs that the printed information be withdrawn from further circulation.

- Recently, the publication by SART of its annual statistics was delayed for several months to allow one of the largest IVF programs in the nation to correct inconsistencies in the original data it had submitted.

- In 1992 (one year before we initiated an audit of our success rates), one of our own programs was taken to task for a few inconsistencies in the IVF data that we submitted to SART. In one case we even misclassified a clinically indicated midtrimester abortion as being a spontaneous midtrimester miscarriage—this happened in a program that is committed to accountability totally. It could not have happened had we been under audit at that time.

So, it was that Pacific Fertility Medical Centers entered into an agreement with the Arthur Andersen accounting firm to perform an audit of its IVF outcomes. This audit, the first of its kind in the United States, was implemented in 1993. Our intent was to continue this process on an annual basis. However, after several meetings between members of SART, Arthur Andersen, and ourselves, we were assured by SART that it would initiate a national audit in 1994. We elected to participate in the proposed SART audit rather than contract with Arthur Andersen that year. The Society elected to work with another auditing firm, at a lower cost and began a data collection process that fell far short of being an audit, which essentially was abandoned before the year ended.

The audit, in fact, did not occur. In protest, Pacific Fertility Medical Centers withheld its data from SART because of a commitment to publish audited data only. We reinstated the Arthur Andersen audit and, accordingly, once again will submit validated data to SART for 1995. Sadly enough, there is still no national audit in place. The Society now intends to work with the Centers for Disease Control and Prevention (CDC) to develop a national audit. We are informed by a reliable source that it is highly unlikely that sufficient funds will be made available to the CDC to complete this project. However, even if the necessary resources were to be made available, enabling groundwork to begin immediately, it is unlikely that audited IVF data would be available to consumers until the next millennium.

It is unconscionable that, in an area of medicine in which the outcome under specified conditions is so clearly definable, as in the field of IVF, after a decade of empty promises our professional representative, SART, has failed to establish a system of true accountability in our field. At what point will consumers be justified in saying enough is enough?

It is not the purpose of this review to convince you of how noble we are at Pacific Fertility Medical Centers. However, as one of the largest providers of IVF services in the country, which with its affiliated programs has been responsible for approximately one of 15 IVF babies conceived in the United States and is an organization that uses marketing techniques to inform patients of our services, we have no choice but to report unimpeachable results to remain above reproach. The audit we are about to describe may not be perfect, but it shows how our patients receive reliable information to help them make informed choices.

All patients undergoing IVF are asked to participate in the audit and sign consent forms authorizing their records to be reviewed by the auditors. Patients requesting total anonymity are assigned numbers that allow the Arthur Andersen accounting firm to track their data.

The audit has three clearly definable objectives. The first is to incorporate each and every IVF cycle. The second is to validate full disclosure of all of our clinical and laboratory data. The third objective is to report outcome in terms of ongoing viable pregnancies that have advanced beyond the 12th week as well as all pregnancy losses that occurred before that time.

The first of two forms is completed before the patient commences fertility hormone therapy. This form serves to provide basic medical information such as age and diagnosis. By identifying all enrollees, the form provides the auditors with the ability to track all IVF cycles initiated. A second form details the IVF cycle, incorporating information such as the number of eggs recovered, fertilization rate, and outcome, which in the case of pregnancy is characterized and confirmed by the patient's obstetrician. Once data collection is completed, auditors visit Pacific Fertility Medical Centers' individual clinics to review patient charts and laboratory records to validate all representations.

Our audit classifies IVF patients on the basis of the woman's age and the absence or presence of significant male infertility and separates IVF cycles using fresh embryos from those in which cryopreserved or thawed embryos are used. Third-party IVF (IVF using donated eggs) also is reported separately. A clinical pregnancy involves ultrasound confirmation of a gestational sac, pathologic or operative evidence of a pregnancy. An ongoing pregnancy is defined as a clinical pregnancy with evidence of fetal cardiac activity and that has progressed beyond the 12th gestational week. We can demonstrate that no more than 5% of all ongoing pregnancies are lost after the 12th week. Accordingly, the expected birthrate is estimated to be 95% of the ongoing pregnancy rate.

Because the outcome of clinical pregnancies conceived late in the year may not be known until the following year, a calculation is made for ongoing pregnancies and live births when the expected birthrate is estimated. Actual birthrates can be calculated after conclusion of all the pregnancies. We choose to report expected birthrates so that we can provide relatively current results.

Our audit has received accolades from our colleagues outside the United States, whereas it has received scathing criticism from our American counterparts. The critics have focused on two details. The first is our use of expected rather than actual birthrates. We agree that the actual birthrate is a more desirable statistic. We chose to report expected birthrates to allow us to publish the audit on a timely basis. Waiting for all pregnancies to end means waiting at least a year to publish the audit. The SART report for a given year presents information relative to IVF that may have been performed up to 2 years prior to publication. In the field of assisted reproduction in which new innovations that improve outcome are almost the order of the day, an undue delay in reporting IVF results may deny consumers access to valuable information for decision making and thus may be misleading. Furthermore, newly established IVF programs hardly can afford a waiting period of 2 years or more to establish credibility through a published SART report.

The second feature of the audit that received criticism was voiced by Dr. Howard Jones of the Jones Institute of Norfolk, Virginia. In a published response to our recent article entitled "Auditing IVF success rates: it can be done," Dr. Jones pointed to the inability of our audit to distinguish the many subtle clinical variables that differentiate patients and the modes of practice in different programs. For instance, he argued that some IVF programs may transfer more embryos than others. Although his concerns are valid, they apply equally to all reporting systems, including that of SART. No system will ever prove perfect. A system that addresses identifiable concerns within existing limitations is a preferable alternative to no system at all. Maintaining the status quo inevitably will lead to consumer apprehension about what we are doing.

Recently, our audit was refined further by the introduction of a real-time computerized data collection system. This program, which we termed the Trouble Shooting Index, was developed to assist in the auditing process, to facilitate ongoing quality assurance, and to permit immediate validation of any representation made by Pacific Fertility Medical Centers at any time.

During the first year of the Arthur Andersen audit, the actual cost ran way over budget. This was due largely to the fact that our record keeping at the individual clinic level had been incomplete. Consider this problem against the background that we were strongly motivated and actively trying to facilitate the auditing process. Imagine the state of affairs in IVF programs that by and large regard data collection as well as reporting to SART as a nuisance. During the second year of our audit, the cost was reduced because our individual clinics were better prepared. We believe that an audit can be performed for approximately $50–60 per IVF cycle.

We have shown how an audit can be implemented successfully given adequate resources, commitment, and good intent. However, previous experience has demonstrated clearly that none of these three requirements for an audit currently exist in our professional governing body, SART. Critics of a true audit claim that although they support the fundamental concept of accountability, deficiencies in the process negate its national implementation. Although all of these concerns may have relevance, they should not preclude going forward without delay. Furthermore, it is unconscionable to use them as a smoke screen to deflect attention from the fundamental issue of accountability, which is both sorely lacking and desperately needed in our field. The only explanation for this duplicity that we can find is that some SART members of good standing may be reluctant and even apprehensive about having their results scrutinized by an objective third party. Given this apparent deadlock and the moral imperative to act quickly, we propose the following solutions for immediate consideration by the CDC and/or the U.S. Federal Trade Commission (FTC):

- As a relatively inexpensive short-term solution, but one that would force immediate accountability by all practitioners of IVF, we suggest that each program be required to provide every patient with an affidavit signed by both the medical and laboratory directors of the IVF program concerned. Such an affidavit would present the couple's expected ongoing pregnancy rate on the basis of the clinic's previous performance record for similar cases for the preceding year. The data would be updated cumulatively every 3 months and ultimately, after minor adjustments for actual birthrates, should correlate with data reported to SART for the same year. Using patient identification codes to protect confidentiality, such affidavits could be held by a responsible body such as the CDC, and lack of compliance or misrepresentations by providers would be subject to public disclosure and have serious consequences. Such an inexpensive process likely would provide a genuine incentive for honest reporting, which should go a long way toward rekindling patient confidence in our discipline.

• Ultimately, a national audit should be mandatory. To address the concerns about the costs of this process, we propose that every IVF patient be required to pay a value-added tax that would be passed on directly to the auditing body. We expect that this tax would cost approximately $50 to 60 per cycle. Concerns that this tax would place an added burden on patients already being asked to pay thousands of dollars for one IVF attempt are like arguing against asking passengers to pay a few extra dollars to improve airline security.

With all due respect, the discussion of all the worthy and lofty issues being deliberated at this meeting leads nowhere unless the issues of accountability and honesty in IVF outcome reporting figure at the forefront of these deliberations.

Let us now consider how audited results affect advertising in the area of IVF. The purpose of advertising is to bring accurate information to potential consumers in a manner that catches their attention. Ethical advertising mandates that all representations are truthful and that all products or services are provided as promised. Backed by an audit and governed by a code of ethics that ensures that IVF is performed only when medically indicated, any IVF program can fulfill the requirements of ethical advertising.

A word of caution, however. As committed as advertising must be to the truth, the very nature of the medium limits the amount of disclosure possible. It is accordingly essential to support all representations by providing detailed printed disclosure, on request, with no strings attached.

We now will focus on one particular marketing strategy that at least five IVF programs have initiated and that has drawn considerable attention and criticism in the medical community. The concept involves linking the cost of IVF services to outcome. Pacific Fertility Medical Centers was one of the first to introduce this approach. Our in vitro fertilization partnership plan, or IVP Plan, refunds 90% of set medical fees to qualifying IVF candidates who do not achieve an ongoing pregnancy after all embryos from a single egg retrieval have been transferred to the woman's uterus through fresh or frozen cycles.

The IVP Plan is designed to spread the risk between the providers and those women who conceive on the first attempt, so that women who need more than one try can afford to do so and couples who do not conceive can choose and afford adoption or any other option. In the process, the IVF program discounts its services and the woman who becomes pregnant the first time she completes the plan pays more.

Taken at face value, any arrangement that attempts to tie medical reimbursement to outcome raises concerns among physicians and ethicists alike. However, certain aspects of IVF lend themselves uniquely to this form of reimbursement, especially in the current environment of managed care and diminishing medical resources.

The first aspect of IVF that justifies an outcome-based fee structure is that the end point of pregnancy or birth is easily definable. This is different from most disease states such as cancer, diabetes, or other chronic debilitating conditions. Although no two patients are exactly alike, IVF patients can be classified into easily definable subgroups that enable realistic prediction of success in a credible and audited program. Whereas there may be no life after failure to respond to treatments for many of these diseases, there is certainly life after infertility, and there are other alternatives, such as adoption.

Unlike virtually every other form of medical treatment in America, IVF largely is not covered by insurance. Furthermore, even in the best centers, most couples require more than one attempt to have a reasonable chance for success. Most people cannot afford enough attempts to shift the odds in their favor. Based on demographic data, there are about 3–4 million infertile couples in America. This translates into an immediate need for the performance of about one million IVF cycles per year. Currently, fewer than 40,000 IVF procedures are performed annually in this country. This discrepancy between supply and demand is largely attributable to lack of affordability and mistrust of the technology. Smaller countries in which reimbursement is available for IVF do much better. For instance, in France, with a quarter of our population, more IVF cycles are performed annually than in the United States, and Australia, whose population is about one twentieth that of ours, performs nearly half the number of IVF cycles that we do per year. Many critics of IVF portray it as a luxury reserved for the rich. In the absence of insurance coverage, outcome-based pricing allows more patients of modest means to avail themselves of the opportunity to go from being infertile to parents.

Furthermore, contrary to statements made by some critics, more than 80% of all IVF candidates would qualify for the IVP plan, using either their own eggs or a donor's. Even severe male infertility, requiring intracytoplasmic sperm injection or testicular biopsy to obtain sperm in certain azoospermic men, or repeated failure to conceive in another IVF program does not preclude a couple's eligibility for the IVP plan. If the woman experiences a first-trimester loss, whether through miscarriage or medically indicated therapeutic abortion, the couple still is entitled to the 90% refund.

To date we have not encountered a single IVF candidate, qualified for the program or not, who has objected to this concept. Patients appear to find it refreshing that an IVF program has a vested interest in their individual success and is willing to back its claims by sharing financial risk. Why is it that much of the IVF medical community raises ethical objections to these plans? What is unethical about supporting audited success rates with a willingness to share the financial risks with the patients?

Pundits point to the American Medical Association's (AMA's) prohibition of physician contingency fees, which reads

Opinion 6.01: If a physician's fee for medical service is contingent on the successful outcome of a claim, such as a malpractice or worker's compensation claim, there is the ever-present danger that the physician may become less of a healer and more of an advocate or partisan in the proceedings. Accordingly, a physician's fee for medical service should be based on the value of the service provided by the physician to the patient and not on the uncertain outcome of a contingency that does not in any way relate to the value of the medical service.

A physician's fee should not be made contingent on the successful outcome of medical treatment. Such arrangements are unethical because they imply that successful outcomes from treatment are guaranteed, thus creating unrealistic expectations of medicine and false promises to consumers.

The first paragraph of the AMA's rejection of contingency fees focuses on situations in which external factors such as the outcome of legal suits or worker's compensation claims would determine medical reimbursement. These situations introduce a conflict of interest that is clearly unethical and that would undermine the inherent value of the medical treatments themselves. In situations in which outcomes stem solely from the inherent value of the medical procedures and are not subject to external factors, contingency fees do not conflict with this part of the AMA's position.

The second part of the statement addresses the issue of uncertain outcomes, the concept that medicine is an art as well as a science. This reflects an overall mistrust of outcome analysis for assessing the benefit of any intervention. Determining reimbursement based on sound actuarial data, when it exists, is morally justified.

The use of the word "guarantee" in the AMA's statement is regrettable. What we are talking about is shared risk. No medical procedure can guarantee success. Perhaps some of our colleagues' objection stems from the confusion of these two concepts. The IVP plan does not guarantee success; instead, it indemnifies against failure by protecting patients from going broke with nothing to show for their emotional and financial investment. Moreover, Pacific Fertility Medical Centers offers its patients the opportunity to choose between conventional fee-for-service and the IVP plan. What could be more ethical than that?

The final criticism presented in the AMA's statement is that outcome-based fee structuring creates false expectations on the part of desperate patients. Given that there can be no dispute over the fact that outcome following IVF is clearly definable, the only remaining issue relates to concerns relative to the authenticity of reported results. And now we are back to the central issue, accountability. When the success rates of a clinic offering outcome-based fees are supported by audited results, patients can form realistic expectations of success.

We believe that the IVP plan provides a window to the future. Already, outcome and reimbursement have been linked in the concept of capitation. In capitation, a doctor or a medical group is paid a lump sum to provide medical care to a predetermined number of people. The provider has a strong incentive to use fewer resources in the pursuit of health maintenance. If the providers succeed in this effort, they profit; if they use too many resources, they lose money.

Using a similar strategy, a group of medical entrepreneurs affiliated with managed care providers offers unlimited infertility services for a 2-year cap fee of approximately $7,000. Medically eligible couples can be readmitted for additional 2-year plans if the woman does not become pregnant. This arrangement raises several questions regarding ethics:

- Where is the incentive for the provider to use the most efficacious treatment modality, regardless of cost?
- Given that participation of providers is not based on validated performance in terms of outcome, on what basis other than financial considerations can the consumer make an informed consent?

Ironically, the IVP plan is more sophisticated than many capitated plans because although it includes most IVF candidates, it helps patients that have little hope of success reevaluate their other options. If the AMA's Council of Ethical Affairs is to carry their policy on contingency to a logical conclusion, they may be pressed to admit that prepaid health plans are based on the very principles that they have labeled unethical.

It is our position that although contingency pricing in medicine is in large part ethically questionable, IVF represents a perfect exception to this objection. The outcome is measurable actuarially, the terms are clearly definable, and the expectations are realistic. In the absence of insurance reimbursement, who is being hurt here? Only those IVF programs that cannot produce success rates that render the plan economically feasible are hurt. We do not advocate the blanket introduction of outcome-based, risk-shared reimbursement in other fields of medicine, in which results may not be as readily definable or measurable as in IVF. In fact, we do not even support its application to IVF if it is not linked to verifiable third-party reporting of success rates. The two must go hand in hand and should be subject to enforceable guidelines.

Objecting to these plans on an ethical basis, when patients uniformly embrace them, promotes a paternalistic image of the medical establishment. The trend in medicine is toward consumer empowerment, and it is the role of medicine to provide patients with informed choices, not to block them. Should consumers be denied access simply because our governing body SART has delayed putting its house in order?

There are those who have argued that outcome-based pricing should be prohibited because unscrupulous IVF providers might use this approach to attract patients. They suggest that programs with poor success rates could advertise receipt of a major refund if no pregnancy occurs, while using the fine print to ensure that only candidates with the greatest chance of success (glibly labeled "easy cases") gain access and the majority of applicants are excluded. We submit that this very argument is a strong indictment of the existing system of nonaccountability. The current situation of fee-for-service in IVF is far worse because unscrupulous providers can charge and receive fees for services while hiding behind claims of success that they may not be able to achieve. If anything, a program such as the IVP plan is likely to discourage poorly performing programs that simply could not survive financially if their IVF birthrates were low and that would be readily identifiable when appropriate guidelines were put in place.

In the absence of true accountability that can be assured only through the implementation of a verifiable third-party audit, the risks of advertising medical services with claims that cannot be substantiated are great. For example, a major university program recently settled a $5 million class-action suit, without contest, after an accusation of misrepresentation of statistics in promotional materials. Similarly, a major provider of IVF services was forced to rescind false claims of success rates publicly. In yet another event, a prominent, well-published leader in the field of IVF was forced to resign from high office and from his IVF program and has left the arena virtually in disgrace because it was discovered that he had grossly misrepresented his success rates. If this sounds bad, consider the individual representations made by many SART member programs that they can achieve national average success rates when in fact they often cannot.

The public debate that has arisen through Pacific Fertility Medical Centers' marketing strategies has served only to promote consumer interest in our services, and we believe our position is ethically sound. It is in spite of this and in full recognition of the consequences that we welcomed the opportunity to address this distinguished body. Honest advertising in medicine, as in any other field, is necessary to promote consumer awareness, and outcome-based pricing has arrived; it is alive, well, and growing. Let us give you a few examples:

- In an effort to drive down the cost of health care, health maintenance and managed care organizations are taking a serious look at outcome-based performance in medicine. This is especially the case in the northeastern United States, and it inevitably will affect fee structuring.
- In 1995, Blue Shield of Northern California approved a policy that would allow subscribers to participate in experimental treatments normally not covered by health insurance. Blue Shield's arrangement with the provider stipulated that payment would be made only if the treatment was deemed "successful."
- In Northern California, Kaiser Permanente offers a partial refund to patients who are dissatisfied after medical consultations.

We hold that the only alternative to outcome-based reimbursement and advertising in the field of assisted reproduction would be the widespread introduction of infertility insurance coverage that motivates qualified physicians to focus on the most efficacious treatments, regardless of cost. We believe that there are two major obstacles to the attainment of this objective:

- First, the current absence of accountability in the field denies insurance companies access to actuarial data on which they could measure their exposure.
- Second, the high incidence of multiple pregnancies associated with IVF often transforms a medical triumph into a costly human catastrophe.

It is poetic justice that by addressing the obstacle of accountability through a verifiable and independent audit, we at Pacific Fertility Medical Centers now can address the issue of multiple births with IVF. Traditionally, IVF outcome has been expressed in terms of the pregnancy or birthrate per transfer of multiple embryos at one time. The Arthur Andersen accounting firm recently sanctioned our reporting pregnancy or birthrates as a function of the number of cycles of ovarian stimulation and egg retrieval as a separate category. This means that we now can transfer one embryo at a time until conception or until the supply of embryos has been exhausted. Once implemented, the single embryo transfer procedure will allow us to refocus on the overall chance of a baby being born following one egg retrieval, regardless of the number of embryo transfers performed.

We maintain that a national audit of all IVF programs will go a long way toward resurrecting the credibility of our discipline and will take us one giant step closer to universal insurance coverage. In the process, it likely would remove the need for advertising and outcome-based pricing altogether.

It is our sincere hope that this presentation will provoke a healthy debate that will focus on the imperative of linking advertising to disclosure and accountability in the field of IVF. To approach ethics from a narrow perspective and sidestep the larger issues of honesty, integrity, and accountability is to create a smoke screen that perpetuates an unacceptable status quo.

Pacific Fertility Medical Centers of California claims the right to continue honest marketing of its services supported by full disclosure and outcome-based fee structures that are linked to fully verifiable performance criteria. We deem such practices to meet the highest standards of morality and ethics and, most importantly, to serve the best interests of our patients.

A Model to Explore
the Ethics of Erotic Stimuli
in Print Advertising

Tony L. Henthorne and Michael S. LaTour

The use of female nudity/erotic stimuli in print advertising has become quite commonplace. Ads characteristic of the genre, such as the continued run of controversial print advertisements for "Obsession" perfume and cologne by Calvin Klein, typically feature a nude couple or solitary female in a suggestively compromising position. Just as memorable are many of the print advertisements for jeans by Calvin Klein. Ads of this type are designed to elicit what the originators hope is a vicarious experience of sensuality without the result being extreme levels of anxiety or discomfort (LaTour and Henthorne, 1993).

The employment of sexual (or erotic) communication appeals in print advertising continues to be a controversial topic, as evidenced by the strength and variability of reactions to its usage. This study evaluates the impact of a sexual appeal by testing a hypothetical model incorporating linkages between the ethical dimensions of the Reidenbach-Robin (1988, 1990) multidimensional ethics scale and resulting attitude toward the ad, attitude toward the brand, and purchase intention.

BACKGROUND

The use of erotic stimuli in print advertising has become almost commonplace in current advertising practices (LaTour and Henthorne, 1994). It is not unusual to find provocatively posed and attired (or unattired) models promoting any number of items in general-interest consumer magazines. This routine use of erotic stimuli in print advertising has resulted in mixed consumer responses. Prior empirical studies have shown both positive reactions and negative reactions from viewers of such ads (see, for example, the works of Alexander and Judd, 1986; Henthorne and LaTour, 1994; LaTour, 1990; LaTour and Henthorne, 1993; Sciglimpaglia *et al.*, 1978). One of the central issues of the erotic stimuli controversy currently facing advertisers is believed to be the perception of continued traditional sex-role stereotyping of women (Boddewyn and Kunz, 1991). This traditional sex-role stereotyping is thought by many social critics to contribute to the perceived continuing injustice and inequality for many women. Additionally, there appears to be no reduction in perceived "sex objectification" in recent years even though female roles have substantially changed to more professional depictions (Ford and LaTour, 1993). Meanwhile, the advertising industry has come under increasing and consistently strong pressure from various outside sources (including well known feminists and feminist groups) who argue that the dignity of women has been lowered by their continued portrayal as sex objects (Kilbourne, 1987; Soley and Kurzbard, 1986). Because the whole issue of sex, sexual innuendo, and what is considered decent, moral, and/or acceptable in a culture or society is in constant evolution (Boddewyn, 1991), advertisers are finding it increasingly difficult to determine whether their viewers will perceive ads containing a relatively high level of female nudity as "sexy" or "sexist" (Lipman, 1991; Miller, 1992). Women's perceptions, in particular, of such female role portrayals have been shown to have a substantial impact upon purchase intention and perceived overall image of the sponsoring corporation (Ford and LaTour, 1993; Lundstrom and Sciglimpaglia, 1977). To assist in coping with this precarious situation, advertising agencies are bringing in increasing numbers of female consultants to provide input on ads which may be viewed as potentially offensive to women (Lipman, 1991). Clearly, with such important and pragmatic concerns at stake, the impact of the use of such advertising on society should be examined.

The Influence of Ethics

One step toward understanding the impact of the use of erotic stimuli in print advertising is to examine the ethical dilemmas emanating from such use. Gould (1994) states that insight into these positive and negative consumer reactions may arise from an investigation of the basic concepts contained in normative ethical theories of moral philosophy. Normative ethical theories of moral philosophy may generally be classified as either deontological or teleological, with the principal difference being in the basic focus of the framework (Murphy and Laczniak, 1981).

Deontological philosophies focus on the specific actions of the individual without regard to the consequences of those actions. The deontological viewpoint is concerned with the inherent rightness of the individual act. Actions should be judged by the actions themselves, without regard to the eventual outcome.

Conversely, teleological philosophies focus primarily on the outcomes and consequences of actions and behaviors in the determination of "worth" (Ferrell and Gresham, 1985). An individual behavior is considered ethical if it produces the greatest balance of good over bad, when compared with all other alternative actions (Hunt and Vitell, 1986). From a teleological perspective, many times the use of erotic stimuli in print advertising is not appealing to viewers and may actually exist in the generation of unintended (i.e., negative) side effects (for example, gratuitous sex). Therefore, these side effects of the use of erotic stimuli in print advertising, as well as the fundamental moral rightness of its use are of interest (Gould, 1994).

Reidenbach and Robin (1988) contend that individuals do not use the clearly defined concepts of deontology or teleology in making specific ethical judgements. They contend that a mixing or combining of the philosophies is more the norm in ethical decision making. This belief is based in the work of Frankena (1963). Frankena (1963) advocated a view blending the seemingly mutually exclusive requirements of teleology and deontology.

The Reidenbach-Robin Ethics Scale

Normative ethical philosophy, containing a number of overlapping theoretical ideals, was used as the basis for the development of the Reidenbach and Robin (1988, 1990) multidimensional ethics scale. (For a detailed discussion of the moral philosophy base of the scale the reader is referred to the work of Reidenbach and Robin [1990].) The scale has typically distilled the three dimensions of "moral equity," "relativism," and "contractualism" (see Table I).

The "moral equity" dimension is composed of four items:

1. Fair–Unfair
2. Just–Unjust
3. Morally right–Not morally right
4. Acceptable to my family–Not acceptable to my family.

According to Reidenbach and Robin (1990), this dimension is believed to be based on lessons from early in life gained through basic institutions (such as

TABLE I   The multidimensional ethics scale

The moral equity dimension
Fair—Unfair
Just—Unjust
Morally right—Not morally right
Acceptable to my family—Unacceptable to my family
The relativistic dimension
Culturally acceptable—Culturally unacceptable
Traditionally acceptable—Traditionally unacceptable
The contractualism dimension
Violates an unspoken promise—Does not violate an unspoken promise
Violates an unwritten contract—Does not violate an unwritten contract

family and religion) regarding such elemental constructs as fairness, equity, and right and wrong. The insights achieved from such institutions are considered decisive in establishing what individuals consider to be decent (positive) or objectionable (negative) in advertising (Gilly, 1988; Reid *et al.*, 1984).

The "relativistic" dimension is composed of two items:

1. Culturally acceptable–Culturally unacceptable
2. Traditionally acceptable–Traditionally unacceptable.

Dimension two is concerned with the social/cultural influences, guidelines, and parameters as they impact the individual. How we work to interpret individual events may be impacted by the items forming this dimension (Reidenbach and Robin, 1990). The possibility of a linkage between the ethical evaluative process and the social/cultural influences on the individual has been examined by Hunt and Vitell (1986). The current level of sex and eroticism in advertising may simply be a mirror of what is now acceptable social behavior (Courtney and Whipple, 1983).

Given the overlapping theoretical dimensions fundamental to the various ethical philosophies utilized in the initial distillation of the scales, it is not surprising to find a high degree of correlation between some of the various constructs. Specifically, dimensions one and two frequently have been shown to combine into a single comprehensive dimension (Reidenbach and Robin, 1990; Reidenbach *et al.*, 1991).

The final dimension, "contractualism," is composed of two items:

1. Violates an unspoken promise–Does not violate an unspoken promise
2. Violates an unwritten contract–Does not violate an unwritten contract.

This dimension is centered around the concept of a "social contract" between the individual and society (Reidenbach and Robin, 1990). Implied obligation or contract is the fundamental issue addressed.

THE HYPOTHETICAL MODEL

Figure 1 reveals the structural relationships posited as linkages between the ethical dimensions of the Reidenbach-Robin conceptualization and the resulting attitude toward the ad (A_{ad}), attitude toward the brand (A_b) and, ultimately, purchase intention (*PI*). Figure 1 displays the two-dimensional structural outcome of the Reidenbach-Robin model. (Preliminary factor analysis of the present study's data supports this structural interpretation.)

It is hypothesized that a perceived lack of "Moral Equity/Relativism" (Lack Morel) associated with the use of the treatment ad will result in a negative relationship with attitude toward the ad (A_{ad}), attitude toward the brand

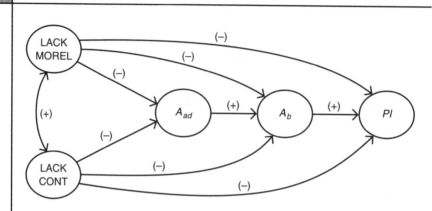

FIGURE 1 Hypothetical model.

(A_b), and purchase intention (PI). In addition to these "direct effects," it is hypothesized some of the negative impact of "Lack Morel" will be indirect. For example, "Lack Morel" may be found to impact purchase intention through the variables of attitude toward the ad (A_{ad}) and attitude toward the brand (A_b). It is further hypothesized the same type of relationships will exist between the endogenous variables and a perceived lack of contractualism. Based on prior research (e.g., Burke and Edell, 1989; LaTour *et al.*, 1990), the present model indicates attitude toward the ad (A_{ad}) should be positively associated with attitude toward the brand (A_b) which, in turn, should be positively linked with purchase intention (PI). This hypothetical model significantly extends previous research by providing a statistical test of linkages between moral philosophical dimensions and advertising response outcomes in one complete model.

The Study

Data Collection and Ad Stimuli

Data were collected by trained interviewers through the use of a mall intercept in a large regional mall located in a culturally dynamic and growing SMSA in the mid-gulf coast region. Following procedures suggested by Nowell and Stanley (1991), data collectors were rotated in random patterns throughout the mall during all hours of the mall's operation over a period of one week. Over 80% of individuals approached agreed to participate in the study. Each respondent completed the questionnaire in private, yet was monitored from a distance by research assistants. The use of the mall intercept as a data collection technique is commonly used in research such as this and has been shown to produce a significant cross-section of respondents (Bush and Hair, 1985). Such a cross-section will include older individuals which may be outside of the target market for youth-oriented products. However, the inclusion of such "non-targeted" individuals in the study is of importance due to their possible exposure to the ad and the resulting unintended social consequences for the advertiser (e.g., the perceived degradation of women) (Gould, 1994).

A high quality copy of a black and white print ad was used in the treatment. The selected ad stimulus was part of a collection of black and white photographs promoting a well known brand of jeans and used in a metropolitan area different from where the current study was being conducted. As part of the treatment selection process, a focus group of adults ranging in age from 21 to 50 was used to select an ad from this promotional outset perceived to contain substantial erotic content and nudity. The focus group selected ad featured a nude female model, with her body up against a chain link fence while at the same time being sexually embraced and kissed by a male model wearing only jeans with the fly unzipped. The ad contained the brand name of the jeans at the bottom. Each respondent was given the ad followed by the questionnaire.

Operationalization

Respondents completed two series of three seven-point items which were summed to measure attitude toward the ad (A_{ad}) and attitude toward the brand (A_b) (see Table II). The items were selected on the basis of focus group research and their use in related advertising research (e.g., Henthorne *et al.*, 1993; LaTour *et al.*, 1990).

In order to evaluate ethical dimensions associated with the ad stimulus, respondents were asked to respond to a series of eight items in terms of their beliefs about the promotional use of the ad they had just seen. As discussed earlier, these eight items were identical to those which were distilled from an earlier instrument based on moral philosophy and validated by Reidenbach and Robin (1988, 1990) (refer again to Table II).

In previous validation research, both a three factor structure solution (Reidenbach and Robin, 1990) and a two factor structure solution (Reidenbach *et al.*, 1991) have been extracted. In the two factor solution, items representing the moral equity and relativism dimensions join to form a single composite dimension. According to Reidenbach *et al.* (1991), a possible explanation to the two dimensional structure may include the effects of a "natural relation expected between what people perceive to be culturally acceptable and what is just (p. 86)." The authors go on to say that the meaning of "fairness" comes to us in part through our culture and that, therefore, such a composite makes intuitive sense.

TABLE II   Variables used in the study

Attitude toward the ad (A_{ad})*	*Attitude toward the brand (A_b)**
1. High quality	1. High quality
2. Interesting	2. Distinctive
3. Appropriate	3. Appealing

Purchase intention*
The next time I purchase jeans I will purchase [brand name] jeans.

Lack morel composite dimension**	*Lack contractualism dimension***
1. Unjust	1. Violates an unspoken promise
2. Unacceptable to my family	2. Violates an unwritten contract
3. Unfair	
4. Not morally right	
5. Not culturally acceptable	
6. Not traditionally acceptable	

*Measured on 7-point scales anchored by "Yes definitely" = 7 and "No definitely not" = 1.
**Measured on 7-point bi-polar adjective item scales.

Next, selected demographic information was collected. Finally, purchase intention was measured by a seven-point item which read "The next time I purchase jeans I will purchase [brand name] Jeans." This scale was anchored by "yes definitely" and "no definitely not."

Preliminary Analysis and Profile of the Sample

Factor analysis indicated the two factor structure (as previously discussed). As in previous research (Reidenbach *et al.*, 1991), a composite dimension (six items) was distilled (entitled "Lack Morel" in the present study) along with the "contractualism" dimension (entitled "Lack Contractualism"). All tests of internal consistency of summed scales indicated adequate levels for basic research (e.g., Cronbach alpha tests greater than or equal to 0.70) (see Bagozzi, 1978; Nunally, 1967).

Table III indicates the per-item average on "Lack Morel" was above the midpoint on a 7-point scale (29.50/6 = 4.91). In contrast, the per-item average on the "Lack Contractualism" dimension was not found to be above the midpoint (7.69/2 = 3.84). Attitude toward the ad per-item average and Purchase Intention per-item average were below the midpoint (9.75/3 = 3.25 and 2.67, respectively). Finally, attitude toward the brand per-item average was found to be above the midpoint (13.26/3 = 4.42). However, all the scales had either sizable standard deviations (refer to Table III) indicating substantial variability in responses. It stands to reason that individuals differ in the degree to which they react to such ad stimuli.

Of the 103 total useable responses, 44 were male and 59 were female. The average age of the sample was approximately 34 years, with a standard

TABLE III   Variable averages

VARIABLE	MEAN	S.D.
Lack morel	29.50	10.68
Lack contract	7.69	3.40
A_{ad}	9.75	5.93
A_b	13.26	5.75
PI	2.67	1.69

deviation of 14.7 years. 19.6% of the sample were African-American, 75.5% were white, 2.9% were Asian, with the remainder indicating "other." Income levels were widely dispersed across several categories and generally reflected the income levels of the population surrounding a ten-mile radius of the mall (as supplied by mall management). The average number of years of education (high school = 12 years) was 13.6 years, with a standard deviation of 2.9 years. As mentioned previously, due to the importance of nontargeted individuals, based on their possible exposure to the ad and the subsequent possible negative social consequences of their viewing of the ad (e.g., perceived debasement of women) (Gould, 1994), no attempt was made to exclude nontargeted individuals from the study.

Results of the Test of the Hypothetical Model

Maximum likelihood estimation was used to model the posited relationship of the variables. Figure 2 reveals strong goodness of fit indices of the data to the parameters specified in the hypothetical model. The chi-square index was non-significant, which in the case of causal modeling is an indicator of good fit. The percentage of variance explained by the structural equations representing the effects of other variables upon A_{ad}, A_b, and PI were 64%, 18%, and 30%, respectively. While this indicates appreciable amounts of variance remaining unexplained, it does establish that the structural relations featured in this model play a major role in these complex variable relationships and that the theoretical linkages were supported.

Analysis of the specific paths reveals a perceived "Lack of Moral Equity/ Relativism" ethical dimension ("Lack Morel") associated with the use of the featured ad. This dimension was strongly negatively associated with A_{ad} (standardized coefficient = −0.795, $p < 0.001$). The relationship between "Lack Morel" and Purchase Intention (PI) was also found to be significant (standardized coefficient = −0.277, $p < 0.001$), but not as strong as the link from "Lack Morel" to A_{ad}. The link between "Lack Morel" and A_b was non-significant. Apparently, the main direct impact of "Lack Morel" is upon the perceptions of the stimulus and, to a lesser extent, perhaps a desire to "boycott" the offending ad sponsor. "Lack Morel" also had a significant (standardized coefficient = −0.388,

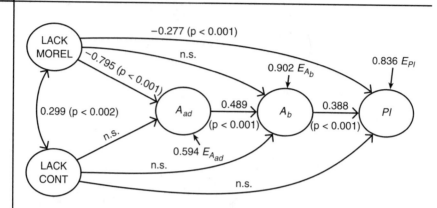

FIGURE 2 Chi-square = 0.828, *p* = 0.36 1 d.f., Bentler-Bonett Normed Fit
Index = 0.99, Bentler-Bonett Nonnormed Fit Index = 1.01,
Comparative Fit Index = 1.00.

$p < 0.001$) negative indirect effect on A_b, through A_{ad} (via the paths from "Lack
Morel" to A_{ad} and from A_{ad} to A_b).

While the correlations between "Lack Contractualism" and Lack Morel"
was positive and significant, none of the paths from "Lack Contractualism"
to the endogenous variables were significant. It seems intuitively reasonable
that the "Lack Morel" composite dimension would be more clearly associated with an advertising issue due to its focus on "moral acceptability" to society. Conversely, violation of an unwritten social promise or contract may
not seem as relevant in this particular context as it is when, for example, a re-
tailer promises some product performance characteristics that are not readily
forthcoming.

As expected, the paths from A_{ad} to A_b, and from A_b to PI were all positive and significant. This supports the well developed arguments found in
the advertising literature (e.g., Burke and Edell, 1989) that such linkage are a
significant part of the "causal chain" of advertising events.

DISCUSSION

The use of female nudity and erotic content in print advertising evokes dynamic reactions from viewers. However, the feelings which result from exposure to such strong stimuli may not be exactly what the advertiser intended
(LaTour and Henthorne, 1994). As product marketers strive to differentiate
and draw attention to their product offering, the use of erotic content has

become increasingly common. It is suggested that such content be used with discretion and caution.

The results of this study indicate that the use of high levels of female nudity/erotic content in print ads may not be perceived as morally right or culturally acceptable to viewers of such ads. While the use of such stimuli may draw additional attention to the ad, the outcome of the use of such high degrees of erotic stimuli may, in fact, be negative. In other words (as indicated by the results of the test of the hypothetical model), the perceived lack of moral equity/relativism associated with the use of high levels of female nudity in print advertising appears to result in negative feelings toward the advertisement and indirectly toward the brand. Additionally, a direct "product boycott" effect from perceived "Lack of Moral Equity/Relativism" is supported. The lack of contractualism impact, at least in the test of this data, does not appear to be relevant to the advertising ethics environment.

Findings such as these should give advertisers pause as they prepare to use prominent levels of erotic content in print advertising. Care and consideration should be directed to predetermining the reaction of their particular target market to print ads containing high levels of nudity and/or erotic content. Additionally, advertisers must consider the likely exposure of individuals outside of the selected target market and the subsequent possible negative social consequences (e.g., perceived sex objectification; Ford and Latour, 1993), perceived degradation of women (Gould, 1994), increased promiscuity (Boddewyn and Kunz, 1991), negative word of mouth (Miller, 1992) to the exposure.

Finally, future endeavors should examine this issue from a cross-cultural perspective. In fact, the controversy surrounding perceptually negative female portrayals in advertising has been shown to be a growing international phenomenon (Ford *et al.*, 1994). As world-wide societal change accelerates due in part to rapidly communicated social norms (such as the roles and portrayals of women in the media) of and among people of widely diverse cultures (Ford *et al.*, 1994), this controversy will become an even more visible and central issue to be deliberated.

References

Alexander, M. W. and B. Judd, Jr.: 1986, 'Differences in Attitudes Toward Nudity in Advertising', *Psychology: A Quarterly Journal of Human Behavior* **23**(1), 27–29.
Bagozzi, R. D.: 1978, 'Salesforce Performance and Satisfaction as a Function of Individual Difference, Interpersonal, and Situational Factors', *Journal of Marketing Research* **15**, 517–531.
Boddewyn, J. J.: 1991, 'Controlling Sex and Decency in Advertising Around the World', *Journal of Advertising* **20**(4), 25–35.
Boddewyn, J. J. and H. Kunz: 1991, 'Sex and Decency Issues in Advertising: General and International Dimension', *Business Horizons*, 13–19.
Burke, M. C. and J. A. Edell: 1989, 'The Impact of Feelings on Ad-Based Affect and Cognition', *Journal of Marketing Research* **26**, 69–83.
Bush, A. J. and J. F. Hair, Jr.: 1985, 'An Assessment of the Mall Intercept as a Data Collection Method', *Journal of Marketing Research* **22**, 158–167.

Courtney, A. E. and T. W. Whipple: 1983, *Sex Stereotyping in Advertising* (Lexington Books, Lexington, MA).

Ferrell, O. C. and L. Gresham: 1985, 'A Contingency Framework for Understanding Ethical Decision Making in Marketing', *Journal of Marketing* **49** (Summer), 87–96.

Ford, J. B. and M. S. LaTour: 1993, 'Differing Reactions to Female Role Portrayals in Advertising', *Journal of Advertising Research* **33**(5), 43–52.

Ford, J. B., M. S. LaTour, E. D. Honeycutt, Jr., and M. Joseph: 1994, 'Female Role Portrayals in International Advertising: Should Advertisers Standardize in the Pacific Rim?', *American Business Review* **12**(2), 1–10.

Frankena, W.: 1963, *Ethics* (Prentice-Hall, Inc., Englewood Cliffs, NJ).

Gilly, M. C.: 1988, 'Sex Roles in Advertising: A Comparison of Television Advertisements in Australia, Mexico, and the United States', *Journal of Marketing* **52**, 75–85.

Gould, S. J.: 1994, 'Sexuality and Ethics in Advertising: A Framework and Research Agenda', *Journal of Advertising* **23**(3), 13–80.

Henthorne, T. L., M. S. LaTour, and R. Nataraajan: 1993, 'Fear Appeals in Print Advertising: An Analysis of Arousal and Ad Response', *Journal of Advertising* **22**(2), 59–69.

Kilbourne, J.: 1987, 'Still Killing Us Softly', (Cambridge Documentary Films, Cambridge, MA).

LaTour, M. S.: 1990, 'Female Nudity in Print Advertising: An Analysis of Gender Differences in Arousal and Ad Response', *Psychology and Marketing* **7**(1), 65–81.

LaTour, M. S. and T. L. Henthorne: 1993, 'Female Nudity: Attitudes Toward the Ad and the Brand, and Implications for Advertising Strategy', *Journal of Consumer Marketing* **10**(3), 25–32.

LaTour, M. S. and T. L. Henthorne: 1994, 'Ethical Judgements of Sexual Appeals in Print Advertising', *Journal of Advertising* **23**(3), 81.

LaTour, M. S., R. E. Pitts, and D. C. Snook-Luther: 1990, 'Female Nudity, Arousal, and Ad Response: An Experimental Investigation', *Journal of Advertising* **19**(4), 51–62.

Lipman, J.: 1991, 'Sexy or Sexist? Recent Ads Spark Debate', *The Wall Street Journal* (Sept. 30), B1.

Lundstrom, W. J. and D. Sciglimpaglia: 1977, 'Sex Role Portrayals in Advertising', *Journal of Marketing* **41**, 72–79.

Miller, C.: 1992, 'Publisher Says Sexy Ads Are OK, But Sexist Ones Will Sink Sales', *Marketing News* **26**(24), 8–9.

Murphy, P. and G. R. Laczniak: 1981, 'Marketing Ethics: A Review with Implications for Managers, Educators and Researchers', *Review of Marketing 1981* (American Marketing Association, Chicago, IL), pp. 251–266.

Nowell, C. and L. R. Stanley: 1991, 'Length-Biased Sampling in Mall Intercept Surveys', *Journal of Marketing Research* **28**, 475–479.

Nunally, J. C.: 1967, *Psychometric Theory* (McGraw-Hill, New York).

Reid, L. N., C. T. Salmon, and L. C. Soley: 1984, 'The Nature of Sexual Content in Television Advertising: A Cross-Cultural Comparison of Award-Winning Commercials', in R. W. Belk (ed.), *AMA Educators' Proceedings* (American Marketing Association, Chicago, IL), pp. 214–216.

Reidenbach, R. E. and D. P. Robin: 1988, 'Some Initial Steps Toward Improving the Measurement of Ethical Evaluations of Marketing Activities', *Journal of Business Ethics* **7**, 871–879.

Reidenbach, R. E., D. P. Robin, and L. Dawson: 1991, 'An Application and Extension of a Multidimensional Ethics Scale to Selected Marketing Practices and Marketing Groups', *Journal of the Academy of Marketing Science* **19**(2), 83–92.

Sciglimpaglia, D., M. A. Belch, and R. F. Cain: 1978, 'Demographic and Cognitive Factors Influencing Viewers' Evaluations of 'Sexy' Advertisements', in William L. Wilkie (ed.), *Advances in Consumer Research*, Vol. 6 (Association for Consumer Research), pp. 62–65.

Soley, L. and G. Kurzbard: 1986, 'Sex in Advertising: A Comparison of 1964 and 1984 Magazine Advertisements', *Journal of Advertising* **15**(3), 45–54, 65.

Information Technology.

Overview.

One of the most dramatic changes in the manner of doing business in recent years relates to the use and influence of the computer and the Internet.

In the late 1950s and 1960s, the computer was a mainframe data processor and by the 1970s provided mainframe support for largely mathematically oriented modeling and applied mathematics, such as engineering. In the late 1980s and early 1990s, the personal computer (PC) market began to grow when DOS-oriented systems received an overlay of pictorial display (as had already been evidenced in Apple systems). The switch to Windows made computer operation user friendly and brought a flood of applications that anyone could use. In short order, personal ownership of PCs and business applications grew exponentially. PCs could be networked and became more powerful and adaptable than the mainframes of only a few decades earlier.

The Internet, a system originally designed for academia, was enhanced by graphics technology that allowed the creation of the World Wide Web. Through the World Wide Web, individuals were able to log on to cyber sites and get information, be titillated, and interact with others.

The speed of these changes makes a person dizzy. Clearly, a difference of "kind" has been achieved so that business must reevaluate how it operates and alter its strategic plans. No company can ignore the new technology and expect to be successful.

In times of such rapid change as experienced during this information technology revolution, the potential for exploitation and abuse exists. Many involved with computers confuse what can be done with what should be done. This applies to all information technology (IT).

Traditional categories of morality apply to the Internet and IT. Businesses must cease to be awed by technology's power and what it might achieve and ask whether each opportunity is a worthy goal consistent with sound professional practice.

In the first article in this section, Duncan Langford summarizes some key jargon and presents some background on contemporary electronic communication. He then identifies two important areas for ethics: individual communication and publication on the Web.

The first area includes both technical action and personal action. Each of these subcategories describes general types of questionable behavior. However, most of the cases he presents seem to result from ignorance and lack of public protocol. Discussion, agreement, and dissemination of such protocol might be able to solve these problems.

The second area includes difficulties with broadcasting, spamming, and intellectual property. This group of problems is more difficult to solve because they are more consciously undertaken. Behavior related to these problems undermines the foundation of freedom on which the Internet was constituted.

The reader is invited to add to these examples and bring to class a list of solutions that can be discussed via their professional practice and ethical content.

In the second article, Peter W. F. Davies advances the thesis that contrary to the idea that technology is a neutral tool, technology actually controls business. This thesis follows from a broad perspective of technology that includes cultural and other values. A person can react to the powerful influence of "can implies ought" either by resigning his freedom or by asserting it. This latter course offers the hope for ethics to check the unbridled expansion of technological influence.

In the third article, Joseph L. Badaracco Jr., and Jerry V. Useem examine a case study concerning Intel's Pentium I chip. In this case, users of this chip detected flaws and utilized the Internet to create an avalanche of public opinion. Intel spent a great deal of money to remedy the problem. These authors discuss whether the Internet should help stakeholders to hold big corporations to a professional level of accountability or to incite a vigilante mentality that stirs up emotion and hostility but has no internal accountability. Managers must consider this important issue when they decide what impact the Internet will have on their company.

In the final article in this section, Michael D. Myers and Leigh Miller suggest that one way to address problems of IT ethics is to use key principle or principles from ethical theory. This is very much in keeping with the pedagogy of this series, *Basic Ethics in Action*.

The authors use a version of Aristotelian ethics in attempting to solve pressing problems in IT ethics concerning privacy, information accuracy, access to information, and intellectual property rights.

I invite the reader to repeat this exercise with one or more of the other major ethical theories and see what differences, if any, are found.

Ethics and the Internet: Appropriate Behavior in Electronic Communication

Duncan Langford

It may fairly be argued that computing is essential to modern life. We use computers in most business activities, from buying an airline ticket to using a credit card, and individuals use a variety of computers, from massive office systems to personal word processors. Even such widely used phrases as "surfing the Internet" and "information superhighway" emphasize the ubiquity of computers. Without them, present-day Western society surely would be impossible to sustain.

Although there are clearly a variety of ethical issues involved in computer use, in this article I am particularly concerned with the consequences of electronic communications and networking. Increasingly, modern computers depend upon wide-scale networking—the linking together of a potentially huge number of individual computers. Linking machines means information may be shared, so whatever data is accessible to one computer becomes, at least theoretically, accessible to all. A networked computer system is therefore infinitely greater than the sum of its parts.

What is ethically appropriate must reflect what is technically possible. In order to consider ethical issues in electronic communication, we must have some understanding of the technical setting. The first part of this article therefore briefly describes the background of computer networking and the Internet. The second section moves on to consider some of the potential ethical problems involved in networked communications.

NETWORKS AND THE INTERNET

When computers are linked together so that they can share files of information, these computers are *networked*. A network can refer to a group of office computers linked to each other by cable. Or, it can refer to the use of a *modem* (a device to connect a computer to a telephone line) to establish links to other computers in distant locations.

For example, through a modem an individual computer might connect to an information provider such as the commercial service CompuServe, which exists to link computer users. Users linked through a single information provider may access the provider's databases or "converse" with other computer users linked to the same provider. Most such providers now also offer a further connection, to the wider Internet community. The Internet is a worldwide mesh of telephone connections through which a computer may be linked to any other computer on the Net, anywhere in the world. There are a growing number of services, public and private, commercial and noncommercial, through which individuals access the Internet. Such access points are often called Internet *sites*. Through most of the Net's history, most sites have been colleges and universities.

Begun as a vehicle for military communication in the mid-1960s, the Internet was originally designed to survive nuclear war. In consequence, there is no central control whatever—any part of it may be removed without damage to the whole. Surprisingly, from such a specialized genesis, the Internet subsequently developed into an essential international infrastructure for communication between academia, business, and individuals.

In attempting to understand how such a devolved system can work, it is essential to appreciate the very strong ethos of the Internet. Its users are very much against external control. In effect, the Internet is a fully functioning anarchy. Until comparatively recently, most actual users of the Internet were technically aware individuals who understood the technical background to this form of networking, and who (because of their experience and background) were perhaps biased in favor of academic freedom and individual autonomy. A recent British government report summarized the position well:

> **13.** The Internet is perceived to have flourished because it was free to evolve without interference from any powerful self-interested groups (these are interpreted as including governments and multinational press corporations). This freedom is greatly cherished by Internet users, who believe that access to the valuable information resources that such freedom makes possible is too important to risk through regulation.

> **14.** Unrestricted data communications are assumed to be vital to the UK's future economic prosperity, and any legislation needs to be framed in this context. Accordingly, the central principle is that everyone should have unfettered freedom to discuss, but not the freedom to harm others, and that individuals must have the appropriate freedom to choose whether they wish to view items or not. Discretion should be the rule, not regulation. (Collaborative Open Group Report, 1995)

As will be discussed in more detail later, it is always important when considering the ethics of electronic communication through the Internet to keep in mind the very unusual background of its development. Of special importance is the widespread conviction on the part of established users of the Internet that individual users can and should be trusted to use the system appropriately and, in particular, that under no circumstances is external supervision or control of the Internet appropriate.

Personal Mail—E-Mail

Once a user has obtained requisite passwords from an information provider, electronic messages may be generated at any computer connected to the Internet and "mailed" or "posted" to any user with a similarly connected computer. All that is needed to send such mail is the electronic "address" of the recipient, an address that details the name, organization name, type of organization, and—if you are not within the United States—the country. My electronic address, for example, is D.Langford@ukc.ac.uk. Decoding is simple: The letters *ukc* represent "University of Kent at Canterbury," *ac* is shorthand for "academic," and *uk* stands for "United Kingdom."

Given the address of your target, electronic mail—known as *e-mail*—can be dispatched in seconds to someone working at the next desk or in the next continent.

Newsgroups

Connection to the Internet also allows access to an enormous number of special interest groups. Known as *newsgroups*, these are electronic notice boards that cover the whole range of human activity. Although those newsgroups concerned with sexual matters may have gained a high profile, there are tens of thousands of others.

Posting an article simply involves sending mail to the electronic address of a relevant newsgroup rather than directing mail to an individual. This process is often facilitated by a utility called a *newsreader*. Not every Internet newsgroup is available from every information provider, but most providers typically accept several thousand groups, all of which are then accessible to their users. Although some newsgroups are moderated, which means a human acts as a filter for postings to them, the huge majority have no such control. What is posted to the newsgroup is then automatically distributed to every Internet site subscribing to it. Posting to an Internet newsgroups is consequently the nearest thing on earth to absolute free speech.

How Newsgroups Work.

There have been demands that the Internet and its newsgroups should be censored. Once the workings of the Internet are understood, however, it will be seen that, even if justified, such censorship is technically impossible.

Basically, messages are constantly being sent along the links between Internet sites. When a site receives a message, it checks to see whether the message's date is current (to prevent swamping of the system, messages are only in circulation for a limited time). If the message has not expired, site software checks that the group to which the message belongs is valid for that site. When checks are complete, a message is made available to a site's individual members; this is done by storing a copy on site. The site also sends another copy of each message onward to the next site in the wider network. Millions of messages are continuously passing around the Internet in this way.

In the example illustrated in Figure 1, a message originates at Site *A* and is then passed to Site *B*, which distributes it not only to its own subscribers but also onward, to Site *C*. Copies of the message then move on to subsequent sites in the network.

What would happen if, instead of passing the message on, Site *B* decided that the message was subversive of morals or authority and refused to circulate either the message or the newsgroup to which it belonged? Clearly,

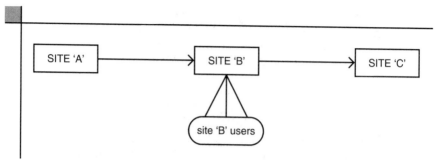

FIGURE 1 **Transmission of typical newsgroup message.**

those users who depended directly upon the site would be unable to access the newsgroup. However, Site C, downstream in Figure 1, would be only temporarily inconvenienced. The Internet is not called *Net* casually. The pattern of its links forms a spider's web; so, if one connection is damaged, information can be obtained from any other. The Internet interprets censorship as damage, and, of course, it was designed from the first to survive massive damage. Site C can consequently easily obtain a censored newsgroup from any other of its connections—or it may readily establish a new connection to an unrestricted news "feed."

This pattern holds true at whatever scale the Internet is viewed. If, for example, a whole country decides to ban a particular newsgroup, at worst this will only affect the country itself. The global Internet community will continue.

It is very important to keep this state of affairs in mind, not only when considering requests for punitive action against publications on the Internet, but when debating appropriate user conduct.

World Wide Web

The ability of an individual to both read and post information is further complicated by the recent explosive growth of a subset of the Internet known as the *World Wide Web*, or WWW. The Web, graphically based and consequently very visual in nature, is inherently easy to use. In structure, it can be considered a static approach to information provision. Here, instead of the contents of a newsgroup being constantly transmitted around the world a message at a time, an individual actually establishes direct contact with a specific remote site that contains desired information and especially accesses it. A great advantage of this system is that Web sites are easily linked to each other, so users of the Web may, by clicking buttons on their personal computers' screens, move between the display of Web sites in different states—or different continents—without realizing they are doing more than moving to the next page of data. Companies and individuals may establish their own Web sites, and people from any connected computer may then read presented information.

Access to Web sites is very easy indeed—they are the simplest way of reading information on the Internet. Although their purposes—location of desired information—may seem similar, Internet Web sites and Internet newsgroups are very different. A newsgroup has no "real" location and cannot therefore be said to exist in any one place, whereas a Web site must, by definition, have a unique home address.

Summary

Anyone with a full Internet connection may post electronic messages to any Internet address anywhere in the world. In addition, they may read from and contribute to Internet newsgroups, which cover the whole range of human activity. Such groups cannot effectively be banned. Graphically based World Wide Web sites also contain information, but such sites, unlike newsgroups, have specific locations. Both rely on the Internet, a paradoxically unorganized and ad hoc arrangement of connected computers that evolved to its present position of global dominance from its origin as a nuclear attack-proof research network.

The underlying ethos shared by long-standing users of the Internet has always been very strongly against external controls and in favor of internal self-regulation.

PROBLEMS IN ELECTRONIC COMMUNICATION

Background

As part of research for a book on computer ethics (Langford, 1995), I sought out the views of professional users of electronic communications. For technical reasons, these respondents were not chosen at random and consequently did not reflect a wide range of users; responses were heavily biased to those with considerable computer experience. Even so, the information provided is of potential interest, particularly because to date there has been little research into the ethical views and opinions of Internet users.

Most contributions came from individuals responding to requests posted to newsgroups directed at professional users of computer systems and of the Internet. Analysis of these replies forms the basis of the following material. For obvious reasons, where specific examples are given, details were changed to prevent identification of respondents.

Two principal areas of computer networking and communications can be considered particularly relevant to ethical examination. The first relates to *individual* communications, defined as messages between people who use an Internet connection to convey information electronically. The second is concerned with *publication*—reading or publishing information more widely, through access to newsgroups and World Wide Web sites.

ETHICAL ISSUES IN INDIVIDUAL COMMUNICATIONS

Ethical issues in individual communication may be further divided, into *technical* and *personal*. Technical issues relate to the abuse of technical knowledge or privileges, whereas personal issues concern individual actions that involve no such technical abuse but which nevertheless have a dubious ethical base. It is not possible to do more than present representative examples in the space available, so it should be kept in mind that cases discussed are illustrative rather than definitive.

Examples of personal actions:

- Misunderstanding of the medium.
- Inappropriate distribution.
- Inappropriate responses.

Examples of technical actions:

- Unauthorized use of superuser privileges.
- Unauthorized access to personal mail.
- Unauthorized access to files or other material held electronically.

Personal: Misunderstanding of the Medium

When moving into new circumstances, it is natural to assume previous experience may be relevant. Consider an apparently simple task, such as writing a letter. It may seem logical to bring to composing and sending an electronic letter an established cognitive model that has worked well in generating personal mail on paper. However, unthinking transference of experience gained from other settings may to lead to serious problems.

One problem for new users lies in mentally classifying an electronic message. Is it, for instance, best treated as a traditional paper memo? There can be similarities, but there are important differences too. Producing a typed office memo involves several stages, at each of which an author may modify the text or even decide to scrap the whole idea. This extended process does not fit the generation of an electronic message, which, in contrast, is very quick and easy to produce. Many people create and send e-mail spontaneously, often without pausing to consider use of tone, language, or even if the message is really appropriate or necessary. Of course, an electronic message can easily be printed as well, so a casual electronic jotting may instantly and unexpectedly achieve the formal authority of a typed memo.

Unlike paper communications e-mail seems to be transitory. A message can flash across a screen and then disappear into electronic limbo. Indeed, with a keystroke or two, it may permanently disappear. However, it is a serious mistake to think of e-mail as temporary. Although messages can certainly be impermanent, the opposite is also true. Once sent, a copy of an unguarded personal message may easily be stored by a recipient for years before, in the phrase of one businessman, "It comes back to haunt you." For example, an outburst such as, "you should stand up to him! If *I* had the sales desk you can be sure old Jones would get told what to do with his policy!" might easily find its way to "old Jones" himself.

Here, individual problems are likely to follow a misunderstanding of the electronic medium, leading to the inappropriate assumption of ethical rules—rules that may have been appropriate in a different setting, but which do not function in a network. For example, sending a paper letter is predicated upon the assumption that its contents will remain personal to the addressee. It is therefore both logical and appropriate to use a paper letter to convey confidential information and to consider that a third party who read it is, normally, acting unethically. Given a very different distribution model and manifold possibilities for inadvertent distribution, transference of such a model to the use of e-mail systems is not appropriate.

Personal: Inappropriate Distribution

A personal e-mail message sent by one individual can easily be distributed to many others. Adding further electronic addresses to the cc (carbon copy) field of an e-mail posting allows the number of recipients to be effortlessly increased. Postings to a *"mailing group"* are forwarded automatically. A mailing group acts as a single point of distribution for every electronic address in the group, so a single message to a group is distributed to every group member. It is very easy to generate vast quantities of electronic "junk mail" simply by circulating and duplicating e-mail unnecessarily.

In this example, there is a high risk of swamping individuals with mail that is of only tenuous interest to them, as well as of passing information to an inappropriately wide audience. Before sending or distributing e-mail, such problems could easily be avoided through proper consideration of individual recipients. However, without encouragement, such consideration is perhaps as unlikely as it is necessary.

Personal: Inappropriate Responses

Additionally, because e-mail is so easily duplicated, once received, a message may also be copied and recopied, with or without the knowledge of the original sender. This means that the eventual readership of a message may be very much more extensive than was originally intended. This may well be important—what you might be prepared to say in private conversation or correspondence, you may understandably be reluctant to repeat in public—and electronic text can be very public indeed.

For example, the development manager of a software company responded to a helpful bug report from a user by sending a rather frank appraisal of the software, which, he felt, had been released too soon. The message was circulated widely, with unfortunate results.

Conventions of behavior have evolved in the "electronic community" that make distribution of personal e-mail in this way generally unacceptable. It is, for example, considered unethical to publish—by posting to a newsgroup—electronic text that has been obtained through private e-mail. Breaking the conventions of user–user distribution by forwarding a message to a mailing list, or other users, is viewed as similarly inappropriate.

Further, as is discussed in more detail later, all persons connected to the Net have the ability to publish whatever they wish to every other Internet-connected individual. Established Internet users belive that this ability is so powerful it must always be limited and used with considerable care and foresight. To act otherwise is to act unethically. Of course, because there is no technical way to prevent global distribution, this restriction is, again, purely an ethical one and may be ignored without legal penalty.

Technical: Unauthorized Use of Superuser Privileges

In order to maintain computer systems, site and system administrators must be allowed awesome privileges. They are able invisibly to read personal mail and to access any data passing through their machine; they can monitor, create, and destroy files, and, in particular, they have the power to electronically "become" any of their users and are then able to behave as if that person's data were their own. Such administrators are known as *superusers.* Although, strictly speaking, this is a network rather than superuser example, consider a list of questions put to one system administrator. His site offered an anonymous access point to a special Internet newsgroup for the survivors of sexual abuse (ASAR, or, more properly, alt.sexual.abuse.recovery). Some abuse survivors understandably prefer anonymity but might nevertheless benefit by drawing support from others with similar experiences. One answer is to post personal e-mail through a special Internet-connected computer system, which maintains a confidential register of identification details but forwards messages to newsgroups or individuals only after removing personal identification.

In this case, by employing superuser powers to read and respond to private e-mail and subtly exploiting "inside" knowledge in other ways, the person responsible for administering the system behaved in a way that was widely perceived as inappropriate. The following questions, directed in an open letter[1] to the system administrator, are taken from a longer posting:

> Is it your responsibility, as a system administrator (particularly on an ASARian system where privacy is so emphasised and needed), to plug the potential holes in your system that may lead to a violation of privacy?
>
> Is it your responsibility, as a system administrator, to not abuse the same holes (if/when found) as a user or as a superuser on the system until they are plugged?
>
> Do you consider yourself to be a system administrator when you are logged on as a superuser?
>
> Do you consider yourself to be a system administrator when you are logged on as a user?
>
> Do you consider yourself to be a system administrator when you are not logged on to [name of anonymous system]?
>
> Is it your responsibility, as a system administrator *AND* as a user of [name of anonymous system], to not breach user's privacy by accessing their files or doing any other activity that would breach their privacy with, or without, their knowing of said actions?

These are serious questions that go to the heart of the responsibilities of an administrator. Their implication should be considered carefully.

Although little or no attention normally is given to the ethics of system management, I suggest that these questions indicate that those who take responsibility for maintaining a networked computer system, especially one connected to the Internet, need to be quite clear about what is expected of them ethically as well as practically. Application of the Golden Rule is the very least that should be done; there is, in my view, a strong case for development of specifically stated ethical standards. These might appropriately build upon the present "Net ethic," aspects of which were touched on in this section. The Net ethic concept, which is surprisingly widely held among computing professionals, is discussed in more detail in the final section.

Summary

In this section I discussed the actions of individuals who communicate electronically or are responsible for the sites and systems that allow electronic communication. I suggest that it is important to apply an appropriate cognitive model to the consideration of electronic communication and proposed that problems may follow inappropriate transference to the electronic world of ethical expectations based upon paper communications. I also mentioned an unwritten ethical code of anticipated behavior, a code that evolved with the

---

[1]Although this posting was public, in view of the special sensitivity of the ASAR newsgroup, specific permission from the writer was obtained before reproducing it.

Internet itself. Elements of this code suggest it is unethical to distribute e-mail inappropriately or to publish personal messages; and that it is particularly inappropriate to use the powers of a systems administrator outside the role of administration.

ETHICAL ISSUES IN NETWORKED COMMUNICATIONS

In addition to the issues concerning personal communication already described, networked computers allow the spreading of information in a way that is directly analogous to traditional broadcasting, or publishing on paper. Once distributed electronically, such "published" information is potentially seen by very large numbers of individuals. Consolidated files of electronic information may be held on Internet-linked computers in "open" directories. They may then be accessed *anonymously* from anywhere in the world by using *ftp*, or "file transfer protocol." The well-established ftp procedure is very similar in its operation to the way the World Wide Web operates, but it lacks the graphical interface that makes the Web so easy to use.

The following examples of inappropriate Internet broadcasting are intended as illustrations rather than definitive cases.

PERSONAL EXAMPLES:

* "Spamming."
* Individual access to "inappropriate" material.

TECHNICAL EXAMPLES:

* Public broadcasting of "inappropriate" material.
* Unauthorized use of copyrighted material.

Personal: Spamming

Sending multiple copies of messages to many different newsgroups is always considered inappropriate. Doing so is called, in Netspeak, *spamming*, after an old Monty Python sketch.

Distributing many hundreds of thousands of copies of your message and presenting it to the readers of every newsgroup might, perhaps, be useful to you, but the disadvantages to everyone else are very clear. Who does this, and why?

The most infamous example was probably the 1994 Green Card Lottery Spam, perpetrated by the law firm of Canter & Siegel in the United States. The firm considered the Internet to be an ideal, low-cost, and perfectly legitimate way to target their advertising to potential clients. Although spreading their "spam" message cost others thousands of dollars and much inconvenience, they had done nothing illegal or, in their view, improper. Among Internet users this was certainly a minority opinion—the reaction of the Internet population was overwhelmingly hostile.

Users in 1994 felt that, first, the Internet was the wrong place to conduct commercial business. Its origins and long-standing academic bias imbued the Net with a long tradition of noncommercialism. Second, use of the Internet was and is not free. For example, several popular newsreaders display variations of the following message before they let news items be posted:

> This program posts news to thousands of machines throughout the entire civilized world. Your message will cost the net hundreds if not thousands of dollars to send everywhere. Please be sure you know what you are doing.

The firm of Canter & Siegel was alleged to have posted to over 6,000 groups, which must surely have involved the expenditure of quite a lot of other people's money.

Finally, in order to be established, newsgroups have individual charters, setting out their aims. Many of the charters of the Internet newsgroups and connected sites specifically prohibit offers to do business. (A few do accept them but restrict buyers and sellers to individuals, not companies.) Of course, being involved with the Internet, such charters have only moral face. Understandably, people reading a particular newsgroup can become very annoyed by irrelevant postings concerning subjects outside the group's charter. This is analogous to a neighborhood group meeting together to discuss the needs of their local school, but being constantly interrupted in its debate by someone trying to sell telephone chat lines.

Respecting the rights of groups and individuals is part of the Internet ethic. People who, for their own purposes, casually override the interests of other users by generating spams are acting unethically.

Personal: Individuals and Inappropriate Material

Newsgroups dealing with sexual matters are among the most heavily trafficked. To one such newsgroup University of Michigan student Joe Baker made three postings. All dealt with brutal rape and murder and were quite extreme, even for a specialist newsgroup. One posting was even more excessive. It used the name of a real person as the victim of the fantasy—a female student who had had the misfortune to share a class with Baker. The FBI arrested Baker, charging him under a U.S. federal statute that makes illegal the transmission across state or international boundaries of a threat to injure the person of another. Although the case was eventually dismissed, there is no doubting the trauma that Baker's actions caused an innocent student. However, the arrest and prosecution of an individual who had done nothing except post written material to the Internet caused a very strong reaction. This reaction came both from advocates of free speech and those concerned with the protection of individuals from sexist threats and potential attack.

The Baker case was certainly extreme, but it encapsulates a central aspect of electronic communication. Are electronic postings to be viewed as exempt from controls, or are they subject to regulation? Can individuals be protected from postings like Baker's? There seems to be urgent need of debate and discussion, although, unfortunately, the issue of what constitute "appropriate" personal postings to the Internet is not one that is likely to be easily resolved.

Technical: "Broadcasting" of "Inappropriate" Material

The Baker case involved an individual making use of an existing newsgroup to post material, but other methods of distributing opinions electronically are also possible. Once a computer is connected to the Internet, running appropriate software on it allows the easy creation of a World Wide Web site. Tens of thousands of such sites exist, and numbers are increasing exponentially. Most such sites are well designed and well conducted—but there are some WWW sites, for example, that exist to distribute pornography, both hard- and soft-core, as well as sites devoted to propagating extremist political views. Such sites are normally packed with color illustrations. All that is needed to view them is the correct electronic address.

As was mentioned earlier, Internet newsgroups are only controllable by refusing to allow news packages to enter an information provider's site. Newsgroup access may also be made more difficult by a "censoring" site's refusal to pass information along the networked chain of computers.

In contrast, a Web site cannot be controlled at all beyond refusing it permission to exist at a particular location. Sites created by individuals but felt to be unsuitable by their information providers have been closed down, but there is no way of forbidding them to exist. A closed site may just spring up somewhere else, from anywhere in the world. Such use is directly analogous to telephone sex lines in the United Kingdom (UK). Although protests resulted in telephone sex lines being banned by UK operators, the lines continued—using numbers located outside the UK.

The ethical issues involved here are both massive and complex, and it would be foolish to pretend there are easy or obvious solutions. The mix of Internet users is increasingly being diluted from its specialist origins by a vast influx of additional users from a range of different backgrounds. The well-established Internet philosophy of open access and free communication is, consequently, in direct conflict with the social and moral mores of many of its new users. If the trend continues, the philosophy itself must, at best, be in a state of flux. What is certain, however, is the inescapable fact that censorship is not possible. Whatever decisions are eventually reached must inevitably reflect this reality.

Technical: Unauthorized Use of Copyrighted Material

Turning a color photograph into a file viewable on a computer is a cheap and straightforward process—a scanner works in a manner similar to a photocopier, but instead of a paper image, it creates an electronic one. Clearly, if individuals are able to include color photographs on their Web pages by simply scanning illustrations from magazines, there is a real danger of copyrighted material being misused. It is also possible, if slightly more trouble, to scan and reproduce text—so printed material is similarly at risk. Copyright laws differ from country to country, so a text may be legally available on an Internet site in the United States but illegal to download elsewhere.

Illegality is of course also a wider issue, particularly obvious where a country with a tradition of free speech meets more repressive regimes. This becomes increasingly likely when an Internet connection becomes a potential link to freedom for political dissidents. Illegality of material is also seen as a problem in parts of Europe. Here, for example, countries with a repressive attitude toward sexual material, such as the UK and Ireland, are within easy electronic reach of countries with sharply different views, such as Holland and France, as well as more geographically distant ones, such as the United States. The problem appears intractable—exactly where does a photograph, legally displayed in the United States, become illegal when accessed from the UK? Halfway across the Atlantic?

Once again, the simple transference to the Internet of an ethical code that works well with older technology may not be appropriate.

THE PROBLEMS

I have so far discussed a selection of examples intended to illustrate some problems in using the Internet. These range from minor difficulties—unexpected responses to personal mail—to the more serious, which potentially involve the abuse or limitation of free speech.

Difficulties faced by new users in attempts to communicate effectively by e-mail are probably typical of the teething problems to be anticipated in the use of most new facilities. Advice to tread warily, together with effective education, should go a long way toward dealing with their problems.

In contrast, the impossibility of exerting effective censorship is difficult for many individuals to understand. Politicians, especially, are understandably reluctant to consider anything other than legislation as the ultimate sanction on behavior. Within the Internet, however, local or even national legislation simply will not work.

There are two main reasons why this is so. First, policing the Internet is technically impossible. Assume a questionable file is being passed across the Internet. Even if it were feasible to screen all Internet messages, which it currently is not, given the huge volume of electronic traffic, it would be very difficult for even the most automated of authorities to identify a needle of suspect material in the mountainous haystack of normal traffic. The situation is rendered impossible by the advent and widespread distribution of effective electronic codes. Their use does not just generate electronic messages that obviously have been coded, although no agency has the funds or resources to randomly decode all such messages on the assumption that some contents may be illegal. The situation is actually even more difficult. Using modern coding techniques, a covert photograph, for example, may be encoded, and the coded material invisibly included as part of an apparently innocent electronic message. Very efficient codes are freely available on the Internet, so, in practice, a suitably coded text might be transmitted without further disguise. The chances of successful interception would still be vanishingly small.

The second reason why policing is impossible lies in the fact that much of the Internet lies beyond the reach of any national police force. This means that any Internet site may make available whatever it likes, provided only that the country *within which it is located* does not object. Although access to such sites from the United States may be officially forbidden, anyone with a computer and telephone may access them. In reality, enforcement is quite impractical.

Given the impossibility of exercising political or technical control over the Internet, the need for appropriate education is growing increasingly urgent. In the past, the Internet worked well; it has done so since it was established. The principal reason we are experiencing problems now lies in a dramatic change in the Internet population. No longer are the majority of users experienced in the use of computers, familiar with an academic approach to free speech, and aware of established expectations of user behavior. Letting loose new users on the Internet without training or education is perhaps analogous to letting loose new drivers without instruction—except that even the worst new driver does not have the ability to inconvenience several million people, a task well within the powers of even a neophyte Internet user.

Quite apart from a massive increase in personal use, we are also seeing an explosion in commercial use of the Internet, principally through the World Wide Web. What was formerly a largely academic network is now a promotional gold rush. Hundreds, if not thousands, of companies from the very large to the very small are racing to seize the enormous potential market represented by those with Internet connections. This commercial rush shows no signs of decreasing—indeed, all the indications are that it will continue to accelerate. What decisions should be taken on defining what is appropriate commercial use of the Internet, and who should be responsible for framing such definitions? How long can the established ethic, which is essentially a shared understanding on the part of users, be sustained under a stunningly rapid dilution of user experience? There appears a real need for the establishment of an updated Internet ethic, if only an acceptable defining body can be found or established.

CONCLUSIONS

In this article I outlined some of the practical and ethical problems concerned with appropriate behavior in electronic communication. I emphasized the impossibility of effective network policing and the associated need for a greatly increased level of education.

Before the advent of the Internet, few individuals could expect to have their views and opinions considered by more than a handful of friends and acquaintances. In contrast, a simple posting to a popular Internet newsgroup may be read by hundreds of thousands of people.

It seems clear that automatically carrying over "small-scale" behavior into a large-scale forum must inevitably lead to difficulties. Such difficulties are likely to be compounded by the greatly increased opportunities the Internet offers for antisocial behavior. Users with even limited knowledge may, for example, employ e-mail to spam newsgroups, and the more technically advanced may use the World Wide Web to distribute extreme political propaganda.

This article was largely based upon the views of a selection of Internet users. Although it may be excessive to take such a collection of loosely defined opinions too seriously, the responses actually indicated a surprising uniformity of belief. Until now, the Internet has worked through acceptance on the part of its users of this belief, which might perhaps be viewed as an evolved general ethic of behavior. Although reflecting what may be a purely pragmatic approach to Internet use, this approach has proved both effective and functional. Of the points discussed, six were particularly emphasized:

- The Internet is very strongly against external control and in favor of self-regulation.
- Rights of groups and individuals should always be respected.
- Individual actions should always reflect awareness of the wider Internet community.
- Person-to-person communications should be private.
- No message should be broadcast without proper cause.
- The ability to post globally is so powerful it must always be voluntarily limited.

Repeatedly mentioned was the well-established Internet philosophy of open access and free communication.

Because the number and variety of new Internet users is constantly increasing, the situation is dynamic, and prediction is risky. However, I strongly suggest there is a case for some form of coordinated encouragement of appropriate ethical standards, ideally founded upon those established during development of the Internet. If such standards are agreed upon, they might then be included in appropriate education of new users of the Internet. New users surely need to demonstrate awareness of the responsibilities, as well as the advantages, of Internet use. Such suggestions may of course be premature; further research into the philosophy of the Internet is essential.

The Internet undoubtedly provides a tremendous global opportunity, analogous to the invention of the printing press in its power to educate and inform. Should it develop without an ethical foundation, we will all surely be the poorer. The exponential growth of the Internet means that time is, however, running out. We must hope that our new electronic culture, rather than repeating the mistakes of the past, can learn from them.

ACKNOWLEDGMENTS

Generous help was given to me by users of the Internet. Permission to reproduce individual personal experiences in the form of case examples was particularly appreciated.

References

Collaborative Open Group Report. (1995). *Collaborative open group on ethical issues final report.* Available by e-mail: a.nainby@ccta.gov.uk
Langford, D. (1995). *Practical computer ethics.* London: McGraw-Hill.

Focus: Technology and Business Ethics Theory

Peter W. F. Davies

"In the modern world, the most dangerous form of determinism is the technological phenomenon. It is not a question of getting rid of it, but, by an act of freedom, of transcending it"

—Jacques Ellul, *The Technological Society*, p. xxxiii

Much of the debate in business ethics is fuelled by differing beliefs about what the purpose and characteristics of business should be, ranging from maximising profits to providing meaningful employment to respecting stakeholders, including the ecological system, to expressing various religious values to cultivating a holistic virtuous approach to the conduct of business.[1] What is common to these various perspectives is their underlying view that there are essentially just two elements involved in business ethics: people, whether as individuals or as groups, and ecology. Technology, it is assumed, is merely a neutral tool in the hands of industry and as such it is rarely highlighted as a separate issue in the business ethics literature, which assumes the real issues can be dealt with by focusing just on people and the ecology as they meet in industry.

Such an approach, I suggest, is inadequate because it completely misunderstands technology's nature and underestimates its transforming power. Hence, as Figure 1 depicts, technology needs to be seen as a third leg alongside humans and the ecology. The triangular relationship between the ecology, humans and technology has had a long and fascinating history,[2] and this tripartite relationship could be said to be the primary defining context in which all business is done; take any one of them away and 'doing business' becomes a meaningless concept. Technology is not only the defining characteristic of our current age (we live in the 'Computer' Age), but it is also the primary way by which we assess past and future civilizations (talk to any archaeologist, or Star Trek fan).[3] As such it seems crucial that we make a serious attempt to understand this phenomenon we call 'technology'. If it takes well over a decade to realise that something as simple as a CFC canister punches a hole in the ozone layer, and if line-production is still in use over 50 years after its detrimental alienating effects have become well known, then what hope have we with genetic engineering and nano-technology? It appears we do not understand our technological creations and this has led to our relating to them in inappropriate ways. Technology, originally the offspring of a human-ecology liaison, has now grown up, left home and is becoming

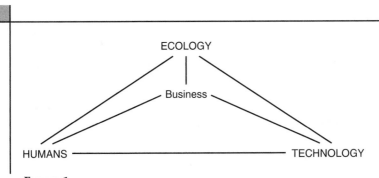

FIGURE 1

independent. Twentieth-century technical developments have put humankind in what the philosopher Hans Jonas calls an 'ethical novum',[4] or a totally new ethical situation. Humankind, through technology as co-ordinated by business, is now a major planetary force; we *have* to be stewards of the whole creation whether we like it or not. For the first time in our global development we have the power to destroy ourselves, and given the ambivalent nature of technology (the continuing discoveries of 'unintended' side-effects) we had better tread carefully, for not only does all human, animal and vegetable life depend on us, so also do the biosphere and planetary stability.

DEFINING TECHNOLOGY

We need here to make a careful definition. The word 'technology' can be used in two senses.[5] One is in the broad sense 'Technological' with a capital 'T', where we mean aspects both *cultural* (goals, values, ethical codes, belief in progress, creativity), and *organisational* (economic and industrial activity, users, structures). The second sense is the narrow one of 'technical', which involves knowledge, skills, techniques, machines, products and so on. Every purely 'technical' decision automatically has characteristic 'Technological' implications, which we are not very good at predicting. Technology is no simple objective transformation of matter; it is a complex and ambivalent form of life which involves "machines, techniques and crisply precise knowledge" ('technical' aspect) as well as always leading to certain "characteristic patterns of organization and imprecise values" ('Technological' aspect).[6] Examples of this latter 'Technological' aspect include hierarchical forms of organisation to control technology, secrecy, social fragmentation, the growth of expertism, and alienation of the user. Every decision about technology is a decision about the way we shall, (and perhaps think we ought to), live.[7]

THE MOMENTUM OF TECHNOLOGY

The difficulty for anyone from an industrialised nation calling technology into question is that technology has reached the status of a god, technological development the status of a world religion and ideology, and our personal dependency on technology is only too apparent. Consider, for example, the negative connotations in English culture surrounding the word 'Luddite', which reveal our modern Western prejudices and blind love affair with technology. So in one sense it should not be surprising that, already well over a century into the 'Technological Age', it was only about 20 years ago that Philosophy of Technology arose as a discipline distinct from Philosophy of

Science.[8] The development of this field owes much to the work of Carl Mitcham[9] and Paul Durbin[10] (for fuller details see Davies[11]).

Furthermore, technology is surrounded by three powerful myths:

- that modern technology is just more of the same;
- that technology is neutral;
- and that technology is progress.[12]

These myths are highly questionable, but they are still believed in and continue to give technology a powerful momentum, so that it acts like some kind of culture-hammer. It might well appear that society is being shaped by technology and that political, cultural, religious, ethical and even economic systems will give way to the 'one best way' as defined by, and driven by, available technologies the world over. It also appears that, apart from obviously destructive technologies, such as biological weapons, there are no real effective mechanisms by which society can seriously question technological developments. Technology, it seems, is only accountable to itself, and this presents a major challenge for ethics, especially since technology does not appear to be evolving into a more humanised version of itself. So if ethics does not rule, then mere technical capability will, with whatever technological implications that has for society.

Has the Means–Ends of the Technology–Business Relationship Been Reversed?

Now, we have to be careful here when saying things like "technology acts . . ."; we are in danger of reifying it and succumbing to technological determinism—the notion that all we humans can do in the face of technological developments is to adapt, or die. What we do have, however, with technology is a kind of reversal of our usual ethical thinking.

Normally, we do not say that 'can' implies 'ought'; just because we can increase profits by getting away with dubious marketing practices, that does not necessarily mean we ought to. But when it comes to technology we tend to reverse such thinking; it appears that there is an unwritten rule that *what technology can do, it ought to do.* Just because we can genetically engineer a 'geep' (half goat and half sheep), then we do. What is going on here in our cultural psychology? Why is it we ever so rarely say 'no' to any technology developments? Partly, I suggest, it is because of technology's sacred and ideological status,[13] and partly because of the promise of technology, both in economic and lifestyle/leisure terms.[14]

It is precisely at this point that technology connects with business ethics. Business provides the micro- and macro-contexts for developing technology, from extracting the raw materials, through processing them, to delivering the final products. Business, then, is really one of two key assets of the technological project, the other being us humans. I suggest, therefore, that business is not essentially about making money, or perpetuating the founder's name, or of providing meaningful employment, or providing goods and services to satisfied customers, or even of oiling the global economic wheels. *Business is the servant of technological development* and to the extent we serve business, so are we. So whilst business people *think* they control technology as a simple neutral means to their ends, in fact the reverse is true.

A LOOK AT THE WORK OF JACQUES ELLUL (1912–1994)

By what reasoning dare we go against received wisdom and propose that it is technology, not money (or love) which makes the world go round? I appeal here to the work of Jacques Ellul, and in particular his trilogy on technology and society which spans 40 years.[15] Ellul's understanding of technology is rooted in his concept of *technique* which he defines as "the *totality of methods rationally arrived at and having absolute efficiency* (for a given stage of development) in *every* field of human activity".[16] *Technique* is the ensemble of technical means which was originally designed to serve humans' ends, but which now is becoming an end in itself and is gradually invading every institution and sphere of human life. Individual technologies are coalescing into a technological *system;* and from business to healthcare to education to our intimate personal relationships *technique* is driving out the normally ethical human aspects of life.

According to Ellul, a civilisation dominated by *technique* will have the outward signs of happiness and choice, but these are bought at the price of dehumanising acquiescence and merely superficial consumer choices—useful distractions ending in a busy but pointless submission to the rule of technique.[17] The contentious point in Ellul's thinking is that there is no grand conspiracy driving *technique*, but that it incrementally feeds on itself—a determinist approach. Ellul would agree with Heidegger's understanding whereby the technology we have is the physical embodiment of a particular mental attitude towards the world, of *bestand*, the desire of having everything "on tap",[18] but Ellul goes even further.

Is all this too pessimistic? Although offering no solutions, Ellul points towards the "Ethics of Non-power". If we never say 'no' to technology, then surely we must accept the determinist viewpoint by default, and also accept whatever type of global society emerges when *technique* has run its course? Certainly in the 1970s and early 1980s there was a genre of literature of "The impact of technology on . . ." variety,[19] offering us little hope but to adapt or die; but this was usefully counteracted with arguments demonstrating how humans did in fact control technology.[20] For Ellul, however, such 'control' is only playing at the edges; we have to go further and have to exercise a radical 'no' vote to *technique* as well as to its concrete embodiment in various technologies, in order to reappropriate our humanity.[21] *Technique* must be desacralised and dethroned. No doubt he might have applauded the example of the Amish communities who provide a fascinating example on a small scale of how to hold at bay the advance of *technique* into personal attitudes and communal relations.[22]

CONCLUSIONS

What then does this exploration into the nature and meaning of technology have for business ethics theory? Culture and Religion each provide value-systems strongly enough embedded to counter *technique* and its associated technologies (consider their role in bringing down communism). Religion, by its aim to help spiritual beings be more human, and culture by its aim to help human beings be more spiritual, both provide a basis for seriously calling technology into question, provided that they themselves are not subverted by *technique*. Culture and religion balance a continual call to the individual's higher self with a reasonable sense of communal relations. For example, they will ask whether, though I am plugged in to the information superhighway, I am any better informed and able to pick out the salient and relevant from amongst the mass of data. Though I speak to people instantly over great distances, does not such *non* face-to-face communication makes our relationship less rich?

Indeed, culture and religion provide a more realistic picture of how to move from data to action; but here there appear to be two diverging routes. One leads to *ethical* action, the other to merely *technically efficient* action, as shown in figure 2.

Technology, then, must not be seen as a collection of individual neutral tools which can be easily controlled and which hence lead to simplistic notions of responsibility, especially when combined with the Anglo-American business ethics emphasis on individuals. Technology has become institutionalised as a technological *system*. It has its own momentum which is driving business, and it therefore requires a response at the same collective and institutionalised level.

In particular, business ethics theory needs to address technological developments by providing a more supportive attitude to culture and religion as two repositories of ethical value-systems which are powerfully embedded enough to question *technique*. Otherwise, business ethicists may end up in a position analogous to the Old Testament bricklayer who worked hard, ethically and conscientiously, was supportive to his colleagues and loyal to his employer. Then on his retirement day he stood back to view what he had been doing all his life—building the Tower of Babel. A thought perhaps for those involved in computerising the world!

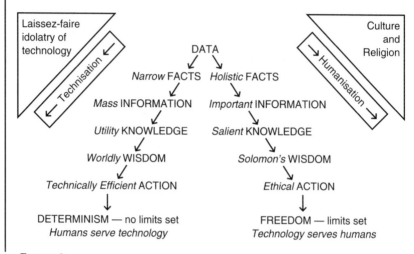

FIGURE 2

NOTES

1. For a detailed study of these various perspectives, see Business Philosophy: Searching for an Authentic Role, in DAVIES, Peter W.F. (Ed.) (1997) *Current Issues in Business Ethics,* London: Routledge.

2. For example see: PACEY, Arnold. (1991) *Technology in World History,* Cambridge, Mass: MIT Press. Also, STAUDENMAIER, John. MSJ. (1986) *Technology's Storytellers: Reweaving the Human Fabric,* MIT Press with the Society for the History of Technology.

3. More academically, consult: MUMFORD, Lewis. (1946) *Technics and Civilization,* London: Routledge & Sons. (first published in 1933).

4. JONAS, Hans. (1982) Technology as a Subject for Ethics, *Social Research,* Winter, 49(4), pp. 891–8. For his larger work, see JONAS, Hans. (1984) *The Imperative of Responsibility: In Search of an Ethics for the Technological Age,* Chicago: Univ of Chicago Press.

5. PACEY, Arnold. (1983) *The Culture of Technology,* Oxford: Basil Blackwell, p. 6.

6. PACEY, Arnold. (1991) Technology: Practice and Culture, in THOMPSON, William B. (ed), *Controlling Technology: Contemporary Issues,* pp. 65–75, at p. 68.

7. WINNER, Langdon. (1986) *The Whale and the Reactor: A Search for Limits in an Age of High Technology,* Chicago: Univ of Chicago Press.

8. PHILOSOPHY OF SCIENCE ASSOCIATION (PSA). (1977) 'Are there any Philosophically interesting Questions in Technology?' *Proceedings of the 1976 biennial meeting of the PSA,* Vol: 2, SUPPE, F. & ASQUITH, P. D. (eds), East Lansing, Mich: PSA, pp. 139–201.

9. In 1973 Carl Mitcham & Robert Mackey produced the *Bibliography of the Philosophy of Technology,* Univ of Chicago Press; this was reprinted in a special supplement to the *Technology and Culture* journal, April 1973, 14(2), pp. S1–S205. They also co-edited *Philosophy and Technology: Readings in the Philosophical Problems of Technology,* The Free Press; first printed 1972, reprinted 1983.

10. Paul Durbin was the initial series editor of *Research in Philosophy and Technology,* 1978–86, JAI Press; subsequently edited by Frederick Ferre, and currently Carl Mitcham. Durbin continues as the series editor of *Philosophy and Technology,* 1987–, Kluwer Academic Press.

11. DAVIES, Peter W.F. (1992) *The Contribution of the Philosophy of Technology to the Management of Technology,* Ph.D. Thesis, Brunel University with Henley Management College.

12. These three myths were the subject of a previous article of mine in this journal; see DAVIES, (1995), Managing Technology: Some Ethical Preliminaries, *Business Ethics, A European Review,* 4, 3 (July 1995), pp. 130–138.

13. ELLUL, Jacques. (1975) *The New Demons,* Oxford: Mowbrays. See also GOUDZWAARD, Bob. (1984) *Idols of our Time,* Downers Grove, Illinois: IVP.

14. BORGMAN, Albert. (1984) *Technology and the Character of Contemporary Life: A Philosophical Inquiry,* Chicago: Univ of Chicago Press.

15. See Ellul's: (1964) *The Technological Society,* NY: Vintage Books, Random House, (1st published in French in 1954 as *La Technique ou L'enjeu du Siècle,* Libraire Armand Colin); (1980) *The Technological System,* NY: Continuum; (1990) *The Technological Bluff,* Grand Rapids, Mich: Eerdmans.

16. ELLUL, (1964), p. xxv. The italics are Ellul's.

17. Ibid, p. viii.

18. HEIDEGGER, Martin. (1977) *The Question Concerning Technology, and Other Essays,* London: Harper.

19. An example of this genre is: EVANS, Christopher. (1979) *The Might Micro: The Impact of the Microchip Revolution,* Hodder & Stoughton.

20. For example: MacKENZIE, Donald & WAJCMAN, Judy (eds). (1985) *The Social Shaping of Technology,* Milton Keynes: OUP. *Also:* PACEY, (1983), note 5 above.

21. ELLUL, Jacques. (1980) 'The Ethics of Non-Power', in KRANZBERG, Melvin (ed), *Ethics in an Age of Pervasive Technology,* Boulder, Colorado: Westview Press, pp. 204–212; a slightly altered version appeared also in 1980 as 'The Power of Technique and the Ethics of Non-Power', in WOODWARD, Kathleen (ed), *The Myths of Information: Technology and Post-Industrial Culture,* London: Routledge & Kegan Paul, pp. 242–247.

22. KRAYBILL, Donald. (1989) *The Riddle of Amish Culture.* London: The Johns Hopkins University Press; especially pp. 141–187. See also: DAVIES, Peter W. F. (1996) 'Negotiating Value Differences across Diverse Cultures: Some Lessons from the Amish Community's Dialogue with Modernity', paper presented to the 9th Annual EBEN conference; Seeheim, Germany, 20th September.

The Internet, Intel and the Vigilante Stakeholder

Joseph L. Badaracco Jr. and Jerry V. Useem

The media is typically an unloved but compelling force in business ethics and corporate social responsibility. From the Ford Pinto controversy to the Tylenol poisoning episodes to the *Exxon Valdez* oil spill, the major networks and newspapers have served as a public court of accountability. Here the scope of a problem is ascertained, corporate conduct and reputation are scrutinized, blame is assessed, and a sentence—ranging from forgiveness to public censure—is handed down. As a result, fear of media exposure can induce companies to behave in socially responsible ways, and advocates of ethical behaviour inside companies are often more persuasive if they say "Let's do it and stay off TV's *60 Minutes*," instead of "Let's do it because it's right."

The most recent media show-trial was the controversy over Intel Corp.'s flawed Pentium chip. Faced with a storm of consumer protest about a bug in the chip and the company's failure to disclose it, Intel was forced into a humiliating reversal of policy, agreeing to replace all the defective chips on request and writing off half a billion dollars in the process. Newspapers and television played an important role in the snowballing of the controversy, but it was a *new form of media*—the Internet, and an obscure corner of it called comp.sys.intel—that was the principal catalyst of these events.

Intel Versus the Internet

Intel is the world's leading chip maker. Its microprocessors are the brains of roughly 80 percent of the world's 150 million PCs, and the company's 56% gross profit margin topped the industry. The company sells most of its chips to a handful of large computer manufacturers—Compaq, Packard-Bell, Gateway 2000 and IBM—who then sell Intel-based PCs under their own brand names. Intel's new, state-of-the-art Pentium chip was selling briskly during 1994, accounting for nearly a quarter of the company's unit shipments. Positioning the chip as suitable for both home and heavy-duty workstation use, Intel coupled the Pentium's release with its $150-million "Intel Inside" advertising campaign designed to heighten consumer awareness of the role of its microprocessor.

In June 1994 Intel engineers discovered a subtle flaw in the way the chip performed division. The Pentium, they discovered, returned inaccurate results in division problems involving long numbers, especially with denominators of nine or more digits, and there was no easy way to tell if the chip had made such a mistake. Intel's engineers, however, concluded that such errors would occur extremely rarely: an average of once every nine billion divides, or once every 27,000 years. "We couldn't imagine anyone ever running into it," remarked Intel President Andy Grove. The errors were also very small. Most occurred in the ninth significant digit or beyond, an inconsequential magnitude for most computer applications. Hence, Intel decided not to inform customers of the bug's existence, and planned to continue selling the "buggy" chips until an updated version could be released in early 1995.

In the spring of 1994, Dr. Thomas Nicely, a mathematics professor at Lynchburg College in Virginia, was using a Pentium-equipped computer as part of a division-intensive research project. On June 13, he noticed that the computer was incorrectly calculating the reciprocals of the numbers 824633702441 and 824633702443. For four months, Nicely scrutinized the operating system and his own programmes for the source of error, all in vain, until finally he came to the startling conclusion that the problem was the Pentium chip itself. Dr. Nicely contacted Intel technical support about the problem in late October, but when Intel failed to provide a meaningful answer within a week, he sent electronic mail messages to several acquaintances and asked them to try replicating the error.

One of the recipients was Andrew Shulman, author of several computer books, who promptly forwarded a copy of the message to Richard Smith, president of Phar Lap Software in Cambridge, Mass. Smith in turn posted the message on Compuserve's Canopus forum. Meanwhile, Alexander Wolfe, a managing editor at the trade journal *Electronic Engineering Times,* saw Smith's posting and immediately e-mailed Terje Mathisen, a computer expert in Norway, asking his opinion on the reported bug. Mathisen wrote a programme to test Nicely's findings and, to his surprise, it confirmed the existence of a division bug on the Pentium. He e-mailed the results back to Wolfe, whose November 7 article in the *EE Times,* although it was the first story to mention the bug, received little mainstream attention. Mathisen then posted a message entitled "Glaring FDIV bug in the Pentium!" to the Internet newsgroup comp.sys.intel.

Newsgroups, one of the most widely used features of the Internet, are forums for information exchange on specialized topics ranging from Barney to bondage to banjo music. Thousands of them exist on the Internet, including company- and product-specific ones devoted to discussing IBM, Chrysler, Denny's, air, travel, cellular telephones or sugar cereals. Intel and its products had inevitably become the focus of a newsgroup: prior to November 1994, comp.sys.intel was a languid newsgroup frequented by computer sophisticates interested in discussing the fine points of Intel hardware. In the weeks after Mathisen's first posting, however, it was transformed into the setting of a heated national—in fact, global—debate, collecting more than 6,000 Pentium-related messages over a six-week period.

At first the discussion was limited to a small band of technical users who confirmed the error and determined its magnitude and frequency of occurrence. Then a slightly wider audience of Pentium-users chimed in, with incensed PhD students asking "How can I publish results that were computed on a defective chip?" The flurry of activity on comp.sys.intel had grown large enough by mid-November so that the controversy began to spill into the national press. It started when Steve Young, a technology reporter for CNN, received e-mail alerting him to the Pentium discussion. Internet newsgroups had recently become popular among reporters as a fishing pond for story leads, and Young logged on to comp.sys.intel several times to read the postings there.

Young's CNN report, which appeared on November 22, initiated a buzz of interest in the print media. Reporters at the *San Jose Mercury* and the San Francisco bureaus of the *New York Times* and *Wall Street Journal* simultaneously started preparing stories on the bug. One of the reporters, who spent time scanning comp.sys.intel with colleagues as he prepared his story, remarked: "Usually when you have a story about consumer beefs, it's hard to track down unhappy customers. But here you had all these inflammatory statements already in text form. You didn't even have to hit the keystrokes—you could just copy the messages onto your computer." The *New York Times* article, which appeared on Thanksgiving day, reprinted a maths problem gleaned from the Internet so customers could test for the error on their computers.

Press coverage of the controversy mushroomed in the following days, and Internet users, alerted to the comp.sys.intel discussion by the mainstream media, logged onto the newsgroup in ever greater numbers. As many as 250 people posted messages each day, while thousands more read their messages as spectators. In contrast to the well informed technical users who dominated the early discussion, many of these new posters were less concerned with the technical elements of the issue than with posting angry, emotional, and sometimes vicious messages attacking Intel for its failure to disclose the bug and its refusal to replace all flawed chips. Since the beginning of the controversy Intel had maintained a policy of granting replacement chips only to high-end users who could demonstrate that they needed a very high level of accuracy in division problems, and these users had to answer questions from Intel representatives before getting a new chip. "I know it's buzzing all over the Net", said Intel spokesman Howard High. "But there are maybe several dozen people that this would affect. So far we've only heard from one. It's reasonably rare." Intel had also initially denied that it was still sending flawed chips to customers, when in fact it was continuing to do so.

On November 27, 1994, faced with a growing chorus of hostility on the Net, Intel's president, Andy Grove, took the unprecedented step of posting his own message on comp.sys.intel. Apologizing for the situation and explaining that "no microprocessor is ever perfect," Grove pointed out that the bug was far less serious than the flaws that had been discovered in early versions of Intel's 386 and 486 chips. He made several blunders. First, because he did not have direct access to the Internet, he posted his message through a subordinate. Because the message did not bear Grove's address, many Internet users doubted the posting's authenticity, thereby fanning their distrust and anger. Secondly, he unflinchingly stood behind Intel's original "one-in-nine-billion" figure—and the idea that the bug was inconsequential for the vast majority of users—when several scientists and mathematicians on comp.sys.intel had posed credible challenges to this assertion. Most importantly, as the technical tone of his message suggests, Grove assumed he was addressing a small colloquium of experienced technical users, when in fact much of his audience was large, growing and diverse, and some of it resembled a lynch mob. Hence, Grove's message added more kindling to the fire. . . .

THE EMPOWERED STAKEHOLDER

. . . Technical experts lend stakeholders legitimacy and power, for they know what they are talking about and they know they deserve to be listened to. The virtual team of mathematicians and scientists who discovered the Pentium bug, documented its effects and later challenged Intel's assertions of probabilities and magnitudes believed their expertise and credibility matched or exceeded that of the Intel team that came up with the "one in nine billion" number and played down the bug's significance. Highly capable experts around the world were willing to spend time scrutinizing Intel's assumptions, rerunning its experiments, challenging its conclusions and finally besting Intel at its own highly technical game, all with clear and detailed explanations. "Usually in situations such as this, companies can give their interpretation of the problem and have it stick," said one reporter who covered the story. "But in this case, there were people that Intel could not snow—mathematicians and technicians—and that's why this issue just wouldn't go away. Intel couldn't give a fully plausible explanation." The nerds had been empowered.

The second way that the Internet can empower stakeholders is by becoming a source of swift and powerful consumer activism—a vehicle for a new Naderism. That is, not only will high-end technical users gain power, but also average customers—in this case Pentium owners or would-be owners. Consumers can find a louder voice through a form of electronic activism that facilitates contacts among like-minded people and allows them to achieve critical mass rapidly.

The Internet worked as a vehicle for consumer activism in two ways. First of all, it provided a meeting point for people who had a common concern. Without a specialized newsgroup like comp.sys.intel, it would otherwise have been quite difficult for dissatisfied Pentium owners to find others like themselves. Secondly, the Internet worked as an amplifier of opinion. That is, once a critical mass of people with a common problem had made contact their efforts to be heard gathered enough momentum that the mainstream press caught wind of the tempest and splashed it across the business pages of the nation's newspapers. The press reports in turn both intensified the Internet storm and afflicted investor confidence enough to move the financial markets; Intel stock weakened as the controversy grew, and the sell-off following IBM's shipment halt was so sharp that the New York Stock Exchange stopped trading in Intel shares for several hours.

Through the consumer activists' discussions on comp.sys.intel, numerous Pentium-owners shared anecdotes about the less-than-cordial treatment they received when calling Intel's 800 number, thereby forming a consensus picture of Intel as a stubborn, arrogant and uncaring corporation. By late November, many comp.sys.intel users were bashing Intel's "Spanish Inquisition" method of interrogating customers before deciding whether to replace their Pentium chips. "COMPANIES THAT SHOW CONTEMPT FOR THEIR

CUSTOMERS ARE SOON LEFT WITH NONE," chided one poster, who entitled his message "Business 101 for slow learners." Other consumer activist messages included:

> Subject: Bug: Issue is about Trust
> From [deleted]
> Date: Tue, 29 Nov 1994 14:53:20 GMT
> Message-ID: [deleted]
>
> In effect, you want us to knowingly accept a defective product and shut up about it.
>
> Understand something about business ethics, or just ethics in general. When a person buys a product, there is an assumption of trust that the product is free of defects and if there is a defect, the vendor or the manufacturer will assume responsibility for its replacement. Pure and simple. That trust is clearly violated.

> Subject: If Intel is to be held accountable . . .
> From [deleted]
> Date: 6 Dec 1994 02:04:02 GMT
> Message-ID: [deleted]
>
> If Intel is to be held accountable, it will have to be by you and me. You need to tell anyone you might think is considering purchasing a Pentium machine in the near future.
>
> No, you cannot just tell your other geeky engineering/compsci/science career friends. Sure they may care the most, but if they are not the ones with the cash, it ain't gonna matter. What must come about is a significant reduction in consumer confidence in Intel. If not, Intel will continue like nothing ever happened. . . .
>
> Spread the word far and wide.

Other posters expressed long-standing complaints about Intel, the prices they paid for hardware and the computer industry in general. "The REAL problem here is that we have a huge industry dominated by a single supplier," wrote one. "[I] suspect that a lot of the pent-up <grin> frustration you see here is due to people being nervous over the fact that Intel has them over a barrel." These messages were accurate, thoughtful and sometimes insightful.

The on-line consumer activism finally culminated in a Net petition organized by Jon Noring, a mechanical engineer at Lawrence Livermore National Laboratory who was in the market to buy a Pentium system. "I . . . firmly believed Intel was in the wrong," he later said, "and I felt it was my 'civic' duty to do something about it." On his own initiative, he drew up and circulated the petition on comp.sys.intel, demanding that Intel replace all Pentiums with no questions asked. "Your actions to downplay the FDIV bug situation have only created confusion and hostility among your loyal customers," said the petition. "We urge you to change course." Noring eventually collected nearly 2,400 signatures before sending it to Intel.

The third way that the Internet might encourage positive "democratic" empowerment is by fostering closer communications links between corporations and customer. In doing so it enables companies to act sooner and respond better. Although Intel was slow to grasp this concept and use it to its advantage, the Pentium episode clearly demonstrated that the Internet can be used very effectively as a focus group, a public relations tool and even a customer hotline. Several months after the affair Grove remarked that on-line services and the Internet "turn out to be very powerful ways to deliver customer support to a segment of our end customers."

The first, and easiest, way that managers can use the Internet to deal with customer issues is simply to read posting pertaining to their company. Once the story had broken in the popular press Intel began monitoring comp.sys.intel as a way to take the pulse of up-to-the-moment popular sentiment. Far more than telephone calls to a customer service line, which companies usually lump into general categories for their records, Internet messages provide companies with lasting, full-text records of customer feedback that capture customers' attitudes, emotions and technical details. It works something like an instant focus group, allowing companies to form a subtle and complex picture of customer issues. . . .

Reflecting on the significance of the Pentium episode, one comp.sys.intel user wrote: "This could turn out to be an historic turning point for the Net, never has it influenced . . . external events in this way. I think this is also the end of the spin doctor, they cannot do their stuff any more; the control of information has left their grasp." This user captured some important shifts in the traditional dynamics of consumer/public relations issues: as information becomes more decentralized and diffuse it is becoming harder for companies to put their "spin" on issues. In this way, too, the Internet has given stakeholders power.

The Internet, in effect, peels away many of the layers and filters that normally modulate company-customer discourse: attorneys, public relations staffs, customer service staffs. Intel acknowledged as much when it started staffing its telephone hotline with chip engineers during the crisis—a practice it decided to continue after the affair was over. Comp.sys.intel hosted an unfiltered, first-person discussion between customers, scientists, and CEOs, perhaps resembling a direct democracy, where every person, no matter how lowly, has the right to be heard.

This decentralization of information is part of what Jack Welch of General Electric has described as the trend toward "boundary-lessness." The Internet helps break down the boundaries of information between the firm and the outside world. Outside experts can get quick access to company-related information and use it to question the company's inside decisions. When Intel and IBM posted press releases or study results on their home pages on the Web Internet users quickly downloaded much of the information and circulated it on comp.sys.intel. At the same time company insiders can monitor and communicate directly with customers, outside experts and even competitors.

With these shifts comes a shift in power. Corporations—this scenario suggests—will get away with less as bottom-up and inside-out information flows replace traditional, top-down control, and as the Internet pokes holes in companies' traditional methods of information control. Increasingly, rather than setting the agenda by holding carefully orchestrated press conferences and issuing meticulously worded press releases, corporations will have the agenda set for them by outsiders who take advantage of the Internet's radical decentralization of power and information. It also does not take too much imagination to conceive of the Internet as a tool for whistle-blowers—the ideal place for employees to post smoking guns and other evidence of corporate misconduct. Companies will find it harder to disappear behind the corporate veil.

In short the optimistic scenario is this: by breaking down the normal channels of communication that companies use to guide and control public understanding of an issue, and by building new ones among customers and experts, the Internet serves a force for truth and justice, acting as a new source of ethical discipline for companies. Interpreted through this scenario the crucial events of autumn 1994 are these: Pentium's division bug, though minor, posed a real problem for a significant number of customers; Intel, in failing to disclose the bug, violated the trust of its immediate customers and its end users; by continuing to downplay the bug after it had been publicized and by refusing to replace the chips, Intel was acting irresponsibly; and finally, Intel got what it deserved when the alliance of comp.sys.intel and IBM forced an expensive capitulation. This, of course, is the interpretation that most comp.sys.intel users gave to the events. "Congratulations to the hundreds if not thousands of comp.sys. internet posts," said one user, "on being the driving force in bringing Intel to finally do the right thing!"

THE VIGILANTE STAKEHOLDER

While the empowerment scenario is quite attractive, there is another, less optimistic view that may capture the essence of the Pentium episode more accurately. On this scenario, the Internet has the tendency of a street mob to run wild—to become electronic barbarians at a cyberspace gate, clamouring to punish competent managers for their supposed misdeeds. As non-issues are fanned into crises by few on-line firebrands, society as a whole loses. The half-billion dollars that Intel wrote off to pay for the Pentium replacement was an amount that could have built several schools or hospitals, or could have been used to create jobs. Such an enormous loss, moreover, would have destroyed most companies, and would have bankrupted Intel a few years earlier, thereby depriving the USA of one of its high-technology champions.

The Pentium controversy, at bottom, revolved around a tiny technical flaw of the sort not uncommon to all computer hardware. It is generally accepted that new microprocessors contain a multitude of glitches—most of them minor—that go undetected until after the chips' release. Early versions of Intel's 486 chips, for example, failed to perform trigonometry correctly. In fact, the article in the *Electronic Engineering Times* November 7 about the bug hardly generated a ripple of discussion at Comdex, the computer industry's annual convention that began November 16, indicating that the flaw was simply not that serious. Thus, by holding companies to unrealistic levels of perfection, customers only cheat themselves, paying higher prices for companies to run lengthy tests on all products and waiting longer for new products to appear on the shelves.

This scenario views the Internet as the latest and most extreme evolution of the modern American media. The Net is not, of course, part of the establishment media, the major television networks and big city papers, nor is it part of the so-called "new media" of radio talk shows, cable television, direct mail, and niche publishing. Rather, the Internet might evolve into another order of media altogether; one that takes the adjectives that describe the "new media"—diffuse, abundant, populist, unpredictable, rapid and less regulated—to their extreme. It could evolve into a kind of hypermedia, with serious negative consequences.

The Internet, for example, wields its power without any restraints or accountability. Even the most outrageous forms of new media are at some level subordinate to the interests of the organization that produces them: TV ratings, government pressure, shareholder sentiment or public image. Comp.sys.intel, by contrast, was a non-organization with no hierarchy, no permanent staff and a budget of zero. In fact it had no physical location other than its existence in the nebulous information web of cyberspace. It lived a virtual, almost metaphysical existence. Thus, while media companies can be irresponsible, the Internet by its very nature is non-responsible: it wields its headless, strategyless, unaccountable power however its users arbitrarily prefer. Moreover, unlike government agencies and conventional interest groups, companies cannot lobby the Internet, do deals with it, wait for a change in its leadership, make strategic political contributions or try to co-opt it—because there is no "it."

The absence of accountability was reflected in the hundreds of angry, unrestrained and often moronic postings that started to overwhelm comp.sys.intel once the Pentium controversy hit the popular press. This was a lunch mob, and the words of one comp.sys.intel user—"THE HELL WITH INTEL"—summarized the content of most of its flame messages. The members of the lynch mob were rather ignorant of both the technical and business aspects of the situation. Like participants in a schlocky TV talk show, they tended to value emotional opinion-airing for its own sake, however ill-informed or exaggerated it may have been. (They could also be flat-out rude: after reading someone else's message, one comp.sys.intel user responded, "Your argument has no substance, and you are a crass idiot.") In fact, on the Internet the more extreme or off-base opinion gets the most attention. And, like members of a lynch mob, the emotional statements of some incited others to even more extreme polemics, reinforcing one another's anger. In contrast to the thoughtful, informative, and reasonable messages of the technical experts and consumer activists, these messages often verged on hysterical.

Subject: ANDY GROVE: RESIGN NOW
From: [deleted]
Date: Thu, 15 Dec 1994 19:52:59 GMT
Message-ID: [deleted]

Andy Grove has proven his utter incompetence running a company and should be asked to step down now.

Subject: Re: EVERYONE GETS A REPLACEMENT!!!!!
From: [deleted]
Date: 14 Dec 1990 01:56:43 GMT
Message-ID: [deleted]

. . . . Lie if you must to get a replacement. Intel's already indicated how much respect they have for you. So screw 'em.

Subject: INTEL–You Disappointed ME!!!!!
    From: [deleted]
    Date: 8 Dec 1994 15:30:58 GMT
    Message-ID: [deleted]

. . . I can't believe Intel would be so petty and treat their customers like sh*t after the SALE! Especially the single user who doesn't have the clout of a major corporation/company. Your chips have a warranty! Whether users have a need or not is none of Intel's concern! What Intel should be concerned with is keeping their customers happy and replacing all of the buggy chips ASAP! This means individual customers as well!

I refuse to get suckered into buying any current buggy pentium machines and going through some ridiculous INTERVIEW where Intel determines if your needs warrant a replacement chip. BULLSH*T!!!!!!

H-E-L-L-Ooooooooo! Who is the paying customer here? Now if Intel were giving away buggy chips, maybe, just maybe I could understand their "profit margin" mentality. Intel . . . after monopolizing the PC chip industry for so long, you disappoint me as a PREVIOUS customer! You have made millions and you still don't understand who got you to where you are/were today . . . THE CUSTOMER!

The new media gets personal. It attacks. Rush Limbaugh has built a following of millions by relentlessly vilifying Bill Clinton, "feminazis," and other individuals and organizations. Just as on the "Rush Limbaugh Show," hype can often dominate reality on the Internet as people deliver ever more hyperbolic and iconoclastic statements in the interests of getting attention. The Internet furthermore is an even more engaging outlet for populist anger than talk shows, for whereas "Rush's" disciples can only get airtime by calling the show and letting Rush use their calls for his own purposes, Netters can express their opinions directly to thousands of other readers and speak in the same forum as Andy Grove. Many use this opportunity to make drive-by attacks against their favourite targets—a sort of hit-and-run vigilantism. . . .

Managers must contemplate and prepare for the day in the not-too-distant future when any disgruntled employee can log on to a bulletin board and complain about their company's labour policies or everyday operations. Information that is not supposed to see the light of day can be paraded before a group of unknown outsiders ranging from nutcases to Nobel laureates, from journalists to members of Congressional staffs. The Internet is a public stage on which just about anything can be posted—a virtual loose cannon on a virtual rolling deck. In this way, it might represent another phase in the decline of restraint and standards in the American media.

Incidentally, the vigilante scenario also places small companies at risk. An engineer at a mid-sized Boston-area software firm said recently that his company was forced into an unwanted programme change after a corporate client posted a vicious letter on the Internet. The software maker had refused the client's requests for the change, believing that the software problem was a "very minor, very obscure situation" and that the proposed change would not be in other clients' best interests. After the client posted its "mean and aggravated" message to the Internet urging other customers to complain to the software firm, however, the company reluctantly agreed to make the revision. "We fear the Internet," said the engineer. "There are now two ways for a customer to get us to do something to a programme: buy obnoxious amounts of software to get some leverage with us, or write to the Internet." He said the company's management also feared its programmers communicating directly with customers via the Internet, bypassing the company's normal communications chain.

IMPLICATIONS FOR MANAGERS

The Pentium case suggests several important lessons:

1. *If companies are not alert to the Internet's multifaceted roles, or attempt to use it clumsily, they can be caught in a meat grinder.* The simultaneous overlapping roles of the Internet thus make it a dangerous place to ignore, and also a dangerous place to play. Managers assuming they are winning a chess match on a single chess board might learn abruptly they are losing a complex game of three-dimensional chess. The incongruity of Intel's politely worded messages on comp.sys.intel, thanking customers for their "continued patience," amidst a frothing sea of anger and denunciation, indicated the feebleness of old-style damage-control in this new volatile mixture.

2. *Histrionic messages may secure disproportionate attention—on the Net and in the media—leading managers to dismiss Internet activism in its entirety and thereby overlooking important hazards and disguising genuine opportunities to develop closer, on-line relationships with their customers.*

3. *Although the two are linked, victories and defeats on the Internet should not be confused with victories and defeats in the marketplace.* Intel stock rebounded strongly after the announcement of the replace-on-request policy, climbing from a low of 57$^{13}\!/_{16}$ on December 19 to 73$^3\!/_8$ on February 6. And sales of Pentium-based computers remained strong through December and January, even continuing to grow during the crisis. IBM, for its part, lost revenue on the sale of its Pentium PCs; as the number of chips that Intel allocated to each of its customers was based on sales of the previous period, IBM's shipment halt restricted its supply of Pentiums for months to come. Thus, another lesson is clear:

4. *The Net's acceleration of information speeds up the decision-making process for companies.* To some extent this is healthy, since the world is moving faster and faster. Matters that might have taken weeks or months to resolve themselves before the advent of high-speed electronic communications can now explode in days. But issues that might not have gathered enough momentum to be noticed by the general public can now quickly snowball and catch companies by surprise, creating a deer-in-the-headlights effect. Managers might find themselves in the position of having to act decisively with only limited information, forcing them into hasty and ill-informed decisions. Intel was thus an unwitting pioneer in a new era of crisis management—one in which high-speed communications accelerate the pace of corporate decision-making to a point that decisions do not receive the care and deliberation they require.

5. *Companies embroiled in Internet controversies may need to rely heavily on close examination of postings, on managers with some "feel" for the Net, and on how the establishment media seems to be interpreting the traffic on the Net.*

6. *Posting by companies and executives are fully public; they can and often will be used against their authors.* Because the Internet is a radical new communications technology, both these scenarios are inevitably speculative. The Net may be to the 21st century what the steam engine was to the 19th century and electricity to the early 20th century. Like all important advances in technology the Internet will bring changes, some marvellous, but some troublesome, some frightening. The most conspicuous evils of the Internet—pornography accessible to children, newsgroups for building bombs—have already received extensive discussion in the mainstream press.

CONCLUSION

There is general jubilation in American whenever the media is made more accessible, populist and flexible. When standards are relaxed and more people are given the chance to express their opinions to a public audience—whether they be talk-show participants, rap artists or publishers of specialty publications—the phenomenon is hailed as democratic, free, open-minded and empowering. Attempts to restrain or filter media content, on the other hand, are often equated with censorship, tyranny and a close-mindedness running contrary to the spirit of the First Amendment. To be sure, a wide-open media plays a vital role in a democratic society, including acting as a watchdog for ethical lapses of the agents of capitalism and giving voice to the concerns of less powerful stakeholders.

But a medium in which filters and standards are removed entirely poses real problems. Perhaps the biggest danger to the American media is not censorship or a tyranny of the Establishment. Perhaps it is the danger of chaos overwhelming truly democratic dialogue; of absolute freedom overwhelming responsibility and accountability; of emotionalism triumphing over reason. The fear of Big Brother has always been lurking somewhere in the American consciousness, but perhaps we should also be concerned about the ability of individuals or small, militia-like groups to wield power without accountability. As the Pentium episode demonstrated, this can easily descend into an irrational tyranny of the few. And highly successful, technically adept and fundamentally *good* companies such as Intel can be the victims. For well *and* ill, the media is a central force in business ethics, and these two scenarios indicate some of these issues that managers and business ethicists will grapple with in the years to come.

NOTE

1. Claire Bernstein, "Consumer power unleashed by the 'Net'," *Toronto Star*, 9 January 1995, p. C3.

Ethical Dilemmas in the Use of Information Technology: An Aristotelian Perspective

Michael D. Myers and Leigh Miller

In recent years, the social and ethical issues associated with the use of information technology have attracted increasing attention (Arnheim, 1990; Bainbridge, 1989; Cliffe, 1991; Higham, 1991; Watson, 1991). As more and more information is stored on computer-based information systems, these systems are having a dramatic impact on people, organizations, and society as a whole. However, the debates in the literature about social control and privacy, security and reliability, and ethics and professional responsibilities (see Dejoie, Fowler, & Paradice, 1991; Dunlop & Kling, 1991; Ermann, Williams, & Gutierrez, 1990) reveal some fundamental disagreements, often about first principles. For example, although some argue that strict regulatory controls should be placed on the keeping of personal records, others argue that legislation restricts personal freedom, and that regulations only add unnecessary costs to businesses and other organizations.

In this article, we suggest that a fruitful and interesting way to conceptualize some of the moral and ethical issues associated with the use of information technology is to apply the principles of Aristotle's ethics to this topic. A number of other ethical frameworks have been suggested for discussing computer-related issues, such as the utilitarian and Kantian theories (see Ermann et al., 1990). However, we believe that framing the moral and ethical choices associated with information technology in Aristotelian terms draws attention to the fact that there are fundamental *dilemmas* to be addressed; there are no simple solutions to the ethical concerns that are being raised, and satisfying one moral principle may only compromise another.

In this article, we discuss the ethical dilemmas associated with the use of information technology. These dilemmas are discussed in relation to the four areas suggested by Dejoie et al. (1991): (a) privacy, (b) information accuracy, (c) access to information, and (d) intellectual property rights. The dilemmas associated with all four areas are illustrated with references to recent legal developments in Australia and New Zealand.

ARISTOTLE'S ETHICS

Aristotle, the Greek philosopher, lived from 384 BC to 322 BC. He wrote about ethics and politics and was a tutor to Alexander the Great (Barker, 1969; More, 1985). As Aristotle's philosophy developed, he more and more came to think of the universe as a vast complex of organisms each striving to attain the end assigned to it by nature.

> It is thought that every activity, artistic or scientific, in fact every deliberate action or pursuit, has for its object the attainment of some good. We may therefore assent to the view which has been expressed that "the good" is "that at which all things aim." (Thomson, 1970, p. 25)

The Greek word for end is *telos*. Hence the Aristotelian system is described as teleological.

Aristotle said that to become a good man you must behave like a good man; then you will know what goodness is. Ethics, he said, is the art of making that discovery. Every activity, artistic or scientific, in fact every deliberate action or pursuit, has as its object the attainment of some good. However, if there is a conflict between the two ends, both of which might be regarded as good, a choice should be made based upon what is the higher or supreme good. Aristotle's philosophy highlights the fact that there are likely to be many such conflicts or ethical dilemmas in human activity.

A fundamental dilemma that Aristotle highlighted is as follows:

> There may be a conflict between the good of the individual and the good of the community.

Aristotle said that in cases where the good of the community conflicts with that of the individual, the good of the community is a greater and more perfect good. This is not to deny that the good of the individual is worthwhile, but what is good for a nation or a city has a higher, diviner quality.

In Aristotelian terms, the terms *morals* and *ethics* can be defined as follows:

- Morals are defined as conformity to socially accepted standards of conduct. Therefore, murder is morally wrong.
- Ethics are defined as conformity to codes of moral principles. Therefore, breaching client confidentiality and trust is unethical in many professions.

We now discuss the ethical dilemmas associated with the use of information technology in relation to four areas: (a) privacy, (b) information accuracy, (c) access to information, and (d) intellectual property rights (see Dejoie et al., 1991).

Four Fundamental Ethical Dilemmas

Privacy

The first fundamental ethical dilemma is related to the issue of privacy. Privacy is an aspect of human dignity, but because information technology is capable of storing and retrieving copious volumes of information about people, questions arise as to citizens' rights to privacy (see Niblett, 1984; Simons, 1982; Tapper, 1983; Wacks, 1980).

In Aristotelian terms, the ethical dilemma with regard to privacy can be stated as follows:

> The information that is kept about people in an information system is property, and as such this property may be very valuable to the owner and user of the system. However, the good of the organization that uses this information may be in conflict with the good of the individual.

In a legal sense, there are four major aspects of privacy that may be applicable here:

1. Intrusion upon an individual's solitude (trespass; nuisance).
2. Public disclosure of confidential information about an individual (breach of confidence).
3. Publicity that places an individual in a bad light in public (defamation).
4. Appropriation of an individual's name or likeness without consent (copyright or character merchandising; the tort of appropriation).

In many countries it is recognized that every individual has an inherent right to privacy and a right to protect him- or herself from the misuse and unlicensed use of personal information. What this right to privacy logically implies is that an individual (data subject) should be able to decide with whom that information is shared and for what purpose that information is given. However, if the owners of a database were required to obtain permission from every single data subject beforehand, data collection could become expensive. Here is a fundamental dilemma with regard to privacy in the use of information technology: The good that accrues to the person or organization that uses the technology may bear an inverse relation to the good of the individual.

This fundamental dilemma can be illustrated with reference to recent developments in New Zealand. The Privacy Commissioner's Act was passed into law in New Zealand in 1992. This law established the office of the Privacy Commissioner to investigate complaints of interferences with privacy. This law, in effect, also authorized data matching between government departments such as the Inland Revenue and Social Welfare Department. This law was justified by the government in collective terms, that is, the government needed to be able to prevent fraud to save money. However, what this law also meant for the data subject was that information given for one specific purpose could be used for another without the data subject's consent.

The Privacy Act was passed into law on July 1, 1993. The Act applies to every person or organization in New Zealand in reference to personal information held in any capacity other than for the purposes of their personal, family, or household affairs. The Act controls how agencies collect, use, disclose, store, and give access to personal information (see Privacy Commissioner, 1993). However, although Information Principle 9 of the Act says that, "An agency that holds personal information that was obtained in connection with one purpose shall not use the information for any other purpose," the Act authorizes some government agencies to undertake information matching programs, providing these programs comply with the restrictions of the Privacy Act.

The New Zealand government has made a clear distinction between the public and private sectors as far as privacy is concerned. Whereas organizations in the private sector are not allowed to engage in any data-matching activities, the Act authorizes data-matching programs by government agencies. The government appears to regard the public good as overriding the individual's right to privacy, but it regards the individual good as more important than the private sector use of personal information. The New Zealand approach is one attempt to address this fundamental dilemma with regard to privacy in the use of information technology.

Information Accuracy

The second fundamental ethical dilemma is related to the issue of information accuracy. As Mason (1991) pointed out, misinformation can have disastrous consequences for an individual, especially when the party with the inaccurate information has an advantage in power and authority. Mistakes can be made, and the consequences may be more than just initial embarrassment; for example, wrongful identification may mean that someone is confused with a bankrupt of the same name.

In New Zealand in the late 1980s, two of the largest credit bureaus attempted to placate public concern about information accuracy in their databases by allowing anyone to inspect his or her file and, if necessary, amend the information. With the Privacy Act of 1993, individuals were given the legal right to have access to personal information held by any agency and to request the correction of such information (Privacy Commissioner, 1993).

We believe that there is a fundamental ethical dilemma related to the issue of information accuracy, however, one that is not so readily solved. This relates to the point in time at which data is collected. Although the data about individuals may be accurate at the time of capture, over time the data subject's circumstances are likely to change. In many systems there is no provision for old data to be updated at regular intervals, nor is there any provision for data to be destroyed. This means that a data subject, by definition, may carry into the future the burdens of the past.

An example of this occurred in New Zealand in 1993. The Social Welfare Department sent a letter regarding a child to the parents, even though the child had died some 2 years earlier. The upset that this caused the parents and the resulting furor was reported extensively in the mass media.

Access to Information

The third fundamental ethical dilemma is related to the issue of information access. The information that is generated by an information system is generally accessible to the user of that system. But should an individual be able to gain access to the information that is held on him or her in a database? One problem here is that not all citizens have the necessary skills or knowledge to be in a position to access the information that may be available. Also, there may be no legal requirement in some countries for public or private organizations to give access to interested persons (although in New Zealand this requirement is enshrined in Principle 7 of the Privacy Act of 1993).

In Western democracies, the free access to information is generally regarded as an inherent right. However, information access usually implies more than just being able to view one's file periodically; it also means having the power to destroy outmoded data or amend the same. The problem here is one of ownership. Who owns the data on an individual? And who is responsible for the accuracy of the data?

Most information systems professionals would no doubt agree that a key aspect of any database is the integrity of the data. For this reason alone, it could be argued that data subjects should have the right to amend or destroy information. However, there are practical problems in effecting this. For example, some individuals (e.g., criminals) might seek to falsify their own records.

We believe that a possible solution to this problem of information access is a commitment to a relevant code of ethics with both national and international standards to protect the data subject. In this regard, the United Kingdom's Data Protection Act of 1984, Australia's Privacy Act of 1988, and New Zealand's Privacy Act of 1993 are examples of legislation in which an attempt was made to regularize the procedures of data collection and data storage (McKeough & Stewart, 1991). In New Zealand, the Privacy Act of 1993 allows for industry codes of practice to be developed. The Privacy Act of 1993 also allows an individual to request the correction of information, but an agency is not required to correct such information if it is unwilling to do so.

Intellectual Property Rights

The fourth fundamental ethical dilemma is related to the issue of intellectual property rights. How can information be protected for the author/owner when that same information can be copied (or pirated) and transmitted to the other side of the world in a matter of seconds? The dilemma here is one of conferring monopoly rights upon individuals or companies while guaranteeing access to information for all.

The difficulties in upholding these monopoly rights can be seen in a recent Australian case from the Federal Court in Adelaide. Here, the ease with which piracy can occur is contrasted with the penalty the judge inflicted. It is worth mentioning that the piracy of software throughout the world costs software developers (the copyright holders) millions of dollars in royalty payments each year.

Irvine v. Carson *(1992)22 IPR 107*

In contravention of both the Copyright Act of 1968 (Commonwealth of Australia) and the Crimes Act of 1914 (Commonwealth of Australia), the unemployed defendant was part of a piracy network with 100 other persons. The network swapped or sold pirated copies of computer programs at a cheap price. In the preceding 12 months, the defendant had sold disks worth approximately A$3,000.00. A total of 2,000 copied programs, photocopies of the operating manuals, and two computers were seized from the defendant's premises by the police.

In his judgment, the judge said:

1. It must be firmly stated that the illegal copying of works protected by copyright and the illegal trading in infringing copies, are serious crimes. When flagrant breaches of copyright protection are detected, the offenders must realize that the consequences will be heavy and that the punishments imposed by the courts will reflect the need, because of the difficulty in detection, to make an example of the offenders by way of general deterrence to others in the community who may also be minded to disregard copyright protection.

2. All of the infringing copies of the computer programs and copies of the operating manuals, plus the two computers, are to be forfeited to the Commonwealth of Australia.

3. The losses that the destruction and forfeiture orders would mean to the defendant are to be taken into account when assessing the penalty.

Although the judge commented on the serious nature of the flagrant breaches of copyright, the punishment inflicted was, in fact, relatively minor.

The defendant was convicted and ordered to perform 120 hours of community service within 8 months and to pay A$500 for the costs of prosecution.

CONCLUSIONS

In this article we suggested that a fruitful and interesting way to conceptualize some of the moral and ethical issues associated with the use of information technology is to apply the principles of Aristotle's ethics to this topic. We argued that there are fundamental ethical dilemmas to be addressed in the areas of privacy, information accuracy, access to information, and intellectual property rights.

In an ideal world, what is desirable is a universal commitment to altruism rather than a narrow commitment to self-interest. In an ideal world, the rights of the individual would be in perfect harmony with the benefits for the whole community. However, in this article we showed that in this not-so-ideal world there are fundamental dilemmas to be addressed by researchers, lawmakers, and those involved with the management of information technology. What is good for a government or company may be in conflict with what is good for the individual. Using examples from Australia and New Zealand, we showed that attempting to balance these different interests within a legal framework is possible, even if extraordinarily difficult.

References

Arnheim, M. (1990). The protection of privacy. *Solicitors Journal, 134*(31), 874–877.
Bainbridge, D. (1989). Computer misuse: What should the law do? *Solicitors Journal, 133*(15), 466–467.
Barker, E. (1969). *The politics of Aristotle.* London: Oxford University Press.
Cliffe, V. (1991). Computer insecurity: A real threat? *The Law Society's Gazette, 6,* 18–20.
Dejoie, B., Fowler, G., & Paradice, D. (Eds.). (1991). *Ethical issues in information systems.* Boston: Boyd & Fraser.
Dunlop, C., & Kling, R. (Eds.). (1991). *Computerization and controversy.* San Diego, CA: Academic.
Ermann, M., Williams, M. B., & Gutierrez, C. (1990). *Computers, ethics and society.* New York: Oxford University Press.
Higham, N. (1991). Software protection versus interoperability. *The Law Society's Gazette, 9,* 27–28.
Mason, R. (1991). Four ethical issues in information systems. In B. Dejoie, G. Fowler, & D. Paradice (Eds.), *Ethical issues in information systems.* Boston: Boyd & Fraser.
McKeough, J., & Stewart, A. (1991). Intellectual property in Australia. Sydney, Butterworths.
More, T. (1985). *Utopia.* London: Penguin.
Privacy Commissioner. (1993). *Privacy Act 1993 fact sheets.* Auckland, New Zealand: Author.
Niblett, B. (1984). Data Protection Act 1894. London: Oyez Longman.
Simons, G. L. (1982). *Privacy in the computer age.* London: NCC Publications.
Tapper, C. (1983). *Computer law* (3rd ed.). London: Longman.
Thomson, J. A. K. (1970). *Aristotle—Ethics.* London: Penguin.
Wacks, R. (1980). *The protection of privacy.* London: Sweet & Maxwell.
Watson, I. (1991). The right client database. *The Law Society's Gazette, 4,* 10–20.

EVALUATING A CASE STUDY:
ASSESSING EMBEDDED LEVELS

The goal in this series is for you to be able to write an essay that critically evaluates a business problem involving ethical issues. Your essay should include an examination of business practice as well as related ethical dimensions. In Chapter 4, we discussed how to bring the ethical dimensions to the fore through the use of detection questions. These were put side by side with the principles of professional practice.

In this chapter, we compare these two types of issues. This comparison can be accomplished in multiple ways; the one offered here invokes a technique that rates professional practice as having three levels of embeddedness: surface, medium, and deep. *Embeddedness* refers to how deeply ingrained a proposition is to the essential nature of the subject area being examined. The level of interaction allows you to see at a glance how professional practice issues, cost issues, and ethical issues conflict.

You need a model of some type to evaluate the professional practice issues, cost considerations, and ethical principles that may conflict. When ethical issues and professional practical issues conflict, you do not *automatically* choose either. Some ethical problems can be solved easily and do not require forgoing the dictates of professional practice. At other times, an ethical problem must be solved in such a way that professional practices must be overridden.

You need a methodology for comparison. The *embedded concept model* is one such methodology. I illustrate how this works with several examples that employ a chart to clarify the ways the concepts conflict. You may also want to use computer technology to chart your responses. A conventional approach is to present these differences through narrative description. The chart is no substitute for solid narrative description, but it simplifies and makes visual the model I propose.

Case 1.

You are vice-president for sales of a life insurance company. You have noticed that many policyholders have been given information regarding future interest rates on universal life policies that have proven to have been too optimistic. As a result, seven to ten years after taking out a policy, policyholders must cut back on their death benefit or pay higher premiums (because the cash values that were projected to accrue and offset higher mortality rates in later years never materialized). Since the cash values were not sufficient to support the policies, a policyholder must pay more or cut back on the benefits of the policy. Both alternatives cause policyholders to feel that they have been cheated.

As a result of this situation, you propose that all of your company's agents project interest rates one-half point *below* what the policies are currently paying when the agents attempt to make a sale. The agents are very reluctant to do this because they believe that they will lose many potential customers to agents from other companies who project rates *even higher* than the policies currently pay. The current professional practice is to quote the current interest rate.

Let us examine this situation via professional practice issues, ethical issues, and cost issues. Each of these areas is important in forming a business decision.

Professional Practice Issues

1. A professional is required only to follow the law and the guidelines of the professional association. Nothing in the insurance industry's standards requires projecting universal life policies at one-half point below current values offered by the company.
2. Going beyond the law and the association's guidelines could be perceived as raising the standard that other insurance companies would be required to follow. Meeting this additional standard could require the use of funds that had not been budgeted.

Ethical Issues

1. A person who buys an insurance policy expects the rates quoted to be accurate projections. Such a policy seems to be a simple example of telling the truth.
2. *Informed* consent is necessary for autonomous decision making.

Cost Issues

1. Stating interest rates one-half point below what is current may result in some lost sales, the problem is not considered serious. In fact, there are sales opportunities for companies associated with honest policies.
2. Additional costs would be incurred in implementing a new system.

Analysis of the Illustration Practices at XYZ Insurance

	Surface	Medium	Deep
Professional Practice Issues			
A professional is required to follow only the law and the professional association's guidelines		x	
The insurance company may be accused of raising the standard	x		
Ethical Issues			
Personal integrity and truthfulness should be followed.			x
Only a truly *informed* consent satisfies the conditions of autonomy			x

	Surface	Medium	Deep
Cost Issues			
New guidelines may affect future sales			x
Additional costs may be incurred in implementing a new system		x	

In this simple case, the ethical issues override those of cost or professional practice. That means that ethical guidelines are "easier" to follow. When a great disparity exists between the embeddedness of one alternative as opposed to the other (meaning deep as opposed to surface), that direction should drive the decision. One should implement the other side as it is possible. For example, in this case, the insurance company should implement the program of projecting life insurance cash values one-half point below the current rate it offers. It should do this because the professional issues are not deeply embedded, the ethical issues are deeply embedded, and the cost issues are not deeply embedded (and the policy may actually become an advantage).

Case 2.

In other cases, the choice is not so simple. You are a regional director of the World Health Organization. One of your duties is to supervise the distribution of birth control devices to women in less-developed countries. The product of choice has been the intrauterine device (IUD) that has proved to be effective and inexpensive. The problem is that in the United States, several hundred users of the IUD have contracted pelvic inflammatory infections that have been linked to use of the IUD. These infections can cause sterility and death.*

ABC Corporation, a large multinational company, has a considerable inventory of IUDs that it cannot sell in the United States. The company would rather not write off its entire inventory and has consequently made a very attractive offer to sell the World Health Organization all of its existing inventory and assist in distributing the product regionally. As regional director, you must decide whether to accept ABC's offer to supply IUDs for the World Health Organization's program for women in less-developed countries.

Professional Practice Issues

1. As a professional in the public health field, your responsibility is to choose the policy that maximizes health and minimizes the health risks in the general population.

---

*I have heard that many of the structural problems with the IUD that caused pelvic inflammatory infection have now been rectified. I am not competent to comment on this; nevertheless, for this case, let us assume that these problems still obtain.

2. Sexual activity without birth control in less-developed countries will lead to an increasing population that, in turn, will lead to severe poverty and mass starvation.

3. Mass starvation kills millions; pelvic inflammatory infections kill hundreds. Thus, it is better to save the many (in the spirit of the profession's mission).

Ethical Issues

1. Each person's life is precious.
2. The end of saving more lives does not justify the means of sacrificing others.

Cost Issues

1. ABC Corporation is willing to give the World Health Organization a substantial price break on its existing inventory of IUDs. This price break will allow the World Health Organization to serve more women of child-bearing age than its original strategic plan had projected. ABC's offer to assist in regional distribution will save the World Health Organization additional money.

2. White knights are not lining up at your door to help you fulfill the mission of this program, and profit is also a part of the company's mission.

Analysis of Population Control in the Third World

	Surface	Medium	Deep
Professional Practice Issues			
Public health mission to preserve the health of as many as possible			x
Sexual activity without birth control leads to mass starvation			x
The end justifies the means			x
Ethical Issues			
Human life is precious			x
The end does not justify the means			x
Cost Issues			
ABC's inventory problem can be used to serve many women			x
ABC's offer can be your gain			x
The World Health Organization needs help from someone or it may be unable to continue this program			x

This case differs from Case 1 because the professional, ethical, and cost guidelines are equal. In this case, the dictates of the ethical imperative must be followed because it is more deeply embedded in a person's worldview than is the imperative of professional practice or cost issues. The components of ethics enter the worldview generally as a feature of a person's humanity.[1] The imperatives of professionalism enter the worldview as one of many modes of personal fulfillment; the imperatives of cost enter the worldview as modes of day-to-day practical consumption. Although many people may create pessimistic scenarios (such as state of nature) to the contrary, most daily practical business decisions will not cause your death or that of a family member. It may cause you to be discharged, drastically affecting your lifestyle. In the United States (at the writing of this book), making such a decision almost never causes an individual to face starvation.[2]

My experience has been that businesspeople are prone to hyperbole when they describe the consequences of an ethical decision that entails the loss of money and worldly goods. This overstatement culture has the effect of blocking businesspeople from taking the right action because they fear exaggerated consequences.[3]

As with scientific theories, the dictates of a universally binding imperative founded on generic structures trump those of a particular person's individual interests. More details on this appear in the "Evaluating a Case Study" section in Chapter Six.

In this essay, the main concern is the ability to assess the levels of embeddedness. Some common problems that my students have made in performing ths assessment follow:

1. *Not giving the imperatives of professional practice or cost issue their due.* Remember that whether you assess embeddedness via a chart or through narrative paragraphs, you are working from your original analysis of the problem. A failure to uncover all the important facets will be reflected in your depiction of embeddedness. You will notice gaps in the reasoning and will feel that something is missing. If this happens, go back over the issues lists. Rewrite the case in your own words; expand or recast the case in some way. By doing this, you become the author and are forced to recognize key elements in the case as presented.

2. *Seeing everything at the same level of embeddedness.* You need to view embeddedness as a way to describe the degree to which the professional

---

[1]For a further discussion of the mechanics, see Chapter One of *Basic Ethics*.

[2]Of course, the dead hero problem applies here. Would one prefer to be a live coward (here understood to mean a moral coward) or a dead hero (here understood to mean someone who has suffered for his or her beliefs)? This is not an easy question and lies at the heart of all discussions of Business Ethics.

[3]It is not the worst thing in the world to have to step back and live on less. It has been my personal experience that the essential elements of personal happiness have no price tag. Truly supported caring relationships cannot be taken away from a person no matter how hard times befall (except through some unrelated event—such as disease or accident).

practice or ethical issues or cost issues, is essential to the case. A less essential issue should be given less consideration. To better understand the essential structure of a professional practice, prepare short justifications of your choice of that element as an issue in the case. As you prepare justifications, think about each element in its relation to the whole. If that relation could not be different without seriously altering the whole, then it is essential. If you can find substitutes that would work just as well, then the relation is incidental.

3. *Listing too many professional, ethical, and cost issues.* This is the flip side to step 1. You have given too much detail that is not essential to the case at hand, or you are listing one issue in a number of different ways. In either event, preparing an essential description of your elements (as in step 2) can help you shorten your issue list to only those required for your evaluation.

Good solid work avoiding these mistakes will enable you to create a more satisfactory result in the argumentative stage, in which you may finally apply your ethical theory to your annotated embeddedness charts.

Macro and Micro Cases*

Macro Case 1. You are the director of human resource development of a Fortune 500 company. You have become aware that the composition of the company's management workforce is almost exclusively white and male. The company has a very high percentage of women and minorities in the lowest-paying jobs so that if the Equal Opportunity Commission reviewed the total numbers, they would look pretty good. However, you brought this issue to the attention of another director, who thought your concerns were crazy: "What does it matter who is running the company? As long as we're both employed and there's no hanky panky going on, what's there to worry about?"

You believe that this director's comments reflect the company's general sentiment. You wonder, however, if the limited managerial diversity may limit the corporate strategic vision. After all, the U.S. marketplace is diverse and having people from varied backgrounds, genders, and races might actually enhance business prospects.

If you put yourself out on the line for an unpopular program, you may be fired. Is this issue worth *that?* You have a comfortable life and a great 401K plan that is filled with company stock, although you have two mortgages on

---

*For more on macro and micro cases, see the overview on p. 105.

your house. Your daughter is headed for college next year. Is discretion the better part of valor?

On the other hand, if you say nothing and a problem should arise, you might be in a difficult position. To clarify your thoughts, write a policy memo addressed to the CEO. In the memo, describe the problem and what you believe should be done to remedy it. After you finish that memo, write a private note that determines whether you should or should not send the memo to the CEO. In each case, be sure to survey professional, practice, ethical, and cost issues.

Macro Case 2. You are the copartner of a famous fashion house, Maria Haut-bas, whose sales figures in the last few years have been lagging. You are considering switching your advertising account from Sacher & Sacher to Mortimer Grunge, Ltd. Sacher & Sacher created an image of elegance that worked for the high end of your line but seemed old-fashioned to younger buyers. As a result, the young market has not had much interest in your line.

Grunge has developed a theme to position you on the "edge." This means that people will notice you, and the contrast from your previous image will draw customers. Grunge suggests doing this by employing anorexic models with a light pallor who appear to be heroin addicts. These women are often in a state of undress or a situation that suggests prostitution as well as drug addiction. However, other aspects of the scene (such as the automobile behind them or the apartment in which they are placed) connote great material wealth.

You understand the concept behind Grunge's campaign. You also believe that it will work. The problem is whether you are doing anything wrong in creating such a campaign. Anorexia is a serious problem among young women. Are you glorifying it? Drug addiction is a terrible situation. Are you promoting it? Prostitution in such a setting connotes an exploitation of women who give up their dignity for money. Is this what being hip really means?

These are serious issues. Consider that this campaign will succeed. Do these possible consequences matter? Perhaps your concerns are overblown. Perhaps viewers of the ads will see them as impossible escapism. What do you think? How conscious should people be about possible implications of their ads?

You must make a recommendation to your partner at Marie Haut-bas about the way to proceed in this ad campaign. Describe the professional practice, ethical, and cost issues involved. Be sure to conclude with a recommendation to proceed or not.

Macro Case 3. You own a small business that employs 65 workers. Your bottom line has been rather sluggish lately. One of the reasons, you believe, is that workers have been wasting time on the Internet and making personal phone calls. Although you believe that you are not an overly controlling person, you have to be sensitive about profits since your core business has been flat.

You have the opportunity to purchase a new product, Employee Scan. It allows you to preset the phone numbers of your clients and those of employees' homes, childrens' schools, and spouses' work places. The software will tell you how often and how long the employee spends on personal calls and lists unidentified numbers called so that they might be checked at your discretion. The software also lists the Internet sites that employees log onto and the time they spend at the site. A number of sex or entertainment sites will be listed in the report, and others can be identified at your discretion.

Even if you do no further checking, this software claims to give you a profile of how an employee uses work hours as far as phone calls and Internet visits are concerned. This sounds beneficial to you since you believe that many employees may be guilty of abusing these devices. However, privacy issues are involved. Even though use of this product breaks no laws, is it ethical to check your employees' behavior? Do they invite such a system if they are abusing your trust?

You want to discuss this situation with your daughter who is vice-president of the company. Write a report outlining a course of action, making sure that you represent professional practice, ethical, and cost considerations.

Macro Case 4. As the head of the Federal Trade Commission, you have been approached by several groups suggesting that your agency should institute certain controls over Internet commerce. You realize that the heart of the Internet has been its freedom to develop unhindered. You also realize that day trading stocks and Ponzi and other schemes have become prevalent on the Net. The great difficulty on the Net is that there seems to be no accountability. The groups have suggested that you regulate the Internet.

You are conflicted as to what to do, so you ask Ms. A to write a report supporting such regulations. In the persona of Ms. A, write this report following professional practice, ethical, and cost considerations.

You have also asked Mr. B to write a report against instituting any regulation of the Internet. In the persona of Mr. B, write this report following professional practice, ethical, and cost considerations.

Be prepared to present the report that you support.

Micro Case 1. You are an assistant at a retail clothing store and provide bookkeeping services as part of your duties. Your immediate supervisor, Mr. Inkster (who works for Mrs. Forest, the owner), has asked you to file certain expenses as marketing costs that really do not fit into that category. For example, he has been spending company money on his girlfriend, Sally Tuls. Mr. Inkster has bought her gifts, paid for hotel rooms, and paid for her expenses on numerous business trips—all out of company money.

This is not marketing money, and you know it. You also know that if it came to your word against his, you would never be believed, but you could make a copy of a selective set of records on disk (in case Mr. Inkster decides to alter the records) and use them to support any accusations you believe should be made. Or you could just look the other way, get the accounting degree you are working on, and hope that this situation will not occur with your next employer.

You are conflicted about what to do. Your mother, with whom you live, is a fair-minded and reasonable person (although a bit oriented toward the practical). Write a letter to her about this situation detailing the problems (professional practice, ethical, and cost) and then explain how you understand each (according to embeddedness). Finally, conclude with plan of action.

Micro Case 2. You are the business manager of an in vitro fertilization (IVF) clinic. Your supervisor, Dr. Mary Reed, has told you to take an ad on local radio stations that you know makes false claims about your agency's success rate with infertile couples. It also implies that insurance carriers may pick up this cost when in your state they do not. The purpose of the ad is to get couples through the door and into consultation. Once they reach this point, the couples will do almost anything to become pregnant (including taking another job just to pay the expenses).

You are conflicted about what to do. You could take a hard stance against Dr. Reed's demands and possibly lose your job. You could take the ad and then tip off a watchdog agency that might confront the clinic. You could do nothing; after all, most of the other agencies in this work exaggerate claims of success. Why should you be any different?

Describe a personal action plan detailing all the issues involved in the professional practice case, the ethical case, and the cost case. Recommend an action plan.

Micro Case 3. You are a regional sales manager of a toy company, Kalon Toys. The company has just come out with a line of toys that encourage building skills. There are concerns about the safety of the toys. Should asthmatic children eat the smallest pieces of the building set and then have several glasses of whole milk, they might experience severe digestive problems. The company has put a warning label on all sets. This problem is expected to affect only seventy-five children.

You realize, however, that claims involving children are always sensitive. A competitor recently was sued on a frivolous claim that cost it millions of dollars. Thousands of people on the Net "chatted" about the claim and spread rumor and innuendo about the product. You want to protect yourself from falling prey to the same situation. Write a report on the actions you might proactively take to protect yourself and the company.

Micro Case 4. You are a software stringer at a major software company. You recently created a modification to the very popular, I Will Take Over the World game. In its 3.0 version, this game sold thousands of copies, but your modifications will triple its sales. However, the game was developed as a result of computer software piracy.

Express your thoughts in writing about why people pirate software, why they should not do so, and the extent of the problem. What ethical theories does piracy involve? What is the general categorization of what is going on? What should society do?

chapter five

Ethical Issues Within the Corporation

GENERAL OVERVIEW.

This chapter address three issues that have ethical implications for corporations: working conditions, affirmative action, and gender. These issues pertain to the environment or corporate culture that affects workers' lives. Each worker has a right to be treated with respect and afforded dignity whenever possible based on any authentically created shared community worldview.

If it is true that work is a substantial part of a person's life and if it is reasonable to assume that everyone wants to create the most meaningful life possible, then these three topics have a vital (although often overlooked) significance for the workplace. No good corporation can ignore them.

Working Conditions.

Overview.

The conditions under which people perform their jobs are very important to them. One reason for this is that each person is an individual with his own worldview. This worldview is connected to that person's sense of individual dignity. It is ethically required that individual dignity be affirmed whenever possible. An employer can do this by making the workplace a safe and healthy environment for employees. Safety is often an issue for manufacturing plants, and it can be an issue even in offices. Workers' physical and mental health must be addressed. Stress; hostile, sexist, or racist company cultures; and the general attitude toward workers as being just replaceable machines contribute to dehumanization, which is immoral. Immanuel Kant phrased a general moral maxim that described this dynamic: "Each rational being should treat himself and all others never merely as a means, but always at the same time as an end in himself."* This maxim forbids exploitation of another, which would be tantamount to treating another person as a means only and would not recognize the person's dignity (as being an end in himself). This Kantian understanding of an "end" is part of what I mean by worldview. Both are connected with recognizing the particularity of *individuals* and providing flexibility and accommodation for this whenever possible.

Employers can affirm a person as an end by paying a fair wage and meeting or exceeding the professional practices of an industry (see "The Principle of Fair Competition," p. 115).

The essays in this section approach the issue of working conditions in different ways. In the first essay, William W. Lowrance questions how we evaluate risk, which he views as something that can be measured. He views safety as the logical complement of risk. In other words, if working in a cotton mill creates a 5 percent risk for lung disease, then our assessment of the risk indicates that a worker is 95 percent safe from lung disease. However, assessment based only on statistical risk has a flaw: we have not defined *acceptable* risk. This issue of acceptability introduces the moral dimension to the question. Lowrance raises several guides to acceptability, but each really begs the question of how much risk is acceptable. The reader is encouraged to look to one of the primary moral theories and the ought-implies-can principle as a guide to evaluate the proper level of risk in the workplace (and, by extension, of safety in the workplace).

In the second article, Sheila M. Neysmith and Jane Aronson address some issues in home care (particularly for the aged). Although their study took place in Canada, the principles can be applied to the United States. (Recently, one workers' compensation study found that that home care was in the riskiest category for back injuries—from lifting elderly patients.)

The article raises many working condition issues. The reader might discern others. Highlighted especially are issues of gender and race and ethnic backgrounds. Caring for others has traditionally been assigned to women in Occidental culture. The care has not been valued although those who need it

---

*Immanuel Kant, *Groundwork of the Metaphysics of Morals* tr. H. J. Paton (London: Hutchinson & Co., 1948), p. 64/428.

certainly value the benefit they receive. When you add to this ingratitude the default bias against women and the factor of race or ethnic bias, a potentially hostile and demeaning environment results.

The third essay, by David M. Schilling, deals with sweatshops. When an employer has the upper hand in a labor market, there is the potential for exploitation. (Note that in "labor-short" environments, excesses can also result, although in our new global economy, companies with the resources will be able to tap the glut of poor people to the companies' advantage.) The reader must make several conclusions about justice to evaluate the sweatshop issue. If there is a willing employer and a willing employee, is there a valid working condition contract? If some fictitious sporting shoe company were to pay a star basketball player $40 million a year in promotional fees and then pay $7.5 million to its 10,000 workers in foreign countries, is something wrong, or is this merely an instance of rewarding according to some system of desert?

The important issue, of course, is whether the average consumer is willing to spend $15 more for a pair of shoes that has been produced under proper working conditions. Is this merely a case of an individual not wanting to work under bad conditions but being willing to pay only the lowest price when it comes to personal shopping decisions?

Of Acceptable Risk

William W. Lowrance

Few headlines are so alarming, perplexing, and personal in their implications as those concerning safety. Frightening stories jolt our early morning complacency so frequently that we wonder whether things can really be *that* bad. We are disturbed by what sometimes appear to be haphazard and irresponsible regulatory actions, and we can't help being suspicious of all the assaults on our freedoms and our pocketbooks made in the name of safety. We hardly know which cries of "Wolf!" to respond to; but we dare not forget that even in the fairy tale, the wolf really did come.

The issues: X-rays, cosmetics, DDT, lead, pharmaceuticals, toys, saccharin, intrauterine contraceptive devices, power lawn mowers, air pollutants, noise. . . .

The questions: How do we determine how hazardous these things are? Why is it that cyclamates one day dominate the market as the principal calorie-cutting sweetener in millions of cans of diet drinks, only to be banned the next day because there is a "very slight chance" they may cause cancer? Why is it that one group of eminent experts says that medical X-rays (or food preservatives, or contraceptive pills) are safe and ought to be used more widely, while another group of authorities, equally reputable, urges that exposure to the same things should be restricted because they are unsafe? At what point do debates such as that over DDT stop being scientific and objective and start being political and subjective? How can anyone gauge the public's willingness to accept risks? . . .

JUDGING SAFETY

. . . Safety is not measured. *Risks* are measured. Only when those risks are weighed on the balance of social values can safety be judged: *a thing is safe if its attendant risks are judged to be acceptable.*

Determining safety, then, involves two extremely different kinds of activities. . . .

> *Measuring risks*—measuring the probability and severity of harm—is an empirical, scientific activity;
>
> *Judging safety*—judging the acceptability of risks—is a normative, political activity.

Although the difference between the two would seem obvious, it is all too often forgotten, ignored, or obscured. This failing is often the cause of the disputes that hit the front pages.

We advocate use of this particular definition for many reasons. It encompasses the other, more specialized, definitions. By employing the word "acceptable," it emphasizes that safety decisions are relativistic and judgmental. It immediately elicits the crucial questions, "Acceptable in whose view?" and "Acceptable in what terms?" and "Acceptable for whom?" Further, it avoids all implication that safety is an intrinsic, absolute, measurable property of things.

In the following two examples, risk-measuring activity is described in Roman type, and safety-judging in italics. . . .

> A scientific advisory committee is charged by the government with recommending radiation exposure standards. The committee reviews all the animal

experiments, the occupational medical record, the epidemiological surveys of physicians and patients exposed to X-rays, and the studies of the survivors of the Nagasaki and Hiroshima explosions. It inventories the modes of exposure; it reviews present radiation standards, including those of other nations and international organizations; and it examines the practical possibility of reducing exposures. *It weighs all the risks, costs, and benefits, and then decides that the allowed exposure has been unacceptably high; it recommends that because the intensity of some major sources, such as medical X-rays, can be reduced at reasonable cost and with little loss of effectiveness, the standards should be made more restrictive.*

Over a three-year period, William Ruckelshaus, administrator of the Environmental Protection Agency, considered many different petitions from the various interested parties before acting on his agency's inquiry into the use of DDT. Finally, in 1972, he ruled that the scientific evidence led him to conclude that DDT is "an uncontrollable, durable chemical that persists in the aquatic and terrestrial environments" and "collects in the food chain," and that although the evidence regarding human tumorogenicity and other long-term effects was inconclusive, there was little doubt that DDT has serious ecological effects. Ruckelshaus reviewed the benefits of DDT in the protection of cotton and other crops and affirmed that other equally effective pesticides were available. *Summing the arguments, then, he ruled that "the long-range risks of continued use of DDT for use on cotton and most other crops is unacceptable and outweighs any benefits. . . ."*[1]

. . . In heading down the slopes a skier attests that he accepts the risks; at a later stage of his life he may reject those very same risks because of changes in his awareness, his physical fragility, or his responsibilities to family or firm. While one woman may accept the side effects of oral contraceptives because she doesn't want to risk pregnancy, another woman may so fear the pill that she judges a diaphragm to be a more acceptable compromise among the several risks. Even though he is fully aware of the mangled fingers, chronic coughs, or damaged eyes or ears of those around him, a worker may accept those risks rather than endure the daily nuisance and tedium of blade guards, respirators, goggles, or ear protectors; but his employer, for reasons of cost, paternalism, or government requirement, may find this risky behavior unacceptable. . . .

Acceptance may be just a passive, or even stoical, continuance of historical momentum, as when people accept their lot at a dangerous traditional trade or continue to live near a volcano. Acceptance may persist because no alternatives are seen, as in the case of automobiles and many other technological hazards. Acceptance may result from ignorance or misperception of risk: variations on "I didn't know the gun was loaded" and "It won't happen to me" show up in every area. Acceptance may be simply acquiescence in a majority decision, such as a referendum-based decision on fluoridation, or in a decision by some governing elite, as with the average person's tacit approval of most public standards. Acceptance may even be an expression of preference for modern but known risks over perhaps smaller but less well understood risks, as with preference for coal- and oil-fired power plants over nuclear plants. . . . It is important to appreciate that such decisions may or may not be—and are certainly not necessarily—fair, just, consistent, efficient, or rational.

There is a great deal of overlap between the two decisionmaking domains implied by our definition of safety. Scientists, engineers, and medical people are called upon by political officials to judge the desirability of certain courses for society. Panels of scientists recommend exposure limits. Physicians prescribe medicines and diets. Engineers design dams, television sets, toasters, and airplanes. All of these decisions are heavily, even if only implicitly, value-laden.

On the other hand, by adopting particular risk data in their deliberations, political and judiciary agents at least implicitly rule on the correctness of measurements. The business of determining risk must often be settled operationally in hearings or other political deliberations, because the day-to-day management of society can't always wait for scientists to complete their cautious, precise determinations, which may take years. Congressional committees and regulatory agencies conduct hearings and issue rulings on the risks of food additives and air pollutants. Courts rule on the dangers of DDT. Risk and its acceptability are weighed by both manufacturers and consumers in the push-and-pull of the marketplace.

Between the two activities—measuring risk and judging safety—lies a discomforting no-man's-land . . . or every-man's-land. Scientists on the fringe of the political arena, attempting to avoid charges of elitism, are looking for more objective ways to appraise society's willingness to accept various risks. At the same time, political officials confronted by scientifically controversial "facts" that never seem to gain the clarity promised by textbooks are exploring the possibilities of advisory assistance, fact-finding hearings, and formal technology assessments.

GUIDES TO ACCEPTABILITY

"Reasonableness." This is by far the most commonly cited and most unimpeachable principle in safety judgments. For instance, the legislative charter of the Consumer Product Safety Commission directs it to "reduce unreasonable risk of injury" associated with consumer goods.[2] Panels of experts frequently invoke a "rule of reason" in rendering advice. The concept of reasonableness pervades economic analyses of hazard reduction and the structures of legal liability.

Unfortunately, reference to reasonableness is in a sense a phantom citation. It provides little specific guidance for public decisionmakers, for whom reasonableness is presumably a requirement for staying in office. Not surprisingly, the Consumer Product Safety Act does not venture to define reasonableness. As guidance, the Safety Commission quotes the description given by the final report of its progenitor, the National Commission on Product Safety:

> Risks of bodily harm to users are not unreasonable when consumers understand that risks exist, can appraise their probability and severity, know how to cope with them, and voluntarily accept them to get benefits that could not be obtained in less risky ways. When there is a risk of this character, consumers have reasonable opportunity to protect themselves; and public authorities should hesitate to substitute their value judgments about the desirability of the risk for those of the consumers who choose to incur it.
>
> But preventable risk is not reasonable
>
> (a) when consumers do not know that it exists; or
>
> (b) when, though aware of it, consumers are unable to estimate its frequency and severity; or
>
> (c) when consumers do not know how to cope with it, and hence are likely to incur harm unnecessarily; or
>
> (d) when risk is unnecessary in . . . that it could be reduced or eliminated at a cost in money or in the performance of the product that consumers would willingly incur if they knew the facts and were given the choice.[3]

The point of safety judgments is indeed to decide what is reasonable; it's just that any rational decision will have to be made on more substantive bases, such as the following, which are in a sense criteria for reasonableness.

Custom of Usage. The Food and Drug Administration has designated hundreds of food additives as "generally recognized as safe" (GRAS). The GRAS list, established in 1958, includes such substances as table salt, vitamin A, glycerin, and baking powder, whose long use has earned them wide and generally unquestioned acceptance.[4] Being classified as GRAS exempts those substances from having to pass certain premarket clearances. From time to time this sanction is challenged, but most critics of the GRAS list have argued not so much that it should be abandoned as that individual items should be subjected to periodic review. In 1969, following its decision to ban the popular artificial sweetener cyclamate (until then GRAS), the Food and Drug Administration initiated a full review of the GRAS list. That review is still in progress, and "so far nothing has been found to lead to any further bans similar to the one on cyclamate."[5]

Prevailing Professional Practice. Long established as the criterion for physicians' clinical practice, this principle is increasingly being invoked in evaluating the protection that engineers, designers, and manufacturers provide their clients. Buildings are said to conform to the "prevailing local standards."

Toys are "of a common design." X-ray machines are operated "at normal intensities." In many instances the wisdom of such deference to convention can be questioned. The underlying assumption is that if a thing has been in common use it must be okay, since any adverse effects would have become evident, and that a thing sanctioned by custom is safer than one not tested at all.

Best Available Practice, Highest Practicable Protection, and Lowest Practicable Exposure. Air and water quality regulations have stipulated that polluters control their emissions by the "best available means." So have noise abatement laws. Obviously, although such a requirement does provide the public regulator with a vague rationale, he must still exercise judgment over what constitutes "best" practice for every individual case and what economic factors should be considered in defining "practicable." Hardware for pollution control or noise abatement may exist, but only at a cost that many allege to be prohibitive; is it to be considered "available"? . . .

"No Detectable Adverse Effect." Although such a principle is applied frequently in our everyday lives, and although it has a certain operational value, it is a weak criterion which may amount to little more than an admission of uncertainty or ignorance. Many hazards now recognized, such as moderate levels of X-rays or asbestos or vinyl chloride, could at an earlier time have been said to have "no detectable adverse effect." . . .

The Threshold Principle. If it can be proven that there is indeed a level of exposure below which no adverse effect occurs, subthreshold exposures might be considered safe. But determining whether there really is a threshold, for the especially vulnerable as well as for the average populace, is usually a nearly impossible task. As we mentioned earlier, for loud noises there are clearly thresholds of annoyance, pain, and ear damage. But whether there are thresholds for effects of radiation, chemical carcinogens, and mutagens has never been firmly established. . . .

ON BEING, AND BEING HELD, RESPONSIBLE

In essence the issue is posed by the following questions: Should technically trained people be expected to bear any social responsibilities different from those borne by others? Why? What are the unique obligations? And further, can all the obligations be met simply by individuals working alone, or are there in addition some responsibilities requiring technical people to act collectively? . . .

Scientists, engineers, designers, architects, physicians, public health experts, and other technically trained people *do* have special responsibilities to the rest of society with respect to personal safety. Some principal kinds of risks which ought to be taken upon the conscience of the technical community are:

1. Technically complex risks whose intricacies are comprehensible only to highly trained people;
2. Risks that can be significantly reduced by applying new technology or by improving the application of existing technology;
3. Risks constituting public problems whose technical components need to be distinguished explicitly from their social and political components so that responsibilities are assigned properly;
4. Technological intrusions on personal freedom made in the pursuit of safety; and
5. Risks whose possible consequences appear so grave or irreversible that prudence dictates the urging of extreme caution, even before the risks are known precisely.

Notice that we have said that these problems *should be taken as matters of conscience* by the technical community. Whether the verb describing the action should be *protecting*, or *watching over*, or *looking out for*, or *issuing a warning*, depends on the situation. The specific response might be doing an experiment, raising an issue before a professional society, blowing the whistle on an employer, exerting political leverage, or aiding a legislator or administrator in untangling the parts of a public issue.

. . . These responsibilities have several deep origins. Basically they arise, in congruence with all major moral philosophies, from the conviction that every person has a general responsibility for the well-being of his fellow men. Reflecting this, the common law has held through the centuries that anyone who becomes aware of the possibility of danger has a responsibility to warn those at risk. But we are obliged to push further and ask whether, in this age of cultural specialization, there isn't more to the issue—for if we don't press, we may be left simply making vague exhortations to virtue.

When we examine what society expects, we find that it does look to the technical community for warning, guidance, and protection, in the kinds of situations we have described and in others as well. Highly trained people are definitely seen as having special status. Given this, a key to developing a compelling ethical argument, and to understanding why the lay public feels as it does, seems to reside in the notion of professionalism.

Over the years a tacit but nonetheless real compact has developed. Society *invests in* training and professional development of scientists and other technical people. It invests heavily; substantial public subsidy of one form or another goes to virtually every college, university, medical school, field station, and research facility in the United States. By and large the professions are left free to govern themselves, control admission to membership, choose their direction of research, enforce the quality of work, and direct the allocation of public funds within their subject area.

Concomitantly, society *invests with* the professions and their institutions certain trusts, among them a trust the professions will watch over the well-being of society, including its safety. As Berkeley sociologist William

Kornhauser has expressed it, "Professional responsibility is based on the belief that the power conferred by expertise entails a fiduciary relationship to society."[6] This "fiduciary relationship," or what we have called a tacit compact, is what gives rise to the ethical "oughts."

... As this century has careened along it has brought an increasing need for a collective shouldering of responsibility. The one-to-one personal relationships that once governed ethical conduct have been supplanted by more diffuse ones involving many intermediaries. Industrial scientists plan their research by committee. Engineers who design tunnels and dams interact with their ultimate public clients only indirectly, through managers, attorneys, and the officials who supervise public contracts. Physicians may still carry the wand of Aesculapius, but they do so in the context of one of the nation's largest businesses. Two sorts of diffuseness enlarge the collective dimension. First, the cliency is expanding, often in the interest of social justice: a national health care system that intends to reach every citizen has quite different ethical dimensions from a free-market private physician system. And second, as we confront hazards that are more diffuse, we often realize that *nobody* has considered that the problem was specifically his concern: there is no International Agency for the Supervision of the Ozone Layer.

We try to manage these problems by government action, building in mechanisms of accountability where possible; and we test the justice of specific actions in the courts, as when people feel that they are being unfairly denied medical care. Beyond that, and usually leading it, we have to depend on action by communities of scholars and coteries of professionals—hence the obligations we listed earlier.

Two current cases exemplify some of the difficulties. Three engineers in California, backed to a limited extent by several engineering societies, have pressed suit against the Bay Area Rapid Transit (BART) system for firing them after they publicly protested that the automatic train control systems their companies were developing for BART were inadequate and not up to the best professional standards with regards to passenger safety. The dispute raises complex questions about how great the risks really were, whether they should have been considered acceptable, how engineers should play their roles, how corporations should handle dissension, and what the professional societies should do.[7] In another case, an international group of biologists has voluntarily convened itself to discuss whether and how to control certain genetics experiments that would have bizarre, disastrous consequences if they ran amok.[8]

There is little precedent for either case, so it is not surprising that neither has been handled with assurance. In the BART case, the engineering societies were not well prepared to act and could muster only limited support. Perhaps for lack of experience and guidance, the three engineers party to the suit were not able to pursue the case through the courts to completion; the case has reportedly had to be settled out of court, thus setting only weak legal precedent. In the genetic experiments case, the scientists involved continue to suffer the anguish of not even being able to reach a firm consensus on the issue, and they are hard pressed to take any action other than to issue stern pronouncements, plead for prudence, and cross their collective fingers that researchers will be careful.

We have developed the above arguments because we believe they are important. They are by no means the sole guide to action. There can be no substitute for honesty, courage, sacrifice, and the other manifestations of high morality. Nor should legal and other sanctions fail to be applied: enforceable building codes can be adopted to supplement voluntary action; duties can be made a matter of contractual responsibility; and falsification of records is cause for lawsuit. There are many obligations in addition to ethical ones. The ethical ones are of a special sort, though, and urgently deserve to be developed.

The great questions of responsibility will remain with us. Is simply providing information or issuing warnings a sufficient response, or ought those with the knowledge do more? How is responsibility passed up through administrative and managerial hierarchies? In what sense is tacit acquiescence in a misleading scheme irresponsible (as when corporate scientists who know better say nothing when their company makes false claims for its products or evades pollution control laws)? To what extent should those who generate scientific and technological innovations be responsible for their subsequent application?

NOTES

1. U.S. Environmental Protection Agency, "Consolidated DDT hearings," 37 *Federal Register*, 13369–13376 (July 7, 1972).
2. Consumer Product Safety Act, *Public Law 82-573* (1972).
3. National Commission on Product Safety, *Final Report*, 11 (1970).
4. 21 *U.S. Code of Federal Regulations*, 121.101 (subpart B).
5. Alan T. Spiner, Jr., "Food ingredient review: Where it stands now," *FDA Consumer*, 23–26 (June 1974).
6. William Kornhauser, *Scientists in Industry*, 1 (University of California Press, Berkeley, 1962).
7. Gordon D. Friedlander, *IEEE Spectrum*, 11, 69–76 (October 1974); Gordon D. Friedlander, "Fixing BART," *IEEE Spectrum*, 12, 43–45 (February 1975).
8. Nicholas Wade, "Genetics: Conference sets strict controls to replace moratorium," *Science* 187, 931–935 (1975); Stuart Auerbach, "And man created risks," *Washington Post* (March 9, 1975.)

Working Conditions in Home Care: Negotiating Race and Class Boundaries in Gendered Work

Sheila M. Neysmith and Jane Aronson

Since the early eighties, industrialized countries have been developing long-term care policies in efforts to respond to the joint realities of population aging, the rising costs of institutionally based care, and the desire expressed by groups of seniors to remain in their communities. Home-based services are seen as basic ingredients in programs designed to meet these three concerns. However, the understanding of care that underlies these models seems to be rooted in familial images where the carer is a spouse or daughter, it is as if formal home care services were simply a paid version of informal care. Such assumptions are at odds with a reality in which service is provided by strangers, usually employed by an agency in which organizational priorities take precedence over those of individual care recipients or their families. Not only are home care workers not family, in Canada they are drawn from low-paid labor pools increasingly made up of immigrant women. Thus, immigration policy determines some of the behavioral and attitudinal distances that have to be traversed when a home care worker and a frail elderly person meet to negotiate the terms and conditions under which care is to be provided and received.

This article focuses on a group of workers who are immigrants from the Caribbean and from the Philippines. The usual ambiguities and conflicts that are part of doing home care work are compounded when the worker is visible as both an immigrant and a woman of color in a racialized society.[1] The experiences of these service workers are important because they provide us with a way of understanding how policy decisions on immigration, health care funding priorities, organizational structures, and community care cumulatively

This work was supported by the Social Sciences and Humanities Research Council of Canada—Women and Change through a research grant (822-92-0015) and a network grant (816-94-0003).

[1]Adjectives such as "racialized" and "gendered" are used as descriptors of social institutions, such as labor markets, where practices reinforce race and gender divisions within a society. In this article the term "women of color" is used because the term includes Caribbean black, East Indian, and Asian women. These groups are frequently referred to by policy makers in Canada as "visible minorities," although group members describe themselves as "women of color."

shape the labor processes and conditions of home care workers and, thus, the care received by elderly clients. . . .

HOME CARE WORKERS: A CHANGING LABOR FORCE

Long-term care policy discourse continues as if home care workers were middle-aged, working-class, white women who fitted in home care work around their own family obligations and shared many cultural similarities with their elderly clients. Maintaining such a stereotype in the face of a rapidly changing home care labor force means that policies and practices will reinforce rather than challenge existent gender, race, and class inequities. Conflicting interests are at work amongst the various players in the home care arena. For instance, minimalist service models mean that community care is limited to services provided in the isolation of people's homes by individual home care workers. The availability of a pool of immigrant women makes it possible for higher income families to hire such persons to do this home-based work. Feminist policy analysts have called for expanding services to care for children and elderly persons. The questions not raised are: who is going to do the work, under what conditions, and who will benefit from increased services? The employment patterns of recent immigrants, combined with the demographic characteristics of Canada's aging population, suggest that it will be low-waged women of color who will do the work. Who will receive the service will vary depending on how the current struggle over the mix of market, voluntary, and public services in the economy of care is resolved.

Examination of the employment patterns of immigrant women shows that services rather than manufacturing is now a major source of jobs (27). Immigration patterns also indicate that service sector employees such as home care workers will increasingly be women of color. This pattern is already quite evident in Canadian as well as in U.S. urban centers (28, p. 17). Immigrants, however, come into a society where established structures determine how newcomers experience class, race, and gender disparities (29–31). Home care policy exists within the broader political economy of a nation and thus reflects the assumptions and institutional practices of that society. The fact that home care workers are women, low-paid, and drawn from an immigrant labor force is not a given but, rather, a social phenomenon that needs to be examined. Home care workers who are women of color move into a type of work that is closely related to traditional domestic service work. Research on domestic workers has documented the oppressive conditions that frequently characterize this work (32–36). This research also shows that women who have worked as domestics are convinced that factory or service jobs in organizations are preferable to domestic service work. They appreciate not being personally subordinate to an individual in that person's household and not having to do that household's dirty work on their property. In long-term care facilities and service agencies, relations with supervisors and clients may be hierarchical but at least they are embedded in impersonal structures governed by more explicit contractual obligations and limits. Also important is the presence of a work group for sociability and support (37, p. 23).

Examining the experiences of home care workers against a backdrop of domestic service research was helpful to us in understanding some of the issues emerging in our study. Furthermore, it provided a useful framework for assessing agency and policy responses to concerns raised by home care workers. Specifically, the parallels between home care work and domestic service reveal how racism unfolds in home-based care work in ways that it does not in institutionally based care work. The parallels are not exact; for example, home care workers are seldom live-ins and they are not hired primarily as domestic servants. However, home care workers' experiences of their work and its location suggest that when home care tasks are done by women of color in private homes, elderly clients and their families may respond as if to domestic servants. Elderly clients' and families' inevitable frustrations at having to rely on home care services were often directed at their individual workers—the only or closest target. All workers in our study, white women and women of color, regularly experienced the diminishment of being referred to as a "cleaning lady." This class-based diminishment certainly affected white workers and was something they strove to resist and, sometimes, reframe with their clients. However, for nonwhite home care workers, clients' frustrations could also be articulated in terms of their ethnoracial characteristics. In other words, an additional discourse, concerned not with class but with race, was available as a medium of expression for clients and families who, variously, sought targets for their complaints about meager home care services or who were, in a more diffuse fashion, struggling with their own diminishment as people deemed dependent and needy. . . .

METHODOLOGICAL CONSIDERATIONS

Racism as ideology exists at the level of daily actions and their interpretations and, at another level, in the refusal by those in the dominant group to recognize and take responsibility for their race privilege. For instance, it is said that to be white in North America means not to have to think about race. This study uses the concept of "everyday racism" developed by Essed (39) to explore how differences between worker and client were structured and experienced at the micro level of providing and receiving help with household and personal needs (see also 40 and 41 for a discussion of race and class bias in research on women). The term "everyday racism" refers to a process in which (*a*) socialized racist notions are integrated into meanings that make these practices immediately definable and manageable by those who encounter them; (*b*) practices with racist implications become in themselves familiar and repetitive and thus rendered invisible; and (*c*) underlying racial and ethnic relations are actualized and reinforced through these routine or familiar practices in everyday situations (39, p. 52). Thus, we would expect home care workers of different ethnoracial groups to experience and talk about their work differently. DeVault's (42) report on interviews with African American nutritionists cautions researchers that adhering to the methodological rule to let findings emerge from the data can result in the researcher failing to hear race-ethnicity in the accounts of informants because it is implicit rather than explicit. Thus, workers' accounts may include personal experiences or knowledge of others' experiences, but in either case women of color place these within a general knowledge of racism to determine whether a specific event is defined as a racist incident. In other words, race, class, and gender disparities are socially constructed systems, but their effect must arise at specific moments, in particular circumstances, and will change as these circumstances change. . . .

The focus groups were held several months after the interviews had been completed and analyzed. Their purpose was to explore more systematically the tensions and conflicts that emerged in the interviews around clients referring to the home care worker as a "cleaning lady." We wanted to get a better understanding of how the domestic service component of home care work was interpreted by women of color, how workers handled the routine racist attitudes and behaviors encountered in carrying out their work assignments, and how this affected the dynamic of relationship maintenance that undergirds home care work. The process for recruiting focus group members was very similar to that used when seeking participants for the interviews. The purpose of the focus groups was announced and volunteers were requested. Participants were remunerated at the rate of $11.25 per hour, the average wage at that time. On the advice of experienced agency workers one group consisted entirely of women from the Caribbean countries, the other group of women from the Philippines. Some focus group participants had taken part in the earlier interviews, others had not. Each focus group had seven members. A group for supervisors was also held. Supervisors represent the bridge between individual workers and the management of home care services, and, ultimately, the link between the daily structuring of home care workers' labor and the overarching policy discourse on meeting the needs of old people. A part of this focus group explored how encounters with racism were dealt with when they were brought to the attention of supervisors. With participants' signed consent, all interviews and focus groups were taped and transcribed. A computer software program (45) allowed us to do word/phrase searches and to code emerging conceptual categories, thus facilitating the practical management of the data.

EVERYDAY RACISM IN HOME CARE WORKERS' WORK

Home care work, like other caring labor, is underspecified and undervalued. Descriptions focus on practical tasks such as cleaning, meal preparation, laundry, bathing, and other aspects of personal care. This emphasis on concrete measurable units of work allows home care work to be classified as semi-skilled labor, basically able to be done by most women with minimal training. Pay scales reflect this. The following excerpts from transcripts of the interviews and focus groups reveal how home care work—carried out in the setting of an old person's home, usually combined with at least a minimum fee for service, but disconnected from the relational assumptions that frame familial care—easily gets categorized as domestic labor. If the home care worker is also an immigrant and a woman of color (the two are often not differentiated) the classification is reinforced. Home care work becomes the site for these women to experience the racism that permeates the larger society. As will become evident, home care workers were regularly called upon to interpret, explain, and respond to the spectrum of racial issues that routinely surface in large multicultural cities.

Dealing with the "Cleaning Lady" Image

Being seen as a cleaning lady emerged as an issue in virtually every interview. Part of the problem seems to be the ambiguous definition of what a home care worker does. She performs some tasks that look like cleaning, are in fact cleaning, but she is there not for the purpose of cleaning but because of the health and social situation of the elderly person. Although home care workers were clear on the purpose and function of their role, they doubted that many elderly clients and their families were (see 46 for a parallel discussion of nanny ambiguity). The trigger for this definitional assignment seems to be the setting—that is, the work is done in an individual's home.

> This is a new kind of job. A lot of ladies and men we visit, they say we're the cleaning lady. They don't know that we have responsibility for everything about them, not just the house. We have to care about them; observe how they are doing; how they are eating; if something is happening.

> In general we are treated as a cleaning lady. You try. You tell them. You talk to them about food, but if the nurse doesn't say it, they don't listen to it.

> She [client] asked him [client's son] who I was. He said "That's the cleaning lady." I said "No, I am not. I'm the homemaker." "That's the same thing," he said. I said, "No, it is not," and I kind of felt upset.

Health and social service professionals were seen as contributing to the confusion by giving mixed messages: "I think it comes about because the

information wasn't given out proper to them by the case worker. Or whoever was interviewing them didn't tell them what it was all about." Home
care workers stated quite clearly that case coordinators and other health
personnel were as much in need of education as clients and their families.

Home care workers are aware that they go along with the cleaning lady
designation rather than continuously battle it. On other occasions they avoid
the issue if they think to do so helps a client.

> I had one lady. She was very depressed. I tried every which way to cheer her up.
> She also thought I was only in there do to the cleaning. I didn't want to be of-
> fensive and make her feel that she couldn't cope. I want to make them feel that
> they are still able to take care of themselves and they just need a little help with
> the cleaning part. Yes, I let them think that way.

Clients are old, and home care workers use this knowledge to explain, but
also excuse, behaviors:

> But I don't blame the people we care for because they are sick, they are in trou-
> ble. Sometimes we explain our work to them; that we are not just cleaning ladies
> and they understand. But some are very confused and we don't have the time.
> So we just forget about it.

The increasingly widespread practice of two rather than three or four
hour work assignments aggravated the situation. The restriction on hours
heightened the emphasis on cleaning—a clear client, if not worker, priority.
This was confirmed in discussions with supervisors:

> Some clients don't like you to call their homes because they think you are hold-
> ing up the homemaker from doing her work [group agrees]. When you phone
> some clients will actually say "She is doing work now, you cannot talk to her."

In the focus group discussions, participants connected being seen as a
cleaning woman to several factors. Most clients had never encountered a home
care worker; while they knew from past experience what physicians, nurses,
and even physiotherapists do, a home care worker is an unfamiliar designation. Furthermore, clients are told by case coordinators that the home care
worker is coming in to help them around the house with such things as meal
preparation and cleaning—a translation into lay language of the professional
category of providing assistance with the activities of daily living. Much more
difficult to convey is the notion of social support that undergirds these surface
activities. Whatever the original intent of the description, it seems that the
elderly person interprets it in terms that are meaningful to her or his lived
experience and current needs. Thus, depending upon class background,
the client can draw on knowledge that someone who helps around the house
is a servant, domestic, or cleaning lady. In addition, the limited physical

capacity of most home care users means that getting cleaning done is a major concern. An elderly person can turn to a nurse or family member to give her a bath, take her for walks, or to do some shopping. Getting someone to do the kind of work that is required to keep even a small apartment clean is more difficult to negotiate. Walker and Warren's (47, p. 156) review of the Neighborhood Support Innovations in the United Kingdom found that the greatest cause of dissatisfaction amongst elderly users was that they gave help with cleaning a high priority whereas the designers of community support services neglected it.

The Meaning of "Immigrant" for Women of Color

If the social support aspect of home care work remains invisible, if cleaning is a priority for elderly service users, and if the home care worker is a woman of color, elderly clients and their families assume she is an immigrant—clearly a negative label for our respondents:

> I'm here 22 years but I'm still an immigrant!

> I have been here since 1981. I did a lot to become an immigrant. I didn't just take it away from anybody. I became a landed immigrant in 1989 and last year I became a citizen.

> I'm here for 5 years. As far as I see, this is the only job you can get.

> Oh yeah, there are a lot of Filipinos in this country, but we're paying taxes, you know, we're working hard.

> There was one lady who said "Well then you should go back to where you come from." You know, immigrants should go where they belong. So I said, "Where did your mother come from?" And she said that she came from such and such. So I said "What does that make you? An immigrant just like me." You do hear it, you know.

We asked homemakers if and how language, culture, and race became issues in their daily routines. Language and cultural differences were fairly easy to negotiate, often recalled with a sense of humor. For instance, a home care worker recalled with a smile her education while cleaning up a kosher kitchen for one elderly couple. Around issues of race, responses were more equivocal:

> They know most Filipinas take jobs in the house. If you are not a nanny, you are a cleaning lady.

> Some people think our jobs are very demeaning. [example] There was a little girl, not a little girl, but she was young looking and she was white—and very pretty. And this lady had a black homemaker going there all the time—and it was ok. But when she saw this white girl she said "What you doing this kind of work for?" It comes back to us. How do you think we feel? We are good enough but

as soon as they see somebody that they feel [pause] then you realize how much they think of you and your job. You know?

Sometimes you can't even describe it but you know it's there. I'm trying to think. "All you people"; a lot say, meaning black people. Not "you people, YOUR people," that's the word—"YOUR PEOPLE." If you say you need a mop to wash the floor, you need modern things, well, "Why should I have to buy a mop when you are not used to a mop in your country?" That kind of thing, little things, you know.

It seems that clients', and their families', reactions to home care workers who are immigrant women of color range from genuine misunderstandings of what home care workers do to racist attitudes toward particular groups.

Negotiating Ethnoracial Tensions

These statements from individual interviews describe and offer some interpretations of the situations encountered by home care workers. In the focus groups, we asked home care workers how they responded to such incidents. Participants observed, with sighs, that they frequently handle them poorly— that is to say, they avoid, ignore, or are angry inside but remain silent. As one participant put it:"You cannot be educating all the time." The examples cited are everyday incidents that are familiar and repetitive:

This lady, she had some candies, and I said "Can I have a candy?" She said "Eenie, meenie, minie, moe, catch a . . ." and she stopped. I guess she was gonna use the nigger word. And she stop and look at me and I just took the candy and walked away. I didn't say anything. She just stopped on "catch a." I didn't make a fuss, no hard feelings. Like I don't hear, I just blank it out. And I'm still going there.

They [the family] were wondering why when they come to visit their sister, I am wearing new clothes. They are wondering where I am getting the money to buy the clothes. I almost said, "I'm receiving $800 every two weeks." But I wanted to finish my job because I had the meeting tonight so I didn't want to have a discussion about it.

On occasion home care workers do respond and counter the interpretations dealt out to them:

She said "Well a white person wouldn't do that [referring to cleaning]." So then I said, "Well, that is why the white person has to go on welfare because they don't wanna do the job. Most of us, I said to her, are employed because we will do the job." That kind of made her think a little bit.

I said [to a client] not all the provinces in the Philippines are poor. All the people who come here are not uneducated because I don't come like that. I answered that there are lots of Philippine people in Canada, but we come here as educated people. We're not all the poorest in the Philippines. It's not like that in our country. [The client] said, "Oh yeah? Are you [educated]?" I said, "Yes, do you want to see my certificate?"

Many Filipino health care professionals emigrate to Canada but their training is not recognized unless they acquire Canadian experience or recertification. Such persons possess skills that are attractive to employers in the home care market. Employees, however, see these jobs as temporary, second-choice options imposed by professional and other dominant interest groups.

In both the interviews and focus groups home care workers attributed much of the negative attitudes and behaviors they encountered to the powerful influence of the media. It was noted that elderly clients watch a lot of television:

> They are older and they don't get out much and they look at that [points to TV]. That's where they get the negative thing about Black people. . . . As soon as you open the door, they say "Did you hear the news?" You can hardly have a conversation without the issue being talked about. We don't bring it up.

> Sometimes they [elderly clients] watch those talk shows, like Oprah, where they are talking about race and stuff. If I feel it's getting too hot I'll just kinda go and find something else to do. I don't really discuss things about that 'cause then I get too touchy and then I'm gonna feel offended or something, or they're gonna feel [voice trails off].

Home care workers from the Caribbean saw as problematic stories on television about black crime. When clients attempted to engage the home care worker in such discussions, a variety of response strategies were used—including some courageous attempts at consciousness raising: "I said 'Well, in all races there are good and bad people. When one person does something you do not have to condemn us all. When a white person does something, we do not condemn all whites.'" Another home care worker pointed out to a client belonging to the same ethnic group as a man who was currently making the headlines for embezzling large sums that his crime and his cultural community were not associated. However, when a crime is committed by a person of color you read about black crime for days. In another case the home care worker explained to an elderly client her reluctance to discuss an incident by saying these things hurt her as a member of that community and thus it was difficult to talk about. . . .

In sum, in everyday home care work and its management, the class, race, and gender disparities existing in the broader society are understood as individual cases of prejudice to be handled on an ad hoc basis. This understanding and the institutional practices that result reinforce the very patterns that perpetuate the problem. This is not intended as a critical comment on the way the cases were handled. Elderly clients, home care workers, and supervisors have no other options when conflicts arising from decreases in service hours, labor market inequities, and prevailing definitions of socially created dependencies must be treated as personal problems rather than public issues. As the above discussion highlights, each incident extracts time, emotional, and mental costs from these three sets of players who, in order to make home care happen, must daily negotiate tensions arising from structural inequities of race, class, and gender. The compromises they negotiate are never satisfactory but represent their best efforts in the face of, seemingly, a complete lack of resources to support alternative resolutions. There are, for example, no policies in place to support or broaden their efforts and no language to politicize or contextualize their individually borne discomforts and struggles. This dearth of institutional and discursive resources raises important questions about the purpose and structure of community-based care. We consider some of these in the following section.

TRANSFORMING COMMUNITY CARE

Revisiting Assumptions in Home Care Models

When policy makers talk about community-based care, they tend to assume that a consensus exists as to its ingredients. The familial model of care that permeates most discussions is justified by appealing to preference statements made by old people that they would like to have their care provided by family members. Limited attention is paid to the fact that elderly respondents, like their younger counterparts, hold idealized images of family. In such images, not only do family members have knowledge of the particular needs and preferences of the elderly person, but they also have the capacity, time, and commitment to provide the desired level of care. An extensive body of research suggests that this is seldom the case. Likewise, taking preference statements at face value fails to recognize that, when trying to respond to questions about how their needs might be met, research participants, like all of us, are limited to concepts and knowledge that are part of their experiences. In the North American context, there is little guarantee of care by sources other than a family member. This situation can be contrasted to that of old people in Norway (48) where home care has been available for over 25 years. There, surveys show, old people prefer not to have family members provide personal care. . . .

Obviously missing from the data presented here are the voices of service users. Bringing their voices in is essential to developing the type of remodeling that we are suggesting. However, if including elderly service users and their families in decision-making is restricted to consumer surveys, we will only get more of what we already know—a list of preferences that reflect an idealized female family carer. If these narrowed preferences become the basis for developing long-term care policy, community-based care in the future will be limited to bolstering the lone carer and promoting opportunities for development of a personal care market for those with the resources to purchase such services. Under such conditions, old people, the family members who care for them (if available), and immigrant women of color who take up such jobs will all be losers. Old people will not have any guarantee of services should they need them. Family carers, primarily women, will bear increasing responsibility with only the hope of some occasional help or relief under a minimalist social policy that shrouds the lack of services to the elderly under the deceptive guise of "helping carers to care." Home care workers will be hired in a low-wage market where training, quality control, and working conditions are of little public concern.

The challenge today is to raise questions about what is required to enable elderly persons to remain a part of their community, however defined. What kinds of supports and guarantees are needed to promote this possibility? Projecting images of youthful active seniors or of severely debilitated elderly persons serenely accepting continuous care by a loving spouse or daughter as the norm is misleading because they are so at odds with the reality facing aging persons. The shape of community care programs is open to debate but can only be meaningful if service users are central to policy decision-making, as distinct from being occasionally consulted (51), and if home care workers can negotiate the content and organization of their work. One writer has phrased it this way: a vision is needed for community care which is both user-centered and worker friendly (52).

CONCLUSION

Redirecting the community care project will take considerable effort because the debates within it are frequently isolated. Feminist literature on caring has concentrated primarily on its effects for unpaid female kin. When formal caring is examined, the focus has been on the specification of tasks, their associated skills or professional expertise, and the organization and funding of services. An understanding of nonfamilial care would transform current models of community care. Recently the caring professions, nursing and social work, have begun to document the skill component of care work and separate it out from an amorphous idea of caring—perhaps most graphically conflated in the idea of caring communities. Caring work is attending physically, mentally, and emotionally to the needs of another and giving a commitment to the nurturing, growth, and healing of that other (53, pp. 18–19). Such a definition allows us to begin to specify what is competence in caring. It indicates that the adequate performance of tasks, such as meal preparation, is not the subject matter of caring; to define it as such misses the relationship-based components of the work. Caring is unpredictable, emotional work which, while not the equivalent of love, does involve commitment to developing and sustaining a relationship (54–57). Such work can occur in a variety of interpersonal relationships and in different institutional contexts. Admittedly, this is difficult to accomplish in bureaucratic work settings or in those that rely on a transient labor force. The recognition of these difficulties highlights just how profoundly care work is affected by the restructuring of health and social services. The long-term care agenda is, currently, the product of a host of economically driven policy directions. At the time of writing, these directions are encouraging new providers in the form of voluntary and paid-for neighborhood service schemes; the development of a mixed economy of care where profit-making agencies compete with public sector and nonprofits for service contracts; and the casualization of the labor force. Until there is a fundamental reexamination of the effects of these policy directions on the three most vulnerable players in home care—old people, their informal carers, and women of color who make up the home care workers labor market—gendered and racist policies will support practices that impede care. We hope that by documenting these effects, this study has taken a step toward this transformative task.

References

1. Benjamin, A. E. An historical perspective on home care policy. *Milbank Q.* 71(1): 129–166, 1993.

2. Szasz, A. The labor impacts of policy changes in home care; how federal policy transformed home health organizations and their labor practices. *J. Health Polit. Policy Law* 15: 191–210, 1990.

3. Burbridge, L. The labor market for home care workers: Demand, supply and institutional barriers. *Gerontologist* 33(1): 41–46, 1993.

4. Estes, C., et al. *The Long Term Care Crisis: Elders Trapped in the No-Care Zone.* Sage, Newbury Park, Calif., 1993.

5. Kenney, G. How access to long-term care affects home health transfers. *J. Health Polit. Policy Law* 18(4): 937–965, 1993.

6. MacAdam, M. Home care reimbursement and effects on personnel. *Gerontologist* 33(1): 55–63, 1993.

7. Daatland, S. Recent trends and future prospects for the elderly in Scandinavia. *J. Aging Soc. Policy* 6(1/2): 181–197, 1994.

8. Special issue on policy issues in care for the elderly in Canada. *Rev. Can. Vieillement/Can. J. Aging* 14(2): 153–446, 1995.

9. Evers, A., and van der Zanden, G. (eds.). *Better Care for Dependent People Living at Home: Meeting the New Agenda in Services for the Elderly.* Netherlands Institute of Gerontology, Bunnick, The Netherlands, 1993.

10. Kraan, R., and Evers, A. (eds.). *Care for the Elderly: Significant Innovations in Three European Countries.* Westview Press, Boulder, Colo., 1991.

11. Lesemann, F., and Martin, C. *Home-Based Care, the Elderly, the Family and the Welfare State: An International Comparison.* University of Ottawa Press, Ottawa, 1993.

12. Wistow, G., and Henwood, M. Caring for people: Elegant model or flawed design. In *Social Policy Review 1990–91,* edited by N. Manning, pp. 78–100. The Longman Group, Harlow, Essex, 1991.

13. Applebaum, R., and McGinnis, R. What price quality? Assuring the quality of case managed in-home care. *J. Case Manage.* 1(1): 9–13, 1992.

14. Eustis, N., Kane, R., and Fischer, L. Home care quality and the home care worker: Beyond quality assurance as usual. *Gerontologist* 33(1): 64–73, 1993.

15. Feldman, P. Work improvements for home care workers: Impact and feasibility. *Gerontologist* 33(1): 47–54, 1993.

16. Kane, R., and Caplan, A. (eds.). *Ethical Conflicts in the Management of Home Care: The Case Manager's Dilemma.* Springer Publishing, New York, 1993.

17. Kramer, A., et al. Assessing and assuring the quality of home health care: A conceptual framework. *Milbank Q.* 68(3): 413–443, 1990.

18. Schmid, H., and Hasenfield, Y. Organizational dilemmas in the provision of home-care services. *Soc. Serv. Rev.* 67: 40–54, 1993.

19. Bartoldus, E., Illery, B., and Sturges, P. J. Job-related stress and coping among home care workers with elderly people. *Health Soc. Work,* August 1989, pp. 204–210.

20. Eustis, N. N., and Fischer, L. R. Relationship between home care clients and their workers: Implications for quality of care. *Gerontologist* 31(4): 447–456, 1991.

21. Kaye, L. W. Worker views of the intensity of affective expression during the delivery of home care services for the elderly. *Home Care Serv. Q.* 7: 41–54, 1986.

22. Mercer, S., Heacock, P., and Beck, C. Nurses aides in nursing homes: A study of caregivers. *J. Women Aging* 6(1/2): 107–121, 1994.

23. Warren, L. We're home helps because we care: The experience of home helps caring for elderly people. In *New Directions in the Sociology of Health,* edited by P. Abbott and G. Payne, pp. 70–86. Falmer Press, London, 1990.

24. Abel, E. Family care of the frail elderly. In *Circles of Care: Work and Identity in Women's Lives,* edited by E. Abel and M. Nelson, pp. 65–91. The State University of New York, Albany, 1990.

25. Dwyer, J., and Coward, R. *Gender, Families and Elder Care.* Sage, Newbury Park, Calif., 1992.

26. Lewis, J., and Meredith, B. *Daughters Who Care.* Routledge, London and New York, 1988.

27. Boyd, M. Gender, visible minority and immigrant earnings inequality: Reassessing an employment equity premise. In *Deconstructing a Nation: Immigration, Multiculturalism and Racism in '90s Canada,* edited by V. Satzewich, pp. 279–321. Fernwood Publishing, Halifax, Nova Scotia, 1992.

28. Foner, N. *The Caregiving Dilemma: Work in An American Nursing Home.* University of California Press, Berkeley, 1994.

29. Anthias, F., and Yuval-Davis, N. (with Cain, H.). *Racialized Boundaries: Race, Nation, Gender, Colour and Class and the Anti-Racist Struggle,* Routledge, London and New York, 1992.

30. Boris, E. The racialized gendered state: The construction of citizenship in the United States. *Social Politics: International Studies in Gender, State and Society* 2(2): 160–180, 1995.

31. Stafford, J. The impact of the new immigration policy on racism in Canada. In *Deconstructing a Nation: Immigration, Multiculturalism and Racism in '90s Canada,* edited by V. Satzewich, pp. 69–92. Fernwood Publishing, Halifax, Nova Scotia, 1992.

32. Arat-Koc, S. In the privacy of their own home: Foreign domestic workers as solution to the crisis of the domestic sphere in Canada. In *Feminism in Action: Studies in Political Economy* edited by M. P. Connelly and P. Armstrong, pp. 149–174. Canadian Scholars Press, Toronto, 1992.

33. Calliste, A. Canada's immigration policy and domestics from the Caribbean: The second domestic scheme. In *Race, Class, Gender, Bonds and Barriers,* Ed. 2, edited by J. Vorst et al., pp. 136–168. Garamond Press, Toronto, 1991.

34. Colen, S. "With respect to feeling": Voices of West Indian child care and domestic workers in New York City. In *All American Women: Lines that Divide, Ties that Bind* edited by J. B. Cole, pp. 3–70. Free Press, New York, 1986.

35. Dill, B. T. "Making your job good yourself": Domestic service and the construction of personal dignity. In *Women and the Politics of Empowerment,* edited by A. Bookman and S. Morgen, pp. 33–52. Temple University Press, Philadelphia, 1988.

36. Donovan, R. Work stress and job satisfaction: A study of home care workers in New York City. *Home Health Serv. Q.* 10: 97–114, 1989.

37. Glenn, E. N. From servitude to service work: Historical continuities in the racial division of paid reproductive labor. *Signs* 18(1): 1–43, 1992.

38. Tellis-Nayek, V., and Tellis-Nayek, M. Quality of care and the burden of two cultures: When the world of the nurse's aide enters the world of the nursing home. *Gerontologist* 29(3):307–313, 1989.

39. Essed, P. *Understanding Everyday Racism: An Interdisciplinary Theory.* Sage, Newbury Park, Calif., 1991.

40. Andersen, M. Studying across difference: Race, class and gender in qualitative research. In *Race and Ethnicity in Research Models,* edited by J. Stanfield II and R. Dennis, pp. 39–52. Sage, Newbury Park, Calif., 1993.

41. Cannon, L., Higginbotham, E., and Leung, M. Race and class bias in qualitative research on women. *Gender and Society* 2(4): 449–462, 1988.

42. De Vault, M. Ethnicity and expertise: Racial-ethnic knowledge in sociological research. *Gender and Society* 9(5): 612–631, 1995.

43. Aronson, J., and Neysmith, S. "You're not just in there to do the work": Depersonalizing policies and the exploitation of home care workers' labour. *Gender and Society* 10(1): 59–77, 1996.

44. Neysmith, S., and Aronson, J. Home care workers discuss their work: The skills required to "use our common sense." *J. Aging Stud.* 10(1): 1–14, 1996.

45. Folio Corporation. FolioVIEWS 2.1. Provo, Ohio, 1992.

46. Gregson, N., and Lowe, M. *Servicing the Middle Classes: Class, Gender and Waged Domestic Labour in Contemporary Britain. Routledge,* New York and London, 1994.

47. Walker, A., and Warren, L. *Changing Services for Older People,* Open University Press, Buckingham and Philadelphia, 1996.

48. Daatland, S. What are families for? On family solidarity and preference for help. *Ageing and Society* 10: 1–15, 1990.

49. Bakan, A., and Stasiulis, D. Making the match: Agencies and the racialization of women's household work. *Signs* 20(2): 303–335, 1995.

50. Razack, S. What is to be gained by looking white people in the eye? Culture, race, and gender in cases of sexual violence. *Signs* 19(4): 894–923, 1994.

51. Aronson, J. Giving consumers a say in policy development: Influencing policy or just being heard? *Can. Public Policy* 19(4): 367–378, 1993.

52. Carpenter, M. *Normality Is Hard Work: Trade Unions and the Politics of Community Care,* Lawrence and Wishart, London, 1994.

53. Davies, C. Competence versus care? Gender and caring work revisited. *Acta Sociol.* 38: 17–31, 1995.

54. Fisher, B., and Tronto, J. Toward a feminist theory of caring. In *Circles of Care: Work and Identity in Women's Lives,* edited by E. Abel and M. Nelson, pp. 35–62. The State University of New York, Albany, 1990.

55. Graham, H. Social divisions of caring. *Women's Studies International Forum* 16: 461–470, 1993.

56. James, N. Care = organization + physical labour + emotional labour. *Sociol. Health Illness* 14: 488–509, 1992.

57. Thomas, C. De-constructing concepts of care. *Sociology* 27(4): 649–669, 1993.

Sneakers and Sweatshops: Holding Corporations Accountable

David M. Schilling

A 12-year-old worker in Pakistan earns 60 cents per day stitching soccer balls that are sold for more than $10 in the United States; an Indonesian worker needs over a month's pay to purchase a pair of shoes she makes for Nike; Mexicans employed by Alcoa must choose between buying food and paying rent.

Although sweatshop conditions in factories throughout the world are not new, they became headline news when the public learned that clothes made under Kathie Lee Gifford's label were sewn by children at Global Fashions, a maquiladora factory (where products are made for export) in Honduras. Gifford, a television talk-show celebrity and children's advocate, was appalled when the National Labor Committee announced that clothes bearing her name were made by girls ages 12 to 14 who were forced to work 13-hour shifts under armed guard for 31 cents an hour. When she found that the charges were true, she convinced Wal-Mart to withdraw its contract from Global Fashions.

It would have been easy for Kathie Lee Gifford to end her involvement there. But she met with Secretary of Labor Robert Reich, who urged her to join the Department of Labor in its effort to end sweatshop conditions in the U.S. and abroad. Since that meeting, Gifford has recruited other celebrities in that effort.

On July 16 the Department of Labor sponsored the Fashion Industry Forum at Marymount University in Virginia. Retailers, buyers, designers, manufacturers, endorsers, contractors, consumers, unions and social responsibility groups gathered to discuss strategies for eradicating sweatshops in the garment industry. As Gifford observed, "The problems are not simple, but insidious and pervasive."

Nancy Penaloza, a sewing machine operator in New York City, described the sweatshop conditions under which she has worked for nine years: "I sew high-quality women's suits priced at $120 or more. I get paid $6 per suit. I work at least 56 hours a week, Monday through Saturday, and get paid $207 a week ($3.75 an hour), off the books. If there are deadlines, we work till the job is done. My boss screams at me all the time to work faster. There is only one bathroom for 100 people. We do not have a union. If you complain, you get fired and someone else takes your job." When Reich asked her, "What if you want to work 40 hours a week, can you?" Penaloza answered, "I have to work the number of hours my boss tells me."

Who is responsible for these substandard labor conditions? Corporate giants in the U.S. apparel industry rarely own the factories that produce their goods. As part of a globalized economy, companies like Levi Strauss, Nike and Reebok contract with suppliers who produce their goods. The working conditions of many suppliers fall far below the most basic standards of fair and humane treatment. Companies typically distance themselves from responsibility for workplace conditions and low wages by contending they do not own or operate these facilities. Yet their orders enable these facilities to operate.

In an interconnected world, both consumers and investors are hearing about child and exploited labor conditions via the evening news or the Internet. Most Americans do not want to purchase a soccer ball made by a Pakistani child who is paid six cents an hour. As both consumers and investors, Americans are pressing U.S. companies and their suppliers to address exploitative work conditions. According to a survey released by Marymount University, more than three-fourths of Americans would avoid shopping at stores if they were aware that the stores sold goods made in sweatshops. The challenge is to make companies enforce their codes of conduct and use their economic power to see that their suppliers observe basic standards of human and labor rights.

The Interfaith Center on Corporate Responsibility (ICCR) has been working with labor groups, companies in the apparel industry, the Department of Labor and the newly formed presidential advisory committee to explore strategies to eradicate sweatshops. ICCR is not new to this work. For 25 years it has been challenging corporations to pay a living wage, provide safe working conditions, and contribute to the communities where they operate. ICCR members have raised their voices in corporate boardrooms and shareholder annual meetings since 1971, when the Episcopal Church filed the first religious shareholder resolution calling on General Motors to divest of its operations in apartheid South Africa. Currently, ICCR has 275 Catholic, Protestant and Jewish institutional investors, including denominations, religious communities, pension funds, dioceses and health-care corporations with combined portfolios worth over $50 billion.

ICCR members combine a principled and pragmatic approach. As religious shareholders, they are "in" but not "of" the corporation—insiders because they are part owners of the company, outsiders because they believe the exclusive focus on bottom-line profits is idolatry. As board member Sister Barbara Aires, S.C., explains, "Economic decisions have profound human and moral consequences. Faith communities measure corporate performance not only by what a corporation produces and its profitability, but also by how it impacts the environment, touches human life and whether it protects or undermines the dignity of the human person. Protection of human rights—civil, political, social and economic—is a minimum standard for corporations seeking to act responsibly."

ICCR, along with two religious counterparts in Great Britain and Canada, has released a draft document titled "Principles for Global Corporate Responsibility: Benchmarks for Measuring Business Performance." This is the first time that religious groups have developed comprehensive global standards for responsible corporate citizenship. The Principles urge companies to envision themselves as one of many stakeholders in the global community and to set high standards for how they treat their employees, the environment and the communities where they operate.

ICCR's approach to corporations involves talking with company officials, filing shareholder resolutions that address changes in policies and practices, running public campaigns focusing on media and public education, and screening out investments in companies whose actions violate members' principles.

In many instances, ICCR uses all these tools at once. Sometimes it takes a public campaign for a company to agree to dialogue. In other cases the filing of a shareholder resolution gets a company's attention and leads to constructive dialogue and change. (In 1996 ICCR members filed 172 shareholder resolutions with 118 companies.)

Like many U.S. corporations, Alcoa operates manufacturing plants in Mexico's maquiladora sector, where goods are assembled for export. In 1965 the Mexican government set up the Border Industrialization Program, creating low-tariff, low-wage export platforms for U.S. companies on favorable terms—long before NAFTA was instituted and made all of Mexico an export platform. U.S. companies shift work to Mexico to cut labor costs. The rapid expansion of this sector has created jobs, but jobs at poverty-wage levels.

ICCR members, along with the Coalition for Justice in the Maquiladoras (CJM)—a broad-based coalition of labor, environmental and religious groups from Mexico, U.S. and Canada—were concerned about Alcoa. Among the concerns were low wages and poor health and safety conditions, including the gas poisonings of Alcoa workers in 1994. In 1995 the Benedictine Sisters of Boerne, Texas, filed a shareholder resolution calling on Alcoa to initiate a review of its maquiladora operations and to recommend changes. Alcoa was urged to participate in a survey to determine the purchasing power of the wages of its Mexican workers. A similar resolution was filed with ten other U.S. companies, including General Electric, Johnson & Johnson and Zenith.

Alcoa and other U.S. companies rationalize paying poverty-level wages in two ways. They point out that wages paid to workers are competitive with what other companies are paying in a specific area and that the wages paid to workers are above the minimum wage set by governments. But workers in Mexico and elsewhere can be paid a competitive wage well above the minimum required by law and still not be able to feed themselves and their families.

Before the 1994 Mexican economic crisis, the average pay of a maquiladora worker was $30 to $50 for a 48-hour week, or barely a subsistence wage. As a result of the peso devaluation and the inflation of over 50 percent that accompanied it, the purchasing power of maquiladora wages plunged below subsistence level.

In January 1996 a group of Alcoa workers in Ciudad Acuña did an informal market study which revealed that basic food items (not including meat, milk, vegetables or cereal) cost $26.87 a week, while wages averaged between $21.44 and $24.60 a week.

How can companies like Alcoa determine what a sustainable wage is, particularly in countries where standardized wage data are difficult to obtain and legal minimum wage levels are so low as to be meaningless? Sister Ruth Rosenbaum, T.C., co-chair of ICCR's Global Corporate Accountability Issue Group and director of the Center for Reflection, Education and Action, has devised an innovative method to determine wage levels. Rosenbaum has developed the Purchasing Power Index Study (PPI), which is based on the standard "market basket" survey similar to the Consumer Price Index done by the U.S. Department of Labor.

The PPI takes the market basket survey an important further step by calculating the intersection of wages and prices documented in the survey. Rosenbaum writes: "Based on wages paid, calculations are performed to determine the number of work minutes required in order to purchase any given item. Since each week contains a limited number of minutes, the calculations reveal how many items the worker can possibly purchase. The purchasing power of the wages is made evident, and the effect of the wage scale upon the life of the worker and the community is clarified in an objective way." (See Rosenbaum, *In Whose Interest?*, January 1996.) A sustainable wage is defined by religious shareholders as one that allows a worker to meet basic needs, set aside money for future purchases, and earn enough discretionary income to support the development of small business in the community.

How has Alcoa responded to religious shareholders? In January the company agreed to come to the U.S.-Mexico border for a meeting with maquiladora workers. But at the same time the Securities and Exchange Commission ruled in the company's favor that the Benedictine Sisters' resolution would be kept off the proxy statement and would not be brought up for a vote at Alcoa's shareholder meeting. Susan Mika, primary filer of the resolution; CJM Executive Director Martha Ojeda; and two Alcoa workers from Mexican plants traveled to Alcoa's annual shareholders' meeting. Workers Juan Tovar and Irma Valadez described the starvation wages, the lack of protective equipment and sanitary conditions and the lack of toilet paper in the workers' bathrooms. The Pittsburgh Labor Action Network on the Americas and the United Steelworkers of America helped draw press attention to the workers' concerns by distributing leaflets outside the meeting.

Mika called on Alcoa CEO Paul O'Neill to meet with the delegation after the annual meeting. O'Neill agreed and promised to review the wages and working conditions in Alcoa's Mexican plants. The combined pressure of religious shareholders, key labor groups, religious investors and maquiladora workers had an impact. In July Alcoa announced that its workers in Ciudad Acuña would receive a 40-pesos-per-week (about $5.25) raise. Said Mika: "This small wage increase, as applied to the reported 5,600 workers in Acuña, would nonetheless represent an additional investment of $30,000 per week in salaries received by workers."

O'Neill visited the plants, checked out workers' allegations, fired a human resources person for not reporting health and safety violations, put soap and toilet paper in plant bathrooms and raised wages.

The next step is to secure Alcoa's participation in a Purchasing Power Index study that could lead to a systematic wage increase for all of Alcoa's Mexican workers. Two U.S. companies that operate maquiladora plants in Mexico—Baxter International and W. R. Grace—have already agreed to participate. If ICCR can persuade a few key companies to raise wages, they can put pressure on all companies to pay a sustainable wage, whether the workers are in Michigan or Mexico, Indiana or Indonesia.

Sometimes work with a corporation produces results in one area but not in another. For example, two years ago General Motors endorsed the CERES Principles on the environment, a major mutual victory for environmental responsibility. In regard to its maquiladora operations in Mexico, however, GM has demonstrated little interest in participating in a study or in raising the wages of its 62,000 workers.

GM executives from Detroit and local GM managers did agree to visit GM workers at their homes in Reynosa, Mexico, which are made from corrugated metal and have no running water or electricity. At the time these workers were making 180 pesos (less than $26) a week in take-home pay. As a result of this trip, GM pledged to raise its workers' standard of living. CEO John Smith announced a housing initiative that "would make affordable housing a reality for thousands of its workers." ICCR supported the initiative but argued for more. "The housing program is a generous and compassionate response to the deplorable living conditions of some of GM's Mexican workers," said Barbara Glendon, O.S.U., of Mercy Consolidated Asset Management Program, for years a key sponsor of GM resolutions. "But compassion without justice is not enough to fulfill the obligations of our company to its employees. We are morally and ethically responsible to provide a sustainable wage to the people whose daily labor benefits us who are GM shareholders." A shift in wage policy from a competitive to a sustainable wage would improve the lives of over 700,000 GM workers worldwide and set a standard for other corporations to meet.

A public campaign over working conditions at a supplier in El Salvador turned into a collaborative relationship between ICCR and The Gap, a San Francisco–based clothing chain. The National Labor Committee Education

Fund in Support of Worker and Human Rights in Central America (NLC) had found violations of The Gap's "Sourcing Principles and Guidelines" at Mandarin International, a shop in San Salvador owned by a Taiwanese firm. Workers had complained to the NLC about the use of child labor, forced overtime, unsafe working conditions, threats to prevent workers from organizing and firing of union leaders. After six months of leafleting at stores, letter writing by religious and community groups and face-to-face discussions, The Gap agreed to explore independent monitoring at Mandarin International and to urge Mandarin to rehire union leaders who had been fired.

Four widely respected Salvadoran institutions agreed to form the Independent Monitoring Group: the secretariat of the Archdiocese of San Salvador, Tutela Legal (the human rights office of the archdiocese), the Human Rights Institute of University of Central America, and CENTRA (a labor research organization). These institutions now monitor Mandarin on a regular basis for worker abuses. In addition, when Mandarin receives enough work orders to restore the workforce to former levels, union leaders will be rehired.

This development is historic. The Gap is the first company to agree to develop an independent monitoring mechanism for its contract suppliers. Other companies have hired third-party consultants (like Ernst and Young, the accounting firm hired by Nike to do social audits of their contractors), but their reports are not independently generated or publicly disclosed. There are signs that independent monitors, made up of respected local institutions committed to human rights, will play a crucial role in ensuring that worker rights are respected, company codes of conduct upheld and sweatshop conditions eliminated.

Individuals and congregations can make a difference by refusing to purchase products made under sweatshop conditions, by writing to companies to inquire about their code of conduct and how it is enforced, by getting the directors of denominational pension funds involved in sweatshop issues and by voting for socially responsible resolutions.

There are companies that are willing to look for ways of doing business responsibly in the global economy; others are reluctant to enter the unknown territory where business operations and human rights intersect. But the consumers' growing concern about conditions under which products are made will not go away. As corporations struggle to do the right thing, we must hold them accountable and support those organizations that are helping to find principled and practical solutions to the challenges posed by the new global economy.

Affirmative Action.

Overview.

Affirmative action is the policy adopted in the late 1960s and early 1970s. Affirmative action has many versions, but in general it involves the assessment of equally qualified candidates for a job, school admission, or government contract that adds a positive selection criterion based on a candidate's membership in a particular race or other identified group or (in some cases) gender (female).

Affirmative action does *not* mean automatically getting a job, admission to school, or contract merely by being a member of one of the identified groups. This would constitute selection based *solely* on membership in a particular group, which might result in unqualified candidates receiving preferences. Instead, affirmative action involves making a selection among a group of qualified candidates and using race, gender, or another characteristic as a positive selection criterion. In other words, all things being equal, this one factor results in the selection of the targeted candidate.

These targeted preferences are not new to the public policy arena. After World War II, veterans were often afforded the same preference as a way to compensate them for the disruption of their lives they experienced while they served their country. These preferences were largely uncontroversial and still exist in certain government jobs.

However, the preferences based on race, gender, and ethnic group have resulted in considerably more controversy. As a result, several states (such as California and Texas) have eliminated affirmative action in academic admissions for public universities and colleges. Other states have reduced efforts on job hiring and contract awards. Some argue against the policy; others argue for its continuation. Clearly, this is a much disputed issue.

To provide readers information about this controversy, I have selected two classics from the beginning of the affirmative action debate (by Thomson and by Simon) and an essay of my own from the contemporary perspective.

Thomson narrows her purview to affirmative action in university hirings. She contends that a problem has existed and continues to exist concerning discrimination against African-Americans and women, a problem she believes should be redressed; she argues that affirmative action is a plausible (albeit imprecise) tool to do so.

Simon's response to Thomson asserts that affirmative action is not an appropriate remedy because it blurs the individual versus the group distinction. (This is a similar dynamic that we examined in the definition of the corporation in Chapter Three.) Did the wrongs of discrimination affect groups or individuals? If the former, then a group remedy is in order. If the latter, then an individual remedy should be made. Affirmative action blurs this distinction and thus, he argues, is an ineffective remedy.

I contend that the governmental policy of affirmative action is grounded in a theory of distributive justice. Many writers on the topic have suggested that the most useful way to view this process is either from the perspective of the small picture (i.e., each individual's personal desert) or from the view of the large picture (i.e., each ethnic, racial, or gender group's share of the total goods and services within the economy). This essay begins with a review of some strengths and weaknesses of each position and then attempts to identify a solution using criteria from a theory of distributive justice and considerations of shared community worldview.

Preferential Hiring

Judith Jarvis Thomson

Many people are inclined to think preferential hiring an obvious injustice.[1] I should have said "feel" rather than "think": it seems to me the matter has not been carefully thought out, and that what is in question, really, is a gut reaction.

I am going to deal with only a very limited range of preferential hirings: that is, I am concerned with cases in which several candidates present themselves for a job, in which the hiring officer finds, on examination, that all are equally qualified to hold that job, and he then straightway declares for the black, or for the woman, because he or she *is* a black or a woman. And I shall talk only of hiring decisions in the universities, partly because I am most familiar with them, partly because it is in the universities that the most vocal and articulate opposition to preferential hiring is now heard—not surprisingly, perhaps, since no one is more vocal and articulate than a university professor who feels deprived of his rights.

I suspect that some people may say, Oh well, in *that* kind of case it's all right, what we object to is preferring the less qualified to the better qualified. Or again, What we object to is refusing even to consider the qualifications of white males. I shall say nothing at all about these things. I think that the argument I shall give for saying that preferential hiring is not unjust in the cases I do concentrate on can also be appealed to justify it outside that range of cases. But I won't draw any conclusions about cases outside it. Many people do have that gut reaction I mentioned against preferential hiring in *any* degree or form; and it seems to me worthwhile bringing out that there is good reason to think they are wrong to have it. Nothing I say will be in the slightest degree novel or original. It will, I hope, be enough to set the relevant issues out clearly.

I

But first, something should be said about qualifications.

I said I would consider only cases in which the several candidates who present themselves for the job are equally qualified to hold it; and there plainly are difficulties in the way of saying precisely how this is to be established, and even what is to be established. Strictly academic qualifications seem at a first glance to be relatively straightforward: the hiring officer must see if the candidates have done equally well in courses (both courses they took, and any they taught), and if they are recommended equally strongly by their teachers, and if the work they submit for consideration is equally good. There is no denying that even these things are less easy to establish than first appears: for example, you may have a suspicion that Professor Smith is given to exaggeration, and that this "great student" is in fact less strong than Professor Jones's "good student"—but do you *know* that this is so? But there is a more serious difficulty still: as blacks and women have been saying, strictly academic indicators may themselves be skewed by prejudice. My impression is that women, white and black, may possibly suffer more from this than black males. A black male who is discouraged or down-graded for being black is discouraged or down-graded out of dislike, repulsion, a desire to avoid contact; and I suspect that there are very few teachers nowadays who allow themselves to feel such things, or, if they do feel them, to act on them. A woman who is discouraged or down-graded for being a woman is not discouraged or down-graded out of dislike, but out of a conviction she is not serious. . . .

II

. . . Suppose two candidates for a civil service job have equally good test scores, but that there is only one job available. We could decide between them by coin-tossing. But in fact we do allow for declaring for A straightway, where A is a veteran, and B is not.[2] It may be that B is a nonveteran through no fault of his own: perhaps he was refused induction for flat feet, or a heart murmur. That is, those things in virtue of which B is a nonveteran may be things which it was no more in his power to control or change than it is in anyone's power to control or change the color of his skin. Yet the fact is that B is not a veteran and A is. On the assumption that the veteran has served his country, the country owes him something. And it seems plain that giving him preference is a not unjust way in which part of that debt of gratitude can be paid.

And now, . . . we should turn to those debts which are incurred by one who wrongs another. It is here we find what seems to me the most powerful argument for the conclusion that the preferential hiring of blacks and women is not unjust.

I obviously cannot claim any novelty for this argument: it's a very familiar one. Indeed, not merely is it familiar, but so are a battery of objections to it. It may be granted that if we have wronged A, we owe him something: we should make amends, we should compensate him for the wrong done him. It may even be granted that if we have wronged A, we must make amends, that justice requires it, and that a failure to make amends is not merely callousness, but injustice. But (a) are the young blacks and women who are amongst the current applicants for university jobs amongst the blacks and women who were wronged? To turn to particular cases, it might happen that the black applicant is middle class, the son of professionals, and has had the very best in private schooling; or that the woman applicant is plainly the product of feminist upbringing and encouragement. Is it proper, much less required, that the black or woman be given preference over a white male who grew up in poverty, and has to make his own way and earn his encouragements? Again, (b), did we, the current members of the community, wrong any blacks or women? Lots of people once did; but then isn't it for them to do the compensating? That is, if they're still alive. For presumably nobody now alive owned any slaves, and perhaps nobody now alive voted against women's suffrage. And (c) what if the white male applicant for the job has never in any degree wronged any blacks or women? If so, *he* doesn't owe any debts to them, so why should *he* make amends to them?

These objections seem to me quite wrong-headed.

Obviously the situation for blacks and women is better than it was a hundred and fifty, fifty, twenty-five years ago. But it is absurd to suppose that the young blacks and women now of an age to apply for jobs have not been wronged. Large-scale, blatant, overt wrongs have presumably disappeared; but it is only within the last twenty-five years (perhaps the last ten years in the case of women) that it has become at all widely agreed in this country that blacks and women must be recognized as having, not merely this or that particular right normally recognized as belonging to white males, but all of the rights and respect which go with full membership in the community. Even young blacks and women have lived through down-grading for being black or female: they have not merely not been given that very equal chance at the benefits generated by what the community owns which is so firmly insisted on for white males, they have not until lately even been felt to have a right to it.

And even those who were not themselves down-graded for being black or female have suffered the consequences of the down-grading of other blacks and women: lack of self-confidence, and lack of self-respect. For where a community accepts that a person's being black, or being a woman, are right and proper grounds for denying that person full membership in the community, it can hardly be supposed that any but the most extraordinarily independent black or woman will escape self-doubt. All but the most extraordinarily independent of them have had to work harder—if only against self-doubt—then all but the most deprived white males, in the competition for a place amongst the best qualified.

If any black or woman has been unjustly deprived of what he or she has a right to, then of course justice does call for making amends. But what of the blacks and women who haven't actually been deprived of what they have a right to, but only made to suffer the consequences of injustice to other blacks and women? *Perhaps* justice doesn't require making amends to them as well; but common decency certainly does. To fail, at the very least, to make what counts as public apology to all, and to take positive steps to show that it is sincerely meant, is, if not injustice, then anyway a fault at least as serious as ingratitude.

Opting for a policy of preferential hiring may of course mean that some black or woman is preferred to some white male who as a matter of fact has had a harder life than the black or woman. But so may opting for a policy of veterans' preference mean that a healthy, unscarred, middle class veteran is preferred to a poor, struggling, scarred, nonveteran. Indeed, opting for a policy of settling who gets the job by having all equally qualified candidates draw straws may also mean that in a given case the candidate with the hardest life loses out. Opting for any policy other than hard-life preference may have this result.

I have no objection to anyone's arguing that it is precisely hard-life preference that we ought to opt for. If all, or anyway all of the equally qualified, have a right to an equal chance, then the argument would have to draw attention to something sufficiently powerful to override that right. But perhaps this could be done along the lines I followed in the case of blacks and women: perhaps it could be successfully argued that we have wronged those who have had hard lives, and therefore owe it to them to make amends. And then we should have in more extreme form a difficulty already present: how are these preferences to be ranked? shall we place the hard-lifers ahead of blacks? both ahead of women? and what about veterans? I leave these questions aside. My concern has been only to show that the white male applicant's right to an equal chance does not make it unjust to opt for a policy under which blacks and women are given preference. That a white male with a specially hard history may lose out under this policy cannot possibly be any objection to it, in the absence of a showing that hard-life preference is not unjust, and, more important, takes priority over preference for blacks and women.

Lastly, it should be stressed that to opt for such a policy is not to make the young white male applicants themselves make amends for any wrongs done to blacks and women. Under such a policy, no one is asked to give up a job which is already his; the job for which the white male competes isn't his, but is the community's, and it is the hiring officer who gives it to the black or woman in the community's name. Of course the white male is asked to give up his equal chance at the job. But that is not something he pays to the black or woman by way of making amends; it is something the community takes away from him in order that *it* may make amends.

Still, the community does impose a burden on him: it is able to make amends for its wrongs only by taking something away from him, something which, after all, we are supposing he has a right to. And why should *he* pay the cost of the community's amends-making?

If there were some appropriate way in which the community could make amends to its blacks and women, some way which did not require depriving anyone of anything he has a right to, then that would be the best course of action for it to take. Or if there were anyway some way in which the costs could be shared by everyone, and not imposed entirely on the young white male job applicants, then that would be, if not best, then anyway better than opting for a policy of preferential hiring. But in fact the nature of the wrongs done is such as to make jobs the best and most suitable form of compensation. What blacks and women were denied was full membership in the community; and nothing can more appropriately make amends for that wrong than precisely what will make them feel they now finally have it. And that means jobs. Financial compensation (the cost of which could be shared equally) slips through the fingers; having a job, and discovering you do it well, yield—perhaps better than anything else—that very self-respect which blacks and women have had to do without.

But of course choosing this way of making amends means that the costs are imposed on the young white male applicants who are turned away. And so it should be noticed that it is not entirely inappropriate that those applicants should pay the costs. No doubt few, if any, have themselves, individually, done any wrongs to blacks and women. But they have profited from the wrongs the community did. Many may actually have been direct beneficiaries of policies which excluded or down-graded blacks and women—perhaps in school admissions, perhaps in access to financial aid, perhaps elsewhere; and even those who did not directly benefit in this way had, at any rate, the advantage in the competition which comes of confidence in one's full membership, and of one's rights being recognized as a matter of course.

Of course it isn't only the young white male applicant for a university job who has benefited from the exclusion of blacks and women: the older white male, now comfortably tenured, also benefited, and many defenders of preferential hiring feel that he should be asked to share the costs. Well, presumably we can't demand that he give up his job, or share it. But it seems to me in place to expect the occupants of comfortable professorial chairs to contribute in some way, to make some form of return to the young white male who bears the cost, and is turned away. It will have been plain that I find the outcry now heard against preferential hiring in the universities objectionable; it would also be objectionable that those of us who are now securely situated should placidly defend it, with no more than a sigh of regret for the young white male who pays for it.

III

One final word: "discrimination." I am inclined to think we so use it that if any-one is convicted of discriminating against blacks, women, white males, or what have you, then he is thereby convicted of acting unjustly. If so, and if I am right in thinking that preferential hiring in the restricted range of cases we have been looking at is *not* unjust, then we have two options: (a) we can simply reply that to opt for a policy of preferential hiring in those cases is not to opt for a policy of discriminating against white males, or (b) we can hope to get usage changed—e.g., by trying to get people to allow that there is dis-criminating against and discriminating against, and that some is unjust, but some is not.

Best of all, however, would be for that phrase to be avoided altogether. It's at best a blunt tool: there are all sorts of nice moral discriminations [*sic*] which one is unable to make while occupied with it. And that bluntness it-self fits it to do harm: blacks and women are hardly likely to see through to what precisely is owed them while they are being accused of welcoming what is unjust.

Notes

1. This essay is an expanded version of a talk given at the Conference on the Liberation of Female Persons, held at North Carolina State University at Raleigh, on March 26–28, 1973, under a grant from the S & H Foundation. I am indebted to James Thomson and the members of the Society for Ethical and Legal Philosophy for criticism of an earlier draft.

2. To the best of my knowledge, the analogy between veterans' preference and the pref-erential hiring of blacks has been mentioned in print only by Edward T. Chase, in a Letter to the Editor, *Commentary*, February 1973.

Preferential Hiring:
A Reply to Judith Jarvis Thomson

Robert Simon

Judith Jarvis Thomson has recently defended preferential hiring of women and black persons in universities.[1] She restricts her defense of the assignment of preference to only those cases where candidates from preferred groups and their white male competitors are equally qualified, although she suggests that her argument can be extended to cover cases where the qualifications are unequal as well. The argument in question is compensatory; it is because of pervasive patterns of unjust discrimination against black persons and women that justice, or at least common decency, requires that amends be made.

While Thomson's analysis surely clarifies many of the issues at stake, I find it seriously incomplete. I will argue that even if her claim that compensation is due victims of social injustice is correct (as I think it is), it is questionable nevertheless whether preferential hiring is an acceptable method of distributing such compensation. This is so, even if, as Thomson argues, compensatory claims override the right of the white male applicant to equal consideration from the appointing officer. For implementation of preferential hiring policies may involve claims, perhaps even claims of right, other than the above right of the white male applicant. In the case of the claims I have in mind, the best that can be said is that where preferential hiring is concerned, they are arbitrarily ignored. If so, and if such claims are themselves warranted, then preferential hiring, while *perhaps* not unjust, is open to far more serious question than Thomson acknowledges.

A familiar objection to special treatment for blacks and women is that, if such a practice is justified, other victims of injustice or misfortune ought to receive special treatment too. While arguing that virtually all women and black persons have been harmed, either directly or indirectly, by discrimination, Thomson acknowledges that in any particular case, a white male may have been victimized to a greater extent than have the blacks or women with which he is competing. However, she denies that other victims of injustice or misfortune ought automatically to have priority over blacks and women where distribution of compensation is concerned. Just as veterans receive preference with respect to employment in the civil service, as payment for the service they have performed for society, so can blacks and women legitimately be given preference in university hiring, in payment of the debt owed them. And just as the former policy can justify hiring a veteran who in fact had an easy time of it over a nonveteran who made great sacrifices for the public good, so too can the latter policy justify hiring a relatively undeprived member of a preferred group over a more disadvantaged member of a nonpreferred group.

But surely if the reason for giving a particular veteran preference is that he performed a service for his country, that same preference must be given to anyone who performed a similar service. Likewise, if the reason for giving preference to a black person or to a woman is that the recipient has been injured due to an unjust practice, then preference must be given to anyone who has been similarly injured. So, it appears, there can be no relevant *group* to which compensation ought to be made, other than that made up of and only of those who have been injured or victimized.[2] Although, as Thomson claims, all blacks and women may be members of that latter group, they deserve compensation *qua* victim and not *qua* black person or woman.

There are at least two possible replies that can be made to this sort of objection. First, it might be agreed that anyone injured in the same way as blacks or women ought to receive compensation. But then, "same way" is characterized so narrowly that it applies to no one except blacks and women. While there is nothing logically objectionable about such a reply, it may nevertheless be morally objectionable. For it implies that a nonblack male who has been terribly injured by a social injustice has less of a claim to compensation than a black or woman who has only been minimally injured. And this implication may be morally unacceptable.

A more plausible line of response may involve shifting our attention from compensation of individuals to collective compensation of groups.[3] Once this shift is made, it can be acknowledged that as individuals, some white males may have stronger compensatory claims than blacks or women. But as compensation is owed the group, it is group claims that must be weighed, not individual ones. And surely, at the group level, the claims of black persons and women to compensation are among the strongest there are.

Suppose we grant that certain groups, including those specified by Thomson, are owed collective compensation. What should be noted is that the conclusion of concern here—that preferential hiring policies are acceptable instruments for compensating groups—does not directly follow. To derive such a conclusion validly, one would have to provide additional premises specifying the relation between collective compensation to groups and distribution of that compensation to individual members. For it does not follow from the fact that some group members are compensated that the group is compensated. Thus, if through a computer error, every member of the American Philosophical Association was asked to pay additional taxes, then if the government provided compensation for this error, it would not follow that it had compensated the Association. Rather it would have compensated each member *qua* individual. So what is required, where preferential hiring is concerned, are plausible premises showing how the preferential award of jobs to group members counts as collective compensation for the group.

Thomson provides no such additional premises. Moreover, there is good reason to think that if any such premises were provided, they would count against preferential hiring as an instrument of collective compensation. This is because although compensation is owed to the group, preferential hiring policies award compensation to an arbitrarily selected segment of the group; namely, those who have the ability and qualifications to be seriously considered for the jobs available. Surely, it is far more plausible to think that collective compensation ought to be equally available to all group members, or at least to all kinds of group members.[4] The claim that although compensation is owed collectively to a group, only a special sort of group member is eligible to receive it, while perhaps not incoherent, certainly ought to be rejected as arbitrary, at least in the absence of an argument to the contrary.

Accordingly, the proponent of preferential hiring faces the following dilemma. Either compensation is to be made on an individual basis, in which case the fact that one is black or a woman is irrelevant to whether one ought to receive special treatment, or it is made on a group basis, in which case it is far from clear that preferential hiring policies are acceptable compensatory instruments. Until this dilemma is resolved, assuming it can be resolved at all, the compensatory argument for preferential hiring is seriously incomplete at a crucial point.

NOTES

1. Judith Jarvis Thomson, "Preferential Hiring," *Philosophy & Public Affairs*, 2, no. 4 (Summer 1973), 364–384.
2. This point also has been argued for recently by J. L. Cowen, "Inverse Discrimination," *Analysis*, 33, no. 1 (1972), 10–12.
3. Such a position has been defended by Paul Taylor, in his "Reverse Discrimination and Compensatory Justice," *Analysis*, 33, no. 4 (1973), 177–182.
4. Taylor would apparently agree, *ibid*, 180.

The Future of Affirmative Action

Michael Boylan

For approximately thirty years, the United States has been struggling with a public policy known as *affirmative action*. Since controversial public policies often have a short life, it is remarkable that affirmative action has lasted as long as it has. In its inception, it was a strategy to reverse the clear and pervasive underrepresentation of African Americans (first) and women (second) in medicine, law, academia, government, and business. Over time, the policy has been expanded to include any clearly defined group that is underrepresented in the most desirable occupational classes, school admission, and government contracts.

Recently, some retrenchment toward affirmative action has occurred. The State of California passed Proposition 209 banning affirmative action in admissions in state colleges and universities. A 1996 court decision, *Hogwood v. Texas*, prohibited the use of racial preferences in determining admissions to state higher education facilities. Thus, two major states have recently discarded affirmative action in their university and college admissions policies. Municipalities are discarding minority set-asides for public contracts. Fewer companies are employing affirmative action criteria in hiring.

Clearly, we are at the crossroads regarding this policy. Either affirmative action will redefine itself and continue into the future, or it will gradually fade away. This essay examines the policy from the point of view of both distributive justice and worldview to suggest which direction the United States should take.

DEFINING AFFIRMATIVE ACTION

For the purposes of this essay, *affirmative action* refers to a policy that gives a preference to individuals based on their membership in designated groups that are underrepresented in the most desirable occupational classes, school admissions, and/or government contracts. This preference can take many forms, including extra point(s) added to some rubric for evaluating candidates, recruiting funds allocated for the expressed purpose of obtaining representation from individuals from a disadvantaged group (even when no rubric credits are given), and special training, education, and/or counseling given to individuals from a disadvantaged group to enable them to compete equally with individuals from advantaged groups.

Individuals from an advantaged group refers here to individuals from some clearly defined socioeconomic, racial, or gender group that is statistically well represented (or overrepresented) in the most desirable occupational classes, school admissions, and government contracts.

Individuals from a disadvantaged group describes individuals from some clearly defined socioeconomic, racial, or gender group that is statistically underrepresented in the most desirable occupational classes, school admissions, and government contracts.

Advantaged describes individuals or groups possessing (or seeming to possess) properties, work habits, general demeanor, and/or work production that are/is valued in the general society by those empowered to make the decisions ("the establishment"). The assumption is that individuals from families that are advantaged will also tend to be advantaged.[1]

Disadvantaged describes individuals or groups not possessing (or seeming not to possess) properties, work habits, general demeanor, and/or work production that are/is valued in the general society by the establishment. The assumption is that individuals from families that are disadvantaged will also tend to be disadvantaged.

Deserving refers to anyone who through *his or her own effort* fulfills some functional requirement of action and as a result achieves a functionally specific result. As an overlay to this basic definition, however, additions and subtractions can be made on the basis of what constitutes "his or her own effort." For example, if A has a 100-piece puzzle that is 80 percent complete and B has the same 100-piece puzzle that is only 10 percent complete, and after some time, A completes the puzzle while B achieves the level of only 80 percent, some adjustment in our calculations is in order.[2] It is true that only A completed the puzzle, but it is also true that B did more of the puzzle than A (and at a stage of it being rather amorphous—which is harder, as any puzzle maker knows).

---

[1]There are certainly many exceptions to this, the most obvious being someone who comes from advantaged parents but has various disabilities that render him disadvantaged or a person from a family that is advantaged but who is given insufficient nurturing measured by that person's needs. In the first case, we have a genetic cause, in the second, we have an environmental cause. In both cases, the paradigm I describe is excepted.

[2]The point of this example is not that B *could not* have finished the puzzle since the last portion is the easiest and if she had been able to complete earlier portions, then she could have completed later portions as well. But there might have been other factors that stopped B from the completion of the task. Let's assume that these factors are beyond her control. Then if we ask who is the better puzzle maker, the issue becomes more difficult. Do we honor results only or process? The former supports A while the latter supports B. My vote is with B because she has exhibited more effort and thus fulfills my definition of deserts.

Thus, A may deserve the title of puzzle finisher, but B deserves of the title of person who completed more of the puzzle and *a fortiori* is more deserving of the title better puzzle maker.[3]

This is a tortured issue, but I believe that A is often given full credit for desert while B is said to be a loser. This is not fair because A and B have been given puzzles at different stages of completion. The work necessary to fulfill the functional requirements for A is markedly less than for B. In this way, "deserts" become skewed.[4]

I suggest a qualitative subtraction of "credit" from A so that we might see his achievement as less than or equal to that of B.

The context of these preferences supposes the following:

1. We are considering only applicants capable of performing the job (i.e., performing work in a profession, doing the academic work at a comparable level, and executing the contract according to the request for proposal.

2. Identically qualified candidates do not exist (so that all such models that refer to them must be fictions). The impact of this requirement is that when we are assessing what it means to fulfill the functional requirements listed in 1, we must have broad enough vision of *how* a candidate might fulfill these requirements. A colleague mentioned to me recently that a position in her department that had been advertised had not been filled because no one had the qualifications of the person who was leaving. This is a common situation. People imagine only one type of person as capable of filling a particular position. What is needed is a broader, more flexible vision.

3. Aptitude tests and other models of prognostication are most effective when applied to individuals from the advantaged rather than the disadvantaged groups (i.e., they may work for those already in the mainstream but are not necessarily good predictors for those out of the mainstream).[5] Thus, to suppose that A (from

---

[3]One of the many difficulties with this type of analysis is that one is never sure whether A *could* have done the same job if he were presented the same puzzle as B. In some ways, this analysis can disadvantage the one who has been given the advantaged position.

[4]For a fine discussion of different senses of "desert," see, Louis P. Pojman and Owen McLeod (eds.), *What Do We Deserve? A Reader on Justice and Desert* (New York: Oxford University Press, 1999).

[5]The ability of aptitude tests to predict how intelligent people are (i.e., to predict success in school or employment) is a very controversial issue. One fundamental underlying issue is whether intelligence tests measure something that is, in fact, invariant. If it does not, it is not an aptitude test. (Achievement tests are rather different and are not at issue here.) The primary candidate for such an invariant factor is some sort of innate intelligence or heritability. It is here that the discussion usually has been engaged. Traditional advocates of the accuracy of such tests include R. M. Yerkes, "Testing the Human Mind," *The Atlantic Monthly* 131 (1923): 358–370; C. C. Bringham, *A Study of American Intelligence* (Princeton, NJ: Princeton University Press, 1923); and L. M. Terman, *The Measurement of Intelligence* (Boston: Houghton Mifflin, 1916). One of the most prominent detractors of the accuracy of such tests during this time period is Horace Mann Bond. For a discussion of his work, see Michael Fultz, "A Quintessential American: Horace Mann Bond, 1924–1929," *Harvard Educational Review* 55 (November 1985), 416–442; and Wayne J. Urban, "The Black Scholar and Intelligence Testing: The Case of Horace Mann Bond," *Journal of the History of the Behavioral Sciences* 21 (October 1989), 323–333.

an advantaged group) is more qualified for some situation because he scored N on some test than B (from a disadvantaged group) because she scored $N–X$ (where $X > 0$) is perhaps to engage in a faulty comparison. The fault occurs because no present testing mechanism exists to measure both A and B on the same methodology.[6]

THE PROBLEM

What problem does the policy of affirmative action seek to redress? There are many candidates.[7] The most persuasive of these refers to past discriminatory actions. Under this view of the problem, a group that has been discriminated against in the past is entitled to reparations of some sort. Thus, if a case could be made that African Americans had been discriminated against in the past, then they are entitled to redress.

However, detractors will contend the following:

1. People who were guilty of causing the most viscous discrimination are not in positions of power today. The people most disadvantaged in the past are not those seeking assistance from affirmative action. Under this scenario, affirmative action may have been an effective strategy in the past but is no longer justified because things are now okay.

Contemporary opinion leans in the opposite direction. The following writers support the link between heritability and intelligence: C. Burt, "The Inheritance of Mental Ability" in *The Discovery of Talent*, ed. D. Wolfe (Cambridge, MA: Harvard University Press, 1969); A. R. Jensen, "How Much Can We Boost IQ and Scholastic Achievement," *Harvard Educational Review* 39 (1969), 1–123; and Richard J. Hernstein, who most recently with Charles Murray, wrote, *The Bell Curve: Intelligence and Class Structure in American Life* (New York: Free Press, 1994). On the other side are N.J. Block and G. Dworkin, "IQ, Heritability, and Inequality" in Block and Dworkin (eds.), *The IQ Controversy* (New York: Pantheon, 1976); S.J. Gould, *The Mismeasure of Man* (New York: Norton, 1981); M.W. Feldman, James Crouse, et al., *The Case Against the SAT* (Berkeley, CA: University of California Press, 1988); and R.C. Lewontin, "The Heritability Hang-up," *Science* 190 (1975), 1163–68. Various environmental variables that might skew results are documented by T.B. Brazelton et al., "The Behavior of Nutritionally Deprived Guatemalan Infants," *Developmental Medicine and Child Neurology* 19 (1977), 364–72; and J. Brozek (ed.), *Behavioral Effects of Energy and Protein Deficits*, NIH Publication No. 79-1906 (Washington, DC: National Institutes of Health, 1979). For some evidence of the most recent scholarship, see Daniel Seligman, *A Question of Intelligence: The IQ Debate in America* (New York: Carol Publishing Group, 1992), and especially Audrey Shuey, *The Testing of Negro Intelligence*, 2d ed. (New York: Social Science Press, 1996).

[6]It is instructive to consider whether this is a practical problem or an "in-principle" problem. I believe that clearly it is, at least, the former (see footnote 5), but it may be the latter as well. This is so because the number of variables that must be considered to generate a definitive response is impossibly high. It is analogous to the "three-ball problem" in Newtonian mechanics being transformed into the "three hundred-ball problem." There is a point where impracticability may become impossibility.

[7]For an excellent summary of most of the arguments in favor of affirmative action, see Louis P. Pojman, "The Moral Status of Affirmative Action" *Public Affairs Quarterly* 6.2 (April 1992), 181–206.

2. Wrongs committed against a group cannot be rectified by individual solutions. This is so because any sampling of individuals from the underrepresented group includes individuals who are not at a disadvantage from being a member of the affected group. In fact, many individuals from this group may be more advantaged than many individuals from the so-called advantaged group.

3. Affirmative action only prolongs the stereotypes of inferiority that have plagued disadvantaged groups from the beginning. To be a "token" hire, student, or contractor does nothing to address the ultimate problem of racism. Therefore, only when all people can be judged by the content of their character rather than by the color of their skin (or other characteristic) can we assert that we are beyond discrimination.

No matter what position a person takes on this issue, most would agree that certain clearly defined socioeconomic, racial, and gender groups are markedly underrepresented in the most desirable occupational classes, school admissions, and government contracts.

What is one to make of these facts? Three common responses follow.

1. Certain groups are just inferior per se.
2. The underrepresentation is a blip in the present statistical environment and will work out differently in the future by some invisible hand.
3. Sociological dynamics distort reality; in fact, everyone at present competes rather well under fair rules. Those who do not succeed do not succeed. They have no one to blame but themselves.

All of these (and other) responses admit to a problem. Response 1 admits to some purported theme of racial, ethnic, or gender superiority, a very difficult claim to assess. The most obvious version of the argument is patently absurd. It smacks of bad science and eugenics. Some modern versions of this argument exist, but I do not believe that they fare better than their ancestors.

Another position seeks to describe different behavioral traits on the model of evolutionary biology. The strongest version of this argument is suggested by the sociobiologists. According to one version, *behaviors* are subject to the same sort of evolutionary pressures as any ordinary phenotypical (physical) trait. This is to say that there is no such thing as a good or a bad trait but only a trait that is adaptive in some environment.

For example, if one were to summarize Kettlewell's classic experiment with moth wing color, the results would be as follows: subspecies (a) has variegated wing color, and subspecies (b) has black wing color. In Environment-1, the trees that constitute the habitat of the moths are variegated in color. In Environment-2, pollution has made the trees black with soot. Kettlewell noticed that the normally populous subspecies (a) [in Enviorienment-1] were giving way to subspecies (b) as a result of industrial pollution [creating Environment-2]. By cleaning the trees, Kettlewell was able to reverse the trend, making subspecies (a) again more populous by re-creating Environment-1.

Does this mean that subspecies (a) is *better* than subspecies (b)? Certainly not, for in Environment-2, subspecies (b) flourished and dominated subspecies (a). All that the experiment shows is that no traits are good or bad per se but are so only within certain environments.

Another example of this can be found in the human realm. Today, young male children are five times more likely than young female children to be diagnosed as being hyperactive, meaning (among other things) that they are easily distracted and will readily move from one task that they are working on to another and another. This often leads to trouble in the first grade (Environment-1). As a result, the teacher may report that these children need to be put on medication right away if they are to be able to make it in the challenging world of the second grade.

However, when a person with this same trait works in a stockbroker's office (Environment-2), things are rather different. The individual who can move on seven planes at once and interrupt himself without a problem to make a trade or to react to fast-breaking market events is a prized commodity. This trait that was deleterious in Environment-1 is highly sought in Environment-2.

In evolutionary biology, phenotypical traits are not good or bad; they simply are. Variation in any species is a dogmatic given. This is what allows the species to survive in changing environments.

If behavioral traits also operate according to the rules of environmental evolutionary biology, then it could be possible that different groups within the human family might be different. To be different does not mean to be *absolutely better* or *absolutely worse*. It refers only to the functional expression of that trait in a given social environment. If Asians outperform Native Americans in competition for the prizes within twenty-first century America, this describes a fact about only certain behavioral traits within this environment but says nothing about how these two groups might fare within a *different* environment.

The crux of this analysis (if correct) is that various groups (as groups, not as individuals) are predisposed (by nature or ethnic nurture) to be more or less successful in different environments. As a result, one must conclude that there may be structural issues of justice and fairness at stake. (These will be addressed in the next section of the essay.)

The second response suggests that the invisible hand of the *market* will solve the problems of job discrimination. I have no doubt that this is true. The question is, however, *how* the problem will be solved. Simply to solve a problem is not enough. Hitler aspired to solve the "problem of the Jews" by killing all of them, which is unacceptable. What is needed is a theory of justice that advocates a solution and a theory (and its application) that are submitted to rational scrutiny.

The third reply is quite common these days. Many claim that problems with discrimination among selected groups in the American experience no longer exist. I reply that this is merely an issue of attentiveness. The so-called invisible person syndrome often affects minority groups. Those who are succeeding at the game may often notice only that their close competitors, the also-rans, are given no heed. This does not mean that they do not exist but merely that they are not noticed. Many fit this category.

Responses to the Problem

The traditional statements of the problem are very complicated. First, they involve individual and group dynamics. Second, they include a theory of "deserts" that gives authority to certain claims for goods. Third, they depend on how goods in a society are allocated. Logically, this is a primary consideration, although it is in the middle of questions about the policy. Fourth, these traditional statements require some assumptions in order to create an action description of the agents including motives, initiative, and other such intentions. Fifth, these statements require some agreement as to the facts about which groups are successful and which are not within the semicapitalist society of the United States in the beginning of the twenty-first century.

I will assess these dilemmas by relating them to an understanding of distributive justice and adding principles of personal and shared community worldview.

Distributive Justice

Each of the many theories of distributive justice[8] makes a different recommendation pertaining to resource allocation. One of the difficulties in theories of justice is that different situations seem to require different theories. This complicates the issue of how to choose a theory of justice. Such an exercise is beyond the scope of this essay; however, I provide a selected sample of theories to make my intended point.

---

[8]A brief survey of positions relevant to this essay include A.W.H. Adkins, *Merit and Responsibility* (Oxford: Oxford University Press, 1960); Claudia Card, "On Mercy" *Philosophical Review* 81 (1972), 182–207; Joel Feinburg, *Doing and Deserving* (Princeton, NJ: Princeton University Press, 1970); Lloyd Fields, "Parfit on Personal Identity and Desert," *Philosophical Quarterly* 37 (1987), 432–40; Alan Goldman, "Real People: Natural Differences and the Scope of Justice" *Canadian Journal of Philosophy* 17 (June 1987), 377–94, Fredrich A. Hayek, *The Constitution of Liberty* (Chicago: University of Chicago Press, 1960); Kai Nielsen, *Equality and Liberty* (Totowa, NJ: Rowman and Allenheld, 1985); C. Perleman, *Justice Law and Argument* (Dordrecht: D. Reidel, 1980); Nicholas Rescher, *Distributive Justice* (Indianapolis, IN: Bobbs-Merrill, 1966); George Sher, *Desert* (Princeton, NJ: Princeton University Press, 1987); Michael Walzer, *Spheres of Justice* (New York: Basic Books, 1983); and Iris Young, *Justice and the Politics of Difference* (Princeton, NJ: Princeton University Press, 1990).

Some major theories of justice that are relevant in this context include *capitalism* (to each according to his production), *socialism* (to each according to her need), *egalitarianism* (to each equally), *aristocracy* (to each according to his inherited station), and *kraterism* (to each according to her ability to snatch what she wants).

Certainly, the last two theories, aristocracy and *kraterism*, would never endorse a policy such as affirmative action. Aristocracy would demur because its very definition supports the status quo concerning the distribution of rank and preferment. *Kraterism* would never accept affirmative action because its mission is to affirm those who are able to grasp the prize. Those who cannot are resigned to the dustbin—end of story.

I contend that the fairest situation is egalitarianism unless situations warrant otherwise.[9] This means that the default system of allocation is always to give to each party equally unless there is a good reason to deviate. If a person were to deviate (on the principle of economic efficiency, for example), then I advocate a mixture of capitalism and socialism (as defined earlier). In a very condensed manner, egalitarianism should be adopted unless compelling reasons indicate that another theory (or mix of theories) is more appropriate. What counts as a compelling reason? It would be a practical need that makes its case in the context of an ethical theory. In my case, that would mean a deontological theory that emphasizes rights and duties.[10]

Since egalitarianism has proved (in a macro sense) to be a very inefficient system on which to base an economy, we would turn to capitalism (modified by socialism). As a matter of fact, this is the direction that all the industrialized countries in the world have taken. The balance between capitalism and socialism is what is at issue. Various countries lean toward rewarding work while others emphasize meeting essential human needs (the so-called cradle-to-grave ideal).

I advocate egalitarianism as the "default" system of justice for it lies at the micro level. At the micro level, a person has many allocation decisions;

---

[9]The reason for this choice comes from a "micro" to "macro" orientation. Like Plato, in the *Republic*, who looked first toward the dymanics of the individual in his familial and interpersonal levels to ground his understanding of the *polis*, I believe that this is the place to start. Barring any other changes in normal operating rules (such as giving one's children a piecework situation in which the family members who do some particular task will get the largest slice of cake or whatever), we should allocate equally. Everyone gets the same helping of dinner unless there are extenuating circumstances such as John is on a diet or Jane must gain weight for lacrosse. This point of view asserts that (on the micro level) the natural system of distribution (justice) is egalitariansim.

[10]I am saying here that a practical need per se is not enough. Of course, some moral theories such as Utilitarianism might make the practical and moral calculations seamless, but the broader point is that a person must present a compelling moral justification for moving away from the default, egalitarian distribution formula. In most macroeconomic situations, this is easily presented, but in individual, micro interactions, this is most often not the best way to allocate goods. Families, small organizations, and community groups are better off beginning with egalitarianism and then arguing for a different allocation method if it is absolutely necessary.

for example, a family must decide how to divide the chocolate cake for dessert. Given that everyone likes chocolate cake equally and no other health considerations exist, the fairest[11] distribution is to give everyone an equal slice. I believe that this is (or should be) the driving principle of distribution among families. If we are allocating clothes, food, or any other desirable good within the family, it should be done equally. Birthday presents, parents' time—everything seems best distributed equally.

If the family is the basic social unit of society, then the principles of justice that hold there ought to hold for other units until some other principle trumps it. Certainly, this thesis is an ambitious one. It could encompass a monograph in itself. But if this brief treatment can be taken as suggestive, then I propose the following process whereby we can link these ruminations to affirmative action.

> *Step One.* We begin with egalitarianism. If we were to allocate in this fashion, then surely underrepresented groups would be compensated (through enhanced access to jobs, schooling, and government contracts) since the strategy is to allocate to each equally.

> *Step Two.* Egalitarianism is not the most efficient macro-allocation strategy. Therefore, in macro cases, it should be replaced with a system of capitalism/socialism (the mixture to be argued for in another venue).

> *Step Three.* The capitalism side of the equation could argue for affirmative action as a sort of investment strategy.[12] Under this scenario, people invest in individuals from disadvantaged groups that are not presently producing at the level one might expect. To each according to his production here must be understood in an Aristotelian *potentiality* sense. We will, as a society, invest in what is potentially a lucrative market (our own people who are underrepresented in the workplace). It is not unusual for capitalism to invest in potential markets. At the writing of this essay, very few information technology (IT) stocks are showing anything close to a profit on Wall Street, yet they are besieged with offers to finance them. People see *actualized* earnings

---

[11]Here I am following a conventional way of describing a value judgment between theories of justice. The normative term *fairest* really means "the best," which presupposes a theory of what constitutes "the best." In this instance (since such a discussion is beyond the scope of this essay), I invoked the Kantian notion of kingdom of ends. The duty to treat others as ends and never as means only is grounded in a theory that counts each person equally and distributes basic rights *equally*. There is some fundamental sense, therefore, that egalitarianism is true with respect to basic moral rights and duties. The next step is into the realm of well-being. This includes distribution of tangible goods. I believe that this sense of egalitarianism carries over here, as well. For an argument on how basic human goods of well-being must also be distributed according to egalitarianism, one need look only to such neo-Kantians as Alan Gewirth, *Reason and Morality* (Chicago: University of Chicago Press, 1978).

[12]Capitalist economies do this all the time. The most recent instance has been the massive support for information technology companies. Throughout history, the United States and other industrialized nations have supported directions that they thought would benefit the country in the long term.

down the road even though some particular company right now has never shown a profit.

If we are willing to gamble in this way on IT and Internet stocks, why can't we gamble on our own people?

Obviously, the depiction of capitalism's acceptance of affirmative action is not acceptable for many people. One criticism of my position might say that a true capitalist would deny any consideration to those who violate the basic formula, to each according to his production,[13] but this begs the question of what society is to do with such individuals (under a capitalist mind-set). These people will not simply vanish; they will not starve to death because they have no employment. At the very least (which should be recognized by even the most ardent free marketer), the disadvantaged will pose a threat to the advantaged because as the gap widens between the groups, anger and frustration accelerate. All of those well-deserved possessions acquired by people who have flourished under the conditions of the present system are in jeopardy if a significant segment of the population decides that it has nothing and therefore nothing to lose. Such people are dangerous to those invested in the status quo. From the macro perspective, societies work best when everyone is brought into the economic picture. The advantaged who ignore the disadvantaged ("let them eat cake!") do so at their own peril.

Thus, even from a nonmoral prudential calculation, it makes no sense to disenfranchise any substantial disadvantaged group. Society needs these people to take a positive role, or society may face severe civil unrest.

The second half of my distribution formula includes socialism, to each according to her needs. All people need work to pay their bills. Thus, they have a rightful claim against society to provide them a proportional share of the most desirable occupational classes, school admissions, and government contracts.

Socialism adds to the equation the aspect that needs must be particularized. The largest flaw in the traditional affirmative action program is that sometimes it has given special help those who did not need it. For example, consider a case of college admissions in which two applicants are striving to obtain a single position at a prestigious college. One applicant is an African-American male from an affluent household earning in excess of $200,000 a year (within the top 2 percent of all wage earners). This student has been to the top private schools and has had every advantage that money can buy (there has always been a strong correlation between income and success within the rules of a society; ergo the popular adage, "the rich get richer and the poor

---

[13]There is, of course, the unexamined issue of the value of work itself. Is all work on a par? Is the invisible hand of the marketplace the only indicator of what is good or bad? Are there no other prescriptive standards in capitalism? I hope to be able to address these important questions in another venue.

get poorer"). The African-American student's parents have terminal post-graduate degrees (the highest degrees in their field) and can provide their child top-notch tutoring and help with schoolwork. The second student is a white male who comes from a family with a combined income of less than $20,000 (within the bottom 10 percent of all wage earners). This student's parents are not very intelligent in ways measured in school. No tutoring is available, and the student must work twenty hours a week to help support the family. Home is often a barren and violent place for him.

Is it fair that the African-American from a prosperous background receive preference over the white male from a disadvantaged background? I say no. The African-American is an individual from a disadvantaged group but happens to be individually advantaged. The other is an individual from an advantaged group but happens to be individually disadvantaged.

It seems to me that individual dynamics ought to take precedent over group dynamics. In other words, being individually disadvantaged is more relevant than being of a group that is disadvantaged. This seems true enough at the extremes; however, the middle (the majority of) cases, are more difficult to judge. Governmental policies must be unambiguous. Therefore, I suggest leaving things as they are in the "great middle" of American life. The goals of affirmative action to help individuals from disadvantaged groups achieve representation in the most desirable occupational classes, school admissions, and government contracts should be maintained. At the extremes, however, a different policy should be adopted because those at the top have already achieved the goal. They have become successful within the environment of modern American life.

Those at the bottom—regardless of their group membership—ought to be helped. Through no fault of their own, they have been born into families for whom succeeding is exceedingly difficult. It is like B with the puzzle mentioned earlier whose task is to complete a larger part of the puzzle.

The practical problem is identifying the individuals in each group. As my example suggests, money is a good indicator; it means that the family has figured out how to succeed in the present socioeconomic environment. As with Kettlewell's biological examples discussed earlier, the winners in the modern environmental struggle in the United States (or any other country) are more likely (through genetics or nurturing) to engender children who also will be winners.

Since the origin of the probable success of these individuals (born into successful families) is not due solely to desert (as defined earlier), they have no real cause to complain that they have had something unfairly taken from them.

If this model is correct, then the issue is to create income parameters for the affirmative action policy for college admissions. These are, subject to debate, of course, but the following set of rules might be created:

1. Applicants who earn more than $100,000 a year themselves or come from a household in which their family income is in excess of $100,000 (pretax gross

personal income) or is (by the same conditions) in the top 20 percent of family incomes—regardless of their membership within a disadvantaged group—cease to be eligible for preference in an affirmative action program.

2. Applicants who earn less than $25,000 a year themselves or come from a household in which their family income (pretax gross income) is less than $25,000 or is in the lower 20 percent of family incomes—regardless of their membership within a disadvantaged group—are eligible for preference in an affirmative action program.

3. For the rest of the population, affirmative action continues to be a policy that gives preference—in one of the ways outlined in the beginning of this essay— to individuals from disadvantaged groups for the most desirable occupations, school admissions, and government contracts.

WORLDVIEW PERSPECTIVES

The perspective of worldview adds further texture to the discussion. I describe *worldview* as encompassing the totality of a person's values about ethics, aesthetics, and truth (including religion). One's positions on these issues shape the vision of reality he endorses.

Obviously, one problem with the multicultural America (world) of today is that there are countless worldviews. These are impossible to embrace comprehensively at the individual level because of the sheer number of people in the world (as many as six billion at last count). Worldview can be discussed meaningfully, but only in some sort of generic sense.[14] In this context, I assert that all people must develop a single comprehensive and internally coherent worldview that is good and that we strive to act out in our daily lives.[15] Thus, at the individual level, each of us is enjoined to examine and come to terms with her many beliefs and values.

If this is correct, then we must find a way to connect individual worldviews. In this context I speak of a shared community worldview imperative to create a common body of knowledge that supports values by which social institutions and their resulting policies might flourish within the constraints of the essential core values: ethics, aesthetics, and truth (including religion). Several key points must be observed about this shared community worldview imperative.

The first point is the necessity to create a common body of knowledge.[16] By the common body of knowledge, I mean the acceptance of certain basic

---

[14]I give an overview of such an analysis in the Introduction to *Basic Ethics* (Upper Saddle River, NJ: Prentice Hall, 2000).

[15]I call this imperative the *Personal Worldview Imperative*. This is argued for in a meta-ethical and normative context in *Basic Ethics* (Upper Saddle River, NJ: Prentice Hall, 2000) and is given further exposition in an applied context in *Medical Ethics* (Upper Saddle River, NJ: Prentice Hall, 2000).

[16]I elaborate on the concept of a common body of knowledge in my book, *The Process of Argument* (Englewood Cliffs, NJ: Prentice Hall, 1988), chap. 1.

facts about reality necessary to make possible a dialogue between individuals of disparate worldviews to forge mutually acceptable principles on which social and/or political institutions might be created. An example of this might be the Constitutional Convention that created the document that governs the United States of America. The members of the Constitutional Convention had various visions of what the newly formed country would be like that often conflicted with each other.

The best way to avoid such deadlocks is to establish a great conversation among the people involved. Sometimes such impasses are "solved" merely by someone gaining a power position over his opposition ("might makes right," a form of *kraterism*).

The best solution for creating a common body of knowledge is to agree to a procedure by which individual issues might be resolved. It is often easier to agree to such a procedure (because it is grounded in an abstract, rational procedure that strips individual interests from its decision-making process) than it is to agree on other points that are more empirical.

However, consensus is not always possible. For example, if Group A had as a part of its worldview that all people of type-x were totally worthless and if Group B had as a part of its worldview that all people of type-x were the most worthy of choice, then, the two could not form a common body of knowledge on that particular issue (unless there were radical compromise or fundamental change by Group A or B or both). The result would probably be that Group A and Group B could not form a shared community worldview. In this case, the only way that social and/or political institutions could be formed would be by the *krateristic* means cited earlier.

The second point is that the institutions and policies that result from those institutions must flourish. This means that impractical proposals are not acceptable. A proposal is impractical if the shared community worldview is so dissonant from the personal worldview of the individual that that individual will not accept ownership of the directives that flow from the shared community worldview. In this case, the individual reacts either in apathy or in defiance (depending on how much force has been used to subvert the oppressed group to the will of those in power).

Thus, to flourish, a significant number of people from all diverse groups within the society must continually strive to renew and to invigorate the great conversation on the fundamental principles that underlie our social and/or political institutions. One way to measure the health of a society is to observe whether the great conversation is ongoing and freely inclusive of all members (the principle of diversity).

The third point to notice about the shared community worldview is that the conversation must take place within the constraints of ethics, aesthetics, and truth (including religion). These are the highest principles by which we live, which are necessary to ensure that the conclusions of the great conversation are good principles. Without this constraint, despotic and repressive regimes could emerge.

Given these principles of personal and shared community worldview, how do they bear on the question of affirmative action? Certainly, one can identify the underlying problem as being one that the great conversation is meant to address (there are clearly identifiable groups based on social, ethnic, racial, and or gender factors that are not participating in the most desirable occupations, educational opportunities, or government contracts).

Diversity and the common body of knowledge are critical here. To engage authentically in the great conversation, we must include all groups. Everyone must be brought into process so that each might make her contribution. This aim at consensus is crucial if all parties are to agree with the result.

Within this context, affirmative action is simply one policy to solve a problem. Other policies may be more or less effective than affirmative action. If people are upset with affirmative action (as presently implemented)—and many are—then they must either revise affirmative action or replace it with something better. Merely to pass a law (such as California's Proposition 209) or take legal action (as in *Hogwood v. Texas*) is not sufficient to solve the problem; it exists and demands a solution.

The worldview perspective offers a foundation to support continued dialogue on problems such as affirmative action within certain constraints that ensure diversity in the process. This dialogue promotes fairness and the practical flourishing called for by shared community worldview.

Perhaps a new policy will emerge from the current debate on affirmative action. If it provides a more effective strategy that is accepted in the fashion described, then so be it. But until a better policy is in effect, I suggest modifying affirmative action at the income extremes as described as the best remedy for this important societal problem.

Since the great conversation is ongoing, we may find ourselves tinkering with this and other public policies in the future. In time, affirmative action may not be needed because the United States will have no severely disadvantaged groups. We are not there yet.

Gender Issues.

Overview.

A myriad of gender issues face the modern U.S. corporation. Integrating women fairly into the corporate community is the ultimate goal. Standing in the way of that goal are latent attitudes, stereotypes, and communication issues. These issues must be addressed both from practical and ethical points of view.

In the first essay, Rekha Karambayya examines issues of race and gender discrimination and the way they affect the day-to-day practice of business. She asserts that these issues are very subtle and create a series of paradoxes for those involved. Overt discrimination (shouts) and subtle discrimination (whispers) are featured as a structural given. "Belonging" is an important element in this equation; we all desire to belong. But what happens when we belong to several groups that pull us in different directions? Do we attempt to break free of such paradoxes or use them to our advantage?

In the second essay, S. Gayle Baugh considers why sexual harassment in the workplace continues if most people, in principle, are against it. Part of this, she suggests, may be attributable to a miscommunication between women and men. What women may consider as nonsexual friendliness is often perceived by men as a come on. This may create a climate in which a woman who is a victim of sexual harassment may be blamed for the problem.

Finally, in the last essay of this section, Ronald J. Burke examines the diversity that women directors bring to a corporation. His study features Canadian companies and suggests that those with women directors are more responsive to issues of importance to women. Since women employees are a large segment of any company and since women directors are able to give uniquely valuable insights into issues that affect them, why are there so few women directors?

In Shouts and Whispers: Paradoxes Facing Women of Colour in Organizations

Rekha Karambayya

Racial discussions tend to be conducted at one of two levels—either in shouts or in whispers. The shouters are generally so twisted by pain or ignorance that spectators tune them out. The whisperers are so afraid of the sting of truth that they avoid saying much of anything at all.

Ellis Cose (1993, p. 9)

While there has been a recent proliferation of research on issues of gender in organizations, there has been relatively little work on issues of race, and even less on the intersections of race and gender (see Bell, Denton and Nkomo, 1993; Bell and Nkomo, 1992; Calas, 1992; for notable exceptions). For the most part, research on women in organizations is based on the implicit assumption that concerns raised are those of all women, and that results generalize to all women. This paper frames the experience of women of colour in organizations as a series of paradoxes, outlining the consequences for individuals and for organizations, and attempts to chart a research agenda for the future.

Bell et al. (1993) point out that research on women in organizations was initiated by the need to correct biases in organizational research. Much of organizational research implicitly excludes or ignores women, yet research on women that was directed at correcting that imbalance is itself guilty of making an "exclusivity error" with respect to women of colour. In framing this paper as dealing with the experience of women of colour I may be accused of making similar oversimplifying assumptions that all women of colour face the same issues and have the same experience. In the interest of simplicity, I refer throughout this paper to women of colour as a group. The issues here are likely to be part of their work lives, to a greater or a lesser degree depending on their unique situations, cultural heritage and identity. However, this discussion of the intersections of race and gender is only the beginning. The concerns raised here may be either magnified or subordinated to others, when factors such as age, class, physical ability and sexual orientation are considered.

For purposes of discussion I have chosen to use the term 'women of colour' rather than 'visible minority'. The latter term has often been perceived as negative (Mukherjee, 1993), at least in part because the term describes how people of colour appear to others, and because it defines them in relation to the majority, thereby reinforcing existing patterns of discrimination and exclusion (Mighty, 1991). The focus of interest here is the organizational experience of women who belong to racial minorities. However, it is important to acknowledge that women of colour are not a homogeneous group, and that this discussion cannot do justice to the diversity of their personal and professional experience. Also important is recognition that for women of colour their gender and racial identity are immediately obvious to those they come in contact with, requiring neither personal disclosure of gender and racial identity, nor significant ethnic influence in their lives. Their interaction with others is inevitably shaped by their gender and race in subtle and pervasive ways.

Bell and Nkomo (1992) point out that much of the research on women in organizations relies on one of two theoretical perspectives. The first of these is the gender-centred perspective in which women are compared to men along various criteria, and usually implicitly or explicitly accorded inferior status. The second is the organization-structure perspective which investigates the ways in which the structural characteristics of organizations restrict and impede women's progress in the workplace. They accuse both perspectives of oversimplifying the issues, the first by creating binary systems of thinking about sex role characteristics, and the second by treating individuals and organizations as separate, rather than interactive, systems.

Bell and Nkomo (1992) suggest using a conceptual framework in which an individual is represented in terms of four core identity elements: gender, race, ethnicity and class. They propose that research be developed based on identity theory by exploring the unique effects that each of these core elements have had on a woman's life. One way that such an approach could evolve is based on the use of individual biographies. This, in their view, would correct some of the limitations of studying the work life of women as if it were divorced from the rest of their life experience. Biographies would provide a way of capturing the interplay among dimensions of a person's identity by offering a "holistic portrayal" of women's lives.

This paper recognizes the importance of such a holistic portrayal, and the critical need to centre research in the individual, unique experiences of women. First, the experiences of women of colour in organizations are portrayed as a series of paradoxes, based on the work of Smith and Berg (1987) on group processes. The organizational experience of women of colour is framed in terms of paradoxes, some occurring at the intrapersonal level, and others at the interpersonal level. With an emphasis on gender and race, this paper points out that organizations and their members socially construct a work environment that poses several double bind situations for women of colour. These paradoxes of organizational membership are raised with a view to drawing attention to their complex nature and the choices they entail. The use of paradox as a conceptual framework reveals the conflicts among dimensions of a person's core identity, and the implications of those conflicts for organizations and their members. Finally, the paper moves on to speculate on how we may begin to pay more explicit attention to the complexity of race and gender issues in organizational research.

The main purpose of this paper is to focus attention on the subtle and unacknowledged ways in which race and gender are woven into the fabric of organizational life. It is also my contention, in line with those of others such as Bell et al. (1993), that organizational research has, for the most part ignored the importance of race, particularly as it shapes the professional lives of women of colour. This paper is an attempt to begin to correct that deficit, and to offer one approach to conceptualizing race and gender in organizations.

On Paradox

A paradox is one or more statements that are self-referential and contradictory, and that taken together trigger a vicious circle. The typical response to a conflict of this nature is to attempt to resolve it by disentangling the contradictions. Paradoxes, however, are beyond most traditional forms of resolution.

Accepting one element of the paradox brings one up against the other which is both contradictory in content, and rooted contextually in the first.

Smith and Berg (1987) used paradox as a conceptual tool to explore the conflicts and tensions inherent in group membership and process. This paper is based on their conceptual framework and its implications for individuals and organizations. Race and gender issues in organizations may be seen as membership in multiple groups whose interests are not entirely compatible. A woman of colour then may belong to groups reflected in her core identity: racial, gender, class, and ethnic. She may concurrently associate herself with professional groups, such as an organizational work unit, a professional association, etc. In that sense, much of what Smith and Berg (1987) describe as tensions between individuals and the groups they belong to may apply to the condition of women of colour in organizations.

In order to set the stage for the discussion that follows, it is necessary to restate some of the underlying assumptions in Smith and Berg's (1987) work on groups. They point out that their use of paradox is not meant to invalidate other concepts and theories of groups. It is instead an attempt to add another perspective for viewing groups and the experience of group life. While paradox may appear to enslave members of groups, and the groups themselves, recognition of their existence may be a necessary step in liberation from vicious circles. Smith and Berg (1987) introduce the possibility that paradox may arise at least partially out of interpretive framing processes, and that the processes of reality creation are central to understanding the behaviour of groups and their members.

This paper makes very similar assumptions about human interaction. First, it assumes that the processes of organizational interaction are influenced by individual and collective psychological processes, some conscious and others unconscious. Second, it acknowledges that this interaction is embedded in a social context that shapes and defines it. Recognition of that social context is critical to any discussion of race and gender in organizations. Finally, the paradoxical perspective applied to the intersections of race and gender is used as a conceptual tool to offer new perspectives on research in this area.

There is no test here of the empirical validity of this framework, and no attempt to develop prescriptions, either for organizations or for individuals. Instead the hope is that we may gain new insight from the use of paradox, and develop alternative research strategies that acknowledge and capture the ways in which race and gender influence organizational experience.

PARADOXES FACING WOMEN OF COLOUR

The nature of the specific paradoxes discussed here do not mirror those of Smith and Berg (1987). While some are similar, others are unique to the ways that issues of race and gender are played out in organizations. No attempt has been made to exhaustively list a series of paradoxes facing women of colour. Instead a few are used for purposes of illustrating how use of paradox may be informative and useful.

Issues of Identity

Smith and Berg (1987) begin their discussion of the paradoxes of group life with what they refer to as the paradoxes of belonging. These paradoxes involve trade-offs around membership in a group. One of these paradoxes is about the tension between individuality and group membership. In order to become a member of a group an individual must experience some degree of similarity with other members, and yet remain separate, unique and maintain some individuality.

Women of colour face a number of circumstances in which the core elements that form their identity are in conflict with each other. They are often faced with explicit or implicit choices between expressing their interests in terms of their gender or in terms of their race, knowing that there are conflicts between the two sets of interests. It has been widely recognized that, for the most part, women's issues in organizations are those of white, middle-class women. Women of colour who draw attention to that fact are often accused of "diluting" the issues (Bell et al., 1993).

Women of colour can then either align themselves with women in organizations, knowing that such association is unlikely to fully address their concerns, or risk alienating white women, who are usually the majority, by creating an alternative forum that more accurately reflects their interests at the intersections of race and gender. Yet they may not have either the strength in numbers or the organizational power to address issues unique to women of colour. So they are faced with a double bind in which each of the available options requires a costly compromise.

The conflicts among core dimensions of one's identity present themselves in other ways as well. Women of colour must decide, either consciously or unconsciously, how they will attempt to "fit in". In order to be recognized as legitimate professionals they may adopt some of the norms of the dominant culture. This may sometimes result in what Bell (1990) calls a bicultural lifestyle, in which women of colour experience the stress of living in a professional world in which they adopt the white male cultural patterns in their work and professional lives, while their private lives remain embedded in their racial/ethnic roots. Aside from the very real problems of managing this participation in two very different cultural worlds, this kind of pattern may be dysfunctional for these women because it involves a suppression or denial of a core part of her identity in each sphere of her life. Cox (1994, p. 58) refers to this as "the cost of acting unnaturally." Not only must these women keep their professional and private lives separate, they are often denied opportunities for expressing themselves fully in each.

The paradox of identity is captured in the experience of a professional black woman interviewed by Cose (1993, p. 64):

> ... Eventually she realized that "I was never going to be vice president for public affairs at Dow Chemical." She believed that her colour, her gender and her lack of a technical degree were all working against her. Moreover, "even if they gave it to me, I didn't want it. The price was too high." Part of that price would have been accepting the fact that her race was not seen as an asset but as something she had to overcome.

Cose reports that this woman drew favourable attention from colleagues because she did not fit racial stereotypes, but in her view she did not achieve her potential. She felt that her colleagues were telling her "You're almost like us, but not enough like us to be acceptable" (Cose, 1993, p. 64).

Attributions of Success, Price of Failure

Associated with issues of identity are patterns of attributions used by women of colour and their organizational colleagues to make sense of success or failure. These attributions and the decisions that arise out of them pose another set of paradoxes.

As proposed in the previous section on identity, women of colour often have to overcome negative stereotypes of their race as well as their gender. They are most often fully aware that their race and gender will inevitably influence organizational decisions. Even when they do achieve success against considerable odds, that success is attributed to their having overcome the limitations of their race and gender, rather than credited to it. Worse, their success may be used by the organization as proof that discrimination does not exist, and that organizational processes are gender and race neutral (Caplan, 1993).

Having achieved success, these women are not always credible role models for other women of colour because they have acquired success through assimilation into the dominant, usually white male, culture. In addition, their behaviour may be interpreted as a denial of one's racial or gender identity by other women of colour. One black lawyer interviewed by Cose (1993, p. 61) said of her success, which was often held up as an exception to the norm, "I don't like what it does to my relationships with other blacks."

If and when attributions involve career failures, characteristics associated with race and gender may play a significant role in explanations. Taken together these patterns suggest that individuals and organizations are socialized into seeing race and gender in a negative light; always associated with failures, never with successes. This set of paradoxes is eloquently summed up by Caplan (1993, p. 71) in her work on women in academia:

> Women—especially those who are targets of multiple forms of discrimination—are less likely than others to be hired; but when they **are** hired, they are assumed to be **less** competent than others and pressured to perform in **supercompetent** ways. (emphasis in original)

Some of the characteristics of managerial jobs may compound this set of paradoxes. In most managerial jobs success and failure involve some interpretation of outcomes, and at least a degree of subjectivity. This subjectivity and uncertainty in performance evaluations may mask gender and race bias, and has been referred to as "static" (Ella Bell as quoted in Cose, 1993) or "yes, but" feedback (Jones, 1973). Previous experience with prejudice or discrimination poses what Cox (1994) calls "attribution uncertainty" for members of minority groups. There is always the problem of trying to untangle discrimination from other factors that might influence performance evaluations. While receiving and responding to performance feedback is necessary for organizational success, women of colour may have to work exceptionally hard to separate legitimate performance feedback from bias. Whether or not bias exists, perceptions that it plays a role may have an effect on responses to it. Joe Boyce, who was interviewed by Cose (1993), speaking about the effects of race said:

> Your achievement is defined by your colour and its limitation. And even if in reality you've met your fullest potential, there's an aggravating, lingering doubt . . . because you're never sure. (p. 59)

This uncertainty is compounded by issues of gender for women of colour. Recent research on appraisal processes in a Fortune 500 company showed that women rated the process lower on fairness despite that fact that on average women in this firm achieved higher appraisal ratings than men during that performance period (Cox, 1994).

There is also the possibility that a self-fulfilling prophesy may be at play in organizational situations (Merton, 1948). The terms refers to an effect whereby expectations of an outcome actually induce the outcome. For instance, with respect to women of colour it is likely that low expectations of performance are communicated by the climate set in the organization, the work assigned to an individual or the nature of feedback offered. If in fact some forms of racial and gender prejudice exist in organizations, the processes by which women of colour are evaluated and selected may predispose them to failure, and reinforce that prejudice.

Faced with attribution uncertainty and the possibility that discrimination and bias still exist in their organizations women of colour must face the difficult dilemma of setting their own expectations for career success. If they allow themselves to be overwhelmed by anger and bitterness they are likely to fail, whatever the circumstances, because they expect nothing else. Yet if they expect race and gender to be inconsequential, and do all the "right things" they are liable to be disillusioned when they find that success is still beyond reach. For many the middle ground has been to measure success relative to the set of options available to them, rather than by comparing themselves to their colleagues who do not face similar biases (Cose, 1993).

SPEAKING OUT AND BEING HEARD

It has been widely acknowledged that there is a curious reluctance to address issues of race in organizations (Bell et al., 1993; Cose, 1993; Nkomo, 1992), even as issues of gender are being raised. From the perspective of the individual woman of colour this may arise out of a hope that despite inequities in the outside world, they will receive fair treatment in the workplace. This need for fairness may be particularly enduring because of the importance of work, and its central role in their personal identity. Eventually, many are forced to realize that "the racial demons that have plagued them all their lives do not recognize business hours" (Cose, 1993, p. 55). Even so there is a pervasive silence about discrimination based on race and gender. Perhaps this reluctance to speak above a whisper stems from a fear that to give expression to the dissatisfaction arising out of unfair treatment would alienate and anger those members of majority groups in whose hands the power lies (Cose, 1993). Women of colour who speak of gender and racial bias would likely face the additional jeopardy of being labelled "shouters" (Cose, 1993) and seen as "troublemakers" (Caplan, 1993).

From the perspective of the organization, it is possible that inequities exist in part because organizations are unaware of them and members of majority groups are blind to their own privilege. These conditions create a paradox in which the organization cannot address issues of race and gender unless they are voiced as concerns by some of their members. Unfortunately, those organizations that are most discriminatory are also those in which such concerns are least likely to be expressed for fear of reprisal (Kabanoff, 1991; Smith and Berg, 1987).

These examples of the paradoxes involved in any consideration of race and gender issues, and their intersections, are merely illustrations of the pervasive and subtle ways in which these factors influence the organizational experience of women of colour. They demonstrate that although race and gender are embedded in organizational life, they are for the most part ignored by those who benefit from their gender and racial identity, and avoided by others who pay a price for theirs. Conceptualizing organizational experience in terms of paradox offers new perspectives on how research may approach race and gender in organizations.

Using Paradox

The use of paradox as a conceptual framework makes several contributions to research on gender and race in organizations. First, articulating the forms that these paradoxes may take draws attention to the multi-level nature of the phenomena at work. Race and gender issues manifest themselves at the intra-personal level, at the interpersonal level and at the organization-person interface. At the intra-personal level they may take the form of conflicting dimensions of an individual's identity, and incompatible demands made by various identity groups. At the interpersonal level they may be reflected in ambiguous or different attributions of success and failure, and in racial and gender stereotypes. Other issues may create paradoxes at the organization-individual interface as in the case of the relationship between speaking out and the organizational distribution of power. These paradoxes may arise either concurrently or sequentially depending on the organization, its membership and context. Any attempt to create egalitarian workplaces will have to recognize the relationships and tensions among these levels of analysis.

Secondly, the use of paradox suggests how and why individuals and organizations may find themselves caught in vicious circles, making compromises that alternatively paralyse them and avoid the real concerns. Any attempts to deal with each horn of a dilemma without awareness of the other is likely to lead to "stuckness" (Smith and Berg, 1987), a phenomenon in which one is endlessly circling the issue without really addressing it.

Smith and Berg (1987) suggest that in order to break out of such a vicious circle, one has to confront the paradox. This response to dealing with contradictions is itself paradoxical. It proposes that the first step in dealing with a significant conflict, usually one that elicits negative emotions, is to move toward rather away from it.

In order to fully engage the paradox, each level at which the paradox exists must explore its own role in it. Individual and groups must attempt to acknowledge their own ambivalence and contribution to the paradox. In the context of this paper that may imply that women of colour, and the organizations that they participate in, must engage in self-reflection and examine how they define themselves and others around them. This approach requires all parties to the paradox to undertake some responsibility for its existence and resolution. The resolution may take on a cyclical nature, moving from one horn of the dilemma to the other. This conceptualization leads us to thinking about race and gender in dynamic, non-linear ways. It also suggests that the issues may be evolving and interactive, never quite reaching a resolution, but moving progressively closer to it.

Viewing the social construction of race and gender in the workplace in terms of paradox also forces us to contend with the processes by which these factors influence organizational life. Research on women of colour has been accused of being concerned with outcomes rather than process (Bell et al., 1993). Using the paradoxical framework highlights the importance of the processes by which these outcomes emerge, and suggests that each woman may have a unique experience of the workplace based on her personal identity and the characteristics of her workplace. It also recognizes how her experience is shaped by the interactive perceptual and interpretive processes that link her to her environment.

It is important to recognize here that at least part of our inability to adequately address race and gender issues, and particularly their intersection, stems from our flaming of organizations and organizational life. We frame organizations as stable, and unchanging, and assume that individuals that participate in them must be willing and able to assimilate into the organizational culture. While the value placed on assimilation suggests that diversity may be dysfunctional for the organization, it also implicitly assumes that organizations are gender and race neutral. Both of those assumptions are highly debatable (Cox, 1994; Nkomo, 1992). At the level of the individual organizational member, such an approach presupposes that gender and race identity may be (or even should be) suppressed, or at least contained, in the interests of organizational success.

One way to address these paradoxes is to reframe them so that the nature of the relationship between women of colour and their employers is reconceptualized as dynamic and interactive (Smith and Berg, 1987). This view recognizes that organizations are both the product of and a significant influence on their members. It also acknowledges the uniqueness of each woman's experience, given her unique situation and identity. At the very least this would suggest that the race and gender issues exist at both the organizational and the individual level, and that each partner in that relationship needs to assume some responsibility for recognizing and responding to them.

References

Bell, E. L.: 1990, 'The Bicultural Life Experience of Career-oriented Black Women', *Journal of Organizational Behavior* **11**, 459–477.

Bell, E. L. and S. M. Nkomo: 1992, 'Re-visioning Women Manager's Lives', in A. J. Mills and P. Tancred (eds.), *Gendering Organizational Analysis* (Sage Publications, Newbury Park, CA), pp. 235–247.

Bell, E. L., T. C. Denton and S. Nkomo: 1993, 'Women of Colour in Management: Toward an Inclusive Analysis', in E. Fagenson (ed.), *Women in Management: Trends, Issues, and Challenges* in *Managerial Diversity*, Vol. 4, 105–130. Women and Work: A Research and Policy Series. Series Editors: L. Larwood, B. A. Gutek and A. Stromberg (Sage Publications, Newbury Park, CA).

Calas, M. B.: 1992, 'An/Other Silent Voice? Representing "Hispanic Woman" in Organizational Texts', in A. J. Mills and P. Tancred (eds.), *Gendering Organizational Analysis* (Sage Publications, Newbury Park, CA), pp. 201–221.

Caplan, P.J.: 1993, *Lifting a Ton of Feathers: A Woman's Guide to Surviving in the Academic World* (University of Toronto Press, Toronto).

Cose, E.: 1993, *The Rage of a Privileged Class* (HarperCollins, New York).

Cox, T.: 1994, *Cultural Diversity in Organizations: Theory, Research and Practice* (Berrett-Kohler, San Francisco).

Jones, E. W.: 1973, 'What It's Like To Be a Black Manager', *Harvard Business Review.* July–August 1973.

Kabanoff, B.: 1991, 'Equity, Equality, Power, and Conflict', *Academy of Management Review* **16**(2), 416–441.

Merton, R. K.: 1948, 'The Self-fulfilling Prophesy', *The Antioch Review* **8,** 193–210.

Mighty, J.: 1991, 'Triple Jeopardy: Employment Equity and Immigrant, Visible Minority Women', *Proceedings of the Administrative Sciences Association of Canada* (Niagara Falls, Ontario).

Mukherjee, A.: 1993, *Sharing our Experience* (Canadian Advisory Council on the Status of Women, Ottawa, Ontario).

Nkomo, S. M.: 1992, 'The Emperor Has No Clothes: Rewriting "Race in Organizations"', Academy of Management Review **17**(3), 487–513.

Smith, K. K. and D. N. Berg: 1987, *Paradoxes of Group Life* (Jossey-Bass, San Francisco).

On the Persistence of Sexual Harassment in the Workplace

S. Gayle Baugh

There is no question that sexual harassment has become an important issue for businesses. Estimates of the percentage of women who have experienced harassment vary from a low of 42% to a high of 90% (e.g., Baldridge and McLean, 1980; Fitzgerald et al., 1988; Safran, 1976; U.S. Meris Systems Protection Board, 1981). It is apparent from these percentages that the problem is not trivial. Further, the human cost of harassment has been highlighted by the publicity accorded to situations like the Clarence Thomas hearings and the Tailhook scandal.

Given the attention focused on the problem of sexual harassment as a result of such incidents, it seems puzzling that sexual harassment apparently continues to be a problem. Indeed, the number of complaints filed with the Equal Employment Opportunity Commission (EEOC) has increased steadily, from 3 661 complaints in 1981 to 5 557 complaints in 1990 (Clark et al., 1991). It seems unlikely that sexual harassment will disappear from the work setting any time in the near future, despite the fact that sexual harassment is generally considered deplorable behavior (Tinsley and Stockdale, 1993).

Incidence studies have also documented that sexual harassment is generally directed toward women and perpetrated by men. Although harassment in other gender combinations does occur, the vast majority of incidents involve a man harassing a woman (e.g., U.S. Merit Systems Protection Board, 1981). This situation conforms with social norms about sex roles in general, and so appears to be "natural" (Hotelling, 1991; Stockdale and Vaux, 1993). It is in part this very "naturalness" of sexual harassment that leads to many of the difficulties in eradicating the behavior that will be delineated here.

Differences in perceptions of sexual harassment between men and women are also implicated in the persistence of harassment in the workplace. It is not too surprising to find that women tend to be more sensitive to sexual harassment concerns, given that women are primarily the targets of harassment, and men are primarily the perpetrators. Gender-based differences in perceptions of sexual harassment will be explored next.

GENDER DIFFERENCES IN PERCEPTIONS OF HARASSMENT

Much of the research documenting gender differences in perceptions of sexual harassment was conducted in university settings. Many of the studies simply asked college students to indicate whether particular behaviors or scenarios should be labeled as sexual harassment, or to rate the severity of the behavior in terms of sexual harassment. With one exception (Terpstra and Baker, 1987), these studies found that female college students rated more behaviors as harassing or rated the harassment as more severe than did male college students (Baker et al., 1990; Fitzgerald and Ormerod, 1991; Kenig and Ryan, 1986; Mazer and Percival, 1989; Murrell and Deitz-Uhler, 1993; Page et al., 1991; Popovich et al., 1986; Powell, 1986).

Another stream of research manipulated specific factors other than respondent gender which could affect perceptions of sexual harassment. Variables studied included the gender of the harasser, the status of the harasser (supervisor vs. coworker), the target's response, or the severity of the behavior. The effect for gender persisted, regardless of the other manipulations included in the studies (Gutek et al., 1983; Jones et al., 1988; Lester et al., 1986; Tata, 1993).

Surveys of working adults offer fairly consistent results with respect to gender differences in perceptions of sexual harassment, as well. One study of state government employees failed to replicate the gender differences apparent among college student respondents (Baker et al., 1990), while the difference was supported in four other empirical investigations (Fok et al., 1995; Gutek et al., 1980; Konrad and Gutek, 1986; Thacker and Gohmann, 1993). Two studies conducted with university faculty, who resemble employed adults more than they do college students, also supported a gender difference (Fitzgerald and Ormerod, 1991; Kenig and Ryan, 1986).

It is also of interest to note that in most of the research cited, severity of the harassing behavior usually attenuated the differences in perceptions between men and women. That is, as the harassing behavior became more severe, to the point of sexual assault, men and women tended to view the behaviors in a similar, negative fashion. Thus, in cases that might be termed "quid pro quo" harassment under the EEOC (Equal Employment Opportunity Commission) guidelines, men and women showed more agreement in their definition of sexual harassment. In the less severe cases, like those that would be termed "hostile environment" harassment, the gender differences in perceptions were more pronounced. These findings suggest that women are least likely to find agreement or support from male coworkers for the types of harassment that they are most likely to experience.

POTENTIAL CAUSES OF GENDER DIFFERENCES IN PERCEPTIONS

Potential explanations for the persistence of gender differences in perceptions of sexual harassment include power differentials, self-serving bias, and different perceptual sets. The first explanation explicitly acknowledges the importance of power differentials in supporting sexual harassment behavior (DiTomaso, 1989; Kuhn, 1984). Because women usually wield less hierarchical power in organizations, and men have more, sexual harassment serves as one method of the powerful asserting control over the powerless (Morrison and Von Glinow, 1990). This suggestion is supported by findings that women are more likely to be harassed when they move into higher levels in organizations or into non-traditional areas (Collinson and Collinson, 1989; DiTomaso, 1989; Gutek and Morasch, 1982; Kissman, 1990; Yoder, 1991).

Power differentials are most apparent when the harasser is the supervisor and the target is the subordinate. But power may also be an explanatory variable in cases of sexual harassment of coworkers. Peers or even subordinates may use sexual harassment in an attempt to gain power over a female coworker (Cleveland and Kerst, 1993) by directing attention to the woman's sex role, rather than to her work role (Gutek, 1989).

While there is no basic incompatibility between sex role and work role for men, women do not believe that they can be viewed simultaneously as competent and as sexual (Gutek, 1989; Sheppard, 1989). Further, women do not have complete control over whether they are perceived through the perspective of their work role or their sex role (Gutek and Dunwoody, 1986). Thus, women must guard carefully against situations which emphasize their sex role at work, and respond in such a way as to direct attention back toward their work role. As a result, women are more sensitive than men to potential harassment, which has the effect of undermining their work competence by highlighting their sex role (Gutek, 1989; Gutek and Dunwoody, 1986; Sheppard, 1989; Tancred-Sheriff, 1989).

Power differentials also serve as an indirect explanatory factor in sexual harassment through the mechanism of selective attention. Individuals with less power tend to be more attentive to individuals with more power than the reverse. This attention is usually an attempt to predict and control the outcomes that are in the hands of the more powerful. More powerful individuals need not focus as much attention on the less powerful, because the less powerful control few valued outcomes (Fiske, 1993).

Further, more powerful individuals have greater demand on their cognitive resources (e.g., more subordinates to be concerned with). Thus, less attention will be focused on understanding the circumstances surrounding behavior for each individual subordinate, making personal attributions more likely than situational ones (Gilbert et al., 1988; Gilbert et al., 1988). The individual with greater power is more likely to believe that an individual is involved in an interpersonal interaction because she wants to be (a personal attribution) than because she feels pressure or potential threat from the more powerful party to the exchange (a situational attribution).

A second potential explanation for persistent differences in perceptions of sexual harassment is self-serving bias. More powerful individuals tend to assume that interaction is non-coerced and is rewarding to both themselves and the less powerful interactants. Lower status individuals tend to be more aware of constraints and the potential for coercion in their relationships with higher-status, more powerful individuals (Brewer, 1982). Thus, higher status individuals are more likely to view an interaction as mutually rewarding, rather than as sexual harassment. Lower status individuals are more likely to perceive some coercion, and thus view the interaction as sexual harassment, leading to differences in views of sexual harassment.

A third explanation for differences in perceptions of sexual harassment is a difference in perceptual sets or behavioral labels. The tendency for men to view fewer behaviors as sexual harassment stems from a tendency to misperceive (or at least to mislabel) friendly behavior on the part of women. On the basis of a laboratory study conducted with college student participants, Abbey (1982) suggested that men tend to view friendliness on the part of women as an expresssion of sexual interest, even when that was not what the woman herself indicated her intentions to be. Additional research has supported the process of misperception on the part of men, but not women (e.g., Abbey, 1987; Johnson et al., 1991; Saal et al., 1989; Shotland and Craig, 1988).

Stockdale (1993) indicates that the tendency to misperceive friendly for sexual behavior among men appears to be linked to a constellation of other beliefs, including traditional sex role attitudes, tolerance for sexual harassment, and beliefs that women express sexual interest by being friendly. Thus, misperceivers seem to be likely candidates for at least the hostile environment form of sexual harassment. Because misperceivers believe that women are expressing sexual interest when they may in fact only be expressing friendship, misperceivers feel that their sexual interest is being reciprocated. This feeling may cause misperceivers to persist in sexual behaviors at work when they are, in fact, unwelcome to the target.

Misperceptions of friendliness as sexual interest may be implicated in the quid pro quo form of harassment, as well. Misperception is linked to a sexually harassing belief system, which has also been shown to be related to the propensity to sexually harass (Murrell and Dietz-Uhler, 1993; Pryor, 1987; Reilly, Lott, Caldwell and De Luca, 1992) and the tendency to rape (Malamuth, 1981). Although the relationship of misperceptions to a sexually aggressive belief system has not yet been empirically tested, misperceptions and sexually aggressive beliefs both seem to be a part of a constellation of beliefs that might lead over time to quid pro quo forms of sexual harassment.

These three possible explanations are not mutually exclusive, and in fact all three can be operative simultaneously. Misperceptions of a female coworker's friendliness may be the result of a tendency to view such behavior as sexual, self-serving attributions, and limited attention due to power differences at the same time.

This suggestion leads to some very serious concerns that the elimination of sexually harassing behaviors in the workplace may prove to be extremely difficult. Because perceptions of sexual harassment are different between men and women, and because people act on the basis of their perceptions, men and women may be acting in the context of very different "realities." The question arises, then, of the extent to which each gender is aware of the differences in perceptions, and whose perceptions are validated and given legitimacy within organizational settings.

AWARENESS OF GENDER BASED DIFFERENCES IN PERCEPTIONS

Given the ample evidence regarding the greater sensitivity of women to sexual harassment in the workplace, it is surprising that little research has focused on exploring awareness of gender-based perceptual differences. A lack of awareness of the differences in definitions or perceived seriousness of sexual behaviors at work has the potential for causing very serious misunderstandings between opposite-sex coworkers. The consistency with which gender-based differences in perceptions are found suggests that recognition of alternative perspectives on the part of each gender may be limited.

The one study exploring this issue (Page and Baugh, 1994) among working adults provided some unexpected results. The authors had suggested that women should be more aware of male definitions and perceptions of sexual harassment than men would be of women's perspectives. This prediction was based on the influence of power differentials, as suggested above. Findings indicated that men and women when responding from their own perspective agreed on severity ratings of both quid pro quo and hostile environment types of harassment.

In addition, when asked to take the perspective of the opposite gender, men accurately perceived women's perspective. Women tended to believe that men would under-rate the severity of quid pro quo types of harassment, despite the fact that men actually rated the severity of these behaviors the same as did women. There appears, then, to be less misunderstanding than might be expected between men and women regarding gender-based perceptions of sexual harassment.

This study tested only the cognitive recognition of sexual harassment behaviors, however. Men and women may still disagree on the appropriate organizational responses to sexually harassing behaviors. A set of studies using working adults as participants suggested that similar cognitive understandings of sexual harassment do not imply similar emotional reactions to its occurrence. While the severity ratings of sexual harassment behaviors were similar between working men and women, the sanctions suggested for those behaviors were not the same. Women suggested that stronger sanctions were appropriate than did men, implying stronger reactions to the situation than men had (Fok et al., 1995).

Perhaps women believe that men view sexual harassment as less serious than they actually do because women do not see appropriate action being taken as a result of incidents of harassment. Although both men and women see sexual harassment as inappropriate at work, women tend to see the behavior as requiring greater sanctions. When those sanctions are not forthcoming, it may seem to women that the problem is being ignored or trivialized. This belief may result in a situation which women feel responsible for managing the harassment on their own, rather than reporting it (Gutek, 1989; Pringle, 1989).

RESPONSES TO SEXUAL HARASSMENT

It seems obvious that sexual harassment has a negative impact on the target of the harassment. Typical responses reported by targets include decreased job satisfaction, decreased organizational commitment, and increased levels of stress (Kissman, 1990; Loy and Stewart, 1984; Morrow, McElroy and Phillips, 1994; Ragins and Scandura, 1995). Female targets also experience tension, anger, and anxiety, while a more limited number experience depression or guilt (Crull, 1982; Jensen and Gutek, 1982). Female targets, more than male targets, may also feel the need for medical or psychological attention (Thacker and Gohmann, 1993). Given the generally negative responses to sexual harassment, it is important to look at what actions women take when they have been harassed, and the effectiveness of those actions (Terpstra and Baker, 1989).

A limited amount of research has explored the mechanisms that women use to cope with sexual harassment. Terpstra and Baker (1989) found that, in response to 18 written scenarios depicting sexual harassment in varying degrees of severity, men and women indicated that they would confront the harasser in a positive manner (24%), report the behavior within the company (20%), or ignore the behavior (15%). Although survey respondents overwhelmingly say that they would confront a harasser (Gutek and Koss, 1993; Rubin and Borgers, 1990), only 46% of actual victims in the U.S. Merit Systems Protection Board study reported objecting to the harassing behavior (Livingston, 1982). Many women chose simply to ignore the behavior (around 12%), and only a very small minority (around 2%) ever filed a formal complaint (Livingston, 1982; U.S. Merit Systems Protection Board, 1988).

Given the uniformly negative effects of sexual harassment on the target, it is interesting that so few individuals choose formal means to seek redress. Why would a victim of sexual harassment not pursue every means possible to eliminate the problem? The failure to pursue formal mechanisms of resolution is particularly surprising given that most targets of sexual harassment are women, and women are slightly more likely than men to prevail in grievances of equivalent severity and viability (Dalton and Todor, 1985).

The reasons usually put forth for the failure vigorously to pursue formal means for resolving sexual harassment complaints are the target's fear of not being believed or fear of repercussions on the job (Cleveland and Kerst, 1993; Gutek and Koss, 1993; Hotelling, 1991; Riger, 1991; Ragins and Scandura, 1995). This fear is not entirely without basis. Of the women in the U.S. Merit Systems Protection Board study who reported taking formal action, fully a third (33%) indicated that the action made the situation worse (Livingston, 1982).

I suggest, however, that the reason that so few instances of sexual harassment are ever formally reported, and the reason that so many of the individuals who do take formal action see the situation as worsening, is more subtle, more widespread, and more pernicious than retribution or simple disbelief. I suggest that there is a pervasive tendency to blame the victim for her own plight by discounting her definitions of sexual harassment or searching for causes of harassment in her own behavior. It is the phenomenon of blaming the victim which reduces formal complaints of sexual harassment to almost nil and perpetuates sexual harassment in the work place, despite laws designed to eradicate the behavior.

BLAMING THE VICTIM OF SEXUAL HARASSMENT

The phenomenon of blaming the victim in sexual harassment cases rests upon differences in perceptions and differences in power between men and women in organizations. The disparity in perceptions causes men and women to define situations in divergent ways. The discrepancy in power, generally favoring men, allows men to legitimize and institutionalize male-biased definitions of sexual harassment (Riger, 1991; Vaux, 1993).

Thus, a woman who attempts to make a claim of sexual harassment is faced with the task of demonstrating to a male-biased, if not male-dominated, power structure the legitimacy of her complaint. The male-biased power structure probably does not share her level of sensitivity to sexually harassing behaviors (Baker et al., 1990; Fitzgerald and Ormerod, 1991; Fok et al., 1995; Gutek et al., 1980; Kenig and Ryan, 1986; Konrad and Gutek, 1986; Mazer and Percival, 1989; Murrell and Deitz-Uhler, 1993; Page et al., 1991; Popovich et al., 1986; Powell, 1986; Thacker and Gohmann, 1993). And even when men and women agree on definitions of sexual harassment, they do not seem to agree on appropriate responses to that behavior (Fok et al., 1995). The woman claimant must make her case and hope for resolution in a system in which her views do not predominate.

In general, sexual harassment has been viewed as a personal issue, not an organizational concern (Gutek, 1989; Kenig and Ryan, 1986). Men are more likely to subscribe to the view that sexual behavior at work is "only natural," and to believe that women simply over-react to that natural behavior (Jensen and Gutek, 1982; Summers and Myklebust, 1992). Indeed, in supporting a legal complaint of a hostile environment form of sexual harassment, a woman must demonstrate that the sexual behavior was "unwelcome," implying that there are instances when sexual behavior at work is viewed as desirable (Paetzold and Shaw, 1994).

This situation can be compared to instances of racial harassment. There is no requirement in such cases that a claimant must demonstrate that racial harassment is "unwelcome" in order to support the case. It is, in fact, difficult to conceive of an instance when a target of racial harassment would consider the behavior desirable, yet the same does not hold true with respect to sexual harassment.

There are a number of factors which can serve to minimize the perceived severity of sexual harassment, or to suggest that the behavior was not entirely unwelcome. Characteristics of the target that have been shown in the laboratory to influence perceptions of sexual harassment include style of dress, use of cosmetics, type of response, and feminist orientation (Abbey et al., 1987; Jones et al., 1987; Pryor and Day, 1988; Summers, 1991; Summers and Myklebust, 1992; Valentine-French and Radtke, 1989; Workman and Johnson, 1991). Factors about the relationship which influence perceptions of harassment include the hierarchical relationship of the perpetrator to the target, career competition between perpetrator and target, and previous history of romance (Gutek et al., 1983; Jones et al., 1987; Lester et al., 1986; Tata, 1993; Summers, 1991; Summers and Myklebust, 1992). Finally, the severity of harassment and persistence of harasser also influence perceptions of harassment (Baker et al., 1990; Pryor, 1985; Tata, 1993). In an organizational setting, determining the credibility of a claim of sexual harassment does not appear to be a simple matter of determining whether the harassing behaviors occurred or not, but also of determining the entire context in which the behaviors occurred and the extent to which the target herself may be seen as culpable.

As a result, there is a great deal of latitude for the phenomenon of blaming the victim to occur. Women in organizational settings are expected to learn to cope with sexual behaviors, and are considered to be less capable if they are unable to do so on their own. Women are prone to see themselves as responsible for controlling the situation, and may be reluctant even to label the situation as sexual harassment (Ellis et al., 1991; Harris, 1990; Stockdale and Vaux, 1993). If behavior which could objectively be labeled as harassing is not identified as such, then sexual behaviors and sexual harassment will continue to be viewed as "natural," rather than as problematic (Felstiner et al., 1980).

Further, when the situation is appropriately identified, and a woman begins to take formal action to eliminate the harassment, she may again find herself the target of an attack. She may find that she herself is viewed as the problem, rather than the behavior which is the focus of her complaint. Because she is pursuing her claim within a system which is predicated on a male-biased perspective of sexual harassment, but which is required nonetheless to take some action as a result of her claim, she is viewed as the "problem." The target who brings sexual harassment to the attention of the organization is seen as the cause of the problem, not the behavior which underlies the complaint.

Because a woman's friendly behavior is sometimes, perhaps even frequently, misperceived as sexual, the woman complainant may be viewed as engaging in token resistance to sexual behavior in which she has been complicitous (Muehlenhard and Hollabaugh, 1988). She may be seen as changing her mind about the nature of the interaction in a self-serving manner, despite the fact that women often are unable immediately to label behavior as sexual harassment (Paetzold and Shaw, 1994). The claim of sexual harassment is seen not just as frivolous, but instead as malicious.

Anecdotal evidence supports the idea that women are often blamed for the occurrence of sexual harassment in the workplace. In one study a woman stated, "Many young women invite this sort of response by their behavior and the type of clothing they wear" (Collins and Blodgett, 1981). Another suggests, "Maybe my businesslike deportment prevents any encouragement of innuendos or allows me to be 'one of the boys'" (Collins and Blodgett, 1981, p. 80). Both quotes strongly suggest that it is the target of sexual harassment who is in control, with the power to discourage harassment with style of dress or deportment. Yet the prevalence and persistence of sexual harassment in the workplace discredits this view.

Beyond being responsible for the harassment itself, claimants are seen as liable for any negative effects that a claim of sexual harassment may have. For example, a claimant who supported her case in court reports, "One woman stopped me in the street and said I probably 'asked for it' and that I'd brought down a good man" (Clark, 1990, p. 64). Finally, one target expressed it this way: "I was the victim of sexual harassment and it was a miserable experience. When I voiced complaints to my so-called feminist male boss and male colleagues, I was made to feel crazy, dirty—as if I were the troublemaker" (Collins and Blodgett, 1981, p. 82).

From the perspective of a male-biased power structure (Collinson and Collinson, 1989), the woman who claims sexual harassment is, indeed, the "troublemaker." It is the woman's non-normative beliefs about the appropriateness of sexual behaviors in the workplace that cause her to take actions that necessitate a response, and sometimes negative consequences. Sexual harassment is viewed as a problem of misunderstanding, rather than a pervasive moral issue with regard to misuse of power (Feary, 1994).

As long as this view of sexual harassment persists, sexual harassment itself will persist. Shifting the focus of attention to the victim, rather than the behavior or the structural factors which facilitate that behavior, serves to make the male bias in organizational systems invisible. As long as the victim, rather than the behavior, is seen as the source of problems, targets of sexual harassment will be reluctant to pursue formal action, or even to label their experiences as sexual harassment. This reluctance enables a male bias to persist without acknowledgement or objection.

The unacknowledged male bias in organizational responses to claims of sexual harassment has a chilling effect on willingness to take action against harassing behavior. The tendency to blame the victim for eliciting sexual behavior serves to perpetuate the problem of sexual harassment. Worse, it also serves to focus attention away from those areas that should prove fruitful in attempts to eliminate sexual harassment from the workplace.

References

Abbey, A.: 1982, 'Sex Differences in Attributions for Friendly Behavior: Do Males Misperceive Females' Friendliness?', *Journal of Personality and Social Psychology* **42**, 830–838.

Abbey, A.: 1987, 'Misperceptions of Friendly Behavior as Sexual Interest: A Survey of Naturally-occurring Incidents', *Psychology of Women Quarterly* **11**, 173–194.

Abbey, A., C. Cozzarelli, K. McLaughlin and R. J. Harnish: 1987, 'The Effects of Clothing and Dyad Sex Composition on Perceptions of Sexual Intent: Do Women and Men Evaluate These Cues Differently?', *Journal of Applied Social Psychology* **17**, 108–126.

Baker, D. D., D. E. Terpstra and B. D. Cutler: 1990, 'Perceptions of Sexual Harassment: A Re-examination of Gender Differences', *Journal of Psychology* **124**, 409–416.

Baker, D. D., D. E. Terpstra and K. Larntz: 1990, 'The Influence of Individual Characteristics and Severity of Harassment Behavior on Reactions to Sexual Harassment', *Sex Roles* **22**, 305–325.

Baldridge, K. and G. McLean: 1980, 'Sexual Harassment: How Much of a Problem Is It . . . Really?', *Journal of Business Education* **56**, 294–297.

Brewer, M. B.: 1982, 'Further Beyond Nine to Five: An Integration and Future Directions', *Journal of Social Issues* **38**, 149–158.

Clark, C. S., M. H. Cooper and R. D. Griffin: 1991, 'Sexual Harassment: Men and Women in Workplace Struggles', *Congressional Quarterly Researcher* **1**, 539–557.

Clark, S. and S. Nelson: 1990, 'My Boss Ordered Me to Sleep with Him', *Redbook Magazine*, April, p. 64.

Cleveland, J. N. and M. E. Kerst: 1993, 'Sexual Harassment and Perceptions of Power: An Underarticulated Relationship', *Journal of Vocational Behavior* **42**, 49–67.

Collins, E. G. C. and T. B. Blodgett: 1981, 'Sexual Harassment . . . Some See It . . . Some Won't', *Harvard Business Review* **69**, (March–April), 76–95.

Collinson, D. L. and M. Collinson: 1989, 'Sexuality in the Workplace: The Domination of Men's Sexuality', in J. Hearn, D. L. Sheppard, P. Tancred-Sheriff and G. Burrell (eds.), *The Sexuality of Organization* (Sage Publications, London), pp. 91–109.

Crull, P.: 1982, 'Stress Effects of Sexual Harassment on the Job: Implications for Counseling', *American Journal of Orthopsychiatry* **52**, 539–544.

Dalton, D. R. and W. D. Todor: 1985, 'Gender and Workplace Justice: A Field Experiment', *Personnel Psychology* **38**, 133–151.

DiTomaso, N.: 1989, 'Sexuality and the Workplace: Discrimination and Harassment', in J. Hearn, D. L. Sheppard, P. Tancred-Sheriff and G. Burrell (eds.), *The Sexuality of Organization* (Sage Publications, London), pp. 71–90.

Ellis, S., A. Barak and A. Pinto: 1991, 'Moderating Effects of Personal Cognitions on Experienced and Perceived Sexual Harassment of Women in the Workplace', *Journal of Applied Social Psychology* **21**, 1320–1337.

Feary, V. M.: 1994, 'Sexual Harassment: Why the Corporate World Still doesn't "Get It"', *Journal of Business Ethics* **13**, 649–662.

Felstiner, W. L. F., R. L. Abel and A. Sarat: 1980, 'The Emergence and Transformation of Disputes: Naming, Blaming, Claiming . . .', *Law and Society* **15**, 631–654.

Fiske, S. T.: 1993, 'Controlling Other People: The Impact of Power on Stereotyping', *American Psychologist* **48**, 621–628.

Fitzgerald, L. F., and A. J. Ormerod: 1991, 'Perceptions of Sexual Harassment: The Influence of Gender and Academic Context', *Psychology of Women Quarterly* **15**, 281–294.

Fitzgerald, L. F., S. L. Shullman, N. Bailyn, M. Richards, J. Swecker, Y. Gold, M. Ormerod and L. Weitzman: 1988, 'The Incidence and Dimensions of Sexual Harassment in Academia and the Workplace', *Journal of Vocational Behavior* **32**, 152–175.

Fok, L. Y., S. J. Hartman and S. M. Crowe: 1995, 'Sexual Harassment Sensitivity and Gender: Clarifying the Differences', unpublished manuscript, University of New Orleans.

Gilbert, D. T., D. S. Krull and B. W. Pelham: 1988, 'Of Thoughts Unspoken: Social Inference and the Self-Regulation of Behavior', *Journal of Personality and Social Psychology* **55**, 685–694.

Gilbert, D. T., B. W. Pelham and D. S. Krull: 1988, 'On Cognitive Busyness: When Person Perceivers Meet Persons Perceived', *Journal of Personality and Social Psychology* **54**, 733–740.

Gutek, B. A.: 1989, 'Sexuality in the Workplace: Key Issues in Social Research and Organizational Practice', in J. Hearn, D. L. Sheppard, P. Tancred-Sheriff and G. Burrell (eds.), *The Sexuality of Organization* (Sage Publications, London), pp. 56–70.

Gutek, B. A. and V. Dunwoody: 1986, 'Understanding Sex in the Workplace', *Women and Work: An Annual Review* **2**, 249–269.

Gutek, B. A. and M. P. Koss: 1993, 'Changed Women and Changed Organizations: Consequences of and Coping with Sexual Harassment', *Journal of Vocational Behavior* **42**, 28–48.

Gutek, B. A. and B. Morasch: 1982, 'Sex Ratios, Sex-role Spillover, and Sexual Harassment of Women at Work', *Journal of Social Issues* **38**, 55–74.

Gutek, B. A., B. Morasch and A. G. Cohen: 1983, 'Interpreting Social-Sexual Behavior in a Work Setting', *Journal of Vocational Behavior* **22**, 30–48.

Gutek, B. A., C. Y. Nakamura, M. Gahart, I. Hanschumacher and D. Russell: 1980, 'Sexuality and the Workplace', *Basic and Applied Social Psychology* **1**, 255–265.

Harris, C.: 1991, August, *The Hostile Environment: An Exploratory Study*. Paper presented at the meeting of the Academy of Management, San Francisco, CA.

Hotelling, K.: 1991, 'Sexual Harassment: A Problem Shielded by Silence', *Journal of Counseling and Development* **69**, (July–August), 497–501.

Jensen, I. W. and B. A. Gutek: 1982, 'Attributions and Assignment of Responsibility in Sexual Harassment', *Journal of Social Issues* **38**, 121–136.

Johnson, C. B., M. S. Stockdale and F. E. Saal: 1991, 'Persistence of Men's Misperceptions of Friendly Cues Across a Variety of Interpersonal Encounters', *Psychology of Women Quarterly* **15**, 463–475.

Jones, T. S., M. S. Remland and C. C. Brunner: 1987, 'Effects of Employment Relationship, Response of Recipient and Sex of Rater on Perceptions of Sexual Harassment', *Perceptual and Motor Skills* **65**, 55–63.

Kenig, S. and J. Ryan: 1986, 'Sex Differences in Levels of Tolerance and Attribution of Blame for Sexual Harassment on a University Campus', *Sex Roles* **15**, 535–549.

Kissman, K.: 1990, 'Women in Blue-collar Occupations: An Exploration of Constraints and Facilitators', *Journal of Sociology and Social Welfare* **17**, 139–149.

Konrad, A. M. and B. A. Gutek: 1986, 'Impact of Work Experiences on Attitudes Toward Sexual Harassment', *Administrative Science Quarterly* **31**, 422–438.

Kuhn, A.: 1984, 'The Power War: Male Response to Power Loss under Equality', *Psychology of Women Quarterly* **8**, 234–247.

Lester, D., B. Banta, J. Barton, N. Elian, L. Mackiewicz and J. Winkelreid: 1986, 'Judgments about Sexual Harassment: Effects of the Power of the Harasser', *Perceptual and Motor Skills* **63**, 990.

Livingston, J. A.: 1982, 'Responses to Sexual Harassment on the Job: Legal, Organizational, and Individual Actions', *Journal of Social Issues* **38**, 5–22.

Loy, P. H. and L. P. Stewart: 1984, 'The Extent and Effects of Sexual Harassment on Working Women', *Sociological Forces* **17**, 31–43.

Mazer, D. B. and E. F. Percival: 1989, 'Ideology or Experience? The Relationship among Perceptions, Attitudes, and Experiences of Sexual Harassment in University Students', *Sex Roles* **20**, 135–147.

Morrison, A. M. and M. A. Von Glinow: 1990, 'Women and Minorities in Management', *American Psychologist* **45**, 200–208.

Morrow, P. C., J. C. McElroy and C. M. Phillips: 1994, 'Sexual Harassment Behaviors and Work Related Perceptions and Attitudes', *Journal of Vocational Behavior* **45**, 295–309.

Muehlenhard, C. L. and L. C. Hollabaugh: 1988, 'Do Women Sometimes Say No When They Mean Yes? The Prevalence and Correlates of Women's Token Resistance to Sex', *Journal of Personality and Social Psychology* **54**, 872–879.

Murrell, A. J. and B. L. Dietz-Uhler: 1993, 'Gender Identity and Adversarial Sexual Beliefs as Predictors of Attitudes toward Sexual Harassment', *Psychology of Women Quarterly* **17**, 169–175.

Paetzold, R. L. and B. Shaw: 1994, 'A Postmodern Feminist View of "Reasonableness" in Hostile Environment Sexual Harassment', *Journal of Business Ethics* **13**, 681–691.

Page, D. and S. G. Baugh: 1994 August, *A Field Investigation of Gender-based Differences in Perceptions of Sexual Harassment*. Paper presented at the meeting of the Academy of Management, Dallas, TX.

Page, D., K. Williams and S. G. Baugh: 1991, 'Sexual Harassment: In the Eye of the Beholder', in D. F. Ray and M. E. Schnake (eds.), *Southern Management Association Proceedings* (Southern Management Association, Atlanta, GA), pp. 196–198.

Popovich, P. M., B. J. Licata, D. Nokovich, T. Martelli and S. Zoloty: 1986, 'Assessing the Incidence and Perceptions of Sexual Harassment among American Undergraduates', *Journal of Psychology* **120**, 387–396.

Powell, G. N.: 1986, 'Effects of Sex Role Identity and Sex on Definitions of Sexual Harassment', *Sex Roles* **14**, 9–19.

Pringle, R.: 1989, 'Bureaucracy, Rationality, and Sexuality: The Case of Secretaries', in J. Hearn, D. L. Sheppard, P. Tancred-Sheriff and G. Burrell (eds.), *The Sexuality of Organization* (Sage Publications, London), pp. 158–177.

Pryor, J. B.: 1985, 'The Lay Person's Understanding of Sexual Harassment', *Sex Roles* **13**, 273–286.

Pryor, J. B.: 1987, 'Sexual Harassment Proclivities in Men', *Sex Roles* **17**, 269–290.

Pryor, J. B. and J. D. Day: 1988, 'Interpretations of Sexual Harassment: An Attributional Analysis', *Sex Roles* **18**, 405–417.

Ragins, B. R. and T. A. Scandura: 1995, 'Antecedents and Work-related correlates of Sexual Harassment: An Empirical Investigation of Competing Hypotheses', *Sex Roles* **32**, 429–455.

Reilly, M. E., B. Lott, D. Caldwell and L. De Luca: 1992, 'Tolerance for Sexual Harassment Related to Self-reported Victimization', *Gender and Society* **6**, 122–138.

Riger, S.: 1991, 'Gender Dilemmas in Sexual Harassment Policies and Procedures', *American Psychologist* **46**, 497–505.

Rubin, L. J. and S. B. Borgers: 1990, 'Sexual Harassment in Universities During the 1980's', *Sex Roles* **23**, 397–411.

Saal, F. E., C. B. Johnson and N. Weber: 1989, 'Friendly or Sexy? It May Depend on Whom You Ask', *Psychology of Women Quarterly* **13**, 263–276.

Safran, C.: 1976, 'What Men Do to Women on the Job: A Shocking Look at Sexual Harassment', *Redbook Magazine*, November, pp. 217–223.

Sheppard, D. L.: 1989, 'Organizations, Power, and Sexuality: The Image and Self-image of Women Managers', in J. Hearn, D. L. Sheppard, P. Tancred-Sheriff and G. Burrell (eds.), *The Sexuality of Organization* (Sage Publications, London), pp. 139–157.

Shotland, R. L. and J. M. Craig: 1988, 'Can Men and Women Differentiate between Friendly and Sexually Interested Behavior?', *Social Psychology Quarterly* **51**, 66–73.

Stockdale, M. S.: 1993, 'The Role of Sexual Misperceptions of Women's Friendliness in an Emerging Theory of Sexual Harassment', *Journal of Vocational Behavior* **42**, 84–101.

Stockdale, M. S. and A. Vaux: 1993, 'What Sexual Harassment Experiences Lead Respondents to Acknowledge Being Sexually Harassed? A Secondary Analysis of a University Survey', *Journal of Vocational Behavior* **43**, 221–234.

Summers, R. J.: 1991, 'Determinants of Judgments of and Responses to a Complaint of Sexual Harassment', *Sex Roles* **25**, 379–392.

Summers, R. J. and K. Myklebust: 1992, 'The Influence of a History of Romance on Judgments and Responses to a Complaint of Sexual Harassment', *Sex Roles* **27**, 345–357.

Tancred-Sheriff, P.: 1989, 'Gender, Sexuality, and the Labor Process', in J. Hearn, D. L. Sheppard, P. Tancred-Sheriff and G. Burrell (eds.), *The Sexuality of Organization* (Sage Publications, London), pp. 45–55.

Tata, J.: 1993, 'The Structure and Phenomenon of Sexual Harassment: Impact of Category of Sexually Harassing Behavior, Gender, and Hierarchical Level', *Journal of Applied Social Psychology* **23**, 199–211.

Terpstra, D. E. and D. D. Baker: 1989, 'The Identification and Classification of Reactions to Sexual Harassment', *Journal of Organizational Behavior* **10**, 1–14.

Terpstra, D. E. and D. D. Baker: 1987, 'A Hierarchy of Sexual Harassment', *Journal of Psychology* **121**, 591–605.

Thacker, R. A. and S. F. Gohmann: 1993, 'Male/Female Differences in Perception and Effect of Hostile Environment Sexual Harassment: "Reasonable" Assumptions?', *Public Personnel Management* **22**, 461–471.

Tinsley, H. E. A. and M. S. Stockdale: 1993, 'Sexual Harassment in the Workplace', *Journal of Vocational Behavior* **42**, 1–4.

U.S. Merit Systems Protection Board: 1981, *Sexual Harassment in the Federal Workplace: Is It a Problem?* (United States Government Printing Office).

U.S. Merit Systems Protection Board: 1988, *Sexual Harassment in the Federal Workplace: An Update* (United States Government Printing Office).

Valentine-French, S. and H. L. Radtke: 1989, 'Attributions of Responsibility for an Incident of Sexual Harassment in a University Setting', *Sex Roles* **21**, 545–555.

Vaux, A.: 1993, 'Paradigmatic Assumptions in Sexual Harassment Research: Being Guided Without Being Misled', *Journal of Vocational Behavior* **42**, 116–135.

Workman, J. E. and K. K. P. Johnson: 1991, 'The Role of Cosmetics in Attributions about Sexual Harassment', *Sex Roles* **24**, 759–769.

Yoder, J. D.: 1991, 'Rethinking Tokenism: Looking beyond Numbers', *Gender and Society* **5**, 178–192.

Women on Corporate Boards of Directors: A Needed Resource[1]

Ronald J. Burke

Less than five percent of the members of boards of directors of private sector organizations are women, about the same percentage as women in senior management ranks. And though women continue to be appointed to boards, they will remain a distinct minority for the foreseeable future. This manuscript indicates reasons why there are so few women on corporate boards of directors and makes the case for increasing the number of qualified women on boards as a necessary corporate resource.

Increasing research attention has been devoted to understanding the roles and responsibilities of boards of directors of North American corporations (Gillies, 1992; Lorsch and MacIver, 1989; Fleischer, Hazard and Klipper, 1988). This has resulted from increased interest in corporate governance, a lowering of the veil of privacy accorded CEOs and board members, scrutiny and criticism of board performance because of specific decisions approved by them, and the generally low level of performance of North American organizations in the international marketplace during the 1980s.

The roles and responsibilities of corporate boards build on a body of legal precedent (Lorsch and MacIver, 1989). Two main themes emerge from this writing. First, board members are legally responsible for the management of the corporation. Second, board members are accountable to shareholders. They have a duty to protect the interests of the shareholders (company owners) and provide an adequate return on investment to them. These statements imply a fairly narrow purpose and constituency which board members serve. Since contemporary corporations interact with a wider variety of stakeholders (employees, suppliers, customers, regulatory groups, etc.) board members must at least be aware of, if not sensitive to, a potentially larger array of constituencies if they are to be effective in their roles.

Initially, boards had honorary or at best advisory roles to CEOs appearing as "ornaments on a corporate Christmas tree" (Mace, 1971). They have also functioned as "old boy's clubs" (Leighton and Thain, 1993). Patton and Baker (1987) are critical of board performance, suggesting that board members do not live up to their responsibilities because of a "let's not rock the boat" mentality. They cite several reasons for this. These include: the dual authority often claimed by CEOs as chiefs of management and Board Chairpersons, the large size of corporate boards which makes good discussion difficult, many board members are themselves CEOs who value each others' friendship and want to keep their seats on the board, and board members are too busy to devote enough time to their board responsibilities. There are also not enough qualified male CEOs to go around. It has been reported that CEOs turn down three invitations to join corporate boards for every one they accept. One way to deal with some of the concerns raised about the effectiveness and relevance of corporate boards of directors is to appoint more women who are qualified to them. Women are developing the necessary experience, track records and abilities to qualify for board membership, though they are often invisible to male CEOs (Schwartz, 1980; Mattis, 1993).

If research on corporate boards has been limited, studies that consider women directors have been few (Burke, 1994). The present study of 278 Canadian women directors examined the following questions, among others:

1. What are the personal, educational and career characteristics of these Canadian women directors?
2. How do they perceive their nomination for board memberships?
3. How much influence do they have on issues relating to women on their boards?
4. What are their views on why there aren't more women on corporate boards?

METHODS

Respondents

Names and addresses of Canadian women directors were obtained from the 1992 Financial Post *Directory of Directors* (Graham, 1991). Each was sent a questionnaire. The final response (N = 278) represents about a fifty percent response rate.

Procedures

An eleven page survey, to be completed anonymously, accompanied by a stamped, self-addressed return envelope, was sent to each woman at either home or office address, depending on the listing in the *Directory of Directors*. A cover letter explained the purpose of the research. A postcard follow-up reminder was mailed out about one month later. All responses were received within slightly over two months of the initial mailing.

RESULTS

Personal and Demographic Characteristics

About ninety percent of the sample were university graduates. About one-quarter of the women had one or more professional designations (e.g., CA). A majority were currently married (71%) with a similar percentage having children. They had an average of 2.4 children. Ages ranged from 28 to 81, with the average being 45. Respondents indicated their annual level of compensation (base pay plus bonus pay) at their current employment. Pay categories ranged from $50,000 or less (N = 21, 8%) to over $400, 000 (N = 9, 4%), the majority fell in the $100,000–$200,000 category (N = 116, 46%) or the $50,000–$100,000 category (N = 78, 31%).

Respondents indicated, for four types of directorships (private sector, public sector, not-for-profit, other), the number they held (0 through 5 or more). Most served on private sector boards (N = 186, 67%) followed in turn by not-for-profit boards (N = 166, 60%), public sector boards (N = 121, 44%) and others (N = 41, 15%). On average, the sample held 1.3 directorships in the private sector, 1.3 directorships in the not-for-profit sector, 0.6 directorships in the public sector and 0.2, other directorships. When all boards were considered together, women service on anywhere from one (66 women) to thirteen boards (one woman) with the average being 3.5 boards.

Respondents indicated their primary occupation, aside from their positions as board directors. Only 26 (9%) had no other paid employment. The majority were full-time employees of organizations (N = 157, 57%), owned their own business (N = 39, 13%), or functioned as consultants, outside directors and freelancers (N = 20, 7%).

Women directors indicated, for three broad categories of background or expertise (the professions, not-for-profit or public sector, business disciplines), those areas in which they had significant background or expertise. Considering the professions first, 54 (19%) had accounting credentials and expertise, 45 (16%) had legal training or legal expertise and 22 (8%) had medical or health care credentials or expertise. Considering next not-for-profit knowledge and experience, 58 (21%) had educational institution knowledge and experience and 47 (18%) had government knowledge and experience. Finally, considering various functional areas of business and management, almost half the women directors (N = 134, 48%) indicated general management expertise, and about one-third (N = 99, 36%) indicated financial expertise. About one-quarter reported public relations (advertising/communication expertise (N = 72, 26%), marketing/sales expertise (N = 66, 24%) and human resources expertise (N = 62, 22%).

These personal and demographic characteristics indicated that Canadian women directors were an impressive and talented group (education, professional designations). In addition, they brought a variety of back-grounds and expertise to their director responsibilities. Many areas of functional business expertise were also represented. Finally, these women served on a variety of boards. In the fall of 1976, the chairman of a major Canadian bank remarked that no women served on his board because none were qualified to do so. It is unlikely that such a statement would be made publicly today.

Nomination and Selection to Boards

Women directors indicated their views on the three most crucial characteristics to attaining directorships from a list of eleven. There was considerable agreement on those characteristics ranked first: a strong track record in one's field or occupation (N = 112, 42%), followed by business contacts (N = 56, 21%) and a good understanding of business (N = 55, 20%).

Women directors also indicated how their names were brought to the attention of the boards on which they serve. The most common method was being recommended by a board member of the company (N = 206, 74%), followed by being recommended by the CEO (N = 162, 58%) and being recommended by someone who knew the CEO or a board member (N = 93, 33%).

Women directors then indicated what they believed was the most important factor from a list of nine in their own board nominations. The most important factor was having the desired areas of expertise and responsibility (N = 158, 34%), holding the appropriate job title or leadership position (N = 81, 17%) and being a woman (N = 58, 12%).

This pattern of findings contained elements suggesting reasons for both optimism and pessimism regarding increasing the numbers of women serving on corporate boards. The optimistic conclusions are based on the importance of a strong track record, business expertise and appropriate position titles in attaining directorships. More and more women are acquiring these credentials. In addition, being a woman was also seen as influencing their appointments to corporate boards. The pessimistic slant on these findings stems from the fact that the nomination process is still pretty much the result of the "old boy's" network. Many qualified women would not be visible to this small, important but insulated group of men.

Impact on Company's Sensitivity to Women's Issues

Women directors indicated how much impact they thought they had on five issues: board sensitivity to issues that affect female employees, shareholders' feelings about investing in the company, female employee's feelings about working for the company, company's ability to recruit women and the representation of women in senior management. In addition, they were asked, in an overall sense, whether they thought they had an impact on their company's sensitivity to issues that affected women.

In general, women directors felt they had limited impact on the five specific issues. They felt that their greatest effect was on making female employees feel more positive about working for the company, followed by increasing board sensitivity to issues affecting female employees.

These conclusions are consistent with findings from the general impact question. Only 25 women (91%) thought they had influenced their companies' sensitivity to a great extent. One hundred and thirty-eight women (52%) thought they influenced their companies' sensitivity to some extent while one hundred and four women (39%) thought they had no impact.

The following comments indicate some of the ways women directors influenced their corporate boards.

> I have been told that discussion around the table of board meetings are of a 'higher tone' (6)
>
> After a commentary on women's issues, they often say 'oh yes, that's right' (16)
>
> They are more aware that women bring a different perspective, but not a bad one, rather just another view. (50)
>
> The first woman controller was appointed in this company's senior position *because* I had raised the issue of the company's policy regarding women in management. (55)
>
> Creating awareness at the Board level of gender word usage and changes required to be made to infrastructure to ensure equal promotional opportunities. Also inputted advice on different recruitment techniques required to search out qualified women. (77)

The few women serving on corporate boards of directors were already having some impact on board performance on women's issues. And as more women get appointed to corporate boards their impact will undoubtedly be greater and more far reaching in these areas. It is also likely that more CEOs/Board Chairpersons will come to realize that appointing a greater number of women to their boards is really a business concern with bottom-line implications (Schwartz, 1980). These involve not only enhanced board decision making, creativity and innovation, but also a number of potential benefits both inside and outside the organization. The former include role-modelling for women managers and professionals, the development of a more women-friendly organizational culture (i.e., policies and practices) and career guidance for high-performing women. The latter include becoming, an employer of choice for women, a service-provider of choice for clients, and an investment of choice for potential and current shareholders.

CEOs and Board Chairpersons need to understand the additional purposes women corporate directors can serve, legitimate such activities on the part of women directors, and negotiate such roles and responsibilities with women directors as they are appointed (Schwartz, 1980).

Why Are There So Few Women Directors?

This research examined the views of women currently serving on corporate boards as to why so few women held directorships. Their unique vantage point, having been selected to serve on corporate boards, and interacting with other board members—both female and male—offered useful insights.

Women directors first expressed their views on the adequacy of the mix of professional experience and backgrounds currently represented on their boards. If they felt the mix was inadequate, they then indicated which people there should be more or less of, from a list of ten possibilities. One hundred and fifty nine women (60%) thought the current mix of experiences and backgrounds was inadequate. One hundred and eighteen women (43%) believed there should be more women; 51 (18%) believed there should be an increase in board members with different ethnic or racial background; 50 (18%) thought more members should have business experiences, 48 (17%) advocated more heads of small companies, and 45 (165) wanted *fewer* directors who were CEOs or presidents or organizations.

These comments provide a flavor of some of this sentiment.

> Most boards are male-dominated—old boy's clubs—most men feel that women do not contribute at a senior level. It is very difficult to make a difference. (268)
>
> I believe that more companies should have a selection committee for board members and that the selection committee should have a broad mandate so that board members are selected from a wider spectrum of people. Over time, this should help to change the makeup of boards and will eliminate the need for a quota system currently used by some corporations. (29)

Women directors then indicated their beliefs as to why more women were not directors of Canadian private sector organizations. Eight reasons were provided and respondents endorsed as many reasons as applied. The most common reason given was that companies do not know when to look for qualified women (N = 143, 51%). This was followed in turn by: companies are not looking to put more women on boards (N = 134, 48%); companies don't think women are qualified for boards service (N = 126, 45%), companies are afraid to take on women who are not already on boards (N = 121, 44%), qualified women are not making it known that they are interested in board service (N = 109, 35%), companies are concerned that women will have a "women's issues" agenda (N = 98, 25%), there are not enough qualified women for board service (N = 70, 25%) and qualified women are not interested in board service. These data are shown in Table I.

Women directors wanted a change in the mix of skills, experiences and backgrounds of board members. In particular women directors wanted more diversity—more women, more ethnic and racial minorities and fewer white male 55 year old CEOs.

TABLE I   Reasons for so few women directors

REASONS	N	%
Think women not qualified	126	45.3
Not enough qualified women	70	25.2
Afraid to take on women not already on boards	121	43.5
Aren't looking to put women on	134	48.2
Don't know where to look	143	51.4
Women did/have a women's agenda	98	35.3
Qualified women not making interests known	109	39.2
Qualified women not interested in serving	10	3.6
Other	67	24.1

Women directors attributed the absence of women on corporate boards primarily to the attitudes of male CEOs and Board Chairmen. Male CEOs were seen as thinking that women were not qualified, they were afraid to take on new and untried women or were fearful that women might have a women's agenda (were feminists?). Some male board members were seen as uncomfortable with women directors (other study data not reported here). In addition, women directors believed that organizations were not looking to put women on their boards or did not know where to look for women. It is almost certain, however, that an organization would know where to look for and how to find someone to fill a senior managerial job in a given function. Women themselves were also seen as shouldering some of the responsibilities for their absence by not making their interests known.

The following comments from women directors illustrate some of their feelings.

> It is with great dismay that I note the lack of women directors in the corporate, particularly resource sectors, at a time when it has become painfully obvious that new and creative solutions are needed. The virtual exclusion of 52% of the population from this sector is a matter of serious national concern. It seems to me no accident that the most progressive and vibrant industries are those that have managed to assimilate males and females into productive work teams. (21)
>
> Over the next 5 to 10 years, there will be an increasing number of women available for board positions—I mean women with advanced education and extensive business skills. Will they get the directorships—probably not to the extent deserved. Why? Because their networks and connections are not as strong as their male counterparts. (33)
>
> In my experience, even the most 'enlightened' boards don't know where to look for women directors. There are very few women CEOs, the normal rank from which to draw directors. They are also afraid to make a mistake. The safe route tends to be to focus on the few women who already sit on Boards and who have developed a good reputation. (56)

There doesn't seem to be any real pressure or perceived need for boards to appoint female directors. Unless a real need is created, I suspect board appointments will continue to primarily via personal/business contacts. (104)

There are a *great* number of women who can make a substantial contribution to corporate Canada and would thoroughly refresh the boardrooms. However, the 'old boy's network' and the 'young boy's network' are great barriers to this. (185)

But women directors, as shown in the following comments, believed that all board appointments should be qualified.

Rightly or wrongly, I choose to serve on boards because of my business background . . . . I do not want to be classified as a 'woman director'; I would rather be a director, who happens to be a woman. I want to serve on a board because I am smart, thorough, well-prepared and because I can make a contribution. (4)

I do not believe in 'token' women directors. If they are not participating professionals on a board, they do more harm than good to the image of women directors. (1)

I think you will find that most women directors of large corporations are too busy doing their job to beat the feminist drum or worry about the politically correct landscape. Margaret Thatcher appeals more than Gloria Steinem or Germaine Greer. If you are good, you will succeed. (60)

These findings suggest that women will continue to be relatively absent from the boards of Canadian private sector organizations for some time to come. There is no obvious punishment for failing to appoint women. The perceived attitudes of male CEOs and Board Chairmen also remain an obstacle to such appointments. For this picture to change, male CEOs and Board Chairman will have to approach the director selection process differently (Leighton and Thain, 1993; Barrett, 1993). This will obviously involve a more extensive search process. Related to this would be looking at levels below the CEO to find qualified but still invisible women. An important question that remains is what role women currently on corporate boards will or should play in this process.

NOTE

1. This research was supported in part by the Faculty of Administrative Studies, York University and the Social Sciences and Humanities Research Council. I would like to thank Mary Mattis and Catalyst for permission to use their survey. Rachel Burke, Doug Turner and Ruth McKay assisted with the collection of the data and Cobi Wolpin helped with data analysis. Bruna Gaspini prepared the manuscript.

References

Burke, R. J.: 1994, 'Women on Corporate Boards of Directors', in J. de Bruijn and E. Cyba (eds.), *Gender and Organizations: Changing Perspectives* (VV University Press, Amsterdam).
Fleischer, A., G. L. Hazard and M. Z. Klipper: 1988, *Boardgames: The Changing Shape of Corporate Power* (Little, Brown & Company, Boston, Mass.).

Gillies, J. G.: 1992, *Boardroom Renaissance* (McGraw-Hill, Toronto).

Graham, J.: 1991, *Directory of Directors* (The Financial Post, Toronto).

Leighton, D. and D. Thain: 1993, 'Selecting New Directors', *Business Quarterly* **57,** 16–25.

Lorsch, J. W. and E. MacIver: 1989, *Pawns or Potentates: The Reality of America's Corporate Boards* (Harvard Business School Press, Boston, Mass.).

Mace, M.: 1971, *Directors: Myth and Reality* (Division of Research, Harvard Business School, Boston, Mass.).

Mattis, M. C.: 1993, 'Women Directors: Progress and Opportunities for the Future', *Business & the Contemporary World* **5,** 140–156.

Patton, A. and J. C. Baker: 1987, 'Why Directors Won't Rock the Boat', *Harvard Business Review 65,* 10–12, 16, 18.

Schwartz, F. N.: 1980, 'Invisible Resource: Women for Boards', *Harvard Business Review* **58,** 16–18.

EVALUATING A CASE STUDY: APPLYING ETHICAL ISSUES

You are finally at the last stage of the process of evaluating ethical cases. By this point, you have (a) chosen a practical ethical viewpoint (including the choice of an ethical theory and practical linking principles, whose point of view you will adopt), (b) listed professional, ethical, and cost issues, and (c) annotated the issues lists by examining how embedded each issue is to the essential nature of the case at hand. What remains is to come to an action decision once these three steps have been completed. The final step is to discuss your conclusions. To do this, you must enter an argumentative phase. In this phase, I suggest that you create brainstorming sheets headed by the possible courses of action open to you. Prepare an argument on each sheet to support that particular course of action utilizing the annotated charts you have already prepared. Then compare what you believe to be the pivotal issues that drive each argument. Use your chosen ethical theory to decide which issue is most compelling. Be prepared to defend your action recommendation.

Let us return to the case of contraception in the less-developed countries. As you may recall, the case discussed in Chapter 4 was as follows.[1] You are a regional director at the World Health Organization. One of your duties is to supervise the distribution of birth control devices to women in less-developed countries. The product of choice has been the intrauterine device (IUD), which has proved to be effective and inexpensive.

The problem is that in the United States, several hundred users of the IUD have contracted pelvic inflammatory infections that have been linked to use of the IUD. Pelvic inflammatory infection can cause sterility and death. As a result, you have seriously considered removing IUDs from the list of approved birth control devices for the population control program.

---

[1] I have heard that many of the structural problems with the IUD that caused pelvic inflammatory infection have now been rectified. I am not competent to comment on this; nevertheless, for this case, let us assume that these problems still obtain.

As discussed in Chapter Four, ABC Corporation, a large multinational company, has a considerable inventory of IUDs that it cannot sell in the United States. The company would rather not write off its entire inventory and has consequently made a very attractive offer to sell the World Health Organization all of its existing inventory and to assist in distributing the product regionally.

As regional director, you must decide whether to accept ABC's offer to supply IUDs to women in less-developed countries.

Remember that in this case, the professional practice, ethical issues and cost considerations were deeply embedded, which creates an intractable conflict; there is no simple way to justify one instead of the other.

What you must do is (a) consult your worldview and see what it dictates that you do and (b) consult the ethical theory of your deepest convictions and see what it dictates that you do. Is there a synonymy between these? If not, then engage in a conversation between your worldview and the professional practice. Let each inform on the other. In the end, you should be able to come to some resolution.[2]

One step in this direction is to examine the arguments that support each position. What are the critical premises in these arguments?[3] In any argument, there is a conclusion. If you want to contrast two arguments, you must begin by contrasting two conclusions. Conclusions are supported by premises that (logically) cause the acceptance of the conclusion. Therefore, what you must do is to create at least two arguments that logically entail different conclusions. To do this, create brainstorming lists on the *key issue(s)* involved in the argument. The key issue of the disputation is that concept that makes all the difference. This case has a number of key issues. Let us try to construct arguments that are both for and against the position.

Sample "Pro" Brainstorming Sheet for the Position

Position to be supported: Accept ABC Corporation's offer and continue to provide IUDs to women in less-developed countries.

Key Thoughts on the Subject

1. As a public health professional, you are enjoined to benefit the greatest number of people possible in your health policy.
2. It is a fact that in less-developed countries, millions die of starvation each year. The simple cause of starvation is too many people for the available food. When you decrease the number of people (given a level food source), more people can eat.

---

[2]This dialectical interaction is described in Chapter Eight of *Basic Ethics*.
[3]See my book, *The Process of Argument* (Englewood Cliffs, NJ: Prentice Hall, 1988, rpt. Lanham, MD: University Press of America, 1995) on the details of this process.

3. There are "blips" on any project. In this case, it is a few hundred or so cases of pelvic inflammatory disease. These casualties pale when compared to the number who will benefit from continuing to provide IUDs.

4. Utilitarian ethical theory dictates that the general good supersedes any individual's good.

5. In less-developed countries, the general good is advanced by continuing to distribute IUDs since more people (by far) benefit than are hurt.

6. ABC Corporation is willing to give a large discount on its present inventory and to provide some assistance in distributing the product regionally This will allow the organization to reach more people than ever before and thus fulfill the agency's mission.

Argument

1. In countries that have a limited amount of food that would feed only a certain population (n), increases in the population ($n + x$) will result in x not having enough food to live—fact.

2. Many less-developed countries experience the conditions mentioned in premise 1—assertion.

3. In many less-developed countries, x increase in population will result in y number of people starving to death—1, 2.

4. Many children who are born are not planned—assertion.

5. If you subtract the number of unplanned births from the total birth rate, the number of births would decrease significantly—assertion.

6. If all children were planned, the number (more than x) of births would decrease significantly—assertion.

7. If all children were planned, less-developed countries would not experience starvation (given constant crop production)—3–6.

8. The IUD is the most effective birth control device in less-developed countries—assertion.

9. The imperative of professional conduct in public health is to help as many people as possible—fact.

10. Public health professional standards dictate that the IUD be provided to women in less-developed countries—7, 8.

11. ABC Corporation is making an offer to provide the World Health Organization with substantial savings on the purchase of its IUD inventory and to assist in distribution—fact.

12. ABC Corporation's offer will allow the World Health Organization to reach more women than previously planned—fact.

13. Cost considerations bolster the professional practice—9–12.

14. The IUD poses potential health risks to some (less than 5 percent)—fact.

15. The ethical imperative of Utilitarianism dictates that the right ethical decision is to advance the cause of the common good—fact.

16. More people in less-developed countries are helped by distributing IUDs than are hurt by doing so—fact.

17. Utilitarianism dictates that IUDs should be provided to women in less-developed countries—14–17.

18. The regional director should accept ABC Corporation's offer and continue to distribute IUDs to women in less-developed countries—10, 13, 17.

Sample Brainstorming Sheet Against the Position

Position to be supported: Reject ABC Corporation's offer and stop selling IUDs in less-developed countries.

Key Thoughts on the Subject

1. As a public health professional, you are enjoined to benefit the greatest number of people possible through your health policy.
2. It is a fact that in less-developed countries, millions die of starvation each year. The simple cause of starvation is too many people for the available food. When you decrease the number of people (given a level food source), more people can eat.
3. There are "blips" on any project. In this case, it is a few hundred or so cases of pelvic inflammatory disease. These casualties pale when compared to the number who will benefit from continuing to provide IUDs.
4. Human life is precious. No amount of practical gain can weigh against one human life.
5. Ends do not justify the means. One may have a very good end in mind, but unless the means to that end are just, the end cannot be willed.

Argument

1. In countries that have a limited amount of food that would feed only a certain population, (n), increases in the population ($n + x$) will result in x not having enough food to live—fact.
2. Many less-developed countries experience the conditions mentioned in premise 1—assertion.
3. In many less-developed countries, x increase in population will result in y number of people starving to death—1, 2.
4. Many children who are born are not planned—assertion.
5. If you subtract the number of unplanned births from the total birth rate, the number of births would decrease significantly—assertion.
6. If all children were planned, the number (more than x) of births would decrease significantly—assertion.
7. If all children were planned, less-developed countries would not experience starvation (given constant crop production)—3–6.
8. The IUD is the most effective birth control device in less-developed countries—assertion.

9. The imperative of professional conduct in public health is to help as many people as possible—fact.

10. Public health professional standards dictate that the IUD be provided to women in less-developed countries—7, 8, 9.

11. The IUD poses potential health risks (less than 5 percent)—fact.

12. It is absolutely ethically impermissible (under Deontology)—no matter what the practical advantage—to knowingly jeopardize the essential health of any person—assertion.

13. ABC Corporation's offer is attractive from a mere cost perspective—fact.

14. It is absolutely ethically impermissible to provide IUDs to women in less-developed countries when they have been shown to be deleterious to the health of Americans—11, 12, 13.

15. In cases of conflict, an absolute ethical imperative trumps an absolute professional standards imperative—assertion.

---

16. The director must reject ABC Corporation's offer and halt the distribution of IUDs to women in less-developed countries—10, 14, 15.

Obviously, the crucial difference in these two arguments is the choice of an ethical theory and the way it is interpreted. Thus, whether a person takes a pro or con position is a function of the underlying value system that person holds. The way a person chooses a value system and the broader practical viewpoint is through the person's worldview and its accompanying baggage.

You must determine how to apply your practical ethical viewpoint. This requires careful attention to the theory and the linking principles you have chosen and the way they affect your evaluation of actual cases. To be an authentic seeker of truth, you must engage in this dialectical process. To do less is to diminish yourself as a person.

You are now ready to evaluate a case study.

Macro and Micro Cases*

Macro Case 1. You are the vice-president of student affairs (dean of students) at a private university. A student group that claims that the company that manufacturers the university's licensed or logo clothing employs sweatshops has protested this practice. You took the group's demands under advisement and decided to research its claims. Your research through two different sources indicates, to your amazement, that the claims are correct. The apparel is manufactured in the United States by illegal workers who are paid less than half the minimum wage for working a 60-hour week in non–OSHA conditions. Your information is from sources that could be used as evidence in court.

---

*For more on macro and micro cases, see the overview on p. 105.

Therefore, you decide to contact the owner of the company, Mr. Big:

"I have heard from sources that the apparel that you are manufacturing for our university is produced in sweatshops."

"Where'd you hear that from, eh? We don't do none of that here. We run a clean business. Made in the U.S.A. What could be better than that?" said Mr. Big.

"Well, would you mind if we had the plant investigated officially so that we might be sure of your compliance?"

"Inspections ain't in our contract. What are you thinking about? You know when you allow inspections, it becomes public record and then your competition comes in and takes advantage of it. I don't think that we're in the mood for that. No, sir. We have a contract with you, and we expect to fulfill it. If you renege on us, we have a battery of lawyers on retainer. They'd love to take you to court and earn an end-of-the-year bonus."

You find that the university has a contract with the company to provide the specified apparel. This contract runs for one more year. If your supplier is in violation of the law, then the contract is broken, but the burden of proof is on the university to prove it. To prove malfeasance, you must conduct an investigation yourself (which is costly) or you must go to the authorities (which might result in a civil suit). Personally, you do not wish to encourage the sweatshops. The board of trustees of the university has shown little interest in this issue. Its concern is the bottom line.

What do you do? How do you justify your decision?

Macro Case 2. You are director of Human Resources Development at a major U.S. auto corporation. Following a recent settlement with a major Japanese auto maker over sexual harassment, the interest in the practices of employees and supervisors at auto manufacturing plant has increased. The problem is that most of the personnel attracted to assembly line jobs have a certain free-wheeling spirit that is often expressed in jokes, discussion, and behavior that many might consider offensive. However, it is impossible to prohibit all off-color jokes, sexist statements, and political and/or social opinions because they are ingrained in the behavior of many employees. They laugh at sensitivity training.

In a recent directors' meeting, someone suggested that the only way to completely "purify" the workplace is to set up a system of secret police who would create a network of informers to identify miscreants. By making an example of key offenders, the company might be able to avoid a potential lawsuit.

You want to create a work environment that is free from harassment, yet you are not sure that the cure is better than the illness. Write a memo to the directors outlining the course of action you believe should be taken and your reasons.

Macro Case 3. You are the city manager of Belleview, North Carolina, population approximately 200,000, located near the Research Triangle. Recently you issued a request for proposals for a new road to be constructed that will link two north-south roads. The cost of the project is $185 million. You had planned to have three companies work on the project. Belleview's municipal guidelines require minority contractors to be a part of the team. You have bids from seven teams, and the top four are from white-owned construction firms. Numbers five and seven are from minority-owned firms. Your feasibility study concluded that three was the best number of firms to work on the job, but a fourth could be added, although it would be inefficient. A fifth is out of the question.

You know that if race were not an issue, the process would be simple. You also know that affirmative action has received strong opposition lately. Federal courts recently released similar communities in a neighboring state from affirmative action requirements.

You are conflicted. You believe in a diverse America that serves and nurtures the needs of all peoples, yet you are a servant of the people of North Carolina and of Belleview. Write a report describing your position using issues of practicality and ethics to draw your final conclusion as to which firms to hire.

Macro Case 4. You are on the board of directors of a small to mid-size company that engineers software designed to solve crucial problems encountered in e-commerce. Since its inception ten years ago, employees of the company have worked extremely long hours and have received very low pay (but generous stock options). The board of directors is about to evaluate a gender bias complaint. It has been suggested that the long hours and hectic schedules discriminate against women since they bear most of the child care responsibilities. Child care is not available for all hours the company is open, nor does it provide for children who are ill or need special attention.

The frenetic pace of this company is not unusual for firms in the industry. If the company responds positively to this complaint, it might open itself to policies contrary to those that have resulted in much of its success. You muse that perhaps some work isn't appropriate for women with families. The men with families at the company are doing well. Is it your company's responsibility to be at the vanguard of some sort of social policy? If the women who made the complaint do not like the working conditions, then they can find work elsewhere; no one is forcing them to stay. However, outsiders might consider this to be gender discrimination. You have to bring up this issue to the board. Write a report highlighting the professional practice, ethical, and cost considerations and use them to support an action plan.

Micro Case 1. You are a store manager at the Zap (a low-priced clothing store that markets to teens and those in their early twenties). You do the ordering for the store. On a buying trip, your visit to a major supplier, X-Z Liners, disturbs you. After you return home, you contact the garment workers union and discover that your fears were well founded—X-Z Liners is running a sweatshop.

At present, 15 percent of your merchandise is from X-Z Liners. You have strong personal and ethical beliefs about sweatshops. However, you realize that if you drop X-Z Liners as a supplier, your average costs will rise. When average costs rise, you risk losing your customers to other stores such as Bald Eagle Outfitters. Your spouse and family depend on your salary to pay the bills. What should you do? Do you bring in another line and risk losing business and your job? Do you forget your values and ignore the situation (after all, other stores buy from X-Z)? You are going to have to discuss this with your spouse. Write a defense of the position you plan to take.

Micro Case 2. You are an African-American male who works in a financial services company as a broker. You have just been informed that a sexual harassment complaint has been filed against you by a female co-worker. This has struck you like a lightning bolt; you cannot imagine what caused this complaint. You immediately think of your uncle who was fired from his position at Eastern-Western State College after forty years of service for supposedly referring to one of his twenty-year-old students as a "girl" (he was sixty-seven at the time).

You are not a ladies' man. You have had sexual relations with only one woman not your wife, and that was before you met your wife. You do not make lewd remarks. You do have fundamentalist Christian values and believe the passages in the Bible about a woman being subservient to her husband. You believe that this is a position dictated by God. Plenty of passages in the Bible support your beliefs.

The complaint states that your attitudes about women (albeit religiously motivated, although the complainant is an atheist) create a hostile work environment.

Write your response to this charge or write the charges that the woman making the complaint might bring.*

Micro Case 3. You are a woman attorney working in a prestigious law firm in a large city. You desire to become a partner, but you have noticed that the firm's partners (and from what you can tell, those at comparable firms) seem to (a) be very aggressive, (b) be highly competitive, (c) be convinced that every dispute must be resolved to the firm's considerable advantage (i.e., equitable resolutions that do not financially benefit the firm are considered to

---

*This case is based on the actual experience of a former student.

be failures), and (d) work long billable hours no matter what the personal cost. This combination does not agree with your personal worldview; you believe in being accommodating (when possible), but you do not believe in structuring deals that benefit one side at the expense of another. You value consensus is based on fairness and working hard, but your job is not your life. There is more to you than being an attorney.

Your problem is that you are in a profession in that seems to demand changing your values to meet the expectations of the norm. What do you do? You love the law and believe that it can work to promote your worldview. However, it appears that if you maintain your values, you will be unsuccessful in your profession (since the other top firms operate in the same fashion). If you change, you will feel that you have sold your soul.

Clarify your thoughts on this issue, and then write a report that examines your options. Then describe a particular action plan.

Micro Case 4. You are a twenty-eight-year-old first-generation Mexican American and are a registered nurse with a master's certification in geriatric care from the top school in your area. You and your husband make about the same salary and are somewhat financially leveraged with respect to your first home mortgage. You and your husband have two children and balance child care responsibilities with some help from your mother-in-law.

You are employed by A-B-C Health Care Corp., one of the nation's largest health insurance companies. A-B-C assigns you to four geriatric cases a day, which is a reasonable number. You go to the insured's home to perform the tasks that fall under your job description. However, there are problems. Your clients are generally economically upper middle class, but few of them have the education you have. Despite this fact, they frequently ask if you understand them, because you speak with a Spanish accent, they assume that you barely speak English, and they talk condescendingly to you. Because of their concept of you, they often ask you to perform tasks that are not in your job description, such as lifting heavy objects and doing housework. You feel sorry for these people, and you have a great affinity for the elderly. But you believe that you should be afforded some respect for who you are and what you do. Sometimes you became so angry that you want to quit. You can talk to your clients, of course, but they respond only to edicts from the company, which they trust because it is 100 percent American. You took this job knowing it would be tough, but sometimes it seems that it is more than you can bear. Jobs are difficult to find. If you go too far, you might lose your job and your salary, which is necessary to meet your mortgage payment.

Before you discuss the situation with your husband, who is very supportive, list the problems and what you plan to do about them.

chapter six

The Context of Business

GENERAL OVERVIEW.

Chapter Five explored issues affecting the corporation from within. In Chapter Six the perspective is from without—the context or environment in which the corporation operates. The chapter examines two contexts. The first concerns national and government regulation. Each national government plays a large role in creating an environment that nurtures or hinders the development of business. Particular policies affect the national business environment.

The second context is the international marketplace. Businesses increasingly have multinational exposures. However, what constitutes proper business practice differs for various cultures. A prominent issue is bribery, which is an acceptable and expected practice in some countries. Until there is international agreement on this issue, business competition will be unfair and confused. This and other ethical problems require action by the international community so that new uniform standards might be adopted to ensure justice and fair competition.

Government Regulation.

Overview.

Few would disagree that every society needs laws and regulations. Since businesses operate within the boundaries of nations, they are subject to regulation, but regulation frequently does not accomplish its goals. That is, a regulation attempts to results in some desired end, x. In a perfect world, regulation p would bring about x. However, government regulations often are bureaucratic and fail to achieve the desired goal—x. In fact, they may cause great net harm at a high social cost. Thus, a principal part of the discussion on regulation is *not* whether regulations are needed, which is a given, but what is the best and most efficient way to accomplish regulation.

Michael J. Clarke argues that the government must always be the entity to ensure compliance with ethical standards. Because of the existence of intense competition in the marketplace, only the government is in the position to bring about needed ethical changes, such as gender equality and proper sales practices. Thus, since the government creates the rules on which businesses operate, government is the most appropriate entity to intervene in the marketplace to establish ethical standards.

John C. Ruhnka and Heidi Boerstler note that government regulation can be expensive and inefficient. They suggest that a strategy that focuses on incentives for self-regulation can be used to accomplish regulatory goals. These incentives can be positive when they encourage desired behavior or punitive when they punish unlawful behavior. The current climate of regulation is overwhelmingly punitive in its approach. This is not the only possible model. The Securities and Exchange Commission, for example, has used positive incentives to encourage self-regulation by the National Association of Securities Dealers, and OSHA and the EPA have used self-regulation. Ruhnka and Boerstler contend that such positive incentives for self-regulation may be the most effective and efficient means to stop the wrongdoing and raise the standards of professional conduct among businesses.

Eric W. Orts concentrates on the specific regulatory arena of environmental protection: How can the government best bring about needed regulations? Orts contrasts two traditional models, the command and control model and the market-based regulation model. The command and control model is punitive and is based on the power of the government to enforce its edicts. Although command and control are necessary for some situations, they are generally neither effective nor efficient modes of regulation.

Marked-based approaches include charges and taxes for pollution, expanding property rights to include the natural environment, tradable pollution rights, and environmental marketing disclosures.

Between these two traditional approaches is the middle model of reflexive law and environmental ethics. By *reflexive,* Orts means that these policies are more interactive among business, government, and other stakeholders and are adaptable to changing situations and shared community value needs. In this way, reflexive and interactive processes can work beyond a mere legal standard and seek to achieve levels of professionalism and integrity.

Focus: Ethics in Need of Regulation

Michael J. Clarke

Discussions of business ethics often tend to concentrate on analyzing moral issues and the dilemmas which they pose for businesspeople. In doing so they take it for granted, as most people do in everyday life, that individuals are informed, guided and motivated by ethical considerations in their conduct. I wish to question this, at least as a realistic account of how ethics can be given an enhanced profile in business life. Rather than seeing ethics, particularly as articulated in public, as a source of motives for conduct, sociologists tend to see it as a source of justifications. They tend to look for motivation in the social context of conduct, whether this is the immediate group surrounding the actor, or the organisation of the institution within which the conduct takes place or the wider social structure of society. This is not to say that ethics is irrelevant to conduct. It is used to give conduct meaning and to negotiate its acceptability to a relevant group or audience. But it justifies rather than motivates, it characterises rather than explains conduct.

THE REAL BUSINESS WORLD

The implications of this for business are important. Most businesspeople think that they are ethical, apart, no doubt, from the occasional misdemeanour or, with hindsight, the occasional misjudgement, and apart from a minority who are brazenly unscrupulous. Business, in a capitalist society at any rate, fosters assertive individualism, even authoritarianism, a capacity to make clear decisions quite rapidly and to insist on their being followed through by subordinates. Managers are aware that business decisions can be tough—that is, have painful consequences—and the businessperson must always be practical and adaptable, and retain a respect for the market and for financial viability. Most importantly, business is competitive, and while market competition is not simply a zero sum game, there are definitely winners and losers, and the notion of market share involves the winners succeeding at the expense of losers. Thus basic institutions—markets—have impact on the conduct of businessmen.

It is not adequate, then, simply to leave matters of ethics to debate and exhortation: this will change little. Some businesspeople may well greet such exhortations with enthusiasm as a welcome remedy to unscrupulousness and duplicity. Others may listen to the debates and acknowledge the points made. The problem is that ethical principles, however lucidly identified, have to be applied in practice, since business is practical, even pragmatic, and vulnerable to the demands of the immediate situation. Long term considerations are fine and not to be ignored, especially by bigger businesses, but you have to get past the obstacles on the way that constantly arise, unpredictably and from all quarters. So, it is not only that businessmen may deride the irrelevance or practicability of ethical arguments (pension rights for part-time workers? you can't be serious, an administrative nightmare and a gross addition to labour costs), but also that, even if the principles are accepted, implementation is a constantly fraught process (now, you started on a one day basis, and then you changed to two and a half, but then you moved to a different department, and then you signed a new contract and that was all before the takeover: so when do we date your pension rights from?)

A COMPLIANCE CULTURE

The answer to these difficulties lies in institutions and regulation, though they are no panacea. Regulation provides the detail on how to implement ethical principles, and, furthermore, it is binding on everyone, so that anxieties about competitive disadvantage are mitigated, though, of course, some people will still cheat. Institutions are developed to administer regulations and to negotiate their constant revision to ensure that they are practical, effective in achieving their purpose and keep up to date with developments. The achievement of changed practice is managed through compliance, that is, the constant implementation of decisions in the light of the regulations, negotiated and reviewed by the relevant institutions. Out of this should arise a compliance culture within which routines are established to ensure that principles are adhered to (part-timers paid in cash without full payslips do not fail to be written into the pension scheme) and that they constitute a regular point of reference in the light of the business subject to the regulation. By this means ethics can be integrated into the life of the enterprise at all appropriate levels and routinized. If regulations and institutions are not well developed, then ethical issues will be left to be dealt with ad hoc, and that means that they will tend either to be ignored altogether or to retain a disruptive character as an additional and unnecessary problem injected into the working life of the business. Those attempting to raise such questions then become subject to such ripostes as 'there isn't time', 'we are not a charity' and that catch-all justification for pragmatism, 'business is business'.

Let me give three examples of how ethical issues in Britain have not been dealt with by business, but have been implemented by regulation, institutions and compliance: equal opportunities for the sexes; corporate governance; and the sale of retail financial services products.

Equal Opportunities

A recent survey by the think tank DEMOS charted the rejection of rigid gender roles by the 18–34 age group, and highlighted their optimism about their futures, including work.[1] Most striking to one who was brought up in the 1950s are the expectations of women in this age group about their working lives. They expect to work and to have successful careers, and many do not anticipate devoting a significant proportion of their lives to the care of children or the elderly. Their expectations of work itself increasingly involve cultural gender equality, in terms not just of promotion prospects but of work cultures with feminine elements such as adaptability, dexterity, consensus and team work.

Only a generation ago it was taken for granted that women were unsuited for all but rather specialised occupations, where their caring nature could be used, notably nursing, teaching and social work. In business their role was as surrogate wives: secretaries and, later, personal assistants. Transformation has not been achieved by ethical debate. Equal pay was only targeted by legislation, equal pension rights are only now being achieved thanks to the European Court, access to closed occupations like law and medicine was only achieved by firm and persistent government pressure. Medical schools in particular had to be instructed that training women as doctors was not a waste of money just because they were likely to bear children. Now female students are more likely to aspire to become solicitors or accountants than teachers or social workers, because of the poor pay, status and working conditions of these traditional female occupations.

Of course, ethical debate took place about gender equality, but in its most visible forms, in the women's liberation movement of the 1970s, it was largely confined to the liberal middle classes where it achieved a hold on parts of the media. These manifestations of ethical debate, however well founded the arguments which were articulated in them, produced derision and avoidance in a large part of the business world. Only as business was compelled to allow women access and to pay them equally with men, and provide them with equal working conditions, did a re-evaluation begin to take place of women's capacities and potential in business. Nor was it achieved by legislative fiat such as the Equal Pay Act. The meaning of equal pay had to be constantly negotiated by court cases, and the role of the Equal Opportunities Commission has been vital in forcefully negotiating increasing degrees of gender equality. A further battle in this campaign is currently being waged on the subject of sexual harassment, a matter which many businesses have refused to acknowledge, by claiming that it does not exist in their company, and that complainants are being oversensitive and unreasonable.

Corporate Governance

Much the same arguments can be put in respect of corporate governance. Ten years ago there was substantial press and academic complaint that directors overpaid themselves, appointed their friends to the board to preclude any serious dissent, leaked information to stockbrokers and others to manage their company's share price and browbeat and deceived their auditors in order to get an annual clean bill of health. Successful industrialists such as Sir James Goldsmith fulminated against demands for greater openness so that shareholders and potential investors could reach informed judgements, and denounced the 'see through society'. At the same time the passive role of the giant financial institutions who control major blocks of shares in leading companies, in relation to such abuses—especially sensitive during contested takeovers—was regularly questioned. The private shareholder is now only a third or a quarter of the market, it was said; the institutions must take responsibility.

I am encouraged by recent research[2] which looked in detail at relations between financial institutions and companies in 1993–4. Ten or fifteen years on, this documents the functioning of quite highly organised relationships following from legislation in several companies acts in recent years specifying and outlawing various abuses. This led to the creation of institutions through the National Association of Pension Funds and the Association of British Insurers, co-ordinating the role of financial institutions as major investors, and to the Cadbury Report on corporate governance specifying good practice and enjoining companies, for example, to separate the roles of chief executive and chairman, establish audit and remuneration committees, limit long-term service contracts for directors and give non-executive directors a clearer and greater role in oversight. At the informal and practical level a system of self-regulation has now emerged in which pressure is brought to bear on companies over specific issues.

The response of business here has been better than with sex discrimination, because the basis existed for the development of influential regulatory institutions in the financial institutions, and these institutions have a common interest in seeing to it that companies in which they have a substantial investment perform well over the long term. The research showed that the financial institutions pursue a dual track policy. In those companies in which their stakes are limited they take less interest, are less disposed to try to exert influence, and respond to conduct of which they disapprove by selling their stake. In the case of larger stake holdings they are able to exert considerable influence, both because they have board membership and because to sell their stake would have severe adverse consequences for the company in terms of wider investor confidence. Once again, ethics does not bite until enshrined in regulation and implemented through powerful, albeit here quite informal, institutions.

Financial Services

My final example is one of an industry which is apparently incapable of accepting new ethical issues, and is benighted to the point that serious damage has been done to it. The sale of retail financial services products—mortgages—life-assurance and pensions, particularly—is now widely identified with abuse of the public. This sector has for long been established, respected and reliable in Britain, and it profited greatly from the post-war rise of affluence and home ownership. With the advent of deregulation and of the property boom and increased foreign competition in the 1980s however, competition for a rapidly expanding market increased dramatically, and formerly conservative and respected institutions threw caution to the winds in a scramble for market share and diversification into new product ranges. The assets of life assurance companies increased by an average of 17.4% in the 1980s and those which were invested in unit trusts and pension funds increased by 25% and 18.9% annually[3]. Mortgages switched from being 80% repayment to 20% endowment in the 1970s to the reverse by the end of the 1980s. Life assurance direct sales staff reached a peak of 200,000; they have now more than halved and are still falling.

Abuses have included overlending on property, so fuelling the boom and leading to a more pronounced crash, with millions of people subsequently facing negative equity and tens of thousands of repossessions annually. Home income plans have left thousands of elderly people facing repossession when bonds purchased with remortgages of their properties failed to produce enough income even to pay the mortgage, let alone the promised surplus income. There has been serious disadvantage to thousands of workers who were induced to opt out of occupational pension schemes by the blandishments of salesmen, following the government's Social Security Act of 1986 and subsequent government propaganda and tax sweeteners favouring private schemes. The abuse of commission has induced salesmen to push products and gain market share at the expense of objective evaluations of their merits in comparison with other products, or their appropriateness to the needs of 'prospects', as customers/investors are called. Low cost endowment mortgages have failed to generate enough on maturity to pay off the loan in some cases. There has been the abuse of early surrenders of endowment insurance which had minimal values and the deliberate boosting of terminal payment bonuses in order to enhance the market rating of products. Other abuses have involved the churning of investors by inducing them to cash in, or should one say, simply abandon, life assurance policies in favour of touted new ones; the selling of insurance as an investment when other forms became more appropriate; and the selling of insurance at rates of premium that could not be afforded, notably, but not exclusively, linked to deferred interest mortgage loans.

Although press and political coverage of such abuses has grown in a crescendo, the most that the financial institutions would admit was that some had made serious errors by rushing into estate agency in the housing boom, and had made losses of up to a third of a billion pounds. The notion that the public was being abused and in some cases driven to distraction and suicide was rejected. It has taken determined action by the Securities and Investments Board even to begin to put things right, action which has been resisted at every step. A large number of household name life assurers have now been fined for failing to meet adequate standards of sales staff training in respect of customers' interests. The length and cost of training, which used to consist of no more than a few days advice on how to sell the product, have rocketed as a result. In 1995 the customer will at last be entitled to be told, in cash terms, what commission the salesman earns from the sale of various products, a position only finally achieved by the intervention of the Chancellor of the Exchequer.

THE NEED FOR INTERVENTION

Practical business ethics, then, is driven by the institutions which dominate it, most of them deriving from the market, and unless there is well organised and empowered intervention the chances of ethical issues making a positive impact are about as great as those of survival in a capsized roll-on/roll-off ferry. Involving business in ethical debate will achieve little; using debate to lay the foundations for regulation and to achieve compliance may be effective.

It should be made clear in this connection that regulation, supported by appropriate institutions and compliance procedures, is not an automatic solution. The retail financial services sector subject to recent abuses has been regulated by LAUTRO and FIMBRA under the supervision of the SIB since 1988, a regime which has clearly been ineffective. Attempts are now being made to improve matters by the establishment of the Personal Investment Authority to replace LAUTRO and FIMBRA, and by sustained pressure for what the head of the SIB has called a 'step change' in standards, backed by constant research and policy recommendations from the Office of Fair Trading. This is not the place to discuss at length the conditions for regulatory effectiveness[4]. Rather, these considerations reinforce the point that ethical considerations will not feature effectively on the business agenda unless they are supported by regulation, institutions and compliance procedures.

NOTES

1. Helen Wilkinson, No turning back: generations and the gender quake, *Demos*, 9 Bridewell Place, London EC4B 6AP.
2. This research was conducted by John Holland of the Department of Accounting, University of Strathclyde, and presented in preliminary form to a conference on Regulation at Hertford College, Oxford, September 1994.
3. See C. Ennew *et al.*, Ethical Aspects of the Marketing for Savings and Investment Products in the UK, *Business Ethics: A European Review*, Vol 3, No 2, 1994, pp. 123–129.
4. For further discussion of these matters see M.J. Clarke, Regulation and Enforcement, *Journal of Asset Protection and Financial Crime*, Vol 1, No 4, 1994, pp. 337–346.

Governmental Incentives for Corporate Self-Regulation

John C. Ruhnka and Heidi Boerstler

INTRODUCTION

It has long been believed that corporate self-regulation offers significant advantages for reducing unlawful or unethical corporate behavior over the alternative of increased direct governmental regulation of corporate activities. The law is limited in its ability to regulate business behavior in situations where the cost of enforcing laws may be too great, or the enforcement of laws would require the violation of higher values in the society, or ethical standards or norms for behavior cannot be easily translated into objective, adjudicable, legal standards (Stone, 1975). Arrow (1973) has pointed out the dilemma of drafting regulations that are flexible enough to meet a wide variety of situations and yet simple enough to be enforceable. Government regulation is also excessively disruptive to corporate enterprise, and corporate self-regulation does not suffer to the same extent from this disability (Pitt and Groskaufmanis, 1990). By corporate self-regulation, we mean a formal, structured program of rules of conduct and associated enforcement mechanisms which is initiated and sanctioned by the highest levels of corporate management to achieve compliance of its operations, managers and employees with applicable legal and regulatory standards governing corporate activities.

The United States has long encouraged lawful corporate behavior through the mechanism of federal and state laws (and associated regulatory rule and enforcement activities) governing corporate behavior. More recently, the federal government and its regulatory agencies, in response to growing resistance to additional direct governmental policing of corporate activities as well as the very significant economic costs both to the government and to business of such supervision, has turned to the mechanism of corporate self-regulation to achieve increased lawful corporate behavior. Rather than wait for voluntary corporate self-regulation mechanisms to develop spontaneously, a number of important actors in the governmental sector including federal regulatory and contracting agencies, federal and state prosecutors, and the U.S. Sentencing Commission have begun to provide "carrot and stick" incentives to encourage the development of self-regulation programs in the private sector. Some of these governmental incentives, most notably in the 1991 Federal Organizational Sentencing Guidelines, have begun to spell out specific features which corporate self-regulation programs must or should incorporate in order to qualify for mitigation of punishment or other benefits. These new governmental incentives thus have the potential both to prod the adoption of corporate self-regulation and to shape the features of such programs.

This article presents a brief overview of traditional legal and regulatory incentives directed at achieving lawful corporate behavior, together with examples of the more recent governmental incentives aimed at encouraging self-regulation activities by corporations, in terms of their use of the "carrot" or the "stick" to influence corporate behavior. In order to provide a picture of the emphasis of different governmental incentives, we have differentiated various incentives as "positive" incentives that benefit corporations for actions that encourage or assist lawful behavior (usually by mitigating negative consequences for violations that would otherwise result), and "punitive" incentives that encourage lawful behavior by punishing corporations for violations of legal or regulatory standards. If one thinks of an incentive as a force for change, the idea of a "punitive" incentive is not necessarily contradictory since governments clearly exert significant pressure on companies to act lawfully by use of the threat of punishment for unlawful behavior.

We next constructed a "prototype" corporate self-regulation program that contains compliance features specified in governmental incentives for corporate self-regulation and applied the same positive versus punitive analysis in order to get an idea of the balance of "carrot versus stick" incentives in the type of corporate compliance program that is presently promoted by governmental incentives. Finally, we address the question of whether governmental incentives for corporate self-regulation are producing an effect on corporations by examining the behavior of the Fortune 1000 companies in enacting or revising corporate codes of conduct, a central feature of virtually every governmentally-encouraged system for corporate self-regulation.

THE GOVERNMENTAL INCENTIVE SYSTEM AND CORPORATE SELF-REGULATION

In the United States, legal and regulatory incentives to produce lawful or ethical behavior in business organizations have traditionally been adversarial and punitive. If a corporation violates the law regulating business conduct it is investigated (usually by the regulatory agencies assigned to monitor compliance with that area of the law) and prosecuted. This style of government regulation has been described as "command and control" regulation (Sigler, 1993), and the resulting fines, penalties and regulatory debarments are intended to send the message "Don't do it again."

The persistence of illegal and unethical corporate behavior in the face of a very extensive system of punitive legal and regulatory incentives has suggested to some regulators that punitive governmental incentives, standing alone, are not able to reduce unlawful corporate behavior to socially desirable levels, at least not without unacceptably intrusive and costly increases in governmental surveillance, investigation, and prosecutorial activities. As a result, a number of governmental actors, with the lead being taken by federal regulatory agencies, have turned to partial "privatization of compliance" as a supplement to, or even a partial replacement for, the traditional system of legal and regulatory penalties to produce lawful behavior.

Beginning in the late 1970's and continuing through the 1990's, at a number of points in the federal legal and regulatory system, positive incentives have begun to appear that are intended to encourage the voluntary adoption of internal compliance mechanisms which will serve to reduce the incidence of unlawful or unethical behavior among corporate actors or reduce the need for more extensive regulatory supervision. These positive incentives are intended to send the message "it can be advantageous to you to organize yourself so that regulatory violations are less likely to occur, or to make our job easier."

Corporations in turn are expected to appreciate that internal compliance systems which produce more lawful and ethical behavior (or reduce the incidence of unlawful or unethical behavior) among the actors on the corporate level, can in turn produce positive benefits (or reduce negative consequences) for the corporate entity on the level of external governmental incentive systems. Since corporate compliance systems by necessity must contain their own positive and punitive incentives for corporate actors (including positive rewards to empower corporate actors to support desired conduct as well as punitive measures to punish transgressors) in order to be effective, they constitute a secondary incentive system for lawful and ethical behavior—which is influenced by and responsive to government regulators. . . .

Legal and Regulatory Standards of Conduct

Federal and state legal and regulatory standards of conduct governing corporate activities, such as the federal antitrust laws, are both long-established and well understood in their effect. The legislature establishes a series of laws governing the activities of corporations and other business entities which are enforced by government prosecutors. Rule-making, monitoring, investigatory and prosecutorial authority is usually devolved to specific regulatory agencies which are responsible for monitoring and enforcement of these specific standards of conduct. Sanctions for breach of legal standards of conduct range from regulatory investigations and prosecutions, to consent orders, civil injunctions against continued unlawful conduct, civil fines, debarments from government contracts or privileges in some cases, and criminal fines. In the most serious cases, government prosecutors may also bring civil or criminal actions against individual corporate officers or agents who were responsible for corporate violations. . . .

Another important legal incentive for lawful corporate behavior is the common-law doctrine of vicarious civil liability and imputed criminal liability which exists in all U.S. jurisdictions. This legal doctrine imposes both civil and criminal liability on a corporation for wrongdoing committed by its employees while acting within the "scope of their employment." In general this means that if an employee acted within the scope of his or her authority and with the intent to benefit the corporation, the corporation may be held legally responsible for the employee's wrongful actions. . . .

Civil Punitive Damage Awards

The common-law doctrine that gives civil juries the power to act as "private attorney generals" and to punish "outrageous" wrongful conduct by corporations or individuals is another powerful incentive for good corporate behavior. So-called "punitive" or "exemplary" damages may be awarded in civil actions in addition to normal compensatory or nominal damages for outrageous conduct. Punitive damages have been justified on the ground that they give a judge or jury the ability to punish a defendant for outrageous conduct, that they deter a defendant from repeating the conduct (beyond the deterrent effect of paying compensatory damages to victims), and that they serve as a deterrent to other potential wrongdoers who are similarly situated. While punitive damages date back to 1791 in U.S. courts, until the 1960's they were rarely awarded and were generally reserved for outrageous acts of libel, slander, defamation, physical brutality or reckless conduct of great consequence. In the past two decades, however, punitive damage awards against corporations by civil juries have increased significantly, including multimillion dollar awards in products liability actions, a $7.5 billion award for alleged interference with contractual obligations in a corporate takeover, and claims for billions of dollars in punitive damages in oil spill litigation.

GOVERNMENTAL INCENTIVES
FOR CORPORATE SELF-REGULATION

Corporate responsiveness to governmental incentives for corporate self-regulation is determined by a number of factors, the most important of which are the *magnitude* of the potential to a specific company for a specific incentive to produce positive benefits for compliance (or negative consequences for non-compliance) and the *certainty* of the potential consequences. Governmental incentives which are of the most potential value to corporations are usually those which can avoid overly broad or ill-suited regulatory requirements and regulatory investigations or compliance actions, along with their associated costs and potential penalties, at the outset. Since no single set of detailed regulatory standards are likely to meet the operating concerns and efficiency requirements of small start-up businesses and large multinational corporations at the same time, the possibility for any "individualization" of regulation is generally welcome. Regulatory agency and contracting agency incentives which can potentially avoid problems at the outset are of more potential value than prosecutorial incentives that operate only *after* serious problems have arisen, or sentencing guideline incentives that operate only *after* a corporation has been both prosecuted and convicted of wrongdoing.

The degree of *certainty* is also important. If a governmental incentive offers corporations identifiable benefits which they "can take to the bank," they are going to be more likely to make the substantial investment in organization, staffing, monitoring (as well as incurring increased exposure to civil liability that may result from self-reporting) that is required. As an example, the Department of Justice has an announced amnesty policy of not criminally prosecuting organizations that are the first to voluntarily disclose antitrust offenses *prior* to any governmental investigation. The certainty of this potential benefit may well justify corporate compliance programs to discover and report antitrust violations, but imagine the difference if the Justice Department only offered to weigh self-reporting of criminal violations in its discretion. As one corporate ethics officer for a Fortune 500 company remarked, "If the government wants a commitment, it must make a commitment in return, not a maybe."

Regulatory and Contracting Agency Recognition of Corporate Compliance Efforts as a Mitigating Factor for Corporate Violations

Regulatory incentives for corporate self-regulation are expanding, and an exhaustive listing of all such incentives is beyond the scope of this article. The following examples give an idea of the general approach and features of some of the most important such incentives.

Securities and Exchange Commission. The U.S. Securities and Exchange Commission (SEC) is significant in that the legislation which created the SEC also formally sanctioned limited self-regulation by securities dealers as a part of the SEC regulatory scheme. Section 15A of the Securities and Exchange Act of 1934 authorized creation of the National Association of Securities Dealers (NASD), a private self-regulatory organization which is responsible for inspection of the offices, books and records, and practices of its member securities dealers for compliance with SEC regulations. NASD regulation and inspection of members (for compliance with SEC regulations) substitutes for direct SEC inspection.

The SEC has also used positive incentives to prompt corporations to voluntarily report and correct corporate misconduct. In 1976 in connection with Internal Revenue Service and SEC investigations of improper off-the-books accounts, bribes, gifts and payments to government officials by U.S. companies, the SEC conducted a "voluntary disclosure program." Voluntary disclosure of questionable domestic or foreign payments by U.S. companies was encouraged by SEC statements that it would be "less likely" to bring enforcement proceedings against companies that voluntarily conducted investigations by Board committees composed of independent directors, publicly disclosed the findings of such investigations, and agreed to forbid any such illegal payments in the future. As the data on enactment of codes of conduct by Fortune 100 companies which appears later in this article indicate, many of the codes of corporate conduct which originated in the 1970's were prompted by this SEC amnesty and the subsequent requirements for internal accounting control systems contained in the Foreign Corrupt Practices Act of 1977 which resulted from these disclosures.

The SEC has also provided positive incentives for securities firms to enact voluntary internal compliance mechanisms in its so-called "Chinese Wall" releases. Chinese Wall procedures are designed to erect a procedural "wall" between the investment banking side (which is often privy to non-public information about pending transactions) and the brokerage side of multiservice securities firms, to forbid exchange of sensitive information between personnel in these two functions, and to monitor potential leakage of information across this artificial wall. While the SEC has not yet explicitly mandated the use of Chinese Wall procedures in multi-function securities firms, it has encouraged such use by its promise of a "safe harbor" to such firms in potential conflict of interest situations where such procedures are in place. The SEC has also sanctioned the use of such protective procedures in its rule governing the relationships between market participants, and in remedial actions accepted by securities firms to settle insider trading cases.

EEOC. The Equal Employment Opportunity Commission (EEOC) guidelines for employers suggest that a meaningful corporate policy against sexual harassment can help to shield an employer against potential vicarious liability for sexual harassment by a supervisor—by implementing a strong and explicit policy against sexual harassment, and by maintaining a confidential procedure with effective remedies for receiving and acting on complaints of sexual harassment which is designed to encourage victims of sexual harassment in the workplace to come forward.

In the case of a civil sexual harassment case, a federal court may make its own assessment of whether an employer's sexual harassment policy was explicit enough, whether channels for employee complaints were sufficient, or whether there was a record of prompt investigation of employee complaints, and meaningful corrective action in the case of meritorious complaints. Since a key question in vicarious corporate liability is whether the employer "knew or should have known of the harassment and failed to take prompt, effective remedial action," when these elements are found to be present, courts are more likely to find that vicarious corporate liability is not warranted.

MONITORED INTERNAL COMPLIANCE PROGRAM REQUIREMENTS

Department of Defense. The Department of Defense (DOD) carries perhaps the biggest "stick" in its arsenal of potential incentives, in that in the case of government contractor violations it can not only apply fines and criminal prosecution to culpable contractors and their responsible officials, but it also can *debar* such firms from eligibility for further government contracts. The DOD has also gone further than other regulatory agencies in spelling out specific features of a "program of internal controls" for defense contractors.

In 1988, the Department of Defense, in order to deflect public criticism for government contracting abuses, stipulated in a DOD regulation that defense contractors *should* develop internal control systems "to promote [high standards of business conduct], to facilitate the timely discovery and disclosure of improper conduct in connection with Government contracts, and assure that corrective measures are promptly instituted and carried out." The carrot proffered to defense contractors was that the existence of such a program would be weighed as a mitigating factor in debarment decisions following a criminal conviction. The DOD regulation indicates that a contractor's internal controls should provide for: (a) a written code of business ethics and conduct and an ethics training program for all employees; (b) periodic review of practices, procedures, policies and internal controls for compliance with requirements of government contracting; (c) a mechanism, such as an ethics hotline, by which employees may report suspected instances of improper conduct, and instructions that encourage employees to make such reports; (d) internal and/or external audits as appropriate; (e) disciplinary action for improper conduct; (f) timely reporting to appropriate government officials of any suspected or possible violations of law in connection with government contracts or other irregularities; and (g) full cooperation with any government agencies responsible for investigation or corrective actions.

The Department of Defense has also negotiated settlements of overcharge claims against defense contractors that have required strengthened corporate ethics programs, and in some cases, required the companies to make periodic progress reports on ethics compliance matters to the government. Similarly, the Federal Trade Commission (FTC) has utilized consent settlements where companies guilty of consumer misrepresentation have been ordered by the FTC to (1) institute new policies to prevent recurrence of the violations, (2) establish an internal monitoring function to ensure compliance with these policies, and (3) maintain detailed records of monitoring and compliance functions which must be made available for FTC inspection to verify future compliance. . . .

REGULATORY "CERTIFICATION" PROGRAMS FOR REGULATED ENTITIES

Whereas most regulatory incentives for corporate compliance efforts provide more favorable treatment in the case of violations than would otherwise be the case, regulatory "certification" programs promise a list of specific benefits to regulated entities that have demonstrated that their internal compliance programs are up to specific regulatory standards. Benefits of regulatory certification can include the right of a certified company to advertise its "certified" status, relief from certain routine regulatory reporting requirements, and relief from certain regulatory inspection requirements. The corporate compliance system, once certified, is permitted to substitute for regulatory inspection and oversight.

OSHA Voluntary Protection Program. A leading example of regulatory "certification" incentives is the Occupational Safety and Health Administration's (OSHA) "Voluntary Protection Program," which provides OSHA certification to industrial plant sites after careful agency review of a company's internal OSHA compliance programs, safety training programs, top management commitment, and employee participation. Firms that achieve the highest level of OSHA certification in the OSHA "Star Program" receive OSHA regulatory certification which carries with it promised relief from certain routine OSHA enforcement requirements, a promised closer working relationship with OSHA, and expedited response to requests for approvals from the agency.

The OSHA Star Program incentives break new ground in the area of regulatory incentives by offering more responsive and less burdensome regulation to those companies that can demonstrate the efficacy of their private compliance programs and efforts. Even so, some commentators (Sigler, 1993) have wondered if the positive incentives offered are sufficient, since the number of U.S. industrial sites certified under the Star Program has grown from nine sites in 1983 when the program was initiated, to only about 90 sites in 1992. This is not a large number in light of the many thousands of applicable industrial operations in the U.S.

Environmental Protection Agency. In 1993, the Environmental Protection Agency (EPA) published notice of proposed EPA "Environmental Leadership Program," a regulatory certification program that would provide additional positive incentives beyond the incentives offered by the OSHA Star Program for agency-certified companies. Proposed EPA incentives for the Environmental Leadership Program include public recognition for companies of their EPA certification, faster EPA permitting of new facilities or processes, "green" product labeling, reduced EPA monitoring, reduced EPA reporting requirements, agency mitigation credit in the case of violations, and arrangements for a designated agency representative to facilitate EPA approvals. After EPA evaluation, companies that were designated as an "environmental leader" could use their own internal environmental compliance program as evidence of EPA compliance, reducing the necessity for periodic reporting to EPA as well as EPA inspections. . . .

INCENTIVE SYSTEMS CONTAINED IN CORPORATE SELF-REGULATORY PROGRAMS

[Table 1] illustrates the elements of a "prototype" corporate compliance program as stipulated by a federal regulatory agency, in this case the suggested "program of internal controls" specified in the 1988 Department of Defense Regulation for defense contractors. This particular set of requirements was selected because it sets out the typical features of a governmentally-encouraged corporate compliance program, and it also conforms with the desired features

TABLE 1

DEPARTMENT OF DEFENSE REQUIREMENTS FOR GOVERNMENT CONTRACTOR INTERNAL CONTROL PROGRAMS	PRIMARY FOCUS	IMPACT
Written code of business ethics and conduct	Employees	Neutral
Ethics training program for all employees	Employees	Neutral
Periodic reviews of practices, procedures and internal controls for compliance with standards of conduct and govt. contracting requirements	Management	Neutral
Ethics Hotlines or other reporting mechanisms for employee reporting of improper conduct plus instructions that encourage employees to make such reports	Employees	Neutral
External and/or internal compliance audits	Employees/ Management	Punitive
Enforcement of sanctions for improper conduct	Employees	Punitive
Prompt reporting of suspected violations of govt. contracting laws to govt. officials	Employees/ Management	Punitive
Full cooperation with govt. agencies in investigations or corrective actions	Management	Punitive

for such programs as specified in the 1991 Federal Sentencing Guidelines for Organizations. The primary focus and impact (positive or punitive) of each of the suggested features of a prototype corporate compliance program has been indicated.

The striking feature about this prototype corporate compliance program is that it is overwhelmingly *punitive* in its intended results, and contains few if any positive incentives to encourage lawful or ethical conduct on the part of corporate employees and managers. In this respect the "private" corporate compliance system promoted by governmental incentives resembles the traditional punitive incentives to prevent unlawful corporate conduct analyzed earlier, far more than the more recent positive regulatory incentives for internal self-regulation systems. For example, nowhere does the prototype compliance system suggest or require that employees or managers completing ethics training or showing exemplary behavior in accordance with the company's code of conduct be rewarded or recognized for such conduct. In short, there do not seem to be any "carrots" for corporate actors who assist a self regulatory system to function effectively. This may prove to be a critical omission in light of the fact that employee insistence on lawful and ethical corporate conduct can sometimes conflict with middle management pressures to overlook such standards in the pursuit of performance goals, as well as the widely-publicized stories of problems that have befallen corporate "whistleblowers."

THE EFFECT OF GOVERNMENTAL INCENTIVES ON CORPORATE SELF-REGULATION

Are the present governmental incentives for corporate self-regulation causing corporations to adopt self-regulation programs? The authors have been working for a number of years to assemble a comprehensive collection of the codes of business conduct for the Fortune 1000 companies (the Fortune 500 Industrial Companies plus the Fortune 500 Service companies). Although this collection is not complete, we presently have the actual codes of conduct in hand for 775 of the Fortune 100 companies. Since the requirement for a written code of corporate conduct that mandates employee compliance with applicable regulatory or legal standards is an essential feature of virtually every governmental incentive discussed above, we hypothesize that governmental incentives for corporate self governance programs, if successful, would prompt companies subject to such incentives to, at a minimum, enact a formal corporate code of conduct that requires employees to adhere to applicable legal and regulatory standards of conduct.

Figure [1] and Figure [2] are time series showing activity in enacting a code of conduct or producing an updated code during the period 1960 through

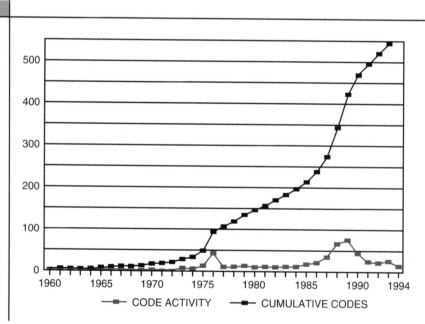

FIGURE 1. **Fortune 500 industrial companies code of conduct activity.**

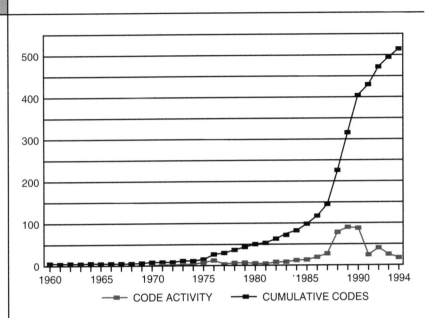

FIGURE 2. **Fortune 500 service companies code of conduct
activity.**

1994 by the Fortune 500 Industrial Companies and the Fortune 500 Service
companies. . . .

Despite . . . limitations of the data, it clearly appears that during the
period 1960 to 1994, many of the Fortune 1000 companies have voluntarily
enacted corporate codes of conduct, and that this activity coincides with the
growth in regulatory, prosecutorial, and judicial incentives for corporate self-
regulation programs during this period. For example the steep rise in code
enactments by the Fortune 500 Industrial companies in 1976 coincides with the
1976 SEC "amnesty" for companies that voluntarily reported illegal foreign
payments and subsequently enacted corporate codes of conduct prohibiting
such activity, as well as the ensuing Foreign Corrupt Practices Act of 1977.
Another bulge of code activity can be seen in 1989 and 1990 coinciding with
the highly-publicized Federal Organizational Sentencing Guidelines, which
became effective January 1, 1991. It can also be seen that these two major governmental incentives for code adoption affected the industrial and service sectors differently. In the mid-1970's Fortune 500 Industrial companies did
substantially more overseas business than did Fortune 500 Service companies, which is reflected by the stronger response of the industrial companies
to the 1976 SEC safeharbor and the 1977 Foreign Corrupt Practices Act. Service firms, on the other hand, seem to have paid less attention to this early

incentive. By 1985 only about 100 of the Service 500 companies had codes in place as compared with over 200 of the Industrial 500 companies. Coming from a lower level of self-regulatory activity the Fortune 500 Service firms appear to have responded more strongly to the Federal Organizational Sentencing Guidelines in 1990 than did the Industrial firms, although at least some of the rapid increase in code activity by Service firms in the late 1980's may have been a response to insider trading enforcement by the large number of banks and financial firms included in the 500 Service group. In the case of both the Industrial and Service firms, code activity did not really "take off" until 1985. This observation is supported by a 1991 Conference Board survey of code activity by 186 U.S. companies that found that 59% of the respondents with codes reported having adopted their code of conduct within the preceding two years (Berenbeim, 1992).

Figure 3 indicates the percentage of Fortune 500 companies in 1991 and in 1994 that presently have codes of conduct, as well as those companies that reported that they do not presently have a code of conduct. This "have code" data includes only those companies for which we have a code in hand (both dated and undated), and does not include situations where a company has claimed to have a code, but refused to release it due to confidentiality concerns. Accordingly, the percentage of Fortune 500 companies presently having codes of

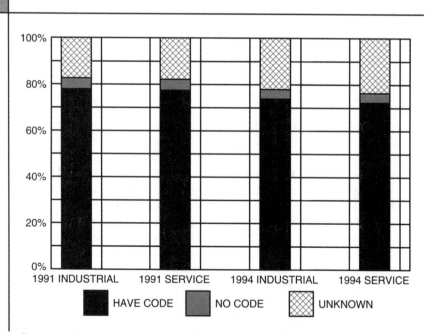

FIGURE 3. **Fortune 500 companies codes of conduct activity.**

conduct probably exceeds 80%. The slight decrease in the percentage of 1994 companies having codes reflects the shorter length of time in which to conduct follow-up requests to the "unknown" category and is probably insignificant.

A key concern of corporations as well as regulators is do corporate compliance programs improve corporate behavior? If we ask if the growth in corporate self-regulation has reduced unlawful or unethical corporate behavior over the situation that would have resulted had such self-regulation programs not been in effect, we have only impressionistic evidence to go on. The lack of accessible direct indicators of ethical corporate behavior means that ethics researchers have generally not examined corporate performance directly, but rather have examined surrogate indicators of corporate ethical behavior such as feelings, opinions, perceptions, orientations, or values held by organizational members (Gatewood and Carroll, 1991). The one notable attempt to date to correlate the existence of corporate codes of ethics with regulatory enforcement actions (FDA, EPA, Consumer Product Safety Commission, and National Highway Traffic Administration violations) involving the subject companies by Mathews (1987), found no effect between regulatory violations and the existence of a code of conduct, due to differences in the length of time the relevant codes of conduct had been in effect, differences in conduct covered by the different codes and in associated enforcement mechanisms, differences in the size and activities of the companies, and difficulties in distinguishing between serious and trivial regulatory violations.

Conclusion

Three questions need to be asked about the present system of governmental incentives for corporate self-regulation. First, is the present uncoordinated system of government incentives sufficient to produce voluntary compliance programs on the corporate level? Second, will the compliance programs which are being developed in response to present governmental incentives be effective in reducing unlawful or unethical corporate behavior? And, third, is the "prototype" corporate self-regulation model which is promoted by present governmental incentives the most effective form of a self-regulation system that can be used to encourage lawful or ethical behavior on the corporate level?

The answer to the first question—are present governmental incentives producing corporate-level compliance programs—appears to be "yes," at least for the largest U.S. corporations, based upon our finding that at least 77.5% and probably more than 80% of the Fortune 1000 companies presently have formal written corporate codes of conduct in place, and that at least some of these codes contain explicit mechanisms for monitoring compliance, employee reporting of code violations, investigation and punishment of violations of such codes. This finding is subject to two significant caveats. First, as architects of corporate compliance programs have pointed out, a code of conduct is *not* a corporate compliance program—it is only part of it, and maybe even not the most important part of a corporate compliance program (Sigler and Murphy, 1988). Many codes of corporate conduct do not presently include detailed (or in many cases, any) information on internal monitoring, compliance and enforcement systems—which are essential elements of an overall corporate compliance system and which are mandated by almost every governmental incentive for such programs. In some companies the associated compliance mechanisms to enforce a code of conduct are contained in corporate procedures manuals or elsewhere. However, in at least some cases these necessary compliance mechanisms may be absent, deficient or inconsistently applied. In other words, the existence of a formal written corporate code of conduct is evidence that a company has *begun* a process of instituting a self-regulation program, but it is not conclusive evidence either that the process has been completed or that it is effective. Second, we have not yet examined the rate of adoption of corporate self-regulation programs by smaller companies below the size of the Fortune 1000 companies. As explicitly recognized by the Federal Organizational Sentencing Guidelines, for smaller companies the cost of instituting formalized and independent code monitoring and compliance mechanisms is relatively higher, and less formal mechanisms may be necessary. Braithwaite (1982) has posited that below a certain size a formal compliance unit answerable directly to top management may be impractical, and that direct regulatory inspections may have to be retained for small businesses.

The second question—will the corporate compliance systems which are being developed in response to present governmental incentives be effective in reducing unlawful or unethical corporate conduct—is much more difficult to answer because of the problems in correlating specific standards of employee conduct, specific compliance programs or specific program features with measurable outcomes, discussed above. Intuitively, an increase in formal corporate codes of conduct of the magnitude indicated by our Fortune 1000 data must be producing *some* positive effect in reducing unlawful corporate behavior over the situation that would exist if such formal codes were not in effect.

The third question—is the corporate self-regulation model promoted by present governmental incentives the most effective system that can be used to encourage lawful or ethical corporate behavior—arises because a "prototype" corporate self-regulation system is emerging from the various governmental incentives for such systems. In broad outline this prototype corporate-level compliance system consists of a formal written code of conduct that contains specific requirements for employee and manager compliance with applicable legal and regulatory standards, coupled with employee ethics training and effective violation reporting mechanisms, compliance audits in some circumstances, and a quasi-independent monitoring and enforcement agency reporting to the highest level of management that consistently investigates and effectively punishes code violations. Our concern is that this governmental model for the privatization of compliance seems to follow the "all stick and no carrot" approach that traditional governmental command and control regulation has traditionally relied upon.

A hypothesis can be constructed that purely punitive legal and regulatory incentives for lawful corporate conduct have been notably *unsuccessful* in reducing unlawful or harmful corporate conduct to a socially-desired level, given the stubborn persistence of unlawful conduct and regulatory violations by U.S. companies in the face of massive increases in punitive laws and regulations in recent decades and the massive increase in the costs of such governmental enforcement activities both to the regulators and to regulated entities. Some critics have argued that punitive incentives tend to freeze regulators and regulated entities into conflictual relationships, and that punishment is not the best means for securing adherence to ethical and legal standards or for maximizing compliance (Sigler and Murphy, 1988). As a result it can be argued that governmental models for private compliance systems should do more than *force* employees to comply with specified legal or ethical standards, they should also help to empower the corporate actors in such "privatized compliance" systems to actively assist in and support such systems to function effectively. We have found evidence that the growing use of *positive* governmental incentives has produced positive results in encouraging corporations to adopt internal self-regulation programs. Could similar *positive* incentives be included for the actors in corporate-level compliance programs, such as positive benefits for employees who facilitate, encourage, assist in, and comply with internal corporate self-governance standards and programs—which in turn could encourage the creation of an ethical corporate climate and make such private programs more effective? This is a question that deserves careful study before governmental regulators settle on a single model of corporate self-regulation to be mandated by future governmental incentives for such programs.

ACKNOWLEDGEMENTS

The authors gratefully acknowledge the assistance of Joseph E. Murphy, Senior Ethics Attorney at Bell Atlantic Corporation and Co-Editor of the *Corporate Conduct Quarterly*, who reviewed earlier drafts of this article and offered many valuable suggestions.

References

Arrow, K. J.: 1973, 'Social Responsibility and Economic Efficiency', *Public Policy* **21**, 303–317.
Berenbeim, R. E.: 1992, *Corporate Ethics Practices* (The Conference Board, Report 11, New York, NY).
Braithwaite, J.: 1982, 'Enforced Self-Regulation: A New Strategy for Corporate Crime Control', *Michigan Law Review* **80**, 1466.

Equal Employment Opportunity Commission, 'Policy Guidance on Sexual Harassment', 8 *Fair Employment Practices Manual* (BNA, 1990) **405**, 6681–6699.

Gatewood, R. D. and A. B. Carroll, 1991, 'Assessment of Ethical performance of Organizational Members: A Conceptual Framework', *Academy of Management Review* **18**(4), 667–688.

Hendricks, W. C.: 1987, 'Memorandum from William C. Hendricks III, Fraud Division Chief to United States Attorneys', reprinted in *A.B.A. White Collar Crime* (American Bar Association, New York, NY, 1988), p. 311.

Mathews, M. C.: 1987, 'Codes of Ethics: Organizational Behavior and Misbehavior', *Research in Corporate Social Performance and Policy* **9**, 107–130.

Perry, W. K., L. S. Dakin and A. Gharakhanian: 1993, 'State Attorneys General Encourage Voluntary Compliance Programs', *Corporate Conduct Quarterly* **2**(4), 49–54, 62.

Pitt, H. A. and K. A. Groskaufmanis: 1990, 'Minimizing Corporate Civil and Criminal Liability: A Second Look at Corporate Codes of Conduct', *Georgetown Law Journal* **78**, 1559.

Sigler, J. A. and J. Murphy: 1988, *Interactive Corporate Compliance* (Greenwood Press).

Sigler, J. A.: 1993, 'Interactive Corporate Compliance', *Compliance Programs and the Corporate Sentencing Guidelines* (Clark Boardman Callaghan, Deerfield, IL), Ch 21.

Stone, C.: 1975, *Where the Law Ends* (Harper & Row, New York, NY), pp. 88–110.

United States Department of Defense: 1988, *Program of Internal Controls for Governmental Contractors*, 48 C.F.R. §203.7000.

United States Department of Justice, *Factors in Decision on Criminal Prosecutions for Environmental Violations in the Context of Significant Compliance or Disclosure Efforts by the Violator* (July 1, 1991), reprinted in *Compliance Programs and the Corporate Sentencing Guidelines* (Clark Boardman Callaghan, Deerfield, IL), Appendix 2.

United States v. Koppers Co., Crim. No. 79–85 (D. Conn., New Haven Div., June 26, 1980), jury instructions.

United States Sentencing Commission, *Guidelines for the Sentencing of Organizations*, 18 USCA App. 4, Ch. 1, Part A, 1 (Supp. 1991).

A Reflexive Model of Environmental Regulation

Eric W. Orts*

Although contemporary methods of environmental regulation have registered some significant accomplishments, the current system of environmental law is not working well enough. First the good news: Since the first Earth Day in 1970, smog has decreased in the United States by thirty percent. The number of lakes and rivers safe for fishing and swimming has increased by one-third. Recycling has begun to reduce levels of municipal waste. Ocean dumping has been curtailed. Forests have begun to expand.[1] One success story is the virtual elimination of airborne lead in the United States. Another is the rapid phase-out of ozone-layer depleting chemicals worldwide.[2] Nevertheless, prominent commentators of diverse political persuasions agree in an assessment that conventional models of environmental law have "failed."[3] Many environmental problems remain unsolved: species extinction, global desertification and deforestation, possible global climate change, and continuing severe air and water pollution in urban areas and poor countries.[4] What is more, successful environmental protection has come only at enormous economic cost. By the year 2000, the Environmental Protection Agency (EPA) estimates that the United States will spend approximately *two percent* of its gross national product on environmental pollution control.[5] Academic economists have pointed out the nonsensical inefficiency of many environmental regulations, but usually to no avail.[6]

A common response to continuing environmental problems is to seek political demons. Depending on one's point of view, the enemies are big business "polluters" or environmentalist "tree huggers" or both. This kind of adversarial environmental politics is counterproductive. Here, I suggest instead that the failures of contemporary environmental law owe more to outmoded regulatory methods than to substantive politics. The next generation of environmental protection requires supplementing conventional methods of regulation with a new model.

I recommend that we should begin to consider seriously a new model of *reflexive environmental law.*[7] This regulatory strategy aims to provide more effective as well as more efficient environmental regulation. In some cases, it may even reduce the need for making tradeoffs between values of economic growth and environmental protection by encouraging new solutions that provide gains for both. This is not to discount the importance of making difficult trade offs between "economy" and "nature." Tradeoffs must be made sometimes. Like many social problems, however, environmental issues are not usually black and white. Complex shades and colors better describe most important environmental issues. The legal problem is to choose the most effective method of addressing them.

By reflexive environmental law, I mean essentially a legal theory and a practical approach to regulation that seeks to encourage self-reflective and self-critical processes within social institutions concerning the effects they have on the natural environment. In other words, reflexive environmental law aims to establish internal evaluative procedures and patterns of decision making within institutions to lessen environmental harm and to increase environmental benefit. The idea is to employ law not directly in terms of giving specific orders or commands, but indirectly to establish incentives and procedures that encourage institutions to think critically, creatively, and continually about how their activities affect the environment and how they may improve their environmental performance.

In referring to "self-reflecting" and "thinking" social institutions, I do not mean to reify them. People, of course, must do the thinking, not abstract social entities. However, to the extent that people have roles within social institutions organized to pursue collective goals or purposes, they direct their thoughts and efforts toward collective ends. It therefore makes sense to consider the manner in which social institutions "think" as shorthand for the thoughts and activities of people following roles or jobs defined within collective groups. Conversely institutions often direct and circumscribe the thoughts and activities of people acting within them.[8]

As a general approach in social theory, Anthony Giddens defines "reflexivity" as "the fact that social practices are constantly examined and reformed in the light of incoming information about those very practices."[9] A theory of reflexive law operationalizes this insight in concrete terms of the governance of institutions. Reflexive law begins from a social theoretical perspective rather than a strictly legal one. Thinking about law only from a legal perspective inevitably truncates analysis, confining it to a narrow perspective of the legal system and its institutions. Reflexive law recognizes the complexity of social life and the diversity of the many institutions created to achieve various ends. It aims to guide rather than to suppress the social complexity of institutions. Reflexive law considers methods by which to embed the quality of reflexivity or self-reflection within institutions. It attempts to off-load some of the burdens of direct regulation to encourage self-regulation of social institutions. The institutions may include a number of voluntary associations, including groups that pursue educational, philanthropic, political, or religious ends.

In the environmental context, public interest and citizens' groups can play an enormously beneficial role. Law can help to structure their contribution. A reflexive model of environmental regulation also involves the economic institutions of business. It seeks to enlist the creative powers of business in finding environmental solutions rather than seeing business always as the "bad guy" who must be stopped or controlled. In this sense, reflexive environmental law breaks free of "the tradition we have developed of labelling different categories of participants in environmental issues as good guys and bad guys—the cowboy hero environmental protection types wearing the white hats versus the sinister despoilers of nature wearing the black hats."[10]

Even with this explanation, I have probably not yet made clear exactly what I mean by reflexive environmental law. In order to flesh out the idea further, let me first provide some perspective by briefly describing the two prevailing models of environmental regulation employed at present. Then I return to describe reflexive environmental regulation in contrast to the two conventional models.

CONVENTIONAL MODELS OF ENVIRONMENTAL LAW

The two basic conventional models or styles of environmental regulation are command-and-control and market-based regulation.

Command-and-control is the most common. As its name suggests, command-and-control achieves environmental protection by ordering regulated individuals and institutions to behave in a specified manner. There are two variations. Performance-based regulation sets limits to emissions of pollutants, usually through a system of government-issued permits. Technology-based regulation mandates the use of pollution-control devices, such as emission-control technology for automobiles.[11]

Although it has had some success, command-and-control has been widely and incisively criticized by legal academics. The main criticism is economic. Command-and-control is not economically efficient in doing the job of protecting the environment.[12] Command-and-control sets broadly gauged standards for environmental performance and requires finely specified pollution-control technology. In doing so, command-and-control becomes inevitably a blunt instrument, even in the hands of experienced administrators. Environmental problems have proven notoriously complex. The problems themselves are often multi-faceted, the science involved is often rapidly changing, the economic and social context is often very finely textured, and the regulatory apparatus itself is increasingly complex. Setting one performance or technological standard to apply across the board does not take account of this complexity. Even when command-and-control works to achieve its environmental goals, the economic cost is often staggering because blunt standards over-deter some and under-deter others without regard to differences in specific circumstances. The inefficiency of command-and-control is not only bad for the economy, it is bad for the environment. Money saved by making regulation more efficient could go to more effective environmental protection, improved economic well-being, or both.

There are a number of other problems with command-and-control in addition to its economic inefficiency. For the sake of brevity, I will just list four of them.

1. *Command-and-control depends too much on administrative agencies, which are vulnerable to changing political winds, capture, and rent-seeking.* Administrative agencies, especially executive agencies, are subject to political forces, such as the election of different Presidents. Recall the infamous influence of former Vice President Quayle's Council on Competitiveness which held up every new environmental regulation deemed to have a potentially adverse effect on economic growth.[13] Another example is the Reagan Administration, which in its first two years cut a quarter of EPA's staff and slashed more than a quarter of its budget.[14]

More subtly, administrative agencies are prone to problems of "capture" by the very businesses they are supposed to regulate. Capture significantly undermines effectiveness. Agencies are also vulnerable to bureaucratic rent-seeking. Bureaucrats may be tempted to use an agency's administrative power to advance their own interests rather than the purposes for which the agency was established.[15] These kinds of limitations lead one to question the long-term efficacy of relying solely on governmental agencies to police environmental protection.

2. *Command-and-control is too static.* Command-and-control establishes performance and technological standards at a given time when the legislation is passed or the regulation adopted. But society changes, the natural environment changes, technology changes, and knowledge changes. Command-and-control is ill-suited to regulating problems that involve fast-changing social and environmental conditions. It is static. Centrally administered through legislatures and agencies, command-and-control cannot easily "learn" from changing circumstances and changing scientific and social knowledge.[16]

3. *Command-and-control becomes too complex and unwieldy.* Environmental regulations stretch out for miles on library shelves. Environmental statutes proliferate. In the United States, there are now over one hundred separate federal environmental statutes and hundreds more state statutes.[17] The texts of the most important federal statutes run to thousands of pages.[18] A few commentators ironically describe the expansion of environmental law as "legal pollution."[19] I refer somewhat less pejoratively to *environmental juridification*.[20] Whatever word is used the phenomenon is the same. The sheer amount of environmental law threatens to clog the wheels of society as a whole. At some point in the escalating process of governments churning out statutes, agencies writing regulations, and courts deciding cases, nobody will be able to say anymore what the applicable legal rules really are or what they are accomplishing. When a body of law becomes so complex and arcane that it cannot even be known, let alone fully complied with or enforced, one cannot hope that its objectives will be realized.

4. *Command-and-control is too harsh and punitive.* As environmental law becomes more complex, its enforcement becomes more difficult. An increasingly detailed law is difficult to police. Legislatures, agencies, and courts gravitate toward imposing heavy penalties on those who are caught in order to preserve the credibility necessary for deterrence. Criminal environmental law is a growth industry.[21] As exponentially increasing numbers of criminal investigators and prosecutors are hired by government, businesses must employ armies of lawyers and auditors to check if they are in compliance with the rules. Even so, one survey found that less than one-third of corporate general counsels believe full compliance with the prolix detail of current environmental law is possible.[22] A large company today cannot avoid the risk of environmental prosecution. Compliance with environmental law becomes more like shooting craps than a rational process.

Under command-and-control, environmental law has taken on a life of its own. It grows like a weed fed by the media, a self-serving bureaucracy, a new class of environmental lawyers, and the ever increasing difficulty and complexity of environmental problems themselves.

This overstates the issue somewhat. Command-and-control is needed in some situations. Intentionally poisoning a river, for example, requires criminal punishment. But critics of command-and-control have argued persuasively for experimenting with a different model, namely, market-based regulation. This second conventional model of environmental law comes in at least four varieties.

1. *Pollution charges and taxes.* The idea here is to require that "polluters pay." Rather than free licenses to pollute contemplated by traditional command-and-control permit systems, this approach allocates "rights" to pollute through a system requiring payment of a fee, a tax, or a charge. Water pollution charges, for example, have been employed in Germany, France, and the Netherlands, but with only mixed success.[23]

There are at least two difficulties with pollution charges and taxes. First, it is not easy for the government to set charges or taxes to achieve the desired results. Government officials must guess how much to charge in order to produce an estimated level of pollution reduction. Calibrating the costs of charges that will achieve the desired overall pollution reduction is tricky. A second difficulty is that taxes, even for a good cause, are very unpopular politically. This is especially true in the United States, as illustrated by the quick death of President Clinton's proposal for an energy tax.[24]

2. *Expanding property rights to include the natural environment.* Some so-called "free market environmentalists" see themselves as following in the footsteps of Ronald Coase.[25] They believe that most environmental problems can be solved if only the system of private property can be expanded to include the natural environment itself. An example is the private ownership of endangered species. If people own an endangered species, such as a rare species of parrots, the human owners will desire to protect them, and the species will survive. If ownership of the rare parrots is not allowed, no human interest will be strong enough to protect the birds from extinction. This strategy may have merit in some situations, such as preserving an endangered species that happens to have a high economic value, such as provided by the wild colors of a pet parrot. But the neo-Coasian approach does not travel very far. Consider air pollution. As Jim Krier notes, air "does not come in marketable packages."[26] Even if technological solutions to the problem of ownership of the air were invented, it would be a terrible world that reduced air to property, although deteriorating air quality in some places may be moving responses in this direction. Several years ago an entrepreneurial environmentalist proposed selling oxygen on the streets of Mexico City for $1.75 per thirty-second shot.[27]

In the end, the neo-Coasian vision of the environmental future reminds me of an old B-52's rock lyric:

Planet Claire has pink air.
All the trees are red.
Nothing ever grows there.
No one has a head.[28]

Nobody really wants Earth to turn into a Planet Claire, not even the most radical free market environmentalist.

3. *Tradeable pollution rights.* This is currently a very popular kind of market-based regulation, although it is actually a variation on command-and-control. This market-based approach simply divides command-and-control permits into units or "rights" and makes them tradeable. The big experiment with this form of regulation is the acid rain permit trading program under the Clean Air Act Amendments of 1990.[29] The jury is still out on this experiment. The best analysis, however, suggests that tradeable pollution rights may work well in cases involving relatively few and relatively large sources of pollution. The acid rain problem seems to meet these conditions. However, the idea of expanding tradeable permits for millions of polluters, for example, millions of automobile drivers, raises significant difficulties in terms of the workability of the system. These difficulties are probably irresolvable in complex situations involving great numbers of polluters.[30]

4. *Environmental marketing regulation.* A fourth type of market-based regulation brings us closer to a different model. Regulation of environmental marketing is of two basic types: (1) truth-in-environmental-advertising, regulated somewhat weakly at present in the United States by the Federal Trade Commission,[31] and (2) government- or privately-sponsored environmental labels.

Examples of government-sponsored environmental labels include the European Union's "Eco-label," Japan's "Eco-mark," Germany's "Blue Angel," and Canada's "Environmental Choice" decal. Privately sponsored environmental labels in the United States include "Green Seal" and "environmental report cards" issued by Scientific Certification Systems. The idea is to establish a kind of Good Housekeeping seal for products that are environmentally beneficial or at least benign. Conversely, environmental labels are often used to warn of environmentally harmful products.[32]

There are technical difficulties with eco-labels. Establishing proper and accurate standards for environmental labelling schemes is very difficult. Most are based on some form of life-cycle analysis, but this is a new science about which there is not yet much to agree.[33] In addition, government-sponsored award schemes may be subject to improper influence through lobbying. Eco-labels might even be used as a method to discriminate against international trade.

Although they have limitations, truth-in-environmental-advertising and environmental labels represent a model of reflexive environmental law. They attempt to provide positive incentives for businesses to improve environmental performance in order to appeal to the environmental preferences of consumers. Product reengineering, creative approaches to manufacturing and production, and invention of new technology are encouraged.

The rub is that consumers must actually care enough about the natural environment to pay an environmental premium that will provide a sufficient incentive for businesses to invest in making environmentally correct products. Environmental marketing regulation acts reflexively, but only through a diffuse market of individual consumers. Its virtue lies in attempting to influence social processes to take account of environmental issues without forcing solutions through direct regulation. However, without widespread environmental education and other measures that would encourage consumers to favor "environmentally friendly" products on a large scale, the regulation of environmental marketing will provide only a limited contribution to environmental protection. Whether environmental marketing regulation will work effectively to improve the overall quality of the natural environment depends directly on the extent to which consumers internalize environmental ethics.

REFLEXIVE ENVIRONMENTAL LAW

Elsewhere, I explore some other areas of law that hint at an emerging model of reflexive environmental law.[34] They include not only environmental marketing regulation, but also the following five examples.

1. *The National Environmental Policy Act (NEPA).*[35] NEPA is one of the oldest federal environmental statutes, and it is also one of the most reflexive. The idea behind NEPA is to encourage governmental institutions to engage in self-reflective and self-critical processes when making decisions that will "significantly affect[] the quality of the natural environment."[36] However, because NEPA applies only to government agencies, its scope is relatively limited. In addition, some critics argue that NEPA does not assure that reflexive decision making actually occurs. They assert that bureaucrats often just go through the motions of complying with NEPA's formal requirements after having already made a substantive decision on other grounds.[37]

2. *Environmental Auditing and Enforcement Policies.* Both the EPA and the Department of Justice have adopted enforcement policies designed to encourage businesses to conduct environmental auditing.[38] In response to criticism that these policies did not go far enough in protecting businesses from investigators and prosecutors seeking to uncover evidence of legal violations through discovery of internal environmental auditing records.[39] The EPA issued a revised *Voluntary Environmental Self-Policing and Self-Disclosure Interim Policy Statement in* April 1995.[40] As the title suggests, the EPA is explicitly attempting to encourage reflexive "self-policing" and "self-disclosure." Whether sufficient incentives and procedures have been put in place to achieve these ends remains debatable. But these enforcement policies are designed to reduce the exposure to command-and-control penalties for businesses that develop strong internal procedures to monitor environmental performance. The enforcement policies are therefore part of an emerging model of reflexive environmental law.

3. *Environmental Sentencing Guidelines for Organizations.* The proposed Environmental Sentencing Guidelines now under review by the U.S. Sentencing Commission also provide an incentive to adopt reflexive environmental auditing and management systems.[41] The proposed guidelines reduce fines for an organization convicted of an environmental crime if it has a qualifying "environmental compliance program." In the absence of a qualifying program, fines are increased. Unfortunately, the kind of compliance programs recognized under the proposed sentencing guidelines strongly emphasize legal compliance rather than a more proactive approach to environmental performance. There is a danger that environmental auditing programs will therefore become overly defensive.[42] But the very fact of including self-evaluative compliance programs as a mitigating and aggravating factor in criminal sentencing represents another manifestation of an emergent reflexive environmental law.

4. *Voluntary Government-Sponsored Programs.* A fourth kind of emerging reflexive environmental law appears in various programs established by EPA under the auspices of the Pollution Prevention Act of 1990.[43] For example, the Industrial Toxics Project or "33/50" program succeeded in significant reductions of emissions of toxic chemicals.[44] The "Green Lights" program reduced electricity consumption through installation of efficient lighting.[45] WasteWi$e, a new voluntary program, promotes the reduction, reuse, and recycling of industrial waste.[46] These programs share the laudable goal of energizing businesses to attack environmental problems creatively. But they also suffer in their inevitably piecemeal effect. Unless systematically encouraged, voluntary programs to encourage environmental management are destined to achieve only very partial results.

5. *Environmental Management and Audit Systems.* The European Union's recently introduced Eco-management and Audit Scheme (EMAS) is systemic in its intended scope.[47] It represents an ambitious attempt to establish a reflexive environmental law. Opting in to the EMAS regulation is voluntary, and businesses may choose not to participate.[48] But unlike the piecemeal voluntary programs experimented with in the United States, the European EMAS has the advantage of involving government in setting up a third-party certification procedure for voluntary environmental auditing and management programs. This approach promises systemic change if enough businesses decide to participate.

The EMAS sets up procedures for businesses that wish to qualify, and there are two essential operative requirements. The first is *public disclosure.* Environmental performance measured through internal auditing must be disclosed in public environmental statements.[49] A second requirement is *third-party certification*. Compliance with the procedures of the EMAS regulation and the accuracy of the public environmental statements based on underlying internal auditing data must be certified by a professionally licensed environmental verifier.[50]

In its emphasis on public disclosure, the EMAS system is analogous to the regulatory strategy of the federal securities laws of the United States. Louis Loss describes the "recurrent theme" in securities regulation as "disclosure, again disclosure, and still more disclosure."[51] Almost from its inception, it was obvious to those who established a federal system of securities regulation that the sheer number of regulated businesses made direct regulation impossible. Even with respect to about 6000 brokers and traders, William O. Douglas declared direct regulation to be "impractical, unwise, and unworkable."[52] Direct regulation of all reporting companies was unthinkable. The alternative hit upon was a self-reporting and largely self-regulating system in which public disclosure figures largely.

Enforcement of disclosure under the securities laws is greatly enhanced by allowing private rights of action by citizens for violations.[53] Third-parties who are harmed by false or misleading statements in publicly disclosed financial documents may sue for damages. The European EMAS does not allow citizen suits for what might be called *environmental fraud*. But future reflexive environmental systems might establish a private right of action for qualified environmental public interest groups to help oversee businesses that participate in an EMAS program.[54]

Third-party certification of the accuracy of public statements is essential to a viable regulatory system based on disclosure. Without a mechanism to assure that public statements about environmental performance are accurate, some companies may make misrepresentations or omissions for the benefit of public relations. Again, securities law provides a useful analogy. Verification of environmental statements is like the well-known requirement of financial auditing of annual reports. The new environmental verifiers are like accountants. Both verifiers and accountants are professional third-parties who audit for the purpose of helping to assure accuracy.

Adding a significant role for third-party verifiers and perhaps even third-party citizen suits helps to break regulatory gridlock by adding a third player to the bilateral regulatory game between government and business, agency and industry. Ian Ayres and John Braithwaite describe this kind of regulatory approach as "tripartism" or "enforced self-regulation."[55] Adding third-parties to the equation helps to overcome the ever-present problems of administrative capture and bureaucratic rent-seeking. In a reflexive system, the government's role changes. Rather than relying on escalating threats of enforcement penalties, a reflexive law relies primarily on disclosure. Enforcement is reserved for backing up the disclosure-based system.

REFLEXIVE LAW AND ENVIRONMENTAL ETHICS

Reflexive environmental law aims to establish environmental ethics in institutions, particularly businesses. As a regulatory model, reflexive environmental law differs from the instrumental approaches of both command-and-control and market-based regulation.[56] Both conventional models use law to impose a foreordained environmental result on the world. In some cases, this is necessary or desirable. For example, criminal regulation must deter intentional endangerment of human life or serious direct harm to the natural environment. Likewise, some otherwise intractable environmental problems, such as acid rain, may succumb most effectively to market-based regulation. Many environmental problems, however, are complex and subtly difficult enough to require a more flexible regulatory approach. For these increasingly common problems, a reflexive model may improve on conventional methods.

Conventional models of environmental law resort to the instruments of the state and the market. Through the direct intervention of the state, command-and-control imposes specific rules on society to achieve environmental protection. However, environmental problems and issues are often too complex for this method to work effectively and efficiently. A place for command-and-control will doubtless remain, but new models are needed. The market-based model improves on command-and-control by providing flexibility in achieving regulatory ends through the use of the market, but it is also instrumental in its reliance purely on economic rationality. Environmental protection should not be limited to conventional instrumental models because solving difficult environmental problems also requires ethical commitment and responsibility.

Conventional models of environmental protection are not sufficient because they act primarily to constrain businesses by threats of lawsuits or economic sanctions. This method of regulation is *negative* in orientation. Conventional models cannot easily succeed in positively motivating businesses to pursue environmentally responsible programs and policies. The conventional regulatory models see businesses as targets on which to impose instrumental punishments. Reflexive environmental law attempts instead to encourage ethical environmental behavior by providing *positive* incentives. Voluntarism, public disclosure, third-party certification, participation by public interest groups, and procedures for institutional self-reflection and self-criticism are the key elements of the reflexive model.

The reflexive model operates at an intermediate level between the state and the market. It seeks to influence the decision making processes of institutions. In this respect, the reflexive model shares similarities with Philip Selznick's notion of "responsive law."[57] As Selznick writes, "there is no escaping the need for institutional self-awareness and self-criticism."[58]

Reflexive environmental law looks to provide regulatory patterns and procedures to encourage the institutionalization of environmental responsibility, particular in business. Holmes Rolston argues persuasively that *"the bottom line ought not to be black unless it can also be green."*[59] However, the structure of society must allow for businesses that respect this principle to survive. Otherwise, businesses with green bottom lines will go bankrupt, and the long-term purposes of environmental protection will not be served. A model of environmental regulation is needed that encourages businesses to adopt environmentally proactive policies and to allow them to prosper in doing so. At the same time, the model must discourage businesses that are environmentally irresponsible.

Rolston also points out correctly that *"[m]orality often exceeds legality."*[60] A fundamental purpose of law, however, is to institute ethical practices. Reflexive environmental law seeks to establish regulatory processes that help to institute environmentally sound management practices. It is consistent with ethical theories that emphasize evolving, flexible group norms coming from the bottom up rather than imposing them from the top down.[61]

If new approaches are not adopted, institutions will inevitably follow the prevailing logic of the market, and economic concerns will drown out voices that call for environmental ethics. Creative and intelligent use of law is central to establishing environmental ethics. Reflexive environmental law aims to challenge and motivate businesses to take environmental performance seriously.

NOTES

*The original version of this paper was given as the Anne M. Ballantyne Lecture at the University of Texas at Austin, Graduate School of Business. For comments, I am especially grateful to Frank Cross, Tom Dunfee, Kinnan Goleman, and Howard Kunreuther. Thanks to David Brady for research assistance and Tamara English and Rae Goodman for secretarial assistance. Thanks also to Paula Murray, Steve Salbu, and Pat Werhane.

1. Gregg Easterbrook, *The Good Earth Looks Better* (New York Times, Apr. 21, 1995), at A31. See also Gregg Easterbrook, *A Moment on the Earth: The Coming Age of Environmental Optimism* (1995) (providing a sanguine view of the success of environmental regulation in developed countries).

2. For airborne lead reduction, see, e.g., Sandra Blakeslee, *Concentrations of Lead in Blood Drop Steeply* (New York Times, July 27, 1994), at A18 (reporting on government study finding 78% decline in the amount of lead in the bloodstreams of Americans over phase-out period of leaded gasoline from 1976 to 1991); Thomas O. McGarity, *Radical Technology-Forcing in Environmental Regulation*, vol. 27, *Loyola of Los Angeles Law Review* (1994), pp. 943, 947–52 (calling the "lead phase down" an "environmental success story"). See also Council on Environmental Quality, *United Nations Conference on Environment and Development: United States of America National Report* (1992), p. 197; Barry Commoner, *Making Peace with the Planet* (4th ed. 1992), p. 22.

For the reduction in the production of ozone-depleting chemicals, see, e.g., William K. Stevens, *Ozone-Depleting Chemicals Building Up at Slower Pace* (New York Times, Aug. 26, 1993), at A1 (recounting that global slowdown of ozone-depleting chemicals in atmosphere can be "attributed to industry's unexpectedly rapid cut in the production of the chemicals even before international agreements to phase them out took full effect"); Philip Shabecoff, *Industry Acts to Save Ozone* (New York Times, Mar. 21, 1988), at A1 (describing industrial efforts to develop substitutes for ozone-depleting chemicals). See also Richard E. Benedick, *Ozone Diplomacy* (1991).

3. See, e.g., Commoner, *supra note* 2, at pp. 19–40 (referring to "the environmental failure"); E. Donald Elliott, *Environmental TQM: Anatomy of a Pollution Control Program That Works!*, vol. 92; *Michigan Law Review* (1994), pp. 1840, 1844 (commenting on "the disappointing record of traditional strategies used in U.S. environmental law to achieve its stated goals"); Lakshman Guruaswamy, *Integrated Environmental Control: The Expanding Matrix*, vol. 22, *Environmental Law* (1992), pp. 77, 83–87 (describing "failures of the existing system"); Cass R. Sunstein, *Paradoxes of the Regulatory State*, vol. 57, *University of Chicago Law Review* (1990), pp. 407, 411 (environmental regulation has "frequently failed").

4. For an overview of the world's continuing environmental problems and an emerging framework for addressing some of them, see Agenda 21, the non-binding agreement drafted at the Earth Summit in Rio de Janeiro in 1992. Agenda 21 is reprinted in Stanley P. Johnson, ed., *The Earth Summit: The United Nations Conference on Environment and Development (UNCED)* (1993), pp. 125–508. See also Christopher D. Stone, *The Gnat is Older Than Man: Global Environment and Human Agenda* (1993), pp. 5–18 (diagnosing some of the continuing basic environmental problems).

5. U.S. EPA, *The Cost of a Clean Environment* (1990), p. v.

6. For an influential argument discussing the inefficiencies of conventional environmental regulation, see Bruce A. Ackerman & Richard B. Stewart, *Reforming Environmental Law*, vol. 37, *Stanford Law Review* (1985), pp. 1333, 1334–40. See also T.H. Tietenberg, *Economic Instruments for Environmental Regulation* in Dieter Helm, ed., *Economic Policy Towards the Environment* (1991), pp. 86, 95–97, tbl. 4.1 (summarizing empirical studies of the high cost of conventional environmental regulation as opposed to least-cost alternatives).

7. My conception of reflexive environmental law is described more fully in Eric W. Orts, *Reflexive Environmental Law*, vol. 89, *Northwestern University Law Review* (1995), p. 1227. For an early development of the theory of reflexive law, see Gunther Teubner, *Substantive and Reflexive Elements in Modern Law*, vol. 17, *Law & Society Review* (1983), p. 239. For recent applications of the idea of reflexive law in the environmental context, see the essays collected in Gunther Teubner, et al. eds., *Environmental Law and Ecological Responsibility: The Concept and Practice of Ecological Self-Organization* (1994). See also Michael Herz, *Parallel Universes: NEPA Lessons for the New Property*, vol. 93, *Columbia Law Review* (1993), pp. 1668, 1689–93 (describing National Environmental Policy Act as an example of reflexive law); Eric Bregman & Arthur Jacobson, *Environmental Performance Review: Self-Regulation in Environmental Law*, vol. 16, *Cardozo Law Review* (1994), p. 465.

8. See Mary Douglas, *How Institutions Think* (1986).

9. Anthony Giddens, *The Consequences of Modernity* (1990), p. 38. *Cf.* Pierre Bourdieu & Loïc J.D. Wacquant, *An Invitation to Reflexive Sociology* (1992), pp. 36–46 (describing various approaches to "reflexive sociology").

10. Kenneth A. Manaster, *Ten Paradoxes of Environmental Law*, vol. 27, *Loyola of Los Angeles Law Review* (1994), pp. 917, 931.

11. See Robert W. Hahn & Robert N. Stavins, *Incentive-Based Environmental Regulation: A New Era from an Old Idea?*, vol. 18, *Ecology Law Quarterly* (1991), pp. 1, 5–6.

12. *Id.* at 6 ("Uniform emissions standards, the dominant policy mechanism chosen to attack a number of environmental problems, tend to lead to inefficient outcomes in which firms use unduly expensive means of controlling pollution. The reason is simple: the costs of controlling pollutant emissions vary greatly among and even within firms. Indeed, the cost of controlling a unit of a given pollutant may vary by a factor of 100 or more among sources, depending upon the age and location of plants and the available technologies."). See also Ackerman & Stewart, *supra* note 6, at 1334–40 (criticizing command-and-control "best available control technology" as wasteful, inefficient, and counterproductive). But see Howard Latin, *Ideal Versus Real Regulatory Efficiency: Implementation of Uniform Standards and "Fine-Tuning" Regulatory Reforms*, vol. 37, *Stanford Law Review* (1985), p. 1267 (defending command-and-control regulation against market-based criticism).

13. See, e.g., Michael Herz, *Imposing Unified Executive Branch Statutory Interpretation*, vol. 15, *Cardozo Law Review* (1993), pp. 219, 223–26 (providing a critical account of the Council on Competitiveness).

14. Kirkpatrick Sale, *The Green Revolution: The American Environmental Movement 1962–1992*, pp. 50–51 (1993).

15. The literature on administrative capture and bureaucratic rent-seeking is vast. For a brief overview of the two problems, see Cass R. Sunstein, *Constitutionalism After the New Deal*, vol. 101, *Harvard Law Review* (1987), pp. 421, 448–51.

16. See Daniel A. Farber, *Environmental Protection as a Learning Experience*, vol. 27, *Loyola of Los Angeles Law Review* (1994), p. 791 (discussing the problem of "learning" in environmental regulation).

17. Council on Environmental Quality, *supra* note 2, app. D (a "selected list" of federal environmental statutes).

18. This total is reached just counting seven statutes: the Clean Air Act, the Clean Water Act, the Federal Insecticide, Fungicide, and Rodenticide Act (FIFRA), the Safe Drinking Water Act, the Toxic Substances Control Act (TSCA), the Resource Conservation and Recovery Act (RCRA), and the Comprehensive Emergency Response, Compensation, and Liability Act (CERCLA). Dallas Burtraw & Paul R. Portney, *Environmental Policy in the United States* in Dieter Helm ed., *Economic Policy Towards the Environment* (1991), pp. 289, 291–97. Not counted are several other important statutes, including the National Environmental Policy Act (NEPA) and the Endangered Species Act.

19. Thomas Ehrlich, *Legal Pollution* (New York Times, Feb. 8, 1976 (Magazine), p. 17); Richard B. Stewart, *Reconstitutive Law*, vol. 46, *Maryland Law Review* (1986), pp. 86, 101.

20. Orts, *supra* note 7, pp. 1239–41.

21. See, e.g., Richard J. Lazarus, *Assimilating Environmental Protection into Legal Rules and the Problem with Environmental Crime*, vol. 27, *Loyola of Los Angeles Law Review* (1994), p. 867 (describing the enormous increases in administrative resources devoted to environmental prosecutions and the controversy surrounding greater reliance on environmental criminal enforcement); Judson W. Starr & Thomas J. Kelly, Jr., *Environmental Crimes and the Sentencing Guidelines: The Time Has Come . . . and It Is Hard Time*, vol. 20, *Environmental Law Reporter* (Environmental Law Institute, 1990) ¶ 10.096 (describing recent reclassification of many offenses under federal environmental statutes from misdemeanors to felonies). See also James M. Strock, *Environmental Criminal Enforcement Priorities for the 1990s*, vol. 59, *George Washington Law Review* (1991), p. 916.

22. Marianne Lavelle, *Environmental Vise: Law, Compliance* (National Law Journal, Aug. 30, 1993), at S1.

23. See, e.g., Eckard Rehbinder, *Environmental Regulation Through Fiscal and Economic Incentives in a Federalist System*, vol. 20, *Ecology Law Quarterly* (1993), pp. 57, 72–74.

24. Michael Wines, *Tax's Demise Illustrates the First Rule of Lobbying: Work, Work, Work*, (New York Times, June 14, 1993), at A1 (recounting the failure of Clinton's proposal for an energy tax even after key concessions were made to various interest groups, including tax breaks for ethanol, diesel fuel, home heating oil, electricity, and even coal).

25. See, e.g., Terry L. Anderson & Donald R. Leal, *Free Market Environmentalism* (1991); Symposium, *Free Market Environmentalism*, vol. 15, *Harvard Journal of Law and Public Policy* (1992), p. 297. Coase's classic article is R.H. Coase, *The Problem of Social Cost*, vol. 3, *Journal of Law and Economics* (1960), p. 1.

26. James E. Krier, *The Pollution Problem and Legal Institutions: A Conceptual Overview*, vol. 18, *UCLA Law Review* (1971), pp. 429, 440.

27. *Oxygen to Go on Sale in Smog-Choked Mexico City* (Reuters, Feb. 7, 1991) (available on LEXIS). For an account of the terrible air pollution problems of Mexico City, see, e.g., Marjorie Miller, *A Day in the Life of Mother Earth: Mexico City's Smog* (Los Angeles Times, May 26, 1992), p. 9.

28. B-52's, *Planet Claire*, B-52's (Island Records 1979).

29. Clean Air Act Amendments of 1990, Pub. L. No. 101-549, § 401, 104 Stat. 2399 (1990). For an overview, see William H. Rodgers, Jr., vol. 1, *Environmental Law: Air and Water Pollution* (Supp. 1994), pp. 64–74. See also Jeanne M. Dennis, Comment, *Smoke for Sale: Paradoxes and Problems of the Emissions Trading Program of the Clean Air Act Amendments of 1990*, vol. 40, *UCLA Law Review* (1993), p. 1101.

30. For a conceptual analysis of this problem, see Dieter Helm & David Pearce, *Economic Policy Towards the Environment: An Overview*, in Dieter Helm, ed., *Economic Policy Toward the Environment* (1991), pp. 1, 15.

31. High profile cases brought by the FTC include enforcement actions resulting in consent decrees concerning advertisements of "chlorine-free" coffee filters made of "recycled" paper, *In re* Mr. Coffee, Inc., 1993 FTC LEXIS 62 (1993), and "biodegradable" trash bags, *In re* North Am. Plastics Corp., 1993 FTC LEXIS 61 (1993); *In re* Mobil Oil Corp., 1992 FTC LEXIS 187 (1992).

32. For further description and an illustration of these environmental labels, see Orts, *supra* note 7, pp. 1246–51, fig. 2.

33. See, e.g., Jamie A. Grodsky, *Certified Green: The Law and Future of Environmental La-belling*, vol. 10, *Yale Journal on Regulations*, vol. 147, (1993), pp. 218–26 (discussing some of the technical problems with life-cycle analysis); Committee on Antitrust and Trade Regulation, Association of the Bar of City of New York, *Private Certification of Manufacturer's Environmental Claims*, vol. 48, *Rec.* pp. 25, 29–30 (Jan.–Feb. 1993) (discussing controversy over life cycle analysis).

34. Orts, *supra* note 7, pp. 1268–1313.

35. 42 U.S.C. §§ 4321-70 (1988).

36. 42 U.S.C. § 4332(2)(c). Michael Herz recognizes and comments on the reflexive aspect of NEPA. Michael Herz, *Parallel Universes: NEPA Lessons for the New Property*, vol. 93, *Columbia Law Review* (1993), pp. 1668, 1689–93.

37. Herz, *supra* note 36, p. 1700, n. 151 (noting "central concern" about whether complying with NEPA's requirements "precedes and informs the agency decision or follows and justifies it"). *Compare* Robertson v. Methow Valley Citizens Council, 490 U.S. 332, 350 (1989) (expressing Supreme Court's view that NEPA is "almost certain" to "affect the agency's substantive decision") *with* Joseph L. Sax, *The (Unhappy) Truth About NEPA*, vol. 26, *Oklahoma Law Review* (1973), p. 239, ("I think the emphasis on the redemptive quality of procedural reform [represented by NEPA] is about nine parts myth and one part coconut oil.") See also *Symposium on NEPA at Twenty*, vol. 20, *Environmental Law* (1990), p. 447.

38. I discuss details of these enforcement policies in Orts, *supra* note 7, pp. 1275–81.

39. Defense lawyers roundly criticized the enforcement policies concerning environmental auditing as unenforceable and even somewhat deceptive. See, e.g., Jed S. Rakoff, et al., *Corporate Sentencing Guidelines: Compliance and Mitigation* (1994), § 8.02[1] ("While ostensibly encouraging audits, [EPA's 1986] Policy Statement [on Environmental Auditing] provides no assurance that the results would not be used against the defendant, nor that the existence of the auditing would create any defense or limitation on liability, nor that the audits would be protected from disclosure at EPA's discretion for use in criminal prosecution."); Terrell E. Hunt & Timothy A. Wilkens, *Environmental Audits and Enforcement Policy*, vol. 16, *Harvard Environmental Law Review* (1992), pp. 365, 370 ("lawyers recommend extreme discretion and caution in the use of environmental audits"). See also Robert W. Darnell, Note, *Environmental Criminal Enforcement and Corporate Environmental Auditing*, vol. 31, *American Criminal Law Review* (1993), pp. 123, 124 ("Executives are now hesitant to authorize audits that the government could, under federal environmental auditing policy, use as a roadmap for establishing knowledge in a criminal prosecution.").

40. 60 Fed. Reg. 16,875 (Apr. 3, 1995).

41. U.S. Sentencing Commission Advisory Panel, *Final Draft Environmental Guidelines* (Nov. 1993). See also John C. Coffee, Jr., *Environmental Crime and Punishment* (New York Law Journal, Feb. 3, 1994), p. 5.

42. For development of this point, see Orts, *supra* note 7, pp. 1281–84.

43. 42 U.S.C. (1994), §§ 13101–09; *Pollution Prevention Strategy*, vol. 56, Fed. Reg. 7849 (1991). See also Stephen M. Johnson, *From Reaction to Proaction: The 1990 Pollution Prevention Act*, vol. 17, *Columbia Journal of Environmental Law*, (1992), p. 153.

44. Participating companies in the 33/50 program voluntarily reduced emissions of seventeen toxic chemicals 33 percent by 1992 and 50 percent by 1995. See, e.g., Seema Arona & Timothy N. Carson, *A Voluntary Approach to Environmental Regulation: The 33/50 Program, Resources* (Summer 1994), p. 6.

45. See, e.g., Bert Black & David H. Hollander, Jr., *Forced Volunteerism: The New Regulatory Push to Prevent Pollution*, vol. 16, *Chemical Regulation Reporter* (BNA) (Jan. 22, 1993), p. 38.

46. *More than 280 Companies Join Effort to Reduce, Reuse, Recycle Waste, EPA Says*, vol. 25, *Environmental Law Reporter* (BNA) (July 22, 1994), p. 529.

47. Council Regulation 1836/93, Allowing for Voluntary Participation by Companies in the Industrial Sector in a Community Eco-management and Audit Scheme, 1993 O.J. (L 168) 1. This regulation went into effect in April 1995. I examine this regulation in detail in Orts, *supra* note 7, p. 1287–1313, and recommend adoption in a revised form of a version of the EMAS in the United States, *id.*, p. 1313–27.

48. Council Regulation 1836/93, art. 1, 1993 O.J. (L 168) 1, 2

49. *Id.* art. 1, at 4.

50. *Id.* arts. 6, 7, at 4–5.

51. Louis Loss, *Fundamentals of Securities Regulation* (1988), p. 7.

52. Joel Seligman, *The Transformation of Wall Street* (1982), p. 185.

53. See, e.g., J.I. Case v. Borak, 377 U.S. 426 (1962); Virginia Bankshares, Inc. v. Sandberg, 501 U.S. 1083 (1991).

54. I advocate allowing citizens' suits in proposed an American EMAS, although it must be kept in mind that adding teeth to a voluntary EMAS system requires corresponding increases in the positive incentives for businesses to participate. See Orts, *supra*, note 7, pp. 1324–27 (discussing enhanced incentives for an American EMAS system, such as strict evidentiary protection of internal environmental audits and perhaps even immunity from criminal prosecution for participating businesses).

55. Ian Ayres & John Braithwaite, *Responsive Regulation: Transcending the Deregulation Debate* (1992), pp. 54–132.

56. *Cf.* Gunther Teubner, *After Legal Instrumentalism?*, in Gunther Teubner ed., *Dilemmas of Law in the Welfare State*, (1986), p. 299.

57. See Philip Selznick, *The Moral Commonwealth: Social Theory and the Promise of Community* (1992); Philip Selznick, *Self-Regulation and the Theory of Institutions* in Gunther Teubner et al. eds., *Environmental Law and Ecological Responsibility: The Concept and Practice of Ecological Self-Organization* (1994), pp. 396–402. See also Phillipe Nonet & Philip Selznick, *Law and Society in Transition: Toward Responsive Law* (1978).

58. Selznick, *The Moral Commonwealth, supra* note 57, p. 236.

59. Holmes Rolston, III, *Environmental Ethics: Duties to and Values in the Natural World* (1988), p. 325 (emphasis in original).

60. *Id.* at 317 (emphasis in original).

61. Assessing competing ethical theories in the context of reflexive environment law lies outside the scope of this article. However, it appears that utilitarian approaches inform both command-and-control and market-based approaches. Contractarian approaches appear highly compatible, at least in spirit, with a reflexive model of environmental regulation. See, e.g., Thomas Donaldson & Thomas W. Dunfee, *Integrative Social Contracts Theory: A Communitarian Conception of Economic Ethics*, vol. 11, *Economics and Philosophy* (1995), p. 85; Thomas W. Dunfee & Thomas Donaldson, *Contractarian Business Ethics: Current Status and Next Steps*, vol. 5, *Business Ethics Quarterly* (1995), p. 173.

The International Marketplace: Bribery.

Overview.

One of the most persistent problems in the international marketplace is that of bribery. This is a nagging problem because making "payments" to various officials to obtain contracts is ingrained in the way business is conducted in much of the world. It is a part of the shared community worldview in these countries. The issue is how U.S. businesses should deal with officials in countries that follow a business standard that differs from U.S. practice and is illegal in the United States.

Issues related to bribery are developed in Michael Philips's article. He argues that in some contexts, accepting a bribe violates no promises or agreements and that in some cases there is no prima facie duty to refrain from offering a bribe.

The force of Philips's argument is to define what constitutes a bribe. His original definitions revolve around the taking of money to disobey the shared community worldview. But what if the shared community worldview were corrupt? This is to suggest that taking and accepting the bribe *simpliciter* are not sufficient for moral condemnation. The only time that this *is not* the case is when the bribe is offered in an environment that is free from taint of prior wrongdoing. Finally, unless there is a clear quid pro quo relationship, the bribe may merely be part of a cultural institution of gift exchange.

Thomas L. Carson replies to Philips by asserting that bribery is essentially wrong because it violates an implicit or explicit promise made to social and political institutions to act in accordance with the rules of that institution. For example, in athletics, the implicit agreement is that the athlete will perform to the best of his or her ability in the pursuit of victory. To do less (e.g., when one is paid money to subvert that compact) is to act immorally. Since the duties involved are prima facie, they may be overridden by more primary moral duties.

An article by Scott Turow ends this section with a legal perspective of this issue. In this article, he offers the following definition: "Bribery occurs when property or personal advantage is offered, without the authority of law, to a public official with the intent that the public official act favorably to the offeror at any time or fashion in the execution of the public official's duties." This is a narrower definition than that used in the previous essays. In this case, the offer (to a public official) is itself sufficient to make the act immoral because all public officials have a duty to treat similar cases the same. Giving a bribe materially changes things. The public official has a new and conflicting interest that is intended to make that public official abrogate her duty to the public at large. Thus, according to Turow, bribery of public officials undermines moral public institutions and threatens any society that claims to be based on ethical principles.

Bribery

Michael Philips

Although disclosures of bribery have elicited considerable public indignation over the last decade, popular discussions of the morality of bribery have tended largely to be unilluminating. One reason for this is that little care has been taken to distinguish bribes from an assortment of related practices with which they are easily confused. Before we can be in a position to determine what to do about the problem of bribery, we need to be clearer about what count and ought to count as bribes. Unfortunately, there is as yet very little philosophical literature on this topic.[1] In this essay I shall remedy this defect by presenting an account of the concept of bribery and by employing that account to clarify matters in three areas in which there is public controversy and confusion.

At least some confusion in discussions of bribery arises from a failure adequately to appreciate the distinction between bribery and extortion. This is true, for example, of accounts of the notorious case of Lockheed in Japan. I shall attempt to show that the morality of this and similar transactions is better assessed if we are clear on that distinction.

A second problem area arises out of the fact of cultural variability. As is generally recognized, the conduct of business, government, and the professions differs from culture to culture. In some places transactions that many Americans would consider bribes are not only expected behavior but accepted practice as well. That is, they are condoned by the system of rule governing the conduct of the relevant parties. Are they bribes? Are only some of them bribes? If so, which?

A third problem arises out of the general difficulty of distinguishing between bribes, on the one hand, and gifts and rewards, on the other. Suppose that a manufacturer of dresses keeps a buyer for a catalog company happy by supplying him with any tickets to expensive shows and athletic events that he requests. Are these bribes? Or suppose that a special interest group rewards public administrators who rule in its favor with vacations, automobiles, and jewelry. May we correctly speak of bribery here?

I

To answer such questions we need to say more precisely what bribes are. A bribe is a payment (or promise of payment) for a service. Typically, this payment is made to an official in exchange for her violating some official duty or responsibility. And typically she does this by failing deliberately to make a decision on its merits. This does not necessarily mean that a bribed official

---

[1]At the time this paper was written there were no references to bribes or bribery in the *Philosopher's Index*. Since that time one paper has been indexed—Arnold Berleant's "Multinationals, Local Practice, and the Problems of Ethical Consistency" (*Journal of Business Ethics* 1 [August 1982]: 185–93)—but, as the title of this short paper suggests, Berleant is not primarily concerned with providing an analysis of the concept of bribery. However, three presentations on the topic of bribery were made at the 1983 "Conference for Business Ethics" (organized by the Society for Business Ethics at DePaul University, July 25–26) and have subsequently been accepted for publication. These are: Kendall D'Andrade's "Bribery" (forthcoming in a special issue of the *Journal of Business Ethics*, devoted to the DePaul conference, 1984); John Danley's "Toward a Theory of Bribery" (forthcoming in the *Journal of Business and Professional Ethics*, 1984); and Tom Carson's "Bribery, Extortion and the Foreign Corrupt Practices Act" (forthcoming in *Philosophy and Public Affairs*, Summer 1984). Where my position on substantive questions differs significantly from D'Andrade's, Carson's, or Danley's, I shall discuss this in the notes.

will make an improper decision; a judge who is paid to show favoritism may do so and yet, coincidentally, make the correct legal decision (i.e., the bribe offerer may in fact have the law on her side). The violation of duty consists in deciding a case for the wrong sorts of reasons.

Although the most typical and important cases of bribery concern political officials and civil servants, one need not be a political official or a civil servant to be bribed. Indeed, one need not be an official of any sort. Thus, a mortician may be bribed to bury a bodyless casket, and a baseball player may be bribed to strike out each time he bats. Still, baseball players and morticians are members of organizations and have duties and responsibilities by virtue of the positions they occupy in these organizations. It is tempting, then, to define a bribe as a payment made to a member of an organization in exchange for the violation of some positional duty or responsibility. This temptation is strengthened by our recognition that we cannot be bribed to violate a duty we have simply by virtue of being a moral agent. (Hired killers, e.g., are not bribed to violate their duty not to kill.) And it is further strengthened when we recognize that we may be paid to violate duties we have by virtue of a nonorganizationally based status without being bribed. (I am not bribed if—as a nonhandicapped person—I accept payment to park in a space reserved for the handicapped; nor am I bribed if—as a pet owner—I accept payment illegally to allow my dog to run free on the city streets.)

Still, it is too strong to say that occupying a position in an organization is a necessary condition of being bribed. We may also speak of bribing a boxer to throw a fight or of bribing a runner to lose a race. These cases, however, are importantly like the cases already described. Roughly, both the boxer and the runner are paid to do something they ought not to do given what they are. What they are, in these cases, are participants in certain practices. What they are paid to do is to act in a manner dictated by some person or organization rather than to act according to the understandings constitutive of their practices. Civil servants, business executives, morticians, and baseball players, of course, are also participants in practices. And their responsibilities, as such, are defined by the rules and understandings governing the organizations to which they belong. At this point, then, we are in a position to state a provisional definition of bribery. Thus, P accepts a bribe from R if and only if P agrees for payment to act in a manner dictated by R rather than doing what is required of him as a participant in his practice.[2]

---

[2]Danley defines "bribing" as "offering or giving something of value with a corrupt intent to induce or influence an action of someone in a public or official capacity." Carson defines a bribe as a payment to someone "in exchange for special consideration that is incompatible with the duties of his position." Both go on to discuss bribery as if it were restricted to officials of organizations. Since these are the most typical and important cases of bribery, their focus is understandable. But it does have at least one unfortunate consequence. For it leads both Danley and Carson to think that the question of whether it is prima facie wrong to offer or accept bribes reduces to the question of whether officials have obligations to satisfy their positional duties. Danley argues that they do not if the institutions they serve are illegitimate. Carson argues that

One advantage of this account is that it enables us to deal with certain difficult cases. Suppose that a high-ranking officer at the Pentagon is paid by a Soviet agent to pass on defense secrets. The first few times he does this we would not hesitate to say that he is bribed. But suppose that he is paid a salary to do this and that the arrangement lasts for a number of years. At this point talk of bribery appears less appropriate. But why should something that has the character of a bribe if done once or twice (or, perhaps, on a piecework basis) cease to have that character if done more often (or, perhaps, on a salaried basis)? In my account the explanation is that the frequency or basis of payment may incline us differently to identify the practice in question. Thus, if an American officer works for the Soviet Union long enough, we begin to think of him as a Soviet spy. In any case, to the extent to which we regard his practice as spying we are inclined to think of the payments in question as payments of a salary as opposed to so many bribes. A similar analysis holds in the case of industrial spies, undercover agents recruited from within organizations, and so forth.[3] We do not think of them as bribed because we do not think of them as full-fledged practitioners of the practices in which they appear to engage.

This practice conception is further supported by the fact that a person may satisfy my account of bribery on a long-term and regularized basis and still be said to be a recipient of bribes. This is so where his continued and regularized acceptance of payments does not warrant any change in our understanding of the practices in which he participates. Thus, we do not think of a judge who routinely accepts payments for favors from organized crime as participating in some practice other than judging, even if he sits almost exclusively on such cases. This may be arbitrary: perhaps we ought rather think of him as an agent of a criminal organization (a paid saboteur of the legal system) and treat him accordingly. My point, however, is that because we do not think of him in this way—because we continue to think of him as a judge— we regard each fresh occurrence as an instance of bribery.

The present account, however, is not entirely adequate as it stands. Consider the following counterexamples: (*a*) an artist is offered $5,000 by

---

they do on the ground that they have made a tacit agreement with their institution to discharge those duties (accepting a bribe, for Carson, is an instance of promise breaking). Whatever the merits of their arguments concerning the responsibilities of officials, both approach the question of the prima facie morality of bribery too narrowly. For different issues seem to arise when we consider bribery outside the realm of officialdom. Clearly it is more difficult for Carson to make his tacit consent argument in relation to the bribed athlete. For it is not clear that a runner who enters a race tacitly agrees to win it (if so, he would be breaking a promise by running to prepare for future races or by entering to set the pace for someone else). Nor is it clear that a boxer who accepts payment not to knock out his opponent in the early rounds violates a tacit agreement to attempt a knockout at his earliest convenience. Danley must expand his account to accommodate such cases as well. For it is not clear what it means to say that a practice such as running or boxing is legitimate.

[3]Such cases present a problem for the accounts of both Danley and Carson. At the very least they must expand their accounts of positional duties such that we can distinguish between a bribe, on the one hand, and a salary paid to a spy recruited from within an organization, on the other.

an eccentric to ruin a half-completed canvas by employing an unsuitable color and (*b*) a parent is paid $500 for the use of his eight-year-old son in a pornographic film.

It might be argued in relation to *a* that it is consistent with the practice of being an artist that one accept payment to produce whatever a client is willing to pay for. However, the conception of a practice that underlies this response seems to me questionable. What seems to me counterintuitive about speaking of bribery in *a* is that the act in question is private. By this I mean, roughly, that it affects no one who is not a party to the transaction. If I pay an artist to ruin a painting that has been commissioned by a museum, the oddity of speaking of bribery disappears. In general, where there is no violation of an organizational duty, we might say that a payment is a bribe only if it affects the interests of persons or organizations who are not parties to the transaction. To forestall counterexamples based on remote or indirect consequences, we must add that the parties affected must be parties whose interests are normally affected by the conduct of the practice in question and that they must be affected in the manner in which they are normally affected.

It is tempting to go further than this and claim that a bribe occurs only when the act agreed to by the bribed party violates the moral rights of some third party or organization. But this seems to me mistaken. We may speak of bribing officers of terribly corrupt institutions (e.g., concentration camps), but it is not at all clear that these officeholders necessarily violate the rights of any person or organization by violating their institutional duties (e.g., by allowing prisoners to escape). Or consider a society in which slaves are used as boxers and masters wager on the bouts. It seems clear that one can bribe a slave to lose a fight here, but it is not at all clear that a slave violates anyone's rights by accepting payment for so doing. (To say this would be to imply that a slave boxer has a prima facie duty to try to win his fight, and this seems to me untenable.)

What, then, of the second counterexample? Why are we reluctant to speak of bribery in the case of parents? One way to deal with this case is to attribute this reluctance to an anachronistic linguistic habit developed and sustained by centuries of thinking according to which children are the property of parents. According to this outmoded way of thinking, either there is no such thing as the practice of parenting or that practice far more resembles an account that Thrasymachus might offer of it than an account most of us would now accept. It sounds odd to speak of bribing parents, then, because our linguistic habits have not caught up with our new vision of parenting. But this is something we should change: we ought to allow that parents may be bribed.

But I am uncomfortable with this reply. Most of us now agree that children have rights which ought to be protected by law and/or community pressure and that parents have duties not to violate these rights. To this extent, we are coming to understand families as organizations. Thus, if we allow that parents are bribed, we will almost certainly hold that they are bribed in the way that members of organizations are typically bribed, namely, they are paid to violate their positional duties. But there is something disturbing about this. For despite our conviction that children have rights, many of us are uncomfortable thinking of the family as just another organization and thinking of a parent as just another functionary. Our reluctance to maintain that parents may be bribed, then, may express a healthy resistance to thinking of a parent on the model of an official. Just how we ought to think of the family, I cannot say; the challenge is to arrive at a conception that acknowledges that children have legally enforceable rights without reducing the family to just another institution.

If we exempt the family from consideration and we build in the condition required by the second counterexample, we are now in a position to present a tentative definition of bribery. Thus, P is bribed by R if and only if (1) P accepts payment from R to act on R's behalf,[4] (2) P's act on R's behalf consists in violating some rule or understanding constitutive of a practice in which P is engaged, and (3) either P's violation is a violation of some official duty P has by virtue of his participation in that practice or P's violation significantly affects the interests of persons or organizations whose interests are typically connected to that practice.

At least two additional important features of bribery deserve mention. The first is a consequence of the fact that bribes are payments. For, like other kinds of payments (e.g., rent), bribes presuppose agreements of a certain kind.[5] That is, it must be understood by both parties that the payment in question is exchanged, or is to be exchanged, for the relevant conduct. In the most typical and important cases, the bribed party is an official and the conduct in question is the violation of some official duty. In these cases we may say simply that an official P is bribed by R when she accepts payment or the promise of payment for agreeing to violate a positional duty to act on R's behalf. This

---

[4]Thus D'Andrade defines bribery as "alienation of agency." In his account bribery occurs when someone is seduced into abandoning his role as an agent of one person or organization and, for a price, becomes the agent of another. This highlights an important feature of bribery that is ignored by Carson and Danley and that was neglected in my own earlier thinking on this subject, namely, that a bribe taker acts on behalf of someone. But D'Andrade's claim that agency is alienated when one accepts a bribe implies that the bribe taker necessarily is committed to act on behalf of some person or organization before he is in a position to accept a bribe. And it is difficult to see what helpful truth this might express in relation to the scientist, runner, or boxer of my examples. Surely it is not helpful to say that a bribe taker begins as his own agent in these cases and, for pay, alienates that agency to another. This applies to anyone who takes a job. Nor is it helpful to say—as D'Andrade did say at one point—that he may begin as an agent of some abstraction (e.g., truth). Surely the point behind this obscure claim is better made by speaking of what is expected of someone as a participant in a practice. It is also worth noting that D'Andrade's alienation of agency account offers no basis for distinguishing between bribed officials, on the one hand, and undercover agents and spies, on the other. For these too alienate agency.

[5]Carson fails to recognize the significance of this feature of bribery. This view of bribery, moreover, is inconsistent with Danley's account. Danley understands a bribe as an attempt to induce or influence someone. In this matter he appears to have most dictionaries on his side (including the OED). However, as I argue in more detail in Sec. IV he is mistaken.

agreement requirement is of great importance. As I shall argue in Section IV, without it we cannot properly distinguish between bribes and gifts or rewards.

Such agreements need not be explicit. If I am stopped by a policeman for speeding and hand him a fifty-dollar bill along with my driver's license, and he accepts the fifty-dollar bill, it is arguable that we have entered into such an agreement despite what we might say about contributions to the Police Benevolence Association. As I shall argue, some of the difficulties we have in determining what transactions to count as bribes may stem from unclarity concerning the conditions under which we are entitled to say an agreement has been made.

It is a consequence of this account that someone may be bribed despite the fact that she subsequently decides not to perform the service she has agreed to perform. Indeed, we must say this even if she has never been paid but has been only promised payment, or even if she has been paid but returns this payment after she decides not to abide by her part of the agreement. I see nothing strange about this. After all, if one accepts a bribe it seems natural to say that one has been bribed. Still, I have no strong objection to distinguishing between accepting a bribe and being bribed, where a necessary condition of the latter is that one carries out one's part of the bribery agreement. As far as I can see, no important moral question turns on this choice of language.

A final interesting feature of bribery emerges when we reflect on the claim that offering and accepting bribes is prima facie wrong. I will begin with the case of officials. The claim that it is prima facie wrong for someone in an official position to accept a bribe is plausible only if persons in official capacities have prima facie obligations to discharge their official duties. The most plausible argument for this claim is grounded in a social contract model of organizations. By accepting a position in an organization, it might be argued, one tacitly agrees to abide by the rules of that organization. To be bribed is to violate that agreement—it is to break a promise—and is, therefore, prima facie wrong.[6] While I concede that this argument has merit in a context of just and voluntary institutions, it seems questionable in a context of morally corrupt institutions (e.g., Nazi Germany or contemporary El Salvador). And even were it technically valid for those contexts, its conclusion would nonetheless be a misleading half-truth.

It is beyond the scope of this paper to discuss, in detail, the problems with the tacit consent argument in a context of corrupt institutions. In brief, my position is that actions which create prima facie moral obligations in just or ideal contexts do not necessarily create comparable obligations in unjust or corrupt contexts. Thus, for example, it does not seem to me that, if I join the Mafia with the intention of subverting its operations and bringing its members to justice, I have thereby undertaken a prima facie obligation to abide by

---

[6]This is Carson's argument.

the code of that organization. Of course, one could say this and add that the obligation in question is typically overridden by other moral considerations. But this seems to me an ad hoc move to defend a position. We use the expression "prima facie duty" to point to a moral presumption for or against a certain type of action. And surely it is strange to insist that there is a moral presumption, in the present case, in favor of carrying out the commands of one's Don.

But even if we grant that there is a prima facie duty here, we must be careful to qualify this assertion. For it is also clear that participants in unjust institutions have a prima facie right to interfere with the normal functioning of those institutions (at least where these functionings can be reasonably expected to produce unjust outcomes). Indeed, where the injustice is great enough they have a prima facie duty to interfere. And in some cases, the strength of this prima facie obligation will exceed the strength of any promise-keeping obligation generated by tacit consent. Thus we may say, other things equal, that the commandant of a concentration camp ought to act in a manner that frustrates the genocidal purpose of that institution. And, assuming that that institution is "rationally" designed to serve its purpose, there will be a strong moral presumption in favor of the violation of his positional duty.

What, then, of the morality of accepting bribes in such cases? If an official has no prima facie duty to satisfy her positional duties—or if the presumption in favor of satisfying them is outweighed by the presumption against so doing—then, other things being equal, it is difficult to see why it is prima facie wrong to accept payment for violating them. After all, there may be serious risks involved. This at least is so where the case against carrying out the purposes of one's organization is strong enough to permit one to violate one's positional duty but is not so strong that one has a prima facie obligation to do this. For it does seem prima facie wrong to make compliance with a prima facie duty contingent on payment (it ought rather to be contingent on an assessment of what one ought to do, all things considered). And it certainly seems wrong to demand payment for doing what is one's duty, all things considered.

Still, this may be too quick. Consider a concentration camp guard who lacks the courage to help inmates escape but who would be courageous enough to undertake the risks involved were he assured of sufficient funds to transport his family to another country and comfortably to begin a new life. If he is in fact reasonably certain that he would be brave enough to do what is required of him were he paid, it seems not improper of him to demand payment. In general, if the wrong of demanding payment for doing one's duty is outweighed by the importance of doing it and if demanding payment for doing it is causally necessary for doing it, then, all things considered, it is not wrong to demand payment.

If it is not wrong for an official to accept a bribe, one does not induce him to do something wrong by offering him one. Thus, we cannot say in all contexts that it is prima facie wrong to offer someone a bribe *because* this is an attempt to induce him to do something wrong or to corrupt him.[7] On the other hand, there may be cases in which it is prima facie wrong to offer a bribe despite the fact that it is perfectly acceptable for the bribed party to accept one. Recall the case of the boxer slave. Despite the fact that the slave has no obligation to try to win, a wagering master may have a prima facie obligation not to pay him to lose. For by so doing the master may gain an unfair advantage over his fellow wagerers. It might be objected that the master's obligation in this case is misleadingly described as an obligation not to bribe. He is obligated, rather, not to fix fights; or, more generally, not to take unfair advantage of his fellow wagerers. This objection raises issues we need not consider here. It is enough to point out that the purpose of offering a bribe is very often to seek some unfair or undeserved benefit or advantage and that this is one reason we are rightly suspicious of the morality of bribe offers.

We are now in a position to state a fifth interesting feature of bribery. Even if it is not prima facie wrong to offer and to accept bribes in all contexts, it is prima facie wrong to do so in morally uncorrupted contexts. Accordingly, a bribe offerer or a bribe taker must defend the morality of his act either by showing that there are countervailing moral considerations in its favor or alternatively by showing that the moral context is so corrupt that the factors that generate prima facie duties in uncorrupted contexts do not apply here. This strategy of moral justifications, of course, is not unique to bribery. It may hold in relation to a wide range of what are ordinarily taken to be prima facie duties. In the case of bribery, however, arguments to the effect that the moral context is corrupted will have a certain characteristic form. Thus, in the most important case—the case of officials—they will be arguments that challenge the legitimacy of an institution.

---

[7]Nor can we say that it is prima facie wrong because it is an attempt to get someone to do something that is prima facie wrong. This argument is flawed in two ways. To begin with, as we have seen, the premise expresses what is at best a dangerous half-truth. Were we to reason from the whole truth we must conclude that there are some contexts in which the presumption in favor of violating one's official duties is stronger than the presumption against it. In the second place, moreover, the inference is invalid: it is not necessarily prima facie wrong to induce someone to do something that is prima facie wrong. Rather, it is prima facie wrong to induce someone to do something that is wrong, all things considered. Thus, if it is prima facie wrong for P to do A, but P ought to do A, all things considered, there is no presumption against my inducing P to do A; I do not need to justify this by appealing to countervailing moral considerations. I require such justification only when it is wrong for P to do so. Cases of this sort are interesting but typically neglected by philosophers. (The following are examples: [a] P is a soldier in a war in which each side has equal claim to justice; R is a guard on the opposite side. Though it might be wrong for R to accept a bribe from P, it is not wrong for P to offer R a bribe. [b] P's father is certain to be convicted of a crime he did not commit because the evidence is overwhelmingly against him. It is permissible for P to offer a bribe to R, an assistant district attorney, to "lose" some evidence; but it is wrong for R to accept the bribe.) In any case, the upshot of this is that even if there were a general moral presumption against accepting bribes it would not follow that there is a comparable presumption against offering bribes.

II

I now turn to the first of three problem areas I shall address in this paper, namely, the problem of distinguishing between bribery and extortion. Compare the following cases:

> *a*) Executive P hopes to sell an airplane to the national airline of country C. The deal requires the approval of minister R. P knows that R can make a better deal elsewhere and that R knows this as well. P's researchers have discovered that R has a reputation for honesty but that R is in serious financial difficulties. Accordingly P offers R a large sum of money to buy from him. R accepts and abides by the agreement.
>
> *b*) The same as *a* except that P knows that he is offering the best deal R can get, and R knows this too. Nonetheless, P is informed by reliable sources that R will not deal with P unless P offers to pay him a considerable sum of money. P complies, and R completes the deal.

According to my analysis *a* is bribery; *b* is not.

The difference between *a* and *b* is clear enough. In *a* P pays R to violate R's duty (in this case, to make the best deal that R can). In *b* P does no such thing. Instead, he pays R to do what is required of R by his institutional commitments in any case. Moreover, he does so in response to R's threat to violate those commitments in a manner that jeopardizes P's interests. Accordingly, *b* resembles extortion more than it does bribery. For, roughly speaking, R extorts P if R threatens P with a penalty in case P fails to give R something to which R has no rightful claim.

If this is true it may be that American corporate executives accused of bribing foreign officials are sometimes more like victims of extortion than offerers of bribes. For in at least some cases they are required to make payments to assure that an official does what he is supposed to do in any case. This is especially true in the case of inspectors of various kinds and in relation to government officials who must approve transactions between American and local companies. An inspector who refuses to approve a shipment that is up to standards unless he is paid off is like a bandit who demands tribute on all goods passing through his territory.

It does not follow that it is morally correct for American companies to pay off such corrupt officials. There are cases in which it is morally wrong to surrender to the demands of bandits and other extortionists. But it is clear that the moral questions that arise here are different sorts of questions than those that arise in relation to bribery. The moral relations between the relevant parties differ. The bribery agreement is not by its nature an agreement between victims and victimizers. The extortion agreement is. Moral justifications and excuses for complying with the demands of an extortionist are easier to come by than moral justifications and excuses for offering bribes.

Of course, the distinction in question is often easier to draw in theory than in practice. An inspector who demands a payoff to authorize a shipment is likely to fortify his demand by insisting that the product does not meet standards. In some cases it may be difficult to know whether or not he is lying (e.g., whether the shipment has been contaminated in transit). And given the high cost of delays, a company may decide that it is too expensive to take the time to find out. In this case, a company may decide to pay off without knowing whether it is agreeing to pay a bribe or surrendering to extortion. Since the morality of its decisions may well turn on what it is in fact doing in such cases, a company that does not take the time to find out acts in a morally irresponsible manner (unless, of course, it is in a position to defend both courses of action).

What sorts of justifications can a company present for offering bribes? It is beyond the scope of this paper to provide a detailed discussion of this question. However, I have already mentioned a number of considerations that count as moral reasons against bribery in a variety of contexts. To begin with, in reasonably just contexts, officials ordinarily are obligated to discharge the duties of their offices. In these cases bribe offers are normally attempts to induce officials to violate duties. Moreover, if accepted, a bribe offer may make it more likely that that official will violate future duties. Accordingly, it may contribute to the corruption of an official. In addition, the intent of a bribe offer is often to secure an unfair advantage or an undeserved privilege. Where this is the case, it too counts as a reason against bribery. To determine whether a bribe offer is wrong in any particular case, then, we must decide: (1) whether these reasons obtain in that case; (2) if they obtain, how much weight we ought to attach to them; and (3) how much weight we ought to attach to countervailing considerations. (Suppose, e.g., that it is necessary to bribe an official in order to meet an important contractual obligation.) It is worth remarking in this regard that, where officials routinely take bribes, the presumption against corrupting officials normally will not apply. Similarly, to the extent that bribery is an accepted weapon in the arsenal of all competitors, bribe offers cannot be construed as attempts to achieve an unfair advantage over one's competitors.

III

It is sometimes suggested that an environment may be so corrupt that no payments count as bribes. These are circumstances in which the level of official compliance to duty is very low, and payoffs are so widespread that they are virtually institutionalized. Suppose, for example, that the laws of country N impose very high duties on a variety of products but that it is common practice in N for importers and exporters to pay customs officials to overlook certain goods and/or to underestimate their number or value. Suppose, moreover, that the existence of this practice is common knowledge but that no effort is made to stop it by law enforcement officials at any level;[8] indeed, that any attempts to stop it would be met by widespread social disapproval. One might even imagine that customs officials receive no salary in N but earn their entire livelihood in this way. One might further imagine that customs officials are expected to return a certain amount of money to the government every month and are fired from their jobs for failure to do so. Finally, one might suppose that the cumulative advantages and disadvantages of this way of doing things is such that the economy of N is about as strong as it would be under a more rule-bound alternative. Are these officials bribed?

In my analysis, the answer to this question depends on how we understand the duties of the customs officer. If the official job description for the customs officer in N (and the written laws of N) is like those of most countries, the customs officer violates his official duties according to these codes by allowing goods to leave the country without collecting the full duty. The question, however, is how seriously we are to take these written codes. Where social and political practice routinely violates them, nothing is done about it, and few members of the legal and nonlegal community believe that anything ought to be done about it, it is arguable that these codes are dead letters. If we find this to be true of the codes governing the duties of the customs officials in country N, we have good reason for saying that the real obligations of these officials do not require that they impose the duties described in those written codes (but only that they return a certain sum of the money they collect to the central government each month). Anything collected in excess of that amount they are entitled to keep as salary (recall that they are officially unpaid). In reality we might say that duties on exports in country N are not fixed but negotiable.

Of course if we decide that the written law of N is the law of N, we must describe the situation otherwise. In that case, the official obligations of the customs officials are as they are described, and the system in N must be characterized as one of rampant bribery condoned both by government and by popular opinion. It seems to me that the philosophy of law on which this account rests is implausible. However, there is no need to argue this to defend my analysis of this case. My position is simply that whether or not we describe what goes on here as bribery depends on what we take the real legal responsibilities of the customs official to be. To the extent that we are inclined to identify his duties with the written law we will be inclined to

---

[8]In D'Andrade's account bribes are necessarily secret, so these could not count as bribes.

speak of bribery here. To the extent that we are unwilling so to identify his duties we will not.[9]

IV

Let us now consider the problem of distinguishing bribes from rewards and gifts. The problem arises because gifts are often used in business and government to facilitate transactions. And to the degree to which a business person, professional person, or government official is influenced in her decision by gifts, it is tempting to conclude that she is violating her duties. In such cases we are tempted to speak of these gifts as bribes.

If I am correct, however, this temptation should be resisted. A bribe, after all, presupposes an agreement. A gift may be made with the intention of inducing an official to show favoritism to the giver, but unless acceptance of what is transferred can be construed as an agreement to show favoritism, what is transferred is not a bribe.

In some cases, of course, the acceptance of what is offered can be so construed. Again, if I offer fifty dollars to a policeman who has stopped me for speeding, he has a right to construe my act as one of offering a bribe, and I have a right to construe his acceptance in the corresponding manner. If I regularly treat the neighborhood policeman to a free lunch at my diner and he regularly neglects to ticket my illegally parked car, we have reason to say the same. Agreements need not be explicit. My point is just that to the degree that it is inappropriate to speak of agreements, it is also inappropriate to speak of bribes.

It follows from this that, if I present an official with an expensive item to induce him to show favoritism on my behalf, in violation of his duty, I have not necessarily bribed him. It does not follow from this, however, that I have done nothing wrong. So long as you are morally obligated to perform your official duty, normally it will be wrong of me to induce you to do otherwise by presenting you with some expensive item. Moreover, if you have any reason to believe that accepting what I offer will induce you not to do your duty, you have done something wrong by accepting my gift. To prevent such

---

[9]A corresponding point holds in relation to bribery outside the realm of officialdom. Consider the case of professional wrestling. Most of us believe that the outcome of professional wrestling matches is determined in advance. Are the losers bribed? (To simplify matters let us assume that they are paid a bit of extra money for losing.) The answer here depends on how we understand their practice. If we take them to be participating in a wrestling competition, we must say that they are bribed. In that case, by failing to compete they violate an understanding constitutive of their practice. It is reasonably clear, however, that professional wrestlers are not engaged in an athletic competition. Rather, they are engaged in a dramatic performance. This being the case the losers are not bribed. They are merely doing what professional wrestlers are ordinarily paid to do, namely, to play out their part in an informal script.

wrongs we have laws prohibiting persons whose interests are closely tied to the decisions of public officials from offering gifts to these officials. And we have laws forbidding officials to accept such gifts.

It might be objected that this account is too lenient. Specifically, it might be argued that wherever P presents Q with something of value to induce Q to violate Q's official duties P has offered a bribe.

But this is surely a mistake. It suggests, among other things, that an official is bribed so long as she accepts what is offered with this intent. Yet an official may accept such a gift innocently, believing that it is what it purports to be, namely, a token of friendship or goodwill. And she may do so with justifiable confidence that doing so will not in any way affect the discharge of her duty.

It may be replied that officials are bribed by such inducements only when they are in fact induced to do what is desired of them. But again, it may be the case that an official accepts what is offered innocently, believing it to be a gift, and that she believes falsely that it will not affect her conduct. In this case she has exercised bad judgment, but she has not been bribed. Indeed, it seems to me that it is improper to say that she accepts a bribe even when she recognizes the intent of the inducement and believes that accepting it is likely to influence her. There is a distinction between accepting a drink with the understanding that one is agreeing to be seduced and accepting a drink with the knowledge that so doing will make one's seduction more likely. To be bribed is to be bought, not merely to be influenced to do something.

From a moral point of view, whenever failure to perform one's official duties is wrong it may be as bad to accept a gift that one knows will influence one in the conduct of one's duty as it is to accept a bribe. And clearly we are entitled morally to criticize those who offer and accept such inducements. Moreover, we are right to attempt to prevent this sort of thing by legally restricting the conditions under which persons may offer gifts to officials and the conditions under which officials may accept such gifts. Nonetheless, such gifts ought not to be confused with bribes. If P accepts a gift from R and does not show the desired favoritism, R may complain of P's ingratitude but not of P's dishonesty (unless, of course, P led him on in some way). If P accepts a bribe from R and does not show the desired favoritism, P has been dishonest (perhaps twice).

This point is not without practical importance. People who work in the same organization or in the same profession often form friendships despite the fact that some of them are in a position to make decisions that affect the interests of others. Here, as everywhere, friendships are developed and maintained in part by exchanges of favors, gifts, meals, and so forth. Were we to take seriously the inducement theory of bribery, however, this dimension of collegial and organizational existence would be threatened. In that case, if P's position is such that he must make decisions affecting R, any gifts, favors, et cetera from R to P should be regarded with at least some suspicion. To guard against the accusation that he has been bribed by R, P must be in a position to offer reasons for believing that R's intent in inviting him to dinner was not to induce him to show favoritism. And for R to be certain that he is not offering P a bribe in this case, R must be certain that his intentions are pure. All of this would require such vigilance in relation to one's own motives and the motives of others that friendships in collegial and organizational settings would be more difficult to sustain than they are at present.

Since decision makers are required to show impartiality they must in any case be careful not to accept gifts and favors that will influence them to show favoritism. Moreover, if they are required by their position to assess the moral character of those affected by their decisions, they may be required to assess the intent with which such gifts or favors are offered. Most officials, however, are not required to assess character in this way. In order to avoid doing wrong by accepting gifts and favors they need only be justly confident of their own continued impartiality. Thus, they are ordinarily entitled to ignore questions of intent unless there is some special reason to do otherwise. If the intent to influence were sufficient for a bribe, however, they would not be at liberty to bestow the benefit of the doubt in this way.

Again, there are cases in which impartiality is so important that decision makers should be prohibited both from accepting gifts or favors from any persons likely to be directly affected by their decisions and from forming friendships with such persons. And they should disqualify themselves when they are asked to make a decision that affects either a friend or someone from whom they have accepted gifts or favors in the reasonably recent past. Judges are a case in point. In other cases, however, institutions and professions should be willing to risk some loss in impartiality in order to enjoy the benefits of friendship and mutual aid. For these are essential to the functioning of some organizations and to the well-being of the people within them. Consider, for example, universities. The practical disadvantage of the inducement account is that it may require us to be unnecessarily suspicious of certain exchanges constitutive of mutual aid and friendship (at least if we take it seriously).

V

An interesting related problem arises in cultures in which a more formal exchange of gifts may be partly constitutive of a special relationship between persons, namely, something like friendship. In such cultures, so long as certain other conditions are satisfied, to make such exchanges is to enter into a system of reciprocal rights and duties. Among these duties may be the duty to show favoritism toward "friends," even when one acts in an official capacity. Moreover, the giver may be expected to show gratitude for each occasion of favoritism by further gift giving. On the face of it, this certainly looks like bribery. Is that description warranted?

To begin with, we need to distinguish between cases in which the special relationships in question are genuine and cases in which they are not. In the latter case certain ritual or ceremonial forms may be used to dress up what each party regards as a business transaction of the standard Western variety in a manner that provides an excuse for bribery. I shall say more about this presently. But let me begin with the first case.

Where the relationships in question are genuine and the laws of the relevant society are such that the official duties of the relevant official do not prohibit favoritism, this practice of gift giving cannot be called bribery. For in this case there is no question of the violation of duty. All that can be said here is that such societies condone different ways of doing business than we do. Specifically, they do not mark off a sphere of business and/or bureaucratic activity in which persons are supposed to meet as "abstract individuals," that is, in which they are required to ignore their social and familial ties. Their obligations, rather, are importantly determined by such ties even in the conduct of business and governmental affairs. Favoritism is shown, then, not in order to carry out one's part of a bargain but, rather, to discharge an obligation of kinship or loyalty. Failure to show favoritism would entitle one's kinsman or friend to complain not that one reneged on an agreement but, rather, that one had wronged him as an ally or a kinsman.

This is not to say that one cannot bribe an official in such a society. One does this here, as elsewhere, by entering into an agreement with him such that he violates his official duties for payment. The point is just that favoritism shown to friends and kinsmen is not necessarily a violation of duty in such societies. Indeed, one might be bribed not to show favoritism.

The official duties of an official, of course, may not be clear. Thus, the written law may prohibit favoritism to kin and ally, though this is widely practiced and condoned and infrequently prosecuted. This may occur when a society is in a transitional state from feudalism or tribalism to a Western-style industrial society, but it may also occur in an industrial society with different traditions than our own. To the extent that it is unclear what the official duties of officials are in such cases it will also be difficult to say what count as bribes. Indeed, even if we decide that an official does violate his duty by showing favoritism to kin and allies who reciprocate with gifts, we may not be justified in speaking of bribery here. For the official may not be acting as he does in order to fulfill his part of an agreement. Rather, he may be acting to fulfill some obligation of kinship or loyalty. Again, his failure so to act may not entitle his kinsmen or allies to complain that he had welched on a deal; rather, it would entitle them to complain that he wronged them as kinsmen or allies.

Of course, all this is so only when the relationships in question are genuine. In some cases, however, the rhetoric and ceremonial forms of a traditional culture may be used to camouflage what are in fact business relations of the standard Western variety. To the extent that this is so, the favoritism in question may in fact be bribery in ethnic dress. The relationships in question are not genuine when they are not entered into in good faith. It is clear, moreover, that when American executives present expensive gifts to foreign businessmen or foreign government officials they do so for business reasons. That is, they have no intention of entering into a system of reciprocal rights and duties that may obligate them in the future to act contrary to their long-term interest. Rather, they perform the required ceremonies knowing that they will continue to base their decisions on business reasons. Their intention is to buy favoritism. And the foreign officials and companies with whom they do business are typically aware of this. This being the case, invitations of the form "First we become friends, then we do business" cannot plausibly be construed as invitations to participate in some traditional way of life. Typically, both parties recognize that what is requested here is a bribe made in an appropriate ceremonial way.

VI

On the basis of this analysis it seems clear that American officials are not always guilty of bribery when they pay off foreign officials. In some cases they are victims of extortion; in other cases, the context may be such that the action purchased from the relevant official does not count as a violation of his duty. The fact that American executives engaged in international commerce are innocent of some of the charges that have been made against them, however, does not imply that those who have made them are mistaken in their assessment of the character of these executives. One's character, after all, is a matter of what one is disposed to do. If these executives are willing to engage in bribery whenever this is necessary to promote their perceived long-term business interests, whatever the morality of the situation, it follows (at very least) that they are amoral.

Bribery and Implicit Agreements: A Reply to Philips

Thomas L. Carson

In a paper that appeared recently in *Ethics*, Michael Philips defends at some length an analysis of the concept of bribery.[1] He also attempts to give an account of the moral status of bribery. Philips attacks several views defended in my paper, "Bribery, Extortion and the 'Foreign Corrupt Practices Act,'" *Philosophy and Public Affairs*, Winter 1985, pp. 66–90. In my paper, I argue that accepting a bribe involves the violation of an implicit or explicit promise or understanding associated with one's office or role and that, therefore, accepting a bribe is always *prima facie* wrong. Philips offers two separate criticisms of this position. (1) He argues that in at least some cases of bribery the person who accepts the bribe does not thereby violate any agreements or understandings associated with any offices or positions that he holds. (2) He argues that in "morally corrupt contexts" there may be no *prima facie* duty to adhere to the agreements or understandings implicit in one's role or position. I shall offer replies to both of these criticisms, although I make some concessions to the first.

(1) Standard cases of bribery involve paying an official of an organization to do things contrary to the obligations of his office or position. The following examples all fit this model of bribery: (1) paying a judge or juror to decide in one's favor, (2) paying a policeman not to give one a traffic ticket, and (3) paying a government official not to report violations of health and safety standards. Philips concedes that in cases in which a bribe is paid to an official it is plausible to suppose that the official's acceptance of the bribe constitutes the violation of a "tacit agreement."[2] However, he claims that there are cases of bribery in which the person being bribed is self-employed and in which his acceptance of the bribe cannot be said to constitute the violation of an agreement or understanding between himself and some other party. (Philips seems to imply that in such cases there is no identifiable party *with whom* one can be said to have made an agreement.) Philips gives the example of bribing a self-employed professional athlete. In such cases, he claims, the acceptance of the bribe cannot to said to constitute the violation of a tacit agreement.

> Clearly it is more difficult for Carson to make his tacit consent argument in relation to the bribed athlete. For it is not clear that a runner who enters a race

tacitly agrees to win it (if so, he would be breaking a promise by running to prepare for future races or by entering to set the pace for someone else). Nor is it clear that a boxer who accepts payment not to knock out his opponent in the early rounds violates a tacit agreement to attempt a knockout at his earliest convenience.[3]

But, Philips to the contrary, athletes, even self-employed athletes who are not members of teams or any other organizations, compete in *public competition* (as opposed to private matches or exhibition matches) on the understanding that they will do their best to win. This understanding constitutes an implicit promise or agreement between the athlete and (i) the sponsors or promoters of the competition, (ii) the spectators, fans, gamblers, and others who follow the competition (they take an interest in the competition only on the assumption that it is serious competition in which each athlete does his best to win), and (iii) his fellow competitors. The runner who enters a public competition tacitly agrees to do his best to win. To run the race with only the intention to 'warm up' for a future race is to violate an implicit agreement. Running so as to 'pace' a teammate violates no understanding, provided that one is competing as a member of a team. In such cases, we can say that one competes on the understanding that one will do the best one can to promote the victory of one's team. The boxer who accepts a bribe not to knock his opponent out in the early rounds violates a tacit agreement to try his best to win. For him to forego early opportunities to knock his opponent out is for him to fail to do his best to win. An athlete who participates in public competition tacitly agrees to do his best to win, short of injuring himself or others or breaking the rules of the sport. The promoters and/or sponsors of the competition, the spectators, and his fellow athletes all act on the assumption that the athletes will do their best to win. Of course, the fact that others *expect* one to do something does not suffice to show that one has consented or agreed to do it. However, there are other features in addition to the mere expectation that the athlete will do his best to win, which permit us to conclude that a tacit agreement exists in this case. The athlete knows that the others expect that he will do his best to win. Further, he knows that they play their roles in this competition only on the basis of this expectation. They would not do what they are doing (or even take an interest in the competiton) if they came to believe that the athletes were not attempting to win.

Philips briefly mentions a somewhat different example that poses serious problems for my position. The case that he mentions is one in which a slave is bribed to lose a boxing match promoted by his master.[4] I find it a bit odd to refer to this as a bribe and am tempted to conclude that a necessary condition of bribery is that the person who receives the bribe accepts the payment in exchange for actions contrary to the duties associated with a position or role that he has accepted voluntarily. However, there are other cases of paying individuals to violate duties attached to positions or roles that they have not accepted voluntarily which we would not be hesitant to describe as bribes. Ordinary usage would allow that it makes sense to speak of bribing a conscripted soldier, even though he has not voluntarily accepted the duties attached to his position. Understandings or agreements entered into by slaves with their masters (or conscript soldiers with the armies of which they are a part) are not voluntary and thus do not create *prima facie* duties in virtue of implicit promises. (Perhaps some conscript soldiers do have a *prima facie* duty to fulfill the obligations of their positions, but these are not duties that they have in virtue of any promises or agreements.) I must, therefore, concede that in such cases the person accepting the bribe has not entered into any agreements or understandings of the sort that could generate a *prima facie* duty not to accept the bribe. However, it is well to note that my account still holds for the vast majority of cases of bribery. In almost all ordinary cases of bribery, the person who accepts the bribe violates duties associated with roles or positions that he has voluntarily assumed. The only exceptions are bribery of conscripted soldiers, some prostitutes, and others held as virtual slaves. The vast majority of us freely choose the roles and offices that we occupy.

(2) Philips argues that, even in those cases of bribery in which the recipient of the bribe is a member of an organization and can be plausibly said to be taking the bribe in violation of some implicit agreement or understanding, this understanding does not necessarily generate a *prima facie* duty not to accept the bribe.

> By accepting a position in an organization, it might be argued, one tacitly agrees to abide by the rules of that organization. To be bribed is to violate that agreement—it is to break a promise—and is, therefore, *prima facie* wrong. While I concede that this argument has merit in the context of just and voluntary institutions, it seems questionable in a context of morally corrupt institutions (e.g., Nazi Germany or contemporary El Salvador). And even were it technically valid for those contexts, its conclusion would nonetheless be a misleading half-truth. . . . Thus, for example, it does not seem to me that, if I join the Mafia with the intention of subverting its operations and bringing its members to justice, I have thereby undertaken a *prima facie* obligation to abide by the code of that organization. Of course, one could say this and add that the obligation in question is typically overridden by other moral considerations. But this seems to me an *ad hoc* move to defend a position. We use the expression "*prima facie duty*" to point to a moral presumption for or against a certain type of action. And surely it is strange to insist that there is a moral presumption, in the present case, in favor of carrying out the commands of one's Don.[5]

I fail to see the force of this argument. Philips thinks it 'dangerous' to suppose that we have a *prima facie* duty to keep all implicit agreements, lest we fail to see that it would be wrong to fulfill our institutional duties in many morally corrupt situations (see Philips' footnote 7). But surely this is not a convincing argument. In general, it is not a valid argument to claim that since it is very clear that *S* ought to do *x* (all things considered), it cannot, in any sense, be his *prima facie* duty not to do *x*. Conflicts of duties aren't necessarily cases in which it is difficult to determine what one ought to do, all things considered. Nor is it an *"ad hoc* move" to say that *prima facie* duties can be overridden by other more important duties. The concept of a *prima facie* duty is derived from Ross. Ross is perfectly prepared to allow that some *prima facie* duties create only a very *weak moral presumption* for certain kinds of acts. He would have no hesitancy to say that implicit promises in the context of morally corrupt institutions create *prima facie* duties—albeit duties that can sometimes be easily overridden by other considerations. If we accept Ross' view that breaking promises (or breaking voluntary promises) is *prima facie* wrong, then we should have no reluctance to say that it is always *prima facie* wrong to accept bribes to do things that are contrary to implicit agreements or understandings into which one has entered *voluntarily*.

NOTES

1. Michael Philips, 'Bribery', *Ethics* **94** (July 1984), pp. 621–636.
2. Philips, p. 623, n. 2.
3. Philips, p. 623, n. 2.
4. Philips, p. 625.
5. Philips, p. 627. Philips attributes this argument to me in his footnote 6.

What's Wrong with Bribery?

Scott Turow

The question on the floor is what is wrong with bribery? I am not a philosopher and thus my answer to that question may be less systematic than others, but it is certainly no less deeply felt. As a federal prosecutor I have worked for a number of years now in the area of public corruption. Over that course of time, perhaps out of instincts of self-justification, or, so it seems, sharpened moral insights, I have come to develop an abiding belief that bribery is deeply immoral.

We all know that bribery is unlawful and I believe that the legal concepts in this area are in fact grounded in widely accepted moral intuitions.

Bribery as defined by the state of Illinois and construed by the United States Court of Appeals for the Seventh Circuit in the case of *United States* v. *Isaacs*, in which the former Governor of Illinois, Otto Kerner, was convicted for bribery, may be said to take place in these instances: Bribery occurs when property or personal advantage is offered, without the authority of law, to a public official with the intent that the public official act favorably to the offeror at any time or fashion in execution of the public official's duties.

Under this definition of bribery, the crime consists solely of an unlawful offer, made or accepted with a prohibited state of mind. No particular act need be specified; and the result is immaterial.

This is merely a matter of definition. Oddly the moral underpinnings of bribery are clearer in the context of another statute—the criminal law against mail fraud. Federal law has no bribery statute of general application; it is unlawful of course to bribe federal officials, to engage in a pattern of bribery, or to engage in bribery in certain other specified contexts, e.g., to influence the outcome of a sporting contest. But unlike the states, the Congress, for jurisdictional reasons, has never passed a general bribery statute, criminalizing *all* instances of bribery. Thus, over time the federal mail fraud statute has come to be utilized as the vehicle for some bribery prosecutions. The theory, adopted by the courts, goes to illustrate what lawyers have thought is wrong with bribery.

Mail fraud/bribery is predicated on the theory that someone—the bribee's governmental or private employer—is deprived, by a bribe, of the recipient's undivided loyalties. The bribee comes to serve two masters and as such is an 'unfaithful servant'. This breach of fiduciary duty, when combined with active efforts at concealment becomes actionable under the mail fraud law, assuming certain other jurisdictional requisites are met. Concealment, as noted, is another essential element of the crime. An employee who makes no secret of his dual service cannot be called to task; presumably his employer is thought to have authorized and accepted the divided loyalies. For this reason, the examples of maitre d's accepting payments from customers cannot be regarded as fully analogous to instances of bribery which depend on persons operating under false pretenses, a claimed loyalty that has in truth been undermined.

Some of the stricter outlines of what constitutes bribery, in the legal view, can be demonstrated by example. Among the bribery prosecutions with which I have spent the most time is a series of mail fraud/bribery cases arising out of corruption at the Cook County Board of Appeals. The Board of Appeals is a local administrative agency, vested with the authority to review and revise local real estate property tax assessments. After a lengthy grand jury investigation, it became clear that the Board of Appeals was a virtual cesspool, where it was commonplace for lawyers practicing before the Board to make regular cash payments to some decisionmakers. The persons accused of bribery at the Board generally relied on two defenses. Lawyers and tax consultants who made the payments often contended that the payments were, in a fashion, a necessity; the Board was so busy, so overcome by paperwork, and so many other people were paying, that the only way to be sure cases would be examined was to have an 'in' with an official whom payments had made friendly. The first argument also suggests the second: that the payments, whatever their nature, had accomplished nothing untoward, and that any tax reduction petition granted by the bribed official actually deserved the reduction it received.

Neither contention is legally sufficient to remove the payments from the category of bribery. Under the definition above, any effort to cause favorable action constitutes bribery, regardless of the supposedly provocative circumstances. And in practice juries had great difficulty accepting the idea that the lawyers involved had been 'coerced' into making the boxcar incomes—sometimes $300 000 to $400 000 a year—that many of the bribers earned. Nor is the merits of the cases involved a defense, under the above definitions. Again, in practical terms, juries seemed reluctant to believe that lawyers would be passing the Board's deputy commissioners cash under the table if they were really convinced of their cases' merits. But whatever the accuracy of that observation, it is clear that the law prohibits a payment, even to achieve a deserved result.

The moral rationale for these rules of law seems clear to me. Fundamentally, I believe that any payment to a governmental official for corrupt purposes is immoral. The obligation of government to deal with like cases alike is a principle of procedural fairness which is well recognized. But this principle is more than a matter of procedure; it has a deep moral base. We recognize that the equality of humans, their fundamental dignity as beings, demands that each stand as an equal before the government they have joined to create, that each, as Ronald Dworkin has put, has a claim to government's equal concern and respect. Bribery asks that that principle be violated, that some persons be allowed to stand ahead of others, that like cases not be treated alike, and that some persons be preferred. This I find morally repugnant.

Moreover, for this reason, I cannot accept the idea that bribery, which is wrong here, is somehow more tolerable abroad. Asking foreign officials to act in violation of moral principles must, as an abstract matter, be no less improper than asking that of members of our own government; it even smacks of imperialist attitudes. Furthermore, even dealing with the question on this level assumes that there are societies which unequivocally declare that governmental officials may properly deal with the citizenry in a random and unequal fashion. I doubt, in fact, whether any such sophisticated society exists; more than likely, bribery offends the norms and mores of the foreign country as well.

Not only does bribery violate fundamental notions of equality, but it also endangers the vitality of the institution affected. Most bribery centers on persons in discretionary or decision-making positions. Much as we want to believe that bribery invites gross deviations in duty, a prosecutor's experience is that in many cases there are no objectively correct decisions for the bribed official to make. We discovered that this was the case in the Board of Appeals prosecutions where a variety of competing theories of real estate valuation guaranteed that there was almost always some justification, albeit often thin, for what had been done. But it misses the point to look solely at the ultimate actions of the bribed official. Once the promise of payment is accepted, the public official is no longer the impartial decision-maker he is supposed to be. Whatever claims he might make, it is difficult to conceive of a public official who could convince anyone that he entirely disregarded a secret 'gift' from a person affected by his judgments.

Indeed, part of the evil of bribery inheres in the often indetectable nature of some of its results. Once revealed, the presence of bribery thus robs persons affected of a belief in the integrity of *all* prior decisions. In the absolute case, bribery goes to dissolve the social dependencies that require discretionary decision-making at certain junctions in our social scheme. Bribery, then, is a crime against trust; and to the extent that trust, a belief in the good faith of discretionary decision-makers, is essential to certain bureaucratic and governmental structures, bribery is deeply corrosive.

Because of its costs, the law usually deems bribery to be without acceptable justification. Again, I think this is in line with moral intuitions. Interestingly, the law does not regard extortion and bribery as mutually exclusive; extortion requires an apprehension of harm, bribery as desire to influence. Often, in fact, the two are coincident. Morally—and legally, perhaps—it would seem that bribery can be justified only if the bribe-giver is truly without alternatives, including the alternative of refusing payment and going to the authorities. Moreover, the briber should be able to show not merely that it was convenient or profitable to pay the bribe, but that the situation presented a choice of evils in which the bribe somehow avoided a greater peril. The popular example in our discussions has been bribing a Nazi camp guard in order to spare concentration camp internees.

The International Marketplace: Universal Codes of Conduct.

Overview.

The most relevant context for business has become the global environment. As our world becomes increasingly economically interdependent, it is the hope that this new order of interests will lessen the possibilities of war. But as with the physical law of thermodynamics, this process will evolve into various stages of equilibrium as nations continued to develop economically. Such a process can be painful as the richer countries continue to watch manufacturing jobs go to poorer nations until those poor nations (having become relatively wealthy), in turn transfer the jobs to others. An example of this is the placement of U.S. jobs with Japan until that country became wealthy. When this occurred, Japan transferred the lowest-wage jobs to other Asian countries.

One difficulty in the international marketplace is that various nations have different shared community worldviews. This nonuniformity can create an unfair competitive environment.

Larry R. Smeltzer and Marianne M. Jennings discuss the problems that cultural relativism creates for international business. For example, the United States has radically different labor laws than Honduras and Bangladesh. Practices that are allowed in some countries (such as bribery and child labor) are not considered to be ethical in the United States. Such dissonance causes real problems. The authors suggest that the best way to work through these problems is to formulate a new global shared community worldview that everyone might accept.

John Blake, Julia Clarke, and Catherine Gowthorpe highlight some issues concerning accounting regulations in different countries. Since accounting is the way businesses record what they do, some standardization of practices is important. One of the key dilemmas for accountants is the economic impact of what they do. Because their actions have clear consequences, there is often an ends-justify-the-means mentality in their work. That is, if the end is the survival or the prosperity of a company, there is pressure on accountants to present a picture that reflects a healthy business.

An ethical perspective can counteract this by urging thoroughness, caution, and an orthodox treatment of various accounting problems across international boundaries. Perhaps (as Smeltzer and Jennings suggest), greater uniformity can be achieved through developing international codes of practices and standards of professionalism.

Finally, Timothy Larrison's article specifies the way a global, macroethical outlook might emerge. This model focuses on agencies promoting international development. First he emphasizes macroeconomic stabilization. A country that is in Rossouw's "survival phase" is not ripe for integrating uniform international standards. Second, after economic stabilization, uniform standards can be introduced. However, Larrison argues that it is important to proceed with microlevel cultural sensitivity. This supports the view that all humans are ends and that such changes can be difficult.

Since development agencies work closely with international businesses, such a plan might in fact be able to develop and implement universal codes of professionalism and conduct.

Why an International Code of Business Ethics Would Be Good for Business

Larry R. Smeltzer and Marianne M. Jennings

INTRODUCTION

In many executive training seminars for international business, executives are taught to honor customs in other countries and "Do as the Romans Do." The emphasis on international business training is on learning how other cultures do business and adapting to their way of business (Wines and Napier, 1992; Paige and Martin, 1983). To some companies, adapting to foreign cultures often requires ethical compromises. That is, companies may conduct international business operations in a manner that is contrary to its standards of conduct in U.S. operation. In fact, some of the conduct in international operations may run contrary to the basic tenets of capitalism. The issue that arises is whether it is possible to successfully conduct business in those countries where cultural issues require ethical compromises that could significantly affect business operations.

Cultures hold significant variations in language, non-verbal communication, and social custom. Anthropologists, historians, and sociologists are intrigued by these differences. Many business people feel that culture differences between countries can make or break business operations between and within particular countries. Business people also discover that cultural norms for doing business in one country often conflict with codes of ethics and other business standards established in the United States. Even divisions within a company can be at odds. A domestic subsidiary may observe that a foreign subsidiary is operating successfully using tactics not permitted within the firm's domestic code of ethics.

A manager for a U.S. title insurer provides a typical example. He complained that if he tipped employees in the U.S. public recording agencies for expediting property filings, he would be violating the company's code of ethics, and could be charged with violations of the Real Estate Settlement Procedures Act, RICO statutes, and state and federal anti-bribery provisions. Yet that same type of practice is permitted, as well as recognized and encouraged, in other countries as a cost of doing business. Paying a regulatory agency in the United States to expedite a licensing process would be bribery of a public official. Yet many businesses maintain that they cannot obtain such authorizations to do business in other countries unless such payments are made. So-called "grease" or facilitation payments are permitted under the Foreign Corrupt Practices Act, so they are classified as legal; however, the issue that remains is whether such payments are ethical (Fadiman, 1986).

Consider three other examples. In India a 10-year old works 12 hours a day weaving a rug. In Honduras 15-year-old girls work 80 hours per week producing Liz Claiborne sweaters. In Bangladesh there are production quotas for nine-year-olds working in shoe factories (Quindlen, 1994). Within these countries' cultures and legal standards, such work schedules and quotas are acceptable. But in the U.S., all three examples would be violations of labor law and contrary to commonly accepted standards of ethics and social responsibility.

An inevitable question arises when national custom and culture in one country clash with ethical standards and moral values adopted by a firm whose primary operations is in another country. Should individual national cultures or should company ethics codes control the firm's ethical decisions for international operations?

Typical business responses to the question of whether cultural norms or company codes of ethics should guide international business operations are: Who am I to question the culture of another country? Who am I to impose my country's standards on all the other nations of the world? Isn't legality the equivalent of ethical behavior? The attitude of businesses is one that permits ethical deviations in the name of cultural sensitivity. Many businesses fear that the risk of offending business people in other countries is far too high to impose its business ethics standards on them.

However, from an economic standpoint as well as from the viewpoint that businesses operate best within certain defined standards, the rote response of cultural imperialism is a short-sighted approach to international business. A culturally imperialistic perspective may prove costly to individual companies as well as an entire national business economy. The purpose of this article is to present an argument supporting a universal framework for ethical operations in international business and offer suggestions for ensuring compliance with that universal orientation.

THE ETHICAL ROOTS OF BUSINESS: TRUST AND OTHER VALUES

Previous work in the area of cross-cultural differences has focused on issues of consistency (Berliant, 1982), international codes of ethics (Schollhammer, 1977), human rights (Donaldson, 1989) and global ethics (Buller, Kohl and Anderson, 1991); however, the successful commercial operations are dependent upon the ethical roots of business. What is this ethical root? TRUST. Nobel Laureate Kenneth Arrow has noted: ". . . a great deal of economic life depends for its viability on a certain limited degree of ethical commitment. Purely selfish behavior of individuals is really incompatible with any kind of settled economic life" (Arrow, 1973). A look at the three major players in all of business establishes that basic trust is a key component in their willingness to interact. The three parties are the risk-takers, the employees and the customers. Risk-takers—those furnishing the capital necessary for production—are willing to take a risk based on the assumption that their products will be judged by customer value. Employees are willing to work in production, to offer input, skills and ideas in exchange for wages, rewards and other incentives. Consumers or customers are willing to purchase products and services as long as they are given value in exchange for their furnishing, through their payment, costs and profits to the risk-takers and employers. To the extent that the interdependency of the parties in the system is affected by factors outside of their perceived roles and control, the intended business system does not function on its underlying assumptions. When the players are uncertain about the underlying assumptions, their willingness to participate is questioned or, at a minimum, the cost of participation is affected.

Ethics in the Capitalistic System

The business system is, in short, an economic system, endorsed by society, which allows risk takers, employees and customers each to allocate scarce resources to competing ends. To the extent that the allocation is based on factors other than the interdependency of these parties with their basic assumptions, the notions of the capitalistic economic system are undermined in favor of systems based, not on value, but on facilitation payments, personal connections and factors other than price, quality, and demand. The purpose of regulating behaviors through legal and ethical standards is to correct and adjust any means of allocation that is not based on the strict interdependence of risk-takers, employees and customers. A study of the Russian Commodity Exchange in which legal enforcement of standards are essentially non-existent, indicates this laissez-fair market works because free market principles of full and complete information for trading commodities are followed (Kolosov, Martin and Peterson, 1993).

Many examples in the U.S. statutory scheme illustrate how regulation has been used to reinstate the basic tenets of the free market assumptions made by economic players. For example, the Securities Exchange Act of 1934 made insider trading a criminal act. Those who have access to non-public information, whether it is obtained through their positions (officer or director) or through bribery (paying insiders for non-public information) are market participants who are making sales and purchases based on information not available to other investors/risk-takers. If investors/risk-takers' perceptions are that there can never be an equitable trading environment for a free market, they are unwilling to invest in such a market. The 1934 Act was thus a correction or adjustment to market practices to restore the interdependent trust necessary for a free market.

Another example of federal regulation used to restore equity for all those involved in the free market, or to reinstate market trust, are the antitrust laws such as the Sherman Act. This act prevents monopolistic practices beyond just building a better mousetrap which consumers are drawn to under the basic tenet of value. Labor laws evolved to control treatment of employees because, as a critical part of the economic flow, they needed to be rewarded appropriately and not taken advantage of or oppressed in order to reduce operating costs. Labor legislation recognized that fairness to employees was required if the economic system was to survive. Rebellion by employees because of unfair treatment has toppled both economic systems and governments. For example, the treatment of workers in Poland not only initiated change in the workplace, it initiated change in the political, economic and social structure of the Eastern European countries. The issues of child labor, minimum wages and maximum hours were the focus of 1930s labor legislation in the United States due to an ever-declining standard of living, the outcry of the public and their demand for legislative response (Bassiry and Jones, 1993).

While the roots of business are primarily economic, even an economic system cannot survive without recognition of some fundamental values. Values here are not defined in the same sense of moral standards or moral norms, which may be culture-specific (Donaldson, 1989). Rather values, as defined here, relate to the equitable means of distribution of benefits and costs or values inherent in a viable economy (Frederick, 1988). Some of the inherent, indeed universal, values built into the capitalistic economic system described earlier are that: (1) the consumer is given value in exchange for the funds expended; (2) employees are rewarded according to their contribution to production; and (3) the risk-takers are rewarded for their investment in the enterprise in the form of a return on that investment. Adam Smith developed his model of a market-driven, consumer-based economic system as an alternative to those systems (mercantilism and others) in which political structures determined supply of goods and services rather than having the structure of the system respond to market forces (Bassiry and Jones, 1993). Smith's model of a capitalistic economy involved decentralized decision-making. Smith also recognized certain universal battles such as no privileges for producers based on political influence, a strong work ethic and, occasionally, government protection for workers.

Beyond just these basic values of capitalism and the free-flow of labor and commerce is the notion that, to a large extent, all business is based on trust. The decision to extend credit, regardless of the credit terms or the level of background check, is still, after all, dependent upon the debtor's honoring the obligation to repay. A consumer commits to purchase on the presumption that a seller can produce. A company invests in plant and equipment on the belief that it will be able to compete. If these assumptions are removed by means of either intended or unintended government intervention in the form of controlling market access, basic assumptions of a system based on business trust are removed. The tenets for doing business are dissolved as an economy moves toward a system in which one individual can control the market in order to maximize personal income.

Suppose, for example, that the sale of a firm's product is no longer determined by perceived consumer value but rather by access to consumers which is controlled by government officials. That is, a company's product cannot be sold to consumers in a particular country unless and until it is licensed within that country. Suppose further that the licensing procedures are controlled by government officials, and those officials demand personal payment in exchange for the company's right to even apply for a business license. Furthermore, payment size may be arbitrarily determined by officials who withhold portions for themselves. The basic values of the system have been changed. Consumers no longer directly determine the demand. Government officials who demand compensation beyond government salaries now determine consumer demand by controlling business within a county. That determination is made not on the basis of product value, but rather on the basis of who is willing to do the most for the government official making the decision to issue licenses to sell. This is not government regulation intended to enhance the market, rather it is government regulation that controls the market. One of the often noted five problems with Smith's capitalistic system is the government intervention that fosters monopolies or awards selective privileges (Wilson, 1989). "Smith's concerns about the evils of monopoly went beyond the unjustified rewards that accrued to the man who was able to rig the market. A still more untoward consequence of monopoly was the ineffective management, that in Smith's view was the likely concomitant of an entrepreneur's being sheltered from the cold winds of competition." (Ginsberg, 1979).

Beyond just the impact on the basic economic system, ethical breaches involving "grease" payments introduce an element beyond a now-recognized component in economic performance: consumer confidence in long-term economic performance. Economist Douglas Brown has described the differences between the United States and other countries in explaining why capitalism works in the U.S. and not in all nations (Brown, 1994). His theory is that capitalism is dependent upon an interdependent system of production. Consumers, risk-takers, and employees must all feel confident about the future, the concept of a level playing field, and the absence of corruption for economic growth to proceed. To the extent that consumers, risk-takers and employees feel uncomfortable about a market driven by the basic assumptions, the investments and commitments necessary for economic growth via capitalism are made (Sherwin, 1983). Significant monetary costs are incurred by business systems based on factors other than customer value discussed previously.

Business Ethics in Economically Developing Countries

In developing countries in which there is the presence of "speed" or "grease" payments and resulting corruption on the part of recipient government officials, the actual money involved in these acts may not be significant in relationship to the nation's economy or culture. However, the so-called Brown impact may be devastating to economic growth. These activities and payments introduce an element of demoralization and cynicism that serves to thwart entrepreneurial activity when these nations most need these risk-takers to step forward.

We cannot deny that several countries that have experienced the most economic expansion in the last five years are nations in which bribery is *de rigeur*. For example, China and Russia are recognized as economic growth successes over the last five years. However, it is important to recognize that there are costs of this economic growth that are not as yet obvious in these still-growing economies. Bribes and *guanxi* (or gifts) in China given to establish connections in the Chinese government are estimated at 3%–5% of operating costs for companies, for a total of $3–$5 billion of 1993's foreign investment in China (Pennar, Galuszka, Lindorff and Jesurum, 1993).

Additionally, China incurs costs that come from the choices government officials make in response to payments. For example, *guanxi* are often used to persuade government officials to transfer government assets to foreign investors at substantially less than their value. Chinese government assets have fallen over $50 billion in value over the same period of economic growth primarily due to the large undervaluation by government officials in these transactions with foreign companies.

Perhaps Italy and Brazil provide the best examples of the long-term impact of foreign business corruption. While the United States, Japan, and Great Britain have scandals such as the savings and loan debacle, political corruption and insurance self-regulation, these scandals are not indicative of the type of corruption that pervades entire economic systems. The same cannot be said about Italy. Elaborate connections among government officials, the Mafia, and business executives have been unearthed with resulting resignations of half the cabinet and the indictments of hundreds of business executives. It has been estimated the interconnections among these three groups have cost the Italian government $200 billion and a resulting financial inability to complete government projects (Pennar, 1993).

In Brazil, the level of government corruption has led to a climate of murder and espionage. Many foreign firms elect not do to business in Brazil because of so much governmental uncertainty and risk, beyond just the normal financial risks of international investment. Why send an executive to a country where officials may use force when soliciting huge bribes from foreign executives?

The *Wall Street Journal* offered an example of how Brazil's corruption has damaged a country's economy despite growth and opportunity in surrounding nations (Kamm, 1994). Governor Ronaldo Cunha Lima of the northeastern Brazilian state of Paraiba was angry because his predecessor, Tarcisio Burity, had accused Lima's son of corruption. Mr. Lima shot Mr. Burity twice in the chest while Mr. Burity was having lunch at a restaurant. The speaker of Brazil's Senate praised Mr. Lima for his courage in shooting Mr. Burity himself as opposed to sending someone else. Mr. Lima was given a medal by the local city council and granted immunity from prosecution by Paraiba's state legislature. No one spoke for the victim, and the lack of support was reflective of a culture controlled by self-interest that benefits those in control. Unfortunately, these self-interests, along with the fears such action creates, preclude economic development.

Paralleling this described moral deterioration has been Brazil's lack of economic advancement despite growth in surrounding South American nations. Economists in Brazil document hyper-inflation and systemic corruption. A Sao Paulo businessman observed, "The fundamental reason we can't get our act together is we're an amoral society" (Kamm, 1994). This business person probably understands capitalism. Privatization that has helped the economies of Chile, Argentina and Mexico cannot take hold in Brazil because government officials enjoy the benefits of generous wages and returns from the businesses they control. The result is that workers are unable to earn enough even to clothe a family, with 20% of the Brazilian population living below the poverty line, and crime at such a level that nightly firefights are accepted. Brazil's predicament has occurred over time as graft, collusion and fraud have become entrenched in the government-controlled economy.

The Loss of Values: Methods of Cultural Corruption

Although bribery is prohibited under the Foreign Corrupt Practices Act, grease or facilitation payments are allowed. Ranging from 30%–10% of licensing fees in various countries, these payments often make business processes proceed quickly for a U.S. company. Thus, a U.S. company can, without violating the law, pay a foreign government official independently of government licensing fees to speed up processing for anything from phone installation to the unloading of goods from a boat docked in a country's waters. Customs clearance can be expedited. Building inspectors can overlook defects in construction and speed up final inspection. An employee can pay a traffic officer and avoid receiving a ticket.

In other countries, such as Russia, government officials actually control market price. Government officials make the determination as to where, when, and for how much goods will be sold. In many countries, government officials permit both businesses and executives to underreport their income for purposes of income taxes in exchange for payments to them. The result is that an individual's control results in higher prices for government contracts.

Decisions to award contracts are based on the amount of payments to officials making the decisions as opposed to the price, quality of the good or service and experience of the bidder. In many of these government contracts, the price of these public service projects can range from 20%–100% higher than what the costs could or should be. For example, the Italian government has experienced a 40% drop in costs of its freeway construction contracts since the removal of government officials who were taking individual payments from construction company executives (Pennar, 1993). Many of the business executives from the construction industry probably rationalized that these payments were a business necessity. In reality, these payments cost the citizens of Italy in the form of premium prices as well as in the resulting lack of freeway completion.

In Russia, police officers and other enforcement officials are paid by businesses to look the other way when they use acts of violence against those who attempt to undersell them in the marketplace. The forms of "doing business" in these countries where government officials profit individually are limited only by the human imagination.

Whether to Do Business:
The Presence of Economic Values

An observation made by many businesses with respect to those countries fraught with individual payoff is: that's the way it has always been done, and you can't do business any other way. It's a way of life. It's the culture. It's international market place reality. When in Rome, Do as the Romans Do!

Given the fact that the basic assumptions of economic systems frequently do not operate in these countries, the initial question a business should ask is not whether to participate in these activities, but whether to do business at all in those countries. The traditional question posed by ethicists is: would you engage in legal forms of corrupt activity in order to conduct business in a country where such payments to individuals is culturally acceptable? The better question is: would you do business at all in a country in which questionable payments are culturally acceptable? Not only is the question presented in a better ethical posture, it represents a more businesslike approach to the problem. Is it going to cost more in the long run to compete in this country because payments to individuals are not defensible and rules vary from situation to situation? Probably yes. Is it going to take more time to establish business there? Without a doubt. The basic value of trust necessary for doing business is missing in countries with standards that include such culturally acceptable practices.

The Levi Strauss Company's decision not to do business in mainland China is an example of a costly financial choice made on the basis that China's current political, social economic environment was too far removed from basic notions of ethics and social responsibility to permit consistent business operations. Concerns about human rights, child labor and the government's role in plant operations caused Levi to forego [*sic*] the potential of a market that would bring them two billion teenager customers between now and the year 2000. Assuming one pair of Levi jeans could be sold to each teenager for a low price of 1 U.S.D. the cost revenues from this ethical choice equal all of Levi's earnings from international operations in 1993.

Why would Levi choose not to do business in China? The uncertainty of labor conditions affects one component of the three basic values of an economic system. Demands and controls by a government that denies basic individual freedoms could be unreasonable, but more importantly, in an economic sense, these practices could deprive Levi of basic financial assumptions about investing in plant and equipment in China. If the rules for business play are uncertain with respect to its citizens, how can the Chinese government provide assurances of fairness to its potential business citizens? In short, the existing cultural atmosphere is not one nurturing to the three values underlying a successful capitalistic economic system.

ESTABLISHING STANDARDS FOR INTERNATIONAL BUSINESS

Once a business has decided to internationalize and determined in which countries it will operate, the next question becomes how the firm will operate in these countries and internationally in general?

Under the school of business thought in which cultural imperialism is touted as the key to international business success, all notions of value, quality and performance are cast aside. Not only are the premises of economic system set aside, the premise of business performance is ignored as all efforts are placed on matters outside the product or business scope. These companies employ any culturally acceptable means in order to infiltrate markets. Their U.S. standards of quality service and the idea of a better mousetrap are ignored with the belief that any culturally acceptable means to success will generally lead to quicker results. Unfortunately, this orientation is contrary to the *Centesimus Annus* of Pope John Paul II. In this document, the Pope addresses the principle characteristics of a just economic order. He concludes that although a pure free market economy is not ideal because of its lack of focus on human needs, an economy that offers opportunity for all and eliminates suffering is desirable over one that benefits the few who accept payments (Sethi and Steidlmeier, 1993).

A company with two sets of values, one for domestic business and another for international business, is a company headed for an ethical crisis. Employees will not see the distinction nor find it justifiable. It is not an issue of how a firm does business in each country, it is a question of *whether* a firm does business in each country. That answer should be dependent upon the business evaluation of the country's atmosphere for competition and its ability to survive without compromising a company's atmosphere for competition and its ability to survive without compromising a company's ethical standards.

Businesses should adopt a code of international ethics for employees so they can better meet its financial goals. Absolutes should exist. For example, no employee should ever pay a government official funds or fees in excess of mandated licensing fees. Such fees are outside the realm of the capitalistic business system.

Other universal values might include prohibitions on commission payments covering factors outside the immediate negotiations. Additionally, monitoring becomes a critical part of preserving international business standards. As a manager becomes familiar with a foreign country's customs, and the practices of competing companies in that country, the tendency is for managers to rationalize behavior. The frequent argument is that forms of business unacceptable in U.S. practices are acceptable in other countries because "everyone else is doing it." This may be particularly true when managers are feeling some pressure to meet quarterly or yearly performance figures. Managers operating in foreign cultures need corporate feedback and reinforcement to be able to maintain ethical and economic standards in countries where such standards are not always practiced, especially by the competition.

Many executives argue that it is impossible to do business without engaging in the types of payments that would be illegal and unethical in the United States. However, a study on levels of international business since the passage of the Foreign Corrupt Practices Act provides some interesting data. U.S. international sales have actually increased dramatically since its passage, as opposed to the opposite prediction that U.S. international sales would decline. The principle of "change your moral standards or lose your markets" has not proven true. The former head of Large Coppee, a French cement maker, has observed, "The conflict over doing right versus doing a deal exists only in the short term. In the long run, companies using ethical practices will win out" (Sasseen, 1993).

Beyond just adopting values related to international operations, companies might consider the adoption of universal values in order to simplify and clarify its ethical posture. These basic values would serve to address the most complex ethical scenarios and could also be used as a framework for the decision process used when a firm is faced with an issue of international expansion into a particular country. Such universal values might include honesty, promise-keeping, fairness, respect for others, compassion and integrity. For example, Pope John Paul's ideal economic system requires the consideration of human and moral factors in a company's method of operation. Under *Centesimus Annus*, a profit made at the expense of workers with their human dignity offended is "morally inadmissible" (Sethi and Steidlmeier, 1993).

An example focusing on safety conditions demonstrates how these basic values related to human dignity and welfare would impact a foreign operations decision. Suppose that a U.S. chemical company is required by OSHA regulations to have employees wear eye protection when they are on the plant floor. The same company operates a plant in India where there are no governmental requirements for eye protection. Honesty would require disclosure of the U.S. standard to the Indian employees. Fairness, respect and compassion would require that the company furnish eye protection for the employees. Dangers for eye injury do not decrease simply because a plant is located outside the U.S. Further, the decision to supply eye protection is an act of integrity. The company is living up to its ethical principles despite the additional costs of these safety measures that may *not* be adopted in competitor's foreign operations.

The issue of international safety standards brings to mind the Union Carbide Bhopal disaster. A plant in complete compliance with Indian government standards caused the deaths and permanent injury of thousands. Just the implementation of the U.S. standard of limiting residences in the area immediately surrounding the plant could have minimized the harm. Again, the standards of honesty, respect for others, compassion, fairness and integrity would have come into play as the decisions were made with respect to plant operations and safety standards. The universality of standards for international operations is again made clear when phrased this way. It is no less dangerous in India to have residences next to a chemical plant than it is in the United States. Further, the decision on operations becomes more clear as we realize that the cost of compliance with U.S. standards for the Indian plant would be far less than the actual and public relations costs incurred by Union Carbide as result of the Bhopal accident.

IMPLEMENTING AN INTERNATIONAL ETHICAL CODE

For those firms struggling with international markets, cultures, and competition, certain basic steps should be taken to ensure that company standards are followed internationally.

1. Train managers on the relationship between capitalism and excessive payments for services.

During a seminar on international business we administer a brief questionnaire. One question asked the managers if they believed strong ethical values led to economic business development. Approximately 50 percent of the 83 managers indicated they believed there was a strong or fairly strong relationship between ethics and business development. However, in subsequent discussions, the seminar participants made strong arguments' for "grease" payments to facilitate operations. But the fact remains that such payments do not increase a product's value. Adding to the personal worth of a government official does not increase anyone's confidence about the future well being of a country's commerce.

When payments to government officials are considered an expense of doing business, education is required. In the U.S., various fees for doing business are used to assure the business meets safety, environmental or humanitarian standards. They are intended to meet the well-being of society. Economic conditions are thus enhanced. In many cultures, "grease" payments are intended to enhance the economic condition of only one or two individuals. Managers must be trained to understand these relationships.

2. Develop a code of universal values.

Let's return to the survey we administered at the international business seminar. Another question asked the participants the extent to which they believed that ethical standards varied among countries. Nearly 75 percent of the participants agreed standards varied. But the next question asked if it would be possible to work under a universal code. Again, over 75 percent of the participants believed it would be possible to work with a universal international code of ethics.

The firm's code of ethics should be based on simple, universal values. Because so many cultures exist, ethical business behavior cannot be culturally specific. In addition to the basic values discussed earlier, employees should be trained with examples involving issues of honesty and fairness. Part of the universal values of honesty and fairness is that no attempt to bribe an individual or make payments beyond those mandated by law will be made. Training should stress that payment may be in the form of actual monetary value or in the form of a *quid pro quo*—An example is that in order to secure business, a company gives a job to the relative of a government official responsible for the contract decision.

3. Conduct cultural, political, economic, and financial evaluations prior to commencing operations in any country.

Most businesses focus on the economic and financial issues as they decide whether to do business in a particular country. However, the cultural and political climates of a country often determine business results. The political climate may be such that the level of trust necessary for market operations is not present. Refraining from conducting business or postponing business in that country could be cost-effective. Further, by evaluating cultural and political norms, a business can establish a baseline. The managers in charge of a country's operation cannot then establish their interpretation of culturally acceptable behavior; the standards are pre-established.

4. Use internal auditors extensively in foreign operations and allow foreign operations as a priority item in the internal audit schedule.

Managers under pressure of deadlines and financial results may stretch the boundaries of acceptable behavior because of cultural or competitive pressure. Regular visits from U.S. managers can serve as a reality check for foreign managers immersed in the culture of foreign operations. Reviewing the financial outcomes of foreign operations is a key checkpoint for spotting deviations from either the legal or economic company standards in foreign operations. Red flags that auditors can spot include excessive commissions, excessive equipment or supply purchases which could be a sign of "bribes" or *quid pro quo* in exchange for contracts. Also, significant consulting contracts and excessive travel expenditures could be a disguise for "grease" payments.

Ethics may vary from country to country; however, an international code of business ethics is possible when based on the tenets of free market operation. Capitalism requires that economic goods enhance product value for all consumers . . . not a select few. What U.S. citizens refer to as corruption is an act that benefits only one or few individuals. These acts undermine the trusting interdependency of parties in the capitalistic system.

The harm that comes from ongoing individual payments in a country ultimately rests upon those who benefitted from the payments—from the paid officials to company executives who enjoyed the rather short-term and short-sighted benefits of the payoffs. Throughout this article, the words corruption, illegal or unethical have been minimized because they are culturally specific terms. What a capitalistic economic society considers unethical or corrupt may be totally acceptable in another society. But the capitalistic economy cannot operate efficiently in a society that circumvents the relationships among risk-takers, consumers and producers.

References

Arrow, K. J.: 1973, 'Social Responsibility and Economic Efficiency', *Public Policy* **21**(3), 300–317.

Bassiry, G. R. and M. Jones: 1993, 'Adam Smith and the Ethics of Contemporary Capitalism', *Journal of Business Ethics*, 185–193.

Butler, P., J. Kohls and K. Anderson: 1991, 'The Challenge of Global Ethics', *Journal of Business Ethics* **10**, 767–775.

Donaldson, T.: 1989, *The Ethics of International Business* (Oxford University Press, New York).

Fadiman, J. E.: 1986, 'A Traveler's Guide to Gifts and Bribes', *Harvard Business Review* (July–August), 122–36.

Frederick W. C., K. Davis and J. E. Post: 1988, *Business and Society*, Sixth Ed. (McGraw-Hill Book Co., New York).

Ginzberg, E.: 1979, 'An Economy Formed by Men', in G. P. O'Driscoll (ed.), *Adam Smith and Modern Political Economy* (Iowa State University Press, Ames, Iowa).

Kamm, T: 1994, 'Why Does Brazil Face Such Woes? Some See A Basic Ethical Lapse', *Wall Street Journal* (Feb. 4, 1994), A1.

Kolosov, M. A., D. W. Martin and J. H. Peterson: 1993, 'Ethics and Behavior on the Russian Commodity Exchange', *Journal of Business Ethics* **12**, 741–744.

Paige, R. M. and J. N. Martion: 1983, 'Ethical Issues and Ethics in Cross-Cultural Training', in D. Landis and R. W. Brislin (eds.), *Handbook of Intercultural Training* vol. 1 (Pergamon Press, New York), pp. 36–60.

Pennar, K., P. Galuszka, D. Lindoff and R. Jesurum: 1993, 'The Destructive Costs of Greasing Palms', *Business Weeek* (Dec. 6, 1993), 133–138.

Quindlen, Anna: 1994, 'Out of the Hands of Babes', *New York Times* (Nov. 23, 1994), A15.

Sasseen, J.: 1993, 'Companies Clean Up', *International Management* (October 1993), 30.

Schollhammer, H.: 1977, 'Ethics in an International Business Context', *MSU Business Topics* (Spring), 54–63.

Sethi, S. P. and Steidlmeier: 1993, 'Religion's Moral Compass and Just Economic Order: Reflections on Pope John Paul's II's Encyclical Centesimus Annus', *Journal of Business Ethics* **12**, 901–917.

Sherwin, D. S.: 1983, 'The Ethical Roots of the Business System', *Harvard Business Review* **61**, 183–192.

Wall Street Journal: August 14, 1994, B1.

Wilson, James Q.: 1989, 'Adam Smith on Business Ethics', *California Management Review* **32**(1) (Fall), 99–117.

Wines, William A. and N. K. Napier: 1992, 'Toward an Understanding of Cross-Cutlural Ethics: A Tentative Model', *Journal of Business Ethics* **11**, 831–841.

Focus: Aspects of Accountancy

The Ethics of Accounting Regulation— An International Perspective

John Blake, Julia Clarke, and Catherine Gowthorpe

OVERVIEW

There is a well established tradition of ethical guidance for the practising accountant. In this paper we argue that ethical issues also arise in relation to the accountant's role in the process of accounting regulation. We:

a. Identify the role of the accounting practitioner in different national modes of accounting regulation;

b. Consider the economic impact issues which arise in accounting regulation and the conflicting views on how accountants should react to these;

c. Review the range of ethical perspectives which have been applied to the question of whether accounting regulators should be influenced by economic impact issues; and

d. Discuss five cases of economic impact issues, considering the relevance of an ethical perspective in each case.

THE ROLE OF THE ACCOUNTING PRACTITIONER IN DIFFERENT NATIONAL MODES OF ACCOUNTING REGULATION

Accounting regulation can come from either the public sector or the private sector; in many countries there is a combination of the two. Most countries have some form of legislation on accounting, whether in the form of 'Company Law', as in the UK, 'Accounting Law', as in Sweden, or 'Tax Law', as in Germany. In addition some countries have governmental bodies with either delegated authority to regulate accounting, as with the "Instituto de Contabilidad y Auditoria de Cuentas" (ICAC) in Spain, or with a formal advisory role to the legislature, as with the Bokföringsnämnden (BFN—Accounting Standards Board) in Sweden. Professional accountants may be among those nominated as members of such a body, either by direct governmental appointment, as with ICAC in Spain, or by nomination of their professional body, as with BFN in Sweden.

Private sector accounting regulation tends to have originated with professional accounting bodies. Examples were the Accounting Principles Board (APB), set up by the American Institute of Certified Public Accountants which led the way in setting recommendations from 1959 to 1973, and the Accounting Standards Committee (ASC), founded by the UK accounting bodies, which set accounting standards from 1970 to 1990. In both countries replacement bodies, in the USA the Financial Accounting Standards Board since 1973 and in the UK the Accounting Standards Board since 1990, have been set up with nominees from a range of interested parties but continued strong representation from the accounting profession.

These private sector standards can be enforced in various ways:

a) In some countries the law may explicitly require companies to comply. Canada is an example. In the UK compliance with accounting standards has effectively been a legal obligation for large companies since 1989.

b) In countries such as the UK, Australia, and New Zealand, which specify some general level of quality that company accounts must achieve such as the 'true and fair view', compliance with accounting standards may be regarded as evidence of achieving that level (see example Renshall & Walmsley, 1990, p. 313).

c) A governmental regulatory body may review standards and require companies to comply with them. This is the procedure of the SEC in the USA.

d) The accounting profession may require its own members, acting as company auditors or directors, to use their influence to secure compliance.

e) The technical quality of private sector pronouncements may be so respected that in practice companies choose to comply with them. This is generally true for pronouncements from Sweden's professional accounting body, which are followed by large Swedish companies. In Spain a private body of accountants, the Asociación Española de Contabilidad y Administración (AECA) issues recommendations which are commonly adopted by companies and frequently form the basis for subsequent official regulations from the governmental body ICAC (see above).

Thus professional accountants may be involved in the process of accounting regulation as members of public sector or private sector regulatory bodies, appointed by government, a professional body, or some other interest group. In the USA concern that members of the accounting standard setting body might be influenced by the interests of their employer led to the structuring of the FASB with seven full-time members, each of whom must sever all links with their previous employer. This contrasts with the previous structure of the APB with part-time members selected to assure a well defined representation of large international CPA firms, other CPA firms, business, and academics. Meyer (1974) examined voting records on the APB and concluded that 'no dominant pattern of voting could be discerned'. Nevertheless Senator Metcalf expressed concern that the (then) "Big Eight" might dominate the accounting standard setting process (US Congress 1976). Studies of voting patterns in the APB (Rockness and Nikolai 1977), the FASB (Brown 1981, Selto & Grove 1982) and a study of both (Newman 1981) have failed to identify any pattern of a "Big Eight" voting block dominating these bodies.

Members of the accounting profession may also become involved in the accounting regulatory process through lobbying the regulators. A former FASB chairman tells us that the large public accountancy firms are regarded as a source of unbiased neutral comment on accounting issues, and so their representations are particularly influential (Armstrong 1977).

Studies of audit firm lobbying to the FASB raise questions as to whether the "Big Eight" firms are biased in representing accounting regulation. Haring (1979) found a positive, though not statistically significant, association between client lobbying and audit firm lobbying, and also found that the likelihood of FASB support for an accounting role is statistically related to accounting firms' preferences. Puro (1984), in an examination of audit firm lobbying, found that on standardisation issues firms tended to favour the position adopted by their clients, while on disclosure issues firms tended to opt for the approach that maximises their own income; i.e., large firms favour increased complexity, small firms oppose it.

Thus the evidence seems to suggest that accounting firms do have a bias in their preferences for certain forms of accounting regulation which influences their lobbying but does not influence the voting pattern of FASB members with former accounting firm links. In view of the apparent reliance placed by accounting regulators on the representations of these firms a question arises as to what ethical constraints should affect their lobbying.

Economic Impact Issues and the Accounting Regulator

Published company accounts are available to a wide range of users. The information that managers provide in those accounts may influence the behaviour of those users. Changes in accounting rules can lead to changes in the information shown in accounts and consequently to changes in the behaviour of the users of the accounts. These changes in behaviour can affect the economy in general and the position of the reporting company and its managers in particular. Thus, changes in accounting rules give rise to potential 'economic consequences', a term which has been defined as follows:

> "Accounting choices have economic consequences if changes in the rules used to calculate accounting numbers alter the distribution of firms' cash flows, or the wealth of parties who use those numbers for contracting or decision making" (Holthausen & Leftwich 1983, p. 77).

The distinction between 'contracting' and 'decision making' is a key point, also termed 'direct' as against 'indirect' (Benston & Krasney 1978), or 'mechanistic' as against 'judgmental' (Blake 1992) issues. This arises because accounts are used in two ways:

1. The numbers in the accounts may define the rights and obligations of the company in line with some regulation or contract. Examples are company borrowing power limits, which are frequently defined as a multiple of share capital and reserves, and director's bonus schemes, which may be based on some proportion of reported profit. These are the 'contracting' or 'mechanistic' issues.
2. The readers of the accounts may take decisions on the basis of the information provided, and managers may change their behaviour in response to their expectations as to users' reaction. Thus, present and potential investors may change their view of share values, governments may change their view as to the tax burden that an industry is able to bear, or employees may adjust their wage demands. These are the 'decision making' or 'judgmental' issues.

The potential economic impact of accounting regulations explains why managers seek to control or influence the process of accounting regulation. As Whittred and Zimmer (1988) argue:

> "These wealth transfers, the economic consequences of accounting method choice, are ultimately the source of the incentive to possess financial rule-making authority, or at least to influence the deliberations of rule-making bodies." (p. 10).

A range of views can be identified on the legitimacy of allowing economic consequences to influence accounting regulation:

1. Awareness of these issues can lead to the argument that "the setting of accounting standards is as much a product of political action as of flawless logic or empirical findings" (Horngren 1973), or perception of accounting regulation as "essentially a political process" (Gerboth 1973).
2. Against this view advocates of 'neutrality', a view that accounting rules should not be chosen by reference to how they might influence a decision or judgement, argue that "the criterion by which rules are to be judged is not the effect they may

or may not have on business behaviour" (Solomons 1978). Here the essential feature of accounting regulation is the provision of "a level playing field" (Solomons 1989), and any other approach means that "the credibility of the information being supplied is lost or damaged" (Stamp 1980).

3. Between these two views a compromise can be identified, a 'mixed strategy' (Rappaport 1977), whereby some form of assessment of economic impact is combined with the development of a 'technical solution' based on a conceptual framework.

THE ETHICAL PERSPECTIVE

As Taylor (1975) observes,

> "One of the most commonly held opinions in ethics is that all moral norms are relative to particular cultures. The rules of conduct that are applicable in one society, it is claimed, do not apply to the actions of people in another society. Each community has its own norms, and morality is entirely a matter of conforming to the standards and rules accepted in one's own culture."

The literature on the application of ethical principles to accounting regulation which we consider here has arisen mainly in the context of the USA, with some contribution from the UK and Australia. We shall consider the relevance of this perspective to issues arising in other cultures in the next section.

Ruland (1984) identifies three perspectives in philosophy which have a bearing on the question as to whether accounting regulators should be guided by economic consequences issues: ends and means; positive and negative responsibilities; and duty to refrain and duty to act.

a) The question as to whether ends justify means involves, in the context of accounting regulation, whether achievement of desirable economic outcomes justifies taking a particular approach to an accounting rule. The deontological point of view is that moral rules apply to the actual actions, the means whereby an end is pursued. The teleological point of view is that an action should be judged on the basis of the moral worth of the outcome. One mechanism that accounting regulators can use to promote a deontological approach is to formulate a conceptual framework laying down the basis on which accounting regulations are to be formulated, and so providing a basis for assessing the quality and consistency of specific accounting regulations. Collett (1995) points out an interesting inconsistency in the Australian Conceptual Framework Statements issued by the Australian Accounting Research Foundation. On the one hand, the formulation of such statements implies a deontological approach, yet the statements specify that all prospective costs and benefits, including by implication economic consequences issues, should be considered in formulating accounting regulations. This implies a teleological approach.

b) The distinction between positive and negative responsibilities. A positive responsibility holds individuals liable for states of affairs which they bring about, while a negative responsibility holds them liable for states of affairs which they allow, or fail to prevent. Thus, positive responsibility holds individuals responsible for the actions they commit, while negative responsibility is impersonal since it makes the individual liable for the acts of others. It is argued that the positive responsibility to produce accounting regulations which result in a fair presentation of business accounts should not be compromised by pursuit of a negative responsibility to avoid certain economic consequences, since these are both uncertain and under the control of other parties.

c) The distinction between a duty to refrain and a duty to act. It is argued that the pursuit of best accounting practice is the explicit duty of the accounting regulator, being a duty to refrain from being distracted by other issues. By contrast, those who argue that economic consequences issues should influence accounting regulation are urging a duty to act. The case for pursuing a duty to refrain rather than a duty to act is based on three issues:

   i) *Relentlessness.* There is an infinite range of economic consequences which can flow from an accounting rule. The full range cannot be comprehended, so that a duty to act cannot be fulfilled.

   ii) *Certainty of outcome.* Ruland (1984) argues that we cannot be certain that, in pursuing a duty to act, the action will achieve or be necessary for the desired outcome, whereas the duty to refrain can demonstrably be fulfilled. Against this, Ingram & Rayburn (1989) argue that many accounting issues do not have a demonstrably superior solution, so that the application of the duty to refrain is as uncertain as the outcome of the duty to act.

   iii) *Responsibility.* Violation of the duty to refrain is clearly the responsibility of the accounting regulator. However, where the regulator chooses to ignore an economic consequences issue, so that an adverse consequence arises, then the responsibility rests with those who have made decisions on the basis of the accounts.

Ingram and Rayburn (1989) interpret the duty to refrain in a different way. They argue:

"we believe that, when it comes to standard setting, the duty to refrain is stronger than the duty to act. Actions, new standards, should be promoted only when there is clear evidence that the benefits to those who are intended to benefit from the standards are greater than the costs." (p. 65).

Ijiri (1983) makes a similar point:

"Stability of the accounting system means that . . . change in the definitions or rules of measurement will not be made unless absolutely necessary. If an accounting system is unstable, the accountor and the accountee sense the risk of relying upon it in developing their agreement and look for other means that are more stable" (p. 79).

SOME SPECIFIC EXAMPLES

We now turn to consider a number of economic impact issues which illustrate the application of an ethical perspective.

The USA

In the USA the emergence of the accounting rules on foreign currency translation offers an example of how an accounting regulation may be changed in response to intensive lobbying. There are two broad approaches to the translation of the accounts of a subsidiary operating in a foreign country and consequently preparing its own accounts in that foreign currency:

a) The temporal method, in historic cost accounts, involves translating non monetary items, such as tangible fixed assets and stock, at the rate of exchange which applied when the item originally entered the accounts, called the 'historic rate'. Monetary items are translated at the rate of exchange at the balance sheet date, called the 'closing rate'.

b) The closing rate method involves translating all assets and liabilities at the closing rate.

These two methods can have substantially different effects on a company's accounts. This is because:

a) Most companies have total assets in excess of total liabilities—a net asset position—but borrowings in excess of cash—a net monetary liability position. Thus, the closing rate method, where the exchange rate applying to all items changes each year, gives the opposite effect to the temporal method, where the exchange rate applied each year changes only in relation to monetary items. Blake offers the following summary of impact together with a fuller explanation:

	Temporal method	**Closing rate method**
Strong foreign currency	Loss	Gain
Weak foreign currency	Gain	Loss

(Blake, 1993, p. 40).

b) The underlying logic of the temporal method tends to identification of the gains or losses on holding individual assets or liabilities as part of the profit or loss for the year. By contrast, the closing rate method, which identifies the gain or loss on the net investment in the subsidiary, is similar in character to a revaluation so that it can justifiably be treated as an adjustment to the reserves rather than appearing on the face of the profit and loss account.

The American Institute of Certified Public Accountants, faced with these two contrasting approaches, commissioned a research study. The result was a firm recommendation for the temporal method (Lorenson, 1972) based on what has been described as 'one of the best pieces of academic research applied to a major practical problem in accounting' (Flower, 1995, p. 360). On the basis of this, an accounting standard prescribing the temporal method, FAS8, was issued in 1975.

The standard proved unpopular with US multinationals because:

a) Through the second half of the 1970's the US dollar tended to weaken, leading to reported losses on translation of foreign subsidiary accounts as we have seen above.

b) Companies like to report 'smooth' rather than fluctuating income figures. Alleman (1982) cites the example of how, under FAS8, in 1986 ITT experienced a virtual halving of profit in one quarter and a doubling in the next because of foreign currency losses and gains.

In 1981, in response to vigorous lobbying, FAS52 was issued prescribing the closing rate method. This satisfied US multinationals. However, Ndubizu (1984) points out that there was a negative economic impact on developing countries. This is because such countries tend to have weak currencies. To minimise the loss which this results in under the closing rate method multinationals tend to reduce their net investment in subsidiaries in developing countries by using local borrowing rather than injecting capital directly. Ndubiza argues that a sharp fall in investment in developing countries can be identified following the issue of FAS52 and concludes (p. 190) "the advanced countries' accounting standard is argued to discourage foreign investments".

This example illustrates the issue of relentlessness identified above. In pursuing a 'duty to act' the FASB responded to the concerns of US multinational enterprises but failed to respond to the less apparent consequences for developing countries.

Spain

A recent Spanish example illustrates the issue of 'certainty of outcome'. In 1990 a new 'Plan General de Contabilidad' (PGC—general accounting plan) was enacted, revising Spanish accounting law in line with the European Union directives on accounting harmonisation. One feature of this 'Plan' was to require capitalisation of finance lease agreements, so that when a company enters into a lease with an option to purchase at a bargain price at the end of the rental period, this should be accounted for as though an asset had been purchased with a secured loan. This is an example of the application of the 'substance over form' concept, whereby a transaction is accounted for in line with economic substance rather than legal form. Application of this concept is well established in the USA and increasingly applied by the Accounting Standards Board in the UK, but is in contrast to the strong legalistic tradition of Spanish accounting.

When this accounting requirement was proposed it was opposed by the Spanish leasing association on the grounds that it would make leasing less attractive to companies because the increase in reported assets and liabilities on the balance sheet would show a higher risk exposure (Vidal, 1992). The association successfully lobbied for classification of leased assets as intangible rather than tangible in the belief that this would solve the problem. Following a survey of Spanish financial managers Blake *et al* (1995) report:

> "The equipment leasing association appears to have been right in its prediction that a finance lease capitalisation requirement would have an adverse effect on the leasing industry. However, given the distaste that company financial managers show for the disclosure of leased assets as intangible rather than tangible, the equipment leasing association would seem to have exacerbated their problem as a result of successfully lobbying for such treatment" (p. 32).

This example shows how a response to an economic impact issue can have a different effect from that intended, thus illustrating the 'certainty of outcome' issue.

Ireland

A number of economic consequences issues arose during the development of an accounting standard on leasing in the UK. The UK and the Republic of Ireland at that time shared a common system for developing accounting standards. In 1981 a proposal to require capitalisation of finance leases included the statement: "By reason of the law at present obtaining in the Republic of Ireland, this exposure draft is not intended to apply to financial statements prepared or audited in the Republic of Ireland".

This provision arose because at that time Irish tax law provided that if a lessee capitalised a finance lease a different, and generally less beneficial, tax treatment would follow. In fact, publication of a mandatory standard on capitalisation of finance leases was delayed by the Institute of Chartered Accountants in Ireland exercising a veto (as reported in *Accountancy Age*, 26.1.84., p. 2) until changes in the 1984 Irish budget changed the position.

In this case the accounting standard setting body appears to have acted on the basis of a 'duty to refrain' in the sense identified by Ingram and Rayburn (1989) cited above. An interpretation of this kind might seem more appropriate for 'mechanistic' consequences, where a specific outcome can be anticipated, than for 'judgmental' consequences, where the outcome is less certain.

Sweden and USA

It is interesting to contrast the role of the accounting profession in two cases where the government introduced unconventional accounting legislation to achieve an economic objective, one in Sweden and the other in the USA. At the end of 1977 Uddeholm A.B., a major Swedish company in steel and forest products, faced a crisis. Major borrowings had been undertaken with a debt covenant provision that total borrowings should not exceed 75% of reported total assets. As a result of a major 1977 loss, the company was in breach of this condition. The Swedish government was minded to rescue this major employer, but it was barred by international agreement from giving a subsidy to a steel producer. Instead the government extended a line of credit to Uddeholm and passed a law effectively requiring the company to treat this line of credit receivable as an asset. The effect was to boost total assets to the point where the company was not in breach of its debt covenant. In the years that followed, the company conducted an orderly realisation of its assets to clear the loans, and in 1985 was taken over by AGA.

Zeff & Johansson (1984) report that this legislation was passed 'much to the displeasure of the leaders of the Swedish accounting profession' (p. 344). In 1980 the opposition in the Swedish parliament called for a report by the parliamentary auditor on this rescue, being concerned with the broad economic issues. Senior members of the accountancy profession drew the auditor's attention to the unconventional accounting treatment, and the ensuing report included a recommendation that in future such accounting legislation should not be enacted until the Swedish accounting standards board had given it impartial consideration. The law was repealed in 1983 and the auditor's recommendation was accepted by the government, so that Zeff and Johansson conclude that "Criticism from the accounting profession had an impact on the political decision makers" (p. 347).

Margavio (1993) summarises the experience in the USA of special accounting treatment formulated in a vain attempt to protect the Savings and Loans institutions. During the 1970s these institutions, long favoured by the US government for their role in providing finance to expand home ownership, were badly hit by inflation and consequent high interest rates. Their problems arose from the practice of lending for long periods at fixed interest rates, while borrowing from depositors on a short term basis at what, of necessity, had to be current market interest rates.

In the early 1980s a series of accounting regulations from the government were enacted to give these institutions the appearance of viability. For example, in 1981 a regulation permitted losses on the sale of portfolios of low interest loans to be carried forward and allocated over the life of the loans rather than being shown as a loss immediately in the accounts. In evidence to the responsible subcommittee of Congress in 1985 a leading critic of these measures observed "The S&L Thrift industry is floating on a sea of tenuous accounting numbers" (Briloff, 1990, p. 8). By the end of the 1980s it had become clear that these measures had failed to give the breathing space necessary for the institutions to recover their stability. Estimates of the cost to the US federal government of underwriting losses in the industry were in excess of $100 billion.

While these regulations come from government rather than the accountancy profession accountants have been criticised for:

a) Failure publicly to identify and criticise the deficiencies of the regulations when they were enacted.

b) Failing as auditors to report on the insolvency of the institutions as it arose. Margavio (1993, p. 2) reports the example of one large firm which has settled claims against it on these grounds for $400 million.

To summarise our comparison of the two cases, in the Swedish example an unorthodox accounting regulation was confined to just one company and prompt action was taken to resolve that company's problems, so limiting the issue of 'relentlessness', while the accounting profession was rigorous in pressing for orthodox accounting treatment. In the US case a series of unorthodox accounting regulations allowed concealment of serious underlying problems which continued to grow with consequent major costs; while the accounting profession failed to give a lead in tackling the issues, and individual audit firms have become involved in major liabilities for their own failure to act.

CONCLUSION

The role of the accountant in the process of accounting regulation raises an ethical issue as to whether to allow 'economic impact' issues to affect technical judgement. A review of the literature on the application of an ethical perspective to this question indicates a case against this. Specific examples of economic impact issues indicate the relevance of the ethical perspective. Overall we would conclude that

1) The ethical perspective does have relevance to the debate on how the accounting regulator should respond to economic impact issues.

2) The ethical perspective would indicate, at the least, a need for care and caution in allowing economic impact factors to influence the development of accounting regulation.

3) There is a separate and distinct question as to the ethical principles which should govern accountants in lobbying on issues of accounting regulation.

References

Alleman, R.H., 'Why ITT likes FAS52', *Management Accounting*, July 1982, pp. 23–29.

Armstrong, M.S., 'The Politics of Establishing Accounting Standards', *Journal of Accountancy*, February 1977, pp. 76–79.

Benston, G.J. and Krasney, M.A., 'The economic consequences of financial accounting standards' in *Economic Consequences of Financial Accounting Standards*. Financial Accounting Standards Board: Stanford, Connecticut, 1978, pp. 161–242.

Blake, J.D., 'A Classification System for Economic Consequences Issues in Accounting Regulation', *Accounting and Business Research*, Vol 22, No 88, 1992, pp. 305–321.

Blake, J., 'Foreign currency translation: A challenge for Europe', *Journal of European Business Education*, May 1993, pp. 30–44.

Blake, J., Amat, O. & Clarke, J., 'Managing the economic impact of accounting regulation: The Spanish case', *European Business Review*, Vol 95 No 6, 1995, pp. 26–34.

Briloff, A.J., 'Accounting and society: A covenant desecrated', *Critical Perspectives on Accounting*, 1, 1990, pp. 5–30.

Brown, P.R., 'A Descriptive Analysis of Select Input Bases of the Financial Accounting Standards Board', *Journal of Accounting Research*, Spring 1981, pp. 232–246.

Collett, P., *Standard Setting and Economic Consequences: An Ethical Issue*, 1995.

Flower, J., 'Foreign currency translation', in Nobes, C. & Parker, R. *Comparative International Accounting*. Hemel Hempstead: Prentice Hall 1995 (4th edition), pp. 348–389.

Gerboth, D., 'Research Intuition and Politics in Accounting Inquiry', *Accounting Review*, July 1975.

Haring, J.R., 'Accounting Rules and the Accounting Establishment', *Journal of Business*, October 1979, pp. 507–519.

Holthausen, R.W. & Leftwich, R.W., 'The Economic Consequences of Accounting Choice: Implications of costly contracting and monitoring', *Journal of Accounting and Economics*, Vol 5, 1983, pp. 77–117.

Ijiri, Y., 'On the Accountability-based Conceptual Framework of Accounting', *Journal of Accounting and Public Policy*, Summer 1983, 75–81.

Ingram, R.W. & Rayburn, F.R., 'Representational Faithfulness and Economic Consequences: Their Roles in Accounting Policy', *Journal of Accounting and Public Policy*, Spring 1989, 57–68.

Lorenson, L., *Accounting research study No 12: Reporting foreign operations of US companies in US dollars*. New York: American Institute of Certified Public Accountants, 1972.

Margavio, G.W., 'The savings and loan debacle: The culmination of three decades of conflicting regulation, deregulation, and reregulation', *Accounting Historians' Journal*, 20, 1, 1993, pp. 1–32.

Myer, F.P.E., 'The APB's Independence and its Implications for the FASB', *Journal of Accounting Research*, Spring 1974, pp. 188–196.

Ndubizu, G.A., 'Accounting standards and economic development: The third world in perspective', *International Journal of Accounting*, Spring 1984, pp. 181–196.

Newman, D.P., 'An Investigation of the Distribution of Power in the APB and the FASB', *Journal of Accounting Research*, Spring 1981, pp. 247–262.

Puro, M., 'Audit Firm Lobbying Before the Financial Accounting Standards Board: An Empirical Study', *Journal of Accounting Research*, 1984, pp. 624–646.

Rappaport, A., 'Economic Impact of Accounting Standards: Implications for the FASB', *Journal of Accountancy*, May, 1977, p. 94.

Renshall, M. & Walmsley, K., *Butterworth's Company Law Guide*, London: Butterworths, 1990.

Rockness, H.O. & Nikolai, L.A., 'An Assessment of APB Voting Patterns', *Journal of Accounting Research*, 1977, pp. 154–167.

Ruland, R.G., 'Duty, obligation and responsibility in Accounting Policy Making', *Journal of Accounting and Public Policy*, Fall 1984, 223–237.

Selto, F.H. & Grove, H.D., 'Voting Power Indices and the Setting of Financial Accounting Standards Extension', *Journal of Accounting Research*, Autumn 1982, pp. 676–688.

Solomons, D., 'The Politicisation of Accounting', *Journal of Accountancy*, November 1978, pp. 65–72.

Solomons, D., *Guidelines for Financial Reporting Standards,* London Institute of Chartered Ac-
    countants in England and Wales, 1989, p. 37.
Stamp, E., *Corporate Reporting: Its Future Evaluation,* Toronto: Canadian Institute of Chartered
    Accountants, 1980.
Taylor, P.W., *Principles of Ethics: an introduction,* Encino, California: Dickenson, 1975.
US Congress, *Senate Sub-Committee on Reports, Accounting, and Management of the Committee on
    Government Operations. The Accounting Establishment: A Staff Study,* (Metcalf Staff Report)
    1976, 94th Congress, 2nd session.
Vidal, C., 'Spain' in Hornbrook, A. (ed), *World Leasing Yearbook 1992,* London: Euromoney, 1992,
    pp. 300–305.
Whittred, G. & Zimmer, I., *Financial Accounting: Incentive Effects and Economic Consequences,* Holt
    Rinehart and Winston, Sydney, 1988.
Zeff, S.A. & Johansson, S.E., 'The curious accounting treatment of the Swedish government loan
    to Uddeholm', *Accounting Review,* April 1984, pp. 342–350.

Ethics and International Development

Timothy K. Larrison

Multinational companies operating in developing countries have continually
been accused of pursuing unethical practices in an effort fully to exploit the
resources of a country or region. The twentieth century is rife with stories of
clearly discernible attempts by multinationals to reap rewards by taking liberties with a vulnerable population and other less conspicuous, often debatable, practices employed in an effort to create benefits for management and
shareholders. The debate about the ethical standards of multinationals in less
developed countries is certainly an interesting one.

A much less understood and discussed topic is that of the ethics of the
international development business. What sort of ethical standards are applied to the army of economists, consultants, volunteers, and evangelical do-
gooders that fight for the elusive goal of development in less developed
countries? Do the same standards apply to the entire development business
community? In an effort to understand further some of the issues that affect
the international development professional this article reflects on several

questions that I have attempted to answer during my own professional experiences in Africa, Central Asia and Eastern Europe.

AID AND DEVELOPMENT

Foreign aid is an instrument used by governments, private non governmental, and multilateral organisations to strengthen the economic, political or social institutions of another country. Development assistance has roots in the language and actions employed in the design and implementation of the Marshall Plan initiated 50 years ago. The field of development assistance or international development has grown to be associated with a wide range of different endeavours. For example, assistance may refer to World Bank structural adjustment loans (macro-economic assistance), water development projects in rural areas, or 'feeding' programmes for children in abject poverty. The 1990 World Bank Development Report states that "External assistance should be more tightly linked to an assessment of the efforts that would-be recipients are making to reduce poverty".[1] Over the last 50 years a multibillion dollar development industry has emerged, employing tens of thousands of professionals around the globe with the objective of alleviating poverty and creating sustainable development in developing countries.

I have had the fortune of working in this industry in three of its primary segments. Initially, I worked for a non-profit, nongovernmental organisation (NGO) participating in water development projects in Africa. I went on to become an Economics Fellow at a policy oriented think-tank in Eastern Europe, and finally worked as a consultant on World Bank and United States Agency for International Development contracts in Central Asia and the former Soviet Union. Through these experiences and six years of higher education focusing on development I have consistently wrestled with the wide range of ethical implications that surround the field.

I offer a two tier framework of ethics with which to analyse the business of international development: macro-ethics and micro-ethics. My argument is split into two sections. The first is an attempt to present the idea of macro-ethics and debunk the relativist approach to ethics, or the "when in Rome" phenomenon, used to describe the unethical or immoral pursuit of development agendas on a global level. This argument implicitly supports the existence of a universal ethical system intricately linked to macro-economic development. Secondly, I argue that a micro-ethic framework involving a degree of cultural sensitivity is necessary when working on the local level. The success or failure of local development initiatives is often decided on the degree to which local rules, culture, and ethical considerations are brought into play in the design and implementation of a project.

LOOKING AT THE LITERATURE

Much of the literature on international business and ethics focuses on the role of the multinational corporation in developing countries. There appears to be little on the ethics of international development. However, I argue that some of the fundamental ethical issues surrounding multinational businesses are linked to the business of international development. In other words, the debate that rages around the organisational and institutional behaviour of multinationals captures many of the same issues about the role of international development and its agents.

In his book *Competing with Integrity in International Business*, Richard T. De George offers three lenses with which to view the question, "Are ethical norms universal or culture-bound?"[2] The first is euphemistically referred to as 'when in Rome do as the Romans do'. The 'when in Rome' approach states that an individual or organisation working in a particular culture should follow the customs, ethics, and rules of each locality. In other words, proponents of this approach believe there are no universal rules and that each country's culture is sacred and must be adhered to when operating in that context. The second view is what De George calls the "righteous American position". This position is centred on the belief that organisations operating abroad should follow the same rules that apply to working in the United States. The final position, the "naive moralist", is that global business should be an ethical 'free-for-all' where no rules apply to individuals or organisations working abroad.

Where De George sets out a broad based framework for analysing the ethics of international business, Mozaffar Qizilbash has attempted to look more closely at the field of international development. In her working paper *Ethical Development,* she indicates that the use of terms such as 'development ethics' or 'ethics of development' have increasingly become reflected in development literature. She argues that the concept of development needs to be redefined to take into account a set of universal ethical standards. Qizilbash claims that development professionals have grown disenchanted with an "economic growth" paradigm of development.[3] She puts forth the term "ethical development" and defines the new paradigm using three strands to describe a revamped concept of development which will:

- give primary import to human beings and consider humans to be the ends rather than the means of development;
- not be consistent with the persistence of, or an increase in, poverty or relative deprivation; and
- give intrinsic importance to freedom.[4]

The three strands make up a new approach during which "Development occurs if and only if there is some overall expansion in human flourishing or the quality of human lives or human well-being consistent with the demands of social justice and freedom".[5]

Throughout Qizilbash's discussion of different philosophies and approaches to ethics and development her belief in a universal ethical standard emerges in her argument for a new paradigm. She stresses that development attempts to answer the philosophical and ethical questions, "What constitutes human well-being or flourishing?" and "What constitutes a free society?"[6] In placing the need to address such questions at the centre of her argument she believes that philosophers, not only economists, must be involved in the debate to redefine development. What is interesting about Qizilbash's argument is that without economic stabilisation and growth, atrophy and chaos may ensue and cause a further suspension of the rights she so wishes to see instilled in the process of development.[7] When she states that development only occurs if there "is some overall expansion in human flourishing[8] . . ." she does not give attention to what has historically preceded human flourishing or human well-being, development linked to sustained economic growth.

Finally, G.J. Rossouw writes in his article *Business Ethics in Developing Countries* that business ethics has become an integral part of the business culture in developed countries but has not expanded to encompass developing countries. Rossouw argues that business ethics is fighting "an uphill battle in becoming part of the business culture in less developing countries".[9] He uses a theoretical model which involves three broad phases of moral development, shown in Table 1. Each phase could apply to an individual, organisation or country. His argument regarding business ethics in developing countries is that many developing countries remain in the survival phase of morality, and therefore do not have the luxury to consider ethical or moral issues when participating in business.

As opposed to Qizilbash, Rossouw argues that moral and ethical development can be viewed as a spectrum. An individual or society moves along the spectrum as conditions in the environment allow for it. One of the major elements lacking in Rossouw's model is the agent or agents responsible for managing changes in society. I argue below that the agent for managing the ethical shifts outlined by Rossouw is a universal development agenda informed by macro-economic development with a global macro-ethics embedded in the process.

TABLE 1. Three Phases of Moral Development[10]

Phase	Attitude	Style	Aim
Survival Phase	Fear of Extinction	Compete	Survival
Reactive Morality	Fear of Rejection	Conform	Acceptance
Pro-Active Morality	Hope	Innovative	Integrity Meaning

ECONOMICS, DEVELOPMENT, ETHICAL STANDARDS:
A CASE FOR MACRO-ETHICS

Economic development is a central component of development. Increasingly universal ideals are being recognised by the international community regarding a set of basic standards that are necessary ingredients in the creation of an effective environment for economic development. Multilateral organisations such as the World Bank and International Monetary Fund (IMF) and bilateral government agencies such as the United States Agency for International Development (USAID) and the Canadian International Development Agency (CIDA) help establish guidelines for international development, investment and industrial growth in developing countries.

The guidelines that are used by the IMF and the World Bank are a reflection of the dominant paradigm in the professional economic and development community. Without question that community is large and diverse. Admittedly, many of the leading experts who define policy for the World Bank and IMF are trained in US academic institutions; however, representatives from all parts of the globe are heard in the on-going debate over policy prescriptions for development. The core of multilateral policy is similar whether applied to Cameroon, Bolivia, Russia or Vietnam. Specifically, economic growth driven by liberalisation in all sectors of the economy is at the heart of international economic development. I argue that the essence of this precept is considered universal by professionals at the multilateral organisations and is receiving ever greater credence from policy makers in developing countries. Increasingly, the importance of investment in human capital and environmentally sustainable economic development are being put forward as critical factors in reaching long term economic development goals.

The emergence of global economic standards for developing countries demands a set of global or macro-ethical standards. Economic liberalisation is often a painful process causing severe cuts in public spending, dislocation and near term increases in unemployment. Although no government wishes to go through the short term difficulties presented by the process of economic liberalisation, the medium term goal of stability and growth is seen as a holy grail regardless of nationality, culture or ethical standards.

I argue that macro-economic stabilisation policies take precedence over other broadbased ethical standards. For without stabilisation there is often severe political and social unrest and a devolution to what Rossouw calls the survival phase of morality. Furthermore, without universal standards such as those described above the underlying reason for international aid and development, the reduction of poverty, would simply not be met.[11] Although ethics are not completely suspended when pursuing macro-economic development, a different set of universal ethics, what I call macro-ethics, should be considered.

I define macro-ethics as the ethical absolutist approach to creating global growth and development. Macro-economics should be approached with a dispassionate analysis and implementation of policy prescriptions that adhere to the fundamentals of stabilisation, liberalisation and growth. For example, corruption may be viewed as a standard, acceptable practice in a given country; however, corruption is rarely efficient economic behaviour. Therefore, corruption is an unacceptable practice. Macro-economics is a science and its practitioners should be removed from any sense of moral or social obligation.[12] A sense of macro-ethics may apply.

LOCAL DEVELOPMENT: A CASE FOR MICRO-ETHICS

Another segment of the international development business is international non-governmental organisations (NGOs). Development NGOs typically work on the local level and are subject to the cultural standards and ethics of the local community. Increasingly development NGOs are based not in Western capitals but in the country in which they work. One very successful, well recognised Kenyan NGO, Green Belt, has a policy of little or no formal contact with Western institutions or organisations for fear of the negative impacts of cultural influence on the activities of the organisation. I argue that local level development needs to take into account micro-ethical standards which are centred around a high degree of cultural sensitivity.

Micro-ethics is a relativist approach to development on the local level. It is close to De George's "when in Rome . . ." approach with one important caveat. Under my definition of micro-ethics the end to the saying would be ". . . listen very carefully to what Romans think is the best (or right) thing to do". The key to local development work is: pay heed to what the people who live there tell you, for it will undoubtedly be the difference between success and disaster.

What happens when NGOs or charitable organisations do not pay heed to the cultural and ethical standards of a community? One of the clearest examples of the disastrous effects of such behaviour is the story of Core, Kenya. In 1989 I was part of a team which visited Core to determine if there was a potential to reclaim land that had been destroyed. Fifteen years prior to my visit Core had been a lush highland area in the midst of the arid desert of Northern Kenya. The population of Northern Kenya is largely nomadic, pastoralist communities that have developed an extremely complex survival strategy over a millennium. A vital part of that strategy is nomadism. In the late 1970s the region was visited by a European missionary who, out of good intentions, decided that a permanent source of water would greatly improve the lives of those who lived in the region. He proceeded to drill a deep well in the heart of the area known as Core, which up until that time had been used exclusively as a dry season feeding ground for livestock. After the bore hole was drilled, creating a permanent source of water, several clans began to settle around the well. As more and more people became attracted by the relative ease offered by the permanent water supply, the land rapidly became overgrazed. Eventually, the once lush area was reduced to sand. Many of those who chose to settle lost their source of wealth, livestock, and shifted from self-reliant, often prosperous, people to being dependent on food aid distributed by the local mission.

The ethics of local development is complex indeed. However, the lessons learned show time and time again that without a high degree of sensitivity, or ethical relativism, local development will not be effective. This approach, micro-ethics, fits under the broad umbrella, along with macro-ethics, of what I believe makes up the ethics of international development.

CONCLUSIONS: TOWARD A MORE SOPHISTICATED UNDERSTANDING OF ETHICS IN INTERNATIONAL DEVELOPMENT

The literature on the ethics of international business is replete with theories and frameworks with which to understand how multinational corporations should (or should not) behave in developing countries. What is interesting is that very little is available regarding the individuals and organisations who influence the environment within which multinationals operate, international development organisations.

I have argued that ethical issues in the business of international development need to be assessed on two levels. The first involves macro-economic considerations. On this level dispassionate ethical absolutism is applied to the use of economic tools to encourage stabilisation, liberalisation and, ultimately, sustainable economic growth and development. The second is a micro-ethical standard. This approach applies to local development efforts and adheres to ethical relativist principles with the most important aspect being a high degree of cultural sensitivity.

NOTES

1. *World Development Report 1990.* World Bank: Oxford University Press, 1990.
2. For a full discussion of De George's three approaches see his book *Competing with Integrity in International Business,* De George also offers a list of guidelines for doing business abroad. Among them is that a multinational should contribute to the host country's development.
3. Qizilbash claims that the economic growth paradigm is simply a rise in per capita income which was often accompanied by the persistence of, or increase in, absolute poverty, a point I strongly disagree with, both in her definition of the economic growth paradigm and in her perceived outcome of per capita GDP growth.

4. Qizilbash, p. 4.
5. Qizilbash, p. 5.
6. Qizilbash, p. 12.
7. Larrison and Moore, p. 5.
8. Qizilbash, p. 3.
9. Rossouw, p. 1.
10. Rossouw, p. 5.
11. Economists often state that economics is a science. J.K. Galbraith refers to the land-mark book by William Stanley Jevons, *The Theory of Political Economy*, in which is stated "Economics, if it is to be a science at all, must be a mathematical science." From a mathematical science moral values are obviously extruded. For a discussion of this moral and ethical detachment see J.K. Galbraith, *A History of Economics*.
12. Again, I refer to J.K. Galbraith.

Bibliography

De George, Richard T. *Competing with Integrity in International Business*, Oxford: Oxford University Press, 1993.
Donaldson, Thomas. *The Ethics of International Business*, Oxford: Oxford University Press, 1989.
Galbraith, John Kenneth. *History of Economics*, London: Penguin Books, 1989.
Kruger, Anne et al. *Aid and Development, Baltimore:* Johns Hopkins University Press, 1989.
Larrison, T.K., and Moore, R.E. Reinventing *Assistance: Lessons for Central and Eastern Europe,* Working Paper, 1993.
Qizilbash, Mozaffar. *Ethical Development,* Working Paper, Department of Economics, University of Southamptom, 1995.
Rossouw, G.J. "Business Ethics in Developing Countries," *Business Ethics Quarterly,* Volume 4, Number 1, January 1994.
Smith, Adam. *Wealth of Nations,* London: Penguin Classics, 1986.
von Hoffman, Nicholas. *Capitalist Fools,* New York: Doubleday, 1992.

EVALUATING A CASE STUDY: STRUCTURING THE ESSAY

In previous sections, you have moved from adopting an ethical theory to weighing and assessing the merits of deeply embedded cost issues and ethical issues conflicts. The process involves (a) chosing an ethical theory (whose point of view you will adopt), (b) determining your professional practice issues and your issues lists, (c) annotating the issues lists by examining how embedded each issue is to the essential nature of the case at hand, (d) creating a brainstorming list that includes both key thoughts on the subject and arguments for and against the possible courses of action, (e) comparing pivotal premises in those arguments using ethical considerations as part of the decision-making matrix, (f) making a judgment on which course to take (given the conflicts expressed in d and e), and (g) presenting your ideas in an essay. The essay is your recommendation about what to do in a specific situation.

This section represents stage (g) in this process. If we continue with the IUD case, your essay might be something like the following.

Sample Essay

Executive Summary. Although my profession would advocate my continuing to distribute IUDs to women in less-developed countries and although cost issues also dictate continuing to distribute them through ABC Corporation's offer, it is my opinion that to do so would be immoral. Human life is too precious to put any one at risk for population control. If IUDs are too dangerous to be sold in the United States, then they are too dangerous to be given to women in poor countries as well. People do not give up their right to adequate health protection just because they are poor. For this reason, I am ordering a halt to the distribution of IUDs until such a time that they can be considered safe again. Furthermore, I will step up efforts to distribute alternate forms of birth control (such as the birth control pill) with better packaging that might encourage regular use.

The Introduction. In this case study, I have chosen the point of view of the regional director. This means that I must decide whether to continue distributing IUDs in less-developed countries despite a health hazard to 5 percent of the women who use this form of birth control. I will present my case against continuing the distribution based on an argument that examines: (a) the imperatives of my profession, public health; (b) cost implications; (c) the imperatives of ethics; and (d) the rights of the women involved. I will contend that after examining these issues, the conclusion must be that IUD distribution in the less-developed countries must cease until they no longer pose a significant problem to women's health.

The Body of the Essay. Develop paragraphs along the lines indicated in the introduction and executive summary.

The Conclusion. Although the dictates of the normal practice of public health and cost considerations seem to suggest that IUD distribution should continue, the ethical imperatives that human life is individually precious and that each woman has a right to safe medical attention overrule the normal practice of the profession. For these reasons, my office will suspend distribution of IUDs until they no longer pose a health risk to the general population.

Comments on the Sample. The sample provides an essay structure that contains a brief epitome and the essay itself. I often encourage my students to come in with their epitome, key issues, arguments for and against, and brainstorming sheets before writing the essay itself. This way I can get an "in-progress" view at the process of composition.

Obviously, the preceding sample represents the briefest skeleton of an essay proposing a recommendation. The length can vary as can any supporting data (charts, etc.) that will support your position. Your instructor may ask you to present your outcomes recommendation to the entire class. When this is the assignment, remember that the same principles of any group presentation also apply here including any visual aid that will engage your audience. It is essential to include your audience in your argument as it develops.

Whether it is a written report or a group presentation, the methodology presented here should give you a chance to logically assess and respond to business problems that contain moral dimensions.

The following are general questions that some of my students have raised about writing the essay, that is, the ethical outcomes recommendation.

What if I cannot see the other side? This is a common question from students. They see everything as black or white, true or false, but truth is never advanced by prejudice. It is important as rational humans to take every argument at its face value and to determine what it says, determine the objections to the key premises, determine the strongest form of the thesis, and assess the best arguments *for* and *against* the thesis.

What is the best way to reach my assessment of the best alternative? The basic strategy of the essay is to take the best two arguments that you have selected to support the conflicting alternatives and then to focus on that single premise that seems to be at odds with the other argument. At this point, you must ask yourself, Why would someone believe in either argument 1 or argument 2? If you do not know, you cannot offer an opinion—yet.

The rational person seeks to inform herself by getting into the skin of each party. You must understand why a thinking person might think in a particular way. If you deprecate either side, you lessen yourself because you decrease your chances to make your best judgment.

The rational individual seeks the truth. You have no need to burden your psyche with illogical beliefs. Therefore, you will go to great lengths to find the truth of the key premises that you wish to examine.

In your final essay, you will focus on one of the argument's premises and find the following:

A. The demonstrated truth of the conclusion depends on the premises that support it.

B. If those supporting premises are false, then the conclusion is not proven.

C. Since we have assumed that the premises are all necessary to get us to the conclusion, if we refute one premise, we have refuted the conclusion.

What if I place professional practice issues, or cost issues, or ethical issues too high in my assessment of the outcome? The purpose of presenting embedded issues analysis is to force you to see that not all ethical issues are central to the problem. Some issues can be solved rather easily. If this is the case, then you should do so. When it is possible to let professional practice issues determine the outcome without sacrificing ethical standards, then it is your responsibility to do so. Clearly, some ethical principles cannot be sacrificed no matter what the cost. It is *your* responsibility to determine just what these cases are and just which moral principles are "show stoppers."

Are ethical values the only values an individual should consider? Each person holds a number of personally important values that are a part of his or her worldview. These must be taken into account in real situations. Often they mean that although you cannot perform such and such an act, it is not requisite that the organization forgo doing whatever the professional practice issues dictate in that situation. For example, you may be asked to perform a task on an important religious holy day. Since your religion is important to you, you cannot work on that day, but that does not mean that you will recommend the company abandon the task that another person who does not share your values could perform.

What happens when you confuse professional practice issues and ethical issues? This often happens among managers at all levels. The problem is that one set of issues is neglected or is too quickly considered to be surface embeddedness. Stop. Go through the method again step-by-step. It may restore your perspective.

Macro and Micro Cases*

Macro Case 1.   You are the secretary of labor. You have become alarmed at the increased amount of apparel—economy brands as well as top-of-the-line labels—that recently has been documented to have been produced in sweatshops. It is obvious that regulations are in order, but you are baffled as to whether the regulations should come from and be enforced by the federal government or be initiated by the industry with internal sanctions and monitoring mechanisms as a positive incentive program with strong government encouragement.

You are conflicted by the arguments for each position. However, you believe that is necessary that your office take a stance, and you put the issue on the agenda for the next senior staff meeting. You must write a report justifying your position; make sure that your report represents both professional practice, ethical, and cost issues and highlights the advantages of the regulation you propose.

Macro Case 2.   As the head of the Federal Trade Commission, you have been beset with requests from parents' groups throughout the country to do something about the violence in computer games. Because of numerous school shootings around the country recently, the issue has received increased support. You, however, are aware of no conclusive studies that link playing (violent) computer games to violent behavior.

You have decided to proactively address the problem at a meeting of the major software companies. At this meeting, you will present your proposal for

---

* For more on macro and micro cases, see p. 105.

regulation consisting of some monitoring or labeling system. There are two choices: creation and regulation of the system by the government or by an industry group.

Write two different proposals and show how each will work and then recommend one of them. State the reason you support this recommendation, be sure to include professional practice, ethical, and cost considerations.

Macro Case 3. You are an executive with a financial services company and are attempting to create a single e-network for all the major world markets. You have already gotten approval from a number of international firms, but you cannot receive it from one Japanese firm that is requiring a hefty bribe before it will enter into serious discussions.

An associate has suggested a way to get around U.S. sanctions on bribery. Although it is perhaps legal (meaning that you will not be jailed if you are discovered), it is certainly against the spirit of the law, but the bribery issue is contrary to your personal worldview. However, you recognize that you are an employee of a publicly owned company and owe the stockholders a fiduciary responsibility.

In your assessment, you have three options: not to offer a bribe and document why, take your associate's advice and do what is necessary to make the deal and cover yourself legally, or resign this position or ask for reassignment to a horizontal position in the company (although such a move is likely to freeze your career).

You are very conflicted about what to do. Part of this conflict concerns how to consider bribes in the ethical sense. Write a report clarifying your ideas on bribery and then on each of the three options. Conclude your report with a clear reason to adopt one of the three options (or another if you devise one) supported (by practical professional practice, ethical, and cost considerations).

Macro Case 4. You are the secretary of commerce. At a recent meeting of the G-8 nations, a proposal was made to establish some basic rules as to international business to be administered by the World Trade Organization (WTO). The WTO already monitors various multilateral trade agreements, but this plan would create new rules to ensure basic economic fairness. It would outlaw bribery and other uncompetitive practices and would include enforcement provisions that would not require an individual country to grant jurisdiction to the WTO.

This theory sounds promising, but one of the uncompetitive practices cited is monopolistic dominance. This means that any overly dominant market entity might be considered a monopoly and its business practices restricted (much as the U.S. Justice Department handles monopolies in the United States). Because the United States has most of these dominant companies, the regulations will benefit smaller countries at the expense of U.S. firms. Although this might fit perfectly in the model of capitalism (as modified in the twentieth century), it will hurt U.S. business, and possibly lower the standard of living (or at least slowing the growth of consumerism).

How should the control of uncompetitive practices such as bribery be balanced against policies that would restrict uncompetitive practices followed by U.S. businesses. Write a letter to the president of the United States describing your position. Be sure to cite professional practice, ethical, and cost issues in your recommendations.

Micro Case 1. You are a branch director of an automobile leasing company with two employees. Your firm does business east of the Mississippi River. A local municipality issued to several auto leasing companies in the region a proposal for a car-sharing program to be part of a welfare-to-work initiative. At a meeting of those intending to submit a bid, you find that most of your competitors plan to provide used cars with a new or remanufactured engine and a new chassis (so they can be registered as new), but these vehicles are *not* new. Although this practice satisfies the law, it seems wrong to you. You are also offended by several of your competitors who joked that these reconditioned vehicles are certainly better than the welfare-to-work persons deserve.

Various government regulations provide sanctions against failing to meet the specifications on a municipal bid. However, you prefer to create a consensus among bidders as to the criteria for making their bid. In other words, you seek regulation of the autos offered in the bid but from within the group.

You mention some of these concerns to your spouse, who asked you to refine your thoughts, which were disorganized. Therefore, your task is to write a report that you will first present to your spouse and then later to the other bidders about the autos that will be included in this bidding process. Do you threaten to go to the authorities? How much emphasis do you give to ethical arguments?

Micro Case 2. You are a telecommunications account executive (salesperson) who has been asked to handle the company's bid on the new telecommunications system for the country of X-Star (an oil-rich eastern European country). Your company is counting on this large contract for its strategic future. Your boss, Dick Sharpe, has given you a considerable wine and dine budget and told you not to skimp on anything you might need.

During the meeting with the U.S. branch procurement officer, Dewey Cheatum, he holds a manila folder in one hand and gestures with the other. Only the two of you are at the meeting:

"You know what I really live for is my boy, Alex" said Mr. Cheatum.

"Yes, sir," you responded.

"He's a talented boy, but you know he just doesn't fit in at the school he's going to. I don't think that he'll ever fit in at a public school. He needs a first-class private school like Excelsior to get that 'edge' in life—know what I mean?"

"Yes, sir," you replied.

"You know it's not how good you are in this world, but it's who you know and what they can do for you that brings success. Yep, that's what brings success. And Excelsior could give that to my Alex."

"So are you going to send Alex to Excelsior?" you naively asked.

"Ha! Fat chance on a civil servant's salary." Mr. Cheatum began hitting his free hand with the manila folder while he talked. "I'd need $45,000 to fall out of the sky to be able to afford four years at *that* tuition. Forty-five thousand. That's how much four years' tuition is at Excelsior."

You nodded as Mr. Cheatum excused himself to use the lavatory. He left the file folder that he had been playing with on the table. Naturally, you opened the folder that held all the specifications and preliminary bids of competitors—in duplicate. Naturally, you took the duplicates and put them in your briefcase. When Mr. Cheatum returned, you talked about several random topics and then you left.

When you got home, you suddenly felt panicked. What had you done? Had you entered into an agreement to pay the costs of Alex Cheatum's prep school education? The total cost was not out of line with your budget, but to put all your eggs in one basket that is the private property of the decision maker concerned you. The problem is that you *took* the information on the telecommunications contract. Suppose the room had a hidden camera.

You decided to take a long walk and think about it. When you got back you resolved to write a memo to yourself that would identify your thoughts on the practical and ethical considerations of the problem. You also need a plan of action. Therefore, after the preliminaries you plan to write out exactly how you should execute your eventual plan of action.

Micro Case 3. You are a newly stationed local official of SAVE THE WORLD, an international development organization. Your organization has convinced several world powers (including the United States) to participate with the World Bank in a key project for the construction of a dam in the western African country in which you are stationed. Your agency is overseeing the dispersal of moneys on the project. When you arrived, you decided to oversee the accounts and discovered that the local official employed a fraudulent accounting system to account for funds. With a little aggressive research, you discover that about half of the money has gone to private individuals and not to the project at hand.

This makes you furious. You do not know how this could have been allowed to transpire. The problem is this:

1. If you make a big deal about this (as fraud), the perpetrators may be caught and punished.

2. If you make a big deal about this (as fraud) and the perpetrators are punished, then your funding sources may pull out leaving a void where there is a legitimate need.

3. If you do not make a big deal of this (putting it all on different accounting methods), it allows the guilty to go free.

4. If you do not make a big deal of this, you (perhaps) become a part of the corruption.

You are conflicted about what to do. If you make the wrong choice it may mean not only your job, but your career in this line of work. Write out a plan of action using both practical issues and ethical issues to support your decision.

Micro Case 4.   You are a bank auditor employed by a major U.S. bank doing business in a Russian republic. You are responsible for doing the taxes for your company. At present, however, the tax collection system in the republic is in its infancy. Large numbers of corporations and individuals simply do not pay. You could pay your fair share according to the regulations that presently exist in the Russian republic. No one else is really doing this, so you would put yourself at a competitive disadvantage with your competitors and perhaps are ignoring your fiduciary responsibility to your stockholders to make them money. You could pay what you think most comparable institutions are really paying on imaginative (a.k.a. fraudulent) accounting practices. In this case, you are doing what most other people in your situation are doing—even though it is contrary to the written law. Or you could take your chances and stiff the system. Worse case scenario on the last option is that you end up paying someone a big bribe (but it would still be less than the cost of option one).

You are not sure what to do. Should you follow one of these three alternatives or another one all together? Should you resign your post?

Write a report that will be directed to the branch manager stating what you plan to do and why. Be sure to cite both ethical and practical considerations.

Internet Resources

The following lists are a beginning for finding interesting material on business ethics on the Internet. Since much of the Internet experience is following associated links to other sites, these brief, annotated offerings will be the first and not the last point in your exploration.

I. More General List

www.luc.edu/depts/business/sbe/index.html   The Society of Business Ethics offers a wide variety of Business Ethics links including scholarly and practical resources.

www.ethics.ube.ca/resources/business/eth-inst.html   The Centre for Applied Ethics offers a very wide list of links to ethical centers that have a primarily global orientation.

www.eben.org/   The European Business Ethics network (EBEN) seeks to offer links that will service both academics and people in business.

www.business-ethics.org/   The International Business Ethics Institute has a linking of business ethics problems along with ways that governments might respond.

II.   Listings with a More Particular Focus

www.ascca.com/INDUST_r/iethics.htm   The Automotive Service Councils of California site provides an example of the principles of business ethics very specifically applied to service stations.

www.perc.com/bppe/   The American Society of Mechanical Engineer's Web site on ethics discusses wider values that engineers should abide by as well as specific professional codes.

www.Php.indiana.edu/~appe/home.html   The Association for Practical and Professional Ethics is a rich resource containing information about academic conferences and links to a wide variety of applied areas.

www.arts.unsw.edu.au/aapae/   The Australian Association for Professional and Applied Ethics Web site resolves around links that relate to the activities of the association. It is thus a bit more academic in its scope.

www.bbb.org/   The mission of the Better Business Bureau is to "promote and foster the highest ethical relationship between businesses and the public." This is a practical site emphasizing everyday issues that concern business.

www.eoa.org/   The Ethics Officer Association Web site is an interactive site that not only lists resources and publications but also has a chat site for association members.

cac.psu.edu/~plc/iabs.html   The International Association for Business and Society is largely dedicated to the needs of its members, there are some interesting abstracts from its journals as well as material on the interrelationship between its member groups and the larger society.

Further Readings

General Business Ethics

Bowie, Norman E. *Business Ethics: A Kantian Approach.* Oxford: Blackwell, 1999.

De George, Richard T. *Business Ethics.* 3d ed. New York: Macmillan, 1990.

Jones, Daniel. *A Bibliography of Business Ethics, 1971–1976; 1976–1980; 1981–1985.* 3 vols. Charlottesville, VA: University Press of Virginia, 1977, 1982, 1986.

Soloman, Robert. *Above the Bottom Line: An Introduction to Business Ethics.* New York: Harcourt Brace, 1997.

Werhane, Patricia, and R. Edward Freeman. *Dictionary of Business Ethics.* Oxford: Blackwell, 1998.

Westra, Laura, Patricia H. Werhane, George Brenkert, and Donald A. Brown. *The Business of Consumption: Environmental Ethics and the Global Economy.* Lanham, MD: Rowman and Littlefield, 1998.

What Is a Corporation?

A. The Corporation as an Individual

Donaldson, Thomas. *Corporations and Morality.* Englewood Cliffs, NJ: Prentice Hall, 1982.

———. *The Ethics of International Business.* New York: Oxford, 1989.

French, Peter A. *Collective and Corporate Responsibility.* New York: Columbia University Press, 1984.

Garrett, J. E. "Redistributive Corporate Responsibility." *Journal of Business Ethics* 8 (1989), 535–45.

Gatewood, Elizabeth, and Archie B. Carroll. "The Anatomy of Corporate Social Response: The Rely, Firestone 500, and Pinto Cases." *Business Horizons* 24 (1981).

McMahon, Christopher. "Morality and the Invisible Hand." *Philosophy and Public Affairs* 10 (1981).

Pfeiffer, R. S. "The Central Distinction in the Theory of Corporate Personhood." *Journal of Business Ethics* 9 (1990), 473–80.

Velasquez, M. "Why Corporations Are Not Morally Responsible for Anything." *Business and Professional Ethics Journal* 2 (1983), 1–18.

B. Stakeholder Theory

Bowie, Norman, and Ronald Duska. *Business Ethics*. 2d ed. Englewood Cliffs, NJ: Prentice Hall, 1991.

Evan, William, and R. Freeman, "A Stakeholder Theory of the Modern Corporation: Kantian Capitalism." In *Ethical Theory and Business* 3d ed. Ed. Tom L. Beauchamp and Norman E. Bowie. Englewood Cliffs, NJ: Prentice Hall, 1988.

Frederick, William, et al. *Business and Society: Corporate Strategy, Public Policy, Ethics*. 6th ed. New York: McGraw Hill, 1988.

Freeman, R. Edward. *Strategic Management: A Stakeholder Approach*. Boston: Pitman, 1984.

Goodpaster, K., and Piper, T. *Managerial Decision Making and Ethical Values*. Cambridge, MA: Harvard Business School Publishing Division, 1989.

Posner, Barry, and Warren Schmidt. "Values and the American Manager: An Update." *California Management Review* (Spring 1984).

Werhane, Patricia. "Engineers and Management: The Challenge of the Challenger Incident." *Journal of Business Ethics* 10 (1991), 605–16.

Competition and the Practice of Business

Dean, P. "Making Codes of Ethics 'Real.' " *Journal of Business Ethics* 11 (1992), pp. 285–90.

Duro, R., and B. Sandstrom. *The Basic Principles of Marketing Warfare*. New York: John Wiley, 1987.

Gordon, I. *Beat the Competition*. Oxford, Blackwell, 1989.

Hamel, G., Y. Doz, and C. Prahalad. "Collaborate with Your Competitors and Win." *Harvard Business Review* 67, no. 1 (1989), pp. 133–39.

McManis, G. "Competitions' Failure Means It's Time for Collaboration." *Modern Health Care*, 20, no. 3 (1990), p. 57.

Paine, Lynn. "Corporate Policy and the Ethics of Competitor Intelligence Gathering." *Journal of Business Ethics* 10 (1991), 423–36.

Ries, A., and J. Trout. *Marketing Warfare*. New York: McGraw-Hill, 1986.

Advertising

Beheish, M. D., and R. Chatov. "Corporate Codes of Conduct: Economic Determinants and Legal Implications for Independent Authors." *Journal of Accounting and Public Policy* 12 (1993), pp. 3–35.

Berman, R. *Advertising and Social Change*. Beverly Hills, CA: Sage Cushman, 1990.

Dyer, G. *Advertising as Communication*. New York: Methuen, 1982.

Gold, P. *Advertising, Politics, and American Culture: From Salesmanship to Therapy.* New York: Paragon, 1987.

Stankey, M. J. "Ethics, Professionalism, and Advertising." In *Advertising in Society.* Ed. R. Howland and G. B. Wilcox. Lincolnwood, IL: NTC Business Books, 1990, pp. 419–36.

Weis, E. B. "What's Ahead for Admen, Starting Third 100 Years." *How It Was in Advertising: 1776–1976.* Chicago: Crain Books, 1976.

Information Technology

Allen, Lori, and Dan Voss. *Ethics in Technical Communication: Shades of Grey.* New York: John Wiley, 1997.

Crandall, Richard, and Marvin Levich. *Logic and Responsibility in the Computer Age.* New York: Springer Verlag, 1998.

Johnson, Deborah G. *Computer Ethics.* Upper Saddle River, NJ: Prentice Hall, 1993.

Migga, Joseph, D. Gries, and F. P. Schneider, eds. *Ethical and Social Issues in the Information Age.* New York: Springer Verlag, 1997.

Pourciau, Lester J., and G. T. Mendina, eds. *Ethics and Electronic Information in the Twenty-First Century.* West Lafayette, IN: Purdue University Press, 1999.

Stichler, Richard N., and Robert Hauptman, eds. *Ethics, Information, and Technology: Readings.* Jefferson, NC: McFarland, 1997.

Weckert, John, and Douglas Adeney. *Computer and Information Ethics.* Westport, CT: Greenwood, 1997.

Working Conditions

Blades, Lawrence, E. "Employment at Will vs. Individual Freedom: On Limiting the Abusive Exercise of Employer Power." *Columbia Law Review* 67 (1967), pp. 1405–35.

Ewing, David W. *Freedom Inside the Organization.* New York: McGraw-Hill, 1977.

Ezorsky, Gertrude, ed. *Moral Rights in the Workplace.* Albany: State University of New York Press, 1987.

Gibson, Mary. *Workers' Rights.* Totowa, NJ: Rowman and Allanheld, 1983.

Jönsson, Berth. "The Quality of Work Life—The Volvo Experience." *Journal of Business Ethics* 1 (1982).

Pfeffer, Richard M. *Working for Capitalism.* New York: Columbia University Press, 1979.

Werhane, Patricia H. *Persons, Rights, and Corporations.* Englewood Cliffs, NJ: Prentice Hall, 1985.

Westin, Alan, F., and Stephan Salisbury, eds. *Individual Rights in the Corporation.* New York: Pantheon Books, 1980.

Affirmative Action

Blackstone, William T., and Robert Heslep. *Social Justice and Preferential Treatment.* Athens, GA: University of Georgia Press, 1977.

Cohen, Marshall, Thomas Nagel, and Thomas Scanlon. *Equality and Preferential Treatment.* Princeton, NJ: Princeton University Press, 1976.

Glazer, Nathan. *Affirmative Discrimination.* New York: Basic Books, 1975.

Greenawalt, Kent. *Discrimination and Reverse Discrimination.* New York: Alfred A. Knopf, 1983.

Gender Issues

Baier, Annette C. *Postures of the Mind: Essays on Mind and Morals.* Minneapolis, MN: University of Minnesota Press, 1985.

Card, Claudia. "Gender and Moral Luck." In *Identity, Character, and Morality: Essays in Moral Psychology.* Ed. Owen Flanagan and Amélie Rorty. Cambridge, MA: MIT Press, 1990.

Collins, Patricia Hill. *Black Feminist Thought: Knowledge, Consciousness, and the Politics of Empowerment.* New York: Routledge, Chapman and Hall, 1991.

Friedman, Marilyn. "Beyond Caring: The De-Moralization of Gender." In *Science, Morality and Feminist Theory.* Ed. Marsha Hanen and Kai Nielsen. Calgary: University of Calgary Press, 1987.

———. "The Social Self and the Partiality Debates." In *Feminist Ethics.* Ed. Claudia Card. Lawrence, KS: University of Kansas Press, 1991.

Gilligan, Carol. *In a Different Voice: Psychological Theory and Women's Development.* Cambridge, MA: Harvard University Press, 1982.

———. "Moral Orientation and Moral Development." In *Women and Moral Theory.* Ed. Eva Feder Kittay and Diana T. Meyers. Totowa, NJ: Rowman and Littlefield, 1987.

Held, Virginia. *Feminist Morality: Transforming Culture, Society, and Politics.* Chicago: University of Chicago Press, 1993.

———, ed. *Justice and Care: Essential Readings in Feminist Ethics.* Boulder, CO: Westview Press, 1995.

Jaggar, Alison. *Feminist Politics and Human Nature.* Totowa, NJ: Roman and Allanheld, 1983.

Noddings, Nel. *Caring: A Feminine Approach to Ethics and Moral Education.* Berkeley, CA: University of California Press, 1984.

O'Brien, Mary. *The Politics of Reproduction.* London: Routledge, 1983.

Rorty, Amélie, ed. *Explaining Emotions.* Berkeley, CA: University of California Press, 1980.

Ruddick, Sara. *Moral Thinking Toward a Politics of Peace.* Boston: Beacon Press, 1989.

Tannen, Deborah. *You Just Don't Understand: Women and Men in Conversation.* New York: Ballantine Press, 1991.

Thomas, Lawrence. "Sexism and Racism: Some Conceptual Differences." *Ethics* 90 (1980), pp. 239–50.

———. *Living Morally: A Psychology of Moral Character.* Philadelphia: Temple University Press, 1989.

Williams, Patricia J. *The Alchemy of Race and Rights.* Cambridge, MA: Harvard University Press, 1991.

Wolf, Susan. *Feminism and Bioethics: Beyond Reproduction.* New York: Oxford University Press, 1996.

Government Regulation

Arthur Andersen and Co. *Cost of Government Regulation Study for the Business Roundtable.* New York: Arthur Andersen, 1979.

Breyer, Stephen. *Breaking the Vicious Circle: Toward Effective Risk Regulation (The Oliver Wendell Holmes Lectures, 1992).* Cambridge, MA: Harvard University Press, 1993.

Buchholz, Rogene. *Business Environment and Public Policy: Implications for Management and Strategy*. 4th ed. Englewood Cliffs, NJ: Prentice Hall, 1992.

Jacoby, Neil, ed. *The Business Government Relationship: A Reassessment*. Pacific Palisades, CA: Goodyear, 1975.

Jones, John Travis, and Frank A. Scott, Jr. *The Economic Impact of Transborder Trucking Regulation*. New York: Garland Press, 1999.

Shleifer, Andrei, and Robert Vishny. *The Grabbing Hand: Government Pathologies and Their Cures*. Cambridge, MA: Harvard University Press, 1999.

International Issues

Barnet, Richard, and Ronald Mueller. *Global Reach: The Power of Multinational Corporations*. New York: Simon and Schuster, 1974.

Beitz, Charles. *Political Theory and International Relations*. Princeton, NJ: Princeton University Press, 1979.

Brown, Peter G., and Henry Shue, eds. *Boundaries: National Autonomy and Its Limits*. Totowa, NJ: Rowman and Littlefield, 1981.

Falk, Richard, Samuel S. Kim, and Saul H. Mendlovitz, eds. *Toward a Just World Order*. Vol. 1. Boulder, CO: Westview Press, 1982.

Meager, Robert F. *An International Redistribution of Wealth and Power*. New York: Pergamon Press, 1979.

Turner, Louis. *Multinational Companies and the Third World*. New York: Hill and Wang, 1973.

Acknowledgments

Chapter One

Interview with Mel Streeter. Used with the permission of Mel Streeter.

Chapter Three

The Corporation as an Individual

Kenneth E. Goodpaster and John B. Mathews Jr., "Can a Corporation Have a Conscience?" Reprinted by permission of *Harvard Business Review*. From "Can a Corporation Have a Conscience?" by Kenneth E. Goodpaster and John B. Mathews Jr., *Harvard Business Review*, 60 (January/February 1982), 132–41. Copyright © 1982 by the President and Fellows of Harvard College. All rights reserved.

Nani L. Ranken, "Corporations as Persons: Objections to Goodpaster's 'Principle of Moral Projection.'" *Journal of Business Ethics* 6 (1987), 633–37. Copyright © 1987. Reprinted with kind permission of Kluwer Academic Publishers.

Peter A. French, "The Corporation as a Moral Person." From *Collective and Corporate Responsibility* by Peter A. French. Copyright © 1984 Columbia University Press. Reprinted by permission of the publisher.

Thomas Donaldson, "Personalizing Corporate Ontology: The French Way," in *Sham, Responsibility and the Corporation*, ed. Hugh Curtler (New York: Haven Publishing, 1986), pp. 101–12. Reprinted by permission of the publisher.

Stakeholders

Kenneth Goodpaster, "Business Ethics and Stakeholder Analysis." *Business Ethics Quarterly* 1 (1991), 52–71. Reprinted by permission of the author.

Stephen Cohen, "Stakeholders and Consent." *Business and Professional Ethics Journal* 14, no. 1 (1995), 3–16. Reprinted by permission of the author.

Chapter Four

Competition and the Practice of Business

Alan Malachowski, "Ethics in Competition: Morality and Competitive Advantage." *Business Ethics: A European Review* 4, no. 4 (1995), 199–201. Copyright © 1995 by Blackwell Publishers Ltd. Reprinted by permission of the publisher.

Advertising

Barbara J. Phillips, "In Defense of Advertising: A Social Perspective." *Journal of Business Ethics* 16 (1997), 109–18. Copyright © 1997. Reprinted with kind permission of Kluwer Academic Publishers.

Geoffrey Sher and Michael Feinman, "Accountability, Representation, and Advertising." *The Jacobs Institute of Women's Health* (1997), 153–61. Reprinted with permission from the Jacobs Institute of Women's Health.

Tony L. Henthorne and Michael S. LaTour, "A Model to Explore the Ethics of Erotic Stimuli in Print Advertising." *Journal of Business Ethics* 14 (1995), 561–69. Copyright © 1995. Reprinted with kind permission of Kluwer Academic Publishers.

Information Technology

Duncan Langford, "Ethics and the Internet: Appropriate Behavior in Electronic Communication." *Ethics and Behavior* 6, no. 2 (1996), 91–106. Copyright © 1996. Reprinted by permission of Lawrence Erlbaum Associates.

Peter W. F. Davies, "Technology and Business Ethics Theory." *Business Ethics: A European Review* 6, no. 2 (1997), 76–80. Copyright © 1997 by Blackwell Publishers Ltd. Reprinted by permission of the publisher.

Joseph L. Badaracco Jr. and Jerry V. Useem, "The Internet, Intel and the Vigilante Stakeholder." *Business Ethics: A European Review* 6, no. 1 (1997), 18–29. Copyright © 1997 by Blackwell Publishers Ltd. Reprinted by permission of the publisher.

Michael D. Myers and Leigh Miller, "Ethical Dilemmas in the Use of Information Technology: An Aristotelian Perspective." *Ethics and Behavior* 6, no. 2 (1996), 153–60. Copyright © 1996. Reprinted by permission of Lawrence Erlbaum Associates.

Chapter Five

Working Conditions

William W. Lowrance, "Of Acceptable Risk." From *Of Acceptable Risk* (Los Altos, CA: William Kauffmann, 1976). Reprinted by permission of the author and publisher.

Sheila M. Neysmith and Jane Aronson, "Working Conditions in Home Care: Negotiating Race and Class Boundaries in Gendered Work." *International Journal of Health Services* 27, no. 3 (1997), 479–99. Copyright © 1997 Baywood Publishers. Reprinted by permission of the publisher.

David M. Schilling, "Sneakers and Sweatshops: Holding Corporations Accountable." Copyright © 1996 Christian Century Foundation. Reprinted by permission from the October 9, 1996 issue of the *Christian Century*.

Judith Jarvis Thomson, "Preferential Hiring." Copyright © 1973 by Princeton University Press. Reprinted by permission of Princeton University Press.

Robert Simon, "Preferential Hiring: A Reply to Judith Jarvis Thomson." Copyright © 1974 by Princeton University Press. Reprinted by permission of Princeton University Press.